INTRODUCTION TO INDUSTRIAL / ORGANIZATIONAL PSYCHOLOGY

Introduction to Industrial / Organizational Psychology

Ronald E. Riggio

California State University, Fullerton

Consulting Editor

Lyman W. Porter

University of California, Irvine

SCOTT, FORESMAN/LITTLE, BROWN HIGHER EDUCATION
A Division of Scott, Foresman and Company
Glenview, Illinois   London, England

To LILA

Library of Congress Cataloging-in-Publication Data

Riggio, Ronald E.
  Introduction to industrial/organizational psychology.

  Includes bibliographical references.
  1. Psychology, Industrial.   2. Organizational change.   I. Title.
HF5548.8.R475   1990   158.7   89–70026
ISBN 0–673–38188–9

Cover illustration: Christopher Gall

Acknowledgments
Acknowledgments for the copyrighted materials not credited on the pages
where they appear are listed in the acknowledgments section beginning on page
483. This section is considered a legal extension of the copyright page.

PREFACE

Introduction to Industrial/Organizational Psychology provides an inviting and comprehensive introduction to the field of industrial/organizational psychology. Two important themes guided the writing of this textbook. First, since I/O psychology is a field with both a strong scientific base and an applied orientation, the book demonstrates the connection between psychological theory and application: Theoretical concepts are shown to lead to useful interventions. Second, this book was designed and written with the student in mind. Whenever possible, the text draws on examples and illustrations from the world of work that students understand. For instance, many work-setting examples include service industries, such as retail chains and fast food restaurants, rather than concentrating solely on traditional office or factory work settings.

Introduction to Industrial/Organizational Psychology is an introductory textbook that appeals to a wide range of students with varying academic backgrounds. It is designed for use in undergraduate survey courses in I/O psychology or in psychology of work behavior courses, and is suited for courses that contain a mix of psychology majors and nonmajors. The text is appropriate for courses at four-year colleges and universities as well as two-year community colleges. While the book is written at a level that makes the material accessible to students who are relatively new to the field of psychology, the coverage of topics is comprehensive. The inclusion of "classic" theories and research along with the latest developments and innovations makes this a thorough and challenging text for advanced psychology students.

Introduction to Industrial/Organizational Psychology is divided into five parts. Part One provides an introduction to the field and an overview of research methods used by I/O psychologists. Beginning with Part Two, the text clarifies the diversity of the field by separating the two sides of industrial/organizational psychology into subcategories. Parts Two and Five concern the industrial side: Part Two deals with personnel issues, including separate chapters on job analysis and job performance, personnel selection, and personnel training; Part Five deals with work environment issues and covers the topics of human factors, work conditions, and work safety. Parts Three and Four concern the organizational side: Part Three covers worker issues, including topics such as worker motivation, job satisfaction, and work stress; Part Four surveys organizational issues, with separate chapters devoted to the topics of communication, group processes, leadership, organizational power and politics, and organizational structure and development. *Introduction to Industrial/Organizational Psychology* emphasizes organizational issues more than other I/O texts because the complex interpersonal processes that occur in work organizations increasingly are topics of research and are of particular interest to many students.

Special features included in each chapter of *Introduction to Industrial/Organizational Psychology* complement the text narrative and provide further illustrations and examples of I/O psychology in the "real world." One of these features, Applying I/O Psychology, takes the theoretical and research material presented in the chapter and shows how I/O psychologists apply this knowledge to make positive changes in actual work settings. A second feature, Up Close (which is particularly student-oriented), provides students with practical information concerning how I/O psychology can increase understanding of everyday work situations. A third feature, On the Cutting Edge, highlights current areas of research or practice in I/O psychology that will likely impact the direction of the field. Inside Tips, found at the beginning of each chapter, draws the various chapters and topics together to help students see the "big picture" of the field of I/O psychology. This feature also provides specific tips for understanding and studying the chapter material.

The chapters are designed to facilitate learning. Each chapter begins with an outline of the topics covered and ends with a chapter summary and a series of study questions and exercises that help students review and think about the chapter material. (End-of-chapter material also includes a suggested reading list.) A marginal glossary of terms appears throughout each chapter, with a more complete alphabetical glossary at the end of the book. The text also includes appendixes dealing with the profession of I/O psychology and information about exploring careers in the field.

The text is complemented by an Instructor's Resource Book prepared by Diane Davis. This manual contains everything needed to create a dynamite course—suggestions for additional lecture material, discussion questions, in-class exercises and demonstrations, a list of appropriate audiovisuals, additional references, transparency masters, and a multitude of test items in various formats.

Acknowledgments. I would like to thank the many reviewers whose valuable input helped shape and improve the text. They are

Caran Colvin, San Francisco State University
Michael Coovert, University of South Florida
Chris Cozby, California State University, Fullerton
Jack Croxton, State University of New York College at Fredonia
Diane Davis, Oakton Community College

Kevin Ford, University of Michigan

Jane Halpert, DePaul University

Douglas Johnson, University of Arkansas at Little Rock

Janet Kottke, California State University, San Bernardino

Diane Krum, College of Lake County

Thomas Lee, University of Washington

Clay Moore, Oakton Community College

Robert Ostermann, Fairleigh Dickinson University

Christopher Taylor, Western Washington University

Robert Vance, Ohio State University

Peter Villanova, Northern Illinois University

Sheldon Zedeck, University of California, Berkeley

Particular thanks goes to Lyman Porter for his expert advice and encouragement. I would also like to express my gratitude to the many people at Scott, Foresman/Little, Brown who helped produce this book. Special thanks to Deb Samyn who has a particular knack for helping rough-draft chapters become a polished product. Thanks also to Joanne Tinsley, Scott Hardy, and Don Hull for their support and their faith in the project. Finally, I would like to thank my wife, Lila, and daughter, Brianna, for their flexibility in allowing me to get the work done and for putting up with all the craziness.

Ronald Riggio

BRIEF CONTENTS

CONTENTS

1

INTRODUCTION:
DEFINITIONS AND HISTORY

CHAPTER OUTLINE

Understanding Industrial/Organizational Psychology

This first chapter is intended to define I/O psychology and to give you a feel for what the field is all about and what I/O psychologists do. The examples drawn from the early history of I/O psychology and the discussion of current trends show how far the field has progressed in a relatively brief period.

Since industrial/organizational psychology is so broad in its scope, it's not easy to gain a good understanding of the entire field by simply learning definitions or studying some of its historical roots; to actually comprehend the scope of I/O psychology you need to get through this entire textbook. Each chapter, from Chapters 3 through 14, presents a general topic and several specialties that I/O psychologists study. As you go through the book, step back and try to see how the various topics fit together. You will then begin to find the threads that hold the field of I/O psychology together.

Finally, to understand I/O psychology fully, you must do some outside reading. For ideas, examine the suggested readings at the end of each chapter and read the appendix dealing with careers for I/O psychologists.

L ike it or not, you and I will spend a big part of our waking lives working. Not only does work take up a large chunk of the day, but it also often governs where we live, how we live, and the kinds of people with whom we associate. It makes sense, then, that we should want to learn more about the world of work and our own work behavior.

Have you ever wondered what motivates people to work, what makes someone a good manager or leader, or why some people are competent, loyal workers, while others are untrustworthy and unreliable? Have you ever considered the ways a particular job might be redesigned to make it more efficient or the processes by which large organizations make decisions? All these and other questions have been studied by industrial/organizational psychologists.

In this chapter, we will define the field of industrial/organizational psychology, study the specialty areas within the discipline, and learn a bit about what industrial/organizational psychologists do. We will then look briefly at the history of industrial/organizational psychology, focusing on some of the important early developments in the field. Finally, we will consider industrial/organizational psychology today to see how the field is progressing and will examine some of the important trends for the near future.

WHAT IS INDUSTRIAL/ORGANIZATIONAL PSYCHOLOGY?

Psychology is the study of behavior and mental processes. Psychologists use systematic scientific methods in an effort to understand more about the hows and whys of behavior and human thought processes. Within the broad field of psychology, there are many specialty areas, each of which focuses on a different aspect of behavior. **Industrial/organizational (I/O) psychology** is the specialty area in psychology that studies human behavior in work settings.

As you might imagine, the study of human behavior in work settings is a large undertaking. Most jobs are quite complicated, requiring the use of a wide range of motor and mental skills. Work organizations are often large and complex entities made up of hundreds or even thousands of workers who must interact and coordinate activities in order to produce some product or service. To better understand how I/O psychologists go about studying the complexity and diversity of work behavior, we will break I/O psychology into categories of problems or issues, which can then be considered individually.

The unifying theme of these various subspecialties within I/O psychology is that all use the same basic methods to study work behavior. Therefore, the first section of this book will deal with the procedures used by all I/O psychologists.

Personnel issues involve the study and analysis of people and jobs. Such issues include the recruitment and selection of workers, employee training and development, and the measurement of job performance. I/O psychologists who focus primarily on personnel issues are likely working in the subspecialty of **personnel psychology.** We will look at personnel issues in the second part of this book.

I/O psychologists also study the psychological processes underlying work behavior, such as why people work and how they react to their jobs, including feelings of job satisfaction and work stress. We will study such employee issues, or *worker issues,* in the third part of this book.

Organizational psychology is the subspecialty within I/O psychology that studies the relationships among workers, including the processes by which work groups interact, the relationships between supervisors and subordinates, and the structure and interdependence of work roles. We will look at *organizational issues* in I/O psychology in the fourth part of this textbook.

Finally, I/O psychologists consider issues relating to how and where workers perform their jobs by looking at the machines and tools, the work procedures and systems, the environmental conditions under which people work, and the physical work settings. Often referred to as engineering psychology, this subspecialty of I/O psychology has more recently been called **human factors psychology** to reflect the emphasis on the human

psychology
the study of behavior and mental processes

industrial/organizational (I/O) psychology
the branch of psychology that is concerned with the study of behavior in work settings and the application of psychological principles to changing work behavior

personnel psychology
the subarea of I/O psychology that deals with the study and analysis of people and jobs

organizational psychology
the specialty of I/O psychology concerned with studying relationships among workers

human factors psychology
the specialty area of I/O psychology concerned with the relationship between the worker and the work task

element in the design of work machines and systems. Human factors psychology attempts to fit workers, machines, and work environment together to maximize efficiency and productivity. We will consider these *work environment issues* in the fifth part of the book.

Within I/O psychology are many separate topics of study, some of which are the following (the order of these topics parallels the chapter sequence):

- *Job analysis:* the processes by which people work and the types of tasks they perform. Job analysis is useful in making decisions about the appropriate level of pay for certain jobs as well as in understanding what a particular job entails in order to appraise job performance effectively.
- *Personnel selection:* the processes by which organizations choose workers. I/O psychologists have assisted companies by developing techniques to help screen job applicants in order to select the most qualified persons.
- *Employee training:* I/O psychologists have participated in the development and execution of methods for employee training. The continuing technological advancements in computers and other sophisticated work machinery means that there is a constant challenge to insure that employees receive training in the skills needed to operate this advanced technology.
- *Worker motivation.* Numerous theories attempt to explain why people work. These theories have led I/O psychologists to develop methods to try to increase worker motivation and productivity.
- *Job satisfaction and work stress.* I/O psychologists have been involved in the measurement of employee satisfaction and stress, which may affect work performance and rates of absenteeism and turnover.
- *Communication and work group processes.* I/O psychologists have examined the interpersonal processes in work organizations. These are very important because employees typically work in interacting groups.
- *Leadership and power:* processes of control and influence in work organizations. I/O psychologists also have examined how organizational structure affects work behavior and work outcomes.
- *Engineering psychology or human factors psychology:* the relationship between worker and machine. I/O psychologists have also explored the related issue of how physical and psychological work conditions affect worker behavior.

In short, just about any important human behavior or thought process that occurs in a work setting can be a target for study by an industrial/

organizational psychologist. I/O psychology has greatly increased our understanding of work behavior and has led to significant improvements in the way that work is conducted, in the types of machines, tools, and procedures used, and in the quality of work life.

THE SCIENCE AND PRACTICE OF INDUSTRIAL/ORGANIZATIONAL PSYCHOLOGY

I/O psychology has two objectives: first, to conduct research in an effort to increase our knowledge and understanding of human work behavior; second, to apply that knowledge to improve work behavior, the work environment, and the psychological conditions of workers. Thus, I/O psychologists are trained to be both scientists and practitioners, although some may operate primarily as one or the other. We will first examine the practice of I/O psychology and then in Chapter 2 will discuss its scientific objective in depth.

When I/O psychologists apply psychological principles to actual work settings, they follow what might be called the **practitioner model.** This model and its methods of practice are similar to those used by physicians, clinical psychologists, and other health care providers. While physicians administer to individual patients or clients, I/O psychologists might deal with an entire organization, department, or group within an organization. The first step in the practitioner model is *diagnosis*. The I/O psychologist, like the physician, engages in detailed, objective observation of the client-organization in order to determine the problem. To aid in diagnosis, the I/O psychologist uses a variety of measurement tools and techniques, such as structured observations, surveys, and tests. The second step involves decisions about a particular "treatment" program, often referred to as an *intervention*. On the basis of the diagnosis of the problem and the information about a variety of possible intervention strategies, the I/O practitioner selects an appropriate program and introduces it into the client-organization. The next step deals with the psychologist's *evaluation* of the effects of the intervention, again using a variety of measurement tools, to see whether the intended results were obtained and to examine for any side effects. If the desired results have not been achieved, the I/O psychologist will reevaluate, perhaps altering the intervention program or trying another strategy. When such a change is made, the evaluation process is repeated.

Consider the following example. An I/O psychologist is called upon to deal with the rising absenteeism rate among workers in a sheet metal factory. The psychologist might begin by examining attendance records to discover the patterns of absences and the reasons given. The psychologist notices that much of the increase results from a rise in the accident rate in

practitioner model
a method of applying psychological principles to changing behavior in work settings through a process of diagnosis, intervention, and evaluation

In this raft-building exercise for executives, communication and leadership—two topics studied in industrial/ organizational psychology—make one group more successful than the other.

the past few months. A careful analysis of these data indicates that newer workers tend to be those more likely to have accidents. Through observation of work procedures and interviews with the workers and supervisors, the I/O psychologist discovers that new workers are not being properly trained in safety procedures. The psychologist's recommendation is thus to institute a safety training program for new employees. Suppose that after the implementation of the program, the rate of absence for injuries is still unacceptable. The psychologist may then suggest additional interventions, such as the posting of safety reminders or an incentive program that rewards departments for accident-free months. Follow-up evaluation indicates that the combined strategies are indeed reducing the accident and absenteeism rates, thereby protecting workers' health and well-being, as well as saving the company a great deal of money.

For more about the work of I/O psychologists and how I/O psychology applies to the world of work, see the Appendix on Careers in I/O Psychology.

THE ROOTS OF INDUSTRIAL/ORGANIZATIONAL PSYCHOLOGY

Around the turn of the century, when the field of psychology was still in its infancy, a few early psychologists dabbled in the study of work behavior. For example, psychology was applied to designing work situations (Munsterberg, 1913) and to advertising (Scott, 1908). But there still was no formal discipline known as industrial psychology (this was the term for the field before the early 1970s, when it was officially changed to industrial/organizational psychology). Surprisingly, the spark that stimulated the beginnings of the field was provided not by a psychologist but by an engineer named Frederick W. Taylor.

SCIENTIFIC MANAGEMENT

Frederick Taylor believed that scientific principles could be applied to the study of work behavior to help increase worker efficiency and productivity. He felt that there was "one best method" for performing a particular job. By scientifically breaking down the job into measurable component movements and recording the time needed to perform each movement, Taylor believed that he could develop the fastest, most efficient way of performing any task. He was quite successful in applying his methods, which became known as **time-and-motion studies.** These time-and-motion procedures often doubled, tripled, and even quadrupled laborer output! Taylor's system for applying scientific principles to increase work efficiency and productivity eventually became known as **scientific management.** In addition to applying time-and-motion procedures, Taylor also incorporated into his system of scientific management other considerations, such as selection of workers based on abilities and the use of proper tools.

According to Taylor, the basic principles of scientific management are as follows:

· Jobs can be scientifically studied to determine the one best method for performing a task.
· There must be a match between the worker's skills and abilities and the type of job the worker is to perform. (Taylor was an early proponent of the idea of "the right person for the right job.")
· Money is a prime motivator. To get workers to increase productivity or to adhere to new work methods, financial incentives must be used.
· Tools and work systems must be designed to fit the requirements of the job and the characteristics of the worker. (For example, Taylor made sure that tall shovelers were provided with extra long-handled shovels to alleviate back strain).

In one application of scientific management, Taylor used his methods to create what he called "the science of shoveling." By experimenting with different shoveling movements, shovel loads, and types and shapes of shovels, he could greatly increase a typical shoveler's productivity. In another series of studies, by considering factors such as worker fatigue, Taylor was able to improve the efficiency of ball-bearing inspectors (Taylor, 1911).

time-and-motion studies procedures in which work tasks are broken down into simple component movements and the movements timed to develop a more efficient method for performing the tasks

scientific management begun by Frederick W. Taylor, a method of using scientific principles to improve the productivity and efficiency of jobs

Frederick W. Taylor, an engineer, was a pioneer in the field of scientific management.

Obviously the increases in productivity provided by the application of scientific management greatly improved the profit picture for companies. Taylor believed that some of these increased profits had to be passed along to the workers to motivate them to adopt the more efficient work procedures and to maintain maximum levels of work output. He was convinced that for the worker, money was the primary motivator; to get people to produce more, he felt, you need only to pay them more. Subsequent research in I/O psychology and perhaps your own observations indicate that this is not always so.

Although the benefits of a systematic and scientific approach to improving work efficiency may seem to be a sensible approach, Taylor's ideas initially met with skepticism and resistance from management and workers alike. Besides being reluctant to try anything new, management did not understand how science could be applied to work, and thus, Taylor spent much of his life trying to convince the working world of the benefits of scientific management. Slowly, however, his ideas began to take hold. He gathered an inspired group of followers, most notably the husband-and-wife team of Frank and Lillian Gilbreth (Lillian Gilbreth was one of the earliest women I/O psychologists), who implemented the principles of scientific management and revolutionized several physical labor jobs by making the accepted work procedures more efficient and productive (see Applying I/O Psychology). Today's followers of Taylor's principles are more commonly referred to as *efficiency experts*. Work efficiency and increased productivity are important to I/O psychologists, but I/O psychology looks beyond efficiency to examine the impact of work procedures and conditions on the working person. Today the issues that scientific management originally addressed are only a small portion of the broader focus of I/O psychology.

Shortcomings of scientific management. Unfortunately, Taylor's philosophy was quite narrow and limited. In his day many jobs involved manual labor and were thus easily broken down and made more efficient through the application of principles of scientific management. Today jobs are much more complex, often demanding sophisticated problem-solving skills or the use of creative thinking. Fewer and fewer people engage in physical labor. Many of these "higher-level" tasks are not amenable to time-and-motion studies. In other words, there is probably not one best method for writing a computer program, developing an advertising campaign, or managing people.

Taylor's ideas about motivation were also somewhat limited. He believed that workers are rational, logical people who will increase their work efforts in order to achieve greater economic gain, but this is not always the case. Often workers are motivated by factors other than money, as we shall see shortly. The narrow focus of Taylor's scientific management approach would be made clear several years later.

Scientific Management

Dramatic Changes in Work Efficiency

From the 1920s to the 1960s, the application of scientific management principles and procedures such as time-and-motion studies greatly improved the efficiency of a wide variety of typical types of jobs, including cabinetmaking, clerical filing, lumber sawing, and the making of reinforced concrete slabs (increased from 80 to 425 slabs per day!) (Lowry, Maynard, & Stegemerten, 1940). It has even been claimed that the efficient procedures used in hospital operating rooms and dental offices are the result of the efforts of the husband-and-wife team of efficiency experts Frank and Lillian Gilbreth. We have all seen the efficient operating room procedure instituted by the Gilbreths: The surgeon shouts, "Scalpel!" and immediately a scalpel is placed in his hand (Gilbreth, 1916).

Even the job of a short-order cook has been improved through scientific management:

> As you wait to be served you watch the sandwich man prepare a group of orders. Everything he needs is within arm's reach. Plates are rising out of a load balanced holder in the counter to his left. His bank of toasters is tipped at an angle on a shelf in front of him . . . [as] the finished product seems to pop up right into his hands.

> Turn your attention to the right for a moment to study the action of the grill cook. He has two work surfaces, an open grill for barbecue-flavored steaks on his left (smoke disappears through a filtered vent at the rear), and next to the open grill, a plate grill for hot cakes, hashed brown potatoes, and similar items. You notice a series of holes cut in the right side of the plate. Refrigerator doors are below the cook surface, and above to the rear is a a shelf stacked with special plates for grill items. The grill cook is preparing four orders of eggs sunny side up, with hashed brown potatoes and ham on the side. As he reaches into the refrigerator for the ham, you notice that each serving has been preseparated with waxed paper. The potatoes are similarly packaged. A cup hangs in their container which is filled with butter patties. . . . No one is working at a killing pace because every move is made to count. Their material, the food, is where the employees need it when they need it. . . . Their equipment is designed for the job, and is properly located in relation to the work place. Clean working conditions are obvious. . . . Everyone is happily busy. (Close, 1960, pp. 4–5)

THE HUMAN RELATIONS MOVEMENT

In the mid 1920s a series of studies was initiated in the Hawthorne, Illinois, plant of the Western Electric Company. Researcher Elton Mayo and his colleagues wanted to study the effects of the physical work environment on worker productivity. In effect, they were carrying on the tradition begun by Taylor and his followers by systematically trying to improve worker efficiency. In the most famous of the experiments, Mayo explored the effects of lighting on worker productivity. Focusing on a group of women who were assembling electrical relay-switching devices, he systematically varied the level of illumination in the room. He expected to be able to determine the optimal level of lighting for performing the task. However, the results were surprising and dramatically changed psychologists' view of the worker from then on. No matter what level the lighting was set at, productivity increased! When lighting was increased, worker output went up. Further increase to very bright illumination resulted in further improvement. Turning the lights down (even to such low levels that it appeared that the women were working in moonlight) also led to increases in productivity. There was a steady increase in workers' output following *any* change in lighting. In other studies, Mayo systematically varied the length and timing of work breaks. Longer breaks, shorter breaks, more or fewer breaks, all resulted in a steady increase in worker output (Mayo, 1933).

Mayo knew that every change in the work environment could not possibly be causing the steady rises in worker productivity. Something else had to be affecting output. Upon closer examination, he concluded that the workers were being affected not by the changes in the physical environment but by the simple fact that they knew they were being observed. According to Mayo, these workers believed that the studies were being conducted in an effort to improve work procedures, and their positive expectations, coupled with their knowledge of the observations, determined their consistent increases in productivity, a phenomenon that has been labeled the **Hawthorne effect.** Although in the first example discovered by Mayo the "Hawthorne effect" was positive, resulting in increased productivity, this is not always the case. In another of his studies, work group productivity *fell* following the introduction of changes in the work environment. Because these workers believed that the results of the studies would lead to more demanding production quotas, they restricted output whenever they were being observed, thus producing a negative Hawthorne effect.

In other studies, Mayo also found, in contrast to the notions proposed by Taylor's scientific management approach, that workers do not always behave in ways that maximize their financial rewards, and, in fact, will sometimes forgo financial considerations for a more pleasant working environment and chances to interact socially with co-workers (Roethlisberger & Dickson, 1939). For example, a worker may pass up a promotion or a more lucrative position with another company to stay in a job that feels comfortable and offers trusted, familiar colleagues.

Although researchers have noted a number of serious flaws in the methods Mayo used to conduct the Hawthorne experiments (see Chapter 2), the general conclusions reached by Mayo and his colleagues resulted in the development of the **human relations movement,** which recognizes the importance of social factors and something called "worker morale" in influencing work productivity. In fact, this movement states that a harmonious work environment, with good interpersonal relationships among co-workers, will be a productive work environment, particularly when

Hawthorne effect
changes in behavior occurring as a function of subjects' knowledge that they are being observed and their expectations concerning their role as research participants

human relations movement
a movement based on the studies of Elton Mayo, that emphasizes the importance of social factors in influencing worker performance

the work itself is boring or monotonous. According to Mayo, workers in repetitive or low-level positions—jobs that do not themselves provide satisfaction—will turn to the social environment of the work setting for motivation.

Some of the basic principles of the human relations movement are as follows:

· Social factors, particularly good interpersonal relationships among workers, are the most important determinants of productivity. In other words, the happy worker is the productive worker.
· In many cases, social factors will outweigh the effects of monetary incentives in determining work performance.
· Workers are often more responsive to their peers' values than they are to those of management. This is the case, for example, when workers restrict their output to maintain some agreed-upon level of productivity (this is called rate-setting).

Shortcomings of the human relations approach. Like Taylor's, Mayo's perspective is too limited and narrow. Mayo overemphasized the role that worker morale, or satisfaction, plays in determining work performance. He believed in the adage, "The happy worker is the productive worker," which, as we shall see, is not always the case. Yes, a pleasant, harmonious work environment is important, but so too are more practical factors such as the money received for performing a job.

Another shortcoming of the human relations approach was that Mayo studied specific groups of workers in a single manufacturing plant who were chiefly engaged in repetitive, tedious work. In this situation, the importance of social relationships among workers in affecting work outcomes may have been magnified. In other jobs, where the type of work is more interesting or varied, the quality of the social environment may not be as important a determinant of job satisfaction or work performance.

COMPARING SCIENTIFIC MANAGEMENT AND HUMAN RELATIONS

Scientific management and the human relations movement represent two radically different views of the worker in the work place. Scientific management sees the worker as a rational, logical being who is motivated by money and will perform to enhance personal economic well-being. The human relations movement, with its emphasis on good interpersonal relationships on the job, stresses the emotional, sometimes nonrational side of the worker. For Mayo and his followers, the worker is a social animal motivated by feelings and by the need to get along with and be accepted by others. Neither approach is necessarily wrong or right, and both de-

A sign reminds a textile worker that he can shut down the line if he spots a defect. Such emphasis on employee decisionmaking stems from the human relations movement.

scribe certain aspects of the worker. Human beings are complex organisms capable of a wide range of behaviors, which are motivated by a number of factors.

In spite of the limitations of their respective viewpoints, Taylor and Mayo were pioneers in the development of industrial/organizational psychology. Throughout this text we will see the continuing influence of their two divergent philosophies. The legacy of scientific management can be seen today in the research that is concerned with designing more efficient tools, machines, and systems that will be compatible with their "human operators." For example, rather than studying, as Taylor did, how shovels could be designed to make a more efficient coal shoveler, today's human factors psychologists might want to redesign the radar display screen to make an air traffic controller's job easier and more efficient. We will examine some of these developments in the final section of the book. The human relations movement may likewise be seen in recent developments in organizational and personnel psychology that focus on ways to improve worker commitment to the organization and stress the increased participation of employees in important work-related decisions. We will study some of these innovations in the sections focusing on personnel and organizational issues. Thus in many ways scientific management and human relations are still with us, but they have evolved into more sophisticated ways of examining human work behavior.

PERSONNEL TESTING AND THE WORLD WARS

While Taylor and Mayo helped shape the emerging field of I/O psychology, psychological tests developed to improve selection and placement of military personnel during the world wars also played an important role in the formation of the field. During World War I, a group of psychologists developed two intelligence tests that could be administered to Army recruits—the Army Alpha, for recruits who could read English, and the Army Beta, for the 30 percent of recruits who were illiterate. More than 1.5 million men were eventually given these tests. Although the war ended before the program could be used to place great numbers of recruits, this intelligence-testing system represented the first large-scale attempt to assess work-related abilities.

When World War II erupted, I/O psychologists played a more important part in the selection and placement of new recruits. The Army General Classification Test, a group-administered pencil-and-paper test, was developed to separate recruits into categories based on their abilities to learn military duties and responsibilities. Screening tests were also created to select candidates for officer training. In addition, psychologists helped the United States Office of Strategic Services (OSS) develop intensive assessment strategies for selecting candidates for dangerous espionage positions. Some of these techniques included "hands-on" situational tests in which candidates had to perform some tasks under difficult and near impossible conditions. The aim was to assess their ability to deal with stressful and frustrating circumstances, which is very important for soldiers involved in military espionage.

The development of these large-scale personnel testing programs and the attention they received led to considerable interest in such testing in the postwar years, and testing and assessment remain major endeavors of personnel psychology, as we shall see below.

INDUSTRIAL/ORGANIZATIONAL PSYCHOLOGY AFTER WORLD WAR II

It was after World War II that I/O psychology truly began to blossom and the specialties discussed above began to emerge and develop unique identities. Personnel psychology became a distinct area, helped in part by the publication of a new journal, *Personnel Psychology,* in 1948. During the cold war years of the 1950s and 1960s the growth of the defense industry spurred the development of engineering psychology, or human factors psychology, through the increased demand for sophisticated weapons systems, which needed sophisticated control systems. Human factors psychologists were called in to help design control systems that were both sensible and easy to operate. In addition, the contributions of sociologists and social psychologists who began studying and performing extensive research in work organizations helped create the specialty of organizational psychology.

One historical event of the postwar years also caused tremendous growth in I/O psychology: the Civil Rights Act of 1964, which banned discrimination in employment practices. Designed to protect underrepresented groups, such as ethnic minorities, from being unfairly discriminated against in work-related decisions, this legislation forced organizations to take a closer look at the ways people were selected for jobs. Particular attention was given to the fairness of employment selection tests and personnel decisions such as promotions and firings. I/O psychologists have played an important part in helping to establish and implement fair employment standards. We will discuss these matters further in Part II.

INDUSTRIAL/ORGANIZATIONAL PSYCHOLOGY TODAY AND IN THE FUTURE

Today, industrial/organizational psychology is one of the fastest growing areas of psychology. I/O psychologists are in the forefront of those professionals who are satisfying the huge demand for information leading to greater understanding of the worker, the work environment, and work behavior. They are involved in nearly every aspect of business and industry, and, as we have seen, the range of topics they research and the varieties of tasks they perform are extensive (for a summary, see Table 1.1).

I/O psychologists hold a variety of positions in businesses, industries, colleges, and government agencies of all kinds. Among the jobs they may hold are positions such as management consultant, director of human relations, vice president of training, affirmative action officer, university professor, manager of manpower development, director of organizational planning, and personnel research specialist.

THE STUDY OF WORK BEHAVIOR: A MULTIDISCIPLINARY, COOPERATIVE VENTURE

Industrial/organizational psychologists are not the only professionals who study work behavior. Researchers in the fields of management,

---

Table 1.1   AREAS OF SPECIALIZATION FOR I/O PSYCHOLOGISTS AND ASSOCIATED TASKS

Selection and placement
    Developing assessment tools for selection, placement, classification, and promotion
      of employees
    Validating test instruments
    Analyzing job content
    Developing and implementing selection programs
    Optimizing placement of personnel
    Identifying management potential

Training and development
    Identifying training and development needs
    Formulating and implementing technical training and management development
      programs
    Evaluating the effectiveness of training and development programs relative to
      productivity and satisfaction
    Career planning

Organization development
    Analyzing organizational structure
    Maximizing the satisfaction and the effectiveness of individuals and groups
    Facilitating organizational change

Performance measurement
    Developing performance criteria
    Measuring utility

Quality of worklife
    Enhancing the productive outputs of individuals
    Identifying factors associated with job satisfaction
    Redesigning jobs to make them more meaningful

Consumer psychology
    Assessing consumer preferences
    Identifying consumer reactions to new products
    Developing market segmentation strategies

Engineering (human factors) psychology
    Designing work environments
    Optimizing operator-machine effectiveness
    Developing systems technologies

---

sociology, political science, organizational communication, economics, and several other social sciences contribute to what we know and understand about the worker and work organizations. Because this research takes place on many fronts, I/O psychologists need to be aware of the recent developments in other fields. A quick look at the titles of journals that publish research of interest to I/O psychologists illustrates the multidisciplinary nature of the study of work behavior. While a great deal of research on work behavior can be found in psychology periodicals such as the *Journal of Applied Psychology, Personnel Psychology, Journal of Occupational Psychology,* and *Annual Review of Psychology,* management journals such as the *Academy of Management Journal* and the *Academy of Management Review* also publish articles of interest to I/O psychologists, as do organizational behavior publications, such as *Organizational Behavior and Human Decision Processes, Organizational Dynamics,* and *Journal of Organizational Behavior.* The *Journal of Communication* and *Human Communication Research,* research publications for communication professionals, may also publish findings that are relevant to I/O psychologists, as do the sociological journal *Human Relations* and the administration-oriented *Administrative Science Quarterly.*

The multidisciplinary nature of the study of work behavior may be illustrated by an issue that is of great concern to many American businesses: the fact that the Japanese are outproducing the Americans (in terms of both quantity and quality) in such products as automobiles, high-tech electronic equipment, and steel. Why is this the case? A psychologist

Japanese-style production teams, now found in many U.S. firms, are an example of a phenomenon that can be best understood from a multidisciplinary perspective.

might focus on differences between the workers or between the work systems of the two countries. An economist might concentrate on the fact that Japan puts a greater proportion of its financial and human resources into these particular industries than does the United States. A political scientist might examine the politics involved, whereas a management researcher might look at differences in management philosophy and style between the two countries. In reality, all of these factors are probably involved, and each approach is valid (see Zussman, 1983). Many work issues are similarly extremely complex and need to be examined from a variety of perspectives. Most importantly, we need to keep an open mind and stay in touch with what other disciplines are doing if we are going to truly understand the working world and human work behavior.

TRENDS AFFECTING THE FUTURE OF INDUSTRIAL/ORGANIZATIONAL PSYCHOLOGY

While the work of I/O psychologists has helped improve behavior at work, other developments in the working world and in the world at large have in turn influenced the field of I/O psychology. The four major trends listed below are strongly influencing the course and character of I/O psychology today and are likely to continue to do so.

cognitive psychology
the area of psychology that studies how people think and process information

First trend: The cognitive explosion.   In the past few decades, psychologists have made tremendous gains in **cognitive psychology,** which tries to understand how people think and process information. The study of how the mind works, or cognition, is having a great impact on I/O psychology in particular, especially in terms of advancements in research on how people make decisions and process information, and in the area of social cognition, which studies how people perceive and understand each other in social situations (see Abelson & Levi, 1985; Markus & Zajonc, 1985; Wickens, 1984).

This impact of such advancements in the study of human cognition is particularly evident in the development and design of sophisticated work machines, especially computers. The microprocessing chip has led to incredible increases in the kinds of tasks that machines can perform. We are now seeing machines that are capable of a limited range of "thinking." Machines can now make simple work-related decisions and can change functions and correct problems by themselves. A small but growing group of cognitive and human factors psychologists have contributed to the development of computer systems and software that are easy to use for the typical person who has not had extensive experience with complex computer systems or languages. Creating such "user friendly" computer systems requires a thorough knowledge of how people think, process information, and make decisions.

Some of the advancements in social cognition involve the study of errors people make in judging others and the biases that affect judgment. We now know that there is a tendency for people to make systematic errors in their judgment of other people and their behavior. Such errors and biases have important implications for how managers perceive and evaluate subordinates in the work setting. For example, certain errors or biases may affect how the performance of workers is evaluated, leading to inaccurate appraisals. Managers are becoming more aware of these potential errors and biases and try to take them into account when evaluating worker behavior or making important work decisions. As a rule, managers are becoming more analytical in the ways they manage their human resources and make their major decisions.

Because workers are thinking, active beings, a better understanding of cognitive processes will lead to a better understanding of the complexity of human behavior at work. This complexity means that there will often not be a simple answer to problems in the work environment. To be able to solve such problems, our approach must be equally sophisticated, taking into account the complex nature of both the problem and the solution.

Second trend: Increasing professionalism of management. Traditionally, managers have always "flown by the seat of their pants," learning (or not learning) how to deal with people on the job. This is now changing because of the recently increasing concern with professional education and training in management. Undergraduate and graduate degrees in management, along with management certification programs, continuing education courses, and workshops for practicing managers, are creating a more highly trained, professional group of work supervisors. Not only is there growing interest in formal training for managers, but the popularity of a variety of books on management techniques and development also indicates that managers are at least somewhat concerned with developing their management skills in order to grow professionally and to help gain a "competitive edge."

I/O psychologists are playing an important role in this trend toward increased management professionalism in two ways. First, they are helping to provide some of the new techniques for improving the management of people at work. For example, in a review and evaluation of theories of leadership, one author claims that many of the more significant advancements in leadership theory and training have been set forth by psychologists (Miner, 1984). Second, I/O psychologists are involved in creating and providing some of the training and development programs offered for practicing managers.

Third trend: An empirical approach to analyzing work behavior. The advent of the computer has not only changed the way people work but has also led to significant advances in our ability to gather, process, and interpret data on work behavior. More and more, organizations are concerned with keeping detailed records on work performance, rates of absenteeism and turnover, employee suggestions, and workers' views about various aspects of the work environment and the organization. Most importantly, this information is being used to help identify potential problems before they happen. Here I/O psychologists are of tremendous assistance in analyzing and interpreting work records and measuring the effectiveness of various work programs. Organizations are always trying new programs designed to improve productivity or working conditions, but these organizations often neglect to evaluate the success or failure of these programs, or they do not understand how to assess program effectiveness. I/O psychologists have played an important role in organizational program evaluation and in stressing the importance of measurement of program outcomes. Their ability to assess the effectiveness of these programs relies on their knowledge of social scientific research methods and statistical analysis.

A thorough grounding in research design and methods is critical if an I/O psychologist is to help organizations collect, analyze, and interpret the mountain of important data that can be gathered about their own operations and those of competitors. More and more, I/O psychologists are called upon to play such a role. We will study their research methods in the next chapter.

Fourth trend: An increasing concern with human resources.   The trend toward increasing concern with the management and maintenance of an organization's human resources that began with Mayo and the human relations movement continues to be important. Since Mayo's time, organizations have become more and more concerned about and responsive to the needs of the work force, because they have learned that employee job dissatisfaction can be linked to outcomes such as increased rates of absenteeism and turnover.

It is likely that in the very near future, work organizations will need to give even greater attention to human resources, for all indicators point to a dwindling supply of skilled workers that will reach bottom at the turn of the century. This means that organizations will have to compete ferociously to attract and keep the best workers. Management will be hit especially hard, as fewer and fewer individuals will possess the knowledge and skills to qualify for entry-level positions. This shrinking pool of skilled labor will mean that employers must place greater emphasis on such areas as employee recruitment and selection procedures and will have to offer more enticing benefit programs to attract and retain workers. In addition, continuing advancements in work technology and the ever-increasing body of knowledge needed by workers to perform their jobs mean that older workers will have to be retrained often to remain contributing members of the work force. All of this suggests the need for

Concerned about human resources, more and more companies are offering special programs such as aerobics to keep employees healthy and happy.

greater focus on personnel issues, such as recruiting, screening, and testing potential workers, and on employee training, development, and compensation programs, all of which are the specialties of personnel psychologists. Only those companies that are willing to spend money and devote attention to developing human resources will be able to survive in the competitive labor market of the future.

Implications of these trends for industrial/organizational psychology. All of these trends deal with areas that are particularly relevant for I/O psychology because each represents a particular sort of skill, knowledge, or expertise possessed by industrial/organizational psychologists. The cognitive explosion has influenced the study of decisionmaking at work and the systematic errors and biases in perceiving and evaluating employees; we will study these topics in more depth in Chapters 9 and 3, respectively. The increasing professionalism of management has led to a greater concern with appropriate training for managers and work group leaders; we will explore these topics in more detail in Chapters 5 and 10. The trend toward a more empirical analysis of work behavior has led to methodological advancements, an issue we will examine in Chapter 2. Finally, the greater concern placed on the recruitment, development, and retention of the human work force will be studied in depth in Chapters 4, 5, and 7. As the developments in I/O psychology unfold over time, we are likely to see greater and greater involvement of I/O psychologists in the work place. The future of the field is very bright indeed.

This book is set up to help you maximize your learning about industrial/organizational psychology. Key terms are set in boldface type when they are first discussed in the chapter, and definitions of these terms appear in the margins next to their first occurrence. You should look over the key terms before you begin reading a chapter and then alert yourself to them as you read. As you move along you can test yourself by using the glossary definitions. Of course, the key terms only deal with major points in each chapter, for there is much more to mastering the material. Not only should you be able to define important terms, but you should also know how they *apply* to work behavior. As you try to learn the important points made throughout the book, stop occasionally and ask yourself such questions as, "How does this apply to the working world that I know?" "Have I seen examples of this concept before?" "How can the material that I am learning be applied in my own working life?" "How can this new information help me to see work and work behavior in a new or different way?"

Each chapter contains three other features, which are set off from the text. The first, entitled Applying I/O Psychology, gives an example of how certain theories or concepts from I/O psychology have been applied to actual work settings. Often they deal with particular programs or intervention strategies that involve successful applications of certain principles derived from I/O psychology. The second, entitled Up Close, offers helpful bits of information, based on research in I/O psychology, that can further your understanding of your past, present, or future world of work. It usually either takes a "how to" approach to improving some area of work behavior or turns to research evidence to explain why some specific work behavior occurs. The third feature, On the Cutting Edge, presents either a recent topic that is being studied by I/O psychologists or an emerging issue that is likely to get a great deal of attention in the future.

Another learning aid, which appears at the beginning of each chapter and is called Inside Tips, is designed to help you understand how the various chapters (and the various areas of I/O psychology) fit together. This section may also offer some suggestions on how to study the information presented in the chapter and may help in relating that material to topics that were presented earlier or will be presented a little further along in the text.

At the end of each chapter is a brief summary of the central concepts. There also are Study Questions and Exercises designed to make you think a little bit more about the topics that were presented and to review what you have learned. The exercises offer opportunities to see how certain concepts may relate to the world of work with which you are familiar. Finally, there are some suggestions for additional reading, which usually include at least one general reference book related to the general theme of the chapter (useful as a starting point for research papers) and a more "popular" reading (for example, an introductory-level book, a magazine, or short journal article) on a particular topic.

SUMMARY

Industrial/organizational psychology is the branch of psychology that deals with the study of work behavior. I/O psychologists are concerned with both the science and practice of industrial/organizational psychology. The scientific goal is to increase our knowledge and understanding of work behavior, while the practical goal is to use that knowledge to improve the psychological well-being of workers. The roots of I/O psychology are found in the work of Frederick Taylor and Elton Mayo and in the contributions of psychologists involved in the testing and placement of recruits during the world wars. Taylor founded the school of *scientific management,* which held that work behavior could be studied by systematically breaking down a job into its components and recording the time needed to perform each. The application of such *time-and-motion studies* increased the efficiency of many manual labor jobs. Elton Mayo and his *human relations movement* emphasized the role that social factors play in determining worker behavior. Through a series of studies he demonstrated the importance of worker morale or satisfaction in determining performance. Mayo also discovered the *Hawthorne effect,* or the notion that subjects' behavior could be affected by the mere fact that they knew they were being observed and by the expectations they associated with being subjects in an experiment. The school of scientific management and the human relations movement, although both narrow and simplistic in their approaches to understanding human work behavior, serve as the foundation of I/O psychology.

During both World War I and World War II, psychologists became involved in the psychological testing of military recruits to determine work assignments. This first large scale testing program was the beginning of formalized personnel testing, which is still an important part of *personnel psychology.* Following World War II, there was tremendous growth and specialization in I/O psychology. The specialties of personnel psychology, engineering, or *human factors,* psychology and *organizational psychology* emerged.

The study of work behavior is a multidisciplinary, cooperative venture. Because I/O psychologists are not the only professionals who study work behavior, they combine their research with that of other social sciences.

Today, industrial/organizational psychology is a rapidly growing field characterized by four trends: the cognitive explosion in psychological theorizing and research, the increasing professionalism of management, a more empirical approach to analyzing work behavior, and a greater concern with human resources.

STUDY QUESTIONS AND EXERCISES

1. After reviewing the specialties and issues studied in I/O psychology, turn to Table 1.1 and try to determine whether each specialty area is a personnel issue, an organizational issue, a work environment issue, and so forth.

2. From what you have experienced or observed, try to recall specific examples of work behavior that support the scientific management philosophy of work behavior and others that support the human relations approach.

3. What are some of the ways in which psychology has contributed to our better understanding of work behavior?

4. Consider the four important trends in I/O psychology today. Are there any ways that these trends have affected your life as a worker or as a student?

SUGGESTED READINGS

Landy, F. J. (Ed.). (1986). *Readings in industrial and organizational psychology.* Chicago: Dorsey. *An edited collection of readings on I/O psychology, grouped by area of specialization. This includes classic articles as well as newer, "state-of-the-art" articles.*

Fretz, B. E., & Stang, D. J. (Eds.). (1980). *Preparing for graduate study: NOT for seniors only!* Washington, DC: American Psychological Association. *An important reference book for students interested in graduate study in I/O psychology or any area of psychology. It also contains helpful information for applying for jobs.*

Dunnette, M. D. (1976). *The handbook of industrial/organizational psychology.* Chicago: Rand McNally. *The classic "encyclopedia" for the field, soon to be published in its second edition. Everything you wanted to know about I/O psychology, and more.*

Society for Industrial and Organizational Psychology, Division 14 of the American Psychological Association. *The Industrial-Organizational Psychologist. The official newsletter of the I/O psychology division of the APA. Although it is actually Division 14's newsletter, it looks more like a journal and contains current information about the field, timely articles, and reviews, as well as job announcements.*

2

RESEARCH METHODS IN INDUSTRIAL/ORGANIZATIONAL PSYCHOLOGY

Measurement of Variables

> Observational Techniques

> Self-Report Techniques

> Measuring Dependent (Outcome) Variables: The Bottom Line

> Key Issues in Measurement: Reliability and Validity

Statistical Analyses of Research Data

> Descriptive Statistics

> Inferential Statistics

> Statistical Analysis of Experimental Method Data

> Statistical Analysis of Correlational Method Data

Interpreting and Using Research Results

Chapter Conclusion

Understanding the Basics of Research Methods and Design

This chapter presents a general overview of selected research methods topics and their use in I/O psychology. Although it is intended to be a general introduction to research methods, some of the material can be quite complicated, particularly if you have not had a course that has introduced you to these concepts. If this is the case, you might want to devote some extra time to this chapter and consider looking at an introductory research methods textbook such as the one in the Suggested Readings.

Many of the concepts discussed in this chapter will be used throughout the book when presenting and discussing theories, interpreting research results, and studying the effectiveness of various interventions used by I/O practitioners.

Because this chapter introduces a number of important terms, you should plan to spend some time studying their definitions and understanding how they are used. In summary, this is an important chapter that serves as a foundation for what is to come.

I magine that you want to find the answer to a work-related question such as what qualities make a person an effective manager. How would you go about answering this question? You might ask people you know, but what if you get conflicting answers? Your father might say that a good manager must have a thorough knowledge of the task and of work procedures. A friend might believe that the most important quality is skill in relating to people. Your boss might answer that the situation determines which type of manager works best. Three people, three answers. Who is correct?

You might then try another strategy: observing some good managers to see for yourself which qualities make someone an effective work group leader. But, how do you know who is a "good" manager? Moreover, how will you determine which characteristics make the good manager effective? The only sound procedure for answering the question of what makes a good manager is to use systematic, scientific research methods.

How would you approach the problem in a more systematic, scientific fashion? First, to determine the most important characteristics of a successful work group manager, you would need to define "success." Is a successful manager one who leads a productive work group, one who is well liked and respected by subordinates, or one who leads a work group that is both productive *and* satisfied? Once you have defined your criteria for managerial success, the next step is to figure out how you will measure such success. It is important that the measurement be accurate and precise to distinguish between truly successful and unsuccessful managers. Next, you must isolate the specific characteristics that are believed to be related to success as a work group manager. From your experience or reading you may have some informed ideas about the kinds of knowledge, abilities, or personality that make a successful manager, but you must test these ideas in some systematic fashion. This is the purpose of research methods in psychology. Research methodology is a set of procedures that allows us to investigate the hows and whys of human behavior and to predict when certain behavior will and will not occur.

In this chapter we will study the basic social scientific research methods used by I/O psychologists to study work behavior. We will learn why the research process is important for industrial/organizational psychology and examine the goals of social science research methods. We will review the step-by-step procedures used in social science research and conclude with a discussion of how research results are interpreted and applied to increase our understanding of actual work behavior.

SOCIAL SCIENTIFIC RESEARCH METHODS

objectivity
the unbiased approach
to observations and
interpretations of be-
havior

One of the prime purposes of the social scientific research methods used by I/O psychologists is to enable the researcher to step back from any personal feelings or biases in order to study a specific issue objectively. **Objectivity** is the overriding theme of scientific research methods in general and of social science research methods in particular. Research methodology is simply a system of guidelines and procedures designed to assist the researcher in obtaining a more accurate and unbiased analysis of the problem at hand. Similarly, statistical analysis is nothing more or less than procedures for testing the repeated objective observations a researcher has collected (as we shall see).

GOALS OF SOCIAL SCIENCE RESEARCH METHODS

Since I/O psychology is a science, it shares the same basic goals of any science: to describe, explain, and predict phenomena (Kaplan, 1964). Because I/O psychology is the science of behavior at work, its goals are to describe, explain, and predict work behavior. For example, an I/O psychologist might attempt to satisfy the first goal by describing the production levels of a company, the rates of employee absenteeism and turnover, and the number and type of interactions between supervisors and workers to arrive at a more accurate picture of the organization under study. The goal of explaining phenomena is achieved when the I/O psy-

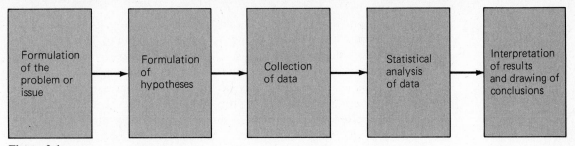

Figure 2.1
STEPS IN THE RESEARCH PROCESS

chologist attempts to discover why certain work behaviors occur. Finding out that a company's employee turnover rates are high because of employee dissatisfaction with the levels of pay and benefits would be one example. The goal of prediction would be addressed when a researcher attempts to use the scores from certain psychological tests to predict which employee would be the best candidate for a management position or uses a theory of motivation to predict how employees will respond to different types of incentive programs.

I/O psychology is also an applied science and therefore has the additional goal of attempting to control or alter behavior to obtain desired outcomes. Using the results of previous research, an I/O psychologist can attempt to alter some aspect of work behavior. For example, there is evidence of a link between employee participation in organizational decisionmaking and levels of job satisfaction. Knowing this, an I/O psychologist might implement a program of increased employee participation in company policy decisionmaking in an effort to improve levels of employee job satisfaction.

STEPS IN THE RESEARCH PROCESS

The process of conducting research typically follows a series of steps (see Figure 2.1). The first step is the formulation of a problem or issue for study. The second step is the generation of hypotheses. The third step is the actual collection of data, which is governed by the particular research design used. The fourth step is the application of statistical analyses to evaluate the data. This leads to the final step, which involves the interpretation of results and the drawing of conclusions based on the results.

Formulation of the problem or issue.   The first step in conducting research is to formulate the problem or issue to be studied. Sometimes, researchers develop an issue because of their interests in a particular area. For example, an I/O psychologist might be interested in the relationships between worker job satisfaction and employee loyalty to the organization, or between worker productivity and the length of time employees stay with a particular organization. Often the selection of a research problem is influenced by previous research. On the other hand, the practicing I/O psychologist-consultant may be provided with an issue because the client company has a particular problem that needs to be alleviated, such as an extraordinarily high level of employee absenteeism.

Generation of hypotheses.   The next step in the process involves the generation of **hypotheses** or statements concerning the supposed relationships between or among things or events, known as **variables.** Variables are simply those elements that a research investigation measures. In the examples of research issues given above, job satisfaction, worker productivity, employee loyalty, employment tenure, and absenteeism are all variables. The hypotheses will later be tested through the analysis of the collected, systematic observations of variables, better known as the collection and analysis of research data.

The role of theorizing in the research process. By testing hypotheses and collecting systematic observations of behavior, a researcher may develop a **theory** or **model,** which is the organization of beliefs that enable us to understand behavior better. In social science, models are representations of the complexity of factors that affect behavior. In I/O psychology, models are representations of the factors that affect *work* behavior.

We have all seen architects' cardboard and plaster models of buildings and the plastic models of aircraft that can be purchased in hobby shops. These are *concrete* models that represent the physical appearance of the actual building or aircraft. The models used in I/O psychology research are *abstract* representations of the factors influencing work behavior. Developing a theory and diagraming that theory are convenient ways to organize our thinking and understanding of complex behavioral processes.

Many people who do not have an understanding of scientific research methodology have misconceptions about theories. They believe that theories are the useless musings of scientists, but this is not true. Theories are important because they help us to represent the complex and often intangible forces that influence human behavior. By using theories as guides, I/O psychologists can develop strategies for altering behavior to improve the work world for all concerned.

Collection of data.   The next step in the research process involves the testing of hypotheses through data collection. A number of strategies can guide this stage. Typically, researchers collect data by following a research design. We shall discuss research designs shortly. However, an important concern in data collection is **sampling,** or selecting a represen-

---

hypotheses
statements about the supposed relationships between or among variables

variables
the elements measured in research investigations

theory/model
the organization of beliefs into a representation of the factors that affect behavior

sampling
the selection of a representative group from a larger population for study

tative group from a larger population for study. In most research, it is impossible to investigate *all* members of a particular population. For example, in preelection polls of preferences, all potential voters cannot be surveyed. Instead a sample is selected, and the results obtained from this subgroup are generalized to the larger population. The process of selection must follow strict guidelines to ensure that the sample is indeed representative of the larger population from which it is drawn. Two such sampling techniques are random sampling and stratified sampling.

With **random sampling** research participants are chosen from a specified population in such a way that each individual has an equal probability of being selected. For example, to choose a random sample of 20 workers from a large company of 200 workers, we would begin with a list of all workers and randomly select 20. If we wanted a random sampling of a particular employee's typical work behavior, we might study different five-minute time periods throughout a typical work day or week.

Stratified sampling begins with the designation of important variables that divide a population into subgroups, or strata. For example, we might want to consider male and female employees and management and nonmanagement personnel as different strata. We then randomly select a specified number of employees in such a way that our research sample mirrors the actual breakdown of these groups in the total population. For example, assume that 40 percent of our total worker population are female and 60 percent are male, while 25 percent are management and 75 percent are nonmanagement. We would want to choose a sample that represented these percentages. Forty percent of our selected sample should be female and 25 percent should be management personnel. We may also want to ensure that the percentages of male and female managers and nonmanagers in our sample are representative of the larger population.

Both these sampling techniques help ensure that the sample is representative of the population from which it is drawn. The random selection procedure also protects against any sorts of biases in the choice of subjects for study.

random sampling
the selection of research participants from a population so that each individual has an equal probability of being chosen

stratified sampling
the selection of research participants based on categories that represent important distinguishing characteristics of a population

Statistical analyses of research data. Once data are gathered, they are subjected to some form of statistical analyses for interpretation. Statistics are simply tools used by the researcher to help make sense out of the observations that have been collected. Some statistical analyses are very simple and are used to help describe and classify the data. Other statistical techniques are quite complex and help the researcher make detailed inferences. For example, some statistics allow the researcher to determine the causes of certain observed outcomes. We will briefly discuss certain statistical analysis techniques later in this chapter.

A researcher who studied management styles in a garment factory would need to be cautious in interpreting the data. Would the same kind of supervision produce the same results in a retail store? in a law firm?

Interpretation of research results. The final step in the research process is to interpret the results. Here the researcher draws conclusions about the meaning of the findings and their relevance to actual work behavior as well as their possible limitations. For example, imagine that a researcher decides to study the effect on work group productivity of two managerial styles: a *directive* style, whereby the manager closely supervises workers, telling them what they should be doing and how they should be doing it, and a *nondirective* style, whereby the manager allows the workers a great deal of freedom in deciding how they will get the work task done. The researcher conducts the study on groups of directive and nondirective front-line managers from several factories manufacturing jet aircraft parts. By collecting and analyzing data the researcher concludes that directive managers lead more productive groups. However, the researcher might want to set some limits for the use of the findings. The psychologist might caution that these results may only apply to managers who are supervising factory work groups and might not pertain to managers of service organizations, such as hospitals or restaurants, or to managers of salespersons. The researcher might also mention that although the directive style appears to be related to productivity, it is not known whether it is related to other important variables, such as employee satisfaction or work quality.

In the next few sections we will examine in depth some of the steps in the research process. First, we will look at the different types of theories or models used by I/O psychologists. Second, we will examine the various research designs used to govern the collection of research data. Third, we will discuss how research variables are measured. Next, we will explore some of the statistical analysis techniques used to interpret research data. Finally, we will discuss some of the problems and limitations of conducting research in I/O psychology and will consider the ways that research results and theories can be applied to the practice of I/O psychology. Research methods are obviously important to practicing I/O psychologists. See the Up Close feature to learn how a knowledge of research methods can help you in your working life.

TYPES OF RESEARCH MODELS

Although I/O psychologists use research models to guide their investigations, models of human work behavior are also the *products* of research. The researcher may use an existing theory or model to develop certain hypotheses about aspects of work behavior and then test those hypotheses through research. These results may then be used to refine the model or to create a new, "improved" model. Because theories are very

How to Use Research Methods in Your Own Life

While a thorough knowledge of social science research methods is critical for an I/O psychologist, how might this knowledge apply to the life of the typical working person?

Perhaps the greatest value of social science research methods is that the general principles of trying to take an objective (unbiased) perspective, using caution concerning cause-and-effect interpretations, and basing interpretations on repeated observations can be extremely useful as guidelines for decisionmaking. Rather than basing important work-related decisions on hunches, previous experience, or personal preferences, approach the problems as a scientist would. Step back from your own biases. Try to collect some objective data to clarify the problems, and base your decisions on the data.

For example, a student approached me about her part-time job, which had been a source of grief to her and to others who worked with her at the customer service desk of a large department store. The problem was that the manager never seemed to schedule hours in a way that satisfied all of the employees. Some seemed to often get the "better" hours, while others were complaining that they consistently had to work the "bad" shifts. The student believed that she had the perfect solution: The employees would all submit their ideal work schedules and possible alternatives, and the manager would arrange them in a way that was satisfactory to everybody.

I suggested that rather than assuming that she had reached a workable solution, she should go back and approach the problem from a research perspective. First, I recommended that she determine the magnitude and scope of the problem. She developed a brief survey that she gave to all of the department employees, asking about their satisfaction with the current work scheduling. The results indicated that the majority of the workers did indeed have difficulties with the scheduling. She next approached the manager to see whether she would be open to suggestions for change, which she was. Rather than relying on just her solution, the student then solicited suggestions for dealing with the difficulties from all the employees. When a new strategy was eventually selected (they did try a variation of her suggestion), it was implemented on a trial basis, with careful assessment of its effects on employee attitudes and on difficulties related to scheduling conflicts. By following this systematic method of relying on data, the workers were thus able to improve their situation.

A sound background in research methods can also assist in the evaluation of new work techniques or management strategies. Whenever you hear of some revolutionary strategy for increasing work performance or efficiency, do what a good social scientist would do. Go directly to the primary source. Find out what research evidence (if any) supports the technique, and read those reports with a critical eye. See if there are serious flaws in the ways that the technique was tested, flaws that might make you doubt whether it really works.

---

important to the science and practice of industrial/organizational psychology and because we will be studying many theories of work behavior throughout this textbook, it will be helpful to discuss the types of research models used by I/O psychologists.

Three types of models are used by I/O psychologists. The first is called a **descriptive model.** Descriptive models do exactly what it sounds

descriptive model
a theory that simply provides an objective account of behavior

Many companies have established day-care centers to attract good employees and reduce turnover. Are such programs successful? A predictive model of benefit programs might offer an answer.
Photo copyrighted by Ken Kerbs Photography, 1989.

like they do: They simply describe the behavior that occurs in a given set of circumstances. They may propose that certain variables are related to one another, but they do not suggest cause-and-effect relationships among variables nor interject any value judgments.

In some ways, a descriptive model represents the first level of theorizing about a phenomenon because it is the result of organizing the initial objective observations of a particular situation into some general representation of the variables. Cultural anthropology is a social science that produces almost exclusively descriptive models of behavior. Cultural anthropologists are unwilling to interject their own values into their interpretation of a foreign culture. The result is simply an objective measurement of specified variables. In a sense, an I/O psychologist going into a new setting may want to behave like a cultural anthropologist by simply observing behavior and organizing these observations into a descriptive model, without initially making any judgments or hypothesizing any cause-and-effect relationships among variables.

For example, a descriptive model might theorize that there is a relationship between employee turnover and company benefit programs, such as health and retirement plans, profit sharing, or paid vacations. This model may be the result of structured interviews with employees who stress the importance of such benefits and the reports of executives who believe that these programs are linked to turnover. However, this descriptive model simply outlines a hypothetical relationship without specifying any cause-and-effect relationship.

Another type of model is the **predictive model,** which attempts to discover the causes of certain behaviors. Predictive models specify cause-and-effect relationships and are most commonly associated with the testing of social scientific hypotheses. Much of the basic research of I/O psychologists and of psychologists in general is guided by predictive models of behavior. However, the development of sound predictive models requires the repeated examination of the relationships among variables under well-controlled circumstances. Most commonly, predictive models result from basic research conducted in controlled settings such as a laboratory. Difficulties can arise, however, when a predictive model, developed in a laboratory or under tightly controlled circumstances in an organization, is applied to an actual work setting.

A predictive model of the relationship between benefits and employee turnover might theorize that the better the benefit package (defined in terms of number of benefits and the dollar value of those benefits), the lower the rate of turnover. Of course, a researcher might try to refine this predictive model by testing different combinations of benefits, under controlled circumstances, to determine whether some are more important to workers than others.

A third type of theory is the **normative model** (also known as the **prescriptive model**). Normative models use the findings of previous research to suggest ways of obtaining certain results. Just as a physician might prescribe a certain drug or treatment to obtain certain positive health results, normative models in a sense prescribe organizational treatments or interventions that will lead to desired work behavior outcomes. It is the normative model that I/O practitioners use when they suggest certain changes in the organization or in organizational behavior to produce certain results. Prescriptive models typically evolve from predictive models. The knowledge gained through the repeated testing of predictive theories eventually leads to suggestions for changing behavior that reflect the results of the basic research. Normative models use predictive models to turn these theories into applications. For example, using the results of the research on the relationships between benefit packages and employee turnover, a normative model might suggest that a certain combination of benefits will reduce turnover rates. A formula might be developed to minimize the turnover with the lowest amount of money invested in particular types of benefits.

This general classification of research models will be useful later when studying the theories of work behavior proposed by research in I/O psychology. Some of these theories will be descriptive models, describing how certain organizational variables relate to one another. Other models will be predictive, showing how one variable affects another and why certain work behaviors occur. When studying treatments and interventions designed to change some aspect of work behavior or work organization functioning, we will be exposed to normative models that propose how to obtain desired outcomes.

RESEARCH DESIGNS

When testing theories and collecting data, researchers generally follow one of two types of research designs: the experimental method or the correlational method. Another way to conduct research is with an in-depth, descriptive investigation of a particular issue or organization. This is known as the case study method. Each of these research designs has its own distinct strengths and weaknesses.

THE EXPERIMENTAL METHOD

The **experimental method** is most commonly associated with research conducted in a laboratory, although it can also be applied in an actual work setting, in which case it is known as a field experiment. The experimental method is designed to give the researcher a very high degree of control over the research setting. In the experimental method, the researcher systematically manipulates levels of one variable, called the

experimental method
a research design characterized by a high degree of control over the research setting to allow for the determination of cause-and-effect relationships among variables

independent variable
in the experimental method, the variable that is manipulated by the researcher

dependent variable
in the experimental method, the variable that is acted upon by the independent variable; the outcome variable

treatment group
the group in an experimental investigation that is subjected to the change in the independent variable

control group
a comparison group in an experimental investigation that receives no treatment

extraneous variables
variables other than the independent variable that may influence the dependent variable

independent variable, and measures its effect on another variable, called the **dependent variable.** The dependent variable is the outcome variable, or the behavior that is of primary interest to the investigator. In the experimental method, other variables in the setting are presumed to be held constant. That is, no elements except the independent variable are allowed to vary. Therefore, any change in the dependent variable is presumed to have been caused by the independent variable. The primary advantage of the experimental method is thus that it allows us to determine cause-and-effect relationships among variables.

To determine whether the manipulation of an independent variable produces any significant change in a dependent variable, researchers following the experimental method usually compare the results of two groups of subjects. One, called the experimental group, or **treatment group,** is subjected to the change in the independent variable. The second, called the **control group,** receives no change. In other words, the second group is not subjected to the treatment. This comparison of treatment and control groups allows the researcher to determine the magnitude of the effect produced by the manipulation of the independent variable (the treatment). Measuring the dependent variable of the control groups allows the researcher to rule out any normal fluctuations that might have occurred naturally in the absence of the treatment. The comparison of treatment and control groups gives the researcher greater confidence that the treatment was (or was not) effective.

For example, imagine that a researcher wants to test the effectiveness of a new training program for sales skills. One group of salespersons are randomly assigned to the treatment group and receive the training. Other salespersons are randomly assigned to the control group and receive no training. A comparison of the two groups' subsequent sales records allows the researcher to determine the effectiveness of the program. In this case, the independent variable is whether the salespersons did or did not receive training; the dependent variable would be the amount of sales. Of course, it is possible to expand the experimental method to include a number of different treatment groups—for example, different types of sales training programs—and to compare the effectiveness of these various treatments with one another and with a control group.

Aside from the specified independent variables, other variables that may be affecting the dependent variable are termed **extraneous variables.** It is these variables that increase the difficulty of conducting research, because they can be anything apart from the independent variables that influences the dependent variable.

Consider, for example, the Hawthorne studies discussed in Chapter 1. In these studies of the influence of lighting and other work conditions on assembly line productivity (the independent variables), the attention paid to the workers by the researchers was an extraneous variable that affected productivity (the dependent variable).

The key to the success of the experimental method is to hold all extraneous variables constant, but this is much easier to do in a laboratory setting than in an actual work setting. Sometimes extraneous variables result from systematic differences in the individuals being studied. For example, if subjects are given the opportunity to volunteer to participate in a particular treatment group (with the nonvolunteers serving as a control group), there may be some motivational differences in the treatment volunteers that might act as a moderating or confounding variable, thus affecting the results. That is, subjects in the treatment group might be more energetic and "helpful" than those in the control group, and it would be impossible to tell whether any differences between the two groups resulted from the treatment or the inherent motivational differences. Many potential extraneous variables can be controlled through the **random assignment** of subjects to the experimental and control groups. This ensures that any motivational differences or other individual characteristics show up in equivalent proportions in both groups.

random assignment a method of assigning subjects to groups to control for the effects of extraneous variables

One of the major drawbacks of the experimental method is its artificiality. A researcher who controls the experimental setting may create a situation that is quite different from the actual work setting. There may thus be some concern about whether the results will apply or generalize to real settings. In field experiments, there is less concern about the generalizability of findings since the subjects are usually representative of those who will be affected by the results. However, any time that a researcher creates an experimental situation, he or she runs the risk of generating artificial conditions that would not exist in the usual work setting.

Two examples of the experimental method. In a recent study, Moriarty and Scheiner (1984) examined the effects of close-set type (type with less space between letters) on reading speed and noticed a trend toward using such type for printed advertisements. The researchers found a lack of previous research on this topic because close-set type is a fairly recent innovation. Their hypothesis was that close-set type would improve reading speed because the words are packed more closely together and thus more quickly read.

The study was conducted using a laboratory experimental method. Two hundred sixty college student volunteers were recruited and randomly assigned to groups. The independent variable was the typesetting. Two groups read the same printed message—a sales brochure for stereo speakers. One group received regular-set type, the other group received close-set type. The dependent variable, reading speed, was measured by having subjects mark the last word they had read at the end of 105 seconds. The results indicated a significant difference in speed, which supported the researchers' hypothesis that close-set type could be read faster than the regular-set type.

Our second example of the experimental method is a field experiment designed to test the effects of vicarious punishment (that is, watching another person being punished) on worker productivity (Schnake, 1986). The subjects were applicants to a university employment office. All were hired for jobs, paying $5.00 per hour, in which they recorded certain stock names and prices from the New York Stock Exchange. Since subjects thought that they were working at real jobs, this study qualifies as a *field experiment*.)

Subjects were randomly assigned to either a control group, a "threat" group, or a "punishment" group. The type of group was the independent variable. Subjects in the threat group watched as the work supervisor, who was actually the researcher's assistant, confronted one of the workers and reprimanded her for poor performance, threatening to cut her pay from $5.00 to $3.50 per hour. In the punishment group, subjects watched as the supervisor actually did punish the poor-performing worker by cutting her pay. In the control condition subjects did not witness any confrontation between the supervisor and the worker. The dependent variable was the work output, measured both before and after the confrontation. The results indicated that the group that observed the punishment produced significantly more than either the control or the threat groups. Moreover, the effects of the punishment continued for the entire week of the experiment.

Although both of these studies are fairly well designed and executed, and produced some useful knowledge, both have limitations. Both used college-age subjects, which raises the question of whether the results would generalize to older workers. As presented, the dependent variables in the studies are fairly limited. (Both studies were presented in simplified format. Additional variables were measured in each.) For example, the reading study found that close-set text was read faster, yet there may be some question as to differences in other potential dependent variables: Did reading comprehension differ between conditions? Were there differences in the number of reading errors? In the punishment study, it appeared that vicarious punishment stimulated workers to produce more, but were there any costs? Would workers learn to fear and mistrust their work supervisor, which could affect future productivity and job satisfaction? Did observing a co-worker being punished cause workers to plan to find jobs elsewhere before they too were punished?

Finally, we might be interested in exploring these findings further in an attempt to answer additional questions concerning the issues under study. For example, we might want to know why one type of text is easier to read or how vicarious punishment affected the workers. These studies answer certain questions, but the results of studies often lead us to pose additional questions. This is the research process. Results of one study may stimulate subsequent research in the same area. Research builds on the results of previous studies, adding and refining, to increase our knowledge of the behavior in question.

THE CORRELATIONAL METHOD

The second major method for data collection, the **correlational method,** looks at the relationships between or among variables as they occur naturally. When the correlational method is used, in contrast to the experimental method, there is no manipulation of variables by the experimenter. A researcher simply measures two variables and then examines their statistical relationship to each other. Because the correlational method does not involve the manipulation of independent variables, distinctions between independent and dependent variables are not nearly as important as with the experimental method. Since the correlational method does not require the rigid control over variables associated with the experimental method, it is easy to use in actual settings. A great deal of the research on work behavior thus uses the correlational method. The major drawback of this method is that we cannot determine cause-and-effect relationships. The most common problem is the tendency of people to try to make causal statements from correlations, which leads to many misconceptions and faulty interpretations of data. Many students of statistics quickly learn that correlation does not necessarily imply causality.

*correlational method
the research method that examines the relationship among or between variables as they occur naturally*

Considerable caution must be exercised when interpreting the results of correlational research. For example, suppose that a researcher finds a relationship between workers' attitudes about their employer and the amount of money they invest in a company stock program. Employees with very positive attitudes tend to use a greater portion of their income to purchase stock. It could be that their favorable attitudes cause them to demonstrate their support for (and faith in) the company by buying stock, but the cause-and-effect relationship could go the other way: Employees who purchase stock at bargain prices may develop more positive attitudes about the company because they now have an investment in it. On the other hand, a third variable (extraneous variable), such as the length of time employees have worked for the company, may actually be the cause of the observed correlation between employee attitudes and stock purchase. Employees with a long tenure may generally have more favorable attitudes about the company than newcomers (over time those with negative attitudes usually leave the organization). These employees are also older and may be able to invest a larger proportion of their incomes in stock options than younger workers, who may be raising families and purchasing first homes. Length of time on the job may thus influence both of the other two variables. The simple correlation between employee attitudes and stock purchases therefore does not lead us to any firm cause-and-effect conclusions.

Two examples of the correlational method. Two researchers studied the ability of certain tests and other assessment methods to predict future managerial success. The subjects were more than 1000 entry-level women managers, all of whom took part in a two-day testing program at an assessment center. The assessment techniques included an interview, some standardized tests, and several scored exercises. (We will discuss assessment centers and employee assessment techniques in Chapter 4.) At the end of the assessment, each woman was rated on a four-point scale of "middle-management potential," with end points ranging from *not acceptable* to *more than acceptable*. Seven years later, measures of the women's "management progress" were obtained. Results indicated "a sizable correlation between predictions made by the assessment staff and subsequent progress 7 years later" (Ritchie & Moses, 1983, p. 229).

In a more recent study, researchers examined the relationship between workers' "typical" job performance—the speed and accuracy of performing a job over an extended period—and "maximum" job performance—the speed and accuracy for brief periods in which workers are asked to perform at their best (Sackett, Zedeck, & Fogli, 1988). Subjects were supermarket checkers using computerized cash registers and price scanning systems. Two measures of performance were used: the number of items checked per minute and the number of checking errors. The results indicated that although the various performance measures were positively correlated, the relationship between typical job performance and maximum job performance was much lower than would be expected. Aside from illustrating the correlational method, the results of this study have important implications for how important variables such as job performance are measured. In other words, people's work behavior under optimum or testlike conditions may differ from their typical, day-to-day behavior.

As mentioned, each of the methods, experimental and correlational, has its own strengths and weaknesses. Sometimes researchers might use both methods in a large-scale investigation. Although the experimental method is most commonly associated with laboratory studies, and correlational research is most often associated with field research, either method can be used in either setting. The key to using the experimental method in a field investigation is to gain control over the environment by manipulating levels of the independent variable and holding extraneous variables constant. Because the correlational method looks at the relationships among variables as they naturally exist, a correlational design may often be easier to implement, particularly in actual work settings.

THE CASE STUDY METHOD

We have stated that there are difficulties in conducting controlled research in actual work settings. Often a researcher or scientist-practitioner will have the opportunity to conduct research in a business or industry but will find it impossible to follow either the experimental or the correlational method. The study may involve a one-time-only assessment of behavior or the application of an intervention to only a single group,

In a recent study using the correlational method, the "maximum" job performance of supermarket checkers showed little relationship to their "typical" performance.

department, or organization. Such research is known as a **case study.** Unfortunately, in some areas of I/O psychology, the bulk of what we know has been obtained through case studies.

The results of a single case study, even if it involves the application of some highly researched intervention strategy, do not allow us to draw any firm conclusions. A case study is really little more than a descriptive investigation. We are unable to test hypotheses or to determine cause-and-effect relationships from a case study because it is like conducting research with only one subject. What may have seemed to work in this one instance may not work in a second or third case. However, this does not mean that the case study method is not valuable, and in fact many exploratory studies follow this method. Case studies can provide rich, descriptive information about certain work behaviors and situations. In some topic areas, where it has been impossible to conduct controlled experimental studies, the results of case studies may be the only evidence that exists. Moreover, such results might inspire the development of hypotheses that will later be tested with experimental or correlational studies.

Two examples of the case study method. An I/O psychologist became interested in a certain organization that had the reputation of being a great place to work. He wanted to know what made this company "special." The company's chief executive officer (CEO) gave the psychologist carte blanche to study the organization from the inside. Through direct observation and interviews with employees, the psychologist developed a detailed account of the dynamics of the company. He discovered a number of policies and management practices that he believed were related to the company's effectiveness and positive reputation. For example, he found that the company encouraged a great deal of social interaction among employees at all levels. Senior managers, junior managers, and lower-level employees got together at company-sponsored picnics, played together on company sports teams, and socialized informally with one another. This led to a great deal of camaraderie, an ability to work well together, and commitment and loyalty to the organization. However, although the psychologist's study produced useful and detailed information about this company, he was unable to test any hypotheses nor generalize his results to other organizations.

In the late 1970s, when unemployment rates were quite high, there was considerable interest in the concept of job sharing, which involves two people, each working part-time, holding a single position in a company. The question arose, "Does job sharing lead to increases in employee productivity?" The rationale was that since each worker only has to work for four hours, fatigue will decrease and job performance will improve. In one case study, a job-sharing program for welfare caseworkers was found to increase productivity as expressed by the number

case study
a descriptive investigation involving a one-time assessment of behavior

In one example of the case study method, a psychologist found that company picnics, games, and other social activities increased employees' loyalty to the organization.

of cases handled by job-sharing workers. In another case study, of job-sharing employees in an assembly plant, there was little improvement in worker productivity. Because these studies represent two isolated examples, we are unable to draw any firm conclusions. The differences in the results could be due to any number of factors, such as the type of work organization (service versus manufacturing) or the way jobs were shared, rather than to the job-sharing program. The case study method, with its lack of control over variables and its examination of only one subject at a time, does not yield the more conclusive information provided in a well-controlled research design.

MEASUREMENT OF VARIABLES

operationalize
the process of defining a variable so that it can be measured or manipulated

One of the more difficult aspects of research is the measurement of variables. A variable must be **operationalized,** that is, brought down from the abstract level to a more concrete level and clearly defined so that it can be measured or manipulated. In the first example of the correlational method outlined above, the variable "middle-management potential" was operationalized as a rating on a four-point scale. In the correlational study of supermarket checkers, performance speed and accuracy were operationalized as the number of items checked per minute and the number of errors made per shift, respectively. Together both variables were considered an operational definition of the more general variable of job performance.

During the process of operationalizing a variable, a particular technique for measuring the variable is usually selected. We will examine two of the variety of techniques used to measure variables in I/O psychology: observational techniques and self-report techniques.

OBSERVATIONAL TECHNIQUES

One procedure for measuring research variables is through direct, systematic observation. This involves the researchers themselves recording certain behaviors that they have defined as the operationalized variables. For example, a researcher might consider the number of items manufactured a measure of productivity or look for certain defined supervisory behaviors, such as demonstrating work techniques to subordinates, giving direct orders, and setting specific work quotas, to assess whether a manager has a task-oriented supervisory style.

The measurement of variables through direct observation can be either obtrusive or unobtrusive. With **obtrusive observation** the researcher is visible to the persons being observed. The primary disadvantage is that the subjects may behave differently because they know that they are a part of a research investigation. This is what happened in the original Hawthorne experiments. Researchers engaging in obtrusive observation must always consider how their presence will affect subjects' behavior and thus the results of the study.

Unobtrusive observation also involves direct observation of behavior, but in this case subjects are unaware of the researcher's presence and do not know that their behavior is being studied. The primary advantage is that the researcher is fairly confident that the recorded behavior is typical. The major drawback to unobtrusive observation lies in ethical concerns about protecting the privacy of the subjects. In one type of unobtrusive observational technique, known as **participant observation,** the researcher poses as a member of a particular group to get the "inside view." Cialdini (1984) conducted research on sales influence techniques by posing as an automobile sales trainee, an applicant for a position as a door-to-door vacuum cleaner salesman, and a novice real estate agent. In these various sales training programs, he learned about the techniques used to hook potential customers and make a sale. For example, he learned that some real estate agents use "set-up" properties—run-down houses that are shown to customers initially to make the later properties appear more desirable. The insights he gained about professional "tricks of the trade" would have been inaccessible to an outsider.

Measurement in research often involves close and systematic observation.

obtrusive observation *research observation in which the presence of the observer is known to the participants*

unobtrusive observation *research observation in which the presence of the observer is not known to the participants*

participant observation *unobtrusive observation research in which the observer becomes a member of the organization being studied*

SELF-REPORT TECHNIQUES

self-report techniques
methods of assessment
relying on the reports
of research subjects
concerning their own
behavior

surveys
a common self-report
measurement technique
in which subjects are
asked to report on their
attitudes, beliefs, or
behaviors

Direct observational measurement techniques are often costly and difficult to obtain, requiring the assistance of trained observers. More commonly, researchers measure variables through **self-report techniques,** which include a variety of methods for assessing behavior from the responses of the research subjects themselves. One of the most popular self-report techniques is **surveys.** Surveys can be used to measure any number of aspects of the work situation, including workers' attitudes about their jobs, their perceptions of the amount and quality of the work they perform, and the specific problems they encounter on the job. Most typically, surveys take the form of pencil-and-paper measures that the subjects can complete either in a group session or on their own time. However, surveys can also involve face-to-face or telephone interviews.

The most obvious problem with surveys is the possibility of distortion or bias of responses (either intentional or unintentional). If the survey is not conducted in a way that protects respondents' anonymity, particularly when it deals with sensitive issues or problems, workers may feel that their answers can be traced back to them and possibly result in retribution by management. In these cases, workers may temper their responses and give "socially desirable" answers to survey questions.

Self-report techniques are also used in I/O psychology research to assess workers' personalities, occupational interests, and management or supervisory style; to obtain evaluations of job candidates; or to elicit supervisors' ratings of worker performance. Compared to observational techniques, self-reports allow the researcher to collect massive amounts of data relatively inexpensively. However, developing sound self-report tools and interpreting the results are not easy tasks and require thorough knowledge of measurement theory as well as research methods and statistics. Many I/O psychologist researchers and practitioners use self-report measures extensively in their work.

MEASURING DEPENDENT (OUTCOME) VARIABLES: THE BOTTOM LINE

There are a tremendous number of independent variables. I/O psychologists have examined how characteristics of workers such as personality, attitudes, and education affect work behavior. As we saw in Chapter 1, factors in the physical and social work environment can be manipulated to see how they affect worker performance and satisfaction. Other variables, such as the amount and frequency of compensation, styles of supervision, work schedules, and incentive programs, also serve as independent variables in research on work behavior.

In contrast, most research considers only a handful of dependent variables: productivity, work quality, employee turnover, employee absenteeism, and employee satisfaction. These key dependent, or outcome, variables represent the "bottom line" in work organizations. Most commonly, changes in these factors result in financial losses or gains for businesses.

Of these important dependent variables, the first two, work productivity and quality, are usually theoretically linked, because a company's goals should be to produce as much as possible while ensuring that the production is of high quality. However, although these variables are linked, they are typically considered separately by many businesses. In fact, in many manufacturing plants the departments responsible for production volume and for quality control are often separate.

On the surface it may seem that the measurement of a variable such as productivity is relatively simple and accurate. This may be true if the task involves production of concrete objects, such as the number of hamburgers sold or the number of books printed. However, for companies that deal with more abstract products, such as services, information, or ideas, the measurement of productivity is not as easy nor as precise.

The accurate measurement of quality is often more difficult. For example, in a department store productivity may be assessed by the dollar amount of sales, which is a fairly reasonable and simple assessment. However, the quality of the salespersons' performance might involve factors such as the friendliness, courteousness, and promptness of their service, which are usually more difficult to measure. Similarly, a writer's productivity might be defined as the number of books or articles the author produced (a straightforward assessment), while the quality of the writing may be more difficult to measure. Thus quality may sometimes be difficult to define operationally.

Although they are distinct variables, employee absenteeism, turnover, and satisfaction are also theoretically tied to one another (Vroom, 1964). In Chapter 1 we saw that Mayo believed that there was a strong relationship between employee satisfaction and productivity. However, this is not always the case; the happy worker is not necessarily the productive worker. There may, however, be a relationship between employee satisfaction and a tendency to show up for work and stay with the job. Specifically, it is thought that higher satisfaction leads to lower absenteeism and turnover. However, this notion about the interrelatedness of job satisfaction, absenteeism, and turnover has recently come under question, primarily because of problems in the accurate measurement of absenteeism and turnover (see Hollenbeck & Williams, 1986; Porter & Steers, 1973). Some forms of absenteeism and turnover are inevitable due to circumstances beyond the employees' control, such as severe illness or a move dictated by a spouse's job transfer. These types of absenteeism and turnover are not likely to be affected by job satisfaction, whereas voluntary absenteeism—playing "hooky" from work—may be caused by low levels of job satisfaction. We will discuss this issue in detail in Chapter 7.

In any case, the interrelationships between job satisfaction, absenteeism, and turnover are important. If negative correlations do indeed exist between employee satisfaction and rates of absenteeism and turnover (they are negative correlations because *higher* satisfaction would be correlated with *lower* absenteeism and turnover), it is important that companies strive to keep workers satisfied. Happy workers may be less likely to be voluntarily absent from their jobs or look for work elsewhere. Reduced rates of absenteeism and turnover can translate into tremendous savings for the company.

Turnover and absenteeism can be fairly easily measured, but the assessment of worker satisfaction is much less precise, since attitudes about a wide range of elements in the work environment must be considered. We will deal more deeply with this point in Chapter 7.

Although these key variables are most commonly considered dependent variables, this does not preclude the possibility that any one could be used as an independent variable. For example, we might classify workers into those who are "good attenders" with very few absences and "poor attenders" with regular absences. We could then see whether there are differences in the good and poor attenders' performance levels or in their attitudes about their jobs. However, certain variables, such as productivity, absenteeism, and turnover, represent the bottom line variables that translate into profits or losses for the company, while job satisfaction tends to be the bottom line variable for the employee. These bottom line variables are most often considered dependent variables.

KEY ISSUES IN MEASUREMENT: RELIABILITY AND VALIDITY

reliability
a concept dealing with the stability of a measurement device over time

Two critical measurement concepts are the reliability and validity of measured variables. **Reliability** refers to the stability of the measurement over time. That is, if we measure a particular variable at two points in time and assume that the variable has not changed during the interval, we should get the same readings of the variable at both time one and time two. Many of the measurement instruments used in I/O psychology research and in social science research in general have less-than-perfect reliability because of the very complex nature of the variables they measure. For example, a researcher might construct a survey to measure consumer attitudes concerning a particular make of automobile. The instrument would contain items such as the following:

Compared to similarly priced cars, how would you rate the overall appeal of the new Chevrolet Thunderbolt?

0 1 2 3 4 5 6 7 8 9

not at all appealing   very appealing

Imagine that one subject circles an 8 on this item. However, a week later he is surveyed again, and, although his attitudes have not changed, this time he responds with a 7. The small fluctuation is most likely due to some unreliability in the measurement scale, not to any actual change in attitude.

Validity deals with the accuracy of measurement. A valid assessment tool is one that measures what it is supposed to measure. Several years ago there was a newspaper article about a woman who claimed that she could assess peoples' personalities from the color of jelly bean they would select from a jar. Red meant that the person was fiery and temperamental, blue meant that the person was depressed, and so on. Of course it is unlikely that this is a valid measure of personality. However, we could test its validity by examining its relationship (correlation) with another measure, such as a standardized personality inventory, that has proven validity.

validity
a concept referring to the accuracy of a measurement instrument

The concepts of validity and reliability refer to the measurement of not only variables but also the research studies themselves. Can the results be obtained again by using the same types of subjects and the same research procedures? Are the interpretations accurate? Have all potential extraneous variables that might alter the conclusions been controlled for or taken into account? These concepts, which we will examine more fully in Chapter 4, must be kept firmly in mind by the researcher. Problems with the validity of research investigations and difficulties in the design and execution of studies can lead to faulty interpretations of research results and of conclusions drawn from the research (see Applying I/O Psychology).

STATISTICAL ANALYSES OF RESEARCH DATA

While a comprehensive treatment of research methods and statistics is beyond the scope of this text, it is important to emphasize that the science and practice of industrial/organizational psychology require a thorough knowledge of methods and statistics and some experience using them. More importantly for our present concerns, it is impossible to gain a true understanding of the methods used by I/O psychologists without some discussion of statistical analyses of research data.

As mentioned earlier in this chapter, research methods are merely procedures or tools used by I/O psychologists to study work behavior. Statistics, which are arithmetical procedures designed to help summarize and interpret data, are also important research tools. We will discuss two types of statistics: *descriptive statistics,* used to summarize recorded observations of behavior, and *inferential statistics,* used to test hypotheses about research data.

The Hawthorne Effect: A Case Study in Flawed Research Methods

The initial Hawthorne studies clearly followed the experimental method because Mayo and his colleagues manipulated levels of lighting and the duration of work breaks. Furthermore, since the studies were conducted in the actual work setting, they also were field experiments. The result, particularly the discovery of the Hawthorne effect, is a classic in the field of I/O psychology. In fact, this effect is studied in other areas of psychology and social science.

While the original Hawthorne studies were set up in the experimental method, the discovery of the Hawthorne effect actually resulted from a breakdown in research procedures. The changes observed in the dependent variable (productivity) were caused not by the independent variable (lighting) but by an extraneous variable that was not controlled by the researchers: the attention the workers received from the observers. While Mayo and his colleagues eventually became aware of this unanticipated variable, which led to the discovery of the Hawthorne effect, there were other methodological problems in the design and implementation of the studies.

Recently researchers have reexamined the data from the original Hawthorne experiments, combing through the records and diaries kept by Mayo and his colleagues. These new investigators found a series of very serious methodological problems that cast doubts on the original conclusions. These reanalyses indicate difficulties with the number of subjects (one of the studies used only five subjects), the experimenters' "contamination" of the subject population (two of the five subjects were replaced because they were not working hard enough), the lack of control or comparison groups, and the absence of appropriate statistical analyses of data (Franke & Kaul, 1978; Parsons, 1974). The I/O psychologist Parsons discovered not only serious flaws in the published reports of the Hawthorne experiments but also a number of extraneous variables that were not considered, further confounding the conclusions. For example:

[U]nlike the big open floor of the relay-assembly department, the test room was separate, smaller, and quieter. . . and the supervisors were friendly, tolerant observers, not the usual authoritarian foremen. . . . Back in their relay-assembly department, the women had been paid a fixed hourly wage plus a collective piecework rate based on the department's total output. In the test room, the collective piecework rate was based on the output of only the five workers, so that individual performance had a much more significant impact on weekly pay. The monetary reward for increased individual effort thus became much more evident and perhaps more effective than in the department setting. (Rice, 1982, pp. 70–74)

All in all, there are significant flaws in the research design and execution of the Hawthorne experiments. Of course this does not mean that a Hawthorne effect does not exist, since we do know that the presence of others can affect behavior. What it does mean is that the original Hawthorne studies were too methodologically muddled to enable researchers to draw any firm conclusions. On one hand, we must forgive Mayo and his associates on some of these issues because their studies were conducted before many advancements in research methodology and design were made. On the other hand, some of the errors in data collection were obvious. In many ways, the Hawthorne studies illustrate some of the difficulties of conducting research and the dangers of drawing conclusions based on flawed research methods.

The moral is that conducting research is a complex but important endeavor. Researchers and users of research must display caution in both the application of methods and the interpretation of results to avoid errors and misinformation.

Table 2.1   PERFORMANCE RATING SCORES OF 60 EMPLOYEES

5	6	6	6	7	4
4	1	7	4	8	6
6	5	8	3	5	9
7	4	5	5	7	5
8	7	4	5	3	4
4	6	6	4	5	5
5	4	2	2	6	3
3	5	9	7	8	6
5	3	5	3	2	4
3	6	2	5	6	5

DESCRIPTIVE STATISTICS

The simplest way to represent research data is to use **descriptive statistics,** which describe data to give the researcher a general idea of the results. Suppose we have collected data on the job performance ratings of sixty employees. The rating scale ranges from 1 to 9, with 9 representing outstanding performance. As you can see in Table 2.1, it is difficult to make sense out of the raw data. A **frequency distribution,** which is a descriptive statistical technique that presents data in a useful format, arranges the performance scores by category so that we can see at a glance how many employees received each numerical rating. The frequency distribution in Figure 2.2 is in the form of a bar graph or histogram.

descriptive statistics
arithmetical formulas for summarizing and describing research data

frequency distribution
a descriptive statistical technique that arranges scores by categories

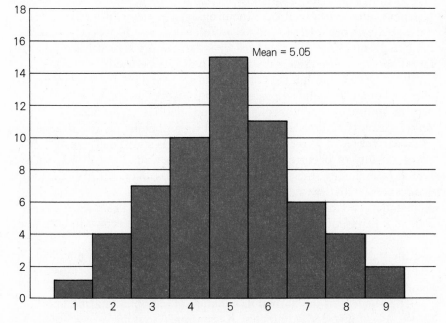

Figure 2.2
FREQUENCY DISTRIBUTION (HISTOGRAM) OF EMPLOYEE PERFORMANCE RATING SCORES

Other important descriptive statistics include measures of central tendency and variability. Measures of central tendency present the center point of a distribution of scores. This is useful in summarizing the distribution in terms of the middle or average score. The most common measure of central tendency is the **mean,** or average, which is calculated by adding all of the scores and dividing by the number of scores. In our performance data, the sum of the scores is 303, and the number of scores is 60. Therefore, the mean of our frequency distribution is 5.05.

Measures of variability show how scores are dispersed in a frequency distribution. If scores are widely dispersed across a large number of categories, variability will be high. If scores are closely clustered in a few categories, variability will be low. The most commonly used measure of distribution variability is the **standard deviation.** In a frequency distribution, the standard deviation indicates how closely the scores spread out around the mean. The more widely dispersed the scores, the greater the standard deviation. The more closely bunched the scores, the smaller the standard deviation. Both the mean and the standard deviation are important to more sophisticated inferential statistics.

INFERENTIAL STATISTICS

While descriptive statistics are helpful in representing and organizing data, **inferential statistics** are used to test hypotheses. For example, assume that we wanted to test the hypothesis that a certain safety program effectively reduced rates of industrial accidents. One group of workers is subjected to the safety program, while another (the control group) is not. Accident rates before and after the program are then measured. Inferential statistics would tell us whether differences in accident rates between the two groups were meaningful. Depending on the research design, different sorts of inferential statistics will typically be used.

When inferential statistics are used to analyze data, we are concerned about whether a result is meaningful, or statistically significant. The concept of **statistical significance** is based on theories of probability. A research result is statistically significant if its probability of occurrence by chance is very low. Typically, a research result is statistically significant if its probability of occurrence by chance is less than 5 out of 100 (in research terminology, the probability, or p, is less than .05; $p < .05$). For example, say that we find that a group of telephone salespersons who have undergone training in sales techniques have average (mean) sales of 250 units per month, while salespersons who did not receive the training have mean sales of 242 units. Based on the difference in the two means and the variability (standard deviations) of the two groups, a statistical test will determine whether the difference in the two groups is statistically significant.

The concept of the **normal distribution** of variables is also important for the use of inferential statistics. It is assumed that many psychological

mean
a measure of central tendency; also known as the average

standard deviation
a measure of variability of scores in a frequency distribution

inferential statistics
statistical techniques used for analyzing data to test hypotheses

statistical significance
the probability of a particular result occurring by chance, used to determine the meaning of research outcomes

normal distribution
a distribution of scores along a continuum with known properties

variables, especially human characteristics such as intelligence, motivation, or personality constructs, are normally distributed. That is, scores on these variables in the general population are presumed to vary along a continuum, with the greatest proportion clustering around the midpoint and proportions dropping off toward the end points of the continuum. A normal distribution of scores is symbolized visually by the **bell-shaped curve.** The bell-shaped curve, or normal distribution, is a representative distribution of known mathematical properties that can be used as a standard for statistical analysis. The mathematical properties of the normal distribution are represented in Figure 2.3. The exact midpoint score, or median, of the normal distribution is the same as its mean. In a normal distribution, 50 percent of the scores lie above the midpoint and 50 percent below. The normal distribution is also divided in terms of standard deviations from the midpoint. In a normal distribution, approximately 68 percent of all scores lie within one standard deviation above or below the midpoint or mean. Approximately 95 percent of all scores in a normal distribution lie within two standard deviations above or below the midpoint.

bell-shaped curve
a graphic representation of a normal distribution

STATISTICAL ANALYSIS OF EXPERIMENTAL METHOD DATA

As mentioned, depending on the research design, different inferential statistics may be used to analyze data. Typically, one set of statistical techniques is used to test hypotheses from data collected in experimental methods, and another set is used to analyze data from correlational research.

The simplest type of experimental design would have a treatment group, a control group, and a single dependent variable. Whether a group receives the treatment represents levels of the independent variable. The

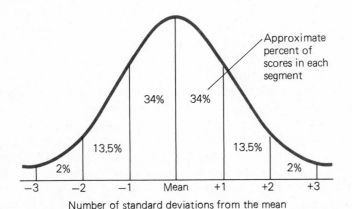

Approximate percent of scores in each segment

Figure 2.3
A NORMAL DISTRIBUTION

t-test
a statistical test for ex-
amining the difference
between the means of
two groups

most common statistical technique for this type of study is the **t-test,** which examines the difference between the means on the dependent variables for the two groups, taking into account the variability of scores in each group. In the example of trained and untrained salespersons used above, a t-test would determine whether the difference in the two means (250 units versus 242 units) is statistically significant, that is, *not* due to chance fluctuations. If the difference is significant, the researcher may conclude that the training program did have a positive effect on sales.

When an experimental design has three or more groups, a statistical method called *analysis of variance,* or ANOVA, is often used. Analysis of variance looks at differences among more than two groups on a single dependent variable. An even more sophisticated technique, *multivariate analysis of variance* (MANOVA), examines data from multiple groups with multiple dependent variables. Understanding how these complex statistical techniques work and how they are calculated is not important for our discussion. These terms are presented only to familiarize you with some of the statistics that you might encounter in research reports in I/O psychology or in other types of social science research.

STATISTICAL ANALYSIS OF CORRELATIONAL METHOD DATA

When a research design is correlational, a different set of statistical techniques is usually used to test hypotheses about presumed relationships among variables. As mentioned, the distinction between independent and dependent variables in a correlational design is not as important as in the experimental method. In a correlational design the independent variable is usually called the predictor, and the dependent variable is often referred to as the criterion. In a simple correlational design with two variables, the usual statistical analysis technique is the **correlation coefficient** which measures the strength of the relationship between the predictor and the criterion. The correlation coefficient ranges from $+1.00$ to -1.00. The closer the coefficient is to either $+1.00$ or -1.00, the stronger the relationship between the two variables. The closer the correlation coefficient is to zero, the weaker the relationship. A positive correlation coefficient means that there is a positive relationship between the two variables, where an increase in one variable is associated with an increase in the other variable. Assume that a researcher studying the relationship between commuting distance of workers and work tardiness obtains a positive correlation coefficient of .75. The greater the commuting distance of employees, the greater the likelihood that they will be late for work. A negative correlation coefficient indicates a negative relationship: An increase in one variable is associated with a decrease in the other. For example, a researcher studying workers who cut out patterns in a clothing factory hypothesizes that there is a relationship between workers' job experience and the amount of waste produced. Statistical analysis indi-

correlation coefficient
the statistical tech-
nique used to deter-
mine the strength of
the relationship be-
tween two variables

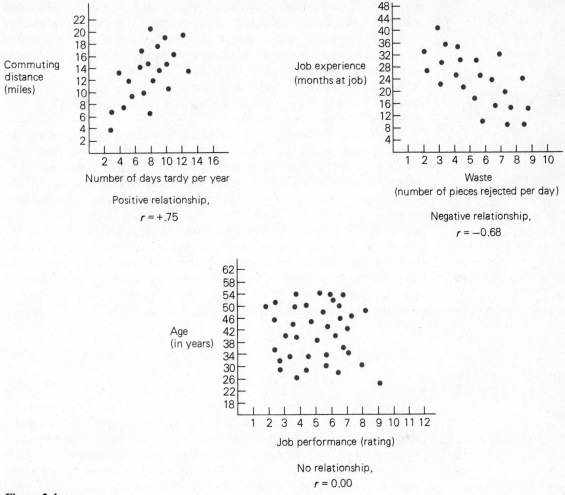

Figure 2.4
PLOTS OF SCORES FOR POSITIVE, NEGATIVE, AND ZERO CORRELATIONS

cates a negative correlation coefficient of − .68: The more experience workers have, the less waste they produce. A correlation coefficient of zero indicates that there is no relationship between the two variables. For example, a researcher measuring the relationship between factory workers' age and their job performance finds a correlation coefficient of approximately .00, which shows that there is no relationship between age and performance. (These relationships are presented graphically in Figure 2.4.)

While the simple correlation coefficient is used to examine the relationship between two variables in a correlational study, the *multiple regression* technique allows a researcher to assess the relationship between a single criterion and multiple predictors. Multiple regression would allow

A study of this insurance office would have external validity if the results could be generalized to other work settings.

a researcher to examine how well several variables, in combination, predict levels of an outcome variable. For example, a personnel researcher might be interested in how educational level, years of experience, and scores on an aptitude test predict the job performance of new employees. With multiple regression, the researcher could analyze the separate and combined predictive strength of the three variables in predicting performance. Again, a detailed understanding of multiple regression is far beyond the scope of this text.

Another statistical method that is often used in correlational designs is *factor analysis,* which shows how variables cluster to form meaningful "factors." Factor analysis is useful when a researcher has measured many variables and wants to examine the underlying structure of the variables or combine related variables to reduce their number for later analysis. For example, using this technique, a researcher measuring workers' satisfaction with their supervisors, salary, benefits, and working conditions finds that two of these variables, satisfaction with salary and benefits, cluster to form a single factor that the researcher calls "satisfaction with compensation." The other two variables, supervisors and working conditions, form a single factor that the researcher labels "satisfaction with the work environment."

INTERPRETING AND USING RESEARCH RESULTS

While statistics can be very powerful tools in the I/O researcher's study and organization of data, it is still the researcher's task to make sense out of the data. To interpret data accurately, an I/O psychologist must be very knowledgeable of methods of data collection and statistical analysis, and be aware of potential research problems and the strengths and limitations of the methods that have been used.

When interpreting results, it is important to consider the limitations of the findings. Of particular concern is the **external validity** of the research results, that is, whether the results obtained will generalize to other work settings. In other words, how well do the findings apply to other workers, jobs, and/or environments? For example, say that the results of research on patterns of interactions in workers in an insurance claims office indicate a significant positive relationship between the amount of supervisor-subordinate contact and worker productivity: The more supervisors and subordinates interact, the more work that gets done. Can these results be generalized to other settings? Maybe, maybe not. These findings might be particular to these workers, related to their specific characteristics. The subjects may be the kind of workers who need a lot of supervision to keep them on task. Other groups of workers might view interactions with supervisors negatively, and the resulting dissatisfaction might lead to a restriction of output. Alternatively, the results might be specific to the

external validity
the degree to which research results will generalize to other settings

Meta-Analysis: A Statistical Technique for Combining the Results of Studies

One problem in reviewing research on a particular topic or a certain hypothesis is that different studies yield different results. One study may find strong support for the hypothesis, another may find weak support, and a third study may find contradictory evidence. How can any conclusions be drawn from the varying and often conflicting results of several independent research investigations?

The answer is found in a statistical technique called **meta-analysis,** which allows the results of a number of studies to be combined and analyzed together to draw a summary conclusion (Wolf, 1986). Depending on the types of studies and their research designs, meta-analysis will use either certain descriptive statistics such as means and standard deviations or reported correlation coefficients to compare and combine the data. Typically, meta-analytic techniques yield a summary statistic. For

example, in meta-analyses of correlational studies, the summary statistic is expressed as a correlation coefficient.

Meta-analytic studies have become quite popular, particularly in I/O psychology. These analyses have addressed such issues as the effectiveness of employment tests and other measures in predicting job performance (Hunter & Hunter, 1984), the relationship between job satisfaction and turnover (Carsten & Spector, 1987), and the validity of certain leadership theories (Strube & Garcia, 1981). In one recent meta-analysis, the results of seventy studies were combined to examine the impact of managerial training programs on manager learning and job performance, and it was found that, in general, such programs were indeed effective (Burke & Day, 1986).

type of tasks in which workers are engaged. Because insurance claims often need to be approved by supervisors, a subordinate must interact with the supervisor to complete the job. Therefore, increased supervisor-subordinate contact may be a sign of increased efficiency. For assembly line workers, however, supervisor-subordinate interactions might be a distraction that reduces productivity, or they might have little effect on output. To know whether research results will generalize to a variety of work settings, results must be replicated with different groups of workers in different work settings (see On the Cutting Edge). Eventually, further research may discover the moderating variables that determine when and where supervisor-subordinate contacts have beneficial effects on work productivity.

External validity is especially important for research conducted under tightly controlled circumstances, such as a laboratory investigation, where the conditions of the research setting may not be very similar to actual work conditions. One solution is to combine the strength of experimental research—well-controlled conditions—with the advantage of real world conditions by conducting experimental research in actual work organizations.

So far, we have been discussing only one objective of research in I/O psychology: the scientific objective of conducting research to understand work behavior more completely. As you recall, in Chapter 1 we mentioned that there are two goals in industrial/organizational psychology:

meta-analysis
a technique that allows results from several research investigations to be combined and summarized

the scientific and the practical, whereby new knowledge is applied toward improving work conditions and outcomes. While some research in I/O psychology is conducted merely to increase the base of knowledge about work behavior, and some I/O practitioners (and practicing managers) use strategies to affect work behavior that are based on hunches or intuition rather than on sound research evidence, the two facets of I/O psychology should work together. To be effective, the applications used by I/O practitioners to improve work behavior must be built on a strong foundation of research. Through sound research and the testing of hypotheses and theories, better applications develop. Moreover, the effectiveness of applications can be demonstrated conclusively only through additional evaluation and research.

CHAPTER 2 CONCLUSION

SUMMARY

The goals of I/O psychology are to describe, explain, predict and then alter work behavior. Research methods are important tools for I/O psychologists because they provide a systematic means for investigating and changing work behavior. *Objectivity* is the overriding theme of the social scientific method used to study work behavior.

The first step in conducting research involves the formulation of the problem or issue. The second step is the generation of hypotheses, which are simply statements about the supposed relationships among variables. Through the systematic collection of observations of behavior, a researcher may develop a set of hypotheses into a more general *theory,* or *model,* which are ways of representing the complex relationships among a number of variables related to actual work behavior. The third step in conducting research is the actual collection of data. This step includes sampling, the methods by which subjects are selected for study. The final steps in the process are the statistical analyses of research data and the interpretation of research results.

Three types of theoretical models guide the research investigations of I/O psychologists. *Descriptive models* describe behavior under study without interjecting value judgments or predictions of cause-and-effect relationships. *Predictive models* attempt to specify cause-and-effect relationships among variables. *Normative models* evolve from predictive models and give prescriptions for obtaining desired behavioral outcomes.

Two basic types of research designs are used by I/O psychologists. In the *experimental method* the researcher manipulates one variable, labeled the *independent variable,* and measures its effect on the *dependent variable*. In an experimental design any change in the dependent variable is presumed to be caused by the manipulation of the independent variable. Typically, the experimental method involves the use of a *treatment group* and a *control group*. The treatment group is subjected to the manipulation of the independent variable, while the control group serves as a comparison. Variables that are not of principal concern to the researchers but may affect the results of the research are termed *extraneous variables*. In the experimental method, the researcher attempts to control for extraneous variables through the *random assignment* of subjects to the treatment and control groups to ensure that any extraneous variables will be distributed evenly between the groups. The strength of this method is the high level of control that the researcher has over the setting, which allows the investigator to determine cause-and-effect relationships. The weakness of the method is that the controlled conditions may be artificial and may not generalize to actual, uncontrolled work settings. The other type of research method, the *correlational method,* looks at the relationships among measured variables as they naturally occur, without the intervention of the experimenter and without strict experimental controls. The strength of this design is that it may be more easily conducted in actual settings. However, the correlational method does not allow the specification of cause-and-effect relationships.

The *case study* is a commonly used descriptive investigation that lacks the controls and repeated observations of the experimental and correlational methodologies. The case study can provide important information but does not allow the testing of hypotheses.

An important part of the research process involves the measurement of variables. The term *operationalization* refers to the process of defining variables so that they can be measured for research purposes. A variety of measurement techniques are used by I/O psychology researchers. Researchers may measure variables through direct *obtrusive* or *unobtrusive* observation of behavior. In obtrusive observation the researcher is visible to the research subjects, who know they are being studied. Unobtrusive observation involves observing subjects' behavior without their knowledge. Another measurement strategy is *self-report techniques,* which yield information about subjects' behavior from their own reports. One of the most widely used self-report techniques is the *survey*. Two important concepts related to the measurement of research variables are whether the measurement is stable over time (*reliability*) and whether the measurement is accurate (*validity*).

Statistics are research tools used to analyze research data. *Descriptive statistics* are ways of representing data to assist interpretation. One such statistic is the *frequency distribution*. The *mean* is a measure of central tendency in a distribution, and the *standard deviation* is an indicator of distribution variability. *Inferential statistics* are used to test hypotheses. Different inferential statistics are typically used to analyze data from different research designs.

When interpreting research results, attention must be given to the *external validity* of the findings, that is, whether they will generalize to other settings. Of critical concern to I/O psychologists is the interrelation of the science and practice of industrial/organizational psychology.

STUDY QUESTIONS AND EXERCISES

1. What are the steps in the research process? What are some of the major problems that are likely to be encountered in each step?

2. How do the goals of social science research methods relate to the types of theories used in I/O psychology?

3. What are the strengths and weaknesses of the experimental and the correlation methods? Under what circumstances would you use each?

4. Consider the various measurement techniques used by I/O psychologists. Why are many of the variables used in I/O psychology difficult to measure?

5. Choose some aspect of work behavior and develop a research hypothesis. Now try to design a study that would test the hypothesis. Consider what your variables are and how you will operationalize them. Choose a research design for the collection of data. Consider who your subjects will be and how they will be selected. How might the hypothesis be tested statistically?

SUGGESTED READINGS

Cozby, P. C. (1989). *Methods in behavioral research* (4th ed.). Mountain View, CA: Mayfield Publishing.   *An excellent and very readable introduction to research methods.*

Kenny, D. A. (1987). *Statistics for the social and behavioral sciences.* Glenview, IL: Scott, Foresman.   *This text examines the basic methods students in the social and behavioral sciences need to analyze data and test hypotheses.*

Miner, J. B. (1983). The unpaved road from theory: Over the mountains to application. In R. H. Kilmann, K. W. Thomas, D. P. Slevin, R. Nath, & S. L. Jerrell (Eds.), *Producing useful knowledge in organizations* (pp. 37–68). New York: Praeger.

Miner, J. B. (1984). The unpaved road over the mountains: From theory to applications. *The Industrial-Organizational Psychologist, 21,* 9–20.   *These two articles discuss the relationship between the research validity of certain I/O psychology theories and their applicability.*

Rice, B. (1982). The Hawthorne defect: Persistence of a flawed theory. *Psychology Today, 16*(2), 70–74.   *A brief but interesting account of the research design flaws in the original Hawthorne experiments.*

3

Job Analysis and Performance

Job Analysis and Job Performance: Establishing a Foundation for Personnel Psychology

The first topic in this chapter, job analysis, is the foundation of nearly all personnel activities. To appraise employee performance, hire the right person for a job, train someone to perform a job, or change or redesign a job, we need to know exactly what the job is. This is the purpose of job analysis. Many of the topics we will discuss in the next two chapters rest on this foundation. For example, when we discuss the recruitment, screening, and selection of applicants for a job, we must understand what a particular job is before we can hire people to fill it.

The analysis of jobs draws heavily on the research methods and measurement issues studied in Chapter 2. In job analysis and in the measurement of job performance we strive to be as objective and precise as possible. For instance, concepts of reliability and validity are critical issues in analyzing job performance.

Because job performance is such an important outcome variable in I/O psychology, it is important to understand the measurement issues concerning this factor. For example, when reviewing studies that discuss effects on job performance, you should investigate how performance was operationally defined and measured. Were hard or soft criteria used? How accurate or inaccurate might the assessments of performance be?

The topics of job analysis and performance also relate to some of the issues discussed in Chapter 1. For example, when Taylor was applying time-and-motion methods to the study of a job, he was in effect conducting a job analysis, and his measures of productivity constituted assessments of job performance. Making connections such as these will help you to see how the various topics that we will be discussing fit together.

personnel psychology
the specialty area of I/O psychology focusing on an organization's human resources

I n the next few chapters, we will be examining the specialty of industrial/organizational psychology referred to as **personnel psychology.** Personnel psychology is concerned with the creation and care of a work force, which includes the recruitment, placement, training, and development of workers; the measurement and evaluation of their performance; and concern with worker productivity and satisfaction. In short, the goal of personnel psychology is to take care of an organization's human resources.

In the past, the personnel department of a traditional organization was primarily a clerical unit, responsible for maintaining employee records—tabulating attendance, handling payroll, and keeping retirement records. Personnel departments were not very high in organizational status and were not considered very important. However, recently this has changed, for as work organizations have become more complex, the importance and scope of personnel departments, and personnel psychology, have expanded. Today, the personnel department is often known as the human resources department, which indicates a more global concern with all aspects of the company's most valuable assets: its human workers. Personnel psychologists are involved in personnel activities such as employee recruitment and selection, the measurement of employee performance and the establishment of good performance review procedures, the development of employee training and development programs, and the formulation of criteria for promotion, firing, and disciplinary action. They may also establish effective programs for employee compensation and benefits, create incentive programs, and design and implement programs to protect employee health and well-being.

JOB ANALYSIS

One of the most basic personnel functions is **job analysis,** or the systematic study of the tasks, duties, and responsibilities of a job and the knowledge, skills, and abilities needed to perform it. Job analysis is the starting point for nearly all personnel functions. Before a worker can be hired or trained and before a worker's performance can be evaluated, it is critical to understand exactly what the worker's job entails. Since most jobs consist of a variety of tasks and duties, gaining a full understanding of a job is not always easy. Therefore, job analysis methods need to be comprehensive and precise. Indeed, large organizations have specialists whose primary responsibilities are to analyze the various jobs in the company and develop extensive and current descriptions for each.

A job analysis leads directly to the development of several other important personnel "products": a job description, a job specification, a job evaluation, and performance criteria. A **job description** is a detailed accounting of the tasks, procedures, and responsibilities required of the worker; the machines, tools, and equipment used to perform the job; and the job output (end product or service). A job analysis also leads to a **job specification,** which provides information about the human characteristics required to perform the job, such as physical and personal traits, work experience, and education. Sample job descriptions and job specifications are presented in Table 3.1. A third personnel "product," **job evaluation,** is the assessment of the relative value or worth of jobs to an organization to determine appropriate compensation, or wages. Finally, a job analysis helps outline performance criteria, the means for appraising worker success in performing a job.

job analysis
the systematic study of the tasks, duties, and responsibilities of a job and the qualities needed to perform it

job description
a detailed description of job tasks, procedures, and responsibilities; the tools and equipment used, and the end product or service

job specification
a statement of the human characteristics required to perform a job

job evaluation
an assessment of the relative value of jobs to determine appropriate compensation

Table 3.1 EXAMPLES OF A JOB DESCRIPTION AND A JOB SPECIFICATION

Partial job description for the job: Engine Lathe Operator—First Class

Job summary: Sets up and operates an engine lathe to turn small airplane fittings from brass or steel bar stock or from unfinished aluminum or magnesium alloy castings, finishing fitting down to specified close tolerances.

Work performed: (1) Sets up lathe; carefully examines blueprints to determine the dimensions of the part to be machined, using shop mechanics to calculate any dimensions not given directly on the print or to calculate machine settings. (2) Sets up lathe to turn stock held in chuck; attaches to lathe the accessories such as chuck and tool holder necessary to perform the machining threading and locking the chuck and the head stock spindle and setting.

Job specification for Engine Lathe Operator—First Class

Minimum two years experience operating engine lathe; experience working with small airplane fittings. Must possess a high school diploma and receive passing score on tests of shop mechanics and blueprint reading. Must be a U.S. citizen, with no criminal record, eligible for security clearance to work on government contracts.

Source: Job description from E. J. McCormick, *Job Analysis: Methods and Applications* (New York: AMACOM, 1979), p. 63.

These products of job analysis are important because they in turn provide the detailed information needed for other personnel activities, such as planning, recruitment and selection programs, and performance appraisal systems (see Figure 3.1). Job analyses and their products are also valuable because of recent legal decisions that make organizations more responsible for personnel actions as part of the movement toward greater legal rights for the worker. Foremost among these laws are those concerned with equal employment opportunities for disadvantaged and minority workers. Employers can no longer make hasty or arbitrary decisions regarding the hiring, firing, or promotion of workers. Certain personnel actions, such as the decisions to hire or promote, must be made on the basis of a thorough job analysis. Personnel decisions that are not so made are difficult to defend in court. Sometimes a job analysis and a job description are not enough. Courts have also questioned the *quality* of job descriptions and the methods used in job analysis by many companies (Ghorpade, 1988).

JOB ANALYSIS METHODS

There are a variety of methods and procedures for conducting a job analysis, including observational techniques, existing data on jobs, interview techniques, and surveys. Each method will yield a different type of information, and each has its own strengths and weaknesses. In certain methods, such as interviewing, the data may be obtained from a variety of sources, such as the job incumbent (the person currently holding the job), supervisory personnel, or outside experts. Moreover, different job analysis methods are often used in combination to produce a detailed and accurate description of a certain job (Levine, Ash, & Bennett, 1980).

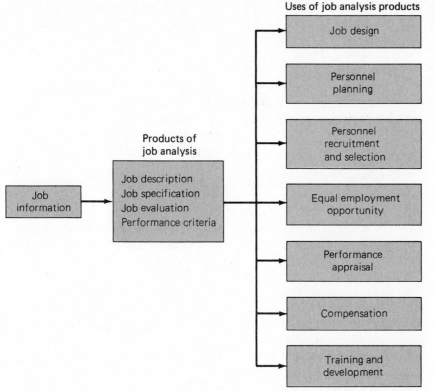

Uses of job analysis products

Job design

Personnel planning

Personnel recruitment and selection

Equal employment opportunity

Performance appraisal

Compensation

Training and development

Products of job analysis

Job description
Job specification
Job evaluation
Performance criteria

Job information

Figure 3.1
LINKS BETWEEN JOB ANALYSIS AND PERSONNEL FUNCTIONS

Source: J. V. Ghorpade, *Job Analysis: A Handbook for the Human Resource Director* (Englewood Cliffs, NJ: Prentice-Hall, 1988), p. 6.

Along with disadvantaged and minority workers, people with handicaps have demanded—and won—greater recognition of their rights and talents. Shown here is John Yeh, whose deafness did not prevent him from founding a major computer-software company.

Observational methods.   Observational methods of job analysis are those in which trained job analysts gather information about a particular job. To do this the analyst usually observes the job incumbent at work for a period of time. Typically, the observer takes detailed notes on the exact tasks and duties performed. However, to make accurate observations, the job analyst must know what to look for. For example, a subtle or quick movement, but one that is important, might go unnoticed. Also, if the job is highly technical or complex, the analyst may not be able to observe some of its critical aspects, such as thinking or decisionmaking. Observational techniques usually work best with jobs involving manual operations, repetitive tasks, or other easily seen activities.

With observational techniques, it is important that the times selected for observation are representative of the worker's routine, especially if the job requires that the worker be engaged in different tasks during different times of the day, week, or year. For example, an accounting clerk may deal with payroll vouchers on Thursdays, may spend most of Fridays updating sales figures, and may be almost completely occupied with preparing a company's tax records during the month of January.

One concern regarding observational methods is whether the presence of the observer in some way influences workers' performance. There is always the chance that workers will perform their jobs differently simply because they know they are being watched (recall the Hawthorne effect discussed in Chapter 1).

Existing data.   Most large, established organizations usually have some information or records that can be used in the job analysis, such as a previous job analysis for the position or an analysis of a related job. Such data might also be borrowed from another organization that has conducted analyses of similar jobs.

Interview methods.   Interviews are another method of job analysis. They can be open-ended ("Tell me all about what you do on the job"), or they can have structured or standardized questions. Since any one source of information can be biased, the job analyst may want to get more than one perspective by interviewing the job incumbent, the incumbent's supervisor, and, if the job is a supervisory one, the incumbent's subordinates. The job analyst might also interview several job incumbents within an organization to get a more reliable representation of the job and to see whether various people holding the same job title in a company actually perform similar tasks.

Survey methods.   Survey methods of job analysis usually involve the administration of a pencil-and-paper questionnaire that the respondent completes and returns to the job analyst. Surveys can consist of open-ended questions ("What abilities or skills are required to perform this job?"), closed-ended questions ("Which of the following classifications best fits your position? a. supervisory, b. technical, c. line, d. clerical''), or checklists (''Check all of the following tasks that you perform in your job.'').

The survey method has two advantages over the interview method. First, the survey allows the collection of information from a number of workers simultaneously. This can be helpful and very cost effective when the analyst needs to study several positions. Second, since the survey can be anonymous, there may be less distortion or withholding of information than in a face-to-face interview. One of the drawbacks of the survey, however, is that the information obtained is limited by the questions asked. Unlike an interview, a survey cannot probe for additional information or for clarification of a response.

SPECIFIC JOB ANALYSIS TECHNIQUES

In addition to these various *general* methods for conducting job analyses, there are also a number of specific *structured* analysis techniques. These techniques have not only been widely used but have also generated a considerable amount of research on their effectiveness. We will consider three of these structured techniques: functional job analysis, the Position Analysis Questionnaire, and the critical incidents technique.

Functional job analysis. **Functional job analysis (FJA)** has been used extensively by organizations in both the public and private sectors (Fine & Wiley, 1971). It was developed in part to assist the United States Department of Labor in the construction of a comprehensive job classification system and to help create the **Dictionary of Occupational Titles (DOT)** (U.S. Department of Labor, 1977), a reference guide that classifies and gives general descriptions for over 40,000 different jobs. The *DOT* classifies each job using a nine-digit code that represents the job classification and gives an idea of the level of work functioning the job requires. The first three digits of the code simply indicate the occupational code, job title, and type of industry or ''industry designation''; the last three digits are an alphabetical ordering of jobs within the same occupational grouping. It is the second three digits that are important for describing the type of work involved in a particular job. These digits represent the job's typical interaction with data, people, and things. *Data* is information, knowledge, and conceptions. Jobs with a great deal of interaction with data involve the use of numbers, words, symbols, and other abstract elements. *People* refers to the amount of contact with others that a job requires. *Things* refers to inanimate objects such as tools, machines, equipment, and tangible work products. Although FJA originally led to the development of the *DOT,* today it uses the *DOT* descriptions as a starting point for more detailed descriptions.

Functional job analysis begins by examining what gets done—the sequence of tasks that must be completed—and how it gets done—the

functional job analysis (FJA)
a structured job analysis technique that examines the sequence of tasks in a job and the processes by which they are completed

Dictionary of Occupational Titles (DOT)
a reference guide that classifies and describes over 40,000 jobs

Table 3.2   HIERARCHY OF WORK FUNCTIONS USED IN FUNCTIONAL JOB ANALYSIS

Data (4th digit)	People (5th digit)	Things (6th digit)
0 Synthesizing	0 Mentoring	0 Setting up
1 Coordinating	1 Negotiating	1 Precision working
2 Analyzing	2 Instructing	2 Operating-controlling
3 Compiling	3 Supervising	3 Driving-operating
4 Computing	4 Diverting	4 Manipulating
5 Copying	5 Persuading	5 Tending
6 Comparing	6 Speaking, Signalling	6 Feeding, Offbearing
	7 Serving	7 Handling
	8 Taking instruction, helping	

Source: U.S. Department of Labor, *Dictionary of Occupational Titles,* 4th ed. (Washington, DC: Government Printing Office, 1977).

processes by which the worker completes the tasks. According to FJA, all jobs require workers to interact with the three components of data, people, and things. Within each of these categories there is a hierarchy of work functions ranging from the most involved and complex functions (given the numerical value of "0") to the least involved and complex (the highest digit in the category; see Table 3.2). These digits are used to classify the functions of specific jobs in the *DOT*. For example, in our sample *DOT* entries in Table 3.3, the job of industrial/organizational psychologist has the numerical code 045.107–030. The three middle digits, 107, refer to the three components of job functions. The 1 means that the job of I/O psychologist requires "coordinating" data. The 0 indicates that I/O psychologists are involved in "mentoring" people, and the 7 shows that their job requires "handling" things. For the punch-press operator, the important digits are 682, meaning that the job involves "comparing" data, "taking instruction, helping" people, and "operating-controlling" things.

In using functional job analysis, the job analyst begins with the general job description provided by the *DOT*. The analyst will then use interviewing and/or observational techniques to conduct a more detailed study of a certain job. FJA is especially helpful when the job analyst must create job descriptions for a large number of positions. It is also quite popular because it is cost effective and because it uses job descriptions based on the *DOT*, which are often considered satisfactory by federal employment enforcement agencies (Mathis & Jackson, 1985).

Position Analysis Questionnaire.   One of the most widely researched job analysis instruments is the ***Position Analysis Questionnaire (PAQ;*** McCormick, Jeanneret, & Mecham, 1969), a structured questionnaire that analyzes various jobs in terms of 187 job elements that are arranged into six categories, or divisions, as follows:

· *Information input:* Where and how the worker obtains the information needed to perform the job. For example, a newspaper re-

Position Analysis Questionnaire (PAQ)
a job analysis technique that uses a structured questionnaire to analyze jobs according to 187 job elements, grouped into 6 categories

Table 3.3 SAMPLE ENTRIES FROM THE *DICTIONARY OF OCCUPATIONAL TITLES*

Job: 045.107–030 Psychologist, Industrial-Organizational

Develops and applies psychological techniques to personnel administration, management, and marketing problems: Observes details of work and interviews workers and supervisors to establish physical, mental, educational, and other job requirements. Develops interview techniques, rating scales, and psychological tests to assess skills, abilities, aptitudes, and interests as aids in selection, placement, and promotion. Organizes training programs, applying principles of learning and individual differences, and evaluates and measures effectiveness of training methods by statistical analysis of production rate, reduction of accidents, absenteeism, and turnover. Counsels workers to improve job and personal adjustments. Conducts research studies of organizational structure, communication systems, group interactions, and motivational systems, and recommends changes to improve efficiency and effectiveness of individuals, organizational units, and organization. Investigates problems related to physical environment of work, such as illumination, noise, temperature, and ventilation, and recommends changes to increase efficiency and decrease accident rate. Conducts surveys and research studies to ascertain nature of effective supervision and leadership and to analyze factors affecting morale and motivation. . . . May adapt machinery, equipment, workspace, and environment to human use. . . .

Job: 615.682–014 Punch-Press Operator III

Operates power press equipped with punch to notch or punch metal or plastic plates, sheets, or structural shapes: Positions, aligns, and clamps specified punch and die set into ram and bed of machine, using feelers, gages, shims, rule, or template. Turns handwheel or installs shims to set depth of stroke. Lifts workpiece onto machine bed or roller table, manually or by using jib or crane. Positions layout marks on workpiece between punch and die. Positions and clamps guide stops to run successive pieces. Starts ram to drive punch through workpiece. May operate machine equipped with two or more punch and die sets. May trace layout marks on workpiece from template. May be designated according to function of machine as Notching-Press Operator.

How to interpret the DOT code: The first three digits indicate the occupational code, title, and industry designations. The next three digits represent the job's typical interaction with data, people, and things (see Table 3.2). The final three digits denote an alphabetical ordering of jobs within the same occupational grouping.

Source: U.S. Department of Labor, *Dictionary of Occupational Titles,* 4th ed. (Washington, DC: Government Printing Office, 1977).

porter may be required to use published, written materials as well as interviews with informants to write a news story. A clothing inspector's information input may involve fine visual discriminations of garment seams.
- *Mental processes:* The kinds of thinking, reasoning, and decision-making required to perform the job. For example, an air traffic controller must make many decisions about when it is safe for jets to land and take off.
- *Work output:* The tasks the worker must perform and the tools or machines needed. For example, a word processor must enter text using keyboard devices.
- *Relationship with other persons:* The kinds of relationships and contacts with others required to do the job. For example, a teacher instructs others, and a store clerk has contact with customers by providing information and ringing up purchases.

· *Job context:* The physical and/or social contexts in which the work is performed. Examples of job context elements would be working under high temperatures or dealing with many conflict situations.
· *Other job characteristics:* Other relevant activities, conditions, or characteristics necessary to do the job.

Each of these job elements is individually rated using six categories: extent of use, importance to the job, amount of time, applicability, possibility of occurrence, and a special code for miscellaneous job elements. The standard elements are rated on a scale from 1, for minor applicability, to 5, for extreme applicability. There is an additional rating for "does not apply" (McCormick, 1979). A sample page from the *PAQ* is shown in Figure 3.2.

The *PAQ* results produce a very detailed profile of a particular job that can be used to compare jobs within a company or similar positions in different organizations. Because the *PAQ* is a standardized instrument, two analysts surveying the same job should come up with very similar profiles. This might not be the case with interview techniques, where the line of questioning and interpersonal skills specific to the interviewer could greatly affect the job profile.

critical incidents technique (CIT)
a job analysis technique that relies on instances of especially successful or unsuccessful job performance

Critical incidents technique. The **critical incidents technique (CIT)** of job analysis records the specific worker behaviors that have led to particularly successful or unsuccessful job performance (Flanagan, 1954). For example, some critical incidents for the job of clerk typist might include: "Produces a manuscript with good margins, making it look like a typeset document"; "Notices an item in a letter or report that doesn't appear to be right, checks it, and corrects it"; "Misfiles charts, letters, etc. on a regular basis"; and "When in doubt, uses a dictionary to check the spelling of a word." All of these behaviors presumably contribute to the success or failure of the clerk typist. Information on such incidents are obtained by questioning, either through interviews or questionnaires, job incumbents, job supervisors, or other knowledgeable individuals. Through the collection of hundreds of critical incidents, the job analyst can arrive at a very good picture of what a particular job—and its successful performance—are all about. An example of a critical incidents interview form is presented in Figure 3.3.

The real value of the CIT is in helping to determine the particular knowledge, skills, and abilities that a worker needs to perform a job successfully. For example, from the critical incidents given for the clerk typist position we know that the successful typist will need to know how to file, use a dictionary, check basic grammar and sentence structure, and set up a typed manuscript page. This technique is also useful in devel-

INFORMATION INPUT

1 INFORMATION INPUT

1.1 Sources of Job Information

Rate each of the following items in terms of the extent to which it is used by the worker as a source of information in performing his job.

Code	Extent of Use (U)
N	Does not apply
1	Nominal/very infrequent
2	Occasional
3	Moderate
4	Considerable
5	Very substantial

1 U_____ Written materials (books, reports, office notes, articles, job instructions, signs, etc.).

2 U_____ Quantitative materials (materials which deal with quantities or amounts, such as graphs, accounts, specifications, tables of numbers, etc.)

3 U_____ Pictorial materials (pictures or picturelike materials used as *sources* of information, for example, drawings, blueprints, diagrams, maps, tracings, photographic films, x-ray films, TV pictures, etc.).

4 U_____ Patterns/related devices (templates, stencils, patterns, etc., used as *sources* of information when *observed* during use; do *not* include here materials described in item 3 above).

5 U_____ Visual displays (dials, gauges, signal lights, radarscopes, speedometers, clocks, etc.).

6 U_____ Measuring devices (rulers, calipers, tire pressure gauges, scales, thickness gauges, pipettes, thermometers, protractors, etc., used to obtain visual information about physical measurements; do *not* include here devices described in item 5 above).

7 U_____ Mechanical devices (tools, equipment, machinery, and other mechanical devices which are *sources* of information when *observed* during use or operation).

8 U_____ Materials in process (parts, materials, objects, etc., which are *sources* of information when being modified, worked on, or otherwise processed, such as bread dough being mixed, workpiece being turned in a lathe, fabric being cut, shoe being resoled, etc.).

9 U_____ Materials *not* in process (parts, materials, objects, etc., not in the process of being changed or modified, which are sources of information when being inspected, handled, packaged, distributed, or selected, etc., such as items or materials in inventory, storage, or distribution channels, items being inspected, etc.).

10 U_____ Features of nature (landscapes, fields, geological samples, vegetation, cloud formations, and other features of nature which are observed or inspected to provide information).

11 U_____ Man-made features of environment (structures, buildings, dams, highways, bridges, docks, railroads, and other "man-made" or altered aspects of the indoor or outdoor environment which are *observed* or *inspected* to provide job information; do not consider equipment, machines, etc., that an individual uses in his work, as covered by item 7).

Figure 3.2

SAMPLE PAGE FROM THE *POSITION ANALYSIS QUESTIONNAIRE (PAQ)*

Source: E. J. McCormick, P. R. Jeanneret, and R. C. Mecham, *Position Analysis Questionnaire* (West Lafayette, IN: Occupational Research Center, Purdue University, 1969), p. 4.

Figure 3.3
CRITICAL INCIDENTS
INTERVIEW FORM

Source: J. C. Flanagan,
"The Critical Incidents Tech-
nique," *Psychological
Bulletin, 51* (1954), p. 342.

"Think of the last time you saw one of your subordinates do something that was very helpful to your group in meeting their production schedule." (Pause till he indicates he has such an incident in mind.) "Did his action result in increase in production of as much as one percent for that day?— or some similar period?"

(If the answer is "no," say) "I wonder if you could think of the last time that someone did something that did have this much of an effect in increasing production." (When he indicates he has such a situation in mind, say) "What were the general circumstances leading up to this incident?"

_____
_____
_____

"Tell me exactly what this person did that was so helpful at that time."

_____
_____
_____

"Why was this so helpful in getting your group's job done?" _____
_____

"When did this incident happen?" _____
_____

"What was this person's job?" _____

"How long has he been on this job?" _____
_____

oping appraisal systems for certain jobs by helping to identify the critical components of successful performance.

Research on job analysis techniques. Several comparison studies of the various job analysis techniques have been conducted. A series of investigations by Levine and his associates (Levine et al., 1980; Levine, Ash, Hall, & Sistrunk, 1983) compared various techniques in terms of their accuracy, level of detail, and cost effectiveness. They found that functional job analysis, the critical incidents technique, and the Position Analysis Questionnaire were all reasonably effective job analysis methods. While FJA and the CIT provided detailed, comprehensive types of analyses, the *PAQ* yielded more limited information, probably because it uses the same general instrument to analyze all types of jobs. The FJA and CIT, by contrast, are tailored to analyze specific jobs. However, the *PAQ* was found to be more cost effective and easier to use than the other methods.

Overall, no one method or technique of job analysis has emerged as superior to all others. It may be that a trained analyst could conduct very good job analyses using any of several methods (Muchinsky, 1987). Obviously, a combination of methods should lead to a more detailed, more reliable, and "better" analysis than one technique alone.

JOB EVALUATION AND COMPARABLE WORTH

As mentioned at the beginning of the chapter, one of the products of a job analysis is a job evaluation, which is the process of assessing the relative value of jobs to determine appropriate compensation. That is, the wages paid for a particular job should be related to the knowledge, skills, abilities, and other characteristics it requires. However, a number of other variables, such as the supply of potential workers, the perceived value of the job to the company, and the job's history, can also influence its rate of compensation.

Detailed job evaluations typically examine jobs on a number of dimensions called **compensable factors.** Examples of compensable factors might be the physical demands of a job, the amount of training or experience required, the working conditions associated with the job, and the amount of responsibility the job carries. Each job may be given a score or weighting on each factor. The summed total of the weighted compensable factors indicates the value of the job, which is then translated into the dollar amount of compensation. Table 3.4 presents two examples of this point system of job evaluation. According to these examples, the job of turret lathe programmer/operator receives a slightly higher point total than the forklift operator position. Therefore, the turret operator should receive a higher rate of compensation.

compensable factors the job elements that are used to determine appropriate compensation

In recent years the issue of how jobs are compensated has created a great deal of controversy. Specifically, there has been a great deal of concern over discrimination in compensation, particularly wage discrepancies for men and women. Two pieces of federal legislation address this issue. The Equal Pay Act of 1963 mandates that men and women performing equal work receive equal pay. Title VII of the Civil Rights Act of 1964 prohibits discrimination in employment practices based on race, color, religion, *sex,* and national origin. In spite of these laws, however, there is considerable evidence that women receive lower wages than men performing the same or equivalent work (Treiman & Hartmann, 1981).

Two issues bear directly on the "gender gap" in wages. The first concerns access to higher paying jobs. Traditionally, many such jobs were primarily held by men, but throughout the 1960s and 1970s the women's rights movement helped increase the access of women to these positions. However, while women are now found in nearly every type of job, there is still considerable sex stereotyping of jobs, which means that many relatively high-paying jobs and professions are still filled mainly by men. For example, men are found in large numbers in skilled craft jobs that receive higher wages than clerical jobs, which are filled mainly by women.

The second issue deals with the fact that women are often paid far

Table 3.4 TWO JOB EVALUATIONS USING A POINT SYSTEM

Job Name: Turret Lathe Programmer/Operator

Compensable Factors	Substantiating Data	Points
Education	Must read work orders, use shop mathematics, use precision measuring instruments and gauges. Equivalent to 2–3 years applied trades training.	42
Experience	Over 4 years, up to and including 5 years	88
Initiative and ingenuity	Plan and perform machine programming and operations. Requires considerable judgment to program, operate, and adjust machinery.	56
Physical demand	Light physical effort. Occasionally lifts or moves average-weight material.	20
Mental demand	Concentrated mental attention required	20
Responsibility for equipment and materials	Careless, negligent, or improper performance could damage tools, equipment, or product	35
Responsibility for safety of others	Improper performance of work may cause others hand, foot, or eye injury	15
Responsibility for work of others	Responsible for 1 or 2 persons 50% or more of time	10
Working conditions	Good. Exposed to office and shop conditions that are not disagreeable.	20
Hazards	Accidents may cause injury to hand, foot, or eye	15
	Total points =	321

Job Name: Forklift Operator

Compensable Factors	Substantiating Data	Points
Education	Must read work orders, use simple mathematics. Grammar school education desirable.	32
Experience	Must learn to operate forklift and hand truck. Two to three weeks on-the-job training.	48
Initiative and ingenuity	Some variety on the job. Uses some discretion in keeping product in order.	38
Physical demand	On feet most of day when not driving forklift. Pushes empty and full pallets with hand truck. Some lifting of heavy boxes.	30
Mental demand	Concentrated mental attention required	20
Responsibility for equipment and materials	Careless, negligent, or improper performance could damage tools, equipment, or product	35
Responsibility for safety of others	Improper performance of work may cause serious injury to others	25
Responsibility for work of others	None	0
Working conditions	In freezer (0°C) for a total of 2–3 hours per day	38
Hazards	Accidents may cause serious injury	25
	Total points =	291

Sources: F. J. Landy, *Psychology of Work Behavior,* 3rd ed. (Homewood, IL: Dorsey, 1985), p. 158. M. L. Rock, *Handbook of Wage and Salary Administration* (New York: McGraw-Hill, 1984), p. 13/6.

less than men for performing equivalent tasks. In the 1980s, this gender-based pay disparity gave birth to the concept of **comparable worth,** or equal pay for equal work. For example, the job of personnel clerk, a traditionally "female" job, and the position of records manager in the production department, a job usually filled by men, both require the workers to perform similar tasks, such as keeping records and managing data files. Because of the similarity in duties, both positions should be paid equal wages.

*comparable worth
the notion that jobs
that require equivalent
knowledge and skills
should be compensated
equally*

Because of its focus on evaluating the worth of work tasks, the issue of comparable worth is tied to the ability of organizations to conduct valid and fair job evaluations, which should reveal instances of equal jobs receiving unequal compensation. However, opponents of the comparable worth movement argue that job evaluation methods may be inaccurate because they do not account for factors like the oversupply of female applicants for certain jobs such as teachers and airline attendants, women's lower levels of education and work experience relative to men, and women's preferences for certain types of "safe" jobs with "pleasant working conditions." Advocates of the comparable worth movement argue that even these factors do not account for the considerable disparity in pay for men and women (Judd & Gomez-Mejia, 1987).

For a number of reasons, women are not paid the same wages for the same level of work. One argument is that society does not value the type of work required by many jobs that are filled primarily by women, such as secretarial, clerical, teaching, and nursing positions. Alternatively, certain jobs that are filled primarily by men may be compensated at higher levels because more value is ascribed to them.

Another reason for gender-based pay disparity is the practice of **exceptioning,** whereby a job evaluation reveals that two jobs, with equivalent duties and responsibilities, receive very different rates of pay, yet no steps are taken to rectify the inequality. In other words, an "exception" is made because it is too costly or too difficult to raise the wages of the lower-paid job. An example of exceptioning is the pay rates for physicians and nurses. The average salary of a physician is three to five times that of a nurse, yet the two jobs have many comparable duties and responsibilities. Although the imbalance in salaries is known to exist, hospitals are financially unable to pay nurses what they are worth, so an exception is made.

The issue of comparable worth has been hotly debated by both business and government officials. Recently, certain cases of sex discrimination in employee compensation have reached the courts, highlighting the issue of comparable worth. For example, in *AFSCME v. State of Washington* (1983), a job evaluation of state employee positions found that women's job classes were paid approximately 20 percent less than comparable men's classes. It was recommended that women state employees should be paid an additional $38 million annually. Because the state of Washington did not act on the recommendation, the women employees' union sued. The court ruled that the state was discriminating against its women employees and awarded them nearly $1 billion.

If the comparable worth movement goes forward and the government decides to take steps to correct pay inequalities, the impact on workers and work organizations will be tremendous. First, job evaluations will have to be conducted for nearly all jobs in the country—a staggering and expensive task. Second, since it is unlikely that workers and unions will allow the wages of higher-paid workers to be cut, the salaries of the lower-paid workers will have to be raised—also an enormous expense. Regardless of what takes place in the next few years, the issue of comparable worth has focused greater attention on job evaluations and job evaluation procedures. It is thus likely that greater attention will be given to improving such procedures in the near future (Risher, 1984).

JOB PERFORMANCE AND PERFORMANCE APPRAISALS

Job analysis allows us to define jobs in terms of their elements and tasks. The next step is to develop ways to assess whether workers are indeed doing their jobs and performing the tasks that lead to work effectiveness. In the next section, we will consider the very important variable of job performance in the context of assessments and evaluations. We will discuss the importance of performance appraisals, procedures for appraising performance, and the difficulties encountered in attempting to appraise performance.

PURPOSES OF PERFORMANCE APPRAISALS

A system of appraising work performance is one of the products that arises from a detailed job analysis, for once the specific elements of a job are known, it is easier to develop the means to assess levels of successful or unsuccessful performance. Typically, in organizations such assessment takes the form of formalized **performance appraisals,** which measure worker performance in comparison to certain predetermined standards.

performance appraisals the formalized means of assessing worker performance in comparison to certain established organizational standards

Performance appraisals are important both to the organization and to the individual worker. To the organization, they provide a means of assessing the productivity of individuals and work units, which is used to make personnel decisions such as promotions, demotions, pay raises, and firings. Performance appraisals can also validate employee selection methods (see Chapter 5) and provide information on the training needs of organizational members (see Chapter 6). Finally, they serve as a basis for evaluating the effectiveness of any type of organizational changes (for example, changes in work design or systems, supervisors, or working conditions). For the individual worker, performance appraisals function as the foundation for career advancement (such as pay increases or promotions), provide feedback to help improve performance and recognize weaknesses, and offer information about the attainment of work goals. Moreover, the formal performance appraisal procedure helps to encourage interaction between workers and supervisors.

THE MEASUREMENT OF JOB PERFORMANCE

Job performance is one of the most important work outcomes. It is the variable in organizations that is most often measured and that is given the most attention. This makes sense, since the success or failure of an organization depends on the performance of its employees. There are many ways to measure job performance. I/O psychologists refer to a measure of job performance as a criterion, the means of determining successful or unsuccessful performance.

One categorization of job performance assessments distinguishes between "hard" and "soft" performance criteria (Smith, 1976). Hard performance criteria involve the measurement of some easily quantifiable aspects of job performance, such as the number of units produced, the dollar amount of sales, or the time needed to process some information. For example, a hard criterion for an assembly-line worker might be the number of products assembled. For an insurance claims adjuster, the average amount of time it takes to process a claim might be a hard measure of performance (see Table 3.5). Such criteria are often referred to as measures of productivity.

Soft performance criteria consist of judgments or ratings done by some knowledgeable individual, such as a worker's supervisor or co-

Table 3.5 EXAMPLES OF HARD JOB PERFORMANCE CRITERIA

Job title	Measure
Typist	Lines per week
Forester	Cords (of wood) cut
Keypuncher	Number of characters; number of errors
Service representative	Errors in processing customer orders
Toll collector	Dollar accuracy/axle accuracy
Clerk	Errors per 100 documents checked; number of documents processed
Wood harvester	Number of cords delivered
Tree planter	Bags of tree seedlings planted
Skateboard maker	Number produced; number rejected
Sewing machine operator	Minutes per operation
Logger	Weight of wood legally hauled
Dentist	Errors in reading radiographs
Inspector	Errors detected in finished product
Tool/die maker	Dies produced
Helicopter pilot	Deviations from proper instrument readings
Bank teller	Number of shortages; number of overages
Air traffic controller	Speed of movement of aircraft through the system; correction of pilot error; errors in positioning aircraft for final approach; errors in aircraft separation

Source: F. J. Landy and J. L. Farr, *The Measurement of Work Performance: Methods, Theory, and Applications* (New York: Academic Press, 1983).

worker. These criteria are often used when hard criteria are unavailable, difficult to assess, or inappropriate. For example, it is usually inappropriate to use hard performance criteria to assess a manager's job since it is difficult to specify the exact behaviors that indicate successful managerial performance. Instead soft criteria, such as subordinate or superior ratings, are used. In addition to hard and soft performance criteria, the assessment of related variables, such as quality of work, attendance records, or numbers of reprimands or complaints, can also be used to measure performance indirectly.

Hard performance criteria offer two main advantages. First, because hard criteria involve objective counts of output or the timing of tasks, they are less prone to bias and distortion than the more subjective, soft performance ratings. Second, hard criteria are usually more directly tied to "bottom line" assessments of an organization's success, such as the number of products assembled or dollar sales figures. It is more difficult to determine the links between soft criteria and bottom line outcomes.

As mentioned, it is often difficult, if not impossible, to obtain hard performance criteria for certain jobs, such as graphic artist, copy writer, and executive vice president. Jobs such as these may best be assessed through ratings or judgments. Another drawback of hard assessments is that they may focus too much on specific objective outcomes. Because many jobs are complex, looking at only one or two objective measures of performance may not capture the total picture of performance. Some aspects of job performance such as work quality, worker initiative, and work effort are difficult to assess objectively. For example, a salesperson might have high dollar sales figures but may be so pushy and manipulative that customers are unlikely to return to the store. Likewise, a machinist may have relatively low output rates because he spends a great deal of time teaching new workers valuable work techniques and helping co-workers solve performance problems. In many cases, collecting hard performance data is time-consuming and costly (although see On the Cutting Edge). By contrast performance ratings are usually easy and relatively inexpensive to obtain and thus may be the preferred method of assessment for many organizations.

Regardless of the criterion used to evaluate performance of a job, there are a number of important criterion concerns or issues that have implications for conducting accurate performance appraisals (Bernardin & Beatty, 1984). A primary concern is **criterion relevance,** the notion that the means of appraising performance is indeed pertinent to job success. A performance appraisal should cover only the specific skills, knowledge, and abilities needed to perform a job successfully. For example, the performance criteria for a bookkeeper should deal with mathematical skills, knowledge of accounting procedures, and producing work that is neat and error-free, not with personal appearance or oral communication skills—factors that are clearly not relevant to effective performance of a bookkeeper's job. However, for a public relations representative personal appearance and communication skills may be relevant performance criteria.

A related concern is **criterion contamination,** the extent to which performance appraisals contain elements that detract from the accurate assessment of job effectiveness. A common source of criterion contamination results from appraiser biases. For example, a supervisor may give an employee an overly positive performance appraisal because the employee has a reputation of past work success or because the employee was a graduate of a prestigious university. Criterion contamination can also result from extraneous factors that contribute to a worker's apparent success or failure in a job. For instance, a sales manager may receive a poor performance appraisal because of low sales levels, even though the poor sales actually result from the fact that the manager supervises a young, inexperienced sales force.

It is unlikely that any criterion will capture job performance perfectly; every criterion of job performance may fall short of measuring performance to some extent. **Criterion deficiency** describes the degree to which a criterion falls short of measuring job performance perfectly. An important goal of performance appraisals is to choose criteria that optimize the assessment of job success, thereby keeping criterion deficiency to a minimum.

criterion relevance
the extent to which the means of appraising performance is pertinent to job success

criterion contamination
the extent to which performance appraisals contain elements that detract from the accurate assessment of job effectiveness

criterion deficiency
the degree to which a criterion falls short of measuring job performance perfectly

The Boss Is Watching: Computerized Monitoring of Employee Performance

Obtaining hard, objective measures of job performance has often been a difficult and time-consuming process, requiring direct observation and the tallying of employee work behaviors by managers. However, in recent years, as more and more workers go "on-line," using computers to perform many activities, the ability of organizations to obtain hard measures of employee productivity is becoming easier and easier. This is especially true when a number of individual terminals are tied into a central computer.

Various computer programs allow an employer to monitor directly the amount and type of computer activities that each employee is engaged in throughout the day. This is particularly true for jobs involving information processing and service jobs in which all customer activities are recorded on computer files. For example, employees in the collections department of a credit card company must maintain computerized records of phone calls, correspondence, and other activity for all accounts. The computerized monitoring system allows supervisors to note the number and length of calls to each account as well as the amount of money collected. Supervisors receive a detailed weekly report of employee computer activities that give a good indication of how the workers spent their time. A hard measure of employee performance is obtained from the amount of money collected from each account.

In some companies and some jobs, this kind of monitoring system is not new. For years, retail employees have had their sales activities monitored through cash register records. What is new, however, is the computer's ability to record a number of work-related activities for several employees simultaneously and to present this information quickly in some summary form. Supervisors are usually given several kinds of breakdowns, providing detailed listings of each employee's activities and making comparisons among employees.

While computerized monitoring can lead to more objective assessments of employee performance, workers have raised certain objections. Some have argued that computer monitoring focuses on only those behaviors that are easily quantified, such as time engaged in a particular activity or dollar sales figures, but ignores measures of quality. Another important consideration is the protection of employees' rights to privacy. There is some question as to when employer monitoring of work activities begins to infringe on the employees' freedom to conduct work activities in a manner they see fit. A related problem is that employee creativity and innovation in work methods may be stifled if the workers know that work activities are being monitored. In any case, computerized monitoring is here to stay and, as systems become more sophisticated, likely to increase.

---

criterion usefulness
the extent to which a
performance criterion
is usable in appraising
a particular job

A final concern is **criterion usefulness,** the extent to which a performance criterion is usable in appraising a particular job in an organization. To be useful, a criterion should be relatively easy and cost-effective to measure and should be seen as relevant by the appraiser, the employee whose performance is being appraised, and the management of the organization.

METHODS OF RATING PERFORMANCE

Because performance ratings play such an important role in performance assessment in organizations, a variety of methods of rating job performance have been developed and researched. However, before we

At some companies, employees using computer terminals are monitored directly through the central computer—a practice that raises questions about workers' right to privacy.

examine the different techniques, we must consider *who* is doing the rating. In the vast majority of cases it is the immediate supervisor who rates the performance of subordinates (Jacobs, 1986). However, performance appraisals can also be made by a worker's peers or by subordinates. Subordinate ratings are most commonly used to assess the effectiveness of persons in supervisory or leadership positions. Because each type of appraiser—supervisor, peer, and subordinate—may see a different aspect of the worker's performance, they all can provide valuable information as well as unique perspectives. Workers' self-appraisals can also help in focusing their attention on their job performance and in getting them to commit to improving future performance. However, and not surprisingly, research indicates that self-appraisals tend to be biased toward more positive, or lenient, appraisals of performance (Thornton, 1980).

The various rating methods of performance appraisals can be grouped into four types: comparative methods, checklists, graphic rating scales, and behaviorally anchored rating scales. Each type has its strengths and weaknesses.

Comparative methods. **Comparative methods** of performance appraisal involve some form of comparison of one worker's performance with the performance of others. One such approach is the ranking technique, whereby supervisors rank order their subordinates from best to worst on specific performance dimensions or give an overall comparative

comparative methods
performance appraisal techniques of comparing one worker's performance with the performance of others

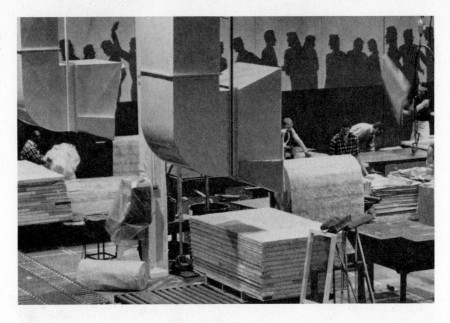

Usually supervisors evaluate their subordinates, but in plants like this wall-panel factory the workers also rate their bosses.

ranking on job performance. Although this is a simple and easy technique that supervisors are not likely to find difficult or time-consuming, it has several limitations. First, although ranking separates the best from the worst workers, there are no absolute standards of performance. This is a problem if few or none of the entire group of workers are performing at "acceptable" levels. In this case, being ranked second or third in a group of fifteen is misleading, because even the highest-ranking workers are performing at below-standard levels. Conversely, in a group of exceptional workers, those ranked low may actually be outstanding performers in comparison to other employees in the organization or workers in other companies.

Another comparative method of performance appraisal is the paired-comparison technique, in which the rater compares each worker with every other worker in the group and then simply has to decide which of the pair is the better performer. Each person's final rank consists of the number of times that individual was chosen as the better of a pair. The drawbacks of this technique are similar to those of the ranking method. However, both these comparative techniques have the advantage of being simple to use and of being applicable to a variety of jobs.

In the comparative method known as forced distribution, the rater assigns workers to established categories ranging from poor to outstanding on the basis of comparison with all other workers in the group. Usually, the percentage of employees who can be assigned to any particular category is controlled to obtain a fixed distribution of workers along the

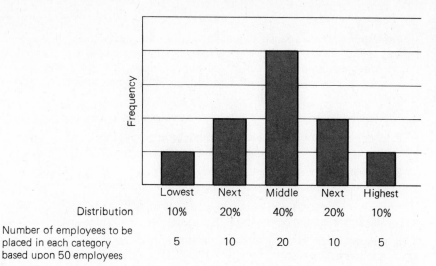

Figure 3.4
A FORCED-DISTRIBUTION
PERFORMANCE RATING
USING FIVE CATEGORIES
WITH A SAMPLE OF FIFTY
EMPLOYEES

	Lowest	Next	Middle	Next	Highest
Distribution	10%	20%	40%	20%	10%
Number of employees to be placed in each category based upon 50 employees	5	10	20	10	5

performance dimension. Most often the distribution is set up to represent a normal distribution (see Figure 3.4). This forced-distribution evaluation technique is similar to the procedure used by an instructor who grades on a normal curve with preassigned percentages of A, B, C, D, and F grades.

Checklists. Performance may also be rated with **checklists,** which consist of a series of statements about performance in a particular job. The statements are derived from a job analysis and can reflect either positive or negative aspects of performance (see Figure 3.5). The rater's task is to check off the statements that apply to the worker being evaluated. Each of the statements is given a numerical value reflecting the degree of effective performance associated with it. The numerical values assigned to the checked items are then summed to give an overall appraisal of the worker's performance.

checklists
performance appraisal
methods using a series
of statements about job
performance

A variation of checklist rating is the forced-choice scale, developed in an attempt to overcome the rater's tendency to give generally positive or negative performance appraisals. While using the forced-choice technique the rater is unaware of how positive an appraisal is being made. This format presents groups of descriptive statements from which the rater must select the one that is either most or least descriptive of the worker (see Figure 3.6). The statements carry different values that are later added to form the overall performance appraisal.

While the checklist methods are easy to use and provide detailed appraisals of performance that are focused on job-related behaviors, they do have some drawbacks. The development of such techniques is expensive and time-consuming, requiring the generation of applicable work-related statements and the assignment of accurate performance values. Also, checklists may limit the focus of a performance appraisal, since the

Figure 3.5

A CHECKLIST RATING
SCALE FOR A PROJECT
MANAGER

Note: This is only a portion
of the checklist. Scores are
derived based on the number
of items checked and the
scale values of those items.
Source: R. R. Jacobs, "Numerical Rating Scales," in
R. A. Berk (Ed.), *Performance Assessments: Methods
and Applications* (Baltimore:
The Johns Hopkins University Press, 1987), pp. 82–99.

Instructions: Below you will find a list of behavioral items. Read each item and decide whether it describes the person being evaluated. If you feel the item does describe the person, place a check mark in the space provided. If the item does *not* describe the person, leave the space next to the item blank.

1. Regularly sets vague and unrealistic program goals   _____

2. Is concerned only with the immediate problems of the day and sees very little beyond the day to day   _____

3. Develops work schedules that allow for completion of projects provided no major problems are encountered   _____

4. Is aware of needs and trends in area of responsibility and plans accordingly   _____

5. Follows up on projects to ensure that intermediate goals are achieved   _____

6. Looks for new markets and studies potential declines in current markets   _____

7. Anticipates and plans for replacement of key personnel in the event of corporate relocation   _____

rater must choose among a finite set of statements that might not capture all aspects of an individual's performance of a particular job.

graphic rating scales
job evaluation methods
using a predetermined
scale to rate the
worker on important
job dimensions

Graphic rating scales. The vast majority of performance appraisals use **graphic rating scales,** which offer predetermined scales to rate the worker on a number of important aspects of the job, such as quality of work, dependability, and ability to get along with co-workers. A graphic rating scale typically has a number of points with either numerical or verbal labels or both. The verbal labels can be simple one-word descriptors, or they can be quite lengthy and specific (see Figure 3.7). Some graphic rating scales use only verbal end points, or anchors, with numbered rating points between the two anchors.

When graphic rating scales are used in performance assessment, appraisals are usually made on anywhere from seven to twelve key job dimensions, which are derived from the job analysis. Better graphic rating scales usually clearly define the dimensions and the particular rating categories. In other words, it is important that the rater know exactly what aspect of the job is being rated and what the verbal labels mean. For instance, in Figure 3.7 examples *f* and *i* define the job dimension, while example *h* defines the rating categories.

Although good graphic rating scales take some time to develop, often the same basic scales can be used for a number of different jobs by simply

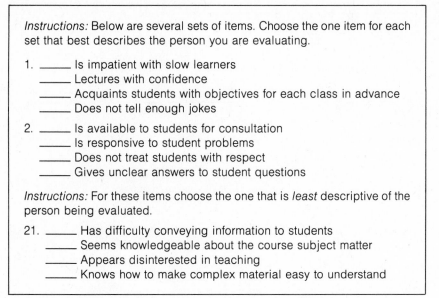

Figure 3.6
A FORCED-CHOICE RATING
SCALE FOR A COLLEGE
PROFESSOR

Source: F. J. Landy, *Psychology of Work Behavior*, 3rd ed. (Homewood, IL: Dorsey, 1985), p. 181.

switching the relevant job dimensions. However, a common mistake made by many organizations is attempting to develop a "generic" set of performance rating scales for use with all persons and all jobs within the company. Because the relevant job dimensions change drastically from job to job, it is critical that the dimensions being rated are those that actually assess performance of the particular job. The major weakness of graphic rating scales is that they may be prone to certain biased response patterns, such as the tendency to give everyone good or fair ratings. Also, limiting ratings to only a few job dimensions may constrain the appraiser and not produce a total picture of the worker's job performance.

Behaviorally anchored rating scales. An outgrowth of the critical incidents method of job analysis, the development of **behaviorally anchored rating scales (BARS),** is an attempt to define clearly the scale labels and anchors in performance ratings (Smith & Kendall, 1963). Rather than having scale labels such as poor, average, or good, BARS have examples of behavioral incidents that reflect poor, average, and good performance in relation to a specific dimension.

Figure 3.8 presents a behaviorally anchored rating scale for appraising the job of Navy recruiter on the dimension of salesmanship skills. Note first the very detailed definition of the job dimension at the top of the scale. On the left are the rating points ranging from 8 to 1. The verbal descriptors to the right of each category give examples of behavioral

behaviorally anchored rating scales (BARS) performance appraisal technique using rating scales with labels reflecting examples of poor, average, and good behavioral incidents

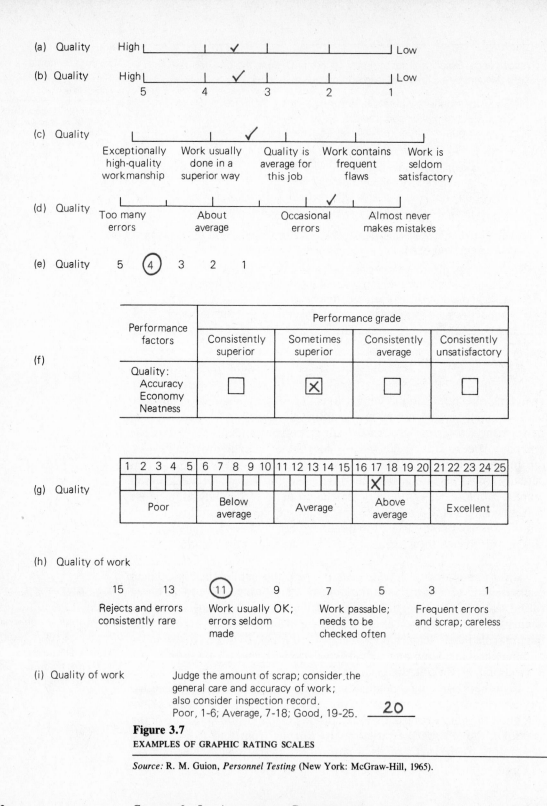

Figure 3.7
EXAMPLES OF GRAPHIC RATING SCALES

Source: R. M. Guion, *Personnel Testing* (New York: McGraw-Hill, 1965).

Figure 3.8
A BEHAVIORALLY
ANCHORED RATING
SCALE (BARS)

Source: W. C. Borman,
''Behavior-Based Rating
Scales,'' in R. A. Berk (Ed.),
*Performance Assessment:
Methods and Applications*
(Baltimore: The Johns Hop-
kins University Press, 1987),
p. 103.

Job: Navy recruiter
Job dimension: Salesmanship skills

Skillfully persuading prospects to join the navy; using navy benefits and opportunities effectively to sell the navy; closing skills; adapting selling techniques appropriately to different prospects; effectively overcoming objections to joining the navy.

8 — A prospect stated he wanted the nuclear power program or he would not sign up. When he did not qualify, the recruiter did not give up; instead, he talked the young man into electronics by emphasizing the technical training he would receive.

7 — The recruiter treats objections to joining the navy seriously; he works hard to counter the objections with relevant, positive arguments for a navy career.

6 — When talking to a high school senior, the recruiter mentions names of other seniors from that school who have already enlisted.

5 — When an applicant qualifies for only one program, the recruiter tries to convey to the applicant that it is a desirable program.

4 — When a prospect is deciding on which service to enlist in, the recruiter tries to sell the navy by describing navy life at sea and adventures in port.

3 — During an interview, the recruiter said to the applicant, ''I'll try to get you the school you want, but frankly it probably won't be open for another three months, so why don't you take your second choice and leave now.''

2 — The recruiter insisted on showing more brochures and films even though the applicant told him he wanted to sign up right now.

1 — When a prospect states an objection to being in the navy, the recruiter ends the conversation because he thinks the prospect must not be interested.

incidents that would differentiate a recruiter's salesmanship skills, from highest levels to lowest.

As you might imagine, the development of BARS is a lengthy and tedious process. The result, however, is a rating instrument that focuses clearly on performance behaviors relevant to a particular job. An appraiser is forced to spend a great deal of time just thinking about what adequate or inadequate performance of a certain job dimension entails, particularly if the rater had a hand in developing the scale. This increased attention on job behaviors helps to overcome some of the general biases and stereotyping that may occur in other performance ratings, for a worker cannot be summarily judged without consideration of how the person's past behavior supports the rating.

A performance assessment technique that is related to the BARS is the use of **behavioral observation scales.** With this method, raters indicate how often the worker has been observed performing key work-related behaviors (Latham & Wexley, 1977). While the BARS focus on expectations that a worker would be able to perform specific behaviors that are typical of certain performance levels, behavioral observation scales concentrate on critical behaviors that were actually performed. Bear in mind that behavioral observation scales do not involve the direct observation and assessment of performance behaviors but rather the recollections of the observers, who may be biased or selective in what they remember.

Narrative methods of performance appraisal. Some performance appraisals are simply open-ended narratives of the worker's performance or listings of specific examples of performance strengths and weaknesses. The advantage of narrative methods is that appraisers have the freedom to describe performance in their own words and to emphasize elements that they feel are important. Their major drawback is that they offer no quantification of performance, which makes it very difficult to compare workers' performance. An additional problem with narrative methods is that the worker may misinterpret the meaning of the report. For example, an appraiser may write that the worker is doing a "fair job," meaning that some improvement is needed, but the worker may interpret the word "fair" to mean "adequate" or "good," with no improvement necessary.

PROBLEMS AND PITFALLS IN PERFORMANCE APPRAISAL

Despite the various performance appraisal tools designed to help obtain more objective assessments, the appraisal evaluation process remains very subjective. Because appraisers selectively observe on-the-job performance and rate what they believe to be an individual's performance level, their judgments are prone to a number of systematic biases and distortions. A great deal of research has helped uncover some of these problems. Understanding these potential errors in the performance appraisal process can make it easier to develop the means to combat them and to produce better and better appraisals of work performance. We will consider several types of such systematic problems, including leniency/severity errors, halo effects, recency effects, attribution errors, and personal biases.

Leniency/severity errors. A **leniency error** in performance ratings occurs when an appraiser tends to judge all workers leniently, routinely

behavioral observation scales
performance appraisal methods that require appraisers to recall how often a worker has been observed performing key work behaviors

leniency error
the tendency to give all workers very positive performance appraisals

giving them very positive appraisals. A **severity error** is the exact opposite, and arises when all workers are placed on the low end of performance scales and are thereby given negative appraisals. For the rater making a severity error, no performance ever seems good enough. There is also a **central tendency error,** whereby the appraiser tends always to use the midpoint of the rating scale. All three of these errors lead to the same problem: a short-circuiting of the appraisal process because the rater's tendency to use only one area of the performance scale does not actually discriminate among poor, fair, and outstanding workers. As shown, some techniques, such as the various comparative methods, help combat such response tendency errors.

Halo effects. A **halo effect** in performance appraisal occurs when appraisers make overall positive appraisals of workers on the basis of one known positive characteristic or action (Nisbett & Wilson, 1977). If a particular worker did an outstanding job on a particular task, the supervisor assumes that all this person's work is also outstanding, regardless of whether it really is. Certain personal characteristics such as physical attractiveness or being labeled a "rising star" may also lead to halo effects (Landy & Sigall, 1974). There is also a "reverse" halo effect, sometimes called the rusty halo or horns effect (Baron, 1986), in which an overall negative performance appraisal is made on the basis of one instance of failure or one negative characteristic. Because halo effects are such a common source of bias in performance appraisals, a number of rater training programs have been developed to try to control for them (Ivancevich, 1979; McIntyre, Smith, & Hassett, 1984; Pulakos, 1984). Much of these training programs involves simply making raters more aware of the phenomenon of halo effects and helping them focus on behavioral dimensions of job performance.

Recency effects. Another potential error in performance appraisals is the tendency to give greater weight to recent performance and lesser value to earlier performance; this can be referred to as the **recency effect.** Because performance assessments usually rely on the appraiser's memory of a worker's past performance, there are bound to be problems related to accurate recall. In general, the greater the delay between the performance and appraisal of work behaviors, the less accurate the appraisal will be (Feldman, 1981; Heneman & Wexley, 1983).

Attribution errors. In performance appraisals the appraiser is attempting to assess not only *what* the level of performance was but also *why* the performance was at a particular level. When performance is at unusually low or high levels, the appraising supervisor would like to know the causes. The process by which people ascribe cause to events or behaviors is known as **causal attribution.**

Research has uncovered a number of systematic biases in causal attribution that have important implications for the accuracy of performance appraisals. One such problem is the tendency for appraisers to give more extreme appraisals if they believe that the cause of a worker's performance is rooted in effort rather than ability (Knowlton & Mitchell, 1980). That is, if an appraiser feels that particularly high levels of performance were the result of great effort on the part of a worker, that worker will receive a more positive performance appraisal than one whose high levels of performance were perceived as resulting from possession of natural ability or talent. Similarly, a performance failure due to lack of sufficient effort will be judged more harshly than a failure believed to be caused by lack of ability.

Another bias in causal attribution, one that is so pervasive as to be referred to as the *fundamental* attribution error, is called the **actor-observer bias** (Jones & Nisbett, 1972). This bias is founded in the belief that in any event there is an actor, the person performing a behavior, and an observer, the person watching and appraising the event and the actor's behavior. In performance appraisals the worker is the actor and the appraiser is the observer. The bias in causal attribution occurs when the actor and observer are each asked to state the cause of the particular event. In the case of performance appraisals, the event could be a particularly successful or unsuccessful work outcome. The actor tends to overemphasize the role that situational factors, such as luck, task difficulty, and the work environment, played in the result. The observer has a tendency to attribute cause to dispositional factors, or personal characteristics of the actor such as ability, effort, and personality. This means the performance appraiser tends to believe that performance is due primarily to qualities in the worker and tends to neglect the role that situational factors played in the performance outcome. Therefore, in certain situations of poor work performance, the supervisor may blame the worker, when the failure was actually due to circumstances beyond the control of the worker. On the other side, the worker is prone to overemphasize situational factors and, in cases of failure, will try to lay the blame elsewhere, for example, by faulting the working conditions or co-workers. The actor-observer bias not only leads to inaccurate perceptions of work performance but is also one of the main reasons that supervisors and subordinates do not always see eye to eye when it comes to performance appraisals (see Applying I/O Psychology).

Personal biases. In addition to these biases and errors that can afflict any appraiser of work performance, the personal biases of any particular appraiser can also distort the accuracy of assessments. The most common personal biases are those based on the worker's sex, race, age, and physical characteristics such as handicaps (Dipboye, 1985; Ferris, Yates, Gilmore, & Rowland, 1985; Kraiger & Ford, 1985). It is no secret that women, ethnic minorities, the elderly, and the handicapped are some-

actor-observer bias
the tendency for observers to overattribute cause to characteristics of the actor and the tendency for the actor to overattribute cause to situational characteristics

Combating the Actor-Observer Bias in Performance Appraisals

The actor-observer bias, or the tendency for actors to make situational attributions and for observers to make dispositional attributions, is a particular problem in performance appraisals that can lead to inaccurate assessments and cause riffs between the evaluating supervisor and subordinates. How can this bias be overcome?

One way to try to combat this problem is to create performance rating forms that require the evaluator to take into account the various situational factors that may have hampered the employee's performance. Although this strategy can avoid some of the observer bias, there may still be some tendencies toward overattributing cause to dispositional characteristics of the worker. An even better remedy is to change the perspective of the observers/evaluators by providing them with direct experience with the actor's job. Because much of the actor-observer bias is the result of the differing perspectives of the actor and the observer, putting the observer/appraiser "in the shoes" of the actor/worker can help the observer see conditions as the actor sees them (Mitchell & Kalb, 1982). A large savings and loan organization has done just that. All supervisors who are responsible for conducting the performance appraisals of customer service representatives—tellers and loan officers—must spend one week during each appraisal period working in customer service. The belief is that because many of these supervisors are far removed from the customer service situation, they are unable to evaluate objectively the pressures that the workers have to deal with, such as difficult or irate customers. Providing appraisers with this direct experience helps them take into account the situational variables that affect employees' performance, thus leading to more accurate assessments.

A common misconception is that the actor-observer bias will be overcome if both supervisor performance appraisals and workers' self-appraisals are obtained. However, if the actor-observer bias is operating, all this will produce is two very discrepant performance appraisals: one from the supervisor, blaming the worker for poor performance, and one from the worker, blaming the situation. Peer evaluations likewise will not be much help, because co-workers are also subject to the actor-observer bias. Peer evaluations will also overattribute cause to characteristics of the person being appraised, because the co-worker is also an observer.

times discriminated against in performance appraisals, in spite of legislation specifically designed to ensure fairness.

Personal biases are deeply ingrained in individuals and are therefore difficult to overcome. As with other biases, one way to deal with personal biases is to make appraisers more aware of them. Since discrimination in personnel procedures has been outlawed through federal civil rights legislation, most organizations and managers are on the lookout to prevent such biases from leading to discrimination. Ironically, programs designed to protect against personal biases and subsequent discrimination may lead to instances of reverse discrimination, a bias toward favoring a member of a particular underrepresented group over members of the majority group.

LEGAL CONCERNS IN PERFORMANCE APPRAISALS

Because performance appraisals are tied to personnel actions such as promotions, demotions, and raises, they are carefully scrutinized in terms of fair employment legislation. Under these legal guidelines, any perfor-

A supervisor can provide performance feedback in a performance appraisal interview or in more informal conversations.

mance appraisal must be valid. Recent court cases have ruled that in order to be considered "valid," appraisals must be based on a job analysis and must be validated against the job duties that the workers actually perform (*Albemarle Paper v. Moody,* 1975; *United States v. City of Chicago,* 1976). Moreover, performance appraisals need to be administered and scored under controlled and standardized conditions (*Brito v. Zia Company,* 1973). Specifically, court cases have ruled that appraisers must receive training, or at least written instructions, on how to conduct performance appraisals, that assessments must focus on performance-related behaviors rather than on performance-related personality traits or other dispositional variables, and that appraisals must be reviewed with the employees (Barrett & Kernan, 1987; Feild & Holley, 1982).

THE PERFORMANCE APPRAISAL PROCESS

The performance appraisal process involves more than just an assessment or rating of worker performance. A good performance appraisal consists of two parts. The first is the performance assessment, or the means of measuring a worker's performance in order to make some personnel decisions. This part we have discussed at length. The second part is **performance feedback,** which is the process of providing information to a worker regarding performance level with suggestions for improving future performance. Performance feedback typically occurs in the context of the performance appraisal interview. Here the supervisor sits down face-to-face with the worker and provides a detailed analysis of the worker's performance, giving positive, constructive criticism and suggestions and guidelines for improvement.

performance feedback *the process of giving information to a worker about performance level with suggestions for future improvement*

Because of the importance of performance appraisals, the appraisal process is likely to have some psychological and emotional effects on the worker. It is crucial that the supervisor be aware of this potential impact of the procedure, and be equipped to deal with the worker's possible reactions. Whether the worker perceives the performance appraisal process positively or negatively and how the worker acts on the information provided in the feedback session are in large part determined by how the information is presented by the supervisor (Ilgen, Fisher, & Taylor, 1979). Research has shown that if the appraiser demonstrates support for the worker and welcomes the worker's input and participation in the assessment process, the performance appraisal is usually more effective (Cederblom, 1982; Wexley, 1986). For example, in one study workers participated in the construction of behaviorally anchored rating scales to appraise their performance. These workers had more favorable perceptions of the appraisal process and were more motivated to try to improve their performance than were workers who did not have a hand in devel-

How to Improve Performance Appraisals

Given the pervasiveness of biases and errors in performance appraisals, how can the appraisal process be improved?

1. Improve performance appraisal techniques

Generally, the more time and energy devoted to the development of detailed, valid instruments for measuring performance, the better the overall quality of the performance appraisal. This means creating different performance appraisal instruments for different job classifications. (You can't, for example, use the same generic rating form for both front-line workers and managerial personnel.) These measures of performance must evolve from detailed job analysis, and should involve relatively straightforward and unambiguous procedures.

2. Train the appraisers

Since conducting good performance appraisals is a difficult process, prone to error and potential bias, it is imperative that appraisers be adequately trained. They must be taught how to use the various appraisal instruments and should be instructed to avoid possible errors, such as halo effects and leniency/severity error (Bernardin & Bulkley, 1981; Pulakos, 1984).

3. Obtain multiple evaluations

One way to increase the reliability of performance appraisals is to use multiple ratings, such as more than one supervisor rating or a combination of supervisor ratings, self-appraisals, and peer appraisals. If the results of the multiple appraisals agree with one another, and if all the appraisers are not influenced by a common bias, it is likely that the result will be a very accurate assessment of performance.

4. Appraise appraisers

Unfortunately, in many organizations supervisors detest conducting performance appraisals because they view the assessments as a difficult and thankless task—extra work piled onto an already heavy work load. To get supervisors to take performance appraisals seriously, it is important that the task of conducting assessments be considered an integral part of their job. This means that the quality of the supervisors' performance appraisals should be assessed and that the supervisors should also receive feedback about their performance of this crucial task. High-quality appraisals need to be rewarded.

5. Conduct performance appraisals regularly and often

Performance appraisals serve not only as tools to assist in personnel decisions but also as a source of feedback for the worker. Frequent and regular assessments are one of the best ways to help the workers learn to overcome problems and improve performance (Cummings & Schwab, 1978).

---

oping their rating instruments (Silverman & Wexley, 1984). Research has also indicated that training programs for appraisers that include training in providing feedback and in dealing with worker's possible reactions to that feedback are effective in improving the entire performance appraisal process (Ivancevich, 1982). (See Up Close for suggestions on how to improve performance appraisals.)

SUMMARY

Job analysis is the systematic study of a job's tasks, duties, and responsibilities and the knowledge, skills, and abilities needed to perform the job. The job analysis, which is the important starting point for many personnel functions, yields several products: a *job description,* which is a detailed accounting of job tasks, procedures, responsibilities, and output; a *job specification,* which consists of information about the physical, educational, and experiential qualities required to perform the job; a *job evaluation,* which is an assessment of the relative value of jobs for determining compensation; and performance criteria that serve as a basis for appraising successful job performance.

Job analysis methods include observation, the use of existing data, interviews, and surveys. One structured job analysis technique is the *functional job analysis (FJA),* a method that has been used to classify jobs in terms of the worker's interaction with data, people, and things. FJA uses the *Dictionary of Occupational Titles (DOT),* a reference book listing general job descriptions for thousands of jobs, and examines the sequence of tasks required to complete the job as well as the process by which the job is completed. Another structured job analysis technique, the *Position Analysis Questionnaire (PAQ),* uses a questionnaire that analyzes jobs in terms of 187 job elements arranged into 6 categories. The *critical incidents technique* of job analysis involves the collection of particularly successful or unsuccessful instances of job performance. Through the collection of hundreds of these incidents a very detailed profile of a job emerges. Research has determined that all of these standardized methods are effective.

Job analysis yields a job evaluation, or an assessment of the relative value of jobs to determine appropriate compensation. These evaluations usually examine jobs on dimensions that are called *compensable factors,* which are given values that signify the relative worth of the job and translate into levels of compensation.

A current topic in the area of job evaluation concerns the "gender gap" in wages. Evidence indicates that women are paid far less than men for comparable work. This inequity has recently given rise to the *comparable worth* movement, which argues for equal pay for equal work. This issue is controversial because of the difficulty and costs of making compensation for comparable jobs equitable.

A thorough job analysis is the starting point for measuring and evaluating actual job performance. *Performance appraisals* involve the assessment of worker performance on the basis of predetermined organizational standards. One way to categorize performance is in terms of "hard" and "soft" criteria. Hard performance criteria are more objective, quantifiable measurements of performance, such as the number of units produced or dollar sales. Soft performance criteria typically involve judgments or ratings of performance. There are a variety of methods for rating performance. *Comparative methods* of appraisal, such as the paired comparison and forced-distribution techniques, compare one worker's performance with that of other workers. *Checklists* and forced-choice scales are easy to use methods of appraisal that require the evaluator simply to check off statements characteristic or uncharacteristic of a particular worker's job performance. The most common method of performance appraisal is *graphic rating scales,* whereby an appraiser uses a standardized rating instrument to make a numerical and/or verbal rating of various dimensions of job performance. A specific type of rating technique, the *behaviorally anchored rating scale (BARS),* uses examples of good and poor behavioral incidents as a substitute for the scale anchors found in traditional rating instruments.

A major problem in rating job performance is caused by systematic biases and errors. Response tendency errors, such as *leniency/severity* or *central tendency errors,* lead to consistently good, bad, or average ratings, respectively. *Halo effects* occur when appraisers make overall positive (or negative) performance appraisals because of one known outstanding characteristic or action. There are also errors caused by giving greater weight to more recent performance, known as *recency effects,* and various attribution errors, including the *actor-observer bias*. The latter may lead an appraiser to place greater emphasis on dispositional factors and lesser emphasis on situational factors that may have affected performance.

Since performance appraisals are important to the worker's livelihood and career advancement, there are considerable legal overtones to the appraisal process. Performance appraisals must be valid procedures, resulting from job analysis, that do not unfairly discriminate against any group of workers.

A good performance appraisal consists of two parts: the performance assessment and *performance feedback*. The feedback should occur in a face-to-face situation in which the supervisor provides constructive information, encouragement, and guidelines for the improvement of the worker's future performance.

STUDY QUESTIONS AND EXERCISES

1. What are the products of a job analysis? How do they in turn affect other organizational outcomes?

2. Compare and contrast the three structured methods of job analysis: functional job analysis, the *Position Analysis Questionnaire,* and the critical incidents technique. What are the strengths and weaknesses of each?

3. Consider your current job, or a job that you or a friend held in the past. How would you begin to conduct a job analysis of that position? What methods would you use? What are the important components of the job?

4. What are the advantages and disadvantages of using graphic rating scales versus comparative methods of performance appraisals?

5. In some organizations, performance appraisals are taken too lightly. They receive little attention and are conducted irregularly and infrequently, and there is little motivation for appraisers to do a good job. Why might this occur? Imagine that your task is to convince the management of one of these organizations to improve their performance appraisal system. What would you say to convince them? What components of a good performance appraisal system would you suggest they implement?

SUGGESTED READINGS

Carroll, S., & Schneier, C. E. (1982). *Performance appraisal and review systems.* Glenview, IL: Scott, Foresman. *An applications-oriented text on the design, implementation, and appraisal of human performance in the work place.*

Dunnette, M. D., & Fleishman, E. A. (Eds.). (1982). *Human performance and productivity: Human capability assessment.* Hillsdale, NJ: Lawrence Erlbaum. *A fairly technical edited book arranged around the theme of research on performance. The various articles illustrate how the variable of job performance relates to nearly every aspect of I/O psychology.*

Gael, S. (Ed.). (1987). *Job analysis handbook for business, industry, and government.* New York: John Wiley & Sons. *An edited book of readings on job analysis.*

Swanson, R. A., & Gradous, D. (1986). *Performance at work: A systematic program for analyzing work behavior.* New York: John Wiley & Sons. *An easy, step-by-step guide to assist managers in analyzing and measuring work performance.*

4

PERSONNEL RECRUITMENT, SCREENING, AND SELECTION

Understanding Personnel Issues and Processes

In this chapter, we continue to build on some of the topics and concepts introduced in the two previous chapters. Personnel screening and selection processes are strongly grounded in research and measurement issues. For example, in our discussion of personnel screening and testing methods, we investigate further issues of measurement reliability and validity first introduced in Chapter 2. The personnel processes discussed in this chapter are also built on a foundation of job analysis and the measurement of performance outcomes presented in Chapter 3. A study hint for organizing and understanding the many screening procedures presented in this chapter is to consider those processes in the context of the measurement issues discussed previously. In other words, much of the strength or weakness of any particular screening method is determined by its ability to predict important work outcomes, which is usually job performance. Issues of validity and reliability of the screening methods are critical here. For example, one of the weaknesses of hiring interviews is the questionable reliability and validity of evaluations of applicants made in such circumstances, while the strengths of standardized screening tests are their established levels of reliability and validity. However, other important considerations for screening methods concern their cost and ease of use, or in other words, their utility. Hiring interviews, for example, are considered to be relatively easy to use, while testing programs are thought to be (rightly or wrongly) costly and difficult to implement.

When considering personnel functions it is important to note the influence exerted by federal legislation and court decisions. Federal guidelines, developed to prevent employment discrimination, have, in a sense, forced employers to take a hard look at the quality of the methods used to recruit, screen, and select employees. This has led to the greater involvement of I/O psychologists in the development of more accurate and fairer personnel screening and selection procedures.

Since personnel issues deal with the care and nurturing of an organization's human resources and since psychology often has a similar concern with human potential, there is a natural link between psychology and personnel work. As a result, many students trained in psychology and other social sciences are drawn to careers in personnel. The use of psychological testing, interviewing procedures, and measurement issues in general also help to connect the two fields.

Organizations spend a tremendous amount of time, money, and energy trying to recruit and select a qualified, capable, and productive work force. As the skilled labor market becomes tighter and tighter with greater competition for the best workers, companies are realizing the importance of developing comprehensive programs for employee recruitment, screening, and selection. Moreover, they are beginning to understand that the costs of hiring the wrong types of workers greatly outweigh the investment of developing good recruitment and screening programs. Depending on the job level, the costs of recruiting, selecting, training, and then releasing a single employee can range from a few thousand dollars to several hundreds of thousands of dollars (Wanous, 1980).

In this chapter we will follow the progression of personnel functions involved in the recruitment and selection of workers. We will begin with an examination of personnel recruitment and then look at the procedures for screening and evaluating job applicants, including standardized tests and hiring interviews. Finally, we will discuss how employers use the information obtained from job applicants to make their selection decisions.

PERSONNEL RECRUITMENT

Personnel recruitment is the process by which organizations attract potential workers to apply for jobs. More and more, organizations are developing strategic programs for recruitment. One of the primary objectives of a successful program is to attract a large pool of qualified applicants. There are a wide variety of recruitment techniques and tactics. Those most familiar to college students are the on-campus recruitment programs conducted by large organizations and the traditional advertisement of job openings in newspapers or trade magazines. Other methods include various media advertising, such as job advertisements on television, radio, or billboards, the use of employment agencies, and referrals by current employees.

*personnel recruitment
the means by which
companies attract job
applicants*

Research has assessed the effectiveness of the various recruitment methods by examining both the quality of newly hired workers and the rate of turnover in new workers. There is evidence that employee referrals and applicant-initiated contacts (that is, "walk-ins") may yield higher quality workers and those who are more likely to remain with the company than newspaper ads or employment agency placement (Breaugh, 1981; Decker & Cornelius, 1979; Taylor & Schmidt, 1983). However, since different methods of recruitment will reach different types of workers, the success of any particular tactic may depend on the sort of job opening and the ability of the method to reach the "right" group of potential job applicants (Swaroff, Barclay, & Bass, 1985). For instance, it is considered common knowledge in many corporations that

On-campus recruitment programs help major companies find qualified new employees.

higher-level management positions are recruited through word-of-mouth or employment agencies but never through newspaper ads, which are considered appropriate for lower-level jobs.

Recruitment is a two-way process: While the recruiting organization is attempting to attract and later evaluate prospective employees, job applicants are evaluating various potential employers. There is considerable evidence that the characteristics of an organization's recruitment program and recruiters can influence applicants' decisions to accept or reject offers of employment (Rynes, Heneman, & Schwab, 1980; Taylor & Bergmann, 1987).

In their efforts to attract applicants, many companies will "oversell" a particular job or their organization. Advertisements may say that "this is a great place to work," or that the position is "challenging" and offers "tremendous potential for advancement." There is no problem if such statements are true, but if the job and the organization are presented in a misleading, overly positive manner, the strategy will eventually backfire. Although the recruitment process may attract applicants, the new employees will quickly discover that they were fooled, and may look for work elsewhere or become dissatisfied and unmotivated. An important factor in the recruitment process that may help alleviate potential misperceptions is the **realistic job preview (RJP),** which is an accurate description of the duties and responsibilities of a particular job. Realistic job previews can take the form of an oral presentation from a recruiter, supervisor, or job incumbent; a visit to the job site; or a discussion in a brochure, manual, or videotape (Colarelli, 1984). Research has shown

realistic job preview (RJP)
an accurate presentation of the prospective job and organization made to applicants

that realistic job previews are important in increasing job commitment and satisfaction and in decreasing initial turnover of new employees (McEvoy & Cascio, 1985; Premack & Wanous, 1985). Some of the positive effect of RJPs is caused by the applicant's process of self-selection. Presented with a realistic view of what the job will be like, the applicant can make an informed decision about whether the job is appropriate. RJPs may also be effective because they lower unrealistically high expectations about the job and may provide an applicant with information that will later be useful in dealing with work-related problems and stress (Porter & Steers, 1973; Wanous, 1980). The implementation of realistic job previews often requires processing more applicants for job openings, because a greater proportion of applicants presented with the RJP will decline the job offer than when no preview is given. However, the usual result is a better match between the position and the worker hired, and a more satisfied new worker.

Another important consideration for any recruitment program is to avoid unintentional discrimination against underrepresented groups, such as women, ethnic minorities, the elderly, and the handicapped. Employers must take steps to attract applicants from such groups in proportion to their numbers in the population from which the company's work force is drawn. In other words, if a company is in an area where the population within a 10 to 20 mile radius is 40 percent white, 30 percent black, 10 percent Asian, and 10 percent Hispanic, the recruitment program should draw applicants in roughly those proportions. We will discuss the topics of employment discrimination and equal employment opportunity later in this chapter.

PERSONNEL SCREENING

Personnel screening is the process of reviewing information about job applicants to select individuals for jobs. A wide variety of data, such as resumes, job applications, employment tests, hiring interviews, and letters of recommendation, can be used in screening and selecting potential employees. If you have ever applied for a job, you have had firsthand experience with some of these.

personnel screening the process of reviewing information about job applicants to choose workers

EVALUATION OF WRITTEN MATERIALS

The first step in the screening process involves the evaluation of written materials such as applications and résumés. Usually, standard application forms are used for screening lower-level positions in an organization, with résumés used to provide biographical data and other background information for higher-level jobs, although many companies require all applicants to complete an application form. The main purpose of the application and résumé is to collect biographical information such as education, work experience, and outstanding work or school accomplishments. Such data are believed to be among the best predictors of future job performance (Owens, 1976).

Most companies use a standard application form. (See the sample application form in Figure 4.1.) As with all employment screening devices, the application form should collect only information that has been determined to be job related. Questions that are not job related, and especially those that may lead to job discrimination, such as inquiries about age, ethnic background, religious affiliation, marital status, or finances, should not be included.

From the employer's perspective, the difficulty with application forms is evaluating and interpreting the information obtained to determine the most qualified applicants. For example, it may be difficult to choose between an applicant with little education but ample work experience and an educated person with no work experience.

There have been attempts to quantify the biographical information obtained from application forms through the use of either weighted application forms or biographical information blanks (BIBs). **Weighted application forms** assign different weights to each bit of information on the form. The weights are determined through detailed research, conducted by the organization, to determine the relationship between specific bits of biographical data and criteria of success on the job (Cascio, 1976). The information that most consistently predicts job success usually deals with level of education and prior work experience (Lawrence, Salsburg, Dawson, & Fasman, 1982).

Biographical information blanks are application forms turned into a forced-choice test. Along with items designed to measure basic biographical information such as education and work history, the BIB might also have questions of a more personal nature, probing the applicant's attitudes, values, likes, and dislikes (Owens, 1976). Biographical information blanks are much longer than traditional application forms and take a great deal of research to develop and validate. Because BIBs are typically designed to screen applicants for one specific job, they are most likely used only for higher-level positions. Research indicates that a BIB is an effective screening and placement tool (Owens & Schoenfeldt, 1979; Reilly & Chao, 1982). Comprehensive BIBs can give a very detailed description and classification of an applicant's behavioral history—a very good predictor of future behavior. (Sample BIB items are given in Figure 4.2.) One potential problem in the use of BIBs concerns the personal nature of many of the questions and the possibility of unintentional discrimination against minority groups because of items regarding age, financial circumstances, and the like. Thus BIBs should only be developed and administered by professionals trained in test use and validation.

weighted application forms
forms that assign different weights to the various information provided on a job application

biographical information blank (BIB)
a personnel screening form that assesses basic biographical information and applicant attitudes and values

APPLICATION FOR EMPLOYMENT
FOR THE POSITION OF

Job Title _____ Job Number _____

1. INSTRUCTIONS

Print in dark ink or type

Applicants failing to complete all sections of this form will be disqualified from consideration for positions.

2. NAME, ADDRESS AND TELEPHONE

Name: Last, First, Middle Initial

Address: Number, Street, Apartment or Space Number

City, State, Zip Code

Home: (   )
Work: (   )
Message: (   )
Ask for:

Area Code   Telephone Number

3. EMPLOYMENT HISTORY

Please show all employment within the last ten years plus other related experience. Include military or volunteer experience. Begin with your current employer. A resume may be attached, but will not be accepted in lieu of completion of any section of this form.

Firm Name (Department)	From: Mo/Yr	Title
Street	To: Mo/Yr	Duties
City, State, Zip Code	Total: Years & Mos	
Telephone (include area code)	Starting Salary	
Supervisor's Name	Final Salary	
Supervisor's Title	Hrs. Worked per Week	Reason for Wanting to Leave

Firm Name (Department)	From: Mo/Yr	Title
Street	To: Mo/Yr	Duties
City, State, Zip Code	Total: Years & Mos	
Telephone (include area code)	Starting Salary	
Supervisor's Name	Final Salary	
Supervisor's Title	Hrs. Worked per Week	Reason for Leaving

Firm Name (Department)	From: Mo/Yr	Title
Street	To: Mo/Yr	Duties
City, State, Zip Code	Total: Years & Mos	
Telephone (include area code)	Starting Salary	
Supervisor's Name	Final Salary	
Supervisor's Title	Hrs. Worked per Week	Reason for Leaving

Name: Last, First, Middle Initial:

Job Title:

Job Number:

4. EDUCATION AND TRAINING

Circle highest level completed: 9   10   11   12   GED   College: 1   2   3   4   5   6   7   8

Institutions of higher education, trade, vocational or professional schools attended (other than high school):

| School | Dates Attended | Major/Concentration | Degree/Certificate |

5. SKILLS, LICENSES, AND CERTIFICATES

Please list all skills related to this position. For licenses and certificates, list the type, class, state, level and expiration date.

6. GENERAL INFORMATION

1. Have you ever been employed under any other name? ☐ No ☐ Yes

   If yes, please indicate name(s):
   (This information will be used to facilitate verification of work records.)

2. May we contact your current employer? ☐ Yes ☐ No   Previous employers? ☐ Yes ☐ No

3. Do you have a current physical or mental disability that would limit your ability to perform the full range of duties in the job for which you are applying? ☐ No ☐ Yes

   If yes, describe what reasonable accommodations could be made: _____

4. Please describe in detail how your experience, knowledges and abilities qualify you for this position:

5. Check all appropriate boxes which indicate your interest:
   ☐ Full-Time ☐ Part-Time ☐ Permanent ☐ Temporary

6. How soon are you available for employment? _____

7. CLERICAL AND SECRETARIAL APPLICANTS ONLY

Indicate which of the following you are skilled in using:
☐ Typewriter _____ (cwpm) ☐ Shorthand _____ (wpm) ☐ Word Processor ☐ Dictating Machine
☐ Other: _____

Figure 4.1
SAMPLE APPLICATION FORM

99

Figure 4.2
SAMPLE BIOGRAPHICAL
INFORMATION BLANK
(BIB) ITEMS

How successful were your teachers in arousing your academic interests?
a. Extremely successful
b. Very successful
c. Somewhat successful
d. Not at all successful

What is your usual state of health?
a. Never ill
b. Never seriously ill
c. About average
d. Feel poorly from time to time
e. Often feel "under the weather"

On the average, how many hours of homework did you do a week in high school?
a. 20 or more
b. 10–20
c. 5–10
d. Less than 5

Which one of the following seems most important to you?
a. A pleasant home and family life
b. A challenging and exciting job
c. Getting ahead in the world
d. Being active and accepted in community affairs
e. Making the most of your particular ability

Do you generally do your best:
a. At whatever job you are doing
b. Only in what you are interested
c. Only when it is demanded of you

PERSONNEL TESTING

After the evaluation of the biographical information available from résumés, application forms, or other sources, the next step in comprehensive employee screening programs is employment testing. As we saw in Chapter 1, the history of personnel testing in I/O psychology goes back to World War I, when intelligence testing of armed forces recruits was used for personnel placement. Today, the use of tests for employment screening and placement has expanded greatly. A considerable percentage of large companies and most government agencies routinely use some form of employment tests to measure a wide range of characteristics that are predictive of successful job performance. For example, some tests measure specific skills or abilities required by a job, while others assess more general cognitive skills or mechanical aptitude believed to be needed for the successful performance of certain jobs. Still other tests measure personality dimensions that are believed to be important for particular occu-

Job applicants at an auto plant are tested for their ability to assemble a circuit board and manage a circuit-assembly business.

pations. Before we discuss specific types of screening tests, however, it is important to consider some issues and guidelines for the development and use of tests and other screening methods.

CONSIDERATIONS IN THE DEVELOPMENT AND USE OF PERSONNEL SCREENING AND TESTING METHODS

As with any measures used in industrial/organizational psychology, personnel screening methods must be reliable and valid predictors of job success. As you recall from our discussion of research methods in Chapter 2, reliability refers to whether a measure will give consistent readings over time, and validity deals with an instrument's ability to measure accurately what it is supposed to measure. Standardized and commercially available psychological tests have typically demonstrated high levels of reliability and validity for use in certain circumstances. However, even with widely used standardized tests it is critical that their ability to predict job success be established for the particular positions in question. It is especially necessary to assure the reliability and validity of nonstandardized screening methods, such as a weighted application form or a test constructed for a specific job.

There are a variety of methods for establishing the reliability of a screening instrument. One technique is **test-retest reliability.** Here a particular test or other measurement instrument is administered to the same individual at two different times, usually a one- to two-week interval. Scores on the first test are then correlated with those on the second test. If the correlation is high (a correlation coefficient approaching +1.0), reliability is established. Of course the assumption is made that nothing has

test-retest reliability a method of determining the reliability of a measurement instrument by administering the same measure to the same people at two different times and then correlating the scores

happened during the administration of the two tests that would cause the scores to change drastically.

A second means of determining the reliability of an employment screening measure is the **parallel forms** method. Here two equivalent tests are constructed, each of which presumably measures the same construct but using different items or questions. Test-takers are administered both forms of the instrument. Reliability is established if the correlation between the two scores is high. Of course the major drawback to this method is the time invested in creating two equivalent tests.

Today, the most common way to establish the reliability of a test instrument is by estimating its **internal consistency.** If a test is reliable, each item should measure the same general construct. Performance on one item should thus be consistent with performance on all other items. Two specific methods are used to determine internal consistency. The first is to divide the test items into two equal parts and correlate the summed score on the first half of the items with that on the second half. This is referred to as split-half reliability. A second method, which involves numerous calculations, is to determine the average intercorrelation among all items of the test. The resulting coefficient is an estimate of the test's internal consistency.

Although there are many ways to determine test validity, the two forms of validity that are most important for the development and use of employment screening tests are content validity and criterion-related validity.

Content validity is the ability of the content of the measurement instrument (that is, the test items) to measure adequately the knowledge, skills, abilities, and other characteristics necessary to perform a job. Typically, content validity is established by having experts such as job incumbents or supervisors judge the appropriateness of the test items, taking into account information from the job analysis. Ideally, the experts should determine that the test content does indeed represent the job content. Content validity is especially important for organizations constructing their own screening tests for specific jobs.

Criterion-related validity is established by determining the relationship between the test scores and some criterion of job success, most often an indicator of job performance such as a measure of work output or quality. There are two approaches to determining criterion-related validity. The first is the follow-up method (often called predictive validity). Here the screening test is administered to applicants without interpreting the scores and without using them to select among applicants. Once the applicants become employees, criterion measures such as job performance assessments are collected. If the test instrument is valid, the test scores should correlate positively with the criterion measure. Once the validity of the instrument is established, test scores are used to select the highest scoring applicants for jobs. The obvious advantage of the predictive validity method is that it demonstrates how scores on the screening

parallel forms
a method of establishing the reliability of a measurement instrument by correlating scores on two different but equivalent versions of the same instrument

internal consistency
a common method of establishing test reliability by examining how the various items intercorrelate

content validity
the ability of the items in a measurement instrument to measure adequately the various characteristics needed to perform a job

criterion-related validity
the accuracy of a measurement instrument in determining the relationship between scores on the instrument and some criterion of job success

instrument actually relate to future job performance. The major drawback to this approach is the time that it takes to establish validity. In the second approach, known as the present-employee method (also termed concurrent validity), the test is given to current employees, and their scores are correlated with some criterion of their current performance. Again, a positive relationship between test scores and criterion scores establishes validity. Once validity is established, a comparison of applicants' test scores with the incumbents' scores is used to select the most qualified applicants. While the concurrent validity method leads to a quicker estimate of validity, it may not be as accurate an assessment of criterion-related validity as the predictive method, since the job incumbents represent a select group. In other words, there is no information about workers who were fired or quit their jobs, or applicants who were not chosen for jobs.

TYPES OF PERSONNEL SCREENING TESTS

The majority of the employee screening and selection instruments are standardized, published tests that have been subjected to research to demonstrate their validity and reliability. Most also contain information to insure that they are administered, scored, and interpreted in a uniform manner. The alternative to the use of standardized tests is for the organi-

Some employment tests involve sophisticated technology, such as this flight simulator used to train and test airline pilots.

zation to construct a test for a particular job or class of jobs, and conduct its own studies of the test's reliability and validity. However, because this is a costly procedure, most employers use standardized screening tests.

Test formats, or the way in which tests are administered, can vary greatly. Several distinctions are important when categorizing employment tests. Formats can be described as individual- versus group-administered tests, speed versus power tests, and paper-and-pencil versus performance tests. Group tests are designed to be given to many individuals simultaneously, while individual tests must be administered one at a time. Usually, tests that require sophisticated apparatus, such as a driving simulator, or tests that require constant supervision are administered individually. Many paper-and-pencil tests can be group administered. Speed tests have a fixed time limit, while power tests allow test-takers sufficient time to complete the entire test. A typing test is an example of a speed test, while many personality tests are power tests, requiring that all test items be completed. Finally, paper-and-pencil tests require some form of written reply. Performance tests, such as tests of manual dexterity or grip strength, usually involve the manipulation of physical objects.

While the format of an employment test is significant, the most important way of classifying the instruments is in terms of the characteristics or attributes they measure: cognitive abilities, mechanical abilities, motor and sensory abilities, job skills and knowledge, or personality traits. (See Table 4.1 for examples of these various tests.)

Cognitive ability tests. Tests of cognitive ability range from tests of general intellectual ability to tests of specific cognitive skills. Group-administered, pencil-and-paper tests of general intelligence have been used in personnel screening for some time. Two such widely used instruments are the Otis Self-Administering Test of Mental Ability (Otis, 1929) and the Wonderlic Personnel Test (Wonderlic, 1945). Both are fairly short and assess basic verbal and numerical abilities. Designed to measure abilities to learn simple jobs, follow instructions, and solve work-related problems and difficulties, these tests are used to screen applicants for positions as office clerks, assembly workers, machine operators, and certain front-line supervisors.

One criticism of using general intelligence tests for employee selection is that they measure cognitive abilities that are *too* general to be effective predictors of specific job-related cognitive skills. However, recent research indicates that such general tests are reasonably good predictors of job performance (Gottfredson, 1986; Hunter & Hunter, 1984).

In the late 1960s and 1970s employers became reluctant to use general intelligence tests for screening job applicants because of fears that they might discriminate against certain ethnic minorities, and there is some evidence that their scores may tend to favor the economically and educationally advantaged. Because certain minorities are at an educational and economic disadvantage, scores on intelligence tests may not fairly esti-

Table 4.1 SOME STANDARDIZED TESTS USED IN PERSONNEL SCREENING
AND SELECTION

Cognitive Ability Tests

Comprehensive Ability Battery (Hakstian & Cattell, 1975–82): Features 20 tests, each designed to measure a single primary cognitive ability, many of which are important in industrial settings. Among the tests are those assessing verbal ability, numerical ability, clerical speed and accuracy, and ability to organize and produce ideas as well as several memory scales.

Wonderlic Personnel Test (Wonderlic, 1983): A 50-item pencil-and-paper test measuring level of mental ability for employment.

Wechsler Adult Intelligence Scale–Revised or *WAISR* (Wechsler, 1981): A comprehensive group of 11 subtests measuring general levels of intellectual functioning. The WAISR is administered individually and takes more than an hour to complete. One of the most widely used intelligence tests.

Mechanical Ability Tests

Bennett Mechanical Comprehension Test (Bennett, 1980): A 68-item pencil-and-paper test of ability to understand physical and mechanical principles in practical situations. Can be group administered; comes in two equivalent forms.

Mechanical Ability Test (Morrisby, 1955): A 35-item multiple-choice instrument that measures natural mechanical aptitude. Used to predict potential in engineering, assembly work, carpentry, and building trades.

Motor and Sensory Ability Tests

Hand-Tool Dexterity Test (Bennett, 1981): Using a wooden frame, wrenches, and screwdrivers, the test-taker takes apart 12 bolts in a prescribed sequence and reassembles them in another position. This speed test measures manipulative skills important in factory jobs and in jobs servicing mechanical equipment and automobiles.

O'Connor Finger Dexterity Test (O'Connor, 1977): A timed performance test measuring fine motor dexterity needed for fine assembly work and other jobs requiring manipulation of small objects. Test-taker is given a board with symmetrical rows of holes and a cup of pins. The task is to place 3 pins in each hole as quickly as possible.

Job Skills and Knowledge Tests

Minnesota Clerical Assessment Battery or *MCAB* (Vale & Prestwood, 1987): A self-administered battery of 6 subtests measuring the skills and knowledge necessary for clerical and secretarial work. Testing is completely computer administered. Included are tests of typing, proofreading, filing, business vocabulary, business math, and clerical knowledge.

Purdue Blueprint Reading Test (Owen & Arnold, 1988): A muiltiple-choice test assessing ability to read standard blueprints.

Typing Test for Business, or *TTB* (Doppelt, Hartman, & Krawchick, 1984): A performance test measuring the skill of applicants in 5 kinds of typing used most often in the work place, such as typing letters, manuscripts, and tables.

Personality Tests

California Psychological Inventory or *CPI* (Gough, 1987): A 480-item pencil-and-paper inventory of 20 personality dimensions. Has been used in selecting managers, sales personnel, and leadership positions.

Hogan Personnel Selection Series (Hogan & Hogan, 1985): This pencil-and-paper test assesses personality dimensions of applicants and compares their profiles to patterns of successful job incumbents in clerical, sales, and managerial positions. Consists of 4 inventories: the prospective employee potential inventory, the clerical potential inventory, the sales potential inventory, and the managerial potential inventory.

Sixteen Personality Factors Questionnaire, or *16 PF* (Cattell, 1986): Similar to the CPI, this test measures 16 basic personality dimensions, some of which are related to successful job performance in certain positions. This general personality inventory has been used extensively in personnel screening and selection.

mate their intellectual abilities and potentials. In certain instances, this may lead to unfair discrimination in personnel selection, a concern we will discuss in the section on legal issues later in this chapter.

Mechanical ability tests. Standardized tests have also been developed to measure abilities in identifying, recognizing, and applying mechanical principles. These tests are particularly effective in screening applicants for positions operating or repairing machinery, for construction jobs, and for certain engineering positions. The Bennett Mechanical Comprehension Test, or BMCT (Bennett, 1980) is one such commonly used instrument. The BMCT consists of sixty-eight items, each of which requires the application of a physical law or a mechanical operation (for examples, see Figure 4.3).

Motor and sensory ability tests. A number of tests measure specific motor skills or sensory abilities. Tests such as the Crawford Small Parts Dexterity Test (Crawford, 1981) and the Purdue Pegboard (Tiffin, 1968) are timed performance instruments that require the manipulation of small parts to measure the fine motor dexterity in hands and fingers required in jobs such as assembling computer components and soldering electrical equipment. For example, the Crawford test uses boards with small holes into which tiny pins must be placed using a pair of tweezers. The second part of the test requires screwing small screws into threaded holes with a screwdriver.

Sensory ability tests include tests of hearing, visual acuity, and perceptual discrimination. The most common test of visual acuity is the Snellen Eye Chart, which consists of rows of letters that become increasingly smaller. Various electronic instruments are used to measure hearing acuity. No doubt you have taken one or more of these in school or in a doctor's office. In employment settings, they are used in basic screening for positions such as inspectors or bus drivers that require fine audio or visual discrimination.

Job skills and knowledge tests. Various standardized tests also assess specific job skills or domains of job knowledge. Examples of job skill tests for clerical workers would be a standardized typing test or tests of other specific clerical skills such as proofreading, alphabetical filing, correcting spelling or grammatical errors, and using a word processor.

Standardized tests of job knowledge include the Computer Competence Tests (Psychological Corporation, 1986), a series of five tests designed to assess competency in several areas of computer knowledge, such as operations, historical development, and the application of technology.

work samples
a job skill test that measures applicants' abilities to perform brief examples of important job tasks

A special sort of job skill test involves the use of **work samples,** which measure applicants' abilities to perform brief examples of some of the

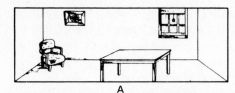

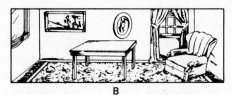

Which room has more of an echo?

Figure 4.3

SAMPLE ITEMS FROM
THE BENNETT TEST
OF MECHANICAL
COMPREHENSION

Source: G. K. Bennett, *Test of Mechanical Comprehension* (New York: Psychological Corporation, 1940).

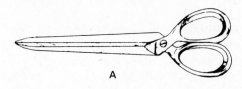

Which would be the better shears for cutting metal?

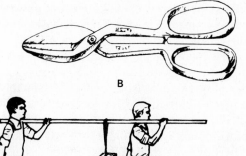

Which man carries more weight? (If equal, mark C.)

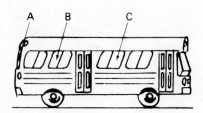

Which letter shows the seat where a passenger will get the smoothest ride?

critical tasks that the job requires. The sample tasks are constructed as tests, administered under standard testing conditions and scored on some predetermined scale. Their obvious advantage is that they are clearly job related. A drawback is that work samples are usually rather expensive to develop and take a great deal of time to administer.

One example of a work sample test was developed for applicants for the job of concession stand attendant at a city park's snack bar. The test required applicants to use the cash register, make change, fill out a report, page someone over a loud speaker, and react to an "irate customer" who was arguing about receiving the wrong change. In addition to being an effective screening device, this work sample also served as a realistic job preview, providing applicants with a good idea of what the job was all about (Cascio & Phillips, 1979).

Personality tests. **Personality tests** are designed to measure certain psychological characteristics of workers. A wide variety of these tests are used in personnel screening and selection to attempt to match the personality characteristics of job applicants with those of workers who have performed the job successfully in the past. In recent years there has been a controversy over the use of such tests because the links between general personality dimensions and the performance of specific work tasks may not be very direct. Indeed, early research indicates that these general tests may not be very accurate predictors of job performance (Ghiselli, 1973; Guion & Gottier, 1965). However, more recent evidence suggests that certain work-related personality characteristics can be reasonably good predictors of job performance, particularly for management and leadership positions (Cascio, 1987).

General personality inventories such as the Minnesota Multiphasic Personality Inventory or MMPI (Hathaway & McKinley, 1970), are also used to screen out applicants who possess some psychopathology that might hinder the performance of sensitive jobs, such as police officer, airline pilot, or nuclear power plant operator. However, most of the time, personality tests are used to assess the "normal" characteristics that are deemed to be important for the performance of certain jobs. For example, personality dimensions such as achievement or persistence might be used to screen applicants for positions in sales jobs, and tests for traits of responsibility and service orientation may be administered to applicants for bank teller positions.

There has been a recent trend toward developing personality tests that more specifically measure job-relevant aspects of personality. For example, Gough (1984, 1985) has derived work orientation and managerial potential scales from the California Psychological Inventory (CPI), a general personality inventory that measures twenty personality dimensions (Gough, 1987) (see Figure 4.4). The work orientation scale of the CPI is a

personality tests *instruments that measure psychological traits of individuals*

Figure 4.4
SAMPLE ITEMS FROM
THE *CALIFORNIA PSYCHO-
LOGICAL INVENTORY*

Note: This is not a "mini-
test". It is simply an illustra-
tive sample of items from the
*California Psychological In-
ventory.*
Source: H. G. Gough,
*California Psychological In-
ventory* (Palo Alto, CA: Consulting Psychologists Press,
1986).

> If you *agree* with a statement, or feel that it is true about you, answer
> TRUE. If you *disagree* with a statement, or feel that it is not true about
> you, answer FALSE.
>
> TRUE   FALSE
>
> People often expect too much of me.
>
> The idea of doing research appeals to me.
>
> It is hard for me just to sit still and relax.
>
> I enjoy hearing lectures on world affairs.
>
> I read at least ten books a year.
>
> I like parties and socials.

predictor of employee performance across positions, while the managerial
potential scale is used in screening and selecting candidates for management and supervisory positions. Hogan and Hogan (1985) have developed
a series of personality scales to measure personality characteristics predictive of employee success in general job categories such as sales, management, and clerical work. These more job-relevant scales are proving to
be better predictors of job performance than the more general personality
inventories.

Miscellaneous tests. In the past, **polygraphs,** or lie detectors, have
also been used in employee selection. Most often polygraphs are used to
screen out "dishonest" applicants for positions in which they would have
to handle cash or expensive merchandise, although they have also been
used by a wide number of organizations to screen and select employees
for almost any position. Polygraphs are instruments designed to measure
physiological reactions, such as respiration, blood pressure, or perspira-
tion, that are presumably associated with lying. As applicants are asked
questions about past honest and dishonest behavior, the examiner looks
for physiological changes that may indicate deception.

Research, however, has questioned the validity of polygraphs. The
major problem concerns the rate of "false positive" errors, or innocent
persons who are incorrectly scored as lying. Because of this questionable
validity and the potential harm that invalid results could do to innocent
people, the federal government has recently passed legislation restricting

polygraph
*an instrument that
measures physiological
reactions presumed to
accompany deception;
also known as a lie
detector*

Testing for Employee Honesty and Integrity: Does It Work?

In recent years there has been great controversy over the use of polygraphs in employee screening, and for other purposes such as attempting to discover the culprit in an incident of employee theft. Much of this controversy stems from studies that have questioned the validity of polygraphs. Estimates of their accuracy range from just over 50 percent, where 50 percent is pure chance that a polygraph subject is either honest or dishonest, to about 90 percent. Because polygraph results are usually dichotomous—you either are dishonest or honest—there is a great deal of concern about such inaccuracies, regardless of their magnitude. In other words, labeling even a small percentage of honest people as liars is a serious error. Moreover, while polygraphs may catch a large percentage of dishonest individuals, a small percentage of thieves will escape undetected. The result of all of this is recent federal legislation that has banned the routine use of polygraphs in employee screening and selection. Polygraphs can now only be used in the screening and selection of persons for sensitive government positions or jobs that involve public security, such as police positions or jobs involving the handling of controlled substances, particularly drugs. Employers may also request employees to submit to a polygraph test only in the case of a specific incident of theft or property damage and only if the employee had access to the property, there is reasonable suspicion of the person, and the employer suffered a financial loss from the incident (Camara, 1988).

While the use of polygraphs in the work place has been restricted, it is unclear whether these restrictions also govern the use of paper-and-pencil tests of honesty or integrity, which is on the rise, even though there has been very little sound research supporting their validity (Sackett & Harris, 1984). Typically, these tests ask about past honest/dishonest behavior or about attitudes condoning dishonest behavior. Typical questions might ask, "What is the total value of cash and merchandise you have taken from your employer in the past year?" or "An employer who pays people poorly has it coming when employees steal. Do you agree or disagree with this statement?" One obvious problem with these tests is the possibility of faking the results and thus "beating" the test, although some of the instruments do include scales to measure if the respondents are distorting their responses. Despite the fact that only a very few individuals would be knowledgeable enough about honesty tests to be able to beat them, this can still cause a problem, since persons motivated to try to beat the test are most likely to be those who have something important to hide. Like polygraphs, these tests also raise the important issue of "false positives," honest persons who are judged dishonest by the instruments. Finally, there is some concern over the cost versus the benefits of honesty testing. In many cases, the dollar amount of employee theft may not be great enough to justify the expense of testing large numbers of employees and the costs of wrongly dismissing those honest individuals who were false positives. Moreover, the use of honesty testing, in any form, may put people on guard and create an air of mistrust. Workers may feel that management has lost faith in them, and in the long run, the general erosion of employee morale and loyalty may be more damaging to the company than the losses incurred because of dishonest employees.

the use of polygraphs in general employment screening (see On the Cutting Edge). However, polygraphs are still allowed for testing employees about specific incidents, such as thefts, and for screening applicants for public health and safety jobs and for sensitive government positions (Camara, 1988).

Another questionable screening "test" is handwriting analysis, or graphology. In graphology, a person trained in handwriting analysis makes judgments about an applicant's job potential by examining the personality characteristics that are supposedly revealed in the shape, size, and slant of the letters in a sample of handwriting. Although used by some companies to screen applicants, the validity of handwriting analysis to assess performance potential is highly questionable (Ben-Shakhar, Bar-Hillel, Bilu, Ben-Abba, & Flug, 1986; Rafaeli & Klimoski, 1983).

Because of the increased use and abuse of drugs in the United States, many organizations are beginning to screen applicants routinely for illegal drug use, particularly marijuana and cocaine. As with polygraphs, a problem with drug testing is the rate of false positives, because current laboratory tests are not completely accurate. Unlike the polygraph, however, today there are few restrictions on drug testing in work settings (Cascio, 1987). Such testing is on the rise and will likely continue to increase.

THE EFFECTIVENESS OF PERSONNEL SCREENING TESTS

The effectiveness of using standardized tests for screening potential employees remains a controversial issue. Critics of testing cite the low validity coefficients (approximately .20) of certain employment tests. (A validity coefficient is a correlation coefficient between the predictor, the test score, and the criterion, usually a measure of subsequent job performance.) However, supporters believe that a comparison of all screening methods—tests, biographical information, hiring interviews— across the full spectrum of jobs reveals that employment tests are the best predictors of job performance (Hunter & Hunter, 1984). Obviously, the ability of a test to predict performance in a specific job depends on how well it can capture and measure the particular skills, knowledge, or abilities required. For example, tests of typing and other clerical skills are good predictors of success in secretarial positions because they do a good job of assessing the skills and knowledge needed to be a successful secretary.

The most effective use of screening tests occurs when a number of instruments are used in combination to predict effective job performance. Because most jobs are complex, involving a wide range of tasks, it is unlikely that successful performance is due to just one particular type of knowledge or skill. Therefore, any single test will only be able to predict one aspect of a total job. Employment screening tests are usually grouped together into a **test battery.** Scores on the various tests in the battery are used in combination to help select the best possible candidates for the job.

We have seen that standardized tests can be reliable and valid screening devices for many jobs. However, two important issues regarding this use of tests must be considered: validity generalization and test utility. The **validity generalization** of a screening test refers to its validity in predicting performance in a job or setting different from the one in which the test was validated. For example, a standardized test of managerial potential is found to be valid in selecting successful managers in a manufactur-

test battery
a combination of personnel tests used to increase the ability to predict job performance

validity generalization
the ability of a screening instrument to predict performance in a job or setting different from the one in which the test was validated

ing industry. If the test is also helpful in choosing managers in a service organization, its validity has generalized from one organization to another. Similarly, validity generalization would exist if a test of clerical abilities is successful in selecting applicants for both secretarial and receptionist positions. Of course, the more similar the jobs and organizations involved in the validity studies are to the jobs and organizations that subsequently use the screening tests, the more likely it is that validity will generalize from the one situation to the other.

High validity generalization of a standardized test will greatly increase its usefulness—and reduce the work load of I/O psychologists because the instrument may not need to be validated for use with each and every position and organization. Some I/O psychologists, such as Schmidt and his colleagues, argue that the validity generalization of most standardized personnel screening procedures is quite high, which means that they can be used successfully in a variety of employment settings and job classifications (Pearlman, Schmidt, & Hunter, 1980; Schmidt & Hunter, 1977, 1981; Schmidt, Hunter, Outerbridge, & Trattner, 1986). At the other extreme is the view that the ability of tests to predict future job success is situation-specific, and validity should be established for each use of a screening instrument. Although few I/O psychologists believe that validity of test instruments is completely situation specific, there is some disagreement over how well their validity generalizes.

Test utility is the value of a screening test in helping to affect important organizational outcomes. In other words, test utility determines the success of a test in terms of dollars gained by the company through the increased performance and productivity of workers selected based on test scores. For example, in one organization a valid screening test was used to select applicants for 600 jobs as computer programmers (Schmidt, Hunter, McKenzie, & Muldrow, 1979). The estimated money gained in one year from the increased speed and efficiency of the chosen workers was more than $97 million. The initial cost of the screening tests was only $10 per applicant, a very good return on investment.

All in all, utility analyses of standardized personnel testing programs indicate that such tests are usually cost effective. Hunter & Schmidt (1982) go as far as to estimate that the U.S. gross national product would be increased by tens of billions of dollars per year if improved personnel screening and selection procedures, including screening tests, were routinely implemented. Utility analyses allow the employer to determine the financial gains of a testing program and then compare them to the costs of developing and implementing the program.

test utility
the value of a screening test in determining important outcomes, such as dollars gained through its use

ASSESSMENT CENTERS

One of the most detailed forms of employment screening and selection takes place in an **assessment center,** which is a detailed, structured evaluation of applicants on a wide range of job-related knowledge, skills,

assessment center
a detailed, structured evaluation of job applicants using a variety of instruments and techniques

The Use of an Assessment Center for Manager Selection and Development

In the 1950s the Bell Telephone Systems created an assessment center to assist in the study of management selection and development. This assessment center and the tools and techniques that it used have served as a model for other centers in a variety of organizations.

The first step in the development of the Bell System assessment center was targeting the specific characteristics and qualities that a successful manager should possess. Among those identified were oral and written communication skills, behavioral flexibility, creativity, tolerance of uncertainty, and skills in organization, planning, and decision-making. Assessment center participants were administered several standardized personality tests. They also completed a contemporary affairs test that measured their knowledge of current events as a means of evaluating cognitive ability. In small groups, participants took part in a management game in which they played the roles of partners in a toy manufacturing company who had to purchase the parts for simple toys, oversee toy assembly, and show a final profit. Participants also took part in a small group discussion, were interviewed, and completed an in-basket exercise. Throughout the various tests, they were observed and evaluated by the assessment center staff, who developed detailed profiles of each participant's performance and management potential. In all, the testing and evaluation took three and one-half days to complete.

A critical component of the Bell System assessment center was the in-basket exercise, which began with the following instructions:

You are now Mr. C. D. Evans, Plant Superintendent of the East District in Division A of the Green Area of the Eastern Telephone Company. You have just arrived in your new job. Mr. I. W. Prior,

your predecessor, died suddenly of a heart attack last Wednesday, March 28. You were notified Friday at 4 P.M. of your new appointment but you could not get here until today, Sunday, April 1.

Today is your first day on your new job and here is what your secretary has left for you. Since it is Sunday no one else is around and you cannot reach anyone on the telephone. You must leave in exactly three hours to catch a plane for an important meeting connected with your previous assignment. . . . In the large envelope in front of you you will find three packets. One contains an organization chart, a map of the district and the division, a copy of the management guide, and a copy of the union contract. The second packet contains the materials your secretary has left on your desk for your attention. These materials include letters, reports, memoranda, etc. Your secretary has attached materials from the files to some of the documents. The third packet contains . . . office forms, memo pads, pencils, and paper. You can use these materials to write letters, memos, notes to yourself, etc. (Bray, Campbell, & Grant, 1974, pp. 24–25)

In the second packet on the hypothetical desk were twenty-five problems that the participants had to address. It is important to note that this detailed exercise was only one component in a very thorough evaluation. As you might imagine, assessment centers such as these are costly and time-consuming to develop and to operate. The result, however, is a very detailed and accurate assessment of each participant's management skill and potential.

and abilities. Because a variety of instruments are used to assess participants, the assessment center makes use of large test batteries. The assessment center approach was developed during World War II by the United States Office of Strategic Services (the forerunner of the CIA) to select spies. Today, they are used primarily to select managers. In assessment centers, applicants are evaluated on a number of job-related variables using a variety of techniques, such as personality and ability tests, that are considered to be valid predictors of managerial success. Applicants also take part in a number of **situational exercises,** which are attempts to approximate certain aspects of the managerial job. These exercises are related to work samples, except that they are approximations rather than actual examples of work tasks. One popular situational exercise is the in-basket test (Fredericksen, 1962), which requires the applicant to deal with a stack of memos, letters, and other materials that have supposedly collected in the ''in-basket'' of a manager. The applicant is given some background information about the job and then must actually take care of the work in the in-basket by answering correspondence, preparing agenda for meetings, making decisions, and the like. A group of observers considers how each applicant deals with the various tasks and assigns a performance score. Another situational exercise is the leaderless group discussion (Bass, 1954). Here applicants are put together in a small group to discuss some work-related topic. The goal is to see how each applicant handles the situation and who emerges as a discussion leader. Again, trained observers rate each applicant's performance.

situational exercises
assessment tools that
require the perfor
mance of tasks that ap
proximate actual work
tasks

The result of testing at the assessment center is a very detailed profile of each applicant as well as some index of how a particular applicant rated in comparison to others. Research indicates that these evaluations are very good predictors of managerial success and that assessment centers are one of the very best selection tools, particularly for managerial positions (Klimoski & Strickland, 1977; Schmitt, Gooding, Noe, & Kirsch, 1984). Of course, the major drawback is the huge investment of time and resources they require, which is the major reason that assessment centers are usually only used by larger organizations and for the selection of candidates for higher-level management positions. (See Applying I/O Psychology for an example of an assessment center.)

HIRING INTERVIEWS

To obtain almost any job in the United States, an applicant must go through at least one hiring interview, which is the most widely used employee screening and selection device. Despite its widespread use, however, the hiring interview unfortunately is not one of the most reliable and valid methods of screening and selection. Reviews of the research all seem to come to the same conclusion: Interviews are not a very effective means for selecting people for jobs (Arvey & Campion, 1982; Hunter & Hunter, 1984; Schmitt, 1976). Part of the problem with their validity is

"WHOEVER YOU ARE, YOU'RE HIRED."

that many interviews are conducted haphazardly. You may have experienced one of these poor interviews that seemed to be nothing more than a casual conversation or in which the interviewer did nearly all of the talking. While you might have learned a lot about the company, the interviewer learned little about your experience and qualifications. In these cases it is obvious that little concern has been given to the fact that, just like a psychological test, the hiring interview is actually a measurement tool.

Because of its popularity, the hiring interview will likely continue to be a central component of employee selection in spite of its questionable validity. For interviews to be effective, however, greater concern must be

How to Conduct More Effective Hiring Interviews

A great deal of research indicates that typical hiring interviews, although widely used, are not very effective predictors of job performance. There are, however, ways to improve their reliability and validity, some of which are outlined below:

- *Use structured interviews.* Structured interviewing, in which the same basic questions are asked of all applicants, is nearly always more effective than unstructured interviewing, because it allows for comparisons among applicants (Arvey & Campion, 1982). The use of structured questions also helps prevent the interview from wandering off course and assists in keeping interview lengths consistent.
- *Make sure that interview questions are job related.* The questions must be developed from a detailed job analysis to ensure that they are job-related. Some researchers have developed situational interview questions (Latham, Saari, Pursell, & Campion, 1980), which are derived from critical incidents job analysis techniques that ask applicants how they would behave in a given job situation. Evidence indicates that situational interviews more accurately predict job success than the traditional interview format (Latham & Saari, 1984).
- *Provide for some rating or scoring of applicant responses.* To interpret the applicant responses objectively, it is important to develop some scoring system. Experts could determine beforehand what would characterize good and poor answers. Another approach is to develop a scale for rating the quality of the responses. It may also be beneficial to make some records of responses to review later and to substantiate employment decisions.
- *Use trained interviewers.* Although the research on whether interviewer training improves the quality of hiring interview decisions is somewhat inconclusive (Heneman, 1975; Vance, Kuhnert, & Farr, 1978; Wexley, Sanders, & Yukl, 1973), it is reasonable to assume that trained interviewers will function better than untrained ones. Interviewers can be instructed in proper procedures and techniques and trained to try to avoid systematic biases (Howard & Dailey, 1979). Because of the public relations function of hiring interviews (the interviewer is representing the organization to a segment of the public), it is also probably a good idea to have all interviewers undergo some training.
- *Consider using panel interviews.* Because of personal idiosyncracies, any one interviewer's judgment of an applicant may be inaccurate. One way to increase interview reliability is to have a group of evaluators assembled in a panel (Arvey & Campion, 1982). While panel interviews may improve reliability, they may still have validity problems if all interviewers are incorrect in their interpretations or share some biases or stereotypes. Also, the use of panel interviews is costly.
- *Use the interview time efficiently.* Many times, interviewers waste much of the time asking for information that was already obtained from the application form and résumé. In one study it was found that previewing the applicant's written materials yielded more information in the hiring interview (Dipboye, Fontenelle, & Garner, 1984). However, information obtained from the written materials should not be allowed to bias the processing of information received during the interview (Dipboye, 1982).

A recent study used a highly structured interview with many of the above properties, including questions based on job analysis, consistent questions and structure for all interviews, rating scales with examples and illustrations to assist in scoring answers, and an interview panel. The results indicated high agreement on decisions made by different interviewers on the same applicants, indicating good reliability of interview evaluations and good prediction of subsequent job performance of applicants hired for entry-level positions in a paper mill (Campion, Pursell, & Brown, 1988).

given to their structure and conduct. Industrial/organizational psychologists have done extensive research on the hiring interview. One of the outcomes of this research is the development of methods to help make the interview a more effective selection tool (see Up Close).

When used correctly as part of an employee screening and selection program, the hiring interview should have three major objectives. First, the interview should be used to help fill in gaps in the information obtained from the applicant's résumé and application form and to measure the kinds of factors that are only available in a face-to-face encounter, such as appearance and oral communication skills. Second, the hiring interview should provide applicants with realistic job previews, which help them decide whether they really want the job and offer an initial orientation to the organization. Finally, since the hiring interview is one way that an organization interacts directly with a portion of the general public, it can serve an important public relations function for the company (Cascio, 1987).

As mentioned, there are serious concerns about the accuracy of judgments made from hiring interviews. Why is this so? Unlike screening tests or application forms, which ask for specific, quantifiable information, hiring interviews are typically more freewheeling affairs. Interviewers may ask completely different questions of different applicants, which makes it very difficult to compare responses. Although hiring interviews are supposed to be opportunities for gathering information about the applicant, at times the interviewer may do the majority of the talking. These interviews certainly yield very little information about the applicant and probably no valid assessment of the person's qualifications.

The reliability of interviewer judgments is also problematic. Different interviewers may arrive at completely different evaluations of the same applicant, even when evaluating the same interview (Arvey & Campion, 1982; Riggio & Throckmorton, 1988). Also, because of nervousness, fatigue, or some other reason, the same applicant might not perform as well in one interview as in another, which further contributes to low reliability.

Perhaps the greatest source of problems affecting hiring interview validity is interviewer biases. Interviewers may allow factors such as an applicant's gender, race, physical attractiveness, or appearance to influence their judgments (Arvey, 1979; Cann, Siegfried, & Pearce, 1981; Forsythe, Drake, & Cox, 1985; Heilman & Saruwatari, 1979). There may also be a tendency for an interviewer to make a snap judgment, arriving at an overall evaluation of the applicant in the first few moments of the interview. The interviewer may then spend the remainder of the time trying to confirm that first impression, selectively attending to only the information that is consistent with the initial evaluation. Another potential source of bias is contrast effects, which can occur after the interview of a particularly good or bad applicant. All subsequent applicants may then be evaluated either very negatively or very positively in contrast to this person.

Hiring interviews are the most common of all screening procedures, but they often provide little help in predicting future performance.

In general, the hiring interview fails to predict job success accurately because of a mismatch between the selection instrument and the information it obtains, and the requirements of most jobs. Receiving a positive evaluation in an interview is related to applicants' ability to present themselves in a positive manner and to carry on a one-on-one conversation (Guion & Gibson, 1988; Hanson & Balestreri-Spero, 1985). For most jobs, however, performance in the interview is in no way related to performance on the job, because the types of skills required to do well in the interview are not the same as those required in many positions.

FOLLOW-UP METHODS: REFERENCES AND LETTERS OF RECOMMENDATION

Two final sources of information for employee screening and selection are references and letters of recommendation. Unfortunately, very little research has examined their validity as selection tools (Muchinsky, 1979). Typically, reference checks and letters of recommendation can provide four types of information: (1) employment and educational history, (2) evaluations of the applicant's character, (3) evaluation of the applicant's job performance, and (4) the recommender's willingness to rehire the applicant (Cascio, 1987).

For a couple of reasons, the use of references and letters of recommendation in applicant screening is on the decline. First, since applicants can usually choose their own sources for references and recommendations, it is unlikely that they will supply the names of persons who will give bad recommendations. Therefore, letters of recommendation tend to be skewed in a very positive direction, so positive that they may be useless in distinguishing among applicants. Second, because of recent litigation against individuals and former employers who provide negative recommendations, many companies are refusing to provide any kind of reference for former employees except for dates of employment. The net result is that many organizations are simply forgoing the use of reference checks and letters of recommendation.

Letters of recommendation are still widely used, however, in applications to graduate schools. In many graduate programs steps have been taken to improve the effectiveness of these letters as a screening and selection tool by including forms that ask the recommender to rate the applicant on a variety of dimensions, such as academic ability, motivation/drive, oral and written communication skills, and initiative. These rating forms often use graphic rating scales to help quantify the recommendation for comparison with other applicants. They also attempt to improve the accuracy of the reference by protecting the recommender from possible retaliation by having the applicants waive their rights to see the letter of reference.

Personnel selection is the actual process of choosing people for employment from a pool of applicants. In personnel selection, all of the information gained from screening procedures, such as application forms, résumés, test scores, and hiring interview evaluations, are combined in some manner to make the actual selection decisions.

personnel selection
the process of choosing applicants for employment

MAKING PERSONNEL SELECTION DECISIONS

Once employers have gathered information about job applicants, they can combine that information in various ways to make selection decisions. All too often such choices are made subjectively, using what is often referred to as the clinical approach. In this approach, a decision-maker simply combines the sources of information in whatever fashion seems appropriate to obtain some general impressions about applicants. Based on experience and beliefs about which types of information are more or less important, a decision is made. Although some good selection decisions may be made by experienced decisionmakers, the subjective, clinical decisions are error-prone and often inaccurate (see Meehl, 1954). The alternative is to use a statistical decisionmaking model, which combines information to select applicants in some objective, predetermined fashion. Each piece of information about job applicants is given some optimal weight that indicates its strength in predicting future job performance.

One statistical approach to personnel decisionmaking is the **multiple regression model,** an extension of the correlation coefficient (see Chapter 2). As you recall, the correlation coefficient examines the strength of a relationship between a single predictor, such as a test score, and a criterion, such as a measure of job performance. However, rather than having only one predictor of job performance, as in the correlation coefficient or *simple* regression model, multiple regression analysis uses several predictors. Typically, this approach combines the various predictors in an additive, linear fashion. In personnel selection, this means that the ability of each of the predictors to predict job performance can be added together and that there is a linear relationship between the predictors and the criterion; higher scores on the predictors will lead to higher scores on the criterion. While the statistical assumptions and calculations on which the multiple regression model is based are beyond the scope of this text, the result is an equation that uses the various types of screening information in combination.

The regression model is a compensatory type of model, which means that high scores on one predictor can compensate for low scores on an-

multiple regression model
a personnel selection method that combines separate predictors of job success in a statistical procedure

other. This is both a strength and a weakness of the regression approach. For example, an applicant's lack of pevious job-related experience can be compensated for by test scores that show great potential for mastering the job. However, in other situations this may be problematic. Take, for example, the screening of applicants for a job as inspector of microcircuitry, a position that requires the visual inspection of very tiny computer circuits under a microscope. From her scores on a test of cognitive ability an applicant might show great potential for performing the job. However, the applicant might have an uncorrectable visual problem that leads her to score poorly on a test of visual acuity. Here, the compensatory regression model would not lead to a good prediction, for the visual problem would mean that the applicant would fail regardless of her potential for handling the cognitive aspects of the job.

multiple cutoff model
a personnel selection method using a minimum cutoff score on each of the various predictors of job performance

A second type of selection strategy, one that is not compensatory, is the **multiple cutoff model,** which uses a minimum cutoff score on each of the predictors. An applicant must obtain a score above the cutoff on each of the predictors to be hired. Scoring below the cutoff on any one predictor automatically disqualifies the applicant, regardless of the scores on the other screening variables. For example, a school district may decide to hire only those probationary high school teachers who have completed a specified number of graduate units and who have scored above the cutoff on a national teacher's examination. The main advantage of the multiple cutoff strategy is that it insures that all eligible applicants have some minimal amount of ability on all dimensions that are believed to be predictive of job success.

The multiple regression and multiple cutoff methods can be used in combination. If this is done, applicants would be eligible for hire only if their regression scores are high and if they are above the cutoff score on each of the predictor dimensions. Of course, using both strategies at the same time greatly restricts the number of eligible applicants, so they are used together only when the pool of applicants is very large.

multiple hurdle model
a personnel selection strategy that requires that an acceptance or rejection decision be made at each of several stages in a screening process

Another type of selection decisionmaking method is the **multiple hurdle model.** This strategy uses an ordered sequence of screening devices. At each stage in the sequence a decision is made to either reject an applicant or to allow the applicant to proceed to the next stage. An example of the multiple hurdle model used for hiring police officers is presented in Figure 4.5. In this example, the first stage or hurdle is receiving a passing score on a civil service exam. If a passing score is obtained, the applicant's application blank is evaluated. An applicant who does not pass the exam is no longer considered for the job. Typically, all applicants who pass all the hurdles are then selected for jobs.

One advantage of the multiple hurdle strategy is that unqualified persons do not have to go through the entire evaluation program before they are rejected. Also, because evaluation takes place at many times on many

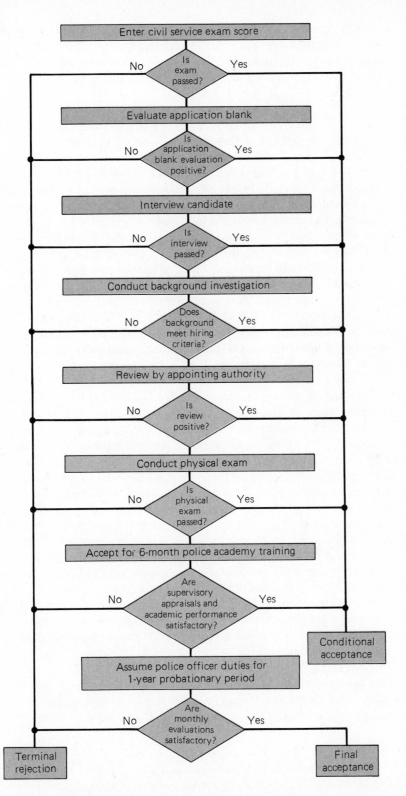

Figure 4.5

MULTIPLE HURDLE
MODEL FOR POLICE
OFFICER SELECTION

Source: W. F. Cascio, *Applied
Psychology in Personnel
Management* (Englewood
Cliffs, NJ: Prentice-Hall, 1987),
p. 282.

levels, the employer can be quite confident that the applicants who are selected do indeed have the potential to be successful on the job. Because multiple hurdle selection programs are expensive and time-consuming, they are usually only used for jobs that are central to the operation of the organization.

EQUAL EMPLOYMENT OPPORTUNITY IN PERSONNEL SELECTION AND PLACEMENT

In 1964 the Civil Rights Act was passed. A section of this major piece of federal legislation, Title VII, was intended to protect against discrimination in employment on the bases of race, ethnic background, sex, or religious preference. Additional laws have since helped protect against age discrimination. This antidiscrimination legislation has led to massive changes in personnel procedures and decisionmaking.

As a result of the legislation a federal agency, the **Equal Employment Opportunity Commission (EEOC)** was created to ensure that employers' personnel selection and placement procedures complied with the antidiscrimination laws. In the 1970s the EEOC (1974, 1978) developed the *Uniform Guidelines on Employee Selection Procedures,* which serves as the standards for complying with antidiscrimination laws. Three concepts are important for understanding the *Guidelines* and their impact on personnel selection procedures.

The first of these concepts is the notion of **protected groups,** which include women, blacks, American Indians, Asians, and Hispanics. Employers must keep separate personnel records, including information on all actions such as recruitment, selection, promotions, and firings, for each of these groups and for whites. If some action is found to discriminate against one or more of these groups, the second concept, **adverse impact,** comes into play. Adverse impact refers to discrimination, either intentional or unintentional, against a protected group by some personnel action by an employer. The *Guidelines* state that if any personnel decision causes a disproportionate percentage of people in a particular group to be hired in comparison to another group, adverse impact exists. For example, if an employer has fifty white job applicants and fifty black applicants and hires 70 percent of the whites but only 40 percent of the blacks, there is adverse impact. In such cases the employer must justify that the decisionmaking procedures were valid. That is, the employer must prove that 70 percent of the white applicants and only 40 percent of the black applicants were indeed qualified for the jobs. In a classic legal decision, *Griggs v. Duke Power Company* (1971), the court ruled that the burden of proof on whether an employment selection test is fair rests with the employer. This means that it is up to employers to show that their screening tests and other selection methods are valid indicators of future job per-

Equal Employment Opportunity Commission (EEOC)
the federal agency created to protect against discrimination in employment

protected groups
groups including women and certain ethnic and racial minorities that have been identified as previous targets of employment discrimination

adverse impact
discrimination against a protected group by an employer's personnel actions

formance. Therefore, it is wise for organizations to validate any and all of their personnel screening instruments to ensure against possible instances of discrimination.

The final important concept from the *Guidelines* is **affirmative action,** the voluntary development of organizational policies that attempt to ensure that jobs are made available to qualified persons regardless of sex, age, or ethnic background. In general, affirmative action programs will hire or promote a member of a protected group over an individual from the majority group if the two are determined to be equally qualified. However, if the protected group member is less qualified than a majority group applicant—usually a white male—the organization is under no obligation to hire the less qualified applicant. Affirmative action programs typically deal with all personnel functions, including recruitment, screening, selection, job assignments, and promotions.

affirmative action
*the voluntary develop-
ment of policies that
try to ensure that jobs
are made available to
qualified individuals re-
gardless of sex, age, or
ethnic background*

SUMMARY

Personnel recruitment is the process of attracting potential workers to apply for jobs. There are a variety of employee recruitment methods, such as advertisements, college recruitment programs, employment agencies, and employee referrals. An important element of the recruitment process is to present applicants with an accurate picture of the job through the use of *realistic job previews (RJPs),* which help increase satisfaction and decrease turnover of new employees.

Personnel screening is the process of reviewing information about job applicants to select individuals for jobs. The first step is the evaluation of written materials such as applications and résumés. Basic background information can be translated into numerical values to compare the qualifications of applicants through the use of *weighted application forms* or *biographical information blanks (BIBs).*

The second step in screening is personnel testing, which typically uses standardized instruments to measure characteristics that are predictive of job performance. Any screening test or method must demonstrate that it is a reliable and valid predictor of job performance. Three methods for establishing reliability are *test-retest reliability, parallel forms,* and *internal consistency.* The two forms of validity that are most important for the development and use of screening tests are *content validity,* or whether the test content adequately measures the knowledge, skills, and abilities required by the job, and *criterion-related validity,* or the relationship between screening test scores and some criterion of job success.

Personnel screening tests vary greatly both in their format and in the characteristics that they measure. Categories of such tests include cognitive ability tests, mechanical ability tests, motor and sensory ability tests, job skills and knowledge tests, personality tests, and miscellaneous in-

**CHAPTER 4
CONCLUSION**

struments such as *polygraphs*. For the most part, the standardized tests are among the best predictors of job performance. Often they are used in combination—in *test batteries*—to help select the best qualified candidates. An important issue regarding the effectiveness of personnel screening tests is *validity generalization,* or a test's ability to predict job performance in settings different from the one in which it was validated. Another concern is *test utility,* an estimate of the dollars gained in increased productivity and efficiency because of the use of screening tests. *Assessment centers* use the test battery approach to offer a detailed, structured assessment of applicants' employment potential, most often for high-level managerial positions.

Employment screening for most jobs includes at least one *hiring interview*. Just like any other selection method, the interview is a measurement tool. Unfortunately, research indicates that the hiring interview, as used, generally has low levels of reliability and validity. Used correctly the interview should help supply information that cannot be obtained from applications, résumés, or tests and should present the applicant with a realistic job preview. However, most interviews are not conducted with this in mind. One of the greatest sources of problems with hiring interviews stems from interviewer biases. The final stage in personnel screening involves follow-up methods, such as references and letters of recommendation. However, the use of these methods is on the decline because they tend to be overly positive and are often noninformative.

Once the screening information has been obtained, a selection decision must be made. All too often, subjective decisionmaking processes are used. Statistical models of decisionmaking include the *multiple regression model,* an approach that allows predictors to be combined statistically; the *multiple cutoff* strategy, a method of setting minimum cutoff scores for each predictor; and the *multiple hurdle* approach, a stringent method that uses an ordered sequence of screening devices.

Regardless of the screening and selection procedures used, an overriding concern of all personnel decisions is to protect against discrimination in employment. The federal *Equal Employment Opportunity Commission (EEOC)* has established guidelines to ensure against discrimination against ethnic minorities and other *protected groups*. To take preventive steps to avoid employment discrimination, many organizations have adopted *affirmative action* plans to ensure that jobs are made available to members of protected groups.

STUDY QUESTIONS AND EXERCISES

1. What are the various steps in the personnel screening process? Consider the strengths and weaknesses of each. For example, what types of information are obtained about applicants at each step? What are some of the dangers or difficulties associated with each stage?

2. Imagine that you are the human resources director for a large company. Design a personnel recruitment, screening, and selection program for your lower-level employees. What elements would you include and why? Design a similar program for recruiting and selecting employees for upper-level management positions. What elements would be included in this program? Why?

3. In what ways has antidiscrimination legislation affected how personnel professionals recruit, screen, and select people for jobs? What are some ways that employers can try to avoid discrimination in personnel decisionmaking?

4. Consider the last job that you applied for. What kinds of screening procedures did you encounter? What were their strengths and weaknesses? How could they have been improved?

5. Consider the different personnel selection methods: multiple regression, multiple cutoff, and multiple hurdle. For each, develop a list of jobs or occupations that would probably require that particular method.

6. It is clear that in much of the hiring that takes place, subjective evaluations of applicants are often the basis for the decisions. Why is this the case? What are some reasons that more objective—and more valid—hiring procedures are often ignored by employers?

SUGGESTED READINGS

Arvey, R. D. (1979). *Fairness in selecting employees*. Reading, MA: Addison-Wesley. *Although somewhat dated, this book is a good reference for issues related to discrimination in personnel selection. It also offers good coverage of research on the strengths and weaknesses of different selection methods.*

Cook, M. (1988). *Personnel selection and productivity*. Chichester, England: John Wiley & Sons. *An overview of current issues in personnel selection that includes chapters on nearly every type of screening and selection method. Written by a British psychologist in an informal, interesting style.*

Personnel and *Personnel Journal*. *These journals have many informative and readable articles discussing issues related to recruitment, screening, and selection.*

Phillips, J. J. (1987). *Recruiting, training, and retraining new employees: Managing the transition from college to work*. San Francisco: Jossey-Bass. *This book was written for human resources professionals to assist in the recruitment, selection, and training of new college graduates. The goal is to lead to a smoother transition for this segment of new employees in an effort to cut down on turnover and the loss of good employment prospects. However, from a student's perspective it is interesting reading. It is encouraging to see that employers do indeed consider college graduates a valuable resource!*

Society for Industrial and Organizational Psychology. (1987). *Principles for the validation and use of personnel selection procedures* (3rd ed.). College Park, MD: Author. *This 44-page handbook is a statement of the principles, adopted by the Society for Industrial and Organizational Psychology, of "good practice in the choice, development, evaluation, and use of personnel selection procedures."*

5

PERSONNEL TRAINING AND DEVELOPMENT

Links Between Learning Theories and Training Methods

This chapter on personnel training has two general objectives. The first is to present the basic theories and processes of learning, with a focus on how workers learn about their jobs. The second goal is to discuss the procedures used in the design, implementation, and evaluation of personnel training programs. Together these two objectives represent the theory and practice of personnel training, respectively. In studying this chapter, try to bear in mind the links between learning theories and training methods.

We will also touch on topics that were introduced in several of the earlier chapters. We return to methodological issues (particularly experimental design issues) when considering the evaluation of training programs. The section on assessing training needs is in some ways related to the discussion of job analysis procedures in Chapter 3, except that now we are assessing what skills and knowledge workers need to perform their jobs rather than analyzing the jobs themselves. Because training relates to many personnel decisions, the same kinds of legal concerns regarding equal employment opportunity that we looked at in Chapter 4 are relevant here too. Considering how personnel training ties in with the other personnel issues studied previously will help you to see the total picture of a very important specialty within I/O psychology: personnel psychology.

Once an applicant has gone through the often arduous process of personnel screening and has actually been selected for a job, that person must next undergo some sort of employee orientation and training. In most organizations, training is not limited to new employees, as various types of training and development programs are offered at all stages of an employee's career. When new machinery or technology is introduced, for example, employees receive some instruction in order to operate the equipment. When new systems or procedures are put into place, workers must learn to adapt. When an employee is promoted to a position of increased responsibility, the individual will be given some training to learn new tasks and to develop the new skills needed. An employee nearing the end of a career may attend a company-sponsored retirement planning workshop to learn of the benefits available and to help plan for the postemployment years. Employee training and development are thus ongoing processes of extreme importance for both the worker and the work organization.

The advent of computers and other high-tech equipment has increased the need for personnel training.

In this chapter we will begin by examining the fundamentals of the learning process and how learning applies to employee training and development. Next, we will look at how employee training needs are assessed and study general training methods. We will then see how training programs are evaluated. Finally, we will examine the various types of training programs offered by work organizations, including employee orientation programs, management training, and employee career development programs.

FUNDAMENTAL ISSUES IN PERSONNEL TRAINING

Personnel training is a planned effort by an organization to facilitate employees' learning, retention, and transfer of job-related behavior. Before we examine the specifics of such programs and methods, and their role in influencing important organizational outcomes such as increased productivity, we must first have some fundamental understanding of basic learning processes.

Learning is a relatively permanent change in behavior that takes place as a result of experience. Learning thus occurs as an interchange of the person and the environment. Through our daily experiences, both on and

learning
a relatively permanent change in behavior that occurs as a result of experience

off the job, we learn new skills, sharpen existing skills, and add to our accumulated knowledge bank. Yet learning is selective, and we do not learn everything to which we are exposed. Exactly when, how, and why we learn are difficult and complex questions to answer.

THEORIES OF LEARNING

To understand the fundamentals of learning more fully, we will briefly consider three basic theories of learning: classical conditioning, operant conditioning, and modeling. Each presents a different view of how learning can take place.

Classical conditioning, also referred to as respondent, or Pavlovian, conditioning, occurs when two events, experienced together in space and time, become associated with each other in the mind of the individual. Classical conditioning is a passive form of learning because it occurs naturally, with little effort from the learner. It begins with a stimulus, termed the unconditioned stimulus (or UCS), which is something in the environment that automatically creates an unconditioned response (or UCR) in the individual or organism. For example, a very loud noise may cause a startle reaction. If you touch it, a hot stove will create pain and cause you to move your hand away. If another event is paired with the unconditioned stimulus, it too can develop an association with the UCS, and the new event—the conditioned stimulus—may then cause the response. For example, if a warning light goes on when the stove is hot, it will probably only take you one trial to learn that when the light goes on, you should quickly move your hand away.

The earliest illustration of the principles of classical conditioning was in a series of experiments by the Russian physiologist Ivan Pavlov. Pavlov was researching the salivation response in dogs when he noticed an interesting phenomenon. In the experiments, the hungry dogs were presented with food (the UCS) to stimulate salivation (the UCR). However, in a short time Pavlov noticed that the dogs would begin to salivate as soon as their handler would enter the room with the food, before it was actually presented. Soon, as the dogs learned to associate the handler's approach with the presentation of food, they would salivate merely upon hearing the footsteps of the handler. The sight or sound of the dog handler had thus become a conditioned stimulus creating the conditioned response of salivation. Pavlov immediately began controlled studies of this learning process. He found that the dogs could be conditioned to salivate to the sound of a bell, a buzzer, or just about anything by merely pairing the presentation of the unconditioned stimulus, the food, with the conditioned stimulus.

Classical conditioning, although important, only deals with a limited range of learning and for the most part has few applications in the work

classical conditioning *learning that takes place when two events are experienced together in space and time and become associated with each other*

world. However, the process does explain some early human learning as well as the learning of very simple tasks, such as responding to warning lights or buzzers while working with new machinery. For example, a college friend who had a summer job working as a spring coiler soon learned that when his coiling machine emitted a low, grinding noise, it meant that the spring wire had been misfed. The noise soon became a stimulus for him to quickly shut off the machine before the misfed wire became hopelessly entangled in the machinery, which required hours of work to fix.

In some police training procedures, recruits are conditioned to be alert and apprehensive to certain seemingly harmless behaviors that might be life threatening in actual police work. For example, in a role-played encounter a trainer may blow a whistle to startle a police cadet in order to condition the trainee to be wary of such behaviors as a car passenger reaching under a seat in a routine traffic stop, which is a signal that the person may be reaching for a weapon.

Classical conditioning illustrates simple, reflexive learning processes that occur naturally, without much thought on the part of the learner. The second type of learning, **operant conditioning,** deals with more voluntary learning of behavior. Operant conditioning begins with the individual's behavior, called the operant, which is followed by some consequence, or an environmental event that follows the performance of a particular behavior. Positive consequences are termed reinforcers or rewards. Negative consequences are punishments. When a positive consequence follows some behavior, it is more likely that the behavior will be exhibited again. A punishment following the performance of a behavior makes it less likely that the behavior will be repeated. Through the rewarding of desirable behaviors and the punishing of undesirable behaviors, a great deal of human learning takes place.

operant conditioning
a learning process in which behaviors are followed by reinforcing or punishing consequences

The work place offers a variety of positive reinforcers, such as pay raises, recognition, and praise, to encourage the learning of desirable behaviors. Moreover, to ensure that employees continue to develop their skills, other rewards are offered, including promotions, awards, and more interesting and challenging assignments. Conversely, a variety of negative consequences, such as reprimands and demotions, can help eliminate undesirable behavior at work.

A third type of basic learning is termed **modeling,** which is imitative learning that occurs through observing and reproducing another person's actions. For example, an employee may learn to operate a piece of machinery or a computer program by watching a supervisor work with the equipment. The concept of modeling and the processes involved are included in Bandura's (1977) **social learning theory,** which holds that four important processes are necessary if learning is to occur. The first process is *attention*. To imitate a particular behavior, attention must be focused on the behavior. A number of factors will increase the probability that a

modeling
learning that occurs through the observation and imitation of the behavior of others

social learning theory
learning theory that emphasizes the observational learning of behavior

potential learner will attend to another's behavior. For example, people are more likely to pay attention to and imitate the behavior of persons who are of higher status, such as supervisors, or who are otherwise respected, such as particularly talented or knowledgeable coworkers. The second process is *retention*. To be modeled, behavior must somehow be processed and recorded in memory, either by forming a mental picture or a step-by-step verbal description. For example, a secretary watching someone demonstrate a word processor might retain the operating instructions verbally: "First, he turned on the power switch. Then he placed a disk in the disk drive. Then he hit the 'return' key. . . . " A third process is the learner's capacity for *motor reproduction* of the behavior. In other words, to learn through modeling, one must have the physical abilities and skill to imitate the exact movements of the model. For example, most of us would be unable to do a good job of imitating the drawing of a talented artist or the swing of a professional golfer through merely watching their movements unless we also possessed some specific artistic or athletic skills and some previous motor experience with the behavior. A final process that affects imitative learning is *motivation:* There must be some reason for learning the observed behavior. For example, you might be more strongly motivated to pay attention to and learn about the various tasks required to perform your boss's job if you aspire to one day hold the position yourself.

The operant and classical conditioning models of learning focus exclusively on the stimulus-response relationship, whereas social learning theory emphasizes the role of cognitive processes in learning and considers the fact that people think about their actions and can consciously monitor and regulate their behavior. We use our experiences to decide on a plan for future behavior. We can learn to improve our performance by comparing our behavior with the results of our own previous performances or those of others. While operant conditioning views learning as taking place through a simple process of worker behavior and subsequent environmental consequences, social learning theory states that work behavior can be best understood in terms of an interaction and a reciprocal cause-and-effect relationship among the individual, the behavior, and the work environment (Davis & Luthans, 1980).

Each of these three learning theories offers different approaches to understanding how learning takes place and encouraging learning in the work place. Sometimes training programs rely heavily on one theoretical approach. For example, a program designed to teach assembly workers to pay closer attention to product quality may apply operant conditioning principles by offering a cash reward to those who reduce the percentage of rejects they produce. Relying on social learning theory, a new employee training program may simply show videotapes of models performing complex work tasks. However, many effective training programs combine the three theories, using paired associations, combinations of rewards and punishments, and modeling techniques.

CRITERIA FOR SUCCESSFUL TRAINING

For learning to translate into positive changes in work performance, a number of considerations should be evaluated when structuring a training program. First, we must consider what could be termed *trainee readiness*. A great deal of research indicates that positive employee attitudes toward training programs is critical for training success (Noe, 1986; Noe & Schmitt, 1986). Is the trainee prepared to learn? Does the trainee feel the need for training and see the usefulness of the material that will be learned? Does the employee possess the basic prerequisites to be a good candidate for learning these new behaviors? In other words, does the trainee have the aptitude to learn? Finally, is the trainee motivated to learn? If an individual has no desire to learn new tasks and to take on new responsibilities, it is unlikely that much learning will take place.

These supermarket trainees learning meat-cutting techniques can see the usefulness of what they are taught—a key factor in successful training.

A second concern is the *structure* of the training program. When and how often does training take place? How long are the training sessions? How much opportunity is there for trainees to practice or apply what they have learned? How much guidance and individual attention does each trainee receive? All evidence indicates that for training programs to be effective, they should be highly structured. Training should also take place on a regular basis, should be thorough, and should continue throughout an employee's career.

Another important concern is the *transfer of training* (Baldwin & Ford, 1988). How well does learning transfer from the training situation to the actual work environment? Since the transfer is influenced by the degree of similarity between the training tasks and the actual job tasks, the most useful training programs directly address the actual tasks that are performed on the job. A transfer of training will be also more likely if the work environment supports the new behaviors that are learned. For the newly learned behaviors to transfer to and remain in the work setting the trainee must be given feedback. Once a trainee moves to the work site, procedures should be set up to determine that the training is working. Feedback concerning training success must be transmitted to the worker if the worker is going to continue to use the new skills. One study found that when trainees set goals for implementing the training strategies and feedback was given concerning the achievement of those goals, the trained behaviors tended to stay in place (Wexley & Baldwin, 1986). Without feedback and reinforcement, learned skills or procedures may deteriorate as workers forget some of their important elements, pick up bad habits that interfere with their application, or lapse into using old work strategies (Marx, 1982). Mechanisms should be put in place to maintain trained behaviors. "Brush-up" or reminder training sessions should follow a few months down the line.

Finally, we must consider the *outcomes* of learning for the trainee. For learning to be applied, there needs to be some sort of reward or incentive to use the learned behaviors. For training to be effective it is important that workers see the connection between the learning of new behaviors and how the use of the new learning will enhance their working lives. In other words, employees must see that learning new work skills helps them to be better, more productive workers, which in turn can lead to promotions and other forms of career advancement.

All of these concerns, along with the basic theories of learning, must be taken into account in the design and implementation of training programs. Before an organization can create a training program, however, there must be some idea of what workers need to know to perform their jobs. Therefore, the starting point of any program is an assessment of training needs.

ASSESSING TRAINING NEEDS

Typically, an assessment of training needs should include analyses on many levels: the organizational level (the needs and goals of the organization), the task level (the requirements for performing the task), and the person level (the skills and knowledge required to do the job). An additional analysis can be done at the demographic level.

ORGANIZATIONAL ANALYSIS

The organizational level of needs analysis considers issues such as the units that need training, long- and short-term organizational goals of the training, the cost-effectiveness of the program, and the general climate for training (that is, the workers' and supervisors' commitment to participation). One strategy for conducting an organizational analysis might involve surveying employees, both workers and supervisors, regarding their perceptions of training needs and their attitudes toward participation in training programs.

TASK ANALYSIS

The task level of analysis is concerned with the knowledge, skills, and abilities that a worker requires to perform a specific job effectively. The starting point for obtaining this information is the job description derived from a detailed job analysis. (As you may recall from Chapter 3, a job analysis is the starting point for just about any personnel operation.) The next and most difficult step involves translating the specific task requirements of the job into the basic components of knowledge and skill that can be incorporated into a training program. For example, a job as department store assistant manager might require the worker to handle customer complaints effectively. However, it may be difficult to determine the specific skills required to perform this task in order to train prospective employees.

In some employee training programs, workers who dropped out of school can earn high school diplomas.

PERSON ANALYSIS

The person analysis of employee training needs examines the current capabilities of the workers themselves to determine who needs what sort of training. Person analysis usually relies on worker deficiencies outlined in performance appraisals for incumbent workers, and information derived from employee selection data, such as screening tests, for new workers. Another important source of information is job incumbents' self-assessments of training needs (Ford & Noe, 1987), which may also help build employee commitment to the training program.

The use of the three levels of training needs analysis can help determine which workers need training in which areas and provide information to guide the development of specific training techniques. Moreover, the organization can consider the impact of a proposed training program in terms of both the potential benefits, such as increased efficiency and productivity, and the potential costs.

DEMOGRAPHIC ANALYSIS

Recently, it has been suggested that training needs analysis may have to be conducted on a fourth level, *demographic* analysis (Latham, 1988). A demographic analysis involves determining the specific training needs of various demographic groups, such as women and men, minorities, and different age brackets. For example, a study of the perceived training needs of workers 40 years of age and older found that the younger workers (aged 40 to 49) believed that they needed training in management skills and the middle-aged group (aged 50 to 59) preferred training in technological skills, while the oldest group (60 years and older) showed little interest in any type of training, perhaps because they felt that they had little to gain from additional training (Tucker, 1985). Another study looking at management training needs found that male and female managers needed training in different types of communication skills. Women managers were perceived by upper level management as requiring training in assertiveness, confidence building, public speaking, and dealing with males, whereas male manager training needs were identified as listening, verbal skills, nonverbal communication, empathy, and sensitivity (Berryman-Fink, 1985).

PERSONNEL TRAINING METHODS

Once specific training needs are identified, the next step is to design a training program to meet them. Such a program can use a wide variety of training methods ranging from the relatively simple and straightforward to the fairly complex and sophisticated, although all involve the basic principles of learning discussed earlier. In actual practice, most comprehensive training programs utilize a combination of several training methods and techniques.

The various methods can be grouped into two broad categories: the on-site methods, or those conducted on the job site, and the off-site methods, or those conducted away from the actual work place.

ON-SITE METHODS

On-site training methods may be further divided into several subcategories, including on-the-job training, apprenticeship, vestibule training, and job rotation.

On-the-job training. One of the oldest and most widely used training methods, **on-the-job training** consists simply of putting an inexperienced worker in the work place and having a more experienced worker teach that person about the job. This technique thus relies on principles of modeling, with the experienced worker serving as the role model. Also, because actual hands-on learning is involved, the worker can receive immediate feedback, be reinforced for successful efforts, and have a chance to learn how to correct errors.

The popularity of on-the-job training is obvious since it requires little preparation and few costs to the organization, aside from the time invested by the experienced worker. Moreover, because the trainee is actually working while learning, certain small levels of output offset the costs of the supervising worker's time. However, problems occur when the organization neglects to consider the abilities and motivations of the expe-

Skilled trades such as carpentry typically require formal apprenticeships.

on-the-job training
a personnel training method of placing a worker in the work place to learn firsthand about a job

rienced workers who serve as trainers. If these trainers do not see the personal benefits of serving as trainers (especially when there are no obvious benefits!), they will not be motivated to do a good job. Also, being a good trainer requires certain qualities, such as patience and an ability to communicate. If the trainer lacks these traits, this can interfere with trainees' learning. Problems can also arise if the trainer does not know or follow proper work procedures. In this case, the trainer may teach the new worker the wrong methods.

On-the-job training is best used when the trainers have been carefully selected because of their ability to teach and have received systematic training to help them be more effective. They must also receive some type of rewards or recognition for performing their training duties. Finally, the organization must accept the fact that during the on-the-job training period, production rates will suffer. It is impossible to expect the trainer-trainee team to do a good job of training while simultaneously maintaining high output rates.

Apprenticeship. Skilled trade professions, such as carpentry, printing, masonry, and plumbing, use a very old type of training program called **apprenticeship.** A typical apprenticeship can last for several years and usually combines some supervised on-the-job training experience with classroom instruction. The on-the-job experience allows the apprentice to learn the mechanics of the profession, while the classroom training usually teaches specific cognitive skills and rules and regulations associated with the profession. For example, an apprentice in the housing construction industry will learn the mechanical skills of building a house while on the job and will learn about building codes and how to read blueprints in the classroom. The obvious advantage of apprenticeship programs is the detailed and long-term nature of the learning process. However, there have been charges from civil rights groups that apprentices are disproportionately chosen from majority groups and that women and members of ethnic minorities have been selectively omitted. In recent years, affirmative action programs in many apprenticed professions have attempted to rectify these problems (Wexley & Yukl, 1984).

A training program for new managers that combines elements of on-the-job training and apprenticeship is **mentoring,** a process by which an inexperienced worker develops a relationship with an experienced worker to promote the former's career development. Much of the learning that takes place in these relationships involves the protégé attempting to imitate the mentor's work and interpersonal style. Modeling thus appears to be the key learning process in mentoring. Mentoring among managers in large organizations is becoming more and more common (see On the Cutting Edge).

Vestibule training. **Vestibule training** is another on-site training method. This method uses a separate training area adjacent to the actual

apprenticeship
a training technique, usually lasting several years, that combines on-the-job experience with classroom instruction

mentoring
a training program in which an inexperienced worker develops a relationship with an experienced worker, who serves as an adviser

vestibule training
training that uses a separate area set up adjacent to the work area to simulate the actual work setting

Mentoring: An Informal Technique for Training New Managers

In certain situations, young, inexperienced workers typically look to older, more experienced workers to help them to "learn the ropes" of the job. Master-apprentice, professor-student, doctor-intern, and coach-athlete are some of the more formalized mentor-protégé relationships.

Recently, there has been considerable research and popular interest in mentoring in management. One study has found that the majority of successful executives surveyed reported having had a mentor in the early stages of their careers. Moreover, those who had had a mentor received higher salaries and bonuses and had more successful career paths than those who had not (Roche, 1979; see also Collins & Scott, 1978). Executives who had had mentors were also more likely to serve as mentors to others later in their careers (the role modeling did indeed transfer!). Additional research has taken a more longitudinal perspective, examining the formation of mentor-protégé relationships and studying their various stages (Kram, 1983). Most recently, research has begun to explore the specific elements of the relationship

that lead to a successful mentoring experience (Noe, 1988).

Mentoring in management appears to be on the rise, and some organizations have formalized programs to encourage its development (Stumpf & London, 1981). Although the majority of mentors in management are men (paralleling the disproportionate number of men in high-level executive positions), more and more women managers are developing mentor-protégé relationships to assist in their career growth (Collins, 1983). Indeed, one author claims that it is nearly impossible for a woman to succeed in top management without the assistance of a mentor (Missarian, 1982).

Although it may appear that the protégé benefits most from the mentoring relationship, there are also payoffs for the mentor and for the organization. The mentor, who may be at a midlife career standstill, may become energized by the chance to assist in the development of an eager young worker's career. The organization also benefits, since mentoring leads to a more well-trained and satisfied young work force.

---

work area to simulate that setting, complete with comparable tools and equipment. Professional trainers teach the new workers all aspects of the job, allowing them hands-on experience in the work simulation area. The main advantage of vestibule training is that there is no disruption of actual production, since trainers rather than experienced workers provide instruction and the novice workers are not in the actual work setting. The major drawback to this method is its costs in terms of the trainers, space, and equipment needed.

job rotation
a method of rotating workers among a variety of jobs to increase their breadth of knowledge

Job rotation. A final on-site training method is **job rotation,** in which workers are rotated among a variety of jobs, spending a certain length of time (usually several weeks to two months) at each. The basic premise behind job rotation is to expose workers to as many areas of the organization as possible so that they can gain a good knowledge of its workings and how the various jobs and departments fit together. Most commonly, job rotation is used to help entry-level management personnel find the positions for which they are best suited. It can also be used to groom managers for higher level positions, presumably making them more effective by enabling them to see the organization from a variety of perspectives. Job rotation has also been used in various team approaches to work task design to increase worker flexibility and commitment to the organization.

OFF-SITE METHODS

Training that takes place in a setting other than the actual work place uses off-site methods. Because of the greater flexibility and control over the situation they afford, off-site methods are more varied and diverse than the on-site techniques. We will consider several off-site methods: lecture, audiovisual instruction, simulation techniques, programmed instruction, and computer assisted instruction.

Lecture. A very common method of employee training, and one that is very familiar to students, is the **lecture,** which typically involves some expert providing job-related information orally in a classroom-like setting. Although this method of training allows a large number of workers to be trained simultaneously at relatively low cost, it has several drawbacks. First, because the lecture is a one-way form of communication, employees may not become highly involved in the learning process. Also, it is unclear whether workers will be able to translate the information they receive from lectures into actual performance of work behaviors. Finally, the lecture method is often only as good as the lecturer. A training program presented by a speaker who is unprepared and speaks in a monotone is unlikely to lead to any significant learning. In fact, one study found that lecturing was one of the least effective employee training methods (Carroll, Paine, & Ivancevich, 1972). Of course, lecturing programs can often be made more effective if the lectures are combined with question-and-answer periods or audience discussion.

lecture
a training method in which an expert provides job-related information in a classroom setting

Audiovisual instruction. **Audiovisual instruction** uses films, slide presentations, videotapes, and closed-circuit television to train workers. Increased access to advanced audiovisual technology means that just about any size organization can afford the equipment needed to create and/or present such training programs. Although there may be some fairly large initial costs, the audiovisual method can be even more cost-effective than traditional lecture techniques if large numbers of employees are going to be trained.

As in lectures, the quality of audiovisual instruction determines its effectiveness as a training tool. In many instances, a film or slide show can be more entertaining than a lecture and may do a better job of attracting the audience's attention. An obvious problem occurs, however, when the informational content is sacrificed for entertainment value.

Audiovisual presentations are especially effective when the information is presented visually rather than verbally. A few minutes of videotape can visually demonstrate manual operations (with instant replay, stop

audiovisual instruction
the use of films, videotapes, slide presentations, and closed-circuit television to illustrate training material

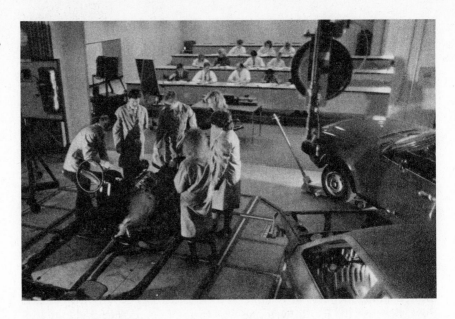

At an insurance company's training facility, claims adjusters are given audiovisual instruction as well as hands-on experience.

action, or slow motion) or can expose workers to a number of different locations and settings, both of which would be impossible in a lecture presentation. Moreover, recorded audiovisual programs can ensure uniformity of training by exposing all workers to the same information. For example, one large printing and publishing company has prepared an audio-slide presentation to give groups of new employees information about company policies, procedures, and employee rights and benefits in a thorough, graphic, and cost-effective manner.

One area in which audiovisual technology has been used in conjunction with another employee training technique is **behavior modeling training** (Decker & Nathan, 1985; Goldstein & Sorcher, 1974). In behavior modeling training, which is based on the social learning theory, trainees are exposed to films or videotapes of role models displaying both appropriate and inappropriate work behaviors as well as their successful or unsuccessful outcomes. Trainees are then allowed an opportunity to try to replicate and practice the positive work behaviors. Research indicates that behavior modeling training, if used correctly, can effectively improve employee job performance (Decker, 1982; Mann & Decker, 1984; Meyer & Raich, 1983).

Simulation techniques. **Simulation** training is a method of replicating job conditions to instruct employees in proper work operations without actually putting them in the job setting. Jet pilots, astronauts, and nuclear power plant operators are all subjected to intensive simulation training before they are allowed to control the complex and dangerous machinery that they will operate on the job. Simulation training allows the worker

behavior modeling training
a training method that exposes trainees to role models performing appropriate and inappropriate work behaviors and their outcomes and then allows them to practice modeling the appropriate behaviors

simulation
training that replicates job conditions without placing the trainee in the actual work setting

hours of practice under conditions that are quite similar to the actual work setting, without allowing the possibility of damaging the equipment, the product, the environment, or themselves.

Most commonly, simulation training uses replications of complex machinery or equipment, such as jet cockpit flight simulators or mock-ups of the control panels used by nuclear power plant operators. Other simulations may be designed to give trainees exposure to what would normally be very hazardous working conditions. For example, a Southern California police department has constructed a mock city (complete with a bank and a convenience store!) for use in training police personnel in simulated emergency conditions. Police trainees attempt to foil simulated robbery attempts and rescue hostages from terrorists using the mock city and blank ammunition. According to the police authorities, the realism of this simulation has led to better preparation of new officers in dealing with actual life-threatening situations.

As you can imagine, simulation training is often very expensive. However, the chance for hands-on experience, immediate feedback, and repeated practice make it a very effective technique.

Programmed instruction. **Programmed instruction** involves the use of self-paced individualized training. Each trainee is provided with materials (usually a printed booklet) to learn and then a series of questions that test how much learning has taken place. When test answers are substantially correct, the trainee is instructed to move on to the next unit. If the questions are answered incorrectly, some review of the previous unit is required. Most of the student study guides that accompany college textbooks are examples of programmed instruction.

programmed instruction self-paced individualized training in which trainees are provided with training materials and can test how much they have learned

The benefits of programmed instruction are that it is efficient, since individuals proceed at their own paces, and that it provides immediate feedback. Furthermore, although the development of such programs is time-consuming, the initial cost diminishes greatly over time if large numbers of employees are trained. A problem can arise, however, in keeping the programs up-to-date, especially in fields where there are rapid changes in technology or in the types of products produced or services performed, which mean that new instruction programs must be created.

Computer assisted instruction (CAI). A more modern approach to individualized employee training is **computer assisted instruction (CAI).** The tremendous power, flexibility, and the recent affordability of computing systems have led to an increase in computer assisted instruction. Although CAI is actually a form of programmed instruction, CAI systems offer the flexibility to change and update the instructional programs continually. CAI also allows for immediate testing of the trainee's learning because the computer can ask questions and instantly score the correctness of responses, automatically returning the trainee to the earlier lesson if the answers are incorrect, and presenting the next unit when the answers are correct. The computer can also generate detailed data on each

computer assisted instruction (CAI) a form of programmed instruction using computers to present material and test trainees

Computer assisted instruction can capture people's attention with enjoyable graphics and immediate feedback.

trainee's performance across all of the lessons. CAI thus offers all of the advantages of programmed instruction, although the initial costs are even greater because of the need for computer hardware and costly software. Another advantage of CAI is that most people find interaction with the computer enjoyable (more enjoyable than working with a printed booklet), although some individuals may have some initial apprehension (Goldstein, 1986; Wexley & Latham, 1981).

A recent development in CAI is computerized, interactive videodisc programs that combine audiovisual techniques, programmed instruction, and simulation techniques. With these programs, a trainee may be presented with a videotape of a work situation. The computer then asks questions about which course of action the trainee would like to take. The response is then used to choose the next videotape segment, where the trainee can see the results of the choice played out on videotape. One such program, used for management training, exposes the trainee to a variety of difficult interpersonal and decisionmaking situations. Through the eye of the videocamera, the trainee is brought into a simulated work situation with actors portraying the roles of co-workers. In one setting, the trainee might need to deal with a subordinate who is angry about having been given a negative performance appraisal. In another situation, the trainee may be asked to play the role of leader of a decisionmaking group and choose one of four possible actions. Choosing the correct management strategies leads to a positive outcome. If an incorrect choice is made, the trainee will view the disastrous results played out by the actors in the subsequent scene. Similar interactive videodisc training programs have been developed to teach medical students diagnosis of illness and treatment decisions.

MANAGEMENT TRAINING METHODS

Because managers are considered to play such a central role in administrative functions, coordinating organizational activities and motivating workers, and because managerial skills are abstract and difficult to learn, most training resources go into the training and development of managers. In fact, a variety of techniques are used almost exclusively in management training.

One common and very popular management training technique is the **problem-solving case study,** which presents trainees with a written description of a real or hypothetical organizational problem. Each trainee is allowed time to study the case individually and come up with a solution. The trainees then meet in small groups to present and critique their solutions and discuss the problem further. One purpose of such studies is to show trainees that there are no single or easy solutions to complex problems. Another goal is to help trainees develop skills in diagnosing and dealing with organizational problems. Although the problem-solving case study is a popular management training method, some doubt its effec-

problem-solving case study
a management training technique that presents a real or hypothetical organizational problem that trainees attempt to solve

tiveness (Argyris, 1980; Campbell, Dunnette, Lawler, & Weick, 1970), specifically whether the learning from the hypothetical situation transfers well to actual management situations.

An extension of this method is to have trainees engage in **role playing** a certain management situation. For example, in a role playing exercise to develop managers' ability to handle difficult interpersonal situations, a trainer may play an irate subordinate who is upset with receiving a poor performance appraisal. The trainee plays the manager, and the trainer may later offer feedback concerning how the situation was handled. In role playing the basic idea is that trainees will become more involved in a problem situation if they act it out. Sometimes, participants will reverse roles to gain a different perspective on the problem situation. An added side effect of role playing may be that management trainees simultaneously learn to develop their presentational and communication skills.

Another management training technique is **management games,** which are usually scaled-down enactments of the management of organizations. They are in many ways similar to some of the more complicated board games that people play at home. In certain management games, participants are presented with a hypothetical organization, budget, and other resources. Various rules and procedures govern the game play. The goal is to make management decisions that will maximize the organization's outcomes, usually expressed in terms of profits. Participants may play either in groups, forming management teams to compete against other teams, or against one another individually. As with case studies, the difficulty is in generalizing learning from the game situation to the actual setting. Also, participants may become so caught up in the game that they do not comprehend the management principles that are being taught.

A final management training technique is the **conference,** or group discussion. Conferences usually involve a very unstructured type of training in which participants are brought together to share ideas and information and solve some shared management problems. The basic goal of conferences is for practicing managers to learn effective management techniques that have been used by other managers. Their main advantage is that they encourage individual participation in the learning process.

As mentioned, full-scale training programs usually include a number of training methods. This is particularly true in management training, in which trainees may attend workshops lasting several days, with participants exposed to training in a variety of areas, including problem solving, decisionmaking, and interpersonal skills, using a number of techniques.

SPECIFIC FOCUSES OF PERSONNEL TRAINING PROGRAMS

Comprehensive employee training and development programs consider the training of all workers at all levels and at all stages of their careers. A comprehensive training program should provide orientation and initial job training for new employees, programs for workers wanting

role playing
a training exercise that requires trainees to act out problem situations that often occur at work

management games
scaled-down enactments of the operations and management of organizations used as a management training technique

conference
an unstructured management training technique in which participants share ideas, information, and problems; also called a group discussion

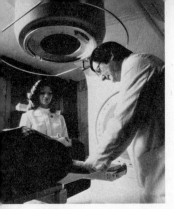

Like many other professionals, doctors and nurses need continuing education to keep abreast of new developments.

to learn new skills and to use new technology, continuing education to keep workers' skills sharp and up-to-date, and ongoing management development, as well as seminars in planning and preparing for retirement. Training, like learning, is a lifelong process, and organizations are beginning to see value in considering and providing for the various training needs of workers. We will examine some of these specific focuses of employee training and development programs.

New employee orientation and training. Orientation programs are typically designed to introduce employees to the organization and its goals, philosophy, policies, and procedures. They can also acquaint workers with both the physical structure and the personnel structure of the organization, such as the chain of supervisory command and the various relevant departments and divisions. During orientation new employees also learn about compensation, benefits, and safety rules and procedures. In short, initial training should provide enough information so that new employees can quickly become productive members of the organization's work force.

Although new employee orientation and training are a large part of most organizations' training programs, many do not give sufficient attention or resources to this area (see Up Close) despite its very important role in creating a productive and dedicated work force. In fact, evidence suggests that employees receiving adequate initial training are less likely to quit during the first six months of a job than workers who receive little initial training (Wanous, Stumpf, & Bedrosian, 1979).

Retraining and continuing education programs. Considerable evidence indicates that a certain amount of the knowledge and skills of workers either erodes or becomes obsolete during their work careers (Landy, 1985). To maintain workers' proficiency, organizations must encourage and support basic "refresher courses" as well as continuing education programs that provide workers with new information. With rapid technological advancements, it is critical that the skills and knowledge of persons employed in jobs that require the use of advanced technology be constantly updated.

Certain professionals, particularly those in licensed health care professions such as medicine, dentistry, and clinical psychology, require some form of continuing education to continue to work in the field. Other professionals, such as managers, lawyers, engineers, and architects, are also increasingly encouraging and supporting continuing education programs.

Training raters to appraise performance. Another rather specialized employee training program is teaching supervisors to rate job performance (Pulakos, 1986; Spool, 1978). Much of the evaluation process involves a somewhat subjective appraisal of worker performances. As dis-

Why Do Some Organizations Give So Little Attention to New Employee Orientation and Training?

Traditionally, some organizations have tended to throw new employees into a work situation with only minimal training and orientation, assuming that they will learn the job by observing and doing. In these instances, there appears to be a strong belief that the really good workers will distinguish themselves by their ability to adapt and survive.

One reason for this "sink-or-swim" treatment of new employees is that employee training and orientation have not been very high priorities for many organizations, particularly smaller businesses and relatively new companies. These organizations are so preoccupied with basic survival—maintaining productivity rates and keeping the size and quality of the work force constant—that training (along with other personnel considerations, such as a program of regular performance appraisals) is put on the back shelf. When conditions stabilize and the company has grown or matured, these personnel functions may be given greater emphasis.

Another reason for the absence of new employee training programs is the lack of assessment of training needs. Many organizations are simply unaware of what new employees need (and want) to know. Those who know the most about new employee training needs are probably the front-line supervisors, who observe firsthand the skill and knowledge deficiencies of new workers. For some reason, however, these training needs are not communicated to the upper-level decisionmakers. Of course it may not be helpful to ask the new workers about their needs, since because they are new they are usually unaware of their training requirements. New workers may also not readily admit to certain skill or knowledge deficiencies in an effort to appear that they are indeed competent. A related problem arises when there is no sound evaluation of existing training programs, for it is unlikely that additional resources will be allocated unless the benefits of such programs have been demonstrated. Finally, inadequate training and orientation may be rooted in the belief that the best way for new workers to learn is by doing. While on-the-job training can be effective, organizations need to consider its costs for new employees, such as reduced levels of production and potential damage to the product, equipment, or the workers. Unregulated on-the-job training may also cause workers to learn poor work habits rather than the proper ones.

cussed in Chapter 3, a number of biases are associated with such ratings. Rater training programs typically focus on teaching appraisers to be more objective and accurate in their observations, and to be aware of and to try to overcome rating errors and biases. Some of these programs simply tell appraisers about specific biases, with the expectation that this knowledge will make them less susceptible to these distortions. Other programs, such as those designed to overcome attributional biases, give raters direct experience with the jobs they are appraising so that they may see the tasks from the workers' perspectives.

Retirement planning and preparation.   In recent years, the training departments of many organizations have begun offering employees assistance in planning and preparing for retirement. Seminars are offered on such topics as making the retirement decision, retirement plans and options, investment and money management, and services and opportunities for retirees and seniors. More general programs aimed at helping retirees

Table 5.1   BENEFITS OF A CAREER DEVELOPMENT SYSTEM

For Managers/ Supervisors	For Employees	For the Organization
Increased skill in managing own careers	Helpful assistance with career decisions and changes	Beter use of employee skills
Greater retention of valued employees	Enrichment of present job and increased job satisfaction	Increased loyalty
Better communication between manager and employee	Better communication between employee and manager	Dissemination of information at all organizational levels
More realistic staff and development planning	More realistic goals and expectations	Better communication within organization as a whole
Productive performance appraisal discussions	Better feedback on performance	Greater retention of valued employees
Increased understanding of the organization	Current information about the organization and future trends	Expanded public image as a people-developing organization
Enhanced reputation as a people developer	Greater sense of personal responsibility for managing career	Increased effectiveness of personnel systems and procedures
Employee motivation for accepting new responsibilities		Clarification of organization goals
Build talent inventory for special projects		
Clarification of fit between organizational and individual goals		

Source: Z. B. Leibowitz, C. Farren, and B. L. Kaye, *Designing Career Development Systems* (San Francisco: Jossey-Bass, 1986), p. 7.

adjust to a nonworking lifestyle are also offered. This increase in preretirement training programs reflects a general trend toward more employee training and greater concern for employees' welfare. Although preretirement programs are becoming quite common, there is little evidence of their effectiveness. Recently, one author issued a challenge to I/O psychologists to devote research to the process of retirement (Beehr, 1986).

Employee career development.   Organizations are becoming more and more aware of the need for greater attention to the development and planning of employees' careers. Helping workers plan their careers can help lead to a more productive, more satisfied, and more loyal work force (Hall & Hall, 1976; Krau, 1981). Many organizations are developing formal career development systems, which benefit all parties involved: workers, managers, and the organization (see Table 5.1).

Career development systems typically offer a variety of programs, including career counseling, courses in career planning, and workshops that provide tools and techniques for helping employees manage their careers. For example, career counseling programs might help individuals set career goals and develop a plan for getting the type of training and

The Career Development System at Disneyland

In the late 1970s a comprehensive career development system was implemented at the Disneyland amusement park in Anaheim, California. Disneyland was particularly concerned with this issue because of the large number of part-time student employees. This, coupled with the fact that the number of employees ranges from 5500 to about 10,000 during the peak summer season, leads to a great deal of turnover and instability in a portion of the work force. The career planning department is staffed by a manager, two full-time career counselors, and clerical personnel.

The goals of the career planning system are as follows:

1. to develop a pool of human resources to staff future expansion and deal with employee turnover;
2. to help minimize mismatches between the employees' career interests and the company's employment needs and availabilities;
3. to assist individuals in their career development, including preparation for promotion and increased responsibility; and
4. to help employees develop and increase their self-awareness and to achieve a better understanding of their own personal abilities and limitations.

To reach these goals, the system offers the following programs:

Disneyland Intern Program.   This program is designed to ensure a constant flow of qualified, high-potential managers. Participants serve as management interns in various departments, receiving a combination of formal and on-the-job training in supervisory skills. Upon completion of the program, they are considered for Disneyland managerial openings.

Employee Career Counseling.   The services of full-time career counselors are available to any employee on request. In the first meeting with a counselor, the employee is encouraged to discuss personal educational objectives, career directions, and possible career changes. The employee may return for additional counseling as often as desired.

Career Planning Workshops.   Disneyland offers a series of workshops to help employees determine career objectives and individual career plans. Topics include goal setting, decisionmaking, job satisfaction, worker effectiveness, résumé preparation, and job interview techniques, complete with videotaped simulations.

Career Resource Library and Job Posting.   Disneyland maintains a library of functional organizational charts, job descriptions for all positions, and a variety of general books on career planning and guidance. A job-posting system announces openings, and a promotion-from-within policy is encouraged.

Skills Inventory.   A computerized skills inventory contains data on all employees' educational levels, work experiences, job classifications, and career interests. When an opening occurs, a listing is produced of those individuals who have been recommended by management for such positions or who have expressed an interest in such jobs. Those people are then invited to interview for the opening.

Career Forum.   Disneyland schedules occasional presentations on career opportunities by company representatives and by their counterparts in other companies. General information is also provided on external job opportunities, particularly aimed at helping the seasonal employees find off-season jobs.

Source: T. G. Gutteridge, "Organizational Career Development Systems: The State of the Practice," in D. T. Hall and Associates, *Career Development in Organizations* (San Francisco: Jossey-Bass, 1986), pp. 82–85.

education necessary to meet those goals. They may also assist in finding jobs for employees who are about to be laid off (see Applying I/O Psychology).

Managers are also becoming more aware of the role that they must play in helping the career development of their subordinates. Time might be scheduled for the manager to discuss each subordinate's past performance, expectations, and career goals. Managers can play the role of career counselor, suggesting ways that the subordinate can help to develop work knowledge, skills, and abilities either through formal education and training programs or on-the-job training. Managers who focus attention on the career development of their subordinates help to create a more highly skilled and productive work force.

THE EVALUATION OF TRAINING PROGRAMS

A crucial component of any employee training program is the evaluation of training effectiveness, for there is no use in investing money and resources in training programs unless they do indeed work. In spite of its importance, however, relatively few programs are actually subjected to rigorous evaluation (Goldstein, 1986).

The evaluation of a training program should first outline the criteria that indicate the program's success and develop the means for measuring these criteria. One framework suggests that there are four types of criteria for evaluating a program's effectiveness (Kirkpatrick, 1959–60; Latham & Saari, 1979):

1. *Reaction criteria:* measures of the impressions of trainees, including their assessments of the program's value, the amount of learning they received, and their enjoyment of the program.
2. *Learning criteria:* measures of the amount of learning that has taken place. Typically, these take the form of some sort of tests assessing the amount of information retained from the program.
3. *Behavioral criteria:* measures of the amount of newly learned skills displayed once the trainee has returned to the job.
4. *Results criteria:* measures of outcomes that are important to the organization, such as increased trainee work output as expressed by production rates, dollar sales figures, or quality of work. Using the results criteria, a cost-benefit analysis can be performed by comparing the costs of the program to the dollar value of the results. This is usually the most important evaluation of a program's effectiveness. However, it is sometimes difficult to translate training outcomes into dollars and cents. For example, if one of the goals is to improve employee attitudes, it may be very hard to place a dollar value on such results.

The important question in the evaluation of programs is whether any measured changes in criteria are indeed the result of training. The methods used in the proper evaluation of a training program are those used to determine the effectiveness of any other type of program introduced into an organization. For a formal evaluation to demonstrate conclusively that training has caused certain outcomes, it should be based on experimental designs. Unfortunately, many evaluations use what might be called "preexperimental designs," which do not allow for proper assessments (Wexley & Yukl, 1984). For example, simply measuring criteria following the completion of a training program does not tell us anything about its effectiveness because we have no basis for any sort of comparison. A **pretest-posttest**—measuring behavior before and after training—is also an inadequate experimental design. Although this approach compares the criterion measures collected before and after the training program, we cannot be sure that the differences from pretest to posttest were due to the program. Consider the example of a training program designed to teach bank tellers to be more friendly and attentive to customer needs. With a simple pretest-posttest evaluation we can never be sure that later observed increases in the quality of customer service was due to training or to other factors, such as a recent pay raise or change in management.

pretest-posttest
a design for evaluating a training program that makes comparisons of criterion measures collected before and after the introduction of the program

To be sure of the effectiveness of a training program, one must apply a more sophisticated, true experimental design that uses at least one treatment group, which receives the training, and one control group, which does not undergo any training. The simplest and most common experimental design for evaluation research uses one training group and one control group, both of which are measured before and after the program. To ensure that there are no unexpected differences in members of the training and control groups, employees are randomly assigned to the two groups. The pretest and posttest scores are then compared. This experimental design makes it clear that any positive changes in the criterion measures of the training group, relative to the control group, are most likely due to the training program.

A more sophisticated experimental design is the **Solomon four-group design** (Solomon, 1949). This method of evaluation uses four groups, two that are trained and two that are not. In the Solomon design, two of the groups are identical to those in the basic experimental design mentioned above. That is, one training group and one control group are measured both before and after the training program. However, the additional training and control groups are measured only *after* the program, which is intended to help rule out the fact that administering a pretraining measure might sensitize employees to what the program is designed to do and might thus produce certain changes in the criterion measures that occur without the benefit of training. For example, if our bank tellers are given a pretraining test of their customer service knowledge, they might realize that management is very interested in this issue, which might cause all

Solomon four-group design
a method of program evaluation using two treatment groups and two control groups

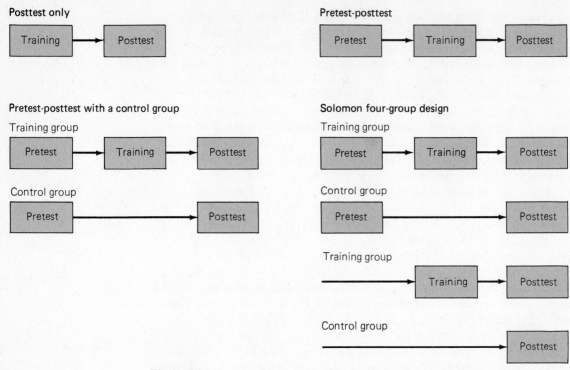

Figure 5.1
FOUR METHODS FOR EVALUATION TRAINING PROGRAMS

tellers to give greater attention to customers, regardless of whether they later receive customer service training. Figure 5.1 summarizes the various evaluation designs.

A comprehensive evaluation of a training program must be well-designed and executed to assure that the training is indeed effective. This means careful consideration must be given to the selection and measurement of criteria, an experimental design with adequate control groups must be used, and the costs versus benefits of the program must be assessed.

EQUAL EMPLOYMENT OPPORTUNITY ISSUES IN PERSONNEL TRAINING

Because training is linked to job performance and can lead to personnel actions such as pay increases, promotions, and firings, several equal employment concerns are related to personnel training (Russell, 1984). One such issue deals with educational or training prerequisites for certain jobs. Because members of underprivileged groups are likely to have less education and formal job training than members of more privileged groups, setting certain levels of education or training as job prerequisites may be considered discriminatory. As mentioned in Chapter 4, equal employment opportunity legislation protects against discriminating against specific groups in providing access to jobs. If access to some jobs requires certain training, employers must take steps to guard against any discrimination in this area by providing remedial education or training for groups of workers who lack the educational prerequisites. For example, some employers are supporting agencies that will train chronically unemployed or underemployed individuals in basic job skills either by making financial contributions or by hiring persons who have undergone the training.

The methods used in employee training programs may also create instances of potential discrimination. For example, the lectures offered in many programs may lead to different rates of learning in different groups of trainees. If certain underprivileged groups lack the education needed to process the information and to perform well on any examinations administered, using the results of such training classes to screen or place workers can lead to unintentional discrimination. A similar case occurs in training courses that require certain strenuous activities, such as lifting and carrying heavy materials, in which women may be at some disadvantage. A recent example was a training course for firefighters that demanded that trainees lift and carry a 150-pound dummy over their shoulders for several yards or down a flight of stairs to simulate carrying an unconscious person from a burning building. A question arose as to whether this part of the course discriminated against women. Critics stated that firefighters rarely carried a person out of a burning building, and the ability to do this was not a critical requirement for adequate performance of their job. Because of the possibility of discrimination and because the fire department could not prove that this was a necessary skill for the position, the training task was eliminated.

Similarly, organizations that require workers to attend and complete some type of training program to gain a position or a promotion must demonstrate that completion of the program is predictive of success in the jobs that trainees will be holding. If not, there is the possibility that certain disadvantaged groups of trainees may not do as well in the program because of unfamiliarity with the training procedures and format. In other words, because of their lack of experience with the classroom situation they may not learn as well as members of the majority group, which can lead to discrimination. For example, if being promoted to a front-line supervisory position in a factory requires attending classes in supervisory skills and passing an examination to complete the course, the organization must prove that completion of the training is related to later success as a supervisor and that the program itself does not discriminate in terms of ability to pass the course. In these cases, the training program is just like any other selection tool. It must be shown to be valid, fair, and job related.

SUMMARY

Personnel training is a planned effort by an organization to facilitate the learning, retention, and transfer of job-related behavior. Three basic *learning* theories describe how learning takes place in personnel training: *classical conditioning,* which involves the paired association of two events; *operant conditioning,* which is learning that occurs as a result of reinforcement or punishment for specific behaviors; and *modeling,* which is imitative learning. The concept of modeling is expressed in *social learning theory,* which holds that for learning to take place, attention must first be focused on a model's behavior and there must be some retention and motor reproduction of the behavior as well as some motivation for performing the behavior.

The first step in an employee training program is the assessment of training needs, which occurs on several levels: Organizational analysis considers the organization's goals, resources, and the climate for training; task analysis evaluates the specific knowledge, skills, and abilities that a job requires; and person analysis examines the capabilities and deficiencies of the workers themselves. Training needs may also have to be conducted through demographic analysis, which is targeted toward assessing the training needs of specific groups, such as males versus females or the old versus the young.

The various training methods can be broken down into two general categories: on-site methods and off-site methods. Of on-site methods, *on-the-job training* is the most widely used, consisting of putting inexperienced workers into the work site under the direction of an experienced teacher-worker. *Apprenticeship* is a much more long-term on-site method, combining classroom training with supervised on-the-job training. *Mentoring* is a third on-site method, in which an inexperienced worker is assigned an experienced mentor who serves as a role model. *Vestibule training* sets up a model training area adjacent to the actual work site, using professional trainers and hands-on experience. *Job rotation* is a training technique designed to broaden workers' experience by rotating employees among various jobs.

Off-site methods include the common *lecture* method, *audiovisual instruction* that provides graphic depictions of work activities, and *simulation* techniques that involve classroom replications of actual work stations. A technique that uses aspects of both audiovisual technology and concepts of social learning theory is *behavior modeling training,* a method of exposing trainees to videotapes of models engaged in appropriate work behaviors and then having them practice the observed behaviors. *Programmed instruction* is a form of self-paced training in which workers can learn at their own pace. A modern, sophisticated version of programmed instruction is *computer assisted instruction (CAI).*

Among the specific methods and techniques used in management training are *problem-solving case studies, role playing,* and *management games,* which all involve simulations of actual management situations. *Conferences,* where participants share ideas or solve shared management problems, is another management training method.

Once training programs have taken place, the evaluation of their effectiveness is very important. The first step is to determine criteria of training effectiveness; four types are typically used: reaction criteria, learning criteria, behavioral criteria, and results criteria. Once the criteria are established, basic research methods and design should be used to evaluate the training programs. The *pretest-posttest* is a common but inadequate means of assessing a program in which measures of criteria are collected both before and after a training intervention, allowing for a comparison of changes in learning or work behaviors. However, this method is inadequate because of the lack of a good comparison group. Better evaluation designs use both a training group and a comparison, or control, group that is not subjected to the training program. A very complex and sophisticated evaluation design is the *Solomon four-group design,* which uses two training groups and two control groups.

Finally, certain legal issues must be considered in the design and implementation of training programs. Training or educational prerequisites and the programs themselves must not unfairly discriminate on the basis of ethnicity, age, or sex.

STUDY QUESTIONS AND EXERCISES

1. Consider the three basic learning theories: classical conditioning, operant conditioning, and modeling or social learning. How is each involved in the type of learning that takes place in work organizations? How do they relate to learning in college classrooms?

2. Consider a work organization that you have had some contact with, either one in which you were employed or in which a friend or relative is working. Based on your knowledge, how might a training needs assessment be conducted? Consider all four levels of assessment: organizational, task, person, and demographic analysis.

3. Compare and contrast the advantages and disadvantages of on-site versus off-site training methods.

4. Consider the various designs for evaluating personnel training programs. Although the more complex and sophisticated designs usually provide better evaluation, what are some of the difficulties of conducting an assessment in actual work organizations?

5. Review the discussion of EEO issues in personnel training. What are the various ways that training programs could discriminate against members of protected groups (ethnic minorities, women, the elderly)?

SUGGESTED READINGS

Casner-Lotto, J. (1988). *Successful training strategies: Twenty-six innovative corporate models*. San Francisco: Jossey-Bass. *This book reviews innovative training and development programs and strategies that are used in major corporations and public organizations throughout the United States.*

Goldstein, I. L. (1986). *Training in organizations: Needs assessment, development, and evaluation* (2nd ed.). Monterey, CA: Brooks/Cole. *A thorough textbook containing just about everything that you would want to know about personnel training. This classic is now in a revised edition.*

Hall, D. T. (1986). *Career development in organizations*. San Francisco: Jossey-Bass. *A book of readings on issues related to employee career development in organizations. This is part of the series on Frontiers in Industrial and Organizational Psychology.*

Mayo, G. D., & DuBois, P. H. (1987). *The complete book of training: Theory, principles, and techniques*. San Diego: University Associates. *A step-by-step guide to training issues designed as a handbook for training professionals.*

Rosow, J. M., & Zager, R. (1988). *Training—the competitive edge: Introducing new technology into the workplace*. San Francisco: Jossey-Bass. *A thorough review of training and development programs as well as strategies used in the work place.*

6

PART THREE

WORKER ISSUES

MOTIVATION

Motivation Within the Context of Industrial/Organizational Psychology

Two areas of I/O psychology involve a tremendous amount of theorizing: motivation and leadership (the topic of leadership will be discussed in Chapter 10). Because both motivation and leadership are extremely complex and important topics in the work world, they are given a great deal of attention by I/O psychologists. This chapter introduces a variety of theories of motivation. Rather than viewing these as isolated models, consider the ways in which they are similar. Some of these similarities are reflected in the grouping of theories into categories such as need theories and job design theories, as shown in the chapter outline. Other similarities can also help draw related concepts together. For example, the need theories emphasize the satisfaction of basic human needs as a key to motivation, while reinforcement theory argues that motivation is caused by positive reinforcement. However, the satisfaction of human needs can be seen as the experience of a positive reinforcement. By understanding similarities such as these you can begin to synthesize what at first appears to be an overwhelming mass of abstract and unrelated ideas.

Because motivation is presumably behind any work behavior, some of the concepts discussed in this chapter also relate to topics that we have already discussed and that we will consider in upcoming chapters. For example, reinforcement theory is linked to the principles of learning presented in Chapter 5. Certain motivational programs, specifically job enrichment and organizational behavior modification, are also used in organizational development, which is introduced in Chapter 12.

Besides looking for similarities among motivation theories and noticing topics that were previously discussed, pay close attention to the last section of the chapter, which emphasizes that motivation is only one of the many variables that can affect work outcomes. This is an important point because it reminds us to consider the "total picture"—the interrelationships among many organizational variables—when studying work behavior.

I n the next two chapters we will examine certain important psychological states that influence employee work behavior: the motivation to work, the satisfaction one gets from a job, and the stress that occurs because of job demands. These three states represent the vital issues of why people work and what happens to them internally because of work rewards and demands. This chapter focuses on motivation.

Work motivation is one of the most widely researched topics in I/O psychology. If you surveyed managers and asked them to list the most difficult aspects of their jobs, odds are that the majority would mention the difficulty in motivating workers as a particular problem. Look around you at work or in school. You will see some people who seem to put more energy and drive into their work, and others who try to get by with minimal effort. When we begin to infer some underlying processes of effort, energy, or drive, we are trying to capture the elusive construct of motivation. Obviously, in any work setting there will be tremendous individual differences in the motivation to work. Why is this the case? What are some of the factors that affect worker motivation? How can we motivate seemingly unmotivated workers?

In this chapter, we will begin by defining motivation. Next, we will examine the various theories of work motivation and see how some of them have been applied in an attempt to increase worker motivation. Finally, we will look at how work motivation relates to work performance.

DEFINING MOTIVATION

According to one definition (Steers & Porter, 1983), **motivation** is a force that serves three functions: It energizes, or causes people to act; it directs behavior toward the attainment of specific goals; and it sustains the effort expended in reaching those goals.

motivation
the force that energizes, directs, and sustains behavior

Since motivation cannot be observed directly, it is very difficult to study. We can only infer motives either by observing goal-directed behavior or by using some psychological measurement technique. Throughout its history, I/O psychology has offered many theories of work motivation. We have already touched on the simplistic models put forth by scientific management and the human relations movement. According to Frederick Taylor, workers are motivated by money and material gains, whereas Elton Mayo stressed the role that interpersonal needs play in motivating workers. Since these early days, more sophisticated theories of motivation have been developed. Some stress the importance of specific needs in determining motivation, and others focus on the role of job design. Still another category of theories argues that motivation is a rational process and that workers cognitively weigh the advantages and disadvantages of expending work energy. Finally, other concepts, including the goal-setting and reinforcement theories, point to work outcomes, such as rewards, as the critical elements behind motivation.

Figure 6.1

NEED THEORIES OF MOTIVATION

needs
physiological or psychological deficiencies that an organism is compelled to fulfill

Several motivation theories assert that people have certain **needs** that are important in determining motivation. Needs involve specific physiological or psychological deficiencies that the organism is driven to satisfy. The need for food and the drive of hunger is a physiological need and drive inherent in all living organisms; the need for human contact is a psychological need. Need theories of motivation propose that motivation is the process of the interaction among various needs and the drives to satisfy those needs. We will examine three need theories of motivation: Maslow's need-hierarchy theory, Alderfer's ERG theory, and McClelland's achievement motivation theory.

MASLOW'S NEED-HIERARCHY THEORY

need-hierarchy theory
a motivation theory, proposed by Maslow, that arranges needs in a hierarchy from lower, more basic needs to higher-order needs

One of the more popular theories of motivation was proposed by psychologist Abraham Maslow and is called the **need-hierarchy theory** (Maslow, 1965, 1970). Maslow maintained that a variety of needs play a role in human motivation and that the categories of needs could be arranged in a hierarchy, ranging from the lower, more basic types to those of a higher order (see Figure 6.1). He proposed a five-tier hierarchy:

1. *Physiological needs:* the basic survival needs of food, water, air sleep, and sex
2. *Safety needs:* the needs for physical safety (need for shelter) and needs related to psychological security
3. *Social needs:* the need to be accepted by others and needs for love, affection, and friendship

To help employees fulfill the sort of social needs identified by Maslow, some firms sponsor weekly parties.

4. *Esteem needs:* the needs to be recognized for accomplishments and to be admired and respected by peers
5. *Self-actualization needs:* the needs to reach one's highest potential and to attain a sense of fulfillment; the highest level of needs

Obviously, many of these human needs can be satisfied in the working environment. A paycheck fulfills the basic survival needs and puts a roof over our heads. Some of the social needs are fulfilled through interactions with co-workers. The recognition and self-satisfaction attained by being successful in a career allows us to satisfy some of the higher level esteem and self-actualization needs.

According to Maslow's theory, certain rules relate to the different levels of needs. First, the lower-order needs must be satisfied before an individual can move on to the higher-order needs. The individual is motivated in a step-by-step process: As each level of need becomes substantially satisfied, it is no longer a motivator, and the next level of need then becomes the predominant motivator. Since the higher-order needs are unlikely to be satisfied in the typical worker, there is also a constant upward striving that explains why, for example, even successful, high-level executives continue to exhibit considerable motivation.

Maslow's theory has received a great deal of attention not only from psychologists but also from professionals in business, education, and other areas. Unfortunately, research has not found much support for the theory, which seems to be a good descriptive model but has fallen short as a predictor of behavior (Rauschenberger, Schmitt, & Hunter, 1980; Wahba & Bridwell, 1976). Moreover, Maslow's theory has not led to any type of useful application (Miner, 1983).

The major contribution of Maslow's theory is that it has expanded the types of needs that are considered important in work motivation. Typically, managers had focused primarily on lower-level needs, such as monetary incentives, to motivate workers. Maslow's work led to the notion that there are higher-level needs related to esteem and self-actualization that can also be important factors in work motivation.

ALDERFER'S ERG THEORY

ERG theory
Alderfer's motivation model that categorizes needs into existence, relatedness, and growth needs

Building in part on Maslow's theory is Clayton Alderfer's (1972) **ERG theory,** which collapses Maslow's five categories of needs into three: existence needs, which are similar to Maslow's basic physiological and safety needs; relatedness needs, which stem from social interaction and are analogous to the social needs in Maslow's hierarchy; and growth needs, which are the highest-order needs, dealing with needs to develop fully and realize one's potential.

Unlike Maslow, Alderfer does not emphasize the strict hierarchical ordering of needs. Instead, individuals may also move downward in the hierarchy, using a lower-level need as a substitute because of frustrated efforts to satisfy a higher-level need. Unfortunately, there has been little research in support of the ERG theory.

All in all, both the ERG theory and Maslow's need-hierarchy theory are extremely general. They tend to be better descriptive and explanatory theories than they are predictive theories, and neither has led to a successful and widely used strategy for improving actual work motivation (Miner, 1983).

MCCLELLAND'S ACHIEVEMENT MOTIVATION THEORY

achievement motivation theory
McClelland's model of motivation that emphasizes the importance of three needs—achievement, power, and affiliation—in determining worker motivation

The concept of needs is also at the core of David McClelland's **achievement motivation theory** (McClelland, 1961, 1975), which states that three needs are central to work motivation: the needs for achievement, power, and affiliation. Unlike the earlier need theories, which were general theories of human motivation, achievement motivation theory deals specifically with *work* motivation. According to McClelland, people are motivated by different patterns of needs, or motives, terms that he uses interchangeably. In other words, the factors that lead to work motivation may differ from person to person, depending on their particular pattern of needs. The three key motives, or needs, in his theory are as follows:

1. *Need for achievement:* the compelling drive to succeed and to get the job done. Individuals with a very high need for achievement are those who love the challenge of work. They are motivated by a desire to get ahead in the job, to solve problems, and to be outstanding work performers.
2. *Need for power:* the need to direct and control the activities of others and to be influential. Individuals with a high need for

power are status oriented and are more motivated by the chance to gain influence and prestige than to solve particular problems or reach performance goals.

3. *Need for affiliation:* the desire to be liked and accepted by others. Individuals motivated by affiliation needs strive for friendship. They are greatly concerned with interpersonal relationships on the job and prefer working with others on a task. They are motivated by cooperative rather than competitive work situations.

This approach emphasizes the differences in these basic needs from person to person. According to McClelland, we all possess more or less of each of these motives, although in each individual a particular need (or needs) tends to be predominant. In his earlier theorizing on motivation, McClelland (1961) emphasized the role of need for achievement in determining work motivation (hence the name, "achievement motivation theory"). However, in more recent analyses, McClelland (1975) has stressed the roles that need for power and affiliation also play in worker motivation. His theory can also be related to leadership, for he argues that a leader must be aware of and be responsive to the different needs of subordinates to motivate workers successfully (see Chapter 10).

To assess an individual's motivational needs, McClelland uses a variation of the **Thematic Apperception Test (TAT).** Respondents are instructed to study each of a series of fairly ambiguous pictures for a few moments and then "write the story it suggests" (see Figure 6.2). The brief stories are then scored using a standardized procedure that measures the presence of the three basic needs to obtain a "motivational profile" for each respondent. The TAT is known as a projective test; that is, respondents project their inner motivational needs into the content of the story they create. One criticism of McClelland's theory concerns the use of the TAT, for its scoring can be quite unreliable, with different scorers possibly interpreting the stories differently.

Thematic Apperception Test (TAT)
a projective test that uses ambiguous pictures to assess psychological motivation

The majority of the research on McClelland's theory has focused on the need for achievement (McClelland, 1961; McClelland, Atkinson, Clark, & Lowell, 1953). Evidence indicates that individuals with a high need for achievement attain personal success in their jobs, but only if the type of work that they do fosters personal achievement. That is, there must be a match between the types of outcomes a particular job offers and the specific motivational needs of the person. For example, people who have a great need for achievement might do best in a job in which they are allowed to solve problems, such as a scientist or engineer, or in which there is a direct relation between personal efforts and successful job outcomes, such as a salesperson working on commission. Those high in the need for affiliation might do best in a job in which they work with others as part of a team. Finally, persons with a high need for power profile should thrive in jobs that satisfy their needs to be in charge. In fact,

Figure 6.2
SAMPLE ITEM FROM A
VARIATION OF THE
THEMATIC APPERCEPTION
TEST (TAT) USED BY
McCLELLAND

research shows that many successful managers are high in the need for power, presumably because much of their job involves directing the activities of others (McClelland & Boyatzis, 1982; McClelland & Burnham, 1976).

The work of McClelland and his associates has led to several applications of the achievement motivation theory to improving motivation in work settings. One strategy is a program to match workers' motivational profiles to the requirements of particular jobs in order to place individuals in positions that will best allow them to fulfill their predominant needs (McClelland, 1980). A second application, effective in positions that require a strong need for achievement, is an achievement training program in which individuals are taught to be more achievement oriented by role playing achievement-oriented actions and strategies and developing plans for setting achievement-related goals (Miron & McClelland, 1979). (But see Up Close for some potential dangers associated with too much need for achievement.) The achievement motivation theory thus not only has been fairly well tested but also has led to these useful intervention strategies (Miner, 1983).

What Is a Workaholic?

According to McClelland, the need for achievement is a continuum ranging from very low to very high levels of achievement. Typically, we consider a high achievement level to be positive, but can we ever have *too much* need for achievement? The answer appears to be yes. When an individual's compelling drive to succeed in a job becomes so great that all other areas of life (family, health concerns, and leisure) are given little or no concern, we may label the person a *workaholic* or "achievement-addicted."

According to researchers, the workaholic is not necessarily motivated by money itself or even by power but by a desire to be number one (Machlowitz, 1976). Money is simply a means of keeping score, although many confirmed workaholics are also very wealthy (see Boroson, 1976). The concept of the workaholic is related in many ways to the hard-driving "Type A," or "coronary-prone," behavior pattern, a topic we will discuss in Chapter 7.

Based on interviews with workaholics, Machlowitz has derived fifteen characteristics common to them all. Look over the list and see how you match up to the definition:

1. An ongoing work style
2. A broad view of what a job requires
3. A sense of the scarcity of time
4. The use of lists and time-saving gadgets
5. Long work days
6. Little sleep
7. Quick meals
8. An awareness of what one's own work can accomplish
9. An inability to enjoy idleness
10. Initiative
11. Overlapping of work and leisure
12. A desire to excel
13. A dread of retirement
14. Intense energy
15. An ability to work anywhere (workaholics can always be spotted taking work into the bathroom)

JOB DESIGN THEORIES OF MOTIVATION

The need theories emphasize the role that individual differences in certain types of needs play in determining work motivation. By contrast, two job design theories, Herzberg's two-factor theory and the job characteristics model, stress the structure and design of jobs as key factors in motivating workers. They argue that if jobs are well designed, containing all elements that workers require from their jobs to satisfy physical and psychological needs, employees will be motivated.

HERZBERG'S TWO-FACTOR THEORY

Influenced greatly by the human relations school of thought, Frederick Herzberg developed a theory of motivation that highlighted the role of job satisfaction in determining worker motivation (Herzberg, 1966; Herzberg, Mausner & Snyderman, 1959). He states that the traditional, single-dimension approach to job satisfaction, with its continuum ends ranging from job dissatisfaction to job satisfaction, is wrong and that job satisfac-

Table 6.1   PROFILE OF HERZBERG'S MOTIVATORS AND HYGIENES

Motivators	Hygienes
Responsibility	Company policy and administration
Achievement	Supervision
Recognition	Interpersonal relations
Content of work	Working conditions
Advancement	Salary
Growth on job	

two-factor theory
Herzberg's motiva-
tional theory that
proposes that two
factors—motivators
and hygienes—are im-
portant in determining
worker satisfaction and
motivation

motivators
elements related to job
content that, when
present, lead to job
satisfaction

hygienes
elements related to job
context that, when
absent, cause job
dissatisfaction

tion and job dissatisfaction are actually two separate and independent dimensions. Herzberg arrived at these conclusions, called the **two-factor theory,** after analyzing the survey responses of many white-collar, professional workers who were asked to describe what made them feel especially good or bad about their jobs. What he found was that the factors clustered into one of two categories. Certain factors, when present, seemed to cause job satisfaction, and Herzberg labeled them **motivators.** Other factors, when absent, tended to cause job dissatisfaction, and he called them **hygienes.** Motivators are factors related to job content; they are inherent in the work itself. The type of work, the level of responsibility associated with the job, and the chances for recognition, advancement, and personal achievement are all motivators. Hygienes are related to the context in which people perform their jobs. Common hygienes include benefits, working conditions (including both physical and social), type of supervision, and company policies (see Table 6.1).

Herzberg's theory indicates that if managers are to keep workers happy and motivated, two things must be done. First, to eliminate job dissatisfaction, workers must be provided with the basic hygiene factors. That is, they must be compensated appropriately, treated well, and provided with job security. However, furnishing these hygienes will only prevent dissatisfaction; it will not necessarily motivate workers. To get workers to put greater effort and energy into their jobs, motivators must be present. The work must be important, giving the workers a sense of responsibility, and should provide chances for recognition and upward mobility.

Research has not been very supportive of Herzberg's theory, however. In particular, the two-factor theory has been criticized on methodological grounds, since subsequent research has not replicated the presence of two distinct factors (Schneider & Locke, 1971). There have also been difficulties in clearly distinguishing hygienes and motivators. For example, salary, which should be a hygiene because it is external to the work itself, may sometimes act as a motivator, since pay can be used to recognize outstanding employees and indicate an individual's status in the organization. It has also been suggested that Herzberg's theory applies more to white-collar than to blue-collar workers (Dunnette, Campbell, & Hakel, 1967). As a result, his model is not currently considered to be a viable theory of motivation.

In spite of criticisms and the lack of supportive research, Herzberg's theory helped stimulate the development of an innovative strategy to increase worker motivation known as **job enrichment,** which involves redesigning jobs to give workers greater responsibility in the planning, execution, and evaluation of their work. When using job enrichment as a motivational strategy, workers may actually take on some of the tasks that were previously performed by higher-level supervisors, such as allocating work tasks, appraising their own work performance, setting output quotas, and making their own personnel decisions (including hiring, firing, giving raises, and the like). These programs typically include the following elements:

job enrichment
a motivational program that involves redesigning jobs to give workers a greater role in the planning, execution, and evaluation of their work

· Increasing the level of responsibility associated with jobs as well as the workers' sense of freedom and independence
· Wherever possible, allowing workers to complete an entire task or function
· Providing feedback so that workers can learn to improve their own performance
· Encouraging workers to learn on the job by taking on additional, more challenging tasks and by improving their expertise in the jobs they perform

For an illustration of job enrichment programs in action, see Applying I/O Psychology.

Although job enrichment programs have been implemented in quite a few large companies in the United States and Europe, their effectiveness is still in question. Since enrichment usually takes place at an organizational or departmental level, it is very difficult to conduct a well-controlled evaluation of the effectiveness of the program. In particular, because the unit of analysis—the subject—is usually the organization or department, it is very difficult to compare the success of various job enrichment programs. Most often, support for or against job enrichment is based on the results of a series of case studies. Moreover, it is clear that some failures are due more to faulty implementation of the program rather than to any weakness in the concept and theory of job enrichment. For example, failures may result if workers or management do not support the program or if jobs are not truly enriched because the level of worker responsibility is not increased. In conclusion, the most that we can say is that job enrichment is an innovative strategy to increase employee motivation by redesigning jobs. Its ultimate success or failure is still in question (Miner, 1983).

Job enrichment means greater responsibility for the worker, such as this employee whose job involves checking and inspecting his own work.

Job Enrichment in a Manufacturing and a Service Organization

In 1971 a decision was made to implement a job enrichment program in a Volvo automobile assembly plant in Kalmar, Sweden, that was suffering from extremely high levels of absenteeism and turnover. First, the traditional assembly-line workers were separated into teams with fifteen to twenty-five members. In keeping with the general principles of job enrichment, each team was made responsible for an entire auto component or function (for example, upholstery, transmission assembly, or electrical system wiring). Each team was given the freedom to assign members to work tasks, to set their own output rates, to order supplies, and to inspect their own work, all of which had previously been performed by supervisors. To encourage team spirit, each group was given carpeted break rooms, and job rotation (rotating workers periodically from one task to another) was encouraged to alleviate boredom. The results of the program indicated a significant decline in both absenteeism and turnover along with improved product quality, although there was a slight decline in productivity and the costs of implementing the program were great. It was also discovered that some workers did not adapt well to the enriched jobs and preferred the more traditional assembly line (Goldman, 1976). However, management proclaimed the program a success and has implemented the strategy in several other plants (Gyllenhammer, 1977; Walton, 1972).

In a more recent example closer to home, a large American financial institution decided to introduce job enrichment into their credit and collec-

tions department, which serviced the company's credit card accounts. The workers maintained account activity, collected on overdue accounts, and dealt with any credit-related difficulties experienced by cardholders, such as changes of address, lost cards, and credit inquiries. In the existing situation, each type of work was handled by a specialist, so that an inquiry on a single account might be handled by several workers. This often led to confusion and to frustration on the part of cardholders, who felt as if they were being passed from worker to worker on even simple service requests. On the employee side, jobs were repetitive and monotonous, which led to high rates of absenteeism and turnover.

The job enrichment program involved dividing the department into two distinct operating units, each composed of a number of two-member teams. One unit dealt solely with actions on current accounts, the other unit only with past due accounts. Rather than assigning work based on the type of task that needed to be performed, each team was now given complete responsibility for certain accounts. This restructuring increased the level of responsibility required of each worker and reduced the routine nature of the jobs. Also, workers were able to receive feedback about their work since they dealt with an action on an account from start to finish. Nine months after the implementation of the job enrichment program, productivity had increased without any increase in staff, collection of past due accounts was more efficient, absenteeism was down 33 percent, and the nine-month turnover rate was zero (Yorks, 1979).

JOB CHARACTERISTICS MODEL

job characteristics model
a theory that empha-
sizes the role that
certain aspects of jobs
play in influencing
work motivation

The **job characteristics model** emphasizes the role of certain aspects or characteristics of jobs in influencing work motivation (Hackman & Oldham, 1976). According to Hackman and Oldham (1976), employees must experience three important psychological states to be motivated: Workers must perceive their work as meaningful, must associate a sense of responsibility with the job, and must have some knowledge of the results of their efforts. Five core job characteristics contribute to a worker's experience of the three psychological states:

1. *Skill variety:* the degree to which a job requires the worker to use a variety of abilities and skills to perform work-related tasks. A job that demands a range of skills is likely to be perceived as challenging and meaningful.
2. *Task identity:* the degree to which a job requires the completion of an entire job or function. The worker needs to see the observable outcome or product of work efforts.
3. *Task significance:* the degree to which a job has a substantial impact on other people within the organization, such as co-workers, or outside of the organization, such as consumers.
4. *Autonomy:* the degree to which the job gives the worker freedom and independence to choose how to schedule and carry out the necessary tasks.
5. *Feedback:* the degree to which the job allows the worker to receive direct and clear information about the effectiveness of performance.

This physical therapist experiences at least two of the psychological states identified by the job characteristics model: she knows her work is meaningful, and she sees the results.

Skill variety, task identity, and task significance all affect the experience of meaningfulness in work; autonomy influences the sense of responsibility associated with the job and with work outcomes; and feedback influences worker experience of work results.

These five core job characteristics can be assessed and then combined into a single motivating potential score (MPS) using the following formula:

$$\text{MPS} = \frac{\text{skill variety} + \text{task identity} + \text{task significance}}{3} \times \text{autonomy} \times \text{feedback}$$

Hackman and Oldham used this formula to show that motivation is not a simple combination of the five job characteristics. In the formula, skill variety, task identity, and task significance are averaged, which means that jobs can have low levels of one or two characteristics but be compensated for by a high score on the third. This average score is then multiplied by the core characteristics of autonomy and feedback. However, if any of the levels of autonomy, feedback, or skill variety plus task identity plus task significance are zero, the MPS will be zero—no motivating potential! For a job to have any motivating potential, it must have both autonomy and feedback and at least one of the other three characteristics.

To summarize the basic job characteristics model, the five core job characteristics influence the three critical psychological states—meaningfulness, responsibility, and knowledge of results—that in turn lead to motivation and certain work outcomes, such as the motivation to work, to improve performance, and to grow on the job (Figure 6.3). Actually, the job characteristics model is more complex. According to Hackman

Figure 6.3

THE JOB CHARACTERIS-
TICS MODEL OF WORK
MOTIVATION

Source: J. R. Hackman and
G. R. Oldham, "Motivation
Through the Design of Work:
Test of a Theory," *Organiza-
tional Behavior and Human
Performance, 16* (1976),
p. 256.

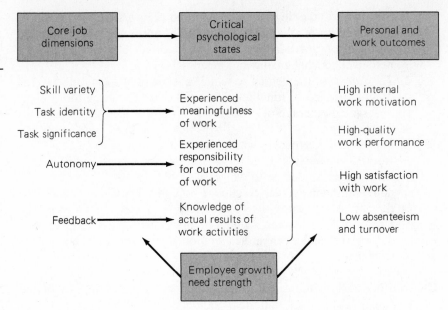

growth need strength
*the need and desire for
personal growth on the
job*

and Oldham, certain "moderators" can affect the success of the model in predicting worker motivation. One such moderator is **growth need strength,** or an individual's need and desire for personal growth and development on the job. In other words, some workers desire jobs that are challenging, responsible, and demanding, while others do not. According to the theory, improving the dimensions of the five core job characteristics should have motivating effects only on those workers who are high in growth need strength. Workers low in this moderator are not likely to be motivated by jobs that offer enriched opportunities for responsibility, autonomy, and accountability.

**Job Diagnostic Survey
(JDS)**
*a questionnaire that
measures core job
characteristics*

Hackman and Oldham (1975) also developed a questionnaire to measure the five core characteristics, called the **Job Diagnostic Survey (JDS).** The JDS and alternative tools, such as the Job Characteristics Inventory (Sims, Szilagyi, & Keller, 1976), have stimulated a great deal of research on the job characteristics model. Generally, the results have been favorable (see, for example, Graen, Scandura, & Graen, 1986; Loher, Noe, Moeller, & Fitzgerald, 1985). For example, a recent meta-analysis of nearly 200 studies of the model found general support for its structure and for its effects on job motivation and related work outcomes (Fried & Ferris, 1987).

As you may have guessed, the job characteristics model is closely aligned with job enrichment. The idea that workers vary in growth need strength indicates that some workers (those high in growth need) will benefit and be motivated by enriched jobs. In effect, the job characteristics theory tries to determine under what conditions and with what workers job enrichment programs and other job design interventions will increase motivation.

RATIONAL THEORIES OF MOTIVATION

The category of rational theories of motivation includes two theories that view workers as rational beings who cognitively assess personal costs and benefits before taking action: equity theory and VIE theory.

EQUITY THEORY OF MOTIVATION

Equity theory states that workers are motivated by a desire to be treated equitably or fairly. If workers feel that they are receiving fair treatment, their motivation to work will be maintained and steady performance can be expected. If, on the other hand, they feel that there is inequitable treatment, their motivation will be channeled into some strategy that will try to reduce the inequity.

Equity theory, first proposed by J. Stacey Adams (1965), has become quite popular. According to this theory, the worker brings **inputs** to the job, such as experience, education and qualifications, energy, and effort, and expects to receive certain **outcomes,** such as pay, fringe benefits, recognition, and interesting and challenging work, in equivalent proportions. To determine whether the situation is equitable, workers make some social comparisons between their own input-outcome ratio and those of **comparison others,** who can be co-workers, people with a similar job or occupation, or the workers' own experience. It must be stressed that equity theory is based on workers' *perceptions* of equity-inequity.

According to equity theory, lack of motivation is caused by two types of perceived inequity. **Underpayment inequity** results when workers feel that they are receiving fewer outcomes from the job in ratio to inputs. Imagine that you have been working at a particular job for over a year. A new employee has just been hired to do the same type of job. This person is about your age and has about the same background and level of education. However, your new co-worker has much less work experience than you. Now imagine that you find out that this new employee is making $1.50 per hour more than you are. Equity theory predicts that you would experience underpayment inequity and would be motivated to try to balance the situation by doing one of the following:

· *Increasing outcomes:* You could confront your boss and ask for a raise, or find some other way to get greater outcomes from your job.

equity theory
a theory that workers are motivated to reduce perceived inequities between work inputs and outcomes

inputs
elements that a worker invests in a job, such as experience and effort

outcomes
those things that a worker expects to receive from a job, such as pay and recognition

comparison others
persons used as a base for comparison in making judgments of equity-inequity

underpayment inequity
workers' perception that inputs are greater than outcomes

- *Decreasing inputs:* You might decide that you needed to limit your work production or quality commensurate with your "poor" pay.
- *Changing the comparison other:* If you find out that the new employee is actually the boss's daughter, she is clearly not a similar comparison other.
- *Leaving the situation:* You might decide that the situation is so inequitable that you are no longer motivated to work there.

Now imagine that you are on the receiving end of that extra $1.50 per hour. In other words, compared to your comparison others, you are receiving greater outcomes from your average-level inputs. This is referred to as **overpayment inequity,** which also creates an imbalance. In this case, equity theory predicts that you might try doing one of the following:

overpayment inequity workers' perception that outcomes are greater than inputs

- *Increasing inputs:* You might work harder to try to even up the input-outcome ratio.
- *Decreasing outcomes:* You might ask for a cut in pay, but this is extremely unlikely.
- *Changing comparison others:* An overpaid worker might change comparison others to persons of higher work status and ability. For example, "Obviously my boss sees my potential. I am paid more because she is grooming me for a management position."
- *Distorting the situation:* A distortion of the perception of inputs or outcomes might occur. For example, "My work is of higher quality and therefore deserves more pay than the work of others."

It is this last outcome, the possibility of psychological distortions of the situation, that weakens the predictive power of this very rational theory of motivation. Equity theory has difficulty predicting behavior when people act irrationally, as they often do.

While most of the research on equity theory has used pay as the primary outcome of a job, other factors may constitute outcomes. For example, one study found that workers would raise their inputs in response to receiving a high-status job title (Greenberg & Ornstein, 1983). In other words, the prestige associated with the title served as compensation, even though there was no raise in pay. There was one catch, however: The workers had to perceive the higher job title as having been earned. An unearned promotion led to feelings of overpayment inequity.

Although equity theory has been well researched, the majority of studies have been conducted in laboratory settings (Greenberg, 1982; Mowday, 1979; although see Carrell, 1978; also see On the Cutting Edge). The most recent research has examined the role of individual differences as moderators of equity. In particular, this research has focused on the construct of equity sensitivity. It has been suggested that individuals vary

Equity Theory and the Two-Tier Wage Structure

In an effort to cut costs and remain financially viable, some large organizations are requesting cost-saving concessions from their union employees. For example, a company may ask the union to take an across-the-board cut in pay or to accept a **two-tier wage structure,** in which the top rates of pay for new employees are substantially lower than those for older employees. Under this system, two employees with the same job titles and the same duties may receive different rates of pay merely because their hiring dates differ.

Because the two-tier structure violates the basic union tenet of equal pay for equal work, it seems a logical place to apply equity theory. A recent study investigated the perceptions and attitudes of nearly 2,000 unionized employees in the retail industry who were under two-tier wage structures (Martin & Peterson, 1987). It was believed that low-tier (newer) employees would use their higher-paid counterparts as a comparison base for pay and thus feel underpayment inequity. It was also hypothesized that high-tier workers would not experience overpayment inequity because their comparison base would not be the low-tier employees but the pay structure before the implementation of the two-tier system. Results tended to be consistent with these predictions made by equity theory. In particular, low-tier employees had perceptions of pay inequity and negative attitudes regarding the union that might have an adverse impact on employee motivation.

in their concern over the equity of input-outcome ratios. In other words, some people are quite sensitive to equity ratios and prefer balance, others may be less concerned with equitable relationships, and still other individuals may prefer to have either an outcome advantage or input advantage, preferring to be overcompensated or undercompensated for their work (see Huseman, Hatfield, & Miles, 1987). In spite of this research, no particular applications have come directly from the equity theory. As Miner (1983, p. 48) states, "The theory has tremendous potential insofar as applications are concerned, but these have not been realized, even though the theory itself has stood the test of research well."

two-tier wage structure
a cost-saving compensation system wherein top rates of pay for new employees are lower than those for older employees

VIE THEORY OF MOTIVATION

One of the most popular motivation theories in recent years is **VIE theory,** which is commonly referred to as expectancy theory. VIE theory is most often associated with Vroom (1964), although there have been some later refinements and modifications (Graen, 1969; Porter & Lawler, 1968). Like equity theory, VIE theory assumes that workers are rational, decisionmaking persons whose behavior will be guided by an analysis of the potential costs and benefits of a particular course of action. Also like equity theory, VIE theory focuses on the particular outcomes associated with a job, which refer not only to pay but also to any number of factors, positive or negative, that are the potential results of work behavior. For example, positive outcomes include benefits, recognition, and job satisfaction, and negative outcomes include reprimands, demotions, and firings.

VIE theory
a rational theory of motivation that states that workers weigh expected costs and benefits of particular courses before they are motivated to take action

valence
the desirability of an outcome to an individual

expectancy
the perceived relationship between an individual's effort and the performance of a behavior

instrumentality
the relationship between performing a behavior and the likelihood of receiving a particular outcome

The name "VIE theory" refers to its three components: valence, instrumentality, and expectancy. **Valence** refers to the desirability (or undesirability) of a particular outcome to an individual. **Expectancy** is the perceived relationship between the individual's effort and performance of the behavior. It is represented as a probability (for example, "If I expend *x* amount of effort I will probably complete *y* amount of work."). **Instrumentality** is the perceived relationship between the performance of a particular behavior and the likelihood that a certain outcome will actually result. VIE theory states that the motivation to perform a particular behavior depends on a number of factors: whether the outcome of the behavior is desirable (valence), whether the individual has the ability, skills, or energy to get the job done (expectancy), and whether the performance of the behavior will indeed lead to the expected outcome (instrumentality). In research and applications of VIE theory, each of the components is measured, and a complex predictive formula is derived.

Consider as an example using VIE theory to study how students might be motivated, or not motivated, to perform exceptionally well in college courses. Choose as the particular outcome acceptance into a prestigious graduate (Ph.D.) program in psychology. First, consider the valence of the outcome; while it may be a very desirable outcome for some (positively valent), it is not for others (negative or neutral valence). Therefore, only those students who view being admitted to a graduate program as desirable are going to be motivated to do well in school to achieve this particular outcome. (Note: This does not mean that there are not other reasons for doing well in school nor that good grades are the only requirements for admission to graduate school.) For those who desire the graduate career, the next component to consider is expectancy. Given what you know about your own abilities, study habits, and effort, what is the probability that you will actually be able to achieve the required grades? Here you might consider your willingness to sacrifice some of your social life to study more as well as considering your past academic performance. Should you say, "Yes, I have the 'right stuff' to get the job done," it is likely that you will be highly motivated. For those individuals unwilling to expend the time and energy required, motivation will be much less. Finally, what about instrumentality? It is well known that there are many more qualified applicants to graduate programs than there are openings. Therefore, the probability of actually achieving the desired outcome, even if you perform at the required level, is less than certain. It is here that motivation might also potentially break down. Some people might believe that the odds are so poor that working overtime to get the good grades is simply not worth it. Others might figure that the odds are not so bad, and thus their motivation will remain strong.

At work, VIE theory might be applied using promotions, the performance of special work projects, or avoiding a supervisor's displeasure as potential outcomes. For example, if an employee's goal is to avoid her supervisor's criticism (avoidance is positively valent), she might consider

VIE theorists favor a clear connection between performance and rewards, as in the case of this employee who earns a raise by demonstrating a new skill.

the expectancy ("Can I perform the job flawlessly so that my supervisor will not be displeased?") and the instrumentality ("Even if I do an error-free job, will my supervisor still voice some displeasure?") before being motivated even to try to avoid having the boss displeased. If the supervisor is someone who never believes that an employee's performance is good enough, it is unlikely that the employee will exhibit much motivation to avoid the displeasure because it is perceived as inevitable.

VIE theory illustrates the notion that motivation is a complex phenomenon, affected by a number of variables. VIE theory looks at factors such as individual goals, the links between effort and performance (expectancy), the links between performance and outcomes (instrumentality), and how outcomes serve to satisfy individual goals (valence). It is one of the most complicated yet thorough models of work motivation. The theory has generated a considerable amount of research, with evidence both supporting (Matsui, Kagawa, Nagamatsu, & Ohtsuka, 1977; Muchinsky, 1977) and criticizing certain aspects of the theory, most notably the measurement of valence, instrumentality, and expectancy (Schmidt, 1973; Schwab, Olian-Gottlieb, & Heneman, 1979; Wanous, Keon, & Latack, 1983). VIE theory continues to be a popular rational model for understanding work motivation. Although there is no single agreed-upon strategy for its application, it does lead to many practical suggestions to guide managers in their attempts to motivate workers, including the following:

· Managers should try to define work outcomes—potential rewards and costs associated with performance—clearly to all workers.

· The relationships between performance and rewards should also be made clear. Workers need to know that if they achieve certain goals, rewards are sure to follow.
· Any performance-related goal should be within the reach of the employee involved.

In sum, both VIE theory and equity theory are based on rational models of motivation. They assume that individuals are constantly aware of important elements in their work environment and that motivation is determined by a conscious processing of the information received. The problem is that some people may simply be more rational than others in their usual approaches to work. The effectiveness of these rational models of motivation is also weakened by the fact that in some situations individuals, regardless of their usual rational approach, may behave in a nonrational manner (for example, when workers become so upset that they impulsively quit their job without considering the implications). Moreover, there is some evidence that even when people are using rational means to evaluate a particular situation, individuals vary in the ways that they process information (see Zedeck, 1977).

GOAL-SETTING THEORY

goal-setting theory
the motivational theory that emphasizes the setting of specific and challenging performance goals

Goal-setting theory emphasizes the role of specific, challenging performance goals and workers' commitment to those goals as key determinants of motivation. Typically, goal-setting theory is associated with Edwin Locke (1968; Locke & Latham, 1984), although theories concerning the establishment of defined performance goals have been around for some time (see, for example, Drucker, 1954; Lewin, 1935).

Goal-setting theory states that for employees to be motivated, goals must be clear, specific, and, whenever possible, quantified. General goals, such as urging employees to do their best or to work as quickly as possible, are not as effective as defined, measurable goals. Moreover, difficult goals will result in greater levels of motivation, as long as the goals have been accepted by the workers (Locke, Shaw, Saari, & Latham, 1981). Of course, goals should not be so high that they are impossible to achieve (Erez & Zidon, 1984). A final consideration is obtaining workers' commitment to goals, for without such commitment, it is unlikely that goal setting will be motivating.

Goal-setting theory has generated a great deal of research, much of it conducted in laboratory settings. The theory itself seems sound and has been well tested (Tubbs, 1986). Most recently, researchers have been examining how the goal setting combines with other factors in creating motivation. There is evidence that if workers participate in goal setting, as opposed to having supervisors set the goals, there is increased motivation as measured by workers setting higher performance goals than those set by supervisors (Erez & Arad, 1986). Research also tends to support the notion that providing feedback to workers en route to the attainment of goals increases motivation to achieve the final goal (Locke et al., 1981). Garland (1984) examined the relationship between workers' expectations concerning their future effort and performance on a task and goal setting—in effect, combining elements of VIE theory and goal-setting theory—and found that both expectations and goals play a role in determining motivation.

A wide variety of motivational techniques and programs, such as incentive programs and management by objectives, or MBO (which we will discuss in Chapter 12), are consistent with goal-setting theory. Goal setting is a relatively simple motivational strategy to implement and thus has become quite popular. Importantly, the research evidence indicates that it is very useful in increasing worker motivation (Miner, 1983).

REINFORCEMENT THEORY

A final model of motivation, **reinforcement theory,** draws on principles of operant conditioning (mentioned briefly in Chapter 5) and states simply that behavior is motivated by its consequences. A consequence that follows a behavior and serves to increase the motivation to perform that behavior again, is a reinforcer. These reinforcers can be of two types. **Positive reinforcers,** more commonly referred to as rewards, are events that are in and of themselves desirable to the person. Receiving praise, money, or a pat on the back are all common positive reinforcers. **Negative reinforcers** are events that lead to the avoidance of an existing negative state or condition. Being allowed to escape the noise and confusion of a busy work area by taking a short break in a quiet employee lounge or working hard at a task to avoid the wrath of a watchful supervisor are negative reinforcement situations. Negative reinforcement increases the motivation to perform the desired behavior again in an effort to keep the aversive negative condition from returning. For example, if a clerical worker feels that being behind schedule is a particularly aversive condition, the individual will be motivated to work hard to avoid the unpleasant state of being behind schedule. It is important to reemphasize that both negative and positive reinforcement can increase the motivation to repeat a behavior.

Punishment is the term used to describe any unpleasant consequence that directly follows the performance of a behavior. The effect of punishment is to weaken the tendency to perform the behavior again. Punishment is applied to behaviors that are deemed inappropriate. Receiving a harsh reprimand from your boss for too much socializing on the job and receiving a demotion because of sloppy work are examples of punish-

reinforcement theory
the theory that behavior is motivated by its consequences

positive reinforcers
desirable events that strengthen the tendency to respond

negative reinforcers
events that strengthen a behavior through the avoidance of an existing negative state

punishment
unpleasant consequences that reduce the tendency to respond

ment. Reinforcement theory argues that reinforcement is a much better motivational technique than is punishment, since the goal of punishment is to stop unwanted behaviors, while reinforcement is designed to strengthen the motivation to perform a particular desired behavior.

Once a particular behavior has been conditioned through repeated reinforcement, removal of the reinforcement will over time weaken the motivation to perform the behavior. Eventually, if reinforcement does not occur again, **extinction,** or the elimination of a conditioned response through the withdrawal of reinforcement, will result.

In principle, the reinforcement model is fairly simple and obvious. We have seen it in operation all of our lives. However, the basic reinforcement model, as presented, is not very useful in actual work situations because it emphasizes what is called a continuous reinforcement schedule: perform a behavior, get a reward. The real work world does not usually operate this way. Reinforcement in the work environment typically takes place on a partial or intermittent reinforcement schedule, which can be of either the interval or ratio type. When interval schedules are used, the reinforcement is based on the passage of time, during which the individual is performing the desired behavior. When ratio schedules are used, reinforcement follows the performance of a number of desired behaviors. Both interval and ratio schedules can be either fixed or variable. Thus there are four reinforcement schedules: fixed interval, variable interval, fixed ratio, and variable ratio. Most typically, in work settings we think of these four types of schedules as representing different schedules of pay.

In the **fixed interval schedule,** the reinforcement occurs after the passage of a specified amount of time. Employees who are paid an hourly or daily wage or a weekly or monthly salary are being reinforced on this schedule, which has two important characteristics. First, the reinforcement is not contingent on the performance of the desired behavior. Of course it is assumed that during the intervening time period, people are performing their jobs. However, reinforcement follows regardless of whether the rate of performing job-related behaviors is high or low. Second, the fixed interval schedule is predictable. People always know when a reinforcement is coming.

A **variable interval schedule** is a somewhat rare means of work compensation. On these schedules, reinforcement is also determined by the passage of time, but the interval varies. For example, a worker for a small business might be paid on the average of once a month, but the exact time depends on when the owner has the funds available. Annual bonuses that are given on the boss's whims are also on a variable interval schedule.

In a **fixed ratio schedule,** reinforcement depends on the performance of a set number of specified behaviors. Examples include workers who are paid for the number of components assembled, baskets of fruit picked, or reports written. This type of fixed ratio payment is commonly referred to as "piecework." The strength of such a schedule is that reinforcement

extinction
the elimination of a conditioned response through the withdrawal of reinforcement

fixed interval schedule
reinforcement that follows the passage of a specified amount of time

variable interval schedule
reinforcement that follows the passage of a specified amount of time, with exact time of reinforcement varying

fixed ratio schedule
reinforcement that is contingent on the performance of a fixed number of behaviors

is contingent on execution of the desired behavior. Individuals on ratio schedules have high rates of responding in comparison to persons on interval schedules who are merely "putting in time."

A **variable ratio schedule** also involves reinforcement that is contingent on the performance of behaviors, but the number of responses required for a particular reinforcement varies. An example of a variable ratio schedule is a salesperson on commission, who is required to give a number of sales presentations (the work behavior) to make a sale and receive a commission (the reinforcement). Imagine a door-to-door salesperson who knows that to make a single sale, approximately ten presentations must be made. However, the payoffs will vary. Sometimes the salesperson will make two consecutive sales, and sometimes twenty or thirty presentations will yield only a single sale, but the overall ratio is one in ten. Variable ratio schedules usually lead to very high levels of motivation because the reinforcement is contingent on performance and because of the "surprise element": you never know when the next reinforcement is coming. Gambling is reinforced on a variable ratio schedule, which is why it is such an addicting behavior.

variable ratio schedule reinforcement that depends on the performance of a specified but varying number of behaviors

Research indicates that different types of schedules lead to various patterns of responding and thus have important implications for using reinforcement to motivate workers. Generally, evidence suggests that ratio schedules result in higher levels of motivation and subsequent task performance than do fixed interval schedules (Pritchard, Hollenback, & DeLeo, 1980; Pritchard, Leonard, Von Bergen, & Kirk, 1976). These findings are important, especially since the majority of American workers are paid on fixed interval reinforcement schedules.

Obviously, reinforcement principles are used informally on a day-to-day basis to motivate workers through compensation systems and other forms of rewards for work outcomes. However, when reinforcement theory is applied formally as a program to increase worker motivation, it most often takes the form of **organizational behavior modification,** in which certain target behaviors are specified, measured, and rewarded. Such programs have been used to motivate workers to be more productive, to produce higher quality work, and to cut down on rates of absenteeism, tardiness, and work accidents by rewarding good performance, attendance, and/or safe work behaviors. In general, organizational behavior modification has been a successful strategy for enhancing worker motivation (Hamner & Hamner, 1976; Miner, 1983).

organizational behavior modification the application of conditioning principles to obtain certain work outcomes

THE RELATIONSHIP BETWEEN MOTIVATION AND PERFORMANCE

Motivation is so central to any discussion of work behavior because it is believed that it is the direct link to good work performance. In other words, it is assumed that the motivated worker is the productive worker.

A car salesman works on a variable ratio schedule of compensation: his earnings depend on the number of successful sales pitches he makes.

Yet this may not always be true, since many other factors can affect productivity independent of the effects of worker motivation. Furthermore, having highly motivated workers does not automatically lead to high levels of productivity. The work world is much more complex than that. As mentioned at the beginning of the chapter, many managers consider motivation to be the primary problem when they see low levels of productivity. However, a manager must approach a productivity problem as a social scientist would. Before pointing the finger at worker motivation, a detailed assessment of all of the other variables that could affect productivity must first be undertaken. These variables can be divided into four categories: systems and technology variables, individual difference variables, group dynamics variables, and organizational variables.

SYSTEMS AND TECHNOLOGY VARIABLES

Regardless of the level of motivation, if workers are forced to work with inadequate work systems, procedures, tools, and equipment, productivity will suffer. Poor tools and systems will affect work productivity independent of employee motivation. This is often seen in the low agricultural production of some Third World countries. A common mistake is to assume that these disadvantaged nations suffer from a lack of worker motivation. A more reasonable (and accurate) explanation is that they lack the appropriate agricultural technology to be as productive as other countries. You may see this in your own life, when having access to a word processor increases your term paper productivity and efficiency without any significant change in your motivational level.

INDIVIDUAL DIFFERENCE VARIABLES

A variety of factors within the individual can affect work productivity regardless of motivation. For example, lacking the basic talents or skills to get the job done will hamper productivity even in the most motivated worker. Perhaps the *least* productive workers in any work setting are also the *most* motivated: new employees. At least initially, the novice employee is energized and determined to make a good impression on the boss. Unfortunately, a total lack of knowledge about the job makes this person inefficient and unproductive in spite of high motivation. Other workers, because of a lack of basic abilities or education or perhaps because of being placed in a job that is incompatible with their own interests and talents, may be particularly unproductive. What may appear on the surface to be a motivational problem is actually a problem of individual abilities.

GROUP DYNAMICS VARIABLES

Rather than working by themselves, most workers are part of a larger unit. For the group to be efficient and productive, individual efforts must be coordinated. While most members may be highly motivated, group productivity can be poor if one or two key members are not good team workers. In these situations motivation effects on productivity become secondary to certain group dynamics variables.

Group dynamics can also affect productivity apart from motivation when rate setting occurs as a work group develops an informal rule to restrict output. A particular rate is set, far below the group's potential output level, and pressure is exerted to keep members from exceeding the rate. Although individual workers may be highly motivated, they usually will adhere to the group rule to avoid being ostracized.

ORGANIZATIONAL VARIABLES

The productivity of an organization requires the concerted and coordinated efforts of a number of work units. High levels of motivation and output in one department may be offset by lower levels in another department. Organizational politics and conflict may also affect the coordination among groups, thus lowering productivity in spite of relatively high levels of motivation in the work force.

Lack of technology, not motivational problems, often limits Third World agricultural production.

As you can see, the role of motivation in affecting work outcomes is important, but limited. The work force is extremely complex. Focusing on a single variable, such as motivation, while ignoring others leads to a narrow and limited view of work behavior. Yet, motivation is an important topic, one of the most widely researched in I/O psychology. However, it is only one piece of the puzzle that contributes to our greater understanding of the individual in the work place.

**CHAPTER 6
CONCLUSION**

SUMMARY

Motivation is the force that energizes, directs, and sustains behavior. The many theories of work motivation can be classified as need theories, job design theories, rational theories, goal-setting theory, and reinforcement theory. Maslow's *need-hierarchy theory* is a popular descriptive theory of motivation that proposes that *needs* are arranged in a hierarchy from the lowest, most basic needs to the higher-order needs. Alderfer's *ERG theory* is another need theory that categorizes needs into three categories: existence, relatedness, and growth needs. McClelland's *achievement motivation theory* proposes that the three needs important in work motivation are achievement, power, and affiliation, which can be measured with a projective test known as the *Thematic Apperception Test*. Unlike Maslow's and Alderfer's need theories, McClelland's theory has been used extensively in work settings to encourage worker motivation.

Job design theories of motivation stress the structure and design of jobs as key factors in motivating workers. Herzberg's *two-factor theory* focuses on job satisfaction and dissatisfaction as two independent dimensions important in determining motivation: *Motivators* are factors related to job content that, when present, lead to job satisfaction. *Hygienes* are elements related to job context that, when absent, cause job dissatisfaction. According to Herzberg, hygienes will prevent job dissatisfaction, but motivators are needed for employee job satisfaction and hence motivation. His theory has led to the development of a strategy for increasing work motivation known as *job enrichment,* which involves redesigning jobs to give workers greater responsibility in the planning, execution, and evaluation of their work. Hackman and Oldham have proposed the *job characteristics model,* another job design theory of motivation, which states that five core job characteristics influence three critical psychological states that in turn lead to motivation. This model can be affected by certain moderators, including *growth need strength,* the notion that certain workers need to grow on their jobs. Workers must be high in growth need strength if programs such as job enrichment are indeed going to produce motivation.

Rational theories of motivation emphasize the role that cognition plays in determining worker motivation. *Equity theory* states that workers are motivated to keep their work *inputs* in proportion to their *outcomes*. According to equity theory, workers are motivated to reduce perceived inequities. This perception of equity-inequity is determined by comparing the worker's input-outcome ratio to similar *comparison others*. *VIE Theory* (representing the three elements of *valence, instrumentality,* and *expectancy*) is a complex model stating that motivation is dependent on expectations concerning effort-performance-outcome relationships.

Goal-setting theory emphasizes challenging goals as a key to motivation, whereas *reinforcement theory* stresses the role that *reinforcers* and *punishments* play in motivation. Reinforcement theory is evident in the various schedules used to pay workers. The theory is applied to increase motivation through *organizational behavior modification* programs.

In spite of the importance given to worker motivation in determining work performance, numerous variables related to systems/technology, individual differences, group dynamics, or organizational factors may all affect work performance directly, without regard to worker motivation. Thus, while motivation is important, it is only one determinant of work behavior.

STUDY QUESTIONS AND EXERCISES

1. How are the need theories and the job design theories of motivation similar? How are they different?

2. Some theories of motivation have led to successful strategies for enhancing work motivation, whereas others have not. What are some of the factors that distinguish the more successful theories from the less successful?

3. Consider the various theories of motivation. Which seems to best describe your own level of motivation at school or at work?

4. Both goal setting theory and reinforcement theory are very general models of work motivation. What are the strengths and weaknesses of such general theories?

5. How would you design a program to improve motivation for a group of low-achieving high school students? What would the elements of the program be? What theories would you use?

SUGGESTED READINGS

Ford, R. N. (1979). *Why jobs die & what to do about it: Job redesign & future productivity.* New York: AMACOM. *Drawing on research in motivation, Ford cites reasons why jobs "die" (such as fragmentation and overspecialization of tasks, and overly rigid and arbitrary work rules), provides a framework for assessing your present job (including checklists and questionnaires), and offers strategies for improving your work situation (ranging from fixing it yourself to getting help from your boss or the organization to getting out!).*

Luthans, F., & Kreitner, R. (1985). *Organizational behavior modification and beyond: An operant and social learning approach.* Glenview, IL: Scott, Foresman. *Uses reinforcement principles and organizational behavior modification to solve a variety of work problems, including motivation, absenteeism, and job dissatisfaction.*

Miron, D., & McClelland, D. C. (1979). The impact of achievement motivation training on small businesses. *California Management Review, 21,* 13–28. *Discusses the research on achievement motivation training programs for small businesses conducted by McClelland and his associates. Gives particulars on their structure and cost-benefits.*

Steers, R. M., & Porter, L. W. (Eds.). (1983). *Motivation and work behavior* (3rd ed.). New York: McGraw-Hill. *A classic overview of theories and research relating to work motivation.*

7

JOB SATISFACTION, WORK STRESS, AND QUALITY OF WORK LIFE

CHAPTER OUTLINE

Job Satisfaction

    Defining Job Satisfaction

    The Measurement of Job Satisfaction

    Job Satisfaction and Job Performance

    Organizational Commitment

    Job Satisfaction, Organizational Commitment, and Employee Attendance

    Increasing Job Satisfaction

    Changes in job structure . Changes in pay structure . Benefit programs

Work Stress

    Defining Work Stress

    Sources of Work Stress

    Organizational sources of work stress . Individual sources of work stress

    Effects of Work Stress

    Coping with Work Stress

    Individual coping strategies . Organizational coping strategies

Quality of Work Life

Chapter Conclusion

Job Satisfaction and Work Stress: How Are They Connected?

Discussing the topics of job satisfaction and work stress in one chapter helps to illustrate the fact that many of the processes that occur in organizations involve a very delicate balance, in this case between positive factors (satisfaction) and negative factors (stress). While the work that we do can be a source of meaning and satisfaction, our jobs also create considerable stress. If someone were to ask us about job satisfaction at any given point, we would probably report some positive feelings of satisfaction with some aspects of our jobs as well as indicating some aspects of the job with which we were dissatisfied. Similarly, work stress involves a balance between the demands that challenge and motivate us and those elements that cause us to feel stress. Much of what I/O psychologists do when considering job satisfaction and work stress is to regulate these ongoing processes by attempting to ensure that satisfaction levels remain fairly high and that stress levels do not get out of hand. Of critical importance is how satisfaction and stress affect the bottom-line variables of performance, productivity, absenteeism, and turnover.

This chapter more than any other pulls together a number of issues and topics from I/O psychology. For example, the discussion of job satisfaction will look at the links between job satisfaction and productivity. This is really an issue of motivation, similar to those examined in Chapter 6. Recall that in Herzberg's two-factor theory, motivation and hence productivity were caused by job satisfaction resulting from increased worker responsibility. This chapter also deals with some measurement issues that were introduced in Chapter 2. Because job satisfaction and work stress are abstract and elusive concepts, they present a number of measurement problems. Much of the difficulty that I/O psychologists have had in studying these phenomena has involved the complexity of measuring them adequately. The discussion of the quality of work life issues in this chapter will emphasize the importance of proper work conditions and employee well-being, which will be covered in depth in Chapter 14. This topic also involves issues relating to group decision-making processes presented in Chapter 9 and crosses over into some of the issues important for organizational change and development discussed in Chapter 12. For example, many techniques designed to enhance the quality of work life involve allowing employees a greater voice in decisionmaking, while programs for organizational development are often implemented as a way of enhancing the quality of work life. This chapter also discusses work stress, which overlaps partially with topics that were considered in the personnel issues chapters (Chapters 3–5), particularly the selection and training of employees. Several strategies for overcoming organizational stress include improving selection and training procedures so that employees feel competent in their jobs. Work stress may also stem from problems in interacting with co-workers, which will be discussed further in Chapter 9.

In short, it is impossible to carve I/O psychology into separate, isolated areas of specialization because there is a great deal of integration and overlap of topics. Keep this in mind as you try to understand the "big picture" of the field.

Sixty years ago, the only compensation that most workers received from their jobs was a paycheck. As time went on, this changed as workers began to demand and receive more from their jobs. Today's workers receive a variety of forms of compensation, including employer-funded health care, retirement, and numerous other benefits and programs. However, one thing that the workers of two generations ago and today's workers have in common is that their jobs constitute a major part of their lives and are one of the greatest sources of personal pleasure and pain. While jobs can be satisfying in some regards, with positive feelings of accomplishment and purpose, they also place heavy demands on workers that can lead to negative states of pressure and strain. In short, nearly all jobs produce some feelings of satisfaction in workers and create some types of work stress.

In this chapter we will examine these two "products" of jobs—job satisfaction and work stress. We will define each and see how each affects important work outcomes such as job performance. We will also study some of the research on job satisfaction and work stress and some of the programs and techniques designed to increase satisfaction and decrease stress. Finally, we will see how job satisfaction and work stress play an important part in determining a worker's quality of work life.

JOB SATISFACTION

In this section, we will begin by defining job satisfaction and discussing how it has been measured. Next, we will examine the links between job satisfaction, job performance, employee attendance, and employee loyalty and commitment. Finally, we will look at various techniques designed to increase job satisfaction.

DEFINING JOB SATISFACTION

As far as management is concerned, the most important outcome variables—the crucial bottom-line variables—are job performance, productivity, work quality, and, to a lesser extent, employee absenteeism and turnover. These are the variables that translate directly into dollars and cents for the organization. However, from the workers' perspective, the most important outcome variable is likely to be job satisfaction. As seen in Chapter 2, job satisfaction, along with productivity, quality, absenteeism, and turnover, is one of the key dependent variables commonly considered (and measured) in research in I/O psychology.

job satisfaction
the positive and negative feelings and attitudes about one's job

Job satisfaction consists of the feelings and attitudes concerning one's job. All aspects of a particular job, good and bad, positive and negative, are likely to contribute to the development of feelings of satisfaction (or dissatisfaction). There are two approaches to conceptualizing job satisfaction. The first is the *global approach,* which considers overall job satisfaction. This way of looking at job satisfaction simply asks if the employee is satisfied overall, using a yes-no response or a single rating scale. The second is the *facet approach,* which considers job satisfaction to be composed of feelings and attitudes about a number of different elements, or facets, of the job. For example, overall satisfaction may be a composite of satisfaction with pay, the type of work itself, working conditions, the type of supervision, company policies and procedures, relations with co-workers, and opportunities for promotion and advancement.

There has been considerable discussion over which approach is better. Proponents of the global approach argue that it is overall satisfaction with a job that is important and that such satisfaction is more than the sum of satisfaction with separate job facets (Scarpello & Campbell, 1983; Schneider, 1985). Advocates of the facet approach maintain that this view provides better, more detailed assessments of job satisfaction. According to the facet approach, a person might be satisfied with one area of their job, such as pay, but dissatisfied with another area, such as the quality of interactions with supervisors and co-workers. Proponents of the facet definition argue that it helps to indicate specific areas of dissatisfaction that can be targeted for improvement (Locke, 1976; Smith, Kendall, & Hulin, 1969). Much of the psychological research on job satisfaction measures from the facet approach.

THE MEASUREMENT OF JOB SATISFACTION

Regardless of the approach, when considering the measurement of job satisfaction, it is important to bear in mind that job satisfaction is an attitude. Since attitudes cannot be directly observed, the measurement of job satisfaction, like the measurement of all attitudes, must usually rely on respondents' self-reports. Strategies for measuring job satisfaction include interviews, group meetings, and a variety of structured pencil-and-paper methods such as rating scales or questionnaires. The obvious advantage of using a rating scale or questionnaire instead of a face-to-face meeting is that the anonymity of responses can often be maintained, particularly if large numbers of employees are surveyed. Generally, the

Sometimes job satisfaction seems obvious, but researchers disagree about the best way of measuring it.

use of anonymous rating scales or questionnaires will protect against some of the distortion of answers by respondents. Some workers, fearing retaliation from management, may not give an accurate representation of their levels of job satisfaction in an interview or meeting and may present an overly positive picture of their feelings. On the other hand, meetings or interviews can provide richer information because the interviewer can ask follow-up questions or request further elaboration or clarification of an answer.

Many organizations develop their own interviews, scales, or surveys to measure employee job satisfaction. While such in-house techniques can be designed to assess satisfaction with specific issues relevant to each company's employees, their results may be difficult to interpret. First, these measures may not be reliable or valid. To construct measures that are reliable and valid, one must have a rather extensive background in survey development and measurement techniques. Moreover, it takes quite a bit of research to establish the reliability and validity of a job satisfaction measure. Many organizations don't have the employees with the skills needed to construct such measures. Second, it is very difficult to know what a particular rating or score means without being able to compare it to some standard. For example, if employees indicate relatively low levels of satisfaction with salary on some scale, does this mean that they are actually dissatisfied with the money they make or that they are merely stating a desire for more money shared by most employees?

Because of these problems in interpreting in-house job satisfaction measures, many companies are using standardized, published surveys. Besides being cost effective, a major advantage of using such standardized measures is that they provide normative data that permit the comparison of ratings with those from similar groups of workers in other companies who have completed the survey. This allows the organization to know whether the job satisfaction levels of its employees are low, high, or in the "normal" range in comparison to other workers in other organizations. The ability to compare scores from standardized job satisfaction measures obtained by different groups of workers in different companies also allows researchers to investigate the various organizational factors that cause job satisfaction and dissatisfaction.

Two of the most widely used standardized surveys of job satisfaction are the **Minnesota Satisfaction Questionnaire (MSQ)** and the **Job Descriptive Index (JDI).** The Minnesota Satisfaction Questionnaire (Weiss, Dawis, England, & Lofquist, 1967) is a multiple-item rating scale that asks workers to rate their levels of satisfaction-dissatisfaction with twenty job facets, including supervisor's competence, working conditions, compensation, task variety, level of job responsibility, and chances for advancement, on a scale from very dissatisfied to neutral to very satisfied. Sample items from the MSQ are presented in Figure 7.1.

The Job Descriptive Index (Smith et al., 1969) is briefer than the MSQ and measures satisfaction with five job facets: the job itself, supervision, pay, promotions, and co-workers. Within each of the five facets are a list of words or short phrases. Respondents indicate whether the word or phrase describes their job, using the answers yes, no, and undecided. Each of the words or phrases has a numerical value that reflects how well it describes a typically satisfying job. Items checked within each scale are summed, yielding five satisfaction scores reflecting the five facets of job satisfaction. These five scores can also be summed into a total score of overall job satisfaction. Since its development in the 1960s, the JDI has been used extensively in research in I/O psychology. Recently, it has been revised and improved, mainly by replacing some of the older scale items with improved items (Smith, Kendall, & Hulin, 1987). Figure 7.2 presents sample items from the JDI.

Both the MSQ and JDI have been widely researched and both have established relatively high levels of reliability and validity (Smith et al., 1969, 1987; Weiss et al., 1967). One obvious difference between the two measures is the number of job satisfaction facets: The JDI measures five facets, the MSQ assesses twenty. An important question is how many or how few facets are needed to measure job satisfaction adequately. Recent research indicates that five facets may be too few and that twenty may be too many. One study suggested that some of the JDI facets could be split in two. For example, the satisfaction with supervision scale could be split

Minnesota Satisfaction Questionnaire (MSQ)
a self-report measure of job satisfaction that breaks satisfaction down into twenty job facets

Job Descriptive Index (JDI)
a self-report job satisfaction rating scale measuring five job facets

On my present job, this is how I feel about	Very Dissatisfied	Dissatisfied	Neutral	Satisfied	Very Satisfied
1. Being able to keep busy all the time	___	___	___	___	___
2. The chance to work alone on the job	___	___	___	___	___
3. The chance to do different things from time to time	___	___	___	___	___
4. The chance to be somebody in the community	___	___	___	___	___
5. The way my boss handles his/her workers	___	___	___	___	___
6. The competence of my supervisor making decisions	___	___	___	___	___
7. The way my job provides for steady employment	___	___	___	___	___
8. My pay and the amount of work I do	___	___	___	___	___
9. The chances for advancement on this job	___	___	___	___	___
10. The working conditions	___	___	___	___	___
11. The way my co-workers get along with each other	___	___	___	___	___
12. The feeling of accomplishment I get from the job	___	___	___	___	___

Figure 7.1

SAMPLE ITEMS FROM THE MINNESOTA SATISFACTION QUESTIONNAIRE

Source: Adapted from D. J. Weiss, R. V. Dawis, G. W. England, and L. H. Lofquist, *Manual for the Minnesota Satisfaction Questionnaire: Minnesota Studies in Vocational Rehabilitation* (Minneapolis: University of Minnesota, Vocational Psychology Research, 1967).

into satisfaction with the supervisor's ability and satisfaction with the supervisor's interpersonal skills (Yeager, 1981). This seems to indicate that the five scales of the JDI do not cover all possible facets of job satisfaction. Other evidence indicates that some of the twenty MSQ scales are highly correlated with one another and could be collapsed into fewer facets (Gillet & Schwab, 1975).

JOB SATISFACTION AND JOB PERFORMANCE

As you recall from our discussion of the human relations movement, Mayo and his colleagues proposed that there was a relationship between one aspect of job satisfaction—employee satisfaction with social relationships at work—and work productivity. While this idea that the "happy worker is the productive worker" might seem to make sense, research studying the links between job satisfaction and performance has shown

Think of your present work. What is it like most of the time? In the blank beside each word given below, write

__Y__ for "Yes" if it describes your work
__N__ for "No" if it does NOT describe it
__?__ if you cannot decide

Work on present job

____ Routine
____ Satisfying
____ Good

Think of the pay you get now. How well does each of the following words describe your present pay? In the blank beside each word, put

__Y__ it it describes your pay
__N__ if it does NOT describe it
__?__ if you cannot decide

Present pay

—— Income adequate for normal expenses
____ Insecure
____ Less than I deserve

Think of the opportunities for promotion that you have now. How well does each of the following words describe these? In the blank beside each word, put

__Y__ for "Yes" if it describes your opportunities for promotion
__N__ for "No" if it does NOT describe them
__?__ If you cannot decide

Opportunities for promotion

____ Dead-end job
____ Unfair promotion policy
____ Regular promotions

Think of the kind of supervision that you get on your job. How well does each of the following words describe this supervision? In the blank beside each word put

__Y__ if it describes the supervision you get on your job
__N__ if it does NOT describe it
__?__ if you cannot decide

Supervision on present job

____ Impolite
____ Praises good work
____ Doesn't supervise enough

Think of the majority of the people that you work with now or the people you meet in connection with your work. How well does each of the following words describe these people? In the blank beside each word below, put

__Y__ if it describes the people you work with
__N__ if it does NOT describe them
__?__ if you cannot decide

People on your present job

____ Boring
____ Responsible
____ Intelligent

Think of your job in general. All in all, what is it like most of the time? In the blank beside each word below, write

__Y__ for "Yes" if it describes your job
__N__ for "No" if it does NOT describe it
__?__ if you cannot decide

Job in general

____ Undesirable
____ Better than Most
____ Rotten

Figure 7.2

SAMPLE ITEMS FROM THE JOB DESCRIPTIVE INDEX, REVISED. (EACH SCALE IS PRESENTED ON A SEPARATE PAGE.)

Source: P. C. Smith, L. M. Kendall, and C. L. Hulin, "Job Descriptive Index," from *The Measurement of Satisfaction in Work and Retirement*. Revised, 1985, Bowling Green State University.

Note: The Job Descriptive Index is copyrighted by Bowling Green State University. The complete forms, scoring key, instructions, and norms can be obtained from Dr. Patricia C. Smith, Department of Psychology, Bowling Green State University, Bowling Green, Ohio 43403.

inconsistent results. Early research reviews concluded that there were no positive relationships between the two (Locke, 1976; Vroom, 1964). In fact, the relationship may actually be more the other way around: Good job performance causes job satisfaction! A model suggested by Porter and Lawler (1968) clarifies how this process might operate. According to them, job satisfaction and performance are not directly linked. Instead,

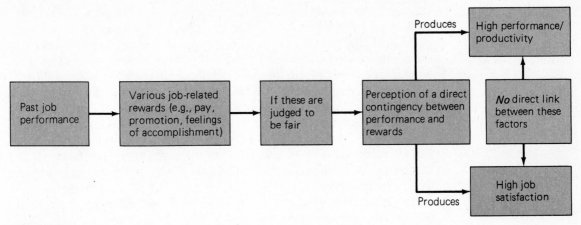

Figure 7.3

THE PORTER-LAWLER MODEL OF THE JOB PERFORMANCE-JOB SATISFACTION
RELATIONSHIP

Source: L. W. Porter and E. E. Lawler, *Managerial Attitudes and Performance* (Homewood, IL:
Dorsey Press, 1968), as adapted by R. A. Baron in *Behavior in Organizations: Understanding and
Managing the Human Side of Work*, 2nd ed. (Boston: Allyn & Bacon, 1986).

effective job performance leads to job-related rewards, such as pay increases, promotions, or a sense of accomplishment. If the process for
offering these rewards is perceived as fair, receiving these rewards leads
to job satisfaction and also to higher and higher levels of performance.
This creates a situation in which job satisfaction and job performance are
actually independent of one another but are linked because both are affected by job-related rewards (see Figure 7.3). Interestingly, the Porter
and Lawler model builds on the equity theory of motivation discussed in
Chapter 6 since notions of equity—fairness in job-related inputs and outcomes—are central to the argument. Specifically, motivation to perform
the job and the satisfaction derived from the job are both caused by the
relationship between what an individual puts into the job and what is
received from the job in terms of rewards. In other words, both motivation and job satisfaction come from the perceived equitable relationship
between the employee's inputs to the job and the job outcomes.

Recently, a number of attempts have been made to study the job
satisfaction–performance relationship. Meta-analyses of dozens of studies examining this relationship indicate that there is a slight positive relationship between the two (Iaffaldano & Muchinsky, 1985; Petty, McGee,
& Cavender, 1984). (Recall that meta-analysis is a technique that allows
researchers to combine the results from several independent investigations in order to summarize the overall findings across all of the studies.)
Although a positive relationship was found between job satisfaction and
job performance, it was weaker than one might expect given the popularly
held belief that the two are closely tied. Why is the relationship not

stronger? One reason is that the relationship is quite complex, and may be moderated by a number of variables, such as the types of jobs being performed, the conditions under which people work, the rewards and recognitions workers receive, and the personal characteristics of the workers. For example, in jobs that require creative skills and ingenuity, a worker who has high levels of job satisfaction may indeed be more productive. However, for dull, routine jobs, levels of satisfaction may not have a direct effect on productivity. Moreover, we may get weaker results if we examine the relationship between overall job satisfaction and general job performance than if we look at the links between satisfaction with certain facets of the job and specific types of performance. For example, satisfaction with the type of work one performs may be related to job performance, but satisfaction with a company's benefit program may not be related to performance.

In summary, both job satisfaction and job performance are important but complex work outcomes. There is some evidence that these two variables are linked, but the relationship is not very strong. This weak link is likely due to the multitude of variables that can moderate the relationship.

ORGANIZATIONAL COMMITMENT

organizational commitment
a worker's feelings and attitudes about the entire work organization

While job satisfaction is the worker's feelings and attitudes about a job, **organizational commitment** is the feelings and attitudes about the entire work organization. Organizational commitment, also referred to as company loyalty, is associated with an acceptance of the organization's goals and values, a willingness to exert effort on behalf of the organization, and a desire to remain with the organization (Porter, Steers, Mowday, & Boulian, 1974). It is similar to job satisfaction since both involve feelings about the work situation. However, because organizational commitment deals specifically with workers' attitudes about the organization, it may be more directly linked to employee attendance variables such as absenteeism and turnover than is job satisfaction. The most widely used organizational commitment measure is a fifteen-item self-report instrument called the Organizational Commitment Questionnaire (OCQ), which is presented in Figure 7.4.

The concepts of job satisfaction and organizational commitment are closely related, although distinct (see Up Close). Research indicates a fairly high positive correlation between the two (Arnold & Feldman, 1982; Stumpf & Hartman, 1984). However, it is conceivable that a worker could be quite satisfied with a job but have low feelings of commitment to the organization or vice versa, although the feelings tend to be positively related. Both are affected by factors such as the type and variety of work, the level of responsibility associated with the job, the quality of the social environment at work, compensation, and the chances for promotion and advancement in the company. Organizational commitment tends to be

Figure 7.4
ORGANIZATIONAL
COMMITMENT
QUESTIONNAIRE (OCQ)

Source: R. T. Mowday,
R. Steers, and L. W. Porter,
"The Measure of Organiza-
tional Commitment," *Journal
of Vocational Behavior, 14*
(1979), p. 228.

Instructions

Listed below are a series of statements that represent possible feelings that individuals might have about the company or organization for which they work. With respect to your own feelings about the particular organization for which you are now working (company name) please indicate the degree of your agreement or disagreement with each statement by checking one of the seven alternatives below each statement.*

1. I am willing to put in a great deal of effort beyond that normally expected in order to help this organization be successful.
2. I talk up this organization to my friends as a great organization to work for.
3. I feel very little loyalty to this organization. (R)
4. I would accept almost any type of job assignment in order to keep working for this organization.
5. I find that my values and the organization's values are very similar.
6. I am proud to tell others that I am part of this organization.
7. I could just as well be working for a different organization as long as the type of work was similar. (R)
8. This organization really inspires the very best in me in the way of job performance.
9. It would take very little change in my present circumstances to cause me to leave this organization. (R)
10. I am extremely glad that I chose this organization to work for over others I was considering at the time I joined.
11. There's not too much to be gained by sticking with this organization indefinitely. (R)
12. Often, I find it difficult to agree with this organization's policies on important matters relating to its employees. (R)
13. I really care about the fate of this organization.
14. For me this is the best of all possible organizations for which to work.
15. Deciding to work for this organization was a definite mistake on my part. (R)

*Responses to each item are measured on a 7-point scale with scale point anchors labeled: (1) strongly disagree; (2) moderately disagree; (3) slightly disagree; (4) neither disagree nor agree; (5) slightly agree; (6) moderately agree; (7) strongly agree. An "R" denotes a negatively phrased and reverse scored item.

What Are the Levels of Job Satisfaction and Organizational Commitment of American Workers?

You have no doubt had ample opportunity to listen to friends, neighbors, and co-workers complain about their jobs. If you consider the incidence of people grumbling about their jobs and the way that jobs are typically portrayed as a tedious source of discontent on television, in songs, and in the movies (for example, *9 to 5* and "Take This Job and Shove It"), you might be led to believe that levels of job satisfaction are generally low. Yet is this true? How do levels of job satisfaction and organizational commitment in the United States compare to those of workers in other countries?

Actually, surveys consistently indicate that more than 85 percent of American employees are generally satisfied with their jobs (Weaver, 1980). Moreover, these levels of satisfaction have remained high and stable throughout recent years (Staw & Ross, 1985). Why the apparent contradiction between the complaints that we hear and the survey results?

Part of the reason may be due to problems in how job satisfaction is measured in these studies. A single-item global indicator is usually used. For example, the surveys may ask such general questions as, "Are you satisfied with your job: yes or no?" or "On the whole, how satisfied are you with the work you do: very satisfied, moderately satisfied, a little dissatisfied, or very dissatisfied?" Such methods can produce an "agreement" tendency or positive response bias. Evidence suggests that posing follow-up questions, rephrasing the questions, or using more indirect questions, such as "Would you like to change jobs: yes or no?," leads to indications of lower levels of job satisfaction, although the majority of respondents do still tend to be generally satisfied with their jobs.

Another explanation is that people report being satisfied with their jobs out of a desire to avoid *cognitive dissonance,* or an unpleasant state of perceived self-inconsistency (Baron, 1986). For example, some workers may be dissatisfied but remain in their jobs even though alternative positions may be available. These respondents would feel cognitive dissonance if they reported that they did not like a job in which they have freely chosen to remain. To avoid this, they report and likely convince themselves that they are indeed satisfied ("I stay in this job; I must like it.").

In spite of the high levels of job satisfaction reported by American workers, there are differences in satisfaction levels among various groups: Persons in higher-status occupations tend to be more satisfied than those in lower-level jobs; older workers are more satisfied than younger workers; and there is a positive association between workers' education and pay and their levels of job satisfaction.

What about the second question? How do the levels of satisfaction and organizational commitment of American and foreign workers compare? Of particular interest in recent years are the workers in Japan, because since the 1970s Japanese productivity has outpaced American productivity. It is popularly believed that Japanese workers are more satisfied and committed to their organizations than their American counterparts, which accounts for the productivity differences and the low levels of turnover in Japan. Surprisingly, research does not support this notion. A survey reported that Japanese workers experienced lower levels of global job satisfaction than American workers! In addition, both Japanese and Korean workers were found to have *lower* levels of organizational commitment than American employees, although the differences were slight (Luthans, McCaul, & Dodd, 1985). The low levels of turnover in Japan were attributed to a system that allows little opportunity for job changes rather than to strong feelings of organizational commitment.

What all of this indicates is that the measurement of job satisfaction and job attitudes is very complex. Job satisfaction can be affected by a number of factors, ranging from the characteristics of the workers to the circumstances under which they work. We must always use caution when interpreting the results of general measures of job satisfaction.

weakened, however, by the perceived chances of finding a job with another company (Bateman & Strasser, 1984; Rusbult & Farrell, 1983).

JOB SATISFACTION, ORGANIZATIONAL COMMITMENT, AND EMPLOYEE ATTENDANCE

Because both job satisfaction and organizational commitment deal with the feelings that workers have about their jobs, the work environment, and the organization in general, it seems likely that both are linked to employee attendance variables such as absenteeism and turnover. Employees who have positive feelings about their jobs and work organizations should be less likely to be absent from work and to leave for a job elsewhere. However, before considering these relationships, we must consider how employee attendance variables are defined and measured (Hackett & Guion, 1985; Stumpf & Dawley, 1981).

Both absenteeism and turnover can be categorized into voluntary and involuntary forms. Voluntary absenteeism is when employees miss work because they want to do something else. Calling in sick to take a three-day weekend or taking a day off to run errands or to go shopping are examples of voluntary absenteeism. Involuntary absenteeism occurs when the employee has a legitimate excuse for missing work, typically illness. Because involuntary absenteeism is inevitable, the organization must be prepared to accept a certain amount of such absences. It is voluntary absenteeism, however, that the organization would like to eliminate. Of course, it is very difficult to distinguish voluntary from involuntary absenteeism, since most employees are unlikely to admit that they were voluntarily absent (Hammer & Landau, 1981). One way that researchers have operationalized the measurement of voluntary and involuntary absenteeism is to use absence frequency (the number of days absent) as a measure of voluntary absenteeism and absence length (the number of consecutive days absent) as an assessment of involuntary absenteeism (Atkin & Goodman, 1984). It is important to note that only voluntary absenteeism is likely to be affected by employee job satisfaction; involuntary absenteeism is beyond the control of the employee.

Indeed, research examining the relationship between job satisfaction and employee absenteeism has produced conflicting findings. Sometimes there is a slight negative relationship between the two (with higher levels of job satisfaction associated with lower rates of absenteeism), and sometimes there is no significant relationship at all (Ilgen & Hollenback, 1977; Porter & Steers, 1973). A recent meta-analysis of a number of studies indicates that job satisfaction and absenteeism are indeed negatively correlated but that the relationship between the two is not very strong (Scott & Taylor, 1985). One reason the relationship is not as strong as one might think stems from problems in measuring absenteeism that cause voluntary and involuntary absenteeism to be lumped together in most of these stud-

Managers may believe that some degree of involuntary turnover is inevitable, but employees often take a different view.

ies. Another problem might be that even though workers are satisfied with their jobs, they may find certain nonwork activities (for example, taking an extra day of vacation or attending a ball game) more interesting or more important (Youngblood, 1984). Finally, employees may be absent because of factors beyond their control, such as health, transportation, or child care problems. Incidentally, difficulties in child care may largely explain why women have higher rates of work absenteeism than men (Markham, Dansereau, & Alutto, 1982).

As with absenteeism, there are difficulties in defining and measuring turnover. Involuntary turnover occurs when an employee is fired or laid off. A certain amount of involuntary turnover is likely to be considered inevitable and possibly even beneficial. Firing workers who are not performing at desirable levels can be viewed as a positive, "weeding" process (Mobley, 1982). Layoffs often occur for financial reasons and thus are likely to be beyond the control of management. Voluntary turnover takes place when a competent and capable employee leaves to work elsewhere. It is this turnover that is costly to the organization, because losing a valued employee means reduced organizational productivity and increased expenses associated with hiring and training a replacement. Voluntary turnover is likely to be influenced by lack of job satisfaction and organizational commitment, while involuntary turnover is not. As with absenteeism, research that does not distinguish between voluntary and involuntary turnover may not find the expected relationships between employee attitudes and turnover simply because the two types of turnover are lumped together. Interestingly, some researchers note that there are also problems in categorizing turnover as either voluntary or involuntary since some poor workers may not be fired but may *voluntarily* choose to leave the organization, which is likely glad to see them go. However, this means that voluntary turnover might be further classified as either dysfunctional or functional, depending on whether it has negative or beneficial outcomes for the organization (Dalton, Krackhardt, & Porter, 1981).

Both job satisfaction and organizational commitment have been investigated as predictors of employee turnover. While there was some inconsistency in the early results, it was generally concluded that the two concepts were slightly negatively correlated. That is, low levels of job satisfaction were related to higher rates of turnover (Mobley, Griffeth, Hand, & Meglino, 1979; Mowday, Koberg, & McArthur, 1984). Similarly, Steers (1977) found that low levels of job commitment were also predictive of employee turnover. Most recently, Williams and Hazer (1986) demonstrated that organizational commitment develops from job satisfaction and in turn influences an employee's decision to remain with or leave the organization. However, while organizational commitment appears to be a predictor of turnover, one of the best predictors of employee turnover is absenteeism, particularly the rate of absences in the years immediately before the employee leaves (Waters & Roach, 1979).

In summary, when examining the relationships between job satisfaction and other outcome variables such as absenteeism and turnover, it is important to consider the type of absenteeism and turnover being measured. Only voluntary absenteeism and turnover are likely to be affected by employee attitudes. Unfortunately, many studies do not distinguish between voluntary and involuntary absenteeism and turnover, which leads to a possible "watering down" of any observed effects.

INCREASING JOB SATISFACTION

As we have seen, job satisfaction is considered important by organizations because it is linked to costly absenteeism and turnover. It is also important to the employee because it reflects a critical work outcome: feelings of fulfillment from the job and the work setting. Because of its significance, organizations have implemented a number of programs and techniques in an effort to increase satisfaction. These programs take many forms. Some change the structure of work, others alter the methods of worker compensation, and still others offer innovative fringe benefit plans and packages. We will examine some of these techniques.

Changes in job structure. Three techniques have been used to try to increase employee satisfaction by changing the structure of jobs. The first technique, **job rotation,** which was introduced in Chapter 5, involves moving workers from one specialized job to another. While job rotation can be used to train workers in a variety of tasks, it can also be used to alleviate the monotony and boredom associated with performing the same

job rotation
the systematic movement of workers from one type of task to another to alleviate boredom and monotony

Job rotation in a department store makes one employee a stock hauler, a cashier, and a salesperson in turn.

work day in and day out. For example, assembly line workers would move from one type of assembly task to another on a weekly or monthly basis, and receptionists in a large company might rotate from the switchboard position to the front desk job to the mail distribution task each week.

Job enlargement is the practice of allowing workers to take on additional, varied tasks in an effort to make them feel that they are more valuable members of the organization. For example, a custodian who is responsible for the cleaning and upkeep of several rooms might progressively have his job enlarged until his duties involve the maintenance of an entire floor. Job enlargement is tricky to implement since it means that workers are required to do additional work, which some might perceive as negative. However, if used correctly, job enlargement can positively affect job satisfaction by giving an employee a greater sense of accomplishment and improving valuable work skills.

Job enrichment, which we studied in depth in Chapter 6, can also be used to increase job satisfaction. Recall that job enrichment involves raising the level of responsibility associated with a particular job by allowing workers a greater voice in the planning, execution, and evaluation of their own activities. For example, in one such program assembly line workers were divided into teams, each of which was given many of the responsibilities that were previously held by front-line supervisors, including ordering supplies, setting output rates, creating quality control inspection systems, and even appraising their own performance. This independence and increased responsibility can go a long way toward increasing motivation and job satisfaction for many workers. While job

job enlargement
the expansion of a job to include additional, more varied work tasks

enrichment and job enlargement seem somewhat similar because both require more work from employees, job enrichment raises the level of tasks, while job enlargement does not raise the level of responsibility associated with the work.

Changes in pay structure.   Although the relationship between pay and job satisfaction is not always a direct, positive one, there is some evidence that employees who are compensated well are less likely to search for jobs elsewhere (Cotton & Tuttle, 1986). While most innovative compensation programs are introduced primarily in an effort to improve job performance, many changes also increase levels of job satisfaction.

One innovative compensation program is **knowledge-based pay,** according to which employees are paid an hourly rate based on their knowledge and skills rather than on the particular job to which they are assigned. In other words, workers are paid for the level of job that they are able to do rather than for the level of the position that they hold. For knowledge-based pay programs to be cost-effective, it is imperative that employees be assigned to jobs that match the levels of their skills and knowledge. Research indicates that workers are more satisfied in organizations that use this system than in those that use conventional pay plans. Particularly satisfied are those who receive knowledge-based pay and who have high levels of ability and motivation (Tosi & Tosi, 1987).

knowledge-based pay a system of compensation in which workers are paid based on their knowledge and skills rather than on their positions

The Porter and Lawler model (see Figure 7.3) suggested that job performance leads to job satisfaction by way of increased rewards, one of the most important of which is pay. If this is the case, then a system of compensation based directly on performance should be an effective strategy for increasing job satisfaction. One such pay-for-performance system is **merit pay,** a plan in which the amount of compensation is directly a function of an employee's performance. In merit pay plans, workers receive a financial bonus based on their individual output. While sensible in theory, such systems do not work well in practice for a number of reasons. First and perhaps most importantly, difficulties in the objective assessment of performance means that it is often impossible to distinguish the truly good performers from the more average performers. This leads to unfairness in the distribution of merit pay and subsequent employee dissatisfaction. Second, most merit pay systems emphasize individual goals, which may hurt the organization's overall performance and disrupt group harmony, especially if jobs require groups to collaborate to produce a product. Finally, in many such plans the amount of merit compensation is quite small in proportion to base salaries. In other words, the merit pay is simply not viewed as a strong incentive to work harder (Balkin & Gomez-Mejia, 1987; see also Pearce, Stevenson, & Perry, 1985).

merit pay a compensation system in which employees receive a base rate and additional pay based on performance

Another strategy for the implementation of pay-for-performance systems is to make pay contingent on effective group performance, a technique termed **gainsharing** (Lawler, 1987). If a work group or department reaches a certain performance goal, all members of the unit receive a

gainsharing a compensation system based on effective group performance

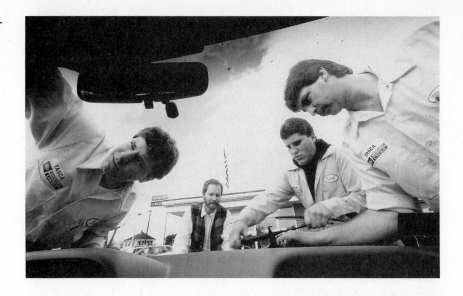

As part of a gainsharing system, this team of auto mechanics competes with other teams for monthly bonuses.

profit sharing
a compensation plan in which employees obtain a share of the organization's profits based on its success

bonus. A more common plan is **profit sharing,** in which all employees receive a small share of the organization's profits (see On the Cutting Edge). One drawback of profit-sharing programs is that it is difficult for employees to see how their individual performances have an impact on the company's total output. Also, there is typically quite a long delay between reaching performance goals and receiving individual shares of the company's profits.

Benefit programs. Perhaps the most common way for employers to try to increase employees' job satisfaction and organizational commitment is through various benefit programs. In recent years, such programs have come to represent about 28 percent of all money paid for employee compensation (Milkovich & Newman, 1987). Benefit programs can include flexible working hours; "cafeteria-style" programs in which each employee chooses from a variety of health care options; retirement plans; profit sharing; career development programs; health promotion and health care options; and employee-sponsored child care. This last program may have the extra advantage of helping to decrease absenteeism caused by employees' occasional inability to find adequate child care.

The effectiveness of programs designed to increase job satisfaction depends on various factors. While most of the techniques intended to increase job satisfaction do indeed appear to do so, there is less evidence that these programs then lead to changes in other important outcome variables such as productivity, work quality, absenteeism, and ultimately

Increasing Organizational Commitment Through Employee Ownership

Although the concept of **employee ownership** of organizations either entirely or in part is not new, in the past few years the number of companies that have implemented some such program has increased dramatically (Rosen, Klein, & Young, 1986). Employee ownership can take one of two forms: direct ownership or employee stock ownership. In direct ownership, the employees are the sole owners of the organization. Employee stock ownership programs, the more common of the two, are considered part of a benefit package whereby employees acquire shares of company stock over time. Each employee eventually becomes a company stockholder and has voting rights in certain company decisions. Proponents of these programs claim that although they are expensive, the costs are offset by savings created by increased employee organizational commitment, productivity, work quality, and job satisfaction and decreases in rates of absenteeism and turnover (Klein, 1987). The basic rationale is that employees will become more committed to an organization of which they are part owners.

Research on the success of employee ownership programs is scanty and somewhat inconsistent (Klein, 1987). For example, one study indicated that employee-owned companies had slightly higher profit levels than did similar conventional firms (Jochim, 1979). However, contrary to predictions, another study found no differences in overall absenteeism rates when companies moved from traditional to employee ownership (Hammer, Landau, & Stern, 1981). More recent research indicates that if employee ownership is going to increase organizational commitment, certain criteria must be met, the most obvious being that the program must be financially rewarding to employees (French & Rosenstein, 1984). A more recent investigation further qualified the conditions required for the success of employee ownership programs. Examining thirty-seven employee stock ownership companies, the study found that rates of employee organizational commitment and satisfaction were highest when the companies made substantial financial contributions to the employee stock purchases, when management was highly committed to the program, and when there was a great deal of communication about the program (Klein, 1987).

It will likely be some time before we know the actual impact of employee ownership programs on organizational commitment and other important outcome variables. However, it is clear that these programs are becoming quite popular and will likely continue to increase in numbers.

---

turnover. If a company implements a program to increase employee job satisfaction and if management is perceived by employees to be taking positive steps to improve the work place in some way, job satisfaction will likely improve immediately after the introduction of the program. However, it may be unclear whether the program actually caused the increase or if it is really a sort of Hawthorne effect in which employees' positive expectations about management's good intentions leads to increases in satisfaction merely because *something* was done. Regardless of the reason for measured improvements following the implementation of some satisfaction-enhancing program, the increases may tend to disappear over time as some of the novelty wears off, which long-term follow-up evaluations would reveal.

employee ownership
ownership of all or part of an organization by its workers, typically through stock purchases

Most workers feel some sense of purpose and accomplishment about their jobs, which can be very rewarding and self-satisfying. However, work can also be a tremendous burden. Deadlines, overload, and difficult bosses or co-workers can all place considerable pressure and strain on workers. Thus, jobs commonly also produce stress, which workers must learn to deal with. In this section, we will define work stress, see how it affects work behavior, examine ways that the individual worker can attempt to cope with it, and consider strategies that organizations can use to try to decrease stress.

DEFINING WORK STRESS

stress
the physiological, emotional, and psychological reactions to threatening events

While **stress** is the physiological, emotional, and psychological reaction to certain threatening environmental events, work stress simply refers to the stress caused by events in the work environment. The physiological reactions to stress include signs of arousal such as increased heart and respiratory rate, blood pressure, and sweating. According to the early stress researcher Hans Selye (1976), these reactions serve a survival function by helping human beings deal with potential dangers. In this response to stress, referred to as the "fight or flight syndrome," the body prepares to deal with the danger either by physical confrontation or by running away (Selye, 1976). The emotional reactions to stress include feelings of anxiety, fear, frustration, and despair. Psychological reactions to stress include appraising or evaluating the stressful event and its impact, thinking about the stressful experience, and mentally preparing to take steps to try to cope with the stress. When an individual is exposed to a **stressor,** an event or thing in the environment that is perceived as a potential threat, the stress reaction occurs.

stressor
an environmental event that causes a stress reaction

In many ways, stress is a perceptual process. An event that one individual perceives to be stressful may not be labeled as such by someone else. Because stress may cause a variety of reactions and feelings, and because perceptions of stress may vary from person to person, stress is not easy to define or measure.

Although we most often think of stress as an unpleasant state, it can have both negative and positive aspects. For example, imagine that you have been working for several years as an assistant manager for a large company and find out that you have just received a promotion to department manager, a position you have been trying to obtain for some time. With your new position comes feelings of stress. Some of these are negative, such as the stress that will result from having to work long overtime hours without additional compensation, to report your ideas regularly to your superiors, and to take the criticism for any problems occurring in your department. On the other hand, there are many positive reactions associated with the promotion, including feelings of accomplishment, anticipation, pride, and challenge. Like the negative aspects, these positive responses also induce physiological, emotional, and psychological changes in the body. Some stress researchers distinguish the negative types of stress, termed *distress,* from the positive kind of stress, called *eustress* (see, for example, Golembiewski, Munzenrider, & Stevenson, 1986).

SOURCES OF WORK STRESS

While people are subjected to a wide range of stressors, only certain types are likely to be encountered at work, including work overload, deadlines and other time pressures, high levels of responsibility, difficulties in relations with co-workers and supervisors, and dangerous work conditions. As you probably know, certain occupations are more likely to subject workers to high levels of stress than are other jobs. For example, air traffic controllers, surgeons, and pilots will experience high levels of stress because the lives of others depend on their performance. Occupations such as policeman or firefighter may be stressful because the lives and safety of the workers themselves are often at risk. Other jobs, such as commodities broker, waiter or waitress, and office manager may experience stress due to constant time pressures and heavy work demands. While some occupations may be relatively low in day-to-day stress levels, nearly every job is likely to expose workers to some form of work stress.

Sources of stress can be divided into two general categories: organizational and individual. Organizational sources come from the work environment and can be broken down into two subcategories: stress derived from work tasks and stress resulting from work roles. Individual sources of stress include a person's history of exposure to stress as well as certain stress-related personality characteristics and behavioral patterns.

Organizational sources of work stress. A great deal of work stress is caused by stressors in the environment of the work organization. Some of this organizational stress is caused by work tasks themselves—the physical and psychological demands of performing a job. Work organizations are also complex social systems in which a worker must interact with many people. The work relationships of various kinds that must be created and maintained for a worker to adequately perform the job can lead to other forms of organizational stress.

Some organizational stress arises from the demands placed on the worker while performing work tasks, which is known as task-based organizational stress. A common source of such stress is **work overload,** which results when the job requires excessive work speed, output, or concentration. Work overload is widely believed to be one of the greatest sources of work stress. However, having too little to do— **underutilization**—can also be stressful (French & Caplan, 1972). Underutilization may also occur when workers feel that the job does not use

Dangerous work conditions are a common source of stress on the job, as in the case of firefighters who risk their lives daily.

work overload
a common source of stress resulting when a job requires excessive speed, output, or concentration

underutilization
a source of stress resulting from workers feeling that their knowledge, skills, or energy are not being fully used

their work-related knowledge, skills, or abilities. Some college graduates in low-level clerical or customer service positions may feel some stress due to underutilization of their knowledge and skills.

Another potential source of stress is **job uncertainty,** which occurs when aspects of a job such as tasks and requirements are not clearly outlined. When workers are unsure of their responsibilities and duties, stress can result (Beehr, 1985). Job uncertainty, and accompanying stress, can also result from a lack of regular performance feedback concerning how well or poorly workers are doing their jobs.

Physical conditions in the work environment also contribute to task-based organizational stress. Jobs that must be performed under extreme temperatures, loud noise, or poor lighting or ventilation can be quite stressful. Dangerous jobs that place workers at risk of loss of health, life, or limb are an additional source of work stress. We will discuss these physical conditions of the work environment and work safety further in Chapter 14.

A second category of organizational stress can be referred to as relationship-based organizational stress. One of the greatest sources of work stress results from difficulties in interpersonal relationships on the job. Such **interpersonal stress** is one type of stress that nearly every worker encounters. Interpersonal stress stems from difficulties in developing and maintaining relationships with other people in the work setting. Having a harsh, critical boss with a punitive management style would likely be stressful for just about anyone. Interpersonal stress can also result when co-workers are placed in some sort of conflict situation. Imagine, for example, that two employees are both being considered for an important promotion. A great deal of stress may be generated if the two individuals must work together while both are competing for the same honor. Whatever its causes, the inability to get along with other workers is one of the most common sources of stress in the work place (Matteson & Ivancevich, 1982).

Another important source of work stress results from workers sensing that they have little control over the work environment and over their own work behavior. Stress resulting from this feeling of **lack of control** is particularly common in lower-level jobs or in highly structured organizations. Jobs that are so constrained and rule-driven that employees are unable to have any sort of input in work decisions and procedures are likely to be stress inducing, particularly for those workers who *want* to have some input. Research indicates that providing workers with a sense of control over their work environment, by techniques such as giving them a voice in decisionmaking processes, reduces work stress and increases job satisfaction (Jackson, 1983).

A final organizational source of stress, one that involves some task-based and some relationship-based stress, is change. People tend to grow accustomed to certain work procedures and certain work structures and they resist change. Most of us prefer things to remain stable and predict-

job uncertainty
a source of stress resulting from ambiguity in the job and work tasks

interpersonal stress
stress arising from difficulties with others in the work site

lack of control
a feeling of having little input or effect on the job and/or work environment that typically results in stress

Table 7.1 CHARACTERISTICS OF JOBS THAT CAUSE STRESS

Work overload (for example, time pressures and too much work)
Underutilization of worker knowledge, skills, ability, or energy
Dangerous work conditions
Responsibility for the health and well-being of others
Difficult or complex work tasks
Unpleasant or uncomfortable physical work conditions
Interpersonal conflict
Decisionmaking
Organizational change
Lack of support from supervisors or co-workers
Lack of control over the work situation
Personal factors (for example, Type A behavior or stress-prone personality)

able. Such stability in our working environments seems comforting and reassuring. Therefore, it should not be surprising that major changes in a work organization tend to cause stress. Some common change situations that lead to work stress include: company reorganizations, mergers of one company with another or acquisitions of one organization by another, changes in work systems and work technology, changes in company policy, and managerial or personnel changes (see Table 7.1).

Individual sources of work stress.   While much of work stress is created by factors in the organization or by features of jobs and work tasks, some is caused by characteristics of the workers themselves. We will consider three such individual sources of work stress: life events history, Type A behavior pattern, and susceptibility to stress and to stress effects.

Research indicates that stress in one area of an individual's life, such as the home or school, can affect stress levels at work (Levi, Frankenhaeuser, & Gardell, 1986; Martin & Schermerhorn, 1983). Particularly important is the worker's experience of traumatic **life events,** which include negative events such as the death of a spouse or loved one, divorce or separation, major illness, and financial or legal troubles as well as positive events such as marriage, the birth of a child, and vacations. These events may bring on stress-related illness and may impair job performance. Measures have been developed to assess a person's stress history. For example, with one measure that is based on a checklist, individuals total the numerical "stress severity" scores associated with the significant life events that they have experienced in the past year (Holmes & Rahe, 1967; see Table 7.2). This provides a personal life events stress index. Research indicates that this score may predict certain work outcomes such as job performance, absenteeism, and turnover. Persons with high personal stress indexes tend to perform more poorly, have higher absenteeism, and change jobs more frequently than persons who experience fewer stressful life events (Bhagat, 1983; Weiss, Ilgen, & Sharbaugh, 1982).

*life events
significant events in a
person's recent history
that can cause stress*

Table 7.2 THE SOCIAL READJUSTMENT RATING SCALE

Life Event	Stress Value
1. Death of spouse	100
2. Divorce	73
3. Marital separation	65
4. Jail term	63
5. Death of close family member	63
6. Personal injury or illness	53
7. Marriage	50
8. Fired at work	47
9. Marital reconciliation	45
10. Retirement	45
11. Change in health of family member	44
12. Pregnancy	40
13. Sex difficulties	39
14. Gain of new family member	39
15. Business readjustment	39
16. Change in financial state	38
17. Death of close friend	37
18. Change to different line of work	36
19. Change in number of arguments with spouse	35
20. Mortgage over $10,000	31
21. Foreclosure of mortgage or loan	30
22. Change in responsibilities at work	29
23. Son or daughter leaving home	29
24. Trouble with in-laws	29
25. Outstanding personal achievement	28
26. Wife begin or stop work	26
27. Begin or end school	26
28. Change in living conditions	25
29. Revision of personal habits	24
30. Trouble with boss	23
31. Change in work hours or conditions	20
32. Change in residence	20
33. Change in schools	20
34. Change in recreation	19
35. Change in church activities	19
36. Change in social activities	18
37. Mortgage or loan less than $10,000	17
38. Change in sleeping habits	16
39. Change in number of family get-togethers	15
40. Change in eating habits	15
41. Vacation	13
42. Christmas	12
43. Minor violations of the law	11

Source: T. H. Holmes and R. H. Rahe, "The Social Readjustment Rating Scale," *Journal of Psychosomatic Research, 11* (1967), pp. 213–218.

When many people think of individuals who are extremely stressed in the work place, they immediately picture the stereotypical hard-driving, competitive executive who seeks a job with a heavy work load and many responsibilities—a person who takes on too much work and never seems to have enough time to do it. Is there any truth to this characterization? The evidence indicates that there is. Researchers have uncovered the

Type A behavior pattern, or Type A personality, which is characterized by excessive drive and competitiveness, a sense of urgency and impatience, and underlying hostility (Friedman & Rosenman, 1974; Rosenman, 1978). This behavior pattern is particularly significant because there is evidence that persons who possess the Type A personality are more prone to develop stress-related coronary heart disease, including fatal heart attacks, than persons who do not have the behavior pattern (Type Bs). While much of the early research found that the relationship between Type A behavior and stress-related illness held for men but not for women, more recent studies have begun to find that the pattern is linked to stress reactions in both sexes (Schmied & Lawler, 1986).

It does not appear that mere possession of the Type A behavior pattern leads to greater levels of self-perceived stress, for although Type As describe their jobs as having heavier work loads and more responsibility than do Type Bs, this is not accompanied by reports of higher stress levels in Type As (Chesney & Rosenman, 1980). In other words, Type As seem to welcome the heavy work loads and responsibilities and do not perceive them as particularly stressful. However, it may be this denial or inattention to stress that leads to greater risk of developing coronary heart disease, since Type As may not realize that their long, intense work style is creating wear and tear on their cardiovascular system. While there are obvious stress-related costs to the Type A behavior pattern, there are also some gains. Studies consistently show that Type As tend to have higher positions and salaries than Type Bs (Chesney & Rosenman, 1980).

Another individual source of stress may stem from the fact that some persons are simply more susceptible to stress while others have stress-resistant, hardy personalities. The concept of **hardiness** was outlined by psychologist Suzanne Kobasa (1982), who argued that hardy personality types are resistant to the harmful effects of stress because of their style of dealing with stressful events. Rather than viewing a stressful situation as a threat, they view it as a challenge. Moreover, they also believe that they can control and influence the course of their lives (recall that a sense of lack of control can contribute to stress) and are committed to their jobs. Conversely, a lack of hardiness is associated with higher levels of self-perceived stress, and there is evidence that such "unhardy" or "disease-prone" persons may be more susceptible to stress-related illnesses and depression (Friedman & Booth-Kewley, 1987; Kobasa & Puccetti, 1983).

Type A behavior pattern a personality characterized by excessive drive, competitiveness, impatience, and hostility that has been linked to greater incidence of coronary heart disease

hardiness the notion that some people may be more resistant to the health-damaging effects of stress

EFFECTS OF WORK STRESS

The topic of work stress and its effects is one of the most rapidly growing research areas in I/O psychology. Much of this interest is due to the very powerful impact that stress can have on workers and work behavior, and most dramatically on employee health.

It is believed that more than half of all physical illness is stress re-

Figure 7.5

RELATIONSHIP BETWEEN
PERFORMANCE AND
STRESS

Source: S. Cohen, "After-effects of Stress on Human Behavior and Social Behavior: A Review of Research and Theory, *Psychological Bulletin, 88* (1980), p. 85.

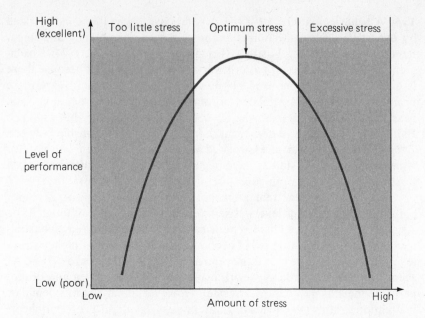

lated. Some common stress-related illnesses are ulcers, colitis, high blood pressure, heart disease, respiratory illnesses, and migraine headaches. Moreover, stress can worsen common colds, flus, and infections, making recovery time longer. These illnesses, attributed in part to work stress, cost billions of dollars annually in health care costs and in employee absenteeism and turnover (Beehr & Bhagat, 1985; Gherman, 1981).

Work stress can also have an adverse impact on employees' psychological states. High levels of stress are associated with depression, anxiety, and chronic fatigue. Stress may also contribute to alcoholism and drug abuse in workers and may influence accident rates on the job (Wolf, 1986; see also Chapter 14).

As you might imagine, stress has strong effects on important work outcomes. Stress is believed to cause decreased work performance and increased absenteeism and turnover. However, the relationships between work stress and these key bottom-line variables are quite complex. For example, it appears that the relationship between stress and performance may often take the form of an inverted U (see Figure 7.5), rather than being direct and linear, with greater stress leading to poorer performance. In other words, very low levels of stress (or no stress) and very high levels of stress are associated with poor work performance, while low to moderate levels of stress seem to be related to better performance (Cohen, 1980). This makes sense, since very high levels of stress will interfere with job performance. On the other end, having little or no stress likely means that workers are not being challenged or motivated. In short, a little bit of stress might not be a bad thing. Of course, both stress and job performance are extremely complex variables, and this inverted U relationship may not hold for all types of stressors and for all aspects of job performance (Beehr, 1985).

The effects of work stress on job performance might also be moderated by other variables. For example, one study showed that the effects of stress on the job performance of nurses was moderated by feelings of depression. That is, work stress caused the nurses to be depressed, and the depression led to decreased quality of patient care and problems with relationships with co-workers (Motowidlo, Packard, & Manning, 1986). If stress is caused by an inability to get along with a certain co-worker, an employee may try to cope with this situation by avoiding all interactions with the individual. This avoidance strategy may impair the employee's job performance if the co-worker has some valuable information that the employee needs to perform his job. In this case, it is not the stress that is causing poor job performance but the coping strategy!

A great deal of evidence suggests that work stress can lead to increased turnover and absenteeism. Gupta and Beehr (1979) found this to be true for a variety of occupations in five organizations. Another study concluded that it was a combination of high levels of work stress and low levels of organizational commitment that predicted voluntary turnover rates for workers in a food processing company (Parasuraman & Alutto, 1984). If stress levels are to blame for certain illnesses, it is a given that stress must be responsible for some absenteeism and some turnover caused by disabling illness.

Employees who are extremely overworked and exposed to other work stressors for extended periods may become victims of **burnout,** a process by which they become less committed to their jobs and begin to withdraw from work. The process of withdrawal may include such reactions as increased tardiness and absenteeism and decreased work performance and quality (Gaines & Jermier, 1983; Maslach, 1982). Burnout usually occurs in three phases. The first phase is emotional exhaustion caused by excessive demands placed on the worker. The second phase is depersonalization, or a cynical, insensitive attitude toward people (other workers or customers) in the work site. The third phase is marked by feelings of low personal accomplishment. Here the burned-out workers feel a sense of frustration and helplessness. They begin to believe that their work efforts fail to produce the desired results, and they may quit trying (Jackson, Schwab, & Schuler, 1986). Research has shown that burnout is especially high in human service professions that involve helping others, such as health care providers (physicians, nurses, counselors), teachers, social workers, and policemen (Cherniss, 1980). A recent study of nurses found that burnout led to decreased organizational commitment and increased negative interactions with supervisors (Leiter & Maslach, 1988).

burnout
a syndrome resulting from prolonged exposure to work stress that leads to withdrawal from the organization

COPING WITH WORK STRESS

The tremendous variety of strategies and techniques designed to cope with work stress can all be categorized into two general approaches: individual strategies and organizational strategies. Individual strategies are those that can be used by individual employees to try to reduce or eliminate personal stress. Organizational strategies are techniques and programs that organizations can implement to try to reduce stress levels for groups of workers or for the organization as a whole.

Individual coping strategies. **Individual coping strategies** are designed to change the worker's physical or psychological condition or change specific behaviors (Newman & Beehr, 1979). The most obvious of such techniques are programs developed to improve the individual's physical condition, such as exercise and diet plans. The primary rationale behind such health programs is to make the body more resistant to stress-related illnesses. Some claim that exercise itself may directly reduce the anxiety associated with stress or have a certain tranquilizing effect on a stressed individual (Jette, 1984). However, it is unclear whether it is the exercise that alleviates the physiological symptoms of stress or whether the positive effects of exercise are primarily psychological. Because exercising and keeping physically fit are valued highly by our culture, it may be that physically active persons feel better about themselves and thus psychologically reduce perceived stress. More rigorous evaluation is needed to determine the precise physiological and psychological influences of exercise and diet programs in alleviating stress.

Another individual coping strategy is the inducement of states of relaxation to reduce the negative arousal and strain that accompany stress. A variety of techniques have been used to achieve this, including systematic relaxation training, meditation, and biofeedback. In systematic relaxation training individuals are taught how to relax all of the muscles of the body systematically, from the feet to the face. Meditation is a deep relaxed state that is usually brought on by intense concentration upon a single word, idea, or object. Supposedly, meditative states are "free of anxiety, tension, or distress" (Sethi, 1984, p. 145). Biofeedback uses some measure of physiological activity, typically brain waves or muscle tension, that is associated with relaxed states. When the person is in the state of relaxation, the measurement machinery provides some sort of feedback, such as a tone. The individual then learns through practice how to enter into the relaxed, stress-free state. While relaxation, meditation, and biofeedback are intended principally to reduce the physiological arousal associated with stress, they may also induce positive psychological reactions to stress.

While these various methods of coping with stress through relaxation processes are widely touted, there has been very little systematic investigation of their effectiveness. In fact, some findings indicate that such

individual coping strategies
techniques such as exercise or meditation that can be used to deal with work stress

Many corporations now sponsor exercise classes to help employees cope with stress.

programs are not very effective at all (Ganster, Mayes, Sime, & Tharp, 1982; Sallis, Johnson, Trevorrow, Hovell, & Kaplan, 1985). One possible reason for their failure is that most of the relaxation techniques require quite a bit of dedication and practice to be used effectively. Not all persons find it easy to induce a deeply relaxed state; others may not be able to adhere to a regular program of systematic relaxation or meditation. Also, many of these programs last only a few hours, not enough time to teach someone difficult relaxation techniques. The timing of the relaxation technique is another problem. Many people would find it difficult (and perhaps inappropriate) to meditate at work, and relaxing before or after work may or may not significantly reduce stress while at work. In short, although any and all of these techniques might be good in theory, they might not function well in practice.

Other individual coping strategies include a variety of techniques to try to fend off work stress through better, more efficient work methods. Courses in time management are often advertised as methods of reducing stress caused by overwork and inefficiency. For example, learning to approach work tasks systematically by budgeting and assigning parcels of time to specific tasks and by planning ahead to avoid last minute deadlines may be quite effective in helping reduce stress for some workers. Again, however, these strategies depend on the individual's commitment to the technique and willingness and ability to use it regularly. (See Applying I/O Psychology for guidelines on how organizations should implement stress management programs.)

Finally, individuals may try to cope with stress by removing themselves, temporarily or permanently, from the stressful work situation. It is not uncommon for workers to exchange a stressful job for one that is less stressful (although many do seek more challenging and *more* stressful jobs). While a vacation may temporarily eliminate work stress, certain trips, such as intense tours of eight European countries in seven days, may create a different kind of stress themselves. The impact of vacations on stress and other important work outcomes is an understudied topic (Lounsbury & Hoopes, 1986).

Organizational coping strategies. While individual coping strategies are steps that workers themselves can take to alleviate personal stress, **organizational coping strategies** are steps that organizations can take to try to reduce stress levels in the organization for all, or most, employees. Since work stress can come from a variety of organizational sources, there are many things that organizations can do to reduce employee stress. These strategies include the following.

Improve the person-job fit. Work stress commonly arises when workers are in jobs they dislike or jobs for which they are ill-suited (French & Caplan, 1972). A mismatch between a worker's interests or skills and job requirements can be very stressful. By maximizing the person-job fit

organizational coping strategies
techniques that organizations can use to reduce stress for all or most employees

Designing Effective Work Stress Management Training Programs

A wide range of programs are used to help employees manage work stress. According to two leading researchers, such programs must follow certain guidelines to ensure their effectiveness: They must be systematic; they must teach knowledge, skills, or attitudes that are useful in coping with stress; and their success must be evaluated and documented (Matteson & Ivancevich, 1987).

The first step in designing a stress management program is the same as in designing any sort of training program: an assessment of training needs. An organizational stress analysis is needed and might include answering such questions as: What are the major producers of stress in the organization? Do these stressors necessarily detract from the accomplishment of organizational goals? (In other words, are they "bad"?) What sort of resources will be committed to the training program?"

According to Matteson and Ivancevich, most stress management programs take one of two forms: knowledge acquisition programs or skill training programs. Knowledge acquisition programs provide participants with some information about stress and a number of coping techniques. An outline of a sample four-part stress knowledge acquisition program is presented below:

1. *Overview of stress and its potential consequences (3 hours):* This might include lecture and readings on facts and myths about stress, the impact of stress on physical and psychological health and on work performance, and potential sources of stress.
2. *Self-analysis: Learning about your personal stress (3 hours):* This section can include assessments of personal stressors using instruments such as the stressful life events scale or workers' self-reports.
3. *Methods of coping with work stress (3 hours):* Here various individual coping strategies are presented and perhaps demonstrated.
4. *Developing a personalized coping plan (3 hours):* In this final part participants work on developing customized programs for managing stress, including setting personal stress management goals and finding means to assess their attainment.

The major advantages of knowledge acquisition programs are that they are relatively inexpensive, do not require a lot of time, and do not place heavy demands on participants. Unfortunately, these "one-shot" training programs may not be as effective as the more involved skill training programs in alleviating work stress.

Skill training programs are designed to improve specific coping skills in areas such as problem solving, time management, communication, social interaction, cognitive coping, or strategies for making changes in life style. An example of a step-by-step problem-solving skill program developed by Wasik (1984) is illustrated below:

1. Identify problem (What is my problem?)
2. Select goals (What do I want to accomplish by solving the problem?)
3. Generate alternatives (What else can I do?)
4. Review the consequences (What might happen?)
5. Make a decision (What is my decision?)
6. Implement the decision (Did I do what I decided?)
7. Evaluate the decision (Does it work?)

This step-by-step program would be conducted in a series of one- to two-hour sessions over many weeks. Participants learn each of the steps, practice them using role playing, and receive feedback concerning their skill development. They are also encouraged to use the skills to deal with actual work problems and then report back to discuss the success or failure of the strategy. The key to these programs is to practice using and applying the coping strategies to real and simulated stressful situations.

The final stage in any stress management program is to evaluate its effectiveness. It has been suggested that an assessment should consider trainees' reactions; how well the program accomplished its immediate objectives; actual behavioral changes; the impact of the program on organizational outcomes such as productivity, absenteeism, morale, and employee health; and the cost effectiveness of the program (Kirkpatrick, 1976).

through the careful screening, selection, and placement of employees, organizations can alleviate a great deal of this stress.

Improve employee training and orientation programs. Perhaps the most stressed groups of workers in any organization are new employees. Although they are usually highly motivated and want to make a good impression on their new bosses by showing that they are hard working and competent, their lack of certain job-related skills and knowledge means that new employees are often unable to perform their jobs as well as they would like. This mismatch between expectations and outcomes can be very stressful for new workers. Moreover, they feel a great deal of stress simply because they are in a new and unfamiliar environment in which there is much important information to be learned. Companies can help eliminate some of this stress by ensuring that new workers receive proper job training and orientation to the organization. Not only does this lead to a more capable and productive new work force, but it also helps to reduce the stress-induced turnover of new employees.

Increase employees' sense of control. We have seen that the lack of a sense of control over one's job can be very stressful. By giving workers a greater feeling of control through participation in work-related decisions, more responsibility, or increased autonomy and independence, organizations can alleviate some of this stress. Programs such as job enrichment, participative decisionmaking, and systems of delegating authority all help increase employees' sense of control over their jobs and the work environment.

Eliminate punitive management. It is well known that humans react strongly when they are punished or harassed, particularly if the punishment or harassment is believed to be unfair and undeserved. The very act of being threatened or punished at work can be very stressful. If organizations take steps to eliminate company policies that are perceived to be threatening or punitive, a major source of work stress will also be eliminated. Training supervisors to minimize the use of punishment as a managerial technique will also help control this common source of stress.

Remove hazardous or dangerous work conditions. In some occupations stress results from exposure to hazardous work conditions, such as mechanical danger of loss of limb or life, health-harming chemicals, excessive fatigue, or extreme temperatures. The elimination or reduction of these situations is another way of coping with organizational stress. We will consider dangerous work conditions more fully in Chapter 14.

Improve communication. Much of the stress at work derives from difficulties in interpersonal relations with supervisors and co-workers. The better the communication among workers, the lower the stress created because of misunderstandings. In addition, stress occurs when workers feel cut off from or uninformed about organizational processes and operations. Proper organizational communication, which will be examined in Chapter 8, can prevent workers from experiencing this stressful sense of isolation.

Both job satisfaction and work stress influence an employee's quality of work life. For example, a worker who feels a great deal of job satisfaction and very little job distress is apt to have a high quality of work life. On the other hand, an employee who feels little satisfaction and a great deal of negative stress will usually have a low quality of work life.

In recent years, I/O psychologists, management professionals, organizational decisionmakers, and the government have become increasingly concerned with workers' quality of work life. **Quality of work life** is determined by the compensation and benefits workers receive, by their chances to participate and advance in the organization, by job security, by the type of work, by the characteristics of the organization, and by the quality of interactions among various organizational members. In short, quality of work life is the state of all aspects of life at work.

In the 1970s, a quality-of-work-life movement was begun in the United States with three interrelated goals: (1) to assess the quality of work life in America by comparing and contrasting the current quality with that of the past and with that of other industrialized nations, (2) to develop strategies to enhance the quality of work life for all workers, and (3) to maintain high rates of productivity and organizational effectiveness through greater participation of workers in organizational processes (Davis & Cherns, 1975; Stein, 1983). This movement aspires to achieve these goals while still improving organizational outcomes. Evidence indicates that enhancing quality of work life can lead to such positive organizational outcomes as increased productivity and quality and decreased absenteeism and turnover (Herrick & Maccoby, 1975).

quality of work life
the evaluative state of
all aspects of work

Table 7.3   THE IMPORTANT FEATURES OF QUALITY OF WORK LIFE

1. Adequate and fair compensation
2. Safe and healthy working conditions
3. Opportunity to use and develop worker capabilities (maximizing the use of workers' knowledge, skills, and abilities; allowing workers control and autonomy over their jobs)
4. Opportunity for continued growth and security (job security; opportunities for promotion and advancement; opportunities to grow on the job)
5. Social environment of the work place (good interpersonal relationships among workers; sense of community in the work organization)
6. Protection of workers' rights (protection against unfair employment decisions; equal opportunity for all workers)
7. Balance of work and nonwork life (adequate work schedules and work demands [for example, not allowing work requirements to interfere with family life]; concern with how work stress affects nonwork life and vice versa)
8. Organizational social responsibility (ethical organizational operations and policies, such as waste disposal, employment practices, and marketing techniques)

Source: R. E. Walton, "Criteria for Quality of Working Life," in L. E. Davis and A. B. Cherns (Eds.), *The Quality of Working Life,* Vol. 1 (New York: Free Press, 1975), pp. 91–104.

Because quality of work life is so complex, made up of a number of interrelated factors, it is very difficult to conceptualize and measure (Lawler, 1982). One comprehensive conceptual model proposes that quality of work life is composed of categories that cover nearly all aspects of working life, including compensation, working conditions, workers' rights, and the opportunity to grow and develop on the job (Walton, 1975; see Table 7.3). However, obtaining the detailed measurements of quality of work life suggested by the Walton model would be extremely difficult and costly. Lawler (1982) suggests that a simpler way for organizations to get some indication of quality of work life is to regularly measure absenteeism, turnover, accident rates, employee satisfaction levels, and dollars spent in employee training and development—variables that are presumed to be related to quality of work life. Regardless of how quality of work life is conceptualized and measured, it is clearly an important organizational issue that is likely to become more and more important.

Some organizations group employees into pairs or teams to enhance the quality of work life.

The goals of having high quality of work life while maintaining high organizational productivity seem on the surface to be somewhat incompatible. The maintenance of work life quality is an expensive burden on the organization's budget. Adequate and fair wages, benefit programs, and safety and health programs are all quite costly. Is it possible to keep these elements at high levels and have sufficient additional resources to cover basic organizational operating expenses? Quality of work life advocates say "yes." In fact, they maintain that it is more costly to organizations *not* to maintain a high quality of work life. Inadequate compensation, lack of opportunity for advancement, and a poor social environment lead to job dissatisfaction and high rates of employee turnover with the accompanying costs associated with the loss and replacement of good workers. Inefficient use of worker skills and a lack of concern with levels of work stress have a direct negative impact on productivity. Unsafe work conditions lead to work place accidents and losses due to absenteeism. Furthermore, organizations that ignore workers' rights and issues of social responsibility face costly lawsuits and the costs of bad publicity. Maintaining a high quality of work life for employees is expensive, but in the long run should lead to a more effective and productive organization.

Organizations have used a variety of techniques to improve quality of work life. While some of the enhancements involve such straightforward changes as paying fair market wages for jobs or passing legislation to protect workers' rights (for example, the rights associated with equal employment opportunity and fair personnel decisions), I/O psychologists have been involved in improving quality of work life through programs that encourage greater employee participation in organizational processes (Lawler, 1986). Some of these participative programs include the development of *work teams,* groups of employees collaborating on a project; the use of *quality circles,* a technique of having workers meet in groups to solve quality-related production problems; and the use of *employee surveys* to obtain input about company operations and policies. We will examine these methods in detail in Chapter 12 as part of our discussion of organizational development. Another participative technique is the introduction of job enrichment, a program mentioned earlier as a method of increasing job satisfaction through heightened job responsibility. Other participative strategies for enhancing quality of work life include allowing workers some flexibility in arranging their own work schedules, which we will discuss in Chapter 14.

The concept of quality of work life and the quality-of-work-life movement help shed light on how job satisfaction and work stress are interrelated processes that occur in all jobs, for both contribute to the overall quality of work life. The quality-of-work-life movement, which is spearheaded by I/O psychologists, also illustrates two important objectives of I/O psychology: to improve the physical and social environment at work in an effort to enhance worker well-being, satisfaction, and work life quality; and to improve organizational outcomes, such as increased productivity, work quality, and reduced absenteeism and turnover, through increasing employee participation in, and commitment to, organizational processes.

SUMMARY

All jobs produce some levels of job satisfaction and work stress. *Job satisfaction,* which is the positive feelings and attitudes about a job, can be conceptualized in overall, or global, terms or in terms of specific components or facets, and can be measured through interviews or self-report instruments. The most widely used self-report measures are the *Minnesota Satisfaction Questionnaire (MSQ)* and the *Job Descriptive Index (JDI).* Research indicates that there is a slight positive relationship between job satisfaction and job performance, although the link may be moderated by a third variable, such as the receipt of work rewards. Job satisfaction is negatively related to rates of employee absenteeism and is associated with *organizational commitment,* or employees' feelings and attitudes about the entire work organization. Both job satisfaction and organizational commitment are negatively correlated with voluntary employee turnover. Programs designed to increase job satisfaction include changes in job structure through techniques such as *job rotation, job enlargement,* and job enrichment. Other satisfaction-enhancing techniques suggest changing the pay structure by using methods such as *knowledge-based pay,* pay-for-performance programs like *merit pay,* or *gainsharing* or *profit sharing,* which are contingent on effective group performance. Still other methods of improving satisfaction involve increasing job-related benefits.

A second product of jobs is *work stress,* which is the physiological, emotional, and psychological reactions to threats from the work environment, termed *stressors.* Work stress can come from organizational sources or individual sources. Organizational sources may include *job uncertainty,* which occurs when job tasks and responsibilities are ambiguous, and *interpersonal stress,* which arises from relations with co-workers. Other sources of stress are derived from workers' feelings of *lack of control* over their jobs from feeling underutilized, or from organizational change. Individual sources of work stress include: the worker's experience of traumatic *life events,* the *Type A behavior pattern,* and the lack of *hardiness,* or resistance to stress-related illnesses. Stress has been shown to be related to certain physical illnesses such as ulcers, high blood pressure, and heart disease. These stress-related illnesses as well as stress itself are tied to rates of employee absenteeism and turnover and to job performance, although the relationship between stress and performance is complex. Long-term stress can lead to *burnout,* a tendency to withdraw from work. Strategies for coping with work stress can be divided into *individual coping strategies* and *organizational coping strategies.* Individual strategies include programs of exercise, diet, systematic relaxation training, meditation, biofeedback, time management, and work planning. Organizational strategies include improving the person-job fit, offering better training and orientation programs, giving workers a sense of control over their jobs, eliminating punitive management behavior, removing hazardous work conditions, and improving organizational communication.

Both job satisfaction and work stress are incorporated into the notion of *quality of work life,* which encompasses all aspects of life at work. The quality-of-work-life movement in America has been involved in the assessment and enhancement of work life quality and the improvement of productivity and organizational performance through increased participation of employees in organizational processes.

STUDY QUESTIONS AND EXERCISES

1. What are some of the difficulties in the measurement of employee job satisfaction? How might I/O psychologists try to deal with these problems?

2. How do job satisfaction and work stress relate to important bottom-line variables (such as performance, absenteeism, and turnover)?

3. What would a good, comprehensive program to increase job satisfaction contain? How would you design a stress-reduction program for a large organization? What elements would you include in each?

4. Consider the relationship between job satisfaction and work stress. What do they have in common? How do they differ?

5. In what ways has the quality of work life of American workers changed over the past fifty years? What sorts of changes do you expect to see in the future?

SUGGESTED READINGS

Gherman, E. M. (1981). *Stress and the bottom line: A guide to personal well-being and corporate health.* New York: AMACOM. *A very readable overview of work stress (and stress in general), including its effects, stress theories, and techniques for managing work-related stress.*

Goodman, P. S., & Atkin, R. S. (Eds.). (1984). *Absenteeism: New approaches to understanding, measuring, and managing employee absence.* San Francisco: Jossey-Bass. *An edited book of readings on all aspects of research on the causes and consequences of employee absenteeism.*

Hall, D. T., & Richter, J. (1988). Balancing work life and home life: What can organizations do to help? *The Academy of Management Executive, II,* 213–223. *A discussion of the interrelations of employee problems, stress, and well-being at work and home. Provides some organizational guidelines for dealing with the spillover of problems from home life to work life and vice versa.*

Matteson, M. T., & Ivancevich, J. M. (1987). *Controlling work stress: Effective human resource and management strategies.* San Francisco: Jossey-Bass. *An up-to-date review of research and practice in dealing with work stress by two active researchers.*

Stein, B. A. (1983). *Quality of work life in action: Managing for effectiveness.* New York: American Management Associations. *This brief publication includes an overview of the quality of work life movement with some guidelines for practicing managers about how to implement programs to improve quality of work life.*

8

COMMUNICATION IN THE WORK PLACE

Communication: A Complex Process in Work Organizations

Communication is a constant process in any work organization. Because organizational communication can take many forms and can occur among any grouping of workers, it is extremely complex and difficult to study. To try to capture communication so that it can be studied, I/O psychologists and other scientists rely heavily on various communication models. This chapter begins with a general model of communication between two persons: sender and receiver. Models of other aspects of communication in the work place are then presented, including communication networks, which are models of group communication; the organizational chart, which is a model of the formal lines of downward, upward, and lateral communication in an organization; and the grapevine, which represents the informal flow of communication. While these various models describe who communicates with whom, they do not explain the type, content, or quality of the communication. Portions of the chapter concentrate on factors that can contribute to or detract from the effective and accurate flow of communication in work settings.

In contrast to the previous chapters, this chapter is more general. The theories and models tend to represent general aspects of communication, and relatively little new terminology is introduced. The research results and practical applications also tend to be focused more on communication in general rather than on specific aspects, largely because communication is a complex process that we are only beginning to understand fully. Therefore, rather than concentrating on learning new terms or specific theories, think about the complexity of organizational communication and the difficulties encountered in trying to measure and understand this important, ongoing process. Consider the number and types of communication you send and receive each day, the various ways that messages are communicated, and the different settings in which this occurs. The sheer amount of communication you encounter in your daily life should give you an idea of the complexity of organizational communication.

P art Three focused on worker issues: the psychological processes, such as motivation, job satisfaction, and work stress, that influence the behavior of the individual. In the next five chapters we will move beyond this focus to examine how workers interact to form work groups and larger work organizations. The study of this interaction is the specialty of the area within I/O psychology known as organizational psychology. In reviewing organizational issues, we will start small, looking at communication between two workers, and finish big, examining how large work organizations are designed and structured.

Most of us do not work alone but rather with others in the context of small groups. In large organizations, these groups are in turn members of larger work groups or departments, which in combination make up the work organization. Depending on the size of the organization, our co-workers may number in the tens, hundreds, or even thousands. Much energy in organizations, particularly from the management perspective, involves coordinating the activities of the various members. In the next few chapters, we will examine work behavior in terms of this organizational interaction. We will investigate the dynamics of work groups—how they coordinate activities and make decisions—as well as the very factors that hold them together. We will see how workers differ in terms of their power and status within the organization, paying particular attention to the relationship between those persons designated as leaders and other workers. We will examine the politics within work organizations and the structure of work groups and larger work organizations. However, before we begin to explore these topics, we must understand one of the most basic processes that occurs among workers in organizational settings: communication.

THE COMMUNICATION PROCESS: A DEFINITION AND A MODEL

Communication can be defined as the transmission of information from one person or group to another person or group. In work settings, communication takes many forms, such as written or spoken orders, informal chatter, printed reports or procedures manuals, discussion among executives in a corporate boardroom, or announcements posted on a bulletin board. Communication is an ongoing process that is the lifeblood of the organization. Communication is also extremely complex and can occur in a variety of ways: through the written or spoken word; through nonverbal means such as gestures, nods, or tone of voice; or through a picture or diagram. We can also communicate in a number of contexts, including in face-to-face conversation, over the phone, in letters or memos, or in a public address. This complexity, coupled with its almost continuous nature (even our silence can communicate), makes communication very difficult to study.

Communication actually involves the process of the exchange of information among two or more parties, which is best represented by a simple model of communication between two persons: the *sender* and the *receiver* (see Figure 8.1). The **sender** (also known as the encoder) is the originator of the communication; the **receiver** (also called the decoder) is the recipient. Communication begins with some information—a mes-

communication
the passage of information between one person or group to another person or group

sender
the originator of a communication, who encodes and transmits a message; also known as the encoder

receiver
the recipient of a communication, who decodes the message; also known as the decoder

Figure 8.1

THE COMMUNICATION
PROCESS

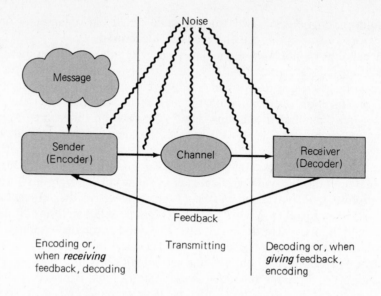

Encoding or,
when *receiving*
feedback, decoding

Transmitting

Decoding or, when
giving feedback,
encoding

sage—that the sender wishes to transmit to a receiver. The sender's task is to take the information and put it into some form in which it can be communicated to the receiver. This process of preparing a message for transmission is referred to as **encoding,** because the sender chooses some sort of shared code as a means of communication. In work settings, this code is usually the shared verbal language, but it might also consist of some common nonverbal code, or "body language."

The next step is for the sender to select a **channel,** the vehicle through which the message will flow from the sender to the receiver. The sender may choose the spoken word, confronting the receiver face-to-face or through the telephone, or the written word, using a memo, or as is becoming increasingly popular, a typed message sent through a computerized mail network (direct from the sender's terminal to the receiver's). Different methods of communication have various advantages and disadvantages (see Table 8.1). For example, face-to-face or telephone communication may be quick and convenient, while formal reports or detailed memos are time-consuming to prepare. However, the more formal, written channels of communication are less likely to be misunderstood or misinterpreted because of their length, detail, and careful preparation. Importantly, the sender must also choose the channel of communication that is appropriate for the situation. For example, personal information is usually conveyed verbally, face-to-face, while an important directive concerning a project deadline might be put in the form of a detailed, typed memo distributed to all relevant parties, with follow-up reminders sent as the deadline nears.

The receiver picks up the message and is responsible for **decoding** it, or translating it in an effort to understand the meaning intended by the

encoding
the process of preparing a message for transmission by putting it into some form, or code

channel
the vehicle through which a message flows from sender to receiver

decoding
the process of translating a message so that it can be understood

Table 8.1 ADVANTAGES AND DISADVANTAGES OF COMMUNICATION CHANNELS

Channel	Advantages	Disadvantages
Telephone	Verbal Permits questions and answers Convenient Two-way flow Immediate feedback	Less personal No record of conversation Message might be misunderstood Timing may be inconvenient May be impossible to terminate
Face-to-face	Visual Personal contact Can "show" and "explain" Can set the mood Immediate feedback	Timing may be inconvenient Requires spontaneous thinking May not be easy to terminate Power or status of one person may cause pressure
Meetings	Can use visuals Involves several minds at once Two-way flow	Time-consuming Time may be inconvenient One person may dominate the group
Memorandum	Brief Provides a record Can prethink the message Can disseminate widely	No control over receiver Less personal One-way flow Delayed feedback
Formal report	Complete; comprehensive Can organize material at writer's leisure Can disseminate widely	Less personal May require considerable time in reading Language may not be understandable Expensive One-way flow Delayed feedback
Teleconference	Saves time for travel Visual Lessens impact of power/ status Makes users be better prepared	Miss interpersonal contact Not good for initial brainstorming sessions Expensive

Source: P. V. Lewis, *Organizational Communication: The Essence of Effective Management,* 3rd ed. (New York: John Wiley & Sons, 1987), p. 9.

sender. Typically, when the receiver has decoded the message, **feedback,** or a response, is transmitted to the sender. The receiver acknowledges receipt of the message and either tells the sender that the message is understood or requests clarification. In the feedback stage of the process, the communication model actually reverses, with the receiver becoming the sender and vice versa. Feedback can be as simple as a nod of the head or as formal as a letter of receipt or the initialing of a memo that is returned to the sender.

Although this model represents communication as a simple and foolproof process, the effective flow of information from sender to receiver can break down at many points. The sender can have difficulty in encoding the message, making comprehension by the receiver difficult. For example, a supervisor might tell an employee, "I would really like you to try to make this deadline" when she really means that the deadline must be met, with no exceptions. On the other side, the receiver may inaccurately decode the message and interpret it in a way wholly different from what

feedback
an acknowledgement that a message has been received and understood

A channel is any vehicle of communication, such as the spoken word via telephone or the written word via fax machine.

the sender had in mind. For example, the employee might interpret the "deadline" statement to mean that the supervisor has now turned entire responsibility for the project over to him and will no longer be available to help meet the deadline. A poor choice of channel may also result in a breakdown of effective communication. For example, giving a co-worker lengthy and detailed instructions about a work task over the telephone rather than in writing may lead to inadequate performance of the job. Furthermore, the work environment may provide any number of distractions that can disrupt the communication process, such as competing conversations, loud machinery, or inconsistent or contradictory messages. Such distractions are collectively called **noise**. Noise may also refer to psychological factors such as biases, perceptual differences, or selective attention that make it difficult for persons to communicate with and understand one another. For example, psychological noise can occur when the receiver ignores the sender because of a belief that the sender "has nothing important to say."

noise
physical or psychological distractions that disrupt the effective flow of communication

RESEARCH ON THE COMMUNICATION PROCESS

Much of the research on the communication process in work settings has focused on factors that can increase or decrease its effectiveness. Among those that can affect the flow of communication from sender to receiver are source factors, channel factors, and audience factors.

source factors
characteristics of the sender that influence the effectiveness of a communication

Source factors. **Source factors** are characteristics of the sender—the source of the message—that can facilitate or detract from the effective flow of communication. One such factor is the status of the source, which can affect whether a message is attended to by potential receivers. Generally, the higher the organizational status of the sender, the more likely that the communication will be listened to and acted upon. For example, messages from the president or owner of a company are usually given top priority. ("When the boss talks, people listen.")

Another source factor is the credibility, or believability, of the sender. If the source is trusted, it is more likely that the message will receive attention. Variables such as the expertise, knowledge, and reliability of the source (i.e., has this person provided truthful information in the past?) contribute to the credibility of the sender (O'Reilly & Roberts, 1976). Employees learn which sources can be trusted and pay closest attention to their messages.

A final source factor is the encoding skills of the sender, or the source's ability to translate an abstract message into some sort of shared code, usually the written or spoken language, so that it can be clearly conveyed to the receiver. In short, these skills include the abilities to speak and write clearly and to select the appropriate channel for transmitting information. Generally, the better the encoding skills of the sender, the smoother and more effective the flow of communication.

Channel factors. **Channel factors,** which are positive or negative characteristics related to the vehicle through which the message is communicated, can also influence the effectiveness of the process. Selection of the proper channel can have an important effect on the accurate flow of communication. For example, using a visual such as a chart or graph to present complex information on sales and profit figures is likely to be a more effective channel than the spoken word. The channel selected can also affect the impact of the message. For example, a face-to-face reprimand from a supervisor might carry more weight than the same reprimand conveyed over the telephone. Whenever possible, using multiple channels to present complicated information will increase the likelihood that it will be attended to and retained.

channel factors
characteristics of the vehicle of transmission of a message that affect communication

Semantic problems are common channel factors that can lead to a breakdown in communication. The difficulties occur because different people may interpret the meanings of certain words differently. For example, if your work supervisor tells you that you are doing a "good" job, you may infer that your performance is well above average. However, if the supervisor defines "good" as work that is barely passable (but really he expects "excellent," "superior," or "outstanding" performance), you may be missing the meaning of the message. Semantic problems may arise through the use of technical language, or **jargon,** the special language that develops within a specific work environment. It typically is filled with abbreviated words, acronyms, special vocabularies, and slang. For example, industrial/organizational psychology could be abbreviated as "I/O Psych." and might be described as the field in which topics such as RJPs, BIBs, and validity generalization are studied. While jargon serves the

jargon
special languages developed in connection with certain jobs; also called technical language

Teleconferencing: Holding Business Meetings over Long Distances

The expansion of many businesses into multiregional or multinational corporations has led to increased costs for the transportation, lodging, and meals involved in holding meetings. An alternative is to use *teleconferencing*, which may take the form of audio conferencing and video conferencing (Barker, Wahlers, Watson, & Kibler, 1987). With audio conferencing, groups of participants may be seated around a multidirectional microphone, using the same telephone line to communicate with another group or individual, or a number of individuals may each be using their own telephone, with lines set up so that they can all hear and speak to one another. Audio conferencing has become a popular, inexpensive, and convenient alternative to face-to-face meetings. However, it has some drawbacks. Participants may have difficulties knowing when to speak and who is speaking. Also, because of the absence of visual, nonverbal cues, some information may be lost, leading to an incomplete and sometimes unsatisfying exchange of messages.

Video conferencing is a recent innovation that offers an improvement over audio conferences. In video conferencing, a two-way television communication system is set up through an arrangement of videocameras, microphones, and monitors. One group can then hear and see the distant participants. With recent advancements in telephone transmissions, there is virtually no delay between sending and receiving messages. Therefore, interaction can take place at a normal pace. Unfortunately, video conferencing also has its problems. Some participants may feel uneasy in front of a camera, which may inhibit their ability to express themselves fully. The interaction may also be more formal, lacking some of the spontaneity and closeness of face-to-face meetings. Furthermore, because of limited camera positioning and framing, some subtle nonverbal information may still be lost. On the positive side, it is easy to make copies of these meetings for future reference or to send to absent participants. Also, the "big production" atmosphere of a video conference may encourage participants to prepare more fully for these meetings, thus leading to a higher-quality interaction.

In spite of certain limitations, the use of teleconferencing (particularly video conferencing) will increase. Research and technological advancements most likely will focus on making it a more effective communication process by more closely modeling the richness of the interaction that occurs in face-to-face encounters.

purpose of speeding up communication between those who speak the language, it can create problems when the receiver is not "fluent" in its use.

The type of channel used to communicate can affect important work-related outcomes, such as job satisfaction. Muchinsky (1977) found that the frequency of face-to-face communication between supervisors and subordinates was positively related to the workers' job satisfaction, while the frequency of written communications was negatively correlated with satisfaction. The type of channel may also have some influence on work performance and efficiency. For example, a company policy of keeping written documentation of all orders and directives rather than simply relying on spoken orders may decrease the likelihood that workers will forget what they are supposed to be doing, which in turn may have positive effects on the productivity and efficiency of the work unit (see On the Cutting Edge).

Video conferencing offers instantaneous, face-to-face communication over long distances.

Audience factors. **Audience factors** are elements related to the receiver, such as the person's attention span and perceptual abilities, that can facilitate or impair the communication process. For example, it is important that training information be presented at a level that matches the audience's ability to perceive and process that information, or much of the communication may be lost. Moreover, it is critical to consider the attention span of the target audience. While all-day classroom training sessions might be appropriate for management trainees who are used to such long sessions, the attention of assembly-line workers might be lost after an hour's lecture because of their unfamiliarity with this format.

The receiver's relationship to the sender can also affect the communication process. For example, if the receiver is subordinate to the sender, the message may be better attended to since the receiver is supposed to listen to superiors. If, however, the situation is reversed, a message from a lower-ranking organizational member may not receive much attention from the higher-ranking employee.

Finally, the decoding skills of the receiver can influence the effectiveness of communication. Workers vary greatly in their ability to receive, decode, and understand organizational messages. While managers are often considered the source rather than the audience of much organizational communication, research has shown that effective managers have good decoding skills in listening and responding to the needs and concerns of their subordinates (Baron, 1986). In fact, because much communication in work settings involves spoken communication, oral decoding skills, often referred to as listening skills, are considered to be the most important of all (Hunt, 1980).

audience factors characteristics of the receiver that influence the effectiveness of a communication

In noisy work settings the best communication may be hand signals or other nonverbal cues.

NONVERBAL COMMUNICATION IN WORK SETTINGS

We commonly think of communication in work settings as taking one of two forms, either written or spoken. However, people can and do use a great deal of **nonverbal communication,** which is sent and received by means other than the written or spoken word. Broadly defined, nonverbal communication can occur through facial expressions, gesture, tone of voice, body movements, posture, and even style of dress, touching, and the physical distance between sender and receiver (Patterson, 1983). We use nonverbal communication to convey a wide range of feelings and attitudes.

nonverbal communication *messages sent and received through means other than the spoken or written word*

To understand the role of nonverbal communication in work settings, we can examine its use from both the sender's and the receiver's perspective. For the sender, nonverbal communication can be used in three ways. First, nonverbal cues can be substituted for verbal communication. Nodding to show approval, shaking your head in disagreement, or gesturing for a person to come closer or to go away are all ways of sending clear, unspoken messages. In particularly noisy work environments or when co-workers are positioned out of hearing range, workers may resort to a set of nonverbal signals instead of verbal communication. The hand signals used by ground crews to guide airline pilots or the gestures used by land surveyors are examples of this. Nonverbal cues can also be used to enhance verbal messages. We often use our tone of voice, facial expressions, and body movements to emphasize what we are saying. If you want to compliment a subordinate for doing an outstanding job, the words will have greater impact if they are accompanied by an enthusiastic tone of voice and an approving smile. A board member who pounds her fist on the table while voicing disagreement with a proposal is going to command greater attention by including this nonverbal emphasizer. Finally, nonverbal cues can be used to convey underlying feelings. In situations in which a person is restricted in what can be said verbally yet wants to get the true message across, the verbal message may be accompanied by a nonverbal "disclaimer" (see Mehrabian, 1981). For example, at a new employee orientation, the trainer may verbally praise the company but with her tone of voice convey that things are not really as good as they seem.

From the perspective of a receiver, nonverbal cues serve two important functions. First, they provide additional information. When verbal communication is limited or when the receiver has reason to mistrust the verbal message, the receiver will look to nonverbal cues as a source of more data. This is particularly likely when the receiver feels that the verbal message may be deceptive, although research has shown that people do not read the nonverbal cues of deception very accurately (DePaulo, Stone, & Lassiter, 1985; Kraut, 1980). Nonverbal cues are also used by receivers in person perception, that is, in making judgments about a person's attitudes, personality, and competence. There is evidence that styles of nonverbal behavior play an important part in person perception (Schneider, Hastorf, & Ellsworth, 1979). This is particularly important in personnel decisions such as hiring. For example, it has been found that persons exhibiting more expressive nonverbal behaviors, such as more smiling and greater eye contact, are more favorably evaluated in hiring interviews than are nonexpressive individuals (Forbes & Jackson, 1980; Imada & Hakel, 1977). However, the relationship between nonverbal cues and interviewing success may be more complex than just simply "more is better" (see Rasmussen, 1984). In other words, rather than looking just at the amount of expressiveness, interviewers or other judges of applicants may look for particular styles of expressive nonverbal behavior that indicate that the person is honest, ambitious, or easy to work with. Other nonverbal cues, such as style of dress, physical attractiveness, and indications of dominance, may likewise play an important role in how people are perceived in work settings (Henley, 1977). For example, it has been shown that attractively dressed and well-groomed individuals make better first impressions in certain work settings than persons who appear sloppy and unkempt (Arvey & Campion, 1982; Cann, Siegfried, & Pearce, 1981).

While nonverbal communication sometimes facilitates the flow of communication in work settings, misinterpreting such messages can also lead to considerable confusion and may disrupt work operations. While there are well-known rules and techniques for learning to use appropriate written and spoken language, there are no firm guidelines governing nonverbal communication. Often the misunderstandings that occur in organizational communication, verbal and nonverbal, are related to the in-

Lateral communication is necessary for co-workers at the same level to coordinate their actions.

adequate skills of the sender or receiver or both. While a great deal of attention is given to trying to improve the verbal and written skills of employees, less concern is focused on nonverbal communication, even though it represents a great deal of the critical communication that takes place in work settings.

THE FLOW OF COMMUNICATION IN WORK ORGANIZATIONS

Just as blood flows through the arteries, giving life to the body, messages flow through communication lines and networks, giving life to the work organization. If you look at the organizational chart of most organizations, you will see positions arranged in a pyramidlike hierarchy. While this hierarchy is most commonly thought of as representing the lines of status and authority within the organization, it also depicts the lines of communication between superiors and subordinates. Formal messages travel back and forth along these routes between the top levels and the lower levels of the organization.

DOWNWARD, UPWARD, AND LATERAL FLOW OF COMMUNICATION

The communication flow in work organizations is usually classified into three types: It can flow downward, through the organizational hierarchy; upward, through the same chain of command; or can flow laterally, from colleague to colleague. Typically, each type of communication flow takes different forms and tends to contain different kinds of messages.

Downward communication consists of those messages sent from superiors to subordinates. Most commonly, they are one of several types: (1) instructions or directions concerning job performance, (2) information about organizational procedures and policies, (3) feedback to the subordinate concerning job performance, or (4) information to assist in the coordination of work tasks (Katz & Kahn, 1966). As you might guess, much of the formal communication that goes on in work organizations involves this downward flow, which makes sense, since the top levels are involved in making important decisions that must be sent to the lower levels.

While much formal communication in organizations is downward, research indicates that most organizations still do not have enough of this communication. A number of studies have found that workers would like more information from their superiors about work procedures and about what is happening elsewhere in the organization. One reason that downward communication is insufficient in some organizations is that superiors may overestimate the amount of information that their subordinates possess and may underestimate the amount they desire (Likert, 1961).

downward communication messages flowing downward in an organizational hierarchy, usually from superiors to subordinates

It also appears that certain types of downward communication may be particularly limited, such as feedback concerning work performance (Baird, 1977). This is especially true in companies that fail to conduct regular performance appraisals. Also, organizations that neglect to provide workers with job descriptions and adequate orientation and training may experience a shortage of downward communication of proper work procedures and company policies.

Upward communication is the flow of messages from the lower levels of the organization to the upper levels. It most typically consists of information managers need to perform their jobs, such as feedback concerning the status of lower-level operations, which could include reports of production output or information about any problems. The upward communication of feedback is critical for managers who must use this information to make important work-related decisions. Upward communication can also involve complaints and suggestions for improvement from lower-level workers, and is significant because it gives subordinates some input into the functioning of the organization.

*upward communication
messages flowing upward in an organizational hierarchy, usually taking the form of feedback*

Unfortunately, in many organizations there is simply not enough upward communication (see Applying I/O Psychology). The upward communication of feedback about problems or difficulties in operations may be restricted, because lower-level workers fear that the negative information might reflect poorly on their abilities, because managers neglect to ask for it, or because subordinates believe that management will not really listen to their suggestions and concerns.

Lateral communication flows between people who are at the same level in the organizational hierarchy and is particularly important when co-workers must coordinate their activities to accomplish a goal. Lateral communication also occurs between two or more departments within an organization. For example, effective lateral communication between the production and quality control departments in a television manufacturer can help the two to coordinate efforts to find and correct assembly errors. Lateral communication between departments also allows the sharing of news and information, and helps in the development and maintenance of interpersonal relationships on the job (Koehler, Anatol, & Applbaum, 1981). While it can help in coordinating worker activities within or between departments, thereby leading to increased productivity, "unauthorized" lateral communication, such as too much socializing on the job, can detract from effective job performance (Katz & Kahn, 1966).

*lateral communication
messages between two parties at the same level in an organizational hierarchy*

BARRIERS TO THE EFFECTIVE FLOW OF COMMUNICATION

The upward, downward, and lateral flow of communication within an organization are subject to various types of information distortion that disrupt communication effectiveness by eliminating or changing key aspects of the message, so that the message that should be sent is not the

Increasing the Upward Flow of Organizational Communication

Most communication problems in work organizations relate to insufficient flow of information that results from a shortage either in downward communication or upward communication. However, since downward communication predominates in most work settings and since it originates from those who have the most power and control over the organizational environment, attention must be given to increasing the flow of communication from those individuals at the bottom of the organization to those at the top, for a shortage of this communication has been associated with employee dissatisfaction and feelings that management is out of touch with employee needs and concerns. Several strategies that can increase upward communication follow.

Employee Suggestion Systems

There are a variety of procedures by which workers can submit ideas for improving some aspect of company operations. The suggestions are then reviewed by company decisionmakers, and beneficial ideas are implemented. Usually, suggestions are encouraged by some sort of incentive, such as rec-

ognition awards or cash prizes that are either fixed amounts or money based on a percentage of the savings that the suggestion produces. This form of upward communication can lead to innovations and improvement in company operations and can increase feelings that lower-level employees can indeed have some influence in the organization. One potential problem with suggestion systems is that employees may use it to voice complaints about conditions that management is unable to change.

Grievance Systems

A related concept is the establishment of formal complaint or grievance procedures. While suggestion systems focus on positive changes, grievances are designed to change existing negative situations and thus must be handled more delicately to protect the employee from the retribution that can result when the complaint concerns mistreatment by someone higher in the organizational hierarchy. Also, to keep communication open and flowing, company officials must acknowledge the receipt of grievances and make it clear what action is to be taken (or why action will not or cannot be taken).

---

filtering
the selective presentation of the content of a communication

one that the recipient receives. Three types of distortion that often occur in work organizations are filtering, censoring, and exaggeration (Gaines, 1980).

Filtering is the selective presentation of the content of a communication; in other words, certain pieces of information are left out of the message. In downward communication, information is often filtered because it is considered to be unimportant to lower-level employees. Often, messages are sent telling workers *what* to do but not telling *why* it is being done. Information from upper levels of the organization may also be filtered because management fears the impact of the complete message on workers. For example, management may send a memo to workers about proposed cost-cutting measures, telling them that these actions are needed to increase efficiency and productivity. However, the fact that these cost-cutting measures are needed for the company to stay financially solvent is filtered out, because management is afraid that this information might cause workers to anticipate layoffs and begin to look

Open-Door Policies

The bottom-to-top flow of organizational communication can also be stimulated if upper-level managers establish an open-door policy by setting aside times when employees can go directly to managers and discuss whatever is on their minds. This procedure by-passes the intermediate steps in the upward organizational chain, ensuring that important messages do indeed get to the top intact. The obvious drawback to the open-door policy is that a lot of the manager's time may be taken up dealing with trivial or unimportant employee concerns.

Employee Surveys

Conducting an employee survey is an efficient and quick way to measure employees' attitudes about any aspect of organizational operations in an effort to target particular problem areas or solicit suggestions for improvement. (We have discussed employee job satisfaction surveys in Chapter 7.) Because surveys offer the added benefit of anonymity, workers can respond honestly without fear of reprisal from management. As in all methods, feedback from management, either in the form of action taken or justification for not taking action, is critical for the program to operate effectively. Many times companies will conduct an employee survey, look at the results, and do nothing. If feedback is not given, respondents will begin to see the survey as a waste of time, and future efforts will not be taken seriously.

Participative Decisionmaking

A number of strategies based on democratic or participative styles of management facilitate the upward flow of communication by involving employees in the process of making important decisions (Harrison, 1985). In participative decisionmaking, employees can submit possible plans and discuss their benefits and drawbacks. They are then allowed to vote on the courses of action the company or work group will take. This strategy covers a wide range of programs and techniques that we will be studying in later chapters. However, any management technique that solicits employee input serves to increase the upward flow of communication.

for jobs elsewhere. Filtering of content in upward communication can occur if the information is unfavorable and if the communicator fears incurring the wrath of the superior. In such cases, the negative information might be altered to make it appear less negative. Filtering in lateral communication can occur when two employees feel that they are in competition with one another for important organizational rewards, such as promotions and recognition from superiors. In such cases, workers continue to communicate but may filter out any important information that is believed may give the other person a competitive edge.

Censoring is the purposeful omission of information presented to another. Whereas in filtering some aspects of the message are omitted, in censoring a choice is made not to send a message. Censoring can occur when a sender believes that the receiver does not need the information because it is unimportant or would be disruptive to the receiver. Davis (1968) examined the censoring of downward communications in a large manufacturing company. In this study, top management presented

censoring
the intentional omission of information from a message or a decision to not transmit particular information

Why Are Communication Breakdowns So Common in Organizations?

In many ways, the success of an organization depends on the efficient and effective flow of communication among its members. Even in very efficient and productive organizations, however, miscommunication seems to occur almost daily. Why are such breakdowns so common?

One answer is that many informal rules (or norms) in organizations appear to work against open and honest communication. Organizational members learn that it is important to engage in impression management, that is, to present oneself in a favorable light to get ahead in the company. It is not considered wise to admit to personal faults or limitations. Likewise, it is believed important to project an air of self-confidence and competence. This may lead to a worker trying to tackle a very difficult task or problem alone, rather than asking for assistance. As we saw in studying hiring interviews, job applicants are particularly concerned with impression management. The resulting restricted communication may lead to a total mismatch between a worker's skills and abilities and the job requirements.

In competitive organizational settings, an air of mistrust of others may arise. As a result verbal messages may not be believed: "What was he *really* saying to me?" Mistrust is often present in organizations that have a history of not dealing honestly and openly with employees. This lack of trust may lead to limited communication, which is a serious problem for organizations whose lifeblood is the open flow of messages.

Another reason for communication breakdowns is employees' feelings of defensiveness, which often develop when their performance is criticized or questioned. Defensive postures by one participant are often followed by a defensive stance in another (Gibb, 1961). For example, when a work group has failed at some task, one group member might act defensively—"It wasn't my fault"—which then causes others to act in the same way. When employees become overly defensive a communication breakdown can result. This defensiveness can also stifle employee creativity as workers become afraid to take chances or to try new things for fear of being criticized.

Organizational communication breakdowns can also be caused by the tendency for people to undercommunicate. Workers generally assume that everyone in the work setting has access to the same information and possesses the same knowledge. Therefore, to avoid redundancy, a communicator may neglect to convey some important information to co-workers, assuming that they already know it. In reality, the others may not have the information or may have forgotten it and need to be reminded. Supervisors and managers are particularly prone to undercommunication, believing that subordinates do not need to be (or should not be) given certain information. This lack of communication flow can seriously disrupt productivity and cause dissatisfaction among workers who feel as if they are left in the dark.

middle-level managers with two messages that were to be sent downward. The first message was important and concerned tentative plans for laying off workers. The second message was relatively unimportant, dealing with some changes in the parking situation. The results indicated that the middle managers censored to whom the information was presented. The important layoff information was passed on to 94 percent of the foremen, who in turn presented it to only 70 percent of the assistant foremen. The censoring of the unimportant message about the parking changes was even greater, with only 15 percent of the assistant foremen eventually getting the message. In this case, censoring took place primarily when the message was believed to be irrelevant to lower-level workers.

Drawing by Ziegler; © 1982 The New Yorker Magazine, Inc.
Spoken messages are especially prone to distortion.

Exaggeration is the distortion of information by elaborating or overestimating certain aspects of the message. To draw attention to a problem, people may exaggerate its magnitude and impact. In downward communication, a supervisor might emphasize that if performance does not improve, subordinates may lose their jobs. In upward communication, workers might present a problem as a crisis to get management to react and make some quick decisions. On the other hand, exaggeration may occur by minimizing the issue, making it seem like less of a problem than it actually is. This can happen, for example, when a worker wants to give the impression of competence and say that everything is under control (see Up Close).

Certain factors increase or decrease the likelihood that distortion will take place in organizational communication. For example, spoken messages are more prone to distortion than are written messages. Regardless of form, a downward-flowing message from a high-status source is less likely to be intentionally altered than a communication originating from a low-status member. O'Reilly (1978) has studied several factors related to communication distortion and specifically found a tendency for the greater distortion of upward messages that are unfavorable in content and less distortion of upward-flowing positive information. He also discovered that low trust in the receiver of a message resulted in a tendency toward distortion, particularly if the information reflected unfavorably on the sender.

exaggeration
the distortion of information by elaborating, overestimating, or minimizing parts of the message

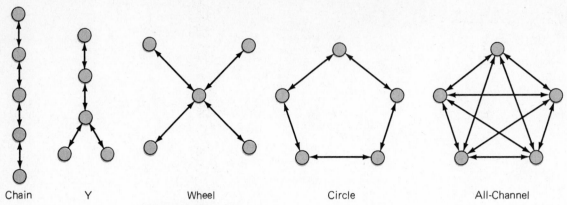

Chain   Y   Wheel   Circle   All-Channel

Figure 8.2
COMMUNICATION NETWORKS

COMMUNICATION NETWORKS

In our discussion of the communication model and the downward, upward, and lateral flow of communication we have been focusing on communication between two individuals, such as superior-to-subordinate or colleague-to-colleague. When we look beyond two-person communication to the linkages among work group, departmental, or organizational members, we are concerned with **communication networks,** which are systems of communication lines linking various senders and receivers.

The flow of organizational communication is regulated by several factors: the proximity of workers to one another, the rules governing who communicates with whom, the status hierarchy, and other elements of the work situation, such as job assignments and duties. Thus communication usually follows predictable patterns, or networks. Considerable research has been conducted on these networks and the properties associated with each. Five major types of communication networks have been studied in depth (Shaw, 1978; see Figure 8.2). The first three are termed **centralized networks** because the flow of information is centralized, or directed, through specific members. The next two are called **decentralized networks** because the communication flow can originate at any point and does not have to be directed through certain central group members. Centralized networks are governed by members' status within the organization; decentralized networks typically are not. Often decentralized networks are controlled by factors such as proximity of members to one another or the personal preferences of the sender.

Centralized networks. The first centralized communication network, which is known as the chain, represents a five-member status hierarchy. A message originates at the top or the bottom of the chain and works its way upward or downward through the different links. An example might

communication networks *systematic lines of communication among various senders and receivers*

centralized networks *networks in which the flow of communication is directed through specific members*

decentralized networks *communication networks in which messages can originate at any point and need not be directed through specific group members*

be a message concerning some changes in the formula for payroll deductions. The director of human resources is the source of the message, which is passed to the payroll manager, who in turn gives the instructions to the assistant payroll manager, who then tells the payroll supervisor. Finally, the payroll supervisor passes the message along to the clerk who will implement the changes. A message that is to go from the clerk to the human resources director must follow the same pattern. As you might guess, the chain is a relatively slow process, but it is direct, with all levels of the hierarchy aware of the message since it must pass through each link.

A related communication network is the Y (which is actually an upside-down Y). The Y is also a hierarchical network, representing four levels of status within the organization, but its last link involves communication to more than one person. The inverted Y is a model of the communication network within a traditional, pyramid-shaped organization: The president issues an order to the chief of operations, who then tells the work supervisor. The work supervisor then gathers the bottom-line workers and gives them the order. In the other direction, the front-line supervisor is responsible for gathering information from bottom-line workers that must be sent upward. The chain and the Y networks are very similar in terms of speed of transmission and the formality of who communicates to whom.

The wheel network involves two status levels: a higher-status member (usually a work supervisor) and four lower-level members. The higher-status member is the hub, or center, through which all communication must pass. In the wheel network there are no direct communication links between the lower-level members. An example might be a sales manager and his four salespersons out in the field, each of whom receives instructions directly from the manager and then sends information about sales activities back to the manager. However, the salespersons do not have any contact with one another unless it is relayed through the supervisor.

Decentralized networks. The circle network, the first of the two decentralized networks, represents communication between members who are immediately accessible to each other, such as workers positioned side by side on an assembly line. Because any member can initiate a communication and no rules govern the direction in which it is sent, it can be difficult to trace the original source of the message in a circle network. Also, since the message can travel in two directions, the circle network has a fairly quick rate of transmission.

The all-channel, or comcon, network allows complete freedom among communication links. Any member can freely communicate with any other, and all members are accessible to each other. In all-channel networks, communication can be rapid, and there is maximum opportunity for feedback. Boards of directors, problem-solving task forces, and employees working as a team are examples of these networks.

A sales manager and two of her salespeople form part of a communication network at Avon.

For creative and complex tasks a decentralized communication network often works better than a centralized one.

There has been extensive research on communication networks, most conducted in laboratory settings. The results indicate that they all have different strengths and weaknesses. For example, the centralized networks (the chain, Y, and wheel) are faster and make fewer errors in dealing with simple, repetitive tasks than do decentralized networks. This makes sense because the central person through whom all messages must pass can coordinate group activities because that individual has all of the information needed to perform the simple tasks. Decentralized networks (circle and all-channel), on the other hand, are better at dealing with complex tasks, such as abstract problem solving (Leavitt, 1951; Shaw, 1964). In general, straightforward, repetitive tasks, such as assembly or manufacturing work, tend to operate well with a centralized communication network, while creative tasks, such as a group working on a product advertising campaign, run best using a decentralized network. One reason that centralized networks may have difficulty in solving complex problems is that the central people may be subject to information overload: They have too much information to deal with efficiently. Because all of the messages cannot be passed on intact to the various network members efficiently and quickly, group performance suffers.

The type of communication network can also affect the satisfaction of network members. Generally, because of the restrictions on who can initiate communication and on who can communicate with whom, members in centralized networks have lower levels of satisfaction than those in decentralized networks (Shaw, 1964). More specifically, in the centralized networks, the persons holding the central positions tend to have high levels of satisfaction due to their role, whereas the noncentral members have extremely low satisfaction (Bavelas, 1950).

Some of the research on communication networks has been criticized for oversimplifying the communication process. Evidence suggests that the differences in the speed and efficiency among the various networks may disappear over time, as the groups learn to adjust to the required communication patterns (Burgess, 1968). For example, members of decentralized networks may learn to cut down on the amount of member discussion to speed up the decisionmaking process. Because most of the research on communication networks has been conducted in controlled, laboratory settings, there is some concern about whether the results of these studies will generalize to communication networks in actual work settings, although the findings do indeed allow us to model (although simplistically) the communication patterns in work organizations.

FORMAL AND INFORMAL LINES OF COMMUNICATION: THE HIERARCHY VERSUS THE GRAPEVINE

So far we have been discussing the *formal* lines of communication, or how organizational members are supposed to communicate with one another. We have also seen that the official lines of communication are illustrated in the company's organizational chart, or **organigram,** which is a diagram of the hierarchy. When official messages must be sent up or down the hierarchy, they typically follow the lines shown in the organigram. The formal lines of communication are usually governed by the organizational status or authority of the different members. However, while every organization possesses formal lines of communication each also has informal communication lines known as the **grapevine.** Just as a real grapevine twists and turns, branching out wherever it pleases, the organizational grapevine can follow any course through a network of organizational members. Throughout the workday, messages are passed from one worker to another along the grapevine. Because much of the daily communication that occurs in work organizations is informal, the organizational grapevine is an important element for I/O psychologists to study.

While the formal communication lines are represented by the organigram, the informal lines of communication among work group or organizational members are illustrated by the **sociogram.** In effect, the sociogram is a diagram of the organizational grapevine. Sociograms are used to study the informal contacts and communications occurring among organizational members (see Figure 8.3).

Baird (1977) suggests that three factors determine the pattern of communication links that form the grapevine: friendship, usage, and efficiency. In the informal communication network people pass information on to their friends, which is only natural. We communicate with those we like and avoid communicating informally with those we do not like. Friendship is thus perhaps the most important factor that holds the grapevine together. In addition, persons who are used as communication links for other purposes will also be used as links in the grapevine. For example, workers who often come into contact with one another for job-related reasons are more likely to start sharing information informally. Finally, the grapevine sometimes develops because it is easier and more efficient for workers to follow their own rather than the formal lines of communication. An organizational member who needs to communicate something immediately may try to get the message through via the grapevine rather than by using the slow and cumbersome formal communication lines. For example, a low-ranking organizational member who wants to get a message to somebody high up in the organizational hierarchy may find it quicker and more efficient to rely on the grapevine to transmit the message rather than going through the formal organizational channels that involve relaying the message through a successive chain of higher-status managers.

In addition to being a substitute network for formal lines of communication, the grapevine also serves a vital function in maintaining social relationships among workers. Because most formal communication tends to be task-oriented, focusing on jobs and job outcomes, the grapevine helps to provide the social communication needs of workers (which Mayo

organigram
a diagram of an organization's hierarchy representing the formal lines of communication

grapevine
the informal communication network in an organization

sociogram
a diagram of the informal lines of communication among organizational members

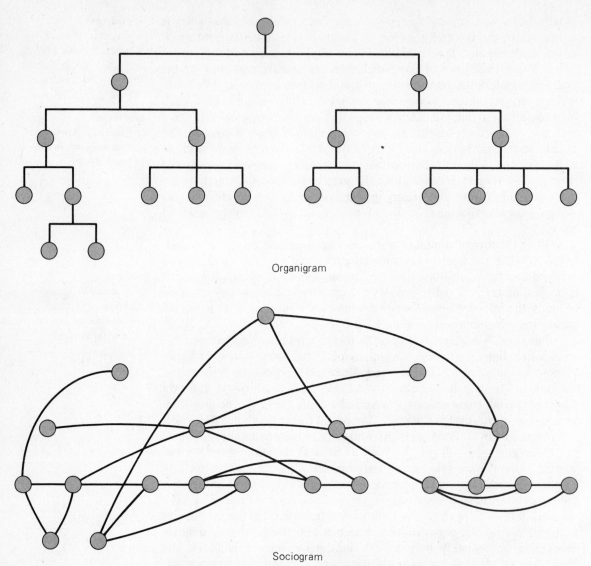

Organigram

Sociogram

Figure 8.3
THE ORGANIGRAM VERSUS THE SOCIOGRAM

and his associates in the human relations movement long ago determined were so important to workers). Through informal communication contacts and the subsequent development of strong work friendships, the grapevine can help to bring workers together and encourage them to develop a sense of unity and commitment to the work group and the organization, which can play a big part in reducing absenteeism and turnover rates (Baird, 1977). The grapevine can also help in reiterating important messages sent through formal communication channels. For example, an employee might be reminded through the grapevine of important deadlines or company policies that were originally announced in memos or bulletins. While the grapevine serves many important functions for the smooth operation of the organization, it can also be perceived as having a somewhat negative function: the transmission of rumors.

Rumors are information that is presented as fact but may actually be either true or false (Davis, 1972). Rumors are based on such things as employee speculations and wishful thinking. Many managers are concerned about the grapevine and attempt to stifle it because they believe that it is the source of false rumors that may be damaging to the company and the work force. However, research indicates that this is a myth. The transmission of false rumors via the grapevine is actually relatively rare, and estimates indicate that the grapevine is accurate over 80 percent of the time (Baird, 1977). In comparison, remember that the messages sent through the formal communication lines may not always be 100 percent accurate.

rumors
information that is presented as fact but may actually be true or false

A false rumor usually results when organizational members lack information about a topic that concerns them. Thus when there is a shortage of information transmitted through the formal channels, rumors may be generated by the informal network (Schachter & Burdick, 1955). The best way for a manager to deal with rumor transmission is to be honest and open, providing sufficient information to employees through the formal lines of communication. Also, rather than trying to uproot the grapevine, the effective manager will be aware of it and its importance to the workers, and may even want to be "tapped into" it as another source of information. When false rumors do occur, the best strategy for combatting them may be to provide accurate information through formal channels of communication *and* through the grapevine, if management is tapped into it (Hersey, 1966; Zaremba, 1988).

ORGANIZATIONAL COMMUNICATION AND WORK OUTCOMES

The effective flow of communication is crucial to an organization's ability to operate smoothly and productively. While I/O psychologists and organizations themselves believe this to be true, very little research has directly examined the impact of communication on organizational performance (Porter & Roberts, 1976). One comprehensive study looked at the relationships among reported organizational communication effectiveness and five independent measures of organizational performance, including the number of clients served, the costs of operation, and the costs of operation per client served, in twelve district offices of a state social services agency (Snyder & Morris, 1984). Questionnaires administered to over five hundred employees assessed perceptions of different types of organizational communication, which included two forms of downward communication—the adequacy of information provided concerning organizational policies and procedures and the skills of supervisors as communicators; a form of lateral communication—the information exchange within the work group; and one type of downward communication—the feedback given about individual performance. The results indicated that the amount of communication, particularly the lateral communication within work groups, and the communication skills of supervisors were related to more cost-effective organizational performance.

While effective communication can lead to bottom-line payoffs in terms of increased productivity, it can also create increased levels of employee satisfaction. Research suggests positive relationships between the amount of upward communication in an organization and feelings of satisfaction in lower-level workers (Koehler et al., 1981). It has also been demonstrated that employees who receive a great deal of information about the organization in the form of downward communication tend to be more satisfied than those who do not. In fact, even employees who were overloaded with so much downward communication that their job performance was hampered tended to be satisfied with more downward communication (O'Reilly, 1980). Moreover, serving as a communication source is also linked to increased levels of satisfaction (Muchinsky, 1977b).

In addition to job performance and job satisfaction, effective communication may also have an impact on absenteeism and turnover rates. While research has not directly addressed the relationship, there may be some theoretical links between certain elements of organizational communication and absenteeism. For example, if workers are more satisfied with their jobs because they communicate well with their co-workers and supervisors, they would logically be less likely to be voluntarily absent from work than workers who are not satisfied with organizational communication. A similar relationship might likewise be expected between the amount of communication and turnover rates. Workers who are satisfied with organizational communication might be more likely to remain with the company than employees who feel that there is not enough communication.

However, there may be some exceptions to these general rules. For example, researchers recently examined the patterns of turnover among workers in three fast food restaurants and found that workers tended to quit their jobs in clusters. Most importantly, the clusters tended to be among workers who communicated freely with one another, a phenomenon that has been termed the "snowball effect" (Krackhardt & Porter, 1986).

All in all, with organizational communication more is usually better, although there may be a few exceptions, as when workers engage in so much nonwork-related communication or are so deluged with messages and other information that job performance is impaired. Although much evidence indicates that it is usually better to keep communication flowing, open, and honest, some researchers claim that, because of organizational politics, at times organizational members might want to close some communication lines and keep certain types of information to themselves (see, for example, Eisenberg & Witten, 1987).

In summary, it appears that many organizations can benefit from greater amounts of communication and that companies can work to make organizational communication more accurate and effective. Top-level managers need to be aware of employees' needs for information and must open the flow of downward communication to provide for these needs. On the other hand, there needs to be greater upward flow of communication in order to make management aware of what is going on at the lower levels of the company and to increase employee participation in and commitment to the organization. It also appears that increased lateral communication plays an important role in work groups' abilities to get the job done, and in the development and maintenance of interpersonal relationships on the job. All of this can lead to more positive outcomes for the individuals, work groups, and organizations involved.

SUMMARY

Communication is crucial for effective organizational performance. The basic communication model begins with the *sender,* who is responsible for *encoding* the message, choosing some mutually understood code for transmitting the message to another. The sender also selects a vehicle for communication, or the *channel.* The task of the *receiver* is to decode the message in an effort to understand its original meaning. The receiver also sends *feedback* to indicate that the message was received and understood. Any factors that disrupt the effective flow of communication from sender to receiver are referred to as *noise.*

Research on the communication process has examined the factors that can influence communication effectiveness. *Source factors* are variables related to the sender, such as status, credibility, and communication skills, that can influence communication. *Channel factors* are variables related to the actual communication vehicle that can enhance or detract from the flow of communication from sender to receiver. In verbal communication semantic problems, or the use of technical language termed *jargon,* can sometimes disrupt the communication flow. *Audience factors,* such as the decoding skills and attention span of the receiver, can also play a role in the communication process.

Nonverbal communication has a subtle but important effect on communication in work settings. It can be used as a substitute for verbal communication, to enhance verbal messages, or to send true feelings. Receivers may also use nonverbal cues as an additional information source or as a means of forming impressions about people.

Communication can flow in three directions through the organizational hierarchy: upward, downward, or laterally. *Downward communication* typically involves messages sent from superiors to subordinates; *upward communication* flows from the lower levels of the organization; and *lateral communication* occurs between persons at the same status level. *Filtering, censoring,* and *exaggeration* are three types of distortion that often disrupt the effective flow of organizational communication.

Much of our knowledge of organizational communication patterns comes from research conducted on *communication networks,* which can be grouped into two types: *centralized,* in which messages move through central members, and *decentralized,* in which communication paths are not directed through specific network members. The formal communication patterns in organizations are represented in the organizational chart, or *organigram.* The informal lines of communication, or *grapevine,* are illustrated in a *sociogram.* The formal lines of communication carry messages that are sanctioned by the organization, whereas the grapevine is an informal network through which messages are passed from worker to worker. Managers are sometimes wary of the grapevine because they see it as a source of *rumors,* although research indicates that the grapevine can be a highly accurate and important information network.

Research suggests that greater and more effective organizational communication is linked to improved levels of performance and job satisfaction. Moreover, there may be links between open, flowing organizational communication and rates of employee absenteeism and turnover.

STUDY QUESTIONS AND EXERCISES

1. What are the steps in the basic communication model? Which factors influence the effective flow of communication at each of the steps?

2. In what ways can nonverbal communication affect the interaction between a supervisor and a subordinate? between two same-status co-workers?

3. Think of an organization with which you have had some contact, such as a work organization, a club or social group, or your college or university. What forms of downward, upward, and lateral communication take place in this organization? How could the flow of each direction of communication be improved?

4. Consider the five types of communication networks. What are the characteristics of each? Can you think of any special work groups that illustrate each network?

5. In what ways will the sources, channels, and audiences of the formal lines of communication and the informal lines of communication (grapevine) in an organization differ?

SUGGESTED READINGS

Hunt, G. T. (1980). *Communication skills in the organization.* Englewood Cliffs, NJ: Prentice-Hall. *A discussion of the importance of communication skills in work settings that contains a great deal of practitioner-oriented material on how to develop communication skill training programs and the like.*

Lewis, P. V. (1987). *Organizational communication: The essence of effective management* (3rd ed.). New York: John Wiley & Sons. *A comprehensive textbook on organizational communication. Contains numerous case studies, exercises, and examples related to work communication.*

Management Communication Quarterly. Sage Publications. *A new journal that contains articles on the theory and practice of management communication. Recent topics include compliance-gaining strategies in upward communication, communication during conflict situations, and measuring communication styles.*

9

GROUP PROCESSES IN
WORK ORGANIZATIONS

Group Processes: The Core of Organizational Psychology

This chapter introduces many of the central concepts in the area of psychology known as group dynamics. A knowledge of group dynamics, or the processes by which groups function, is central to understanding how work organizations operate, since they are made up of smaller work groups. This chapter builds on Chapter 8's discussion of work place communication, for it is communication that holds people together in work groups. This chapter also sets the stage for the next three chapters on organizational processes. In particular Chapter 10, on leadership, studies a very important ongoing process in work groups: the relationship between the leader and the other members of the group. Chapter 11, which examines influence, power, and politics, continues the discussion of group processes presented in this chapter by considering how these three social processes operate in work groups and larger work organizations. Chapter 12 moves to the next level—the design and structure of work organizations—to explore how work groups link up to form larger organizations.

You may already be familiar with some of the concepts presented in this chapter. For example, conformity, roles, norms, and conflict are central not only in industrial/organizational psychology but in other specialty areas of psychology and in other behavioral sciences. Here, however, we will be applying these concepts specifically to the study of behavior in work settings. Other topics, such as organizational socialization and interorganizational conflict, are more particular to I/O psychology. This chapter represents a blending of some older, traditional concepts with some newer ones.

Many of the issues involved in describing group processes are particularly complex. Specifically, the concept of groupthink, with its many interrelated symptoms, merits attention. The different levels of conflict described in this chapter also have similar-sounding names that can be confusing. An inside tip is to remember that the prefix intra- *means "within," while the prefix* inter- *means "between" or "among." Therefore,* intragroup *means within a group, whereas* intergroup *means between groups. Another potential difficulty involves distinguishing between the concept of competition as a motivating process in work groups and the strategy of competition as a means of resolving conflict. At first glance, using the same term to describe two different processes can be confusing, but special attention to these terms should help clarify the situation.*

Work organizations are made up of individuals, and these individuals are tied together by their membership in particular work groups. A work group might be a department, a job classification, a work team, or an informal group of co-workers who socialize during lunch and after work. Groups are very important to the functioning of work organizations, for the members of a group can pool their talents, energy, and knowledge to perform complex tasks. Work groups also help provide professional identities for members and satisfy human needs for social interaction and the development of interpersonal relationships on the job. Finally, groups help establish rules for proper behavior in the work setting and play a part in determining the courses of action that the work group and the organization will follow.

In this chapter, we will study work groups and their processes. We will begin by defining groups, examining the different roles within groups, and considering what holds groups together. Next we will study the processes of cooperation, competition, and conflict, which are regular parts of work group functioning. Finally, we will look at how work groups affect organizational decisionmaking and how group decisionmaking affects organizational outcomes.

DEFINING WORK GROUPS

group
two or more individuals engaged in social interaction to achieve some goal

A **group** can be defined as two or more individuals, engaged in social interaction, for the purposes of achieving some goal, which in work settings is usually work related, such as producing a product or service. However, groups at work may form merely to develop and maintain social relationships. Work groups can be either formal—put together by the organization to perform certain tasks and handle specific responsibilities—or informal, developing naturally. Informal work groups might include groups of workers who lunch together, socialize on weekends, or play on a company-sponsored athletic team.

ROLES

roles
patterns of behavior that are adopted based on expectations about the functions of a position

role expectations
beliefs concerning the responsibilities and requirements of a particular role

Within work groups, members can play various **roles,** or patterns of behavior that are adopted on the basis of expectations about the functions of a particular position. Group roles are important because they help provide some specific plan for behavior. When a worker is playing a particular role within a group, that person usually knows something about the responsibilities and requirements of the role, or the **role expectations.** In most work groups, members are quite aware of the various expectations associated with each of the different positions within the group.

As a work group develops, the various members learn to become responsible for different aspects of its functioning. In other words, mem-

As a civilian analyst, the woman plays a clearly defined role in this military group, identifying tactical problems and possible solutions.

bers begin to play different roles within the work group. This process whereby group members learn about and take on various defined roles is called **role differentiation.** For example, a new worker who enters a work group may immediately fall into the role of novice worker. However, the person may later develop a reputation for having a good sense of humor and thus begin to play the role of jokester, providing levity when situations get too tense or when boredom sets in.

role differentiation the process by which group members perform various roles

One important role that is clearly differentiated in most work groups is that of leader. The leader in a formal work group or department plays an important part in directing group activities, being spokesperson for the group, and in deciding which courses of action the group will follow. Because of its significance, we will consider the topic of leadership in great depth in Chapter 10.

The various roles in work groups are often created based on factors such as position or formal job title, status within the group, or the possession of some particular work skill or ability. For example, employees who are designated as assistant supervisor, senior mechanic, or communications specialist perform specific roles and engage in certain behavior consistent with these job titles. While workers can be designated as playing certain usual roles within the work group, they can perform different functional roles at different times. Two early researchers outlined a wide range of work roles, which they grouped into three categories (Benne &

Table 9.1   THE VARIOUS ROLES INDIVIDUALS PLAY IN WORK GROUPS

Group Task Roles

Initiator-contributor: recommends new ideas about, or novel solutions to, a problem

Information seeker: emphasizes getting facts and other information from others

Opinion seeker: solicits inputs concerning the attitudes or feelings about ideas under consideration

Information giver: contributes relevant information to help in decisionmaking

Opinion giver: provides own opinions and feelings

Elaborator: clarifies and expands on the points made by others

Coordinator: integrates information from the group

Orientor: guides the discussion and keeps it on the topic when the group digresses

Evaluator-critic: uses some set of standards to evaluate the group's accomplishments

Energizer: stimulates the group to take action

Procedural technician: handles routine tasks such as providing materials or supplies

Recorder: keeps track of the group's activities and takes minutes

Group Building and Maintenance Roles

Encourager: encourages others' contributions

Harmonizer: tries to resolve conflicts between group members

Compromiser: tries to provide conflicting members with a mutually agreeable solution

Gatekeeper: regulates the flow of communication so that all members can have a say

Standard setter: sets standards or deadlines for group actions

Group observer: makes objective observations about the tone of the group interaction

Follower: accepts the ideas of others and goes along with group majority

Self-Centered Roles

Aggressor: tries to promote own status within group by attacking others

Blocker: tries to block all group actions and refuses to go along with group

Recognition seeker: tries to play up own achievements to get group's attention

Self-confessor: uses group discussion to deal with personal issues

Playboy: engages in humor and irrelevant acts to draw attention away from the tasks

Dominator: attempts to monopolize the group

Help seeker: attempts to gain sympathy by expressing insecurity or inadequacy

Special interest pleader: argues incessantly to further own desires

Source: K. D. Benne and P. Sheats, "Functional Roles of Group Members," *Journal of Social Issues, 4* (1948), pp. 41–49.

Sheats, 1948; see Table 9.1). The first category, group task roles, is related to getting the job done. Group task roles are given such titles as information giver, procedural technician, and evaluator-critic. For example, a machinist in a cardboard container factory who outlines the steps necessary for the work group to construct and assemble a new type of box is playing the procedural technician role. The second category of functional roles is group building and maintenance roles. These deal with the maintenance of interpersonal relations among group members and include such roles as encourager, harmonizer, and compromiser. A worker who plays an active part in settling an argument between two co-workers may be taking on the harmonizer role. The third category, called self-centered roles, involves satisfying personal rather than group goals. Titles of these roles include recognition seeker, aggressor, and help seeker. Employees who look to others for assistance in completing their own work assignments are playing the help-seeker role. The fact that there are so many different roles that members can play in work group functioning illustrates the complexity of the processes that occur daily in work groups.

In organizations, persons often are expected to play more than one role at a time. In some cases, the behaviors expected of an individual due to one role may not be consistent with the expectations concerning another role. Instances such as these give rise to **role conflict.** Role conflict is quite common, particularly in positions that require workers to be members of different groups simultaneously. For example, imagine that you are the supervisor of a work group. One of your roles involves holding the group together and protecting members' interests. However, you are also a member of the organization's management team, and in this role you are ordered to transfer a very talented and very popular work group member, against her wishes, to another department. Because you cannot satisfy the two incompatible goals of holding the team together while carrying out the organization's plan to transfer the worker, you experience role conflict, a form of stress that can have negative effects on job satisfaction, performance, and mental and physical well-being.

role conflict
conflict that results when the expectations associated with one role interfere with the expectations concerning another role

NORMS

While work groups contain various members, each playing different roles, all members, regardless of their role, must adhere to certain group rules. **Norms** are the rules that groups adopt to indicate appropriate and inappropriate behavior for members. Group norms can be formalized as written work rules, but are most commonly informal and unrecorded. Norms can govern any work activity, including the speed with which a person should perform a job, proper modes of dress, acceptable topics for group conversation, and even who sits where in the employee lunchroom. According to Feldman (1984), norms develop in a number of ways. They can come from explicit statements made by supervisors or co-workers. For example, a supervisor might tell group members, "No one goes home until the work area is spotlessly clean." This leads to a norm that all workers stop working fifteen minutes before quitting time to clean up the work area. Group leaders or powerful group members often play an important role in such norm formation. Norms can also evolve from the group's history. For example, if a certain work procedure leads to a disastrous outcome, the group may place a ban on its use. In other instances, norms may be carried over from past situations. When a member changes groups, norms from the old group may be imported to the new

norms
rules that groups adopt governing appropriate and inappropriate behavior for members

one. For example, a sales supervisor was transferred from the corporate office to a regional sales office. On her first day in the new office, she commented on the casual dress of employees by saying, "At the corporate office, men always wear suits and ties and women always wear skirts or dresses." From the next day on, a new dress code of more formal attire developed.

Norms serve many important purposes for groups. First and foremost, they are established to help the group survive. A group must be able to produce enough to ensure the economic success of the group and the organization. Therefore, some norms will develop to facilitate group production. On the other hand, if members feel that production rates are too high and will lead to layoffs of some of them, norms to restrict group output (rate-setting) will arise. Norms also help increase the predictability of members' behavior. For example, norms regarding speaking turns and the length of time that one may hold the floor in group meetings may ease the flow of the meetings and avoid embarrassment. Finally, norms provide a sense of identity for the group by giving members a chance to express their shared values and beliefs. If an advertising agency believes that they are responsible for setting advertising trends, a norm for producing advertisements that are unique or novel may develop (Feldman, 1984; Katz & Kahn, 1978).

In summary, both roles and norms help provide a structure and plan for group members' behavior. They play an important part in regulating group activities and in helping group members to achieve shared goals.

ORGANIZATIONAL SOCIALIZATION: LEARNING GROUP ROLES AND NORMS

organizational socialization
the process by which new employees learn group roles and norms, and develop specific work skills and abilities

A critical area of research that has recently received increased attention from I/O psychologists is **organizational socialization,** or the process by which new employees become integrated into work groups. Organizational socialization includes three important processes: (1) the development of specific work skills and abilities, (2) the acquisition of a set of appropriate role behaviors, and (3) adjustment to the work group's norms and values (Feldman, 1981; Schein, 1968). The first process—learning specific work skills and abilities—is the main goal of personnel training, which was discussed in depth in Chapter 5. The other two processes—the acquisition of roles and role behaviors, and the learning of group norms—are of particular interest here. New employees learn about group roles and norms in the same way that they learn new job skills, specifically by observing and imitating the behaviors of others. Newcomers may look to established workers as role models and try to copy their successful work behaviors. For example, a novice trial attorney may watch the way that a seasoned senior partner handles herself in court and at firm meetings to learn about the expected role behaviors for the firm's successful attorneys. New employees may also learn about group norms by being reinforced for performing appropriate behaviors and being punished for inappropriate actions. A new salesperson in a busy clothing store may learn about norms for appropriate employee dress and the usual procedures for handling impatient customers through receiving a reinforcing smile and nod, or a disapproving frown, from the sales manager.

Typically, organizational socialization occurs in stages, as one moves from being a newcomer to a fully functioning and contributing member of the work group (Wanous, Reichers, & Malik, 1984). One model outlines three stages in the socialization of new employees (Feldman, 1976a, 1976b). The first is anticipatory socialization. Here newcomers develop a set of realistic expectations concerning the job and the organization and determine if the organization will provide the right match with their abilities, needs, and values. The second stage in the process is accommodation. In this stage, new employees learn about the various roles that work group members play and about their own specific roles in the group. They also begin to "learn the ropes" as they discover important work group norms and standards. In this second stage, the newcomers begin to develop interpersonal relationships with other group members. In the third stage, role management, newcomers make the transition to regular members or insiders, mastering the tasks and roles they must perform. As they move through this stage, they eventually have a thorough knowledge of all facets of work group norms and operations.

Group norms not only define appropriate work behavior but also influence such personal matters as clothing and hair style.

Although all new employees are likely to pass through the same stages in the organizational socialization process, the most recent research indicates that employees may be socialized at different rates, depending on the characteristics of the workers and of the work environment (Reichers, 1987). For example, workers who are forced to move from an old, established work group or organization to a new setting because of layoffs or geographical moves may have a more difficult time becoming socialized than workers who voluntarily make the move. In short, newcomer attitudes and willingness to become a part of the new work group can play an important function in how quickly and smoothly socialization occurs.

Organizations can also greatly facilitate the socialization of new employees. Good employee orientation and training programs are essential to the process, as are the work group's openness and willingness to welcome new members. One technique for encouraging employee socialization is to link newcomers with established, knowledgeable workers, an approach similar to the mentoring concept discussed in Chapter 5. The more quickly new employees are socialized into the work group and organization, the faster they will become productive and valuable workers. Research also indicates that effective socialization is related to reduced employee turnover, increased organizational commitment, and employee career success (Wanous, 1980).

Group cohesiveness grows more readily if the members have similar backgrounds and status.

BASIC GROUP PROCESSES

Several basic social processes that occur in all work groups help to hold the groups together, regulate group behavior, coordinate group activities, and stimulate action by group members. In the following section we will consider four of these processes: conformity, cohesiveness, cooperation, and competition. A final group process, conflict, will be considered under a separate heading because of its importance.

CONFORMITY

Conformity is the process of adhering to group norms. Because these norms are so important to a group's identity and activities, groups exert considerable pressure on members to follow them. Violation can result in subtle or overt pressure to comply with the rules, which can take the form of a look of disapproval, verbal criticism, or isolation of the offending individual (giving the person the "silent treatment"). Once the violator conforms to the norm, the pressure is removed and the person is again included in normal group activities. Generally, conformity to norms is very strong, and helps maintain order and uniformity in the group's behavior.

Because pressure to conform to group norms is so strong, we need to consider the circumstances in which an individual might choose to violate a norm. Usually, someone will not conform to a group norm if the individ-

conformity
the process of following group norms

ual's goals are different from those of the group. For example, imagine that a manufacturing group has a norm of steady but less than optimal production. If a worker within the group wants to be noticed by management as an exceptionally hard worker who would be a good candidate for a promotion to a supervisory position, that person might break the group's production rate norm. Of course, the group will exert pressure in an effort to get the "rate-buster" to conform. Extreme and repeated cases of norm violation may eventually lead to ostracism from the group (Scott, Mitchell, & Birnbaum, 1981). An individual might also resist the pressure to conform to demonstrate that the member believes that the norm is incorrect and should not be followed. Generally, members who have more power and influence in the group, such as the leader, will have a better chance of resisting the group's conformity pressure and persuading the group to change or eliminate the norm. Also, if the violator has a past history of being a "good," conforming member, the nonconformity will be tolerated better than if it is done by a member known for repeated norm violations (Feldman, 1984).

GROUP COHESIVENESS

Another basic group process, cohesiveness, is the "glue" that holds people together in groups. **Cohesiveness** refers simply to the amount or degree of attraction among group members. It is cohesiveness that explains the team spirit that many work groups possess. It is generally assumed that cohesive groups are more satisfied and more productive than noncohesive groups because their members tend to interact more, participate more fully in group activities, and accept and work toward the groups' goals (Cartwright, 1968; Hare, 1976). In fact, however, while cohesive groups are usually more satisfied than noncohesive groups, they are not necessarily more productive (Shaw, 1981). For a cohesive group to be productive, the reason for the cohesiveness must be work related. In other words, one of the goals of the group must be to do a good job. However, a group may be cohesive yet have as a goal to do as little work as possible. In this case, cohesiveness is high and group satisfaction may be high, but productivity is likely to be very low (Tziner, 1982).

Because group cohesiveness is theoretically linked to member satisfaction and, under certain circumstances, productivity, there has been considerable research on the factors that increase group cohesiveness. The most important of these factors are the size of the group, the equality of status of members, member stability, member similarity, and the existence of a common threat or enemy.

Generally, the smaller the group, the more cohesive and the more satisfied its members. This makes sense, since small groups offer many more chances to interact with members and to form closer ties than do large groups. As smaller businesses become larger, gaining more and

cohesiveness
the degree of attraction among group members

Most organizational conflict occurs behind the scenes, but in extreme instances the dispute becomes public.

more employees, cohesiveness often declines. Older workers often lament the strong cohesiveness of the earlier, smaller work group ("In the old days it used to be like a family around here"). One way to regain some of the cohesiveness is to break the large group into smaller work teams.

The more equal the status of group members, the greater the cohesiveness. When a status hierarchy exists, the lower-status members may feel resentful of those of higher status, which leads to disharmony. Conversely, the higher-status members may try to use their authority to direct or control the activities of the lower-status members, which can also erode group cohesiveness. Many team approaches, such as job enrichment, attempt to eliminate status differences in groups to increase cohesiveness. For example, in many job enrichment programs team members are all given the same work classification and job title.

The stability of group membership can also have positive effects on cohesiveness. Generally, the more stable the membership, the more time members have to develop strong ties to one another. New members may often disrupt group harmony because they are unaware of group norms and may unwittingly violate them as they try to learn the ropes. Thus high rates of member turnover and the presence of many new members can be detrimental to group cohesiveness.

Another factor that affects group cohesiveness is the similarity of group members. The more similar their characteristics, the more cohesive the group is likely to be. If members have similar backgrounds, education, and attitudes, it is reasonable to assume that they will develop closer ties to one another. Years of research on group processes indicate that member similarity is a very powerful force in determining social ties; we tend to be attracted to, and establish close relationships with, persons who are similar (Forsyth, 1983).

The presence of an external threat or enemy can likewise increase the cohesiveness of a work group. When a group perceives itself as under attack, the members tend to pull together. Cohesiveness of this type is often referred to as the **we-they feeling** ("We're the good guys, they're the bad guys"). One smaller computer company has recently attempted to increase cohesiveness (and hence productivity) within their organization by fostering the notion that the number one computer company is an ominous threat, which they have begun to call "Big Blue." The smaller company is hoping that the increased cohesiveness will result in greater productivity as the workers pull together in an effort to "beat Big Blue." Unfortunately, within organizations this we-they feeling often develops between the workers and management. This can lead to increased cohesiveness within the work group but can be disruptive in coordinated efforts to achieve organizational goals if the workers perceive management as the enemy.

In sum, all these factors tend to increase group cohesiveness, which can in turn be related to improved work outcomes, particularly increased

we-they feeling
intragroup cohesiveness created by the existence of a common threat, which is typically another group

levels of member satisfaction and reduced rates of absenteeism and turn-over. Moreover, regardless of the actual relationship between group cohesiveness and group productivity, many managers believe that cohesiveness is critical for work group success.

COOPERATION AND COMPETITION IN WORK GROUPS

We have mentioned that the main purpose of work groups is to facilitate the attainment of personal and organizational work goals. This often requires that people work together, coordinating their activities, cooperating with one another, and sometimes helping each other. Yet work groups are also rife with competition as workers try to outperform one another to attain scarce bonuses, raises, and promotions. Competition may also be encouraged when one employee's performance is compared to that of others. Incentive programs are specifically designed to increase motivation by inducing competition—pitting one worker against another. These two seemingly incompatible processes, cooperation and competition, exist simultaneously in all work groups. Because they are such important group processes, we will consider each in depth.

Strong interdependence among work groups can be seen in the airline industry, where flight crews rely on the efforts of the ground personnel.

Cooperation. Surprisingly, cooperation in work groups is an under-studied topic. Perhaps because work groups are *supposed* to cooperate, it is assumed that mutual cooperation in work settings is the "normal" state of affairs, which it often is. Consider three employees in a bookstore as an example. The employees take turns performing the tasks that their jobs require. At any time, two are at the front desk serving customers. The third worker is opening boxes of books, pricing them, and putting them on the appropriate shelves. The workers are coordinating their efforts in an attempt to meet the organizational goals of selling books and providing good customer service. If one of the workers at the front desk goes on a lunch break, the person stocking shelves moves to the front to help customers. If an employee does not know the answer to a customer's question, he may turn to a more knowledgeable and experienced co-worker for assistance. The store employees also coordinate their time off, developing a mutually agreeable vacation schedule (see On the Cutting Edge).

For the most part, such cooperation among work group members is the rule rather than the exception, chiefly because it is often difficult to achieve work goals alone. As long as workers hold to the same goals, they will usually cooperate with one another. Employees might also go out of their way to help each other because of the **reciprocity rule** (Gouldner, 1960), which is illustrated by the sayings, "One good turn deserves another," and "Do unto others as you would have them do unto you." Thus workers help each other because they believe that when they need assistance, they will be paid back in kind. The reciprocity rule is very strong, and people do indeed tend to reciprocate helping behaviors.

reciprocity rule
the tendency for persons to pay back those to whom they are indebted for assistance

Groupware Creates Computerized Work Teams

In the very near future, a work group may conduct regular business meetings, share information and data, and work together on developing a shared product without ever meeting one another face-to-face. The group will be held together not by regular social interactions but through sophisticated computer software called groupware (Richman, 1987), which is designed to link the activities of the members.

Each member will have a desktop terminal with the computer program coordinating members' schedules and conveying messages among them. Meetings will be held through computer-run teleconferences, with participants viewing one another through interactive video hook-ups. Pictures will be controlled by the computer, which will guide the discussion and help keep the meetings on track. The computer system will also automatically record the proceedings and take notes for each of the group members.

Computer software companies have already started developing groupware. For example, one currently available program allows a team of up to sixteen members to collaborate on writing, review-

ing, and editing documents simultaneously. The group can develop a common document, such as a business plan, by adding text, making comments, suggesting revisions, and making changes. Another program helps coordinate group activities by sending messages to members, reminding them of the aspects of the group product for which they are responsible, announcing deadlines, reporting on other members' activities, and updating all on the group's collective progress.

Groupware is designed to increase the efficiency and productivity of work groups by allowing members to share information quickly and by keeping meetings and communications focused on the work task. However, the key to successful groupware will likely be programs that can improve group productivity but still allow for the important human interaction that occurs in work groups. Most groupware will enable members to communicate with one another informally, privately, and off the record. Developers claim that while the systems might change some aspects of how groups of employees work together, the basics of group dynamics will remain intact.

Group members also cooperate because achieving organizational goals can lead to payoffs for the individual workers in terms of raises, bonuses, and promotions. Assisting others can also build up "social debts" that can be collected later when the individual needs help. But does cooperative behavior ever occur without any expected individual payoffs? Are workers ever altruistic, acting unselfishly for the good of other workers or of the organization? This question of altruistic, or *prosocial*, behavior has been studied by social scientists for more than two decades (Latane & Darley, 1970), although its study in work settings is relatively new.

Brief and Motowidlo (1986) define organizational prosocial behaviors as those that go beyond specific work role requirements. They are behaviors performed to promote the welfare of the work group or the organization. Protecting an organization from unexpected dangers, suggesting ways for organizational improvement without expecting a payoff, undertaking deliberate self-development, preparing oneself for higher levels of organizational responsibility, and speaking favorably about the organization to outsiders are all forms of prosocial behavior. Not only do such actions affect the coordination of efforts among work group members, but there is also evidence that they influence job satisfaction (Smith, Organ, & Near, 1983).

In short, cooperation among work group members seems to be an almost natural process. Most workers do indeed learn to get along well with their fellow employees. However, while cooperation is quite common in work groups, members also tend to compete with one another as they strive to attain scarce organizational rewards.

Competition.   **Competition** is also a natural behavior that commonly arises in group dynamics. While cooperation involves group members working together toward shared common goals, competition within groups involves members working against one another to achieve individual goals, often at the expense of other members. For example, in a sales competition, all members of a sales group compete with one another, but only one can be named top salesperson. Most work groups are rife with competition as members struggle to get ahead.

Because both cooperation and competition are very natural, human processes, they often both exist side by side in work groups, and work organizations and work culture actually encourage both. The very fact that work organizations exist indicates that there must be some advantage in having workers cooperate by pooling their efforts to perform some complex tasks. At the same time, the compensation systems adopted by American organizations emphasize the rewarding of individual efforts, which breeds competition. Much of this competition is viewed as healthy because it often motivates people to improve their work performance. Indeed, in the United States and many other industrialized Western nations, being competitive is a highly valued characteristic that is considered imperative for individual and organizational success.

CONFLICT IN WORK GROUPS AND ORGANIZATIONS

While competition refers to a motivating state, **conflict** is used to describe competitiveness of individual workers or work groups that becomes exposed. Conflict is behavior by a person or group that is purposely designed to inhibit the attainment of goals by another person or group (Gray & Starke, 1984). There are many typical instances of conflict between members of an organization: two delivery persons arguing over who gets to drive the new company truck, union and management representatives in heated negotiations over a new contract, or two applicants competing for a single job. Conflict in work organizations and in other areas of everyday life is indeed a common state of affairs.

The key element in the definition of conflict is that the conflicting parties have incompatible goals. Thus both delivery persons cannot drive the same truck, the union cannot attain its goals unless management is willing to give up some of its goals, and two people cannot hold the same

competition
the process whereby group members are pitted against one another to achieve individual goals

conflict
behavior by a person or group intended to inhibit the attainment of goals by another person or group

job. Because in its extremes conflict can lead to a variety of negative behaviors, such as shouting, name calling, and acts of aggression, and perhaps because there is often a "loser" in conflict outcomes, it is commonly believed that conflict is bad. However, this is not necessarily true. Conflict is a natural process that occurs in all work groups and organizations. It can have negative, destructive consequences, but it can also be constructive and lead to positive outcomes for work groups and organizations. Generally, the only way to determine when conflict is bad or good is to examine whether it has positive or negative consequences for the conflicting parties and for the work group or organization as a whole. Although the consequences of conflict are very important, we must first examine the different levels of conflict that occur in organizations and the potential sources of conflict.

Levels of conflict. Conflict can occur at four levels within a work organization: intraindividual conflict, interindividual conflict, intragroup conflict, and intergroup conflict. At the larger level, interorganizational conflict can occur between work organizations.

We typically think of conflict as occurring between two people or two groups. However, the first level of conflict, **intraindividual conflict,** occurs when one person is faced with two sets of incompatible goals. This is what happens when someone is in role conflict: The goals associated with one of the individual's roles conflicts with the goals of another. In such cases, the two roles represent the two conflicting parties. For example, the business owner who hires her son is going to be faced with serious internal conflict when dealing with him as a work employee. Her role as mother and as work superior may come into conflict.

Conflict between two people, or **interindividual conflict,** is quite common in work groups and organizations. Two persons vying for the same promotion would create interindividual conflict, because the person who gets the promotion would block the other from attaining the goal. A disagreement between two machinists over a particular work procedure is also interindividual conflict. Many of the interpersonal problems on the job stem from such conflict.

The next level of conflict, **intragroup conflict,** occurs between one person or faction within a group and the other group members. An individual who violates a group norm is creating intragroup conflict, as are members of a work group who disagree over the course of action for the group. Assume, for example, that a legal firm is trying to decide how to conduct their billing operations. Some of the attorneys favor hiring someone in-house who will handle billing, while others believe that billing should be contracted with an outside agency. Until the group settles on one of the plans, the firm will experience high levels of intragroup conflict.

When two groups are in conflict with each other, **intergroup conflict** exists. Such conflict occurs annually in many organizations when departments are asked to submit their budget requests for the upcoming year.

intraindividual conflict
conflict that occurs when an individual is faced with two sets of incompatible goals

interindividual conflict
conflict that occurs when two individuals are striving to attain their own goals, thus blocking the other's achievement

intragroup conflict
conflict that arises when a person or faction within a group attempts to achieve a goal that interferes with the group's goal attainment

intergroup conflict
conflict that occurs between two groups trying to attain their respective goals

Usually, the sum of the requests greatly exceeds the total amount of money available, which creates a great deal of intergroup conflict as each department tries to achieve its budgetary goals at the expense of those of the others. Some departments within an organization experience ongoing intergroup conflict because of incompatible goals. A classic example of this occurs between the production department and the quality control department in a manufacturing organization. The production group is concerned with meeting certain output quotas, usually expressed as number of components produced. Quality control's goal, on the other hand, is to only pass those components that meet certain specifications and standards. Each time the quality control inspectors reject a component, they interfere with the goal attainment of the production department, leading to ongoing intergroup conflict.

While each of these four levels of conflict takes place *within* a particular organization, **interorganizational conflict** occurs *between* organizations. Businesses that are fighting over the same consumer market are likely to engage in interorganizational conflict as each organization tries to achieve its sales goals at the expense of those of the other. Most businesspersons would agree that, for the most part, interorganizational conflict is a good thing; it is the cornerstone of the free enterprise system. It is the competitive marketplace, spurred on by interorganizational conflict, that helps organizations compete to provide better goods and services for consumers.

interorganizational conflict
conflict between organizations with incompatible goals

Sources of conflict.   Conflict in work groups and organizations comes from many sources. Sometimes it is caused by the organizational structure. For example, status differences are a common source of conflict. Sometimes conflict results because of simple disagreements between two parties over the appropriate work behavior or course of action. Although it would be difficult to list all potential sources of conflict, we will examine some of the more common causes.

A scarcity of important resources—money, materials, tools, and supplies—is perhaps the most common source of conflict in work organizations. It is a rare organization that has enough resources to satisfy the needs of all of its members. When members are forced to compete with one another for these resources, conflict usually follows. Generally, the scarcer the desired resources, the greater the potential for conflict.

Individuals and work groups usually must rely on the activities of other persons and groups to get their own jobs done. Therefore, individual and group interdependence is an important source of conflict. Generally, the greater the interdependence of work activities, the greater the potential for conflict (Walton & Dutton, 1969). For example, in the airline industry, flight crews must depend on the maintenance crews, luggage handlers, and passenger boarding personnel to do their jobs in servicing and loading the aircraft before they can do their job. Intergroup conflict can result if one group does not feel that another is doing its job. If the flight crew feels that the luggage handlers are too slow, causing delays in takeoff, the fact that the flight crew may be blamed for the delays creates a potential conflict situation. The strong interdependence among all workers on an assembly line also opens up the door for intragroup conflict, because the ability of any single person to perform the job correctly is governed by how others further up the line performed theirs. If an assembled product is rejected and it is another person's fault, the individual's work is also rejected.

We have seen that the we-they feeling plays a large role in fostering group cohesiveness; nothing can draw a group together better than having a common enemy to fight. However, a problem occurs when the "enemy" is within your own organization. This is what often causes the conflict in wage negotiations between workers and managers. The workers ask for a wage increase, while management, in an effort to keep costs down, rejects the request. What commonly results is that each group views the other as an enemy blocking its goal attainment. Although the common enemy helps draw the members together within their respective groups, it also tends to draw the two groups further and further away from each other. Thus while the we-they feeling can increase group cohesiveness, it may also cause intergroup conflict.

One of the most common sources of conflict is not related to the availability of resources, the structure of the organization, or the formation of work groups but rather results from the fact that certain individuals simply do not get along with each other. This important source of conflict thus comes from *interpersonal* sources. Two organizational members who dislike each other may refuse to cooperate. This sort of interpersonal conflict can be very disruptive to the larger work group and the organization in general, especially if the problem is between two powerful people, such as two department heads who may turn their subordinates against members of the other department. What was once a conflict between two persons can thus escalate into conflict between two groups.

Research evidence also suggests that some people are more conflict prone than others. Differences in personality and temperament mean that certain persons may be likely to engage in conflict. Indeed, studies have shown that some people try to stir up interindividual conflict because of their desire to gain at others' expense (McClintock, Messick, Kuhlman, & Campos, 1973; see also Knight & Dubro, 1984).

A final characteristic that can be a potential source of conflict is age. A good deal of evidence indicates that younger workers are more conflict prone than older workers, presumably because they have less to lose and more to gain from the outcomes of conflict situations (Robbins, 1974).

Conflict outcomes. It has been stated that conflict in work settings can produce both positive and negative outcomes. Attention is usually given to how conflict affects the important organizational outcomes of job performance or productivity, job satisfaction, and employee attendance.

Thus, conflict is most often labeled as positive or negative from the standpoint of the organization. First, we will examine the positive outcomes of conflict.

A primary question is how conflict within a work group or organization relates to performance. One way that conflict can indirectly affect performance is by increasing the motivation and energy level of group members. A little bit of conflict seems to energize members, which in turn may increase their motivation to perform their jobs. The complete absence of conflict in work groups can cause workers to become complacent and unmotivated. (It can also be very dull.)

Another positive outcome of conflict is that it can stimulate creativity and innovation. When people challenge the existing system, a form of conflict results. But out of this type of conflict come new, and often better, ideas. For example, in many groups, workers continue to use the same old, "tried and true" work procedures. When a worker suggests a new, improved method, there may be some initial conflict as members resist having to learn a new technique. However, if the new procedure is effective, group productivity may increase. Thus although people tend to resist changes, when change is for the better, the organization and its members benefit.

Another performance-related positive outcome of conflict occurs when conflict improves the quality of decisions. Giving all members of a group some input into the decisionmaking process leads to conflict because the group must consider a wide range of opposing views and opinions. Conflict occurs as each member tries to be heard and pushes for what he or she thinks is right. The positive result of all of this, however, is that decisions made are usually of high quality, being the result of a very critical process. (We will return to a discussion of group decisionmaking processes later in this chapter.)

Conflict can also positively affect other important organizational outcomes such as absenteeism, turnover, and job satisfaction. For example, it was mentioned that a little bit of conflict can stimulate interest in the work group, which can motivate workers not only to perform their jobs but also to come to work. Some conflict can make the work setting a more interesting place to work, which may reduce employee absenteeism and turnover. Conflict can also have a positive effect on group member satisfaction when it leads to an airing of problems. When interpersonal conflicts exist between employees but are not brought out and dealt with, an underlying state of tension can result which may harm member satisfaction. By definition, bringing these problems to the surface creates group conflict. However, acknowledging such problems is the first step in resolving them. When these interpersonal conflicts are resolved, the satisfaction levels of the interactants can be improved.

In Chapter 7 and 8, we saw that employees who feel that they have an active role in affecting group or organizational processes tend to be more satisfied than those who have no influence. Being able to communicate freely with co-workers, having a voice in decisionmaking, and being allowed to make suggestions or criticize group or organizational operations are all ways in which workers can have some impact on group processes. Although some conflict is likely to arise every time workers are allowed to introduce their own opinions, the fact that they can take part in this positive, productive type of conflict is associated with greater group member satisfaction. Therefore, some forms of conflict can be directly associated with member satisfaction and commitment to the work group.

Among the various negative outcomes of conflict, one of the most obvious is the reduction of group cohesiveness. While a little bit of conflict can energize group members, too much can erode cohesiveness and, in extremes, diminish the members' ability to work with each other. This may contribute to increased voluntary absenteeism and eventually employee turnover.

Conflict can also hamper effective group performance when it retards communication. People who are in conflict may avoid communicating with each other, making it difficult to work together. Conflict can also be destructive to group member satisfaction when conflicting parties begin to send misleading or deceptive messages to one another or when false and disparaging rumors are started. Evidence also suggests that when a great deal of interpersonal conflict occurs among work group members, supervisors may begin to avoid allowing subordinates to participate in decisionmaking processes, thus shutting down this type of communication, presumably in an effort to avoid further conflict (Fodor, 1976). Conflict is especially damaging to performance when it allows group goals to become secondary to the infighting. Sometimes members direct so much energy to the conflict situation that they neglect to perform their jobs. When winning the conflict becomes more important than reaching work-related goals, the outcomes are negative for the individuals and for the organization (Robbins, 1979).

In summary, neither too much nor too little conflict is beneficial for the work group members and the organization. This means that there must be some optimal level of conflict. Because conflict is so pervasive in work groups and organizations, it would be very difficult to assess whether all forms of conflict were at their optimal levels at any given time. However, at times the conflict has obviously gone too far, becoming detrimental to the operations of the work group as a whole. Likewise, at other times the work group has become too complacent and needs some conflict to get the members more active and involved. Since some excess or shortage of conflict is inevitably going to exist, the smart thing to do at all times in all work groups is to learn to manage conflict.

Managing conflict. To manage conflict—to keep it at an optimal level—one of two things must be done. If the conflict becomes too great, leading to severe negative outcomes, it must be resolved. If, on the other hand, the level of conflict is too low, conflict stimulation is needed.

There is little doubt that too much conflict can have devastating consequences on the work group and the organization. Therefore, a great deal of attention has been given to the development and application of various conflict resolution strategies, which can be of two types: Individual conflict resolution strategies are those that the conflicting parties can use themselves to try to resolve the conflict; managerial conflict resolution strategies are steps that managers or other third parties can take to encourage conflict resolution. Thomas (1976) has identified five individual conflict resolution strategies:

1. **Competition:** persisting in the conflict until one party's goals are achieved at the expense of those of the other. This can be labeled a win-lose strategy: One party wins, the other loses.
2. **Accommodation:** giving in or acting in a self-sacrificing manner to resolve the conflict. This is a lose-win strategy. Sometimes this strategy of appeasement is done to cut losses.
3. **Compromise:** each party must give up something. This is a lose-lose strategy. Compromise is typical in bargaining situations. For example, in union-management negotiations, management may offer a $.50-an-hour raise, while the union wants a $1.50 raise. They compromise at $1.00, but neither group has achieved its complete goal. They have each lost something from their original position.
4. **Collaboration:** the parties try to cooperate and reach a mutually beneficial solution. This is a win-win situation. Unfortunately, this is not always possible, particularly when the conflict is over scarce resources and there is not enough to satisfy both parties' needs.
5. **Avoidance:** suppressing the conflict, not allowing it to come into the open, or simply withdrawing from the situation. While this strategy avoids open conflict, the differences between the two parties still exist and will likely continue to affect their ability to work with one another.

competition
a conflict resolution strategy of persisting in a conflict until one party attains personal goals at the expense of the other's

accommodation
a conflict resolution strategy of making a sacrifice to resolve a conflict

compromise
a conflict resolution strategy in which both parties give up some part of their goals

collaboration
a conflict resolution strategy in which the parties cooperate to reach a solution that satisfies both

avoidance
withdrawing from or avoiding a conflict situation

While the two conflicting parties can take such steps to try to resolve their differences, managers, because of their status and power in the organization, can play a major role in resolving conflict between subordinates (Blake, Shepard, & Mouton, 1964). Managers may try to force an end to the conflict by deciding in favor of one or the other parties. While this may end the conflict, resentment may be built up in the losing person that may surface later in actions against the manager or the co-worker. Managers can also act as arbitrators or mediators to resolve conflict in a way that may satisfy both parties. For example, in a furniture factory, two workers were constantly fighting over a particular tool that each occasionally needed to perform their jobs. When one worker needed the tool, it always seemed that the other person had it, which led to constant arguments. When the shop manager became aware of the problem, he instantly resolved it by simply purchasing another tool.

One managerial conflict resolution strategy, outlined in a series of studies by Sherif and his colleagues (Sherif, Harvey, White, Hood, & Sherif, 1961), deals with resolving intragroup conflict by stimulating intragroup cohesiveness through the introduction of a common, **superordinate goal** that is attractive to both parties. When a group is split over some minor issue, introducing a more important superordinate goal may draw the two sides together as they strive to attain the common end. For example, commissioned salespersons in the men's clothing section of a large chain department store were constantly fighting over who would be the first to grab a customer who walked into the area. The manager helped to resolve much of this conflict by introducing a bonus program that pitted the department's overall sales against those of men's departments in other stores. By focusing on pooled sales figures, the employees became oriented toward beating the other stores rather than beating each other.

Managers can also help resolve conflict in group decisionmaking. For example, they may use their authority to call an issue to a vote, which means that the majority of workers will win the conflict situation. However, there may be a disgruntled minority of losers, who may then carry on the conflict by refusing to follow the elected plan or by some other means. The manager will need to deal with this residual conflict if it is deemed serious enough to require resolution.

The key to successful conflict resolution from the managerial perspective is to maintain a broad perspective, trying to find a workable solution and considering the potential side effects, such as disgruntled losers, that may result from the resolution process (see Applying I/O Psychology).

In certain situations, such as when group members appear to have become complacent and disinterested in work activities, managers may feel that some specific types of conflict are needed. A number of strategies can be used to stimulate conflict. One tactic is simply to ask for it. Asking employees for their suggestions or for complaints about the organization and its policies may lead to some conflict as employees critically evaluate the organization and management. However, this type of conflict will hopefully lead to constructive change and improvement. When top management feels that work groups have become *too* cohesive, to the detriment of the groups' energy and motivational levels, they may decide to break up that cohesiveness and inject a little stimulating conflict by making personnel changes such as bringing in new employees or rotating workers to different departments or work sites. Restaurant and retail chains use this strategy when they rotate managers among stores.

Sales or performance competition programs are another way of stimulating some positive group conflict. The key to a successful competition program, however, is to ensure that members do not engage in dysfunc-

Reducing Management-Union Conflict

A common type of intergroup conflict in large work organizations exists between management and unions. The behavioral scientists Blake, Mouton, and Sloma (1964) outline a case in which such conflict was reduced through a two-day workshop designed to refocus the two groups' efforts on common work-related goals. The company was a large electronics manufacturing plant with over 4,000 employees. Because there was a history of disagreement between management and the labor union, one of the most difficult tasks for the behavioral scientists was to get both sides to agree to the "experiment." Finally, however, they agreed that the hostility between the two groups was so high that something needed to be done.

The scientists believed that the key to reducing conflict was to get the two groups to increase their understanding of each other and to see that in many ways they had compatible rather than competing goals. The workshop intended to achieve this was broken down into eight phases, as follows:

Phase	Activity	Time (Hours)
1	Orientation; purposes of workshop explained	½
2	Intragroup development of own images and images of other group	5
3	Exchange of images across groups	1
4	Clarification of images	2
5	Intragroup diagnosis of present relationship	4
6	Exchange of diagnoses across groups	3
7	Consolidation of key issues and sources of friction	2
8	Planning of next steps to be taken	1

In the first few phases, the management and union representatives wrote down their images of themselves, particularly in their relationship with the other group, and their images of the other side. These images were exchanged, and heated discussion ensued. In these early discussions, the two groups continued their intense conflict. For example, one manager said, "I can't even talk with these union officials. I just 'see red' and clam up every time I see one of them coming."

Eventually, however, as the groups moved through the middle phases of the workshop, they began to gain insight into each other's positions and some of the misunderstandings began to disappear. This was helped along by the fifth phase in which both groups' task was to try to discover why the conflict had become what it was. In the discussion that followed, the two sides began to find that they had some common goals:

> The employee relations manager, who had been listening intently all this time, stood up with a look of disbelief on his face. He didn't seem to realize he was on his feet. "Do you mean to say you people are really interested in production?" He had listened to the union say this for two days, but he had just "heard" it for the first time. His next question was a simple one, but it triggered an hour-long discussion. He asked, "What could management do to use people more effectively?" (Blake, Mouton, & Sloma, 1964, p. 189)

By finding that they shared common goals, the two groups set an agenda to work together not only to reduce the management-union conflict further but also to develop some cooperative strategies for dealing with work-related problems. From this workshop arose a plan of action for creating better lines of communication between the two groups and for implementing strategies that would increase plant efficiency and productivity for the benefit of all.

tional behaviors, such as sabotaging others' work activities, in an effort to win the competition. Ideally, a good program should allow all participants to achieve a goal. For example, a bonus should be given to each employee who reaches a certain performance level, instead of only to the top performer.

A widely used conflict stimulation strategy that can often lead to positive outcomes is to move from centralized decisionmaking procedures to a group decisionmaking process in which all group members have a say in certain work-related issues. Although this automatically increases conflict by allowing each worker to state his or her opinion and argue for a particular course of action, it is presumed that this type of conflict will yield positive results because it allows for consideration of a wider range of plans and greater critiquing of the various possible decisons.

GROUP DECISIONMAKING PROCESSES

One of the most important processes in work groups is group decisionmaking, which includes establishing group goals, choosing among various courses of action, selecting new members, and determining standards of appropriate behavior. The processes by which groups make these decisions have been of interest to I/O psychologists for many years.

Groups can make work-related decisions in a number of ways. The simplest and most straightforward strategy, known as **autocratic decisionmaking,** is when the group leader makes decisions alone, using only the information that the leader possesses. The major advantage of autocratic decisionmaking is that it is fast. Decisions are made quickly by the leader and are then expected to be carried out by group members. However, because the decision is made based only on what the leader knows, the quality of the decision may suffer. For example, suppose a leader of a group of office workers has to decide which word processing system to buy. If the leader actually knows which system is the best for the group, there will be no drawback to the autocratic approach. If, however, the leader cannot make an informed choice, the decision may be faulty. In this case, input from the group members would be helpful. A variation on the strict autocratic decisionmaking approach occurs when the leader solicits information from group members to assist in reaching a decision but still holds the final say. In the word processing decision, soliciting input from group members about which systems they favor might lead to a higher quality decision.

A very different strategy is **democratic decisionmaking,** in which all group members are allowed to discuss the decision and then vote on a particular course of action. Typically, democratic decisionmaking is based on majority rule. One advantage of this approach is that decisions are made using the pooled knowledge and experience of all of the group

autocratic decisionmaking
a process by which group decisions are made by the leader alone, based on information the leader possesses

democratic decisionmaking
a strategy by which decisions are made by the group members based on majority-rule voting

For important decisions many executive groups strive to achieve consensus.

members. Moreover, because all members have a chance to voice an opinion or suggest a different course of action, a greater number of alternatives are considered. Also, because group members have a role in the decisionmaking, they are more likely to follow the chosen course.

The most obvious drawback to democratic decisionmaking is that it is time-consuming. Because it encourages conflict, it can also be inefficient. While the democratic, majority-rule approach results in a satisfied majority who will back the decision, there may be a disgruntled minority that resists its implementation.

A strategy that overcomes some of the weaknesses of democratic decisionmaking is to make decisions based on **consensus,** which means that all group members, without exception, have agreed on the chosen course of action. Because consensus decisionmaking is especially time-consuming, it is usually only used for very important decisions. For example, juries use this strategy because the decision affects the freedom and future of the accused. Some company executive boards may strive for a consensus when making major decisions about changes in the direction of the organization or in organizational structure or company policy. As you might imagine, the outcome of consensus decisionmaking is usually a high-quality, highly critiqued decision, backed by all members of the group. The obvious drawback is the tremendous amount of time it may take for the group to reach a consensus. In fact, in many situations arriving at a consensus may be impossible, particularly if one or more group members is strongly resistant to the majority's decision (the courtroom analogy would be a hung jury).

consensus decisionmaking based on 100 percent member agreement

Table 9.2   ADVANTAGES AND DISADVANTAGES OF GROUP DECISIONMAKING

Advantages	Disadvantages
Based on broad knowledge base	Slow (can be a problem in crisis situations)
Decision is accepted by members	Creates intragroup conflict
Decision is highly critiqued	Potential for groupthink and group polarization
Aspects of the problem can be divided among group members	Certain members, such as leaders, may dominate the decisionmaking process

EFFECTIVENESS OF GROUP DECISIONMAKING

In recent years, organizations have been turning more and more to group strategies for making important work-related decisions. Part of this is fueled by beliefs in the inherent advantages of group over individual decisionmaking. However, while group decisionmaking has many positive aspects, it also has some drawbacks (see Table 9.2). The key is to know not only *how* group-made decisions can be more effective than those made by individuals but also *when* group decisionmaking is superior.

As mentioned, the major advantage of group decisionmaking is it offers increased knowledge and experience on which to base the decision. But do groups actually make better decisions than individuals? Research does give the edge to group decisionmaking, *on the average*. The average group will make a higher-quality decision than the average individual. However, the best decisionmaking individual—one who possesses all the information needed to make a high-quality decision—will be able to perform as well as or better than a group (Hill, 1982; Miner, 1984). Moreover, certain members, such as a group leader or respected individual, may have more influence in affecting the outcome and may be able to sway a group toward accepting a particular course of action. If the influential member is not knowledgeable or well-informed about the alternatives, the group may be led to make a poor decision.

We have also seen that group decisionmaking tends to be slower than individual decisionmaking, which can be a problem in situations such as an emergency or crisis. At these times, it may be better for an individual to take charge and make decisions for the group (Tjosvold, 1984a). However, if a problem is complex and multifaceted, with many steps required to arrive at a decision, a group may make the decision faster than an individual, because the various aspects of the problem can be divided among group members.

Perhaps the strongest argument in support of group decisionmaking is that it tends to lead to increased member satisfaction and greater member commitment to the course of action than does individual decisionmaking. But what happens if the group-made decision is a bad one? Research indicates that when this occurs, members may increase their commitment

What Is Brainstorming, and Does It Work?

In the 1950s an advertising executive developed a technique to encourage groups to come up with creative ideas (Osborn, 1957). The technique, termed brainstorming, involved six to ten group members throwing out ideas in a noncritical and nonjudgmental atmosphere as a means of trying to generate as many creative ideas or solutions to a problem as possible. Since its invention, brainstorming has become very popular, and tremendous claims have been made regarding its success.

The basic rules in brainstorming sessions are: (1) No idea is too far out; (2) criticism of any idea is not allowed; (3) the more ideas the better; and (4) members should try to build on each other's ideas. The technique has been widely used in a variety of businesses, but does it work? Evidence from nearly twenty years of research indicates that, despite its popularity, brainstorming is not as effective as its proponents might lead one to believe (see, for example, Bouchard, Barsaloux, & Drauden, 1974; Taylor, Block, & Berry, 1958; Yetton & Bottger, 1982). The problem is that in spite of the rules, group dynamics are too powerful; the creativity of people in the brainstorming groups is often inhibited (Diehl & Stroebe, 1987). The research indicates that individuals are equal to or better than the brainstorming groups in generating creative ideas. The moral is that just because a technique sounds logical or is popular, this does not mean that it will necessarily work.

to the poor decision (Bazerman, Giuliano, & Appleman, 1984). If the poor decision was made by an individual, group members will not be as committed and may be more likely to see its faults and try another course of action.

In summary, although group decisionmaking has certain limitations, it offers many advantages over individual decisionmaking, particularly in improving the quality of decisions and increasing the commitment to decisions once they are made. Recent trends toward encouraging greater involvement of workers in organizational processes mean that group decisionmaking is likely to increase in the future (see Up Close).

GROUP DECISIONMAKING GONE AWRY: GROUPTHINK AND GROUP POLARIZATION

When making important work decisions, particularly those that have a major impact on the work procedures or working lives of group members, group decisionmaking may be preferred over decisionmaking by high-ranking members of the organization. This is done in an effort to increase the amount of relevant information available and to encourage member commitment to the eventually chosen course. However, psychologists have discovered two situations in which the usual advantages of group decisionmaking may not be forthcoming: One is known as groupthink, and the other is termed group polarization.

Groupthink. Groups generally arrive at high-quality decisions because the alternative courses of action have been subjected to critical

Self-censorship and the illusion of unanimity are symptoms of groupthink.

"*All those in favor say 'Aye.'*"
"*Aye.*"   "*Aye.*"   "*Aye.*"
"*Aye.*"   "*Aye.*"

Drawing by H. Martin; © 1979 The New Yorker Magazine, Inc.

groupthink
a syndrome characterized by a concurrence-seeking tendency that overrides the ability of a cohesive group to make critical decisions

evaluation. This is particularly true in consensus decisionmaking, since even one dissenting member can argue against a plan favored by all the rest. There is, however, an exception to this rule. A complex set of circumstances can sometimes occur in consensus decisionmaking that retards the critical evaluation process. What results is a complete backfiring of the normal, critical decisionmaking that results in a premature, hasty, and often catastrophic decision. This situation is termed **groupthink.** Groupthink is a syndrome that occurs in highly cohesive, decisionmaking groups, where a norm develops to arrive at an early consensus, thereby reducing the effectiveness of the group's ability to make high-quality, critical decisions.

The concept of groupthink was researched by psychologist Irving Janis (1972; Janis & Mann, 1977). According to Janis, groupthink usually occurs only in highly cohesive groups in which the members' desire to maintain cohesiveness overrides the sometimes uncomfortable and disruptive process of critical decisionmaking. A course of action is laid out on the table, and without it being adequately critiqued, the members rapidly move toward a consensus to adopt the plan.

In developing his theory of groupthink, Janis studied a number of poor decisions made by high-level decisionmaking groups, such as U.S. presidential administrations and boards of directors of large companies, the consequences of which were so bad that he labeled them "fiascoes." Janis investigated a number of historical fiascoes such as the Kennedy administration's failed Bay of Pigs invasion, the Truman administration's decision to cross the thirty-eighth parallel in the Korean War, and the Johnson administration's decision to escalate the Vietnam War. He also studied catastrophic business decisions, such as the decision to market the drug Thalidomide, which led to thousands of birth deformities; the Buffalo Mining Company's decision about dam construction, which caused the deaths of 125 people; and the Ford Motor Company's decision to market the Edsel, one of the greatest failures in American automotive history (Wheeler & Janis, 1980). By studying the decisionmaking processes in each of these cases, Janis noticed certain similarities that he has termed the "symptoms of groupthink," specific group factors that work toward preventing the critical evaluation usually present in decisionmaking groups (see Table 9.3).

To understand how the symptoms of groupthink interfere with critical decisionmaking processes, consider the following example. A board of directors of an international air freight service must decide whether the company should enter a cost-cutting war with their competitors. The board begins its decisionmaking meeting with the chairperson's loaded question, "Should we enter into this foolish price war, or just keep rates the way they are?" By labeling the price war as "foolish," the chairperson has already indicated her preferred course of action: Keep the rates as they are. Normally, the critical decisionmaking process would involve a great deal of discussion of the relative strengths and weaknesses of the various alternatives, and the decision that would result should be of high

Table 9.3 THE EIGHT SYMPTOMS OF GROUPTHINK

1. *Illusion of invulnerability:* the highly cohesive decisionmaking group members see themselves as powerful and invincible. Their attraction to and faith in the group leads them to ignore the potential disastrous outcomes of their decision.
2. *Illusion of morality:* members believe in the moral correctness of the group and its decision; related to the first symptom. Derived from the we-they feeling, members view themselves as the "good guys" and the opposition as bad or evil.
3. *Shared negative stereotypes:* members have common beliefs that minimize the risks involved in a decision or belittle any opposing viewpoints.
4. *Collective rationalizations:* the members explain away any negative information that runs counter to the group decision.
5. *Self-censorship:* members suppress their own doubts or criticisms concerning the decision.
6. *Illusion of unanimity:* members mistakenly believe that the decision is a consensus. Since dissenting viewpoints are not being voiced, it is assumed that silence indicates support.
7. *Direct conformity pressure:* when an opposing view or a doubt is expressed, pressure is applied to get the dissenter to concur with the decision.
8. *Mindguards:* some members play the role of protecting or insulating the group from any opposing opinions or negative information.

quality. However, in groupthink situations this does not occur. The symptoms of groupthink, themselves manifestations of such basic group processes as cohesiveness, stereotyped and rationalized views, and conformity, can counteract the critical evaluations that should be made. If groupthink does indeed occur, the consequences may be devastating, particularly because the group believes that the chosen action is the result of a critical and well-conducted decisionmaking process, when it is not.

If groupthink takes place at the air freight company, the board of directors would likely manifest three symptoms—the *illusion of invulnerability*, the *illusion of morality*, and the presence of *shared negative stereotypes*—that result from the we-they feeling that is typically present in highly cohesive groups. The members believe that they and their organization are powerful and good. Negative stereotypes about nonmembers or other groups (the enemy) also stem from the we-they feeling. Examples of these three symptoms might be seen in the board members' statements that they believe the group and the company are invulnerable ("We're the number one company in this business") and morally good ("We always provide the best possible service to our customers"). Other comments suggest that they hold shared negative stereotypes about the competition ("With their inept management and poor equipment, they will never be able to offer the kind of service that we do"). These three groupthink symptoms thus begin a tendency toward seeking concurrence, as the members strive to stick together and agree with one another (Janis, 1972).

Additional groupthink symptoms—*collective rationalizations* of opposing viewpoints, a tendency for members to engage in *self-censorship*, and the *illusion of unanimity*—lead the group to arrive at a premature consensus. Suppose that one of the board members suggests an alternative to the plan to keep rates as they are that the board is moving toward adopting. The dissenter wants to keep rates the same while starting an advertising campaign that tells customers, "You get what you pay for," thus emphasizing the company's higher quality of service. Collective rationalizations of members immediately put down the alternative plan ("People never listen to advertisements anyway," and "That will cost us more than lowering our rates!"). Other board members may see the merit in the alternative plan, but since it appears that most of the others, because of their silence, do not like it, they engage in self-censorship and keep their opinions to themselves. The fact that no one speaks up leads to the illusion of unanimity, the notion that everybody is for the original plan.

If dissenters do speak up, two additional groupthink symptoms operate to stifle the critical decisionmaking process even further. *Direct conformity pressure* might be applied to force dissenters to keep their opinions to themselves and not break up the group's agreement. Some members may even play the role of *mindguards*, taking it upon themselves to keep dissenting opinions from reaching the ears of the group leader and other members. The member advocating the advertisement plan, for example, might be told by a self-appointed mindguard to not bring the plan up again, "for the good of the group."

Janis believes that groupthink can be combated by breaking up some of the cohesiveness of the group through the interjection of productive conflict. This might involve using strategies such as bringing in outsiders to offer different viewpoints or having some members play the role of critical evaluators—"devil's advocates"—who are highly critical of any plan of action that is brought before the group. Also, because groupthink is partly brought on by a sense of time urgency, if the group begins with the idea that they need to come up with the best possible decision, regardless of how long it takes, groupthink may be avoided.

Group polarization. The quality of group decisions may also be adversely affected by **group polarization,** or the tendency for groups to make decisions that are more extreme than those made by individuals (Myers & Lamm, 1976). Early research found evidence of the effects of group polarization when decisions carried a high degree of risk. In these studies individuals were asked to make a decision between an attractive but risky course of action and one that was less attractive but also less risky. After making the decision, the respondents were put into groups and asked to come up with a group decision. It was found that the groups tended to make riskier decisions than the average individual (Wallach, Kogan, and Bem, 1962). This effect became known as the risky shift and was the topic of much research and theorizing. It had major implications for the making of important decisions in business and government, since it suggested that group decisions might be more dangerous than decisions made by individuals. However, subsequent research began to challenge these early findings, failing to find a risky shift in some decisionmaking groups and occasionally finding evidence of a *cautious* shift. What we now know is that groups tend to move toward more extreme decisions, which is the group polarization effect.

How does group polarization relate to decisions made in work situations, and why does it occur? Imagine that a company must choose which of several new products it should introduce. Some of the products are costly to develop and market, but if successful could bring large profits. Other products are less costly but will lead to smaller financial gains. An individual who makes the decision might choose to introduce a product of medium-level risk and payoff. However, if the person is put into a group that is leaning toward marketing a risky product, the group's decision would be more extreme than the individual's. If, on the other hand, the group is leaning toward the side of caution, the group might shift to a more cautious choice than the typical individual would choose.

Two explanations for group polarization have been offered. The first is that in the group, the individual is presented with persuasive arguments by other members that bolster the individual's tendency toward making

group polarization
the tendency for groups to make decisions that are more extreme than those made by individuals

either a risky or cautious decision. After hearing others argue for a cautious strategy, it makes the individual more sure that caution is needed, and there is a tendency for the group to become more cautious. The other explanation is that individuals adopt the values of the group in regard to level of risk or caution. If the group is leaning toward caution, the individuals go along with the group, becoming even more cautious than they would be alone. If the group is inclined toward risk, the individuals will become risk takers to demonstrate that they endorse the group's values. Regardless of why it occurs, the fact that some group decisions may be more extreme than those of individuals is a reason for some concern, particularly when extreme risk or caution may be detrimental to the attainment of the group's goals.

CHAPTER 9 CONCLUSION

SUMMARY

A *group* is two or more individuals, engaged in social interaction to achieve some goal. Within work groups, members play various *roles*, which are patterns of behavior adopted based on *expectations* held about the function of a position. Work groups also develop *norms*, or rules to help govern member behavior. The process of *organizational socialization* refers to the integration of individuals into work groups and organizations through learning work procedures, work roles, and organizational and group norms.

Certain basic processes occur in all work groups. One is *conformity*, the process of adhering to and following group norms. Another basic process, *cohesiveness*, is the degree of attraction among group members. A number of factors, such as size, status, member stability, and member similarity can influence group cohesiveness.

Two common yet opposing forces that are evident in all groups are cooperation and competition. Cooperation is critical to coordinating the activities of work group members. *Competition* can lead to *conflict*, which is behavior by one party that is designed to inhibit the goal attainment of another party. Conflict can occur at a number of levels within work organizations, taking the form of *intraindividual, interindividual, intragroup, intergroup*, or *interorganizational conflict*. It can arise from various sources, most notably from a scarcity of desired resources and from individual and group interdependence. The effect of conflict can be both positive and negative; it is positive when it motivates workers or stimulates them to be creative or innovative, and negative when it disrupts group work activities and social relationships. Managing conflict involves regulating the level of conflict, resolving it when it is negative and stimulating it when it is positive or productive. A number of conflict resolution and conflict stimulation strategies are used in organizations.

An important function in work groups is group decisionmaking, which has several advantages and disadvantages over individual decisionmaking. While group decisionmaking is slow and conflict ridden, it can lead to high-quality decisions and greater member satisfaction with and commitment to the decision. A type of breakdown in the effectiveness of decisionmaking groups is termed *groupthink,* which is a concurrence-seeking tendency that overrides the ability of a cohesive group to make critical decisions. *Group polarization* is the tendency for groups to make more extreme decisions, either more risky or more cautious, than individuals.

STUDY QUESTIONS AND EXERCISES

1. Consider a work or social group of which you are a member. What are the various roles that members play? What roles have you played? What are some of the norms that are particular to this group?

2. In what ways can group cohesiveness facilitate goal attainment in work groups? How might cohesiveness hinder their attainment?

3. List the levels of conflict that occur in work groups. Give specific examples to illustrate each.

4. Discuss the ways in which cohesiveness and conflict can be seen as opposite forces in work groups.

5. What are some of the potential positive and negative outcomes of conflict? Using a work or social group with which you have had contact, think of examples of conflict that led to negative outcomes. How might these situations have been managed to reduce their negative impact?

6. Consider the eight symptoms of groupthink. What steps can decisionmaking groups take to try to avoid each of them?

SUGGESTED READINGS

Forsyth, D. R. (1983). *An introduction to group dynamics.* Monterey, CA: Brooks/Cole.   *A textbook providing a comprehensive overview of group dynamics.*
Tjosvold, D. (1986). *Working together to get things done: Managing for organizational productivity.* Lexington, MA: Lexington Books.   *A very readable book that gives suggestions for developing work teams. Contains chapters such as "Making Conflict Productive" and "How to Develop Cooperative Goals."*
Zander, A. (1982). *Making groups effective.* San Francisco: Jossey-Bass. Zander, A. (1985). *The purposes of groups and organizations.* San Francisco: Jossey-Bass.   *Zander, a leading researcher in group dynamics, has written these two guides for achieving greater understanding of the processes for improving the performance of work groups.*

10

LEADERSHIP

Understanding Leadership Theories

This chapter presents some of the many theories of leadership in work organizations in more or less chronological order, beginning with the earliest (and simplest) theories and progressing to the more current (and complex) models. While each of these theories takes a somewhat different perspective in examining work group leadership, there are common threads. Specifically, most of the more recent models build on the behavioral theories of leadership, which focus on the behaviors displayed by effective leaders. The behavioral theories' dichotomy of leader behavior—task-oriented and relationship-oriented—is used as a starting point for developing more complex theories. Later theories of leadership, called contingency theories, look at the interaction of leader behavior and situational circumstances. All of these theories involve some measurement of leader characteristics or behavior coupled with some measurement of the leadership situation.

Because of their complex analysis of specific situations, contingency theories provide useful approaches to improving leader effectiveness. However, the interventions suggested will depend on the theories' assumptions about leader behavior. As you will see, the contingency theories have one of two orientations: Leader behavior is considered to be either relatively fixed, as characterized by Fiedler's model, or flexible. These two opposing views lead to very different strategies for applying the theories. If leader behavior is viewed as fixed, the situation must be changed to fit the leader if leader effectiveness is to be improved. If leader behavior is seen as flexible, leaders can be trained to fit situational requirements better.

The theories of leadership introduced in this chapter are directly related to topics discussed previously and also provide a background for upcoming chapters. Specifically, the topic of leadership follows the discussion of group processes in Chapter 9, as the relationship between leaders and other members of the work group is itself an important group process. Leadership and the leadership role are also linked to organizational communication (Chapter 8), particularly the downward flow of communication in organizations. Finally, this chapter will link up with the discussion of influence, power, and politics in Chapter 11, for it is clear that the most influential and powerful members of work groups are usually the leaders.

In Chapter 9 we saw that individuals play various roles in work groups and organizations. One of these roles is that of leader, which in many groups is viewed as the key position. Rightly or wrongly, many people believe that the success or failure of a particular group is largely dependent on the leader and the type of leadership demonstrated. The importance placed on leadership has made it a major topic in politics, the military, and work organizations. Organizations spend millions of dollars annually trying to select managerial personnel who possess the qualities necessary to be effective leaders of work groups. Millions more are spent on training employees to be more effective leaders and to develop important leadership characteristics. Before we can study the qualities of leaders, however, we must define leadership.

Leadership is defined as the ability to direct a group toward the attainment of goals. Leaders play a central role in helping to facilitate a group's goal attainment. It is often assumed that the terms "leader" and "manager" are synonymous in work groups and organizations. However, while the leader in a work group is often the person who holds a particular position or title, such as supervisor, manager, vice-president, or leadperson, a work group leader may also be a person with no official title or status. These informal leaders emerge because they have some characteristics that the group members value. Furthermore, the fact that a manager or supervisor holds a position of responsibility does not necessarily make that person a true leader. Leadership, if we look closely at the definition, is the ability, regardless of position or title, to lead groups to the attainment of goals. Of course, in work organizations, a powerful position or title can provide a strong starting point for a person to become an effective leader, but a position or title alone will not make an effective leader. Therefore, our definition deals with *effective* leadership. We may all know (or have worked under) managers who were not effective leaders. They may have done nothing to help the group achieve work goals, or they may have actually hindered the group's work. Such leaders are "leaders" in name only. This chapter will concentrate on theories of effective leadership.

I/O psychology has long had tremendous interest in the topic of leadership; theories and research on this subject abound. As we shall see, there is some consistency to the various theories. They all tend to build on one another, with later models using components of earlier theories and expanding on or using them in new ways. The discussion will begin with the earliest theories, which are known as universalist theories because they were attempts to uncover the universal characteristics of effective leaders. The second category is the behavioral theories, which focus on the behaviors of effective leaders. The third and largest category is the more complex contingency theories, which examine the interaction between leader characteristics and elements of the work situation. Throughout the discussion relevant research and applications of the theories will

leadership
the ability to guide a group to the achievement of goals

Lee Iacocca, chairman of Chrysler Corporation, is credited with reviving the company's fortunes.

also be presented. In particular, we will compare and contrast the contingency theories. Finally, we will discuss how leadership theories can be used to improve the effectiveness of leadership in work organizations.

UNIVERSALIST THEORIES OF LEADERSHIP

Universalist theories of leadership search for the one key characteristic or a cluster of key characteristics held by effective leaders, arguing that leaders with these traits will be successful regardless of the situation. Universalist theories represent the earliest and simplest approaches to the study of leadership. We will discuss three of these theories: the great man-woman theory, the trait theory, and McGregor's Theory X and Theory Y.

universalist theories
theories that look for the major characteristic common to all effective leaders

GREAT MAN-WOMAN THEORY

The **great man-woman theory,** which is much older than any of the formal social science disciplines, reflects the adage that "great leaders are born, not made." Rather than being a formal theory, this theory is a belief that personal qualities and abilities make certain great persons natural leaders. Proponents of the great man-woman theory would state that if important historical leaders such as Julius Caesar, Alexander the Great, or Joan of Arc were alive today, they would again rise to positions of leadership because of their natural abilities. Of course this is mere speculation, and there is little evidence to support the theory, but this does not mean that people do not still believe in it. The fact that in certain countries the relatives of great leaders are also put into positions of power may indicate that there is some general faith in this notion of in-born leadership ability.

great man-woman theory
a universalist theory of leadership that maintains that great leaders are born, not made

TRAIT THEORY

In the early part of this century, psychologists made many attempts to isolate the specific **traits,** or consistent and enduring personality attributes, associated with leader success. The **trait theory** of leadership refers to several of these investigations. Much of this research involved identifying effective and ineffective leaders, measuring them in terms of certain personality traits, and isolating those that distinguished the effective from the ineffective leaders. Some of the more commonly studied traits were extraversion, dominance, psychological adjustment, and intelligence (Hollander, 1985). It was presumed that those who were more extraverted, dominant, better adjusted, or more intelligent would be more likely to do well as leaders. Unfortunately, the results of these studies

traits
enduring attributes associated with an individual's personality

trait theory
attempts to discover the traits shared by all effective leaders

have been inconclusive; there is no solid evidence of any single trait or group of traits common to all effective leaders (Hollander, 1985; Stogdill, 1948).

The major problem with the trait approach to leadership is that it is too general. It is unlikely that any one trait will be associated with effective leadership in all situations, with all kinds of tasks, and among all groups of followers. The world of work, with the variety of workers and work settings, is much too complex and diverse for any one type of leader to be universally successful.

McGREGOR'S THEORY X AND THEORY Y

Theory X
a leader orientation characterized by the view that workers are basically unmotivated, disinterested in work, and need to have their activities directed and controlled

Theory Y
a leader orientation characterized by respect for and trust in subordinates, and a belief that workers are self-motivated and desire responsibility

Another universalist theory of leadership is McGregor's Theory X and Theory Y approaches to management. In his model, the key to effective leadership is the leader's assumptions and beliefs about subordinates. According to McGregor, leaders can have one of two basic orientations. Those with a **Theory X** approach, which is the traditional and outdated management viewpoint, believe that workers inherently dislike work and will avoid work if possible. They also maintain that workers must be coerced into working and that their activities must be controlled and directed by management. Finally, Theory X leaders feel that the average worker shuns responsibility and has little ambition to grow in the job and no desire to achieve organizational goals (McGregor, 1960). On the other hand, leaders with a **Theory Y** orientation believe that workers find work as natural a part of their lives as play or rest. They are accordingly believed to be self-motivated, to desire responsibility, and to be committed to the organization and its goals.

McGregor argued that Theory X assumptions are apparent in many aspects of more traditional work organizations. For example, the fact that most organizations are arranged in an authority hierarchy with each individual's activities directed and controlled by someone higher up suggests the presence of Theory X, as does the widespread use of punishment and other coercive tactics by managers. McGregor believed that work leadership would be improved if some fundamental changes were made in managers' views of workers. In other words, modern-world, effective leaders need to have a Theory Y orientation. According to McGregor, because Theory X has stifled employee motivation and initiative, Theory Y would encourage worker initiative and greater participation in work group activities and thus would be universally associated with leader effectiveness.

McGregor's general, descriptive model outlines two very different leader orientations. Like the great man-woman theory and the trait models, Theory X and Theory Y are too simplistic and in reality represent very different extremes of a continuum of leaders' beliefs about subordinates. Many managers may not be strictly Theory X or Theory Y, although they may lean slightly toward one or the other. Still, there is little evidence to support McGregor's contention that Theory Y managers make more effective work group leaders.

The general failure of the universalist theories to isolate the characteristics associated with leader effectiveness led to a change in focus. Rather than trying to measure characteristics in the leader's orientation or personality, researchers began to examine the actual behavior of effective leaders to determine what kinds of behavior led to success. In the late 1940s and throughout the 1950s, two research projects, one conducted at Ohio State University and the other at the University of Michigan, investigated the behaviors exhibited by effective leaders. Both projects arrived at some very similar conclusions concerning leaders, their behavior, and effective leadership. Theories based on these studies and focusing on the particular behaviors that lead to effective leadership are called **behavioral theories of leadership.**

behavioral theories of leadership
theories derived from studies at Ohio State and the University of Michigan that focus on the behaviors common to effective leaders

OHIO STATE LEADERSHIP STUDIES

Using self-reports and detailed observations of leader behavior from both the leaders themselves and their subordinates, researchers at Ohio State University accumulated a list of hundreds of leader behaviors. Using a statistical process called factor analysis, they found that these hundreds of behaviors could all be narrowed into two general categories: initiating structure and consideration (Halpin & Winer, 1957). (Recall from Chapter 2 that factor analysis examines how variables are related to each other and clusters them together to form meaningful categories, or factors.) **Initiating structure** includes leader activities that define and organize, or *structure*, the work situation, such as assigning specific tasks, defining work group roles, meeting deadlines, making task-related decisions, and maintaining standards of work performance. **Consideration** describes behaviors that show a genuine concern for the feelings, attitudes, and needs of subordinates by developing rapport with them and showing them mutual respect and trust. Such activities include asking subordinates for their opinions and input, showing concern for the feelings of workers, encouraging communication from and between subordinates, bolstering workers' self-confidence and job satisfaction, and implementing their suggestions.

initiating structure
leader behaviors that define, organize, and structure the work situation

consideration
leader behaviors that show a concern for the feelings, attitudes, and needs of subordinates

The Ohio State researchers concluded that these two dimensions, initiating structure and consideration, were independent of each other. That is, a leader's score on one did not relate to the score on the other. This means that *both* categories of leader behavior are associated with effective leadership but that they do not necessarily coexist. In other words, some effective leaders are high on initiating structure alone, others display only consideration behaviors, and still others exhibit both.

To assess various leader behaviors, the Ohio State group developed several questionnaires. One, the Leader Opinion Questionnaire (LOQ), was designed to gain insight into what the leader thinks is correct leader

Figure 10.1
ITEMS FROM
THE LEADERSHIP OPINION
QUESTIONNAIRE

Source: E. A. Fleishman,
*Leadership Opinion Question-
naire* (Chicago: Science Research Associates, 1960).

Structure	Consideration
1. Put the welfare of your unit above the welfare of any person in it.	1. Back up what persons under you do.
2. Emphasize meeting of deadlines.	2. Get the approval of persons under you on important matters before going ahead.

behavior. It consists of a series of statements representing initiating structure and consideration behaviors. Leaders then indicate whether they believe each is an appropriate leader behavior. Another instrument, the Leader Behavior Description Questionnaire (LBDQ), asks the subordinates to rate how a leader behaves in varying situations. The original LBDQ contained forty items representing various initiating structure and consideration behaviors (there have been many subsequent revisions of the LBDQ). Workers indicate how well each item describes their leader. These instruments both measure the amount of initiating structure and consideration behaviors particular leaders tend to display. Although these measures have been used primarily as research tools, they may also indicate that a leader who displays low levels of either or both dimensions needs some training to learn effective leader behaviors. (See Figure 10.1 for sample items from the LOQ and LBDQ.)

A great deal of research has been conducted using the LOQ and LBDQ, some of which has tested the soundness of the initiating structure and consideration dimensions. Generally, the results show that most leader behavior can indeed be grouped into one of the two categories (Bass, 1981; Fleishman & Harris, 1962; Stogdill & Coons, 1957). The LOQ and LBDQ have also been used to assess leadership behavior patterns to determine whether leaders are prone toward a style of behavior that is high in one or both dimensions (Schriesheim & Kerr, 1974). Additional studies have looked at how the two categories are related to the important outcome variables of work performance and job satisfaction (Kerr & Schriesheim, 1974; Yukl, 1971). Initiating structure has been found to be correlated with effective work performance but also with lower group member job satisfaction and corresponding increases in turnover. On the other hand, consideration leader behaviors tend to be positively related to job satisfaction but may be unrelated to or even negatively correlated with work productivity (Bass, 1981; Locke & Schweiger, 1978). However, these results are inconsistent. For example, one study found that the size of the work group affected the relationships between initiating structure and consideration leader behaviors and member satisfaction. Initiating structure was positively related to satisfaction in large groups but negatively related in small groups. The opposite relationships held for leader consideration: positively correlated with satisfaction in

Mikhail Gorbachev has boldly led the Soviet Union in political and economic reform.

small groups and negatively related in large ones (Schriesheim & Murphy, 1976). The inconsistencies probably arise because the effectiveness of specific leader behaviors is likely to be dependent on a number of other factors that serve as moderating variables that can determine whether a particular behavior will be related to a certain outcome, such as group performance or satisfaction, in a given situation. For instance, in the example above the size of the work group is the moderating variable, affecting the relationship between leader behavior and specific work outcomes.

While the Ohio State behavioral approach stimulated a great deal of research on effective leader behaviors, it, like the universalist theories, is too simplistic. The Ohio State investigations leave us with two categories of leader behavior, both of which may or may not be related to certain indicators of leader effectiveness. While the results had the positive effect of stimulating research on leader behaviors, it is clear that the Ohio State studies fall short when it comes to making firm predictions about the relationships between leader behaviors and specific work outcomes in all types of working situations.

As the publisher of influential magazines like Ebony *and* Jet, *John H. Johnson helps to shape opinion on a national scale.*

UNIVERSITY OF MICHIGAN LEADERSHIP STUDIES

At about the same time as the Ohio State studies were being conducted, researchers at the University of Michigan were also focusing on the behaviors characteristic of effective leaders and came up with quite similar results. Studying leaders in a number of large industrial organizations, the Michigan researchers found that successful leaders tended to exhibit patterns of behavior that were labeled task-oriented, sometimes also called "production-oriented," and relationship-oriented, also referred to as "employee-oriented" (see Kahn & Katz, 1960). **Task-oriented behaviors** are concentrated on performing the job that the work group faces and are thus similar to those of the initiating structure factor. The leader is concerned with setting work standards, supervising the job, and meeting production goals. **Relationship-oriented behaviors** are focused on maintaining social relationships in the work place and thus resemble consideration behaviors. Relationship-oriented leader behaviors include showing concern for employees' well-being and involving them in decisionmaking processes. The primary difference between the Ohio State and Michigan studies was that the Michigan results tended to consider relationship-oriented leader behaviors to be more effective than task-oriented behaviors (Likert, 1967). One of the most famous Michigan studies examined the behavior of leaders in a large insurance company. The findings indicated that both task-oriented and relationship-oriented leadership behavior patterns were positively related to work group performance. However, subordinates of relationship-oriented leaders tended to be more satisfied and had lower turnover rates than employees who were managed by task-oriented leaders (Morse & Reimer, 1956; see also Up Close: How to Be an Effective Leader).

task-oriented behaviors
leader behaviors focused on the work task

relationship-oriented behaviors
leader behaviors focused on maintaining interpersonal relationships on the job

How to Be an Effective Leader

It is very likely that sometime in the near future you will find yourself in a leadership role. You may serve as a formal manager of a work group, you may be elected to serve as a leader of a club or civic organization, or you may be appointed head of some work task force. In any case, the research on leadership as well as other findings that we have studied in the areas of communication and group dynamics can help you to do a better job. Of course, as you should know by now, there is no one best way to lead. There are, however, some general principles that you can follow to increase your chances of success:

Become a More Effective Communicator

It has been estimated that as much as 80 percent of a manager's job involves communication (Mintzberg, 1973). As we saw in Chapter 8, communication is essential for the effective functioning of work groups and organizations. The better the channels of communication beween the leader and followers, the more likely it is that the two will be able to cooperate to get the task done. It is particularly important to listen to subordinates and be sensitive to their needs and concerns. The leader who steals away behind closed doors will be unable to meet these needs, which may lead to breakdowns in productivity and in work group satisfaction.

Be Both Task-Oriented and Relationship-Oriented

As the research indicates, both task-oriented and relationship-oriented behaviors are related to leader effectiveness. Therefore, leaders who are able to display concern for both the task and the people are more likely to be successful. Gaining insight into your own leader behavior patterns will help you to realize if you have a deficit in either area.

Give Careful Attention to Decisionmaking

One of the leader's most important tasks is decisionmaking. As we have seen, in addition to reaching a good and workable solution, the process itself is also important. For example, involving subordinates in the decision can increase their levels of satisfaction but usually also leads to slower decisionmaking. The decision making leadership model emphasizes flexibility—adapting the leader's decisionmaking style to the situation. Certain decisions may call for more autocratic decisionmaking; others demand a participative approach. Being able to determine what process to use in what situation is the key. However, since evidence indicates that subordinates are generally satisfied with participative decisionmaking, when in doubt it may be wise to use this style.

Remember That Leadership is a Two-Way Street

While leaders influence their followers, followers also influence their leader. A leader can be truly effective only if that person has the support of followers. An effective leader knows what his or her own needs are and works to satisfy those needs, but the effective leader is also in tune with, and responsive to, the needs of followers.

Learn to Delegate

Effective leaders learn to delegate certain challenging and responsible tasks to subordinates, which often not only develops their work skills and abilities, thus making them more valuable to the leader and to the organization, but also gives the leader more time to work on other duties, leading to higher levels of productivity.

Be Flexible

Effective leadership means doing the right thing in the right situation. Effective leaders are thus flexible or adaptable. One way to be more flexible is to step back and objectively analyze a situation before you act. Leaders should also be objective about their own feelings, behaviors, attitudes, and biases, and how they may negatively affect leadership ability. Sometimes, leaders fall into comfortable patterns of behavior, using the same leadership style in all situations simply because it is easier than adapting behavior to fit the situation. However, it is the objective, adaptable leaders who are successful.

Source: R. A. Baron, *Behavior in Organizations: Understanding and Managing the Human Side of Work,* 2nd ed. (Boston: Allyn & Bacon, 1986), pp. 288–289.

EVALUATION OF THE BEHAVIORAL THEORIES OF LEADERSHIP

While initiating structure (task-orientation) and consideration (relationship-orientation) seem to be reliable dimensions describing leader behavior, the behavioral approach has one major shortcoming: The two dimensions represent very different types of leader behavior, yet both have been linked to effective management (Bass, 1981; Morse & Reimer, 1956). If we believe the universalist contention that there is one set of effective leader characteristics or one best leadership style, such divergent leader behaviors simply cannot represent a single, effective leader. The most likely explanation is that other variables, particularly those related to the type of tasks or the characteristics of the work group, determine whether certain leadership behaviors will be effective. In other words, a task-oriented leader might be effective in certain situations under specific circumstances, while a relationship-oriented leader might be effective in another situation. Indeed, research since the time of the Ohio State and Michigan studies has taken this approach, looking at the interaction of leader behavior and the situation (see Applying I/O Psychology).

A charismatic labor organizer, Cesar Chavez has led the struggle to improve the lives and working conditions of farm workers.

CONTINGENCY THEORIES OF LEADERSHIP

The next stage in the evolution of leadership theories produced **contingency theories,** which examine the interaction of characteristics of the leader and the situation, stating that effective leadership depends on the proper match between the two. Many of the contingency theories do, however, build on the behavioral theories, using the leader behavior dichotomies—task-oriented/initiating structure and relationship-oriented/consideration—as a starting point. However, contingency theories recognize no one best style of leadership behavior. Rather, leader effectiveness depends, or is *contingent* upon, the interaction of leader behavior and the situation. We will examine four of the more popular contingency theories of leadership: Fiedler's contingency model, the path-goal theory, Vroom and Yetton's decision making model, and the leader-member exchange model.

contingency theories
theories that look at the interaction of characteristics of both the leader and the situation

FIEDLER'S CONTINGENCY MODEL

The leadership theory proposed by psychologist Fred Fiedler (1967) is so popular that it is often simply referred to as *the* contingency model. But, as outlined, the term "contingency model" actually specifies a certain category of theory. **Fiedler's contingency model** argues that effective leadership depends on a match between a leader's behavioral style and

Fiedler's contingency model
a leadership theory that maintains that effective leadership depends on a match between the leader's style and the degree to which the work situation gives control and influence to the leader

The Managerial Grid®: The Marketing of Leadership Theory

One of the more successful and widespread applications of leadership theory to business is Blake and Mouton's (1985) **Managerial Grid.** This leadership intervention program encompasses two core dimensions—people emphasis and production emphasis. These are attitudinal in character and are to be distinguished from the behavioral dimensions identified in the research originating at the Ohio State and Michigan studies. The basic premise of the Managerial Grid is that the best leaders are those who show both high concern for the task (task orientation) and high concern for people (relationship orientation). Each manager is rated on two nine-point scales, the first assessing the manager's task orientation, the second measuring the leader's relationship orientation. The best leader receives a score of 9,9, meaning someone high in both task and relationship orientation (labeled a "team manager"); the worst leader receives a 1,1 rating, meaning someone low in both task and relationship orientation (labeled an "impoverished manager"; see the accompanying diagram). By stating that there is one best leadership style (the 9,9 leader), the Managerial Grid takes a universalist approach, which is a departure from the results of the Ohio

State studies indicating that either task orientation or relationship orientation could be related to leader effectiveness (see Figure 10.2).

The Managerial Grid has been criticized primarily because of its universalist approach. Most researchers advocate that there is no one best leadership style and that effective leadership depends on how the leader's style fits with the particular work situation. In spite of some criticisms, the Managerial Grid has had significant impact. According to the authors, the program has "boosted productivity and profits for thousands of corporations worldwide"; they claim that Managerial Grid training has been provided to more than a quarter of a million leaders and managers. In fact, the program has been so well packaged that its name is a registered trademark. Still, there has been little systematic research on the theory behind the grid by persons other than its authors, although Tjosvold (1984b) recently found that leaders who were task-oriented and also demonstrated a relationship orientation by expressing leader warmth led groups that were more productive than those led by leaders who lacked both of these orientations.

the degree to which the work situation gives control and influence to the leader. In other words, the leader's style of behavior must fit with the amount of control and power the leader will have in the work situation.

Building on the Ohio State and Michigan behavioral approaches, Fiedler's theory divides leaders into two basic types based on their behavioral styles—task-oriented and relationship-oriented—that he sees as relatively fixed and stable. In other words, leaders are either task-oriented or relationship-oriented. To measure a leader's orientation or style, Fiedler developed a self-report measure referred to as the **LPC** measure, which stands for **least preferred co-worker.** The LPC requires leaders to rate the person with whom they had "the most difficulty in getting a job done." These ratings are done using sixteen bipolar adjective rating scales, such as pleasant-unpleasant and friendly-unfriendly (see Figure 10.3). The LPC is scored by summing the ratings on the sixteen scales. This total score indicates whether a person is a task-oriented or relationship-oriented leader. Persons scoring relatively low on the LPC measure, giving their

least preferred co-worker (LPC)
a measure that assesses leaders' task or relationship orientation by having them rate the fellow worker with whom they had "the most difficulty in getting a job done"

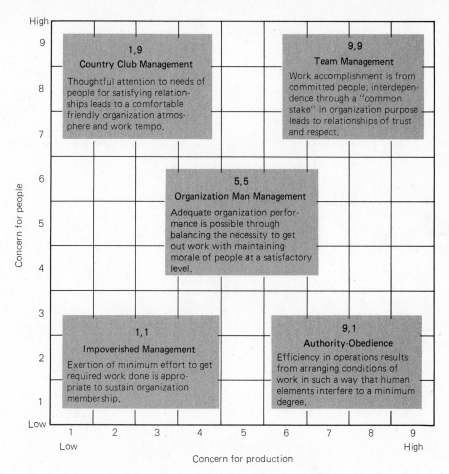

Figure 10.2
MANAGERIAL GRID

Source: Robert R. Blake and
Jane Srygley Mouton, *The
Managerial Grid III: The Key
to Leadership Excellence*
(Houston: Gulf Publishing
Company, 1985), page 12.

least preferred co-workers very harsh ratings, are task-oriented leaders. Individuals who rate their least preferred co-worker somewhat leniently, leading to relatively high LPC scores, are considered to be relationship-oriented. Scores from normative populations help determine what are low and high LPC scores. The rationale behind this scoring system is that a task-oriented leader will be very critical of a poor worker because they value task success. A relationship-oriented leader, on the other hand, values interpersonal relationships and is likely to rate the least preferred co-worker more leniently (Rice, 1978). According to Fiedler, task-oriented leaders with low LPC scores link a worker's poor performance with undesirable personality characteristics, while relationship-oriented leaders with high LPC scores can separate the least preferred co-worker's personality from the individual's work performance (Fiedler, 1967).

Determining a leader's task or relationship orientation with the LPC

Managerial Grid
an application of the
findings from the be-
havioral theories of
leadership that stress
that effective leaders
should be both task-
oriented and relation-
ship-oriented

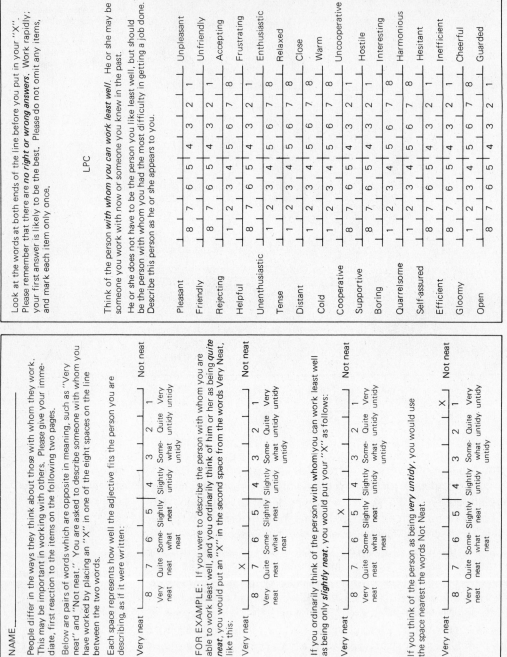

NAME

People differ in the ways they think about those with whom they work. This may be important in working with others. Please give your immediate, first reaction to the items on the following two pages.

Below are pairs of words which are opposite in meaning, such as "Very neat" and "Not neat." You are asked to describe someone with whom you have worked by placing an "X" in one of the eight spaces on the line between the two words.

Each space represents how well the adjective fits the person you are describing, as if it were written:

Very neat | 8 | 7 | 6 | 5 | 4 | 3 | 2 | 1 | Not neat
Very neat / Quite neat / Some-what neat / Slightly neat / Slightly untidy / Some-what untidy / Quite untidy / Very untidy

FOR EXAMPLE: If you were to describe the person with whom you are able to work least well, and you ordinarily think of him or her as being *quite neat*, you would put an "X" in the second space from the words Very Neat, like this:

Very neat | 8 | 7(X) | 6 | 5 | 4 | 3 | 2 | 1 | Not neat
Very neat / Quite neat / Some-what neat / Slightly neat / Slightly untidy / Some-what untidy / Quite untidy / Very untidy

If you ordinarily think of the person with whom you can work least well as being only *slightly neat*, you would put your "X" as follows:

Very neat | 8 | 7 | 6 | 5(X) | 4 | 3 | 2 | 1 | Not neat
Very neat / Quite neat / Some-what neat / Slightly neat / Slightly untidy / Some-what untidy / Quite untidy / Very untidy

If you think of the person as being *very untidy*, you would use the space nearest the words Not Neat.

Very neat | 8 | 7 | 6 | 5 | 4 | 3 | 2(X) | 1 | Not neat
Very neat / Quite neat / Some-what neat / Slightly neat / Slightly untidy / Some-what untidy / Quite untidy / Very untidy

Look at the words at both ends of the line before you put in your "X". Please remember that there are *no right or wrong answers*. Work rapidly; your first answer is likely to be the best. Please do not omit any items, and mark each item only once.

LPC

Think of the person *with whom you can work least well*. He or she may be someone you work with now or someone you knew in the past.

He or she does not have to be the person you like least well, but should be the person with whom you had the most difficulty in getting a job done. Describe this person as he or she appears to you.

Pleasant	8	7	6	5	4	3	2	1	Unpleasant
Friendly	8	7	6	5	4	3	2	1	Unfriendly
Rejecting	1	2	3	4	5	6	7	8	Accepting
Helpful	8	7	6	5	4	3	2	1	Frustrating
Unenthusiastic	1	2	3	4	5	6	7	8	Enthusiastic
Tense	1	2	3	4	5	6	7	8	Relaxed
Distant	1	2	3	4	5	6	7	8	Close
Cold	1	2	3	4	5	6	7	8	Warm
Cooperative	8	7	6	5	4	3	2	1	Uncooperative
Supportive	8	7	6	5	4	3	2	1	Hostile
Boring	1	2	3	4	5	6	7	8	Interesting
Quarrelsome	1	2	3	4	5	6	7	8	Harmonious
Self-assured	8	7	6	5	4	3	2	1	Hesitant
Efficient	8	7	6	5	4	3	2	1	Inefficient
Gloomy	1	2	3	4	5	6	7	8	Cheerful
Open	8	7	6	5	4	3	2	1	Guarded

Figure 10.3
LEAST PREFERRED CO-WORKER (LPC) MEASURE

Source: F. E. Fiedler, *A Theory of Leadership Effectiveness* (New York: McGraw-Hill, 1967), pp 40–41.

is only the first part of Fiedler's contingency model. The next step is defining characteristics of the work situation to find the proper match between leadership style and the situation. The characteristics of a work situation are defined using three variables—leader-member relations, task structure, and position power—that combine to create circumstances that are either very favorable, very unfavorable, or neither favorable nor unfavorable for the leader.

Leader-member relations is the relationship between the leader and followers, in other words, how well liked, respected, and trusted the leader is by subordinates. According to Fiedler, this dimension can be measured on a scale ranging from good to poor by having group members indicate their loyalty for and acceptance of the leader.

leader-member relations
the relationship between leader and followers

The second dimension, **task structure,** assesses how well a job is structured by considering such factors as whether the group's output can be easily evaluated, whether the group has well-defined goals, and whether clear procedures for reaching those goals exist. Tasks can either be structured or unstructured.

task structure
an assessment of how well elements of the work task are structured

The third dimension that Fiedler uses to define the situation is **position power,** or the leader's authority over subordinates, which is usually defined as the leader's ability to hire, fire, discipline, and reward. Position power ranges from strong to weak. It is usually easy to determine position power, because it is clearly outlined in company policies.

position power
a leader's authority to punish or reward subordinates

Recall that according to Fiedler's contingency model, the key to effective leadership is the leader's control and influence in a specific situation. Obviously, the situation that is going to be most favorable for the leader is one in which the leader-member relations are good, the task is structured, and the leader has strong position power. Research indicates that task-oriented leaders with low LPC scores are most effective in situations that are either highly favorable or highly unfavorable for the leader—the two extremes of the continuum. Relationship-oriented leaders are more effective in "middle situations" in which the leader's control and influence are neither low nor high.

According to Fiedler, task-oriented leaders with low LPC scores are successful in very unfavorable situations because their take-charge style puts some structure into the circumstances and may encourage the group to perform the job. In other words, in an extremely unfavorable situation, the task-oriented leader has nothing to lose. Taking a firm hand, and focusing on task performance and task-related goals may produce results, which is what is needed in such a crisis. At these times followers might walk all over a relationship-oriented leader. In very favorable situations, groups are already likely to be productive because the task is straightforward and structured, relations between leader and members are good, and the leader has the power to reward for good performance. According to Fiedler (1967), in these settings low-LPC leaders actually shift from their dominant, task-oriented style and focus more on relationship-oriented behaviors, which is an effective strategy. Although it may seem that high-

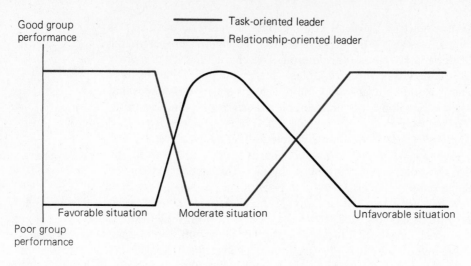

Figure 10.4
FIEDLER'S CONTINGENCY MODEL PREDICTIONS

Leader-member relations	Good	Good	Good	Good	Poor	Poor	Poor	Poor
Task structure	Structured	Structured	Unstructured	Unstructured	Structured	Structured	Unstructured	Unstructured
Position power	Strong	Weak	Strong	Weak	Strong	Weak	Strong	Weak

LPC leaders would be more effective in very favorable situations, such persons are actually less effective than low-LPC leaders because, according to Fiedler, they retreat from the dominant, relationship-oriented style and actually become task-oriented.

Relationship-oriented leaders are more successful when their situational control and influence are neither very high nor low. In these "middle" circumstances, it is important that leaders be well equipped to deal with the interpersonal conflicts that inevitably arise. This is the specialty of the high-LPC, relationship-oriented leaders. Because such situations may lack one of the three situational variables, a leader who shows increased concern for workers and allows them to voice opinions may increase group member satisfaction levels and even job performance. By contrast, being task-oriented in these situations may be counterproductive, alienating members and decreasing levels of satisfaction, because the leader appears to care only about the task. Fiedler also argues that high-LPC leaders may be more cognitively complex, or better able to deal with complex situations. Situations that are neither clearly favorable nor clearly unfavorable for the leader are best handled by such a person.

Figure 10.4 is a graphic representation of the predictions made by the

Fiedler model. The graph shows that task-oriented leaders (color line) have higher group performance when in very favorable or very unfavorable situations. Relationship-oriented leaders (black line) lead higher performing groups in situations of moderate favorability.

Although some studies have failed to find the predictions made by Fiedler's theory (Vecchio, 1977), others have generally supported the model (Strube & Garcia, 1981). However, the predictions hold up better in laboratory studies than in studies conducted in actual work settings (Peters, Hartke, & Pohlmann, 1985). Critics have focused primarily on the use of the LPC measure, arguing that it is not clear exactly what it measures since it only infers a leader's orientation from feelings about a co-worker rather than directly assessing task and relationship orientation (Ashour, 1973; Schriesheim, Bannister, & Money, 1979). Another criticism concerns individuals who score near the middle of the LPC scale. In fact, one researcher divided the ratings into high, low, *and* middle scores and found that the middle LPC leaders seemed to be effective in a range of situations (Kennedy, 1982). Another weakness in Fiedler's predictions concerns the assessment of situations, for it is not clear how actual work situations would break down in terms of their favorableness for the leader. In other words, we do not know how many real world situations would be favorable or very unfavorable for the leader and thus demand a task-oriented leader. Nor do we know how many situations are moderately favorable for the leader or what distinctions there are between moderately favorable situations (i.e., are there "low moderate" and "high moderate" favorable situations?).

In spite of these criticisms, the Fiedler contingency model is important for many reasons. First, it was the first highly visible leadership theory to present the contingency approach. Second, its detailed attention to the situation emphasized the importance of both situation and leader characteristics in determining leader effectiveness. Third, Fiedler's model stimulated a great deal of research, including tests of its predictions and attempts to improve on the model, and inspired the formulation of alternative contingency theories. Finally, it also led to the development of a program by Fiedler and his colleagues (Fiedler & Chemers, 1984) to apply his theory to actual leadership situations. Known as Leader Match, their program consists of a workbook containing an LPC measure, leadership problems that the leader must analyze and solve, directions on how to assess elements of the leader's situation, guidelines for changing elements of the situation, and suggestions for helping subordinates improve performance. Basically, Leader Match teaches managers to recognize their own leadership orientation using the LPC and then trains them to recognize those situations in which they are most likely to succeed. If a mismatch is discovered between the leader's orientation and the work situation, suggestions are made for changing one or more of the three situational variables to provide a more appropriate fit. For example, if a low-LPC, task-oriented leader is in a situation of moderate favorability in

Katharine Graham headed the influential Washington Post *during that newspaper's ground-breaking investigation of the Watergate scandals.*

Leader of Poland's Solidarity movement, Lech Walesa has helped propel his country toward democracy.

which leader-member relations are fair, the task is unstructured, but position power is strong, an attempt might be made either to improve leader-member relations or to make the group work task more structured to increase the favorability of the situation and thus make it more compatible with the leader. The Leader Match program holds that it is more effective to change the situation or to fit certain types of leaders to appropriate situations than it is to try to change the leader's style of behavior.

Leader Match has been widely used. Fiedler claims that is has been used by more than forty thousand managers. Although the program has been shown to be quite successful in increasing managers' leadership effectiveness (Leister, Borden, & Fiedler, 1977), it is not without its critics, who argue that at times Leader Match does not follow the predictions made by the theory (Jago & Ragan, 1986; Kabanoff, 1981).

In sum, Fiedler's contingency model was one of the first detailed theories of leadership. It makes certain predictions about the situations in which certain types of leaders will be effective, and has been a straightforward and widely used intervention for improving leader effectiveness.

THE PATH-GOAL THEORY

Expanding on the definition of leadership presented at the start of this chapter, the **path-goal theory** states that a leader's job is to help the work group attain the goals that they desire (House, 1971; House & Mitchell, 1974). The leader is accordingly seen as a facilitator, or guide, who helps the group overcome the various barriers and roadblocks they may encounter on the way to achieving their goals. Usually these goals involve increasing worker motivation to perform the job and attempting to gain increases in worker satisfaction.

To help the group reach its goals, the leader may adopt one of four categories of behavior—directive, achievement-oriented, supportive, and participative—the selection of which depends on the characteristics of the situation. **Directive behavior** provides instructions and suggestions for getting the job done. Examples include giving workers specific guidelines and procedures, setting up schedules and work rules, and coordinating work group activities. **Achievement-oriented behavior** focuses on specific work outcomes and may involve setting challenging goals for the group and measuring and encouraging improvements in performance. **Supportive behavior** concentrates on the interpersonal relations among group members by showing concern for workers' well-being and providing a friendly work environment. Finally, **participative behavior** encourages members to take an active role in work group planning and decisionmaking through actions such as soliciting information from workers about how to do the job and asking for opinions and suggestions. These four types of leader behaviors outlined in the path-goal theory offer a more detailed breakdown of the initiating structure (task-oriented) and consideration (relationship-oriented) behaviors: Directive and achievement-

path-goal theory
a theory that states that a leader's job is to help the work group achieve their desired goals

directive behavior
leader behavior that provides instructions and suggestions for performing a job

achievement-oriented behavior
leader behavior concentrated on particular work outcomes

supportive behavior
leader behavior focusing on interpersonal relationships and showing concern for workers' well-being

participative behavior
leader behavior that encourages members to assume an active role in group planning and decision making

oriented behaviors are two kinds of initiating structure behavior, while the supportive and participative behaviors are two kinds of consideration behaviors.

The choice of leader behavior is contingent on the type of work task and the characteristics of the subordinates. For example, if a task is routine and easy to understand and if the work group is made up of experienced, self-motivated individuals, the directive style of leadership would probably not be needed since subordinates can perform the job without much supervision. Instead, supportive behavior might be called for to maintain a harmonious work setting, or participative behavior may be necessary to encourage employees to suggest ways to improve work procedures and the work environment. On the other hand, if the task is fairly complex and the workers are somewhat inexperienced, a directive style might be appropriate.

The results of research on the path-goal theory have been mixed. While there has been some support for the model (see, for example, Downey, Sheridan, & Slocum, 1976; House & Dessler, 1974), its general approach and its inability to make specific and precise predictions in actual work settings have been criticized (Shriesheim & Kerr, 1977). While the theory does offer some idea of how leaders must change their behavior to fit the situation, the biggest disappointment is that to date it has not led to a specific type of intervention for use on the job (Miner, 1983). On the positive side, like Fiedler's contingency model, the path-goal theory offers a rather detailed assessment of the situation in an effort to relate the leader's behavior to the characteristics of a specific situation. It also goes a step beyond the simple dichotomy of task orientation and relationship orientation in defining leader behavior. In terms of the history of leadership theories, the path-goal theory is a relative newcomer. It is likely that additional research and applications may prove productive.

Already a legend in the computer field, Steven Jobs co-founded Apple Computer, guided development of the Macintosh, and then moved on to introduce the Next line of computers.

VROOM AND YETTON'S DECISION MAKING MODEL

As seen in Chapter 9, one of the major tasks of a work group leader is to preside over important work-related decisions. Vroom and Yetton (1973) have developed a contingency theory of leadership that is based on the premise that leaders are basically decisionmaker. Their **decision making model** is sometimes referred to as the normative model because it is a prescriptive theory (see Chapter 2) that not only makes predictions about proper leader behavior in making decisions but also actually gives prescriptions for the decisionmaker to follow. The decision making theory holds that a leader can make work decisions using a number of strategies, ranging from acting alone (purely autocratic decisionmaking) to arriving at a decision on the basis of group consensus (completely participative decisionmaking). In the latter type of decisionmaking the leader is just another group member. The five decisionmaking styles used in the Vroom and Yetton model are presented in Table 10.1.

To define the decisionmaking situation, the theory provides a series

*decision making model
a theory that matches characteristics of the situation with leader decisionmaking strategies*

Table 10.1 FIVE DECISION-MAKING STRATEGIES: THE VROOM AND YETTON MODEL

Decision-Making Strategy	Process
1. Autocratic decision I	The leader makes the decision alone, using information available only to the leader.
2. Autocratic decision II	The leader obtains information from subordinates and then makes the decision alone.
3. Consultative decision I	The leader shares the problem with relevant subordinates and gets their ideas and input individually, but makes the decision alone.
4. Consultative decision II	The leader shares the problem with subordinates as a group, gets their collective input, but makes the decision alone.
5. Group decision	The leader shares the problem with subordinates as a group and together they make a consensus decision.

Source: V. H. Vroom and P. W. Yetton, *Leadership and Decision-Making* (Pittsburgh: University of Pittsburgh Press, 1973), p. 13.

of seven yes-no work-related questions that a leader must ask before adopting a particular strategy. For example, the first question is whether or not a high-quality decision is needed. If the leader answers yes, it is likely that a more participative style is needed; if the answer is no, it is likely that a more autocratic style is appropriate. Of course, the decision making style chosen is a composite of all seven questions. The Vroom and Yetton model presents a decision tree framework for the leader to follow, with each of the seven questions representing a choice point that eventually leads to the correct behavior for the decision that needs to be made (see Figure 10.5). Consider, for example, the manager of the parts department of an automobile dealer who must purchase a computerized inventory system for the department. A number of systems are available, each with its own advantages and drawbacks. The leader answers each of the questions on the decision tree as follows:

A. Yes, there is a need for quality—a computer system that will work best in our department.
B. No, the leader doesn't have enough information to make a quality decision alone.
C. No, the problem is not structured, because there is no clear-cut way to decide among the various systems.
D. Yes, subordinates will be using the system and need to accept it.
E. No, if subordinates did not like the computer system they might avoid using it.
F. Yes, workers do share organizational goals (they want a computer system that will do the job).
G. Not applicable.

This framework suggests that the leader should use a group strategy to arrive at a consensus. Since the department is small and the workers are

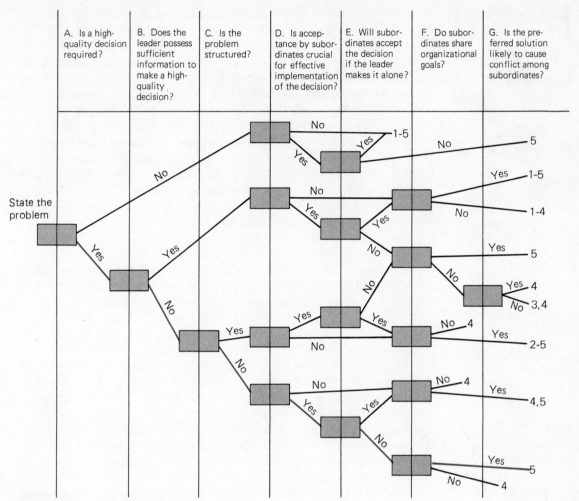

Figure 10.5

DECISION TREE FLOW CHART (NUMBERS AT THE END OF THE TREE CORRESPOND TO
THOSE OF THE STRATEGIES IN TABLE 10.1)

Source: V. H. Vroom and P. W. Yetton, *Leadership and Decision-Making* (Pittsburgh: University of
Pittsburgh Press, 1973), p. 194.

A dynamic speaker, former congresswoman Barbara Jordan is known for her leadership in civil rights and other social issues.

involved in their jobs, they can contribute a great deal to the decisionmaking process, and it is critical that they accept the decision.

Research has largely supported this decision making model (Field, 1982; Margerison & Glube, 1979). For example, a study found that the effective strategies used by actual managers to solve important work-related decisions were consistent with the Vroom and Yetton prescriptions (Vroom and Jago, 1978). Because of the normative nature of the model, it is also a unique combination of theory and application. As a contingency model, it is effective because it considers how a leader's individual behavior fits with the dynamics of a specific situation. Moreover, it provides a very detailed definition of the situation, as outlined by the seven questions. The major problem with the model is its complexity, which may make it difficult for managers to understand and to learn to use. This occurs to theories in general: As they get closer to modeling real world complexity, they may also become harder to apply. There is a general tendency for people to look for simple solutions to problems. Thus, while complex contingency models, such as the decision making model, might be sound and accurate, they may not be widely used or accepted in actual work settings due to their complex nature.

THE LEADER-MEMBER EXCHANGE MODEL

leader-member exchange model
the theory that effective leadership is determined by the quality of the interaction between the leader and particular group members

The previous contingency models of leadership, including Fiedler's model and the path-goal theory, fit the leader's behavior to various characteristics of the work situation. Fiedler's model also considers the amount of power a leader has in a given situation, while the decision making theory weighs a variety of characteristics related to a situation. The **leader-member exchange model** takes a different approach and considers that effective leadership is determined by the quality of the interaction between the leader and a particular work group member (Dansereau, Graen, & Haga, 1975). According to this theory, the worker *is* the situation. Basically, the model (which was formerly called the vertical dyad linkage model) states that the types of one-on-one, or dyadic, relationships that develop between the leader and each follower will be somewhat different. In any work group, the leader tends to develop better relationships with a few subordinates (the ingroup), while the rest receive less attention or concern from the leader (the outgroup). The character of the leader-member exchange can range from low quality, in which the leader has a negative image of the subordinate and the subordinate does not respect or trust the leader, to high quality, in which the leader has a positive view of the worker and the worker feels that the leader is supportive and provides encouragement. Of course, such differences affect important outcomes such as work performance and job satisfaction (Graen, Novak, & Sommerkamp, 1982).

The notion that leaders develop different types and quality of relationships with subordinates makes sense. For example, the president of a large company may have to interact with a number of department managers. Some of them may be the trusted advisers with whom the president interacts quite frequently and to whom he gives an important role in establishing company policy. The president's relationships with other managers may not be close at all, and they may in fact have very little actual contact with the president. Naturally, and as the leader-member exchange model predicts, the motivation to perform and the levels of satisfaction of the ingroup managers are likely to be high, while the outgroup managers may not be very motivated or satisfied.

The authors of the leader-member exchange theory claim that their approach is an improvement over other leadership theories because previous models assume that leaders act in a relatively uniform way toward all subordinates. Because these traditional approaches look only at typical, or average, leader behavior and ignore the nontypical behavior displayed in very good or very poor leader-member exchanges, a focus on specific leader-member relations will lead to better predictions of the effects of that leader behavior on work outcomes (Dansereau et al., 1975; Graen, 1976; see also Vecchio, 1982). In other words, rather than looking at how the leader's behavior influences a particular outcome in subordinates, the leader-member exchange approach generally emphasizes how a leader's particular behavior with particular subordinates—both ingroup and outgroup members—affects their specific job outcomes.

Although this model is quite new, it shows a great deal of promise and has generated a considerable amount of research. A recent review and critique concluded that this theory "has identified an aspect of leadership that has been overlooked in the past and deserves continued study" (Dienesch & Liden, 1986, p. 631). While these authors see potential in the model, they also note that in its present form it is oversimplified. Dienesch and Liden argue that the leader-member exchange process is complex and needs to be more fully researched and defined, work that is currently underway. For example, recent research has been attempting to refine the ways of measuring ingroup/outgroup membership (Duchon, Green, & Taber, 1986).

The strategy for applying the leader-member exchange model to improving leader effectiveness seems relatively straightforward: Improve the quality of leader-member relationships. Initial tests of leadership training programs aimed at this goal have been encouraging. For example, in one study of eighty-three computer-processing employees of a large service organization, a program that trained leaders to listen and communicate their expectations to subordinates led to a 19 percent increase in work group productivity and significant increases in subordinates' job satisfaction (Scandura & Graen, 1984).

Elizabeth Hanford Dole, a cabinet member in the Reagan and Bush administrations, is a powerful voice in Washington.

Leadership Traits: A Reconsideration

In the early days of leadership research, the trait approach—searching for characteristics common to effective leaders—proved to be unfruitful. There did not appear to be any stable leader traits that were effective in all situations. The contingency theories of leadership helped indicate why this search was futile, for many of them argue that effective leaders must change their behavior to fit particular situations. Therefore, it seems impossible that certain traits could be successful in all settings. However, recent research indicates that this may not be altogether true and that certain characteristics may in fact be important not only in achieving success as a leader but also in attaining such a position (Kenny & Zaccaro, 1983; Lord, DeVader, & Alliger, 1986).

Many contingency models state that to be effective, a leader must be able to change behavior, which in some cases must be quite drastic, as in changing from being task-oriented in one situation to being relationship-oriented in another. This requires a great deal of *flexibility* from the leader. It may be that flexibility is the trait that is common to effective leaders, although we don't usually think of it as a trait. Leader flexibility does not refer to an arbitrary change of behavior but rather to an adaptive process by which the *perceptive* leader

changes behavior to fit the particular situation. Kenny and Zaccaro (1983, p. 678) describe this characteristic as "the ability to perceive the needs and goals of a constituency and to adjust one's personal approach to group action accordingly." As such, leader flexibility may not be a single trait but instead a very complex set of abilities to perceive and understand social situations, to communicate effectively, and to act wisely in a variety of social settings (Marlowe, 1986; Riggio, 1986) that might be better termed "social intelligence" or "social competence" (see Hollander, 1978, p. 125). The socially intelligent or competent leader can diagnose what kinds of leader behavior a particular situation requires and then act accordingly. A group of employees working together on some task is a complex social situation in which a socially intelligent leader will likely be more effective than one who lacks such competence.

There is little evidence that traditional personality traits play an important role in leader effectiveness. However, certain characteristics, such as a leader's social intelligence, may be significant in predicting leader success, although these key leader qualities are probably more complex and multifaceted than those investigated in the early leadership research.

COMPARISON OF THE CONTINGENCY THEORIES OF LEADERSHIP

Each of the contingency theories of leadership presents a different way of examining leader effectiveness by focusing on the leader-situation interaction. To better understand the perspectives that these theories take in predicting leader effectiveness, we need to compare the various models.

One obvious difference among the contingency theories is how they view the leader's primary task. For example, Fiedler's model sees the leader as determining the course the work group should take; the path-goal theory considers the leader as merely a facilitator who helps the group achieve their goals; the Vroom and Yetton model sees the leader's main job as work-related decisionmaking; and the leader-member exchange theory focuses on the leader's role with subordinates. The models also differ in how they define effective leadership. In Fiedler's contingency model, in contrast to the other models, the leader's style is seen as relatively fixed and unchangeable. Thus, the leader must seek out or create situations that are compatible with the leader's behavioral orientation. All of the other contingency models assume that leaders are more flexible and require leaders to change their behavior in accordance with the situation. For example, according to the decision making model, a leader should be participative and democratic in dealing with decision-making in one situation, and be more autocratic and directive in another. Likewise, according to the path-goal theory, a leader may change roles from time to time to meet the varying goals of the work group. As we shall see, this notion of the flexibility or stability of leader behavior is very important to the application of leadership theory (see On the Cutting Edge).

APPLICATIONS OF LEADERSHIP THEORIES

The various leadership theories suggest several possible interventions for improving leaders' effectiveness. For example, Fiedler's Leader Match program offers suggestions for changing a work situation to fit with the leader's behavioral orientation; the decision making theory prescribes the appropriate decisionmaking strategy for any situation; and the leader-member exchange model advocates teaching leaders to be more attentive and responsive to group members. The most common suggestion by far is trying to change the leader's behavior. Spurred by this, tremendous energy and resources have gone into programs to train leaders. From the other perspective, some effort has also gone into ways of redesigning jobs to fit particular leaders' styles. It should be noted that these approaches apply equally to male and female leaders; research has shown essentially no difference between the sexes in behavioral orientation (see Up Close: Are There Differences Between Male and Female Leaders?).

As chairman of the Federal Reserve Board, Alan Greenspan probably exerts more influence on the nation's economy than any other person.

LEADERSHIP TRAINING

Leadership training programs take a number of forms, although most follow two general approaches. The first approach teaches leaders diagnostic skills, that is, how to assess a situation in order to determine the type of leader behavior that will work best. The assumption is that a leader who knows the particular behavior that a situation requires will be able to adjust behavior accordingly. The path-goal and decision making theories emphasize such diagnosis. The path-goal theory requires leaders to determine the goal expectations of the work group, while the decision making model asks the leader to perform a detailed assessment of a situation before adopting a decisionmaking strategy. The second approach teaches leaders specific skills or behaviors that they lack. For example,

Are There Differences Between Male and Female Leaders?

There is considerable evidence of discrimination against women in gaining leadership positions in work organizations (*Work in America,* 1973). Furthermore, when women do attain such positions, they may discover discrimination in terms of the distribution of rewards (Larwood & Wood, 1977; Nieva & Gutek, 1981). While discrimination in work settings certainly exists, are there any actual differences in the effectiveness of female and male leaders or even in female and male leadership behaviors?

Recent research has found no differences in the effectiveness of female and male leaders and virtually no differences in their leadership behaviors (Bass, 1981; Rice, Instone, & Adams, 1984). For example, one review of seventeen studies found that male and female leaders exhibit equal amounts of task-oriented and relationship-oriented leader behaviors (Dobbins & Platz, 1986). The few relatively insignificant sex differences that do emerge in some studies seem to be limited to research on leadership in simulated laboratory settings with college students or manager trainees role playing leader situations. These small differences do not appear in studies of actual leaders.

It thus appears that the belief that female and male leaders behave differently is a myth. As Nieva and Gutek (1981, p. 81) wrote, "contrary to popular beliefs, female leaders are not more emotional and suggestible, or less decisive, aggressive, and objective than male leaders. Also contrary to notions about sex specialization in leadership styles, women leaders appear to behave in similar fashion to their male colleagues."

such programs might train task-oriented leaders to be more relationship-oriented or teach relationship-oriented leaders to focus more on work procedures and performance. Probably a combination of both approaches—teaching diagnostic skills plus increasing the leader's behavioral repertoire—is likely to be most effective.

Organizations invest a great deal of time and money in programs designed to train their leaders to be more effective. While research indicates that many of these programs are successful (Burke & Day, 1986; Latham, 1988), a number of factors must be considered to maximize the chances of such effectiveness.

First, as in all types of training programs, training needs must be determined (see Chapter 5). In leadership training it is important to identify the specific behaviors or diagnostic skills that the trainee lacks. A second, related concern is the leader trainee's openness and acceptance of the training program. If a leader is to be successful in a program that involves a substantial change in behavior, the leader must be willing to accept the change. The leader must see the merit in learning new leadership behaviors and perhaps abandoning past leadership behaviors. If the leader is not committed to the program, it is likely to fail. This is a problem in many training programs that managers are "forced" to attend. When leadership training programs are mandatory, the program may fail because of resistance from the participants. Third, the more time and energy invested in the program, the more successful it is likely to be. Changing the behavior of practicing managers is neither quick nor easy, for old leadership patterns have likely become deeply ingrained. If the change that needs to take place in leader behavior is great—for example, teaching a task-oriented, autocratic leader to become more participative—it is unlikely that a program lasting a few hours or even a weekend is going to be very effective.

Another important consideration is whether the particular leadership behaviors taught in the training program will be accepted in the work group and organization. In many cases, when the leaders try to use their newly acquired leadership behaviors in the work environment, they meet with resistance from both subordinates and colleagues. The new behaviors may be incompatible with the usual operating procedures within the organization or the work group, and the new leadership style may not fit the expectations of group members. For example, a training program that taught police sergeants to replace task-oriented, authoritarian styles with participative behaviors was a spectacular failure. Although the sergeants accepted the change, it was met with considerable resistance by their subordinates, who felt that the program had made their leaders "soft," a condition that they perceived as dangerous in the life-and-death situations that policemen often face. Thus for leadership training to be effective, the organization must accept and support the new leader behavior.

Finally, sound evaluations of leadership training programs must be conducted routinely to determine whether the programs are indeed successful. Such evaluations include measuring the effects of leadership training programs on organizational outcomes such as work group productivity, work quality, and member satisfaction. Training programs that deal with these various concerns can improve the quality of leadership in work groups and organizations.

JOB REDESIGN

Certain critics, such as Fiedler, suggest that leadership training may be ineffective and a waste of organizational resources. Because Fiedler believes that a leader's orientation is inflexible, he argues that organizations should concentrate on changing the job to fit the leader rather than vice versa (Fiedler, 1965). The most obvious example of this approach is his Leader Match program, which offers suggestions for altering the work situation to fit the leader's predominantly task-oriented or relationship-oriented pattern, usually by increasing or decreasing task structure or position power. The main problem with this approach is that many work situations may be unchangeable. In such cases, Fiedler (1973) suggests that it may be easier to transfer the leader to a situation that is more compatible with the leader's orientation than to try to alter the leader's behavioral orientation. However, changing the situation to fit the leader's style may prove to be quite successful.

Research in redesigning jobs indicates that in certain instances leaders may be unnecessary (Kerr & Jermier, 1978). For example, a group that is cohesive and has very structured norms for operation may have no need for a leader. Examples of such leaderless groups include some of the job enrichment teams mentioned in Chapter 6, in which all members have equal status and authority, as well as groups of professionals such as physicians or real estate agents who all have high levels of ability, experience, training, and knowledge. In addition, a leader would be redundant in a situation in which the task is well-structured and routine and the work is intrinsically satisfying to workers, since there would be no need for direction or for encouragement. Finally, it has been suggested that a form of self-leadership, or self-management, might substitute for the traditional supervision provided by a formal leader (Manz, 1986; Manz & Sims, 1980). However, while some work groups may be able to operate well without formal leaders, such groups probably represent a small proportion of work groups. It is likely that leaders will remain an important part of most work groups.

**CHAPTER 10
CONCLUSION**

SUMMARY

Leadership is the ability to direct a group toward the attainment of goals. Leadership theories can be divided into three categories: *universalist theories, behavioral theories,* and *contingency theories.* The *great man-woman theory,* a universalist theory, holds that some people are natural, born leaders. The *trait theory* specifies certain personality *traits,* or characteristics that are common to all effective leaders. According to McGregor's *Theory X,* leaders view subordinates as unmotivated and irresponsible, whereas *Theory Y* leaders see followers as self-motivated and responsible. These universalist theories suffer from the facts that they are simplistic and that they focus on individual leader characteristics.

The behavioral theories of leadership are typified by studies conducted at Ohio State and Michigan that looked directly at leader behavior, rather than at inferred leader characteristics. Two dimensions of leader behavior emerged: *initiating structure* (also called *task-oriented behaviors*), which focuses on work task production, and *consideration* (also known as *relationship-oriented behaviors*), which emphasizes interpersonal relationships among workers. The *Managerial Grid* is an application of the findings from the behavioral theories—a program that stresses both task-oriented and relationship-oriented behaviors as the keys to leader success.

The latest and most popular theories of leadership are the *contingency theories. Fiedler's contingency model* states that effective leadership depends on a match between the leader's style and the favorableness of the work situation. Leader style is assessed through the *least preferred co-worker (LPC)* measure. Task-oriented leaders are most effective in either very favorable or very unfavorable situations, while relationship-oriented leaders do better in moderately favorable situations. The favorability of situations in Fiedler's model is determined by three variables: *leader-member relations, task structure,* and the leader's *position power.* The *path-goal theory* asserts that the leader is a facilitator who chooses the type of behavior that will most help the work group to achieve their goals. According to the path-goal theory, the leader can adopt four types of leader behavior: *directive, achievement-oriented, supportive,* or *participative.* The Vroom and Yetton *decision making model* sees the leader's main role as making work-related decisions. This prescriptive model contains a decision tree framework for the leader to follow to decide the appropriate decision-making strategy (ranging from autocratic to democratic) to use in a particular situation. Finally, the *leader-member exchange model* examines the quality of the relationship between the leader and each subordinate, which leads to a more precise determination of work outcomes.

The application of leadership theories involves one of two strategies: instituting leadership training programs or redesigning the job to fit the leader. The majority of the theories advocate leadership training, either by teaching specific leader behaviors (for example, task-oriented or relationship-oriented) or by training leaders to diagnose situations that call for task-oriented or relationship-oriented behaviors. Job redesign usually involves changing characteristics of the situation to fit the leader's typical style or orientation. However, work situations that are amenable to such job redesigns may be limited.

STUDY QUESTIONS AND EXERCISES

1. Discuss the limitations of the universalist leadership theories. Why do you suppose they had such popular appeal?

2. Consider the distinction between task-oriented (initiating structure) and relationship-oriented (consideration) leader behaviors. How are they used in the various contingency theories?

3. Think of a leader of a work or social group whom you have known. How would you characterize this person's leadership style or orientation? What theory of leadership best describes and explains this person's leadership situation?

4. All contingency theories of leadership measure some characteristics of both the leader and the work situation. How do the different theories—Fiedler's, path-goal, decision making, leader-member exchange—define characteristics of the work situation?

5. What considerations should be made to maximize the effectiveness of leadership training?

SUGGESTED READINGS

Bass, B. M. (1981). *Stogdill's handbook of leadership: Revised and expanded edition*. New York: Free Press. *A comprehensive review of theory and research on leadership from the earliest days through the late 1970s.*

Kerr, S., Hill, K. D., & Broedling, L. (1986). The first-line supervisor: Phasing out or here to stay. *Academy of Management Review, 11,* 103–117. *An interesting article that claims that because of increases in participative decisionmaking and in the autonomy of many work groups, the front-line supervisor's role is changing from a task orientation to a relationship orientation.*

McCall, M. W., Lombardo, M. M., & Morrison, A. M. (1989). *The lessons of experience: How successful executives develop on the job*. Lexington, MA: Lexington Books. *A book on the development and success of high-level business leaders that presents "how-to" information for creating a leader development program.*

Smith, P. B., & Peterson, M. F. (1988). *Leadership, organizations, and culture*. Newbury Park, CA: Sage Press. *A book that offers a cross-cultural look at leadership and seeks to answer questions such as, "How important is leadership?" and "How does the concept of leadership differ from culture to culture?"*

11

INFLUENCE, POWER, AND POLITICS

Defining and Differentiating Influence, Power, and Politics

This chapter presents and discusses three topics: influence, power, and organizational politics. While each is a distinct concept, they are also three facets of the same general process, for all involve one party trying to affect the behavior of another. However, it is important to be able to distinguish among the three. Influence is an informal process by which an individual uses personal skills and abilities to affect the behavior of others. Power can come from a position held in an organization or from the possession of important work resources or work-related abilities. Most research on power looks specifically at the types of power, which are commonly called power bases. Politics, which is self-serving behavior, is the most difficult concept to distinguish, partly because both influence and the use of power can be labeled political behaviors if they are self-serving. Thus certain forms of influence and uses of power can be subsets of the category of political behavior, depending on how they are used. This is an important point that will help in understanding how the three concepts are different and similar.

Because the study of influence, power, and politics in work organizations is relatively new, there is less theory and less terminology in this chapter than in many of the others. However, this does not mean that these topics are less important. Indeed, influence, power, and politics are extremely significant and pervasive processes in all work groups and organizations. Power and influence in particular are important aspects of leadership (see Chapter 10), because leaders use their power and influence to help work groups attain their goals. Influence, power, and politics are also important factors in group processes, which we discussed in Chapter 9. For example, conformity to group norms will occur only if the group can influence members to follow the rules. Also, managers can use their power and authority to help resolve conflicts among group members. Furthermore, group decisionmaking, by its very nature, is a political process. Finally, because certain forms of power are linked to the very structure of the organizational hierarchy, our discussion in this chapter will provide some groundwork for examining organizational structure in Chapter 12.

I n Chapters 9 and 10 we examined important processes and relationships that occur in work groups. In this chapter we will continue to study key group processes, specifically influence, power, and politics, which are the forces by which individuals and work groups affect the behavior of other persons and groups.

Work organizations are filled with individuals who are trying to succeed, but simply being a dedicated, hard-working employee is usually not enough. People advance in organizations partly due to their talents and energy but also partly due to their ability to gain influence and power over others. As an individual moves up the ladder, authority and power typically increase. However, two managers at the same level in a company may not be equal in terms of their power and influence. For example, one may be more powerful because she is well liked and respected by subordinates and superiors, and because she understands the politics of the company and knows how "to play the game."

Although influence, power, and politics are ongoing processes in the day-to-day life of any work organization, with important implications for organizational performance and employee satisfaction, these topics have only recently been studied in depth by social scientists (Pfeffer, 1981). The concepts of influence, power, and politics are also closely intertwined with the topics of group processes and leadership that were discussed earlier. For example, individuals in work groups use influence and power to affect and alter the behavior of other members. Leaders also use their power and influence to achieve group goals. Moreover, they must often act politically to gain and hold their powerful leadership positions, and individuals may also engage in politics to improve their position in the organization. Influence, power, and politics likewise play a major role in group decisionmaking processes. For example, a powerful, influential member can have an important impact in deciding the courses of action a group will take. Democratic decisionmaking, by its very nature, involves political behaviors such as lobbying for and voting on particular plans. Moreover, because influence, power, and politics affect the behavior of others, they can help determine the amount of conflict and coordination within work groups.

DEFINING INFLUENCE, POWER, AND POLITICS

In one sense, influence, power, and politics are similar, because all three involve getting others to do something. There are, however, some important differences among them.

Influence is a form of social control or social power. It is an individual's ability to get another person to perform a certain action. Usually, influence is exerted by using informal strategies such as persuasion, peer pressure, or compliance techniques. For example, an individual might use persuasive influence in trying to obtain a loan from a friend or when attempting to persuade a co-worker to help complete a work task. Peer pressure influence might take the form of a worker's plea to a colleague to break a company rule because "everybody does it." Influence might also involve the use of compliance techniques. For example, an executive

influence
the ability to use social forces to affect the behavior of others

At a typical business meeting, influence, power, and politics may all come into play.

might use flattery or the offer of a favor to get a typist to work overtime to finish typing a report. In this definition, the term might be called "social influence," which is a more restricted usage than the more general notion of influence as any process of affecting behavioral change in others (Allen & Porter, 1983).

Power in the work place is a more formal process that can be defined as the use of some aspect of a work relationship to force another person to perform a certain action despite resistance. For example, a company president can give an order to a vice-president and expect it to be carried out because of the power associated with the status relationship. A safety inspector may be able to demand that operators shut down a piece of machinery that has a potentially dangerous malfunction by virtue of the person's position as an acknowledged safety expert. While influence resides primarily in the individual, power usually derives from the relation-

power
the use of some aspect of a work relationship to compel another to perform a certain action despite resistance

ship between two parties. For example, a co-worker might use persuasion skills—a form of influence—to try to get an unmotivated worker to increase work output by appealing to the worker to "pull his own weight." However, a supervisor, by virtue of the status relationship that gives the person authority over the worker, can use power to order the worker to improve productivity or face the consequences. Thus, power resides in the relationship between parties or in their positions, rather than in the individuals themselves.

Organizational politics is a very different process that involves any actions taken to influence the behavior of others to reach personal goals. The one thing that distinguishes political behaviors from power and influence is the fact that organizational politics are *always* self-serving, while power and influence are not necessarily self-serving.

The following shows how a person might use influence, power, and politics to achieve a certain outcome: Marilyn James has a problem. The vacation schedules at her company, Mackenzie Electronics, have been set up for several months. However, she has just found out that her husband's vacation will come two weeks earlier than they had anticipated. She now needs to exchange her vacation time with Dan Gibbons, who will be taking his vacation during the two weeks she needs. Marilyn could use influence by trying to persuade Dan to change his plans; she might promise to do him a favor, or she might simply make an appeal to Dan's generous nature and willingness to help. Marilyn would be using power if she ordered a change in the vacation schedule, which she could do because she is assistant manager of the marketing department and Dan is a newcomer, far down in the departmental hierarchy. Finally, she might use politics to get what she wants. Marilyn could encourage the marketing director to assign an important project to Dan, saying, "He's a real hard worker, and he deserves to handle this assignment." The project would require that Dan make a formal presentation on August 24, right in the middle of his vacation. Later, when Dan mentions that he needs to trade vacation times to work on the assignment, Marilyn would be ready to jump right in and offer to switch. In short, Marilyn could use any one of these methods—influence, power, or politics—to affect Dan's behavior.

Influence, power, and politics are pervasive processes in all work organizations that involve efforts by some organizational members to control the actions of others. However, the means exerted in using each process are quite different and thus will be examined separately.

organizational politics
self-serving actions
designed to affect the
behavior of others to
achieve personal goals

INFLUENCE: THE USE OF SOCIAL CONTROL

People often attempt to persuade, cajole, convince, or induce others to provide assistance, change an opinion, offer support, or engage in a certain behavior in both work organizations and everyday social life. A

Table 11.1 CATEGORIES OF INFLUENCE TACTICS

Assertiveness

Making orders or demands
Setting deadlines and making sure they are met
Emphasizing rules that require compliance

Ingratiation

Using praise or making the other person feel important
Showing a need for the other person's help
Being polite and/or friendly

Rationality

Using logic to convince someone else
Writing a detailed justification of a plan
Presenting information to support a request along with the request

Sanctions

Withholding salary increases
Threatening to fire someone or to give a poor performance evaluation
Promising or giving a salary increase

Exchanges

Offering an exchange of favors
Reminding another of past favors
Offering to make some personal sacrifice in exchange for a favor

Upward appeals

Obtaining the support of superiors
Sending the target person to see superiors
Filing a report about the target person to superiors

Blocking

Threatening to stop working with the other person
Ignoring the other person or withdrawing friendship
Engaging in a work slowdown

Coalitions

Obtaining co-workers' support of a request
Making a request at a formal conference
Obtaining subordinates' support of a request

Source: D. Kipnis, S. M. Schmidt, and I. Wilkinson, "Intraorganizational Influence Tactics: Explorations in Getting One's Way," *Journal of Applied Psychology, 65* (1980), pp. 445–448.

study by Kipnis, Schmidt, and Wilkinson (1980) attempted to classify the various influence tactics used in the work place by having 165 lower-level managers write essays describing incidents in which they influenced either their superiors, co-workers, or subordinates. The 370 tactics were put into 8 categories: assertiveness, ingratiation, rationality, sanctions, exchanges, upward appeals, blocking, and coalitions (see Table 11.1). In addition to trying to influence others by being assertive or by using logical arguments, one might also employ **ingratiation** by increasing one's personal appeal through such tactics as doing favors, praising, or flattering another. Other categories of influence are offering exchanges of favors or threatening the other person with negative sanctions, such as a demotion

ingratiation
influencing others by increasing one's personal appeal to them

CHAPTER 11 INFLUENCE, POWER, AND POLITICS

or firing. The final three categories of influence are making appeals to persons higher in the status hierarchy; engaging in behaviors that block, interfere with, or prohibit the others' work activities; or building coalitions by getting the support of co-workers or subordinates.

The study found that the choice of influence tactic was determined by the situation, the status of the individuals involved, and other characteristics of the organization such as size and whether or not the organization was unionized. For example, higher-status persons were more likely to use assertiveness or sanctions, while lower-status individuals used rational appeals to influence superiors. Co-workers commonly employed ingratiation and exchange when attempting to influence one another and to obtain personal favors, while rational and coalition tactics were often used to institute changes in the work or the work context. Interestingly, there were no sex differences in the use of the various influence tactics. Men and women seem to use the same tactics in the same ways.

Other studies have found that subordinates use different upward influence tactics with superiors, depending on whether they were seeking personal goals, such as a pay raise or promotion, or organizational goals, such as gaining the supervisor's approval of a new, more efficient work procedure. When seeking personal goals, subordinates tended to use tactics such as ingratiation. When seeking organizational goals, they favored strategies such as upward appeals and rational persuasion to try to influence superiors (Ansari & Kapoor, 1987; Schmidt & Kipnis, 1984). Moreover, subordinates' influence tactics varied depending on whether the superior was autocratic and task-oriented, or participative and relationship-oriented. Subordinates tended to use ingratiation, blocking, and upward appeal techniques with autocratic managers but rational persuasion strategies with participative superiors (Ansari & Kapoor, 1987).

Like individuals, groups will also use a wide variety of tactics to exert influence. For example, groups tend to use influence to get members to conform to group norms. As we saw in Chapter 9, if a member is in violation of a group norm, pressure will be exerted in the form of criticism, isolation (the "silent treatment"), or, in extreme cases, expulsion. Such pressure to conform is a very common and very important influence process in work groups and organizations (Feldman, 1984; Moscovici, 1985; see Up Close).

POWER: A MAJOR FORCE IN WORK ORGANIZATIONS

Power, in contrast to influence, is a more formal force in work organizations that derives from an individual's role or position or from some specific characteristics of the individual, such as work-related expertise or admirable leadership qualities. Whereas influence depends on the skill of the influencer in affecting another person at a particular place or time,

How to Resist Social Influence Tactics

Social psychologist Robert Cialdini (1988) has discussed the various uses of social influence tactics by "compliance professionals," such as salespersons, advertisers, and con artists, who are those people whose job it is to get others to do something. Using the technique of participant observation (see Chapter 2), he infiltrated such groups by posing as a door-to-door vacuum cleaner salesman, a car dealer, and a telephone fundraiser. Through his research, Cialdini was able to identify the most frequently used influence tactics. Three of the more common strategies are the *reciprocity rule,* the *rule of commitment and consistency,* and the *scarcity principle.* With the reciprocity rule, a "favor" is done to get something in return. The rule of commitment and consistency is used in getting people to commit to a small initial request and then hitting them with a larger request. The most infamous example of this is the "foot-in-the-door" tactic used by salespersons or people seeking donations. The compliance professional might begin with the question, "You are concerned about the plight of the whales, aren't you?" Answering affirmatively commits you to agreeing with the next question: "Then you would like to make a donation to the Save the Whales Fund, wouldn't you?" The scarcity principle is used to create the illusion of a limited supply, as is done by advertisements that read, "Act now, supply is limited." In work settings, these same tactics can be used by co-workers or bosses to influence people to do what they might not otherwise do. For example, reciprocity is often invoked by management after workers are given a cost of living raise. Workers, feeling as if management has just done them a favor, may be more compliant than usual, even though the raise was tied to some factor other than management's generosity. A company may try to use the commitment and consistency rule to increase company loyalty and cut down on voluntary turnover. For example, each month the company might hold a contest in which employees submit essays about why the company is a great place to work. Winning essays could be published in the company newsletter. This may make it tougher for employees to consider leaving for work elsewhere when they have made such a public act of loyalty. An organization might employ the scarcity principle in performance incentive programs by encouraging employees to work hard to obtain one of a very few scarce rewards.

Cialdini maintains that the best way to combat unethical use of influence tactics is to be able to recognize them. By understanding that people are trying to use these strategies to take unfair advantage of you, you may be able to resist them simply by seeing such obvious exploitation attempts for what they really are.

---

power is a consistent force that is likely to work across situations and time. In organizations, power is a fairly stable capacity or potential that can consistently affect the behavior of others, as long as the power remains with the individual. In other words, the use of influence strategies to affect the behavior of others is sometimes successful, but the use of power is *almost always* successful.

organizational power *power derived from a person's position in an organization and from the control over important resources afforded by that position*

POWER SOURCES

Power can take many forms and is derived from a variety of sources that are of two main types. Most often, power comes from the organization. **Organizational power** comes from an individual's position in the organization and from the control over important organizational resources conveyed by that position. These organizational resources can be tangible, such as money, work assignments, or office space, or more intangible, such as information and communication access to other people. **Individual power** is derived from personal characteristics, such as particular expertise or leadership ability, that are of value to the organization and its members.

Astley and Sachdeva (1984) outline three important sources of organizational power. One is the *hierarchical structure* of the organization. Power derived from the status hierarchy is inherent in one's position in the organization. Workers lower in the hierarchy often obey their superiors simply because they believe that their higher position gives them the right to exercise power. Organizational power can also result from *control of important resources* such as money, fringe benefits, knowledge, and work-related expertise. Finally, organizational power can come from being in a position of *network centrality* that is crucial to the flow of information. Persons in such positions may have access to information that others do not possess and may develop social relationships with important individuals or groups within the organization. For example, an executive's secretary may have low levels of power due to ranking in the organizational hierarchy and little control over resources, but may still be powerful because of a position of network centrality that involves contact with important people and information.

French and Raven (1959) looked at different types of power that they called **power bases,** which are the sources of a person's power over others in the organization. They specify five important power bases: coercive power, reward power, legitimate power, expert power, and referent power.

Coercive power is the ability to punish or to threaten to punish others. For example, threatening to fine, demote, or fire someone are all means of exercising coercive power, as is assigning a person to an aversive work task. An individual may possess coercive power by holding a position in the organization that allows the person to punish others. However, any individual, regardless of position, can use coercive power by threatening to harm someone either physically or psychologically with tactics such as damaging a reputation by spreading false rumors.

We have seen that the use of coercive power, with its punishment and threats of punishment, carries certain risks since it may create anger and resentment in the subject. Coercive power must be exercised carefully, with awareness of the potential strengths and weaknesses of punitive strategies. For example, while coercive threats may get quick action, the threatened person may try to retaliate later.

In many ways, **reward power** is the opposite of coercive power, for while coercive power is the ability to do harm, reward power is the ability to give something positive, such as money, praise, promotions, and interesting or challenging work assignments. The ability to reward others is

individual power
power derived from personal characteristics that are of value to the organization, such as particular expertise or leadership ability

power bases
sources of power possessed by individuals in organizations

coercive power
the use of punishment or the threat of punishment to affect the behavior of others

reward power
power that results from having the ability to offer something positive, such as money or praise

a very common source of power in work organizations, where it often derives from having control over the resources that others value. Having the ability to administer pay raises, bonuses, promotions, or coveted work tasks can be an extremely strong power base.

Legitimate power involves the formal rights or authority that an individual possesses by virtue of a position in an organization. Titles such as manager, foreman, director, or vice president are all bases for legitimate power. When employees carry out a request simply because "the boss" asked them to do it, they are responding to such power. In work organizations, legitimate power is typically combined with the reward and coercive power bases. That is, most persons with legitimate authority also have the power to reward or punish subordinates. These three power bases are usually, although not always, tied together. There can be some rare instances in which persons are given some formal position that is not accompanied by reward and coercive power—a position of power in name only. Such is the case of the vice president for public affairs in a relatively small insurance company. The organizational chart for this company reveals that this vice president probably lacks much reward or coercive power to back up his legitimate title because he is the sole employee in the department, with no subordinates!

Expert power is one of the strongest power bases an individual can possess, since it results from the possession of some special work-related knowledge, skill, or expertise. Such power is becoming even more important in today's work settings because of the increasing sophistication of technology. The advancing computerization and robotization of many types of work tasks means that the people who have the knowledge and expertise to design, operate, and maintain this sophisticated technology are going to be very important—and very powerful—in the organization. Expert power is also the source of power behind many health care professionals. For example, you are willing to take the advice of a physician because you believe that this individual has some special knowledge concerning your health.

A very different type of power base is **referent power,** which develops because an individual is respected, admired, and liked by others. Because the person is liked or admired, workers respond to the person's wishes in an effort to please the person and to gain favor. The most dramatic illustration of referent power is the charismatic political leader who can spur an entire population to action merely because of their admiration and respect for that person. Certain leaders in work settings may also have a strong referent power base and thus be very influential in controlling the activities of others.

In sum, the different power bases indicate that power can indeed take many forms and arise from many sources. For example, expert power and referent power reside within the individual and thus are forms of individual power. More often than not, legitimate, reward, and coercive power are derived from organizational rather than personal sources and thus are

legitimate power
the formal rights or authority that an individual has due to a position in an organization

expert power
power that derives from having certain work-related knowledge or skill

referent power
power resulting from the fact that an individual is respected, admired, and liked by others

Expert power—the control wielded by an individual who has special skills or expertise—is increasingly important as technology advances.

types of organizational power. A great deal of research has been conducted on power dynamics, or on how the different power bases operate in work settings and how they affect work outcomes.

POWER DYNAMICS IN WORK ORGANIZATIONS

Despite its importance (Bacharach & Lawler, 1980), the topic of power in work settings has only recently been studied in depth by behavioral scientists (Gandz & Murray, 1980). This research, although limited, has uncovered certain findings concerning the dynamics of power in work organizations. For example, researchers have investigated such issues as the distribution of power in work organizations, the attempts of organizational members to increase power, power and dependency relationships, and the effects of power on important organizational outcomes—specifically job performance and satisfaction.

Differences in power distribution.   We know that power, because of its many forms, is unevenly distributed in work settings. Usually, organizations are arranged in a power hierarchy, with people at the upper levels possessing great power and those at the bottom having relatively little power. However, individual differences in the expert and referent power bases ensure that no two people, even those at the same status level, have exactly equal power. Therefore, although persons high in the hierarchy tend to possess more power than those at lower levels, even a low-ranking member can wield considerable power because of personal sources of power, such as expert power and referent power.

*"I have to take one three times a day to curb
my insatiable appetite for power."*

Drawing by Dana Fradon; © 1977 The New Yorker Magazine, Inc.

McClelland (1975) has shown that people place different values on the gain and use of power, with some people being high in the need for power and others having a low need for power (see Chapter 6). Thus organizations may have some individuals who are "power hungry" and others who have little interest in gaining much power. However, although people may differ in their needs for power, once individuals have obtained power, they are usually reluctant to give it up (Kipnis, 1976). This makes sense, since it is power that enables organizational members to satisfy their various work-related goals.

Ways to increase power. One way for an organizational member to increase power is to gain work-related expertise or knowledge (Mechanic, 1962). Learning to solve complex problems, being able to operate or repair sophisticated machinery, and knowing complicated procedures are all linked to an expert power base. Low-power individuals may also increase their organizational power by developing a relationship with a higher-ranking member. Protégés often benefit from their association with a mentor, leading to greater organizational status and power. Low-ranking members may also gain power by forming a **coalition,** which is a group of low-level workers banding together to achieve common goals. A coalition can be a very powerful force because of its ability to slow or shut down organizational operations. A group of low-level workers acting to-

coalition
*a group of individuals
who band together to
combine their power*

CHAPTER 11 INFLUENCE, POWER, AND POLITICS

gether as a unit can become very powerful by sheer virtue of their numbers. In other words, a few workers may be easily replaced, but an entire line of workers cannot. A strong coalition can be created when employees join a union, which can exercise its power by threatening to strike or by actually striking.

Power and dependency relationships. When a nonreciprocal dependency relationship exists such that party A is dependent on party B, but B is not dependent on A, B will have power over A. In work settings, it is very common for certain individuals or groups to depend on others for certain resources needed to do a job. If the dependency does not go both ways, the individuals or groups who control the scarce resources will have power over the have-nots (Hickson, Hinings, Less, Schneck, & Pennings, 1971). Workers who have a great deal of expertise often have such power because those without the expert knowledge must rely on them to perform their jobs correctly. Because expert power is based in the individual, the dependent party sometimes has higher status than the expert. For example, in the military, commissioned officers attain their positions by attending officer training school. Although they have more formal education than noncommissioned officers, they have virtually no on-the-job experience. Thus, when junior lieutenants receive their first assignments, they quickly find out who holds the expert power—the noncommissioned officers, especially the master sergeants, who have many years of experience. A dependency relationship develops. A lieutenant who does not learn to get along with the master sergeants is in trouble and will be unable to command effectively because of a shortage of expert knowledge. Similar situations exist in business when a new manager may have to rely on the expertise of a long-time employee to get the job done.

Businesses strive to avoid dependency relationships on the organizational level. For example, a company will try hard not to have to rely on a single supplier for needed materials because such sole dependency gives the supplier power over the company. One famous fast-food chain has eliminated most dependency relationships by controlling the supply within the company. This restaurant chain owns their own cattle ranches to supply meat, farms to supply grain products, and even paper mills to make bags and containers. The resulting independence allows the company to increase its power over competitors who may be hurt if, for example, their meat suppliers go on strike.

Power and work outcomes. The possession and use of power bases can be directly related to important organizational outcomes such as performance and job satisfaction. For example, expert power is generally related to effective job performance (Bachman, Bowers, & Marcus, 1968), because expert power is based on knowing how to do the job. Referent power, on the other hand, is consistently linked to member satisfaction with the person wielding the power. This should not be surprising, because referent power results from the subjects' willingness to submit to the power of someone they admire and respect. In contrast, coercive power tends to decrease the attractiveness of the power wielder and may lead to decreased job satisfaction in work group members. Moreover, the use of coercive power may erode the individual's referent power base. In other words, we lose respect for people who consistently punish or threaten us. In practice, the exercise of coercive power more often involves threats of punishment rather than actual punishment. While drastic threats can be effective means for gaining compliance, the person who makes such threats runs the risk of having someone "call the bluff" and refuse to comply. The exerciser is now faced with a dilemma: If the person does not follow through with the punishment, some coercive power will be lost because the subject learns that it is an empty threat. On the other hand, the exerciser who administers the punishment risks infuriating, or in the case of threats to fire, losing the employee. In many instances, the use of coercive power is a no-win situation. While it may be used to threaten workers into higher levels of performance, satisfaction is likely to decrease, and the organization may lose in the long run through increases in voluntary absenteeism and turnover in the dissatisfied work force.

power corollary
the concept that for every exercise of power, there is a tendency for the subject to react with a return power play

The power corollary.   One aspect of power dynamics is known as the **power corollary** (Robbins, 1979), which states that for every use of power, there is a tendency for a corollary use of power—a return power play by the subject ("for every action there is a reaction"). In other words, when people are the subject of an obvious power play, they tend to try to assert their own power. According to French and Raven (1959), this is why it is important to possess a legitimate power base when exercising other power bases, particularly coercive power, for the combination will limit the form a corollary use of power can take. For example, if a co-worker tries to use coercive tactics on you, you might respond in kind, with threats of your own. However, if the person using coercive power is your supervisor, your response options are limited. In other words, it is unlikely that you will directly threaten someone who has legitimate authority.

Power and leadership.   The concepts of power and leadership are closely intertwined. Leaders use their power to help followers attain desired goals. Ideally, to be effective, a leader should possess a number of power bases. Having high levels of all five would be ideal (although it is likely rare), because the various power bases often complement one another. As we have seen, legitimate power tends to validate the use of reward and coercive power. Expert power should also exist in legitimate power positions, because the most qualified persons are usually the supervisors. Finally, if the work group is committed to doing a good job, and if they have a leader who is high in legitimate and reward power and has the expert power to lead a group to high levels of productivity, the leader is likely to develop a strong referent power base as well.

Looking back to some of the concepts of leadership presented in Chapter 10, we can see the importance of power in leader effectiveness. Power is either explicitly or implicitly a crucial part of some of the contingency theories of leadership. For example, the decisionmaking model views leaders as possessing the power to make major work-related decisions alone or to delegate some of the decisionmaking power to subordinates. Decisionmaking power can be a form of legitimate power. The leader-member exchange model focuses on the quality of leader-member relations as a key to effective leadership. Referent power is important here because the quality of leader-member relations may depend on the leader's referent power. Perhaps the leadership theory that is most strongly linked to notions of power and specific power bases is Fiedler's (1967) contingency model. According to Fiedler, a leader is effective when the leader's style—task-oriented or relationship-oriented—matches the leader's power and control in a given situation. Recall that Fiedler outlines three dimensions for defining the leadership situation: position power, leader-member relations, and task structure. Two of these are strongly linked to certain power bases. Position power deals with the leader's power to reward and punish subordinates. It actually refers to a combination of the three types of organizational power: legitimate, reward, and coercive power. Leader-member relations refers to the quality of the relationship between leader and followers, which represents the leader's referent power. In short, power is a key element in theories of leadership because the role of leader, by its very nature, must be accompanied by some form of power over followers (see Applying I/O Psychology).

ORGANIZATIONAL POLITICS

The use of politics occurs daily in all organizations at all levels (Schein, 1977). For example, a qualified individual is passed over for a promotion that goes to a co-worker who is clearly less qualified; organizational members say that it was a political decision. Two office workers who have a history of never getting along suddenly file a joint formal complaint about a mutually disliked supervisor; observers explain that their collaboration is due to office politics. A junior-level manager gives up a planned weekend trip to stay at home and take care of the boss's dog while the executive is out of town. The manager's motivation? Obviously political. Anyone who has had the chance to observe the operations of an organization has seen organizational politics in action.

Although the study of organizational politics is relatively new in industrial/organizational psychology, it is very important because politics in

The Empowerment Process: A Key to Organizational Success

Recently, researchers have begun to explore the concept of **empowerment,** which is the process by which organizational members are able to increase their sense of power and personal control in the work environment. Workers can be empowered by managers or other persons in authority positions, or by increasing important work-related skills or responsibilities. While a manager can empower subordinates by giving them some decisionmaking power or assigning some legitimate power, workers can also be empowered when conditions in the work environment that make them feel powerless are removed. Individual workers can also become empowered by developing a sense of **self-efficacy,** which is the belief that they have the abilities and energy to accomplish a particular task or goal (Bandura, 1986; Conger & Kanungo, 1988). Other ways in which leaders can empower workers include the following:

- *Express confidence in subordinates' abilities and hold high expectations concerning their performance.* Considerable evidence suggests that supervisors who have high expectations about their work group's performance may subtly communicate these feelings to the workers and thus positively influence their behavior.
- *Allow workers to participate in decisionmaking processes.* Workers who share in decisionmaking are more committed to the chosen courses of action (see Chapter 9).
- *Allow workers some freedom and autonomy in how they perform their jobs.* For example, let workers be creative or innovative in work methods. The job enrichment programs discussed in Chapter 6 can empower workers by giving them increased responsibility over how their jobs are performed and evaluated.
- *Set inspirational and/or meaningful goals.* Again, there is considerable evidence that goal setting is an important motivational

strategy (see Chapter 6). Also, according to the path-goal theory of leadership (see Chapter 10), setting meaningful goals is one of the important moves that leaders can make to help work groups be more effective.
- *Use managerial power in a wise and positive manner, such as to limit the use of coercive tactics.* Our discussion of the use of different power bases emphasized that coercive power can lead to dissatisfaction in the targets of the power and a reduction in the power user's referent power base. By contrast, reward, expert, and referent power bases allow workers greater choice and flexibility in following the power user. They can decide to strive for the reward or can choose to follow someone who is knowledgeable or admired. These are generally more effective strategies for achieving positive work group outcomes.

The empowerment process can have very positive effects on organizational outcomes. For example, empowering workers can help lessen the impact of demoralizing organizational changes. If workers feel that they have some sort of personal control over aspects of the work environment, and if they have had a say in some of the organizational changes, they can more easily adapt to and accept the changes (Greenberger & Strasser, 1986). Empowered workers may also be better able to deal with certain types of organizational stress, particularly stress that results from a sense of lack of control (see Chapter 7). There is considerable evidence that empowerment and feelings of self-efficacy play an important role in motivating workers to achieve challenging work-related goals (Gist, 1987), especially if they have a hand in setting the goals and feel that the goals are within reach. Finally, empowered workers are more likely to persist at a task in spite of difficult organizational or environmental obstacles (Block, 1987; Conger & Kanungo, 1988).

organizations is common, occurs at all levels, and has significant effects on job performance, satisfaction, and turnover. However, before we begin to explore the effects of organizational politics, we must start by clearly defining the term.

DEFINING ORGANIZATIONAL POLITICS

Earlier definitions stated that organizational politics involved the self-serving, or selfish, use of power or influence to achieve desired outcomes. This covers a very wide range of behaviors; in fact, just about any behavior can be interpreted as being political. Typically, the types of political behaviors in which we are interested involve the use of power or influence that is not part of one's position or role within the organization (Mayes & Allen, 1977). Because political behaviors are not "sanctioned" by the organization, it is assumed that organizational politics are bad or harmful to the organization's functioning, but this is not always true. Although a worker may act politically to satisfy selfish goals, using means that are not considered acceptable organizational procedures, the outcome might actually be favorable to the organization. In other words, political behaviors sometime lead to successful organizational outcomes. Such behavior might be called **functional politics**—behaviors that assist the organization in attaining its goals. On the other hand, political behavior that inhibits the attainment of organizational goals is **dysfunctional politics.** The same political behavior may be either functional or dysfunctional depending on how it affects the goals of the organization. For example, a salesman may use high-pressure tactics to make a sale, despite an organizational policy that frowns on such techniques. However, if the sale is made and the customer is satisfied, the tactics are functional because the goals of both the salesperson and the organization have been met. However, if the salesperson uses the unapproved techniques and makes the sale but the customer is unhappy with being subjected to high-pressure tactics and vows never to buy another of the company's products, the political behavior can be termed dysfunctional. The salesperson's goals have been met, but the organization's goal of keeping customers happy and loyal has been thwarted. It is not always easy to distinguish between functional and dysfunctional political behavior because the difference between the two depends on the outcome of the behavior (Cavanagh, Moberg, & Velasquez, 1981).

Ideally, if political behavior is going to occur in organizations (and it is), it should be functional. However, in any organization some of the political behavior will be functional and some will be dysfunctional. Figure 11.1 shows how political behavior that operates in the individual's self-interest can sometimes overlap with the organization's goals. The political behavior that satisfies the goals of both is functional; the behavior that satisfies the goals of the individual but not of the organization is dysfunctional.

empowerment
the process by which organizational members can increase their sense of power and personal control in the work setting

self-efficacy
the belief that a worker has the abilities and energy needed to perform a certain task or goal

functional politics
political behaviors that help the organization to attain its goals

dysfunctional politics
political behaviors that detract from the organization's ability to attain its goals

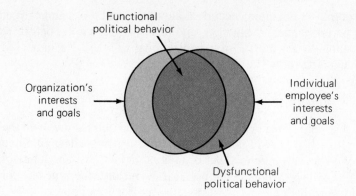

Figure 11.1

POLITICAL BEHAVIOR

Source: S. P. Robbins, *Organizational Behavior: Concepts and Controversies* (Englewood Cliffs, NJ: Prentice-Hall, 1979), p. 404.

Functional political behavior

Organization's interests and goals

Individual employee's interests and goals

Dysfunctional political behavior

When people think of politics or politicians, they often conjure up a less than positive image. It can be argued that it is dysfunctional political behavior that has given politics in general a bad name. For example, a politician from a region with many oil companies—who incidentally contribute to the politician's campaign funds—might push hard to have a wildlife preserve opened for oil exploration. If this behavior is viewed to be in the best interests of the politician but not of the general population, which wants drilling in protected lands banned, the politician's behavior may be judged negatively. The politics of a worker who reports any sort of misbehavior by co-workers to management and who later gets a promotion because of it might also be judged negatively. Political behavior that operates to further the individual's own ends, without considering its effects on others, is likely to be viewed negatively by others.

While some of the political behavior that takes place in government and work organizations is dysfunctional, oriented toward achieving personal goals to the detriment of organizational goals, much political behavior is actually functional, helping both the individual and the organization achieve respective goals. However, it is the dysfunctional politics that often gains the most attention because it sometimes violates the organization's codes of ethical and moral behavior. For example, in one organization reporting negative information about another worker to management might be considered a breach of ethics, while in another organization such political behavior might be more accepted. In one company, management might view workers' unionization as an acceptable political practice, while the management of a rival organization might see it as mutiny.

TYPES OF POLITICAL BEHAVIORS

Political behavior was defined as any self-serving behavior. This means that politics includes many different types of behaviors. To better understand organizational politics, it is important to have some scheme for classifying political behaviors. Farrell and Petersen (1982) have sug-

gested that political behaviors can be grouped along three dimensions: internal-external, lateral-vertical, and legitimate-illegitimate.

The internal-external dimension refers to whether political behavior involves only members of the organization or if it extends beyond the boundaries of the organization to include outside people and resources. Examples of external political behaviors would be bringing a lawsuit against an organization or organizational member, consulting with members of competitor organizations, or leaking secret company information to the press. The lateral-vertical dimension concerns whether the political behavior occurs between members of the same status within the organization or if it crosses vertical status levels. Political behaviors involving superiors and subordinates would be an example of vertical politics, while two co-workers campaigning for the same promotion are engaging in lateral politics. If a subordinate by-passes the typical chain of command and goes to someone higher in the organization to complain about an immediate supervisor, this is vertical politics. Several co-workers of the same status who form a coalition are engaging in lateral politics. The third dimension is whether a particular political behavior is legitimate or illegitimate. This legitimate-illegitimate dimension concerns whether the behavior is "normal everyday" politics or some extreme form of political behavior that violates the generally accepted "rules of the game." As mentioned, organizations and work groups establish their own codes of what is appropriate, or legitimate, and what is unacceptable, or illegitimate. Illegitimate political behavior is most likely to be used by alienated members of the organization who feel that they have no other alternatives and nothing to lose, such as a worker who is about to be fired. For

Scapegoating—pointing out someone to blame—is one form of organizational politics.

"*Okay, what's happened now?*"

© Punch/Rothco

example, slowing down work output—rate setting—may be a legitimate form of political behavior in many organizations, whereas sabotage, such as purposely breaking an important piece of work equipment, will almost always be considered illegitimate.

Interestingly, the distinction between whether a particular political behavior is legitimate or illegitimate, acceptable or unacceptable, or good or bad is in large part a value judgment. The same type of behavior may be considered unacceptable in one situation but acceptable when performed in another. Imagine that two employees are being considered for the same promotion. One of the workers brings up some negative information about the other—the fact that the person was arrested for a burglary many years ago. It might be considered that one candidate is trying to gain an advantage by mudslinging, a practice considered unacceptable in this organization. However, suppose that the promotion is to the position of chief of company security. In this situation, the same act might be viewed more favorably, because the candidate is seen as acting to protect the interests of the organization. Thus, the interpretation of a particular political act often depends on how it is perceived and evaluated by others.

Table 11.2 ORGANIZATIONAL POLITICAL BEHAVIORS: THE GOOD, THE BAD,
AND THE UGLY

Good	Bad	Ugly
Forming coalitions	Striking	Rioting
Blame placing (pointing out who is legitimately at fault)	Passing the buck (avoiding personal blame)	Scapegoating (blaming an individual who is likely not at fault)
Image building (making yourself look good by emphasizing your positive attributes)	Discrediting others (pointing out others' faults so that you look good in comparison)	Mudslinging (bringing up negative and possibly false information about another person)
Making demands and bargaining	Blackmailing	Sabotaging
Limiting communication	Withholding information	Lying
Refusing to comply	Stalling	"Stonewalling"
Forming alliances	Displaying favoritism	"Brown-nosing"

The same basic political behavior, which may initially be seen as "good" or acceptable, can be misused or can be seen as being misused and can be labeled "bad." Certain political behaviors can be taken to extremes that can be very dysfunctional to the organization and its functioning.

It is also true that political behaviors performed by certain organizational members might be approved, while the same behavior in other workers may be disapproved. For example, political behaviors are usually considered a way of life at the top levels of an organization, while such behaviors among the lower-level members are often labeled subversive and potentially dangerous to the organization. The perspective of the person making the judgment also affects whether a political behavior is considered acceptable or unacceptable. What one person considers to be a perfectly reasonable action, another may consider to be dirty politics. Moreover, actions that many might agree are reasonable political behaviors can, if taken to extremes, lead to very negative and very dysfunctional ends. For example, forming coalitions can be seen as a good way for low-ranking members to gain some collective power and influence within the organization. However, management may perceive such coalitions as precursors to negative outcomes such as work stoppages and striking. At extremes, striking workers may engage in activities to disrupt organizational operations by forming picket lines to keep "scab" workers out, destroying company property, and rioting. The same basic process can be thus perceived as either good or bad depending on the timing, the circumstances, and the people involved (see Table 11.2).

CAUSES OF ORGANIZATIONAL POLITICS

Organizational politics are attempts by organizational members to use their influence and power to achieve personal goals such as increased pay and career advancement. Often in order to achieve these goals, workers must engage in certain types of political behaviors. To understand organizational politics, which is an inevitable, ongoing process with important implications for the operations of work organizations, we need to explore the factors that contribute to increasing the incidence of political behaviors in work organizations. These include such things as competition for power and scarce resources, difficulties in measuring important work outcomes, compensation for worker inadequacies, and increased group decisionmaking.

Competition for power and resources. When resources, such as money, promotions, and status are scarce, people may try to exercise their power to obtain what they need to satisfy their goals. The scarcer the resources and the more difficult they are to obtain due to "red tape" or arbitrary allocation procedures, the greater the potential that organizational members will act politically to get what they want. For example, an individual who forms a relationship with someone in the organization who has control over distributing important resources may be able to get a larger share of the resources (and to get them more quickly). In a publishing company, a manager noticed that new word-processing equipment was often distributed first to persons who were friendly with the departmental manager rather than to those who needed them most. In a city government, an employee saw that the incidence of political behaviors increased whenever the city obtained a large state or federal grant as each department lobbied for a greater share of the money. Generally, competition for power resources increases the incidence of organizational politics.

Subjective performance appraisals. When job performance is not measured objectively, it means that performance may be unrelated to career success. When personnel decisions, such as pay raises and promotions, are based on subjective criteria, workers will resort to political tactics such as forming alliances, discrediting others, and lobbying to gain favor with the appraisers and get ahead. This can be extremely dysfunctional for the organization since the best workers may not be recognized and encouraged for their efforts. Even worse, poor performers who are good politicians will occasionally be placed in positions of responsibility.

When criteria other than performance, such as dressing a certain way or espousing company philosophy, are emphasized in personnel decisions, workers may make efforts to look good rather than to perform well. When managers make comments like, "He looks like a real company man," they are likely giving weight to factors that are unrelated to good work performance.

Delay in measurement of work outcomes. In many jobs, particularly white collar positions, workers are faced with a variety of tasks. Some tasks see immediate results, while with others the results may not be observed for a long time. A problem occurs when management wants periodic appraisals of workers' performance. Workers who are involved in long-term activities will be at a disadvantage over those engaged in "quick-and-dirty" tasks. This means that workers faced with long-term jobs have two choices: Focus their energy into short-term tasks or engage in political behaviors to convince management that they are indeed good workers. Either case can be dysfunctional for the organization, since it directs effort away from the long-term tasks, which are often very important to the organization. University professors are subject to this delay in measurement with their research activities. Although both longitudinal and field research projects are valuable, they often require a great deal of time, often even several years to complete. Meanwhile, professors are under pressure to "publish or perish." This leads many to abandon valuable long-term projects for simpler laboratory studies in which the results, and the subsequent publications, appear more quickly.

Compensation for inadequacies. When jobs are ambiguous and workers do not know how to perform them correctly, there is the potential for dysfunctional political behavior as the workers try to look as if they know what they are doing. Defining jobs and work procedures clearly and orienting new employees well eliminates a good deal of this problem and reduces the likelihood that workers will engage in political behaviors to compensate for being confused or inadequate.

According to one management theory, there is a tendency for members in an organizational hierarchy to be continually promoted upward until they reach a level at which they have exceeded their abilities to perform the job well. This has been labeled the "Peter principle" (Peter & Hull, 1969), which basically states that employees will eventually rise to their level of incompetency. If this is true—and it probably is more true for some employees than for others—then these workers who have "peaked out" must engage in organizational politics to maintain their positions and to make further upward progress. This obviously is very dysfunctional for the organization.

In certain instances, workers may engage in politics to cover up another's inadequacies. This might occur if a worker, out of pity, helps and covers up for someone who does not have the skills to perform a job. In other instances, subordinates may protect a leader who is incompetent because of strong positive feelings for that person. However, covering up for a leader who is under legitimate attack is a form of dysfunctional politics. While subordinates may feel that they are being loyal to their boss, having a poor leader can be very harmful for the organization.

Increased group decisionmaking. The more group decisionmaking procedures are used in organizations, the greater the potential for politics. Group decisionmaking is basically a political process, with members lobbying for certain courses of action and engaging in a variety of exchanges of favors and support to obtain certain outcomes. For the most part, group decisionmaking, when properly regulated, leads to functional out-

Group decisionmaking can be a very political process, but in the right environment it can function smoothly and harmoniously.

comes. However, if the process begins to break down so that high-quality decisions are not being accepted because of opponents' political savvy and power, the results can be dysfunctional. In extremes, group members may begin to focus more and more energy into the political process, ignoring the implementation of decisions, which is also dysfunctional.

It is clear that politics can be stimulated by a number of factors in work organizations and that political behaviors take many forms. An important concern is how to manage organizational politics. This is difficult to answer. Research on organizational politics is still fairly new. It is hard enough to try to isolate and classify the multitude of political behaviors that occur without even considering the means to stifle or control them. The management of organizational politics is probably much like the management of conflict that was discussed in Chapter 9: The first step is simply to know when it occurs. Learning the causes of political behavior—particularly factors that are likely to lead to dysfunctional political behavior, such as inappropriate performance measures, inadequate job descriptions and procedures, or poor training for new employees—can help to ensure that conditions do not encourage too much political behavior. On the other hand, a certain amount of politics is natural and may even lead to functional outcomes for the organization (see On the Cutting Edge). Group decisionmaking processes, workers' critiques of estab-

Organizational Power and Politics: Toward a Contingency Approach

The use and effectiveness of organizational power and politics depends on a number of factors. We have seen that individuals vary in their tendencies, abilities, and willingness to use power and politics. We also know that ability to use power effectively is related to the characteristics of those who are the subject of the power play. Moreover, organizations and work groups differ in the extent to which they will allow certain types of power and political maneuvering by members. All of this indicates that power and politics in work organizations are extremely complex phenomena that are best explained and understood through a contingency approach, which looks at the interaction of characteristics of the individual or group and factors related to the situation in which the individual or group is behaving.

Recently, researchers have attempted to put power and politics into contingency frameworks. Gray and Ariss (1985) propose that politics vary across the stages of an organization's "life cycle." That is, the political behaviors observed in a very new organization (termed the "birth and early growth stage") are very different than those occurring in a more "mature," established organization. According to this model, appropriate political behaviors are critical for success in managing an organization effectively. The man-

ager must be able to adapt political strategies to those appropriate to the organization and its particular life-cycle stage (see also Mintzberg, 1984; Salancik & Pfeffer, 1977). For example, in the earliest stages of an organization, the manager is actually the entrepreneur who founded the organization. At this point, the manager should wield absolute power, controlling and distributing resources as the manager sees fit. The entrepreneur-manager also controls decisionmaking power and aligns the organization's goals with the manager's self-interest. In other words, the organization is created in the image and likeness of the manager. As the organization moves toward maturity, the manager will switch to more of a "bargaining" political strategy of exchanging resources for favors.

In another contingency approach, Cobb (1984), building on the work of Porter, Allen, & Angle (1981), proposes an "episodic model of power" that examines power episodes, or the use of power in actual work settings. (See the figure below.) The episodic model includes consideration of aspects of the exerciser, or agent, of power and the subject, or target, as well as elements of the power situation. For example, in trying to understand the use of power, this model looks at three factors related to the agent of power. The first, *psychological*

continued

Factors Considered in Cobb's Episodic Model of Power

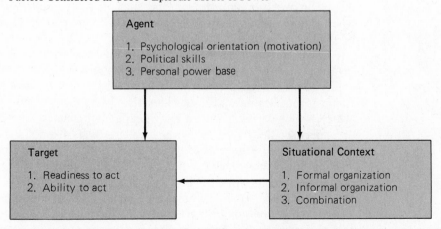

continued

orientation, is the motivation to use power. The second, *political skills,* is the agent's understanding of organizational politics and ability to act politically. Finally, *personal power base* is the amount and types of power a person possesses. The model also considers two factors related to the target of power: the *readiness* to act and the *ability* to act. Readiness is defined as the extent to which the target is inclined to act in a manner consistent with the agent's desires. Ability is whether the target can indeed perform the act the agent desires. Finally, this model looks at the power situation, examining whether the "power episode" occurs in the context of the formal organization, the informal organization, or in both. If the power episode is a formal situation, the agent's legitimate power and authority will likely play a greater role in influencing the target than will the agent's political skills. However, if the situation is informal, the agent's influence skills may be more important than legitimate power bases. This model thus attempts to integrate the scattered research on power in organizations to offer a broad and complex approach to understanding power dynamics.

In sum, the topics of power and politics in organizations are still fairly new, although they have been the focus of a great deal of research in the past few years. The contingency models briefly presented here represent future directions in the study of organizational power processes.

lished work procedures and suggestions for alternatives and improvements, and competition among workers may all result in functional political behaviors and improved organizational outcomes.

CHAPTER 11 CONCLUSION

SUMMARY

Influence, power, and politics are important processes in work groups and organizations. *Influence* is the use of informal social strategies to get another to perform specific actions. *Power* is the use of some aspect of a social relationship to compel another to perform an action despite resistance. *Organizational politics* is the use of power to achieve selfish, or self-serving, goals. A wide variety of influence tactics are commonly employed in work organizations. One such strategy, *ingratiation,* occurs when an individual tries to influence others by increasing personal appeal by doing favors or flattering them.

There are five major *power bases,* or sources: *coercive power,* which involves the use or threat of punishment; *reward power,* which is the ability to give organizational rewards to others; *legitimate power,* which is the formal rights and authorities that accompany a position; *expert power,* which derives from an individual's work-related knowledge, skill, or expertise; and *referent power,* which comes from the fact that an individual is respected and admired by others. Research indicates that the various power bases have different effects on important organizational outcomes such as work performance and job satisfaction.

Organizational political behaviors can be divided into two categories: The first, *functional politics,* is political behavior on the part of an organizational member that helps the organization to attain its goals. The second, *dysfunctional politics,* inhibits the organization's goal attainment. Organizational politics arises from a variety of sources, including competition for power and resources, subjective performance apraisals, delay in measurement of work outcomes, compensation for inadequacies, and increased group decisionmaking. Research has attempted to categorize political behaviors and recognize conditions under which they are likely to occur. One goal of management is to try to eliminate much of the dysfunctional political behavior by eliminating conditions that give rise to it.

STUDY QUESTIONS AND EXERCISES

1. In what ways are influence, power, and organizational politics different? In what ways are they similar?

2. Consider the five power bases described by French and Raven (1959). Give examples of how a manager might use each to increase work group productivity.

3. Recall some instances in which you observed power used in a work or social group. Which power bases were used in each case? How effective were they in influencing others' behavior?

4. What is the distinction between functional and dysfunctional political behavior? Give examples of each.

5. What are some of the potential causes of political behaviors?

SUGGESTED READINGS

Allen, R. W., & Porter, L. W. (Eds.) (1983). *Organizational influence processes.* Glenview, IL: Scott, Foresman. *A collection of readings on all aspects of influence, power, and political processes in work organizations.*

Cialdini, R. B. (1988). *Influence: Science and practice.* (2nd ed.). Glenview, IL: Scott, Foresman. *An enjoyable explanation of how social influence is used by compliance professionals to affect the behavior of others.*

Kipnis, D. (1976). *The powerholders.* Chicago: The University of Chicago Press. *A look at the use of power in organizations by one of the leading researchers on the subject.*

McClelland, D. (1975). *Power: The inner experience.* New York: John Wiley & Sons. *An investigation of individual differences in the need for power and applications to industry, mental health, and everyday life.*

12

ORGANIZATIONAL STRUCTURE AND DEVELOPMENT

Organizational Structure and Development: Unifying Concepts in Industrial/Organizational Psychology

In this chapter, we view organizations at the most general level—the organizational structure—which can tell a great deal about the worklife of the typical worker. For example, in rigid, rule-driven, traditional organizations, it is likely that employees will be expected to adhere closely to strict company regulations and policies. By contrast, in nontraditional organizations, there is a lack of rigid structure and rules, which means that workers will have quite a bit of freedom and are expected to take on responsibility and to demonstrate initiative. Knowing about the structure of an organization can help us to better understand and analyze the work behavior that occurs within the organization.

Although this chapter focuses on organizational structure, the concept of structure has been touched on previously. For example, in Chapter 8, we saw that the organizational chart, or organigram, illustrates the lines of formal communication within an organization, or the organization's communication structure. In this chapter we will focus more on the organization's authority structure, since the organizational chart also represents the formal lines of status and authority. The general concept of authority was also discussed in Chapter 11 when the topic of legitimate power was introduced. There are strong ties between the concept of power and the structure of organizations because organizations can be viewed as power structures. Finally, because people in authority are often the decisionmakers, the lines of organizational structure can also tell something about the typical decisionmaking patterns within the organization. Recall that decisionmaking is an important factor in the dynamics of group processes (Chapter 9) and leadership models (Chapter 10).

The field of organizational development (OD), which is introduced in this chapter, is concerned that organizations must take steps to keep up with the changing world around them. Organizational development is an eclectic area of I/O psychology, for it draws on many theories and applications from a variety of topics within the broader field, and uses them to help organizations change. For example, OD consultants are usually strongly grounded in social science research methods (Chapter 2). They use survey instruments, interviews, and observational techniques to diagnose organizational problems. Many OD programs use interventions that try to heighten employee motivation (Chapter 6) or improve employee job satisfaction and organizational commitment (Chapter 7). Others focus on improving communication in the work setting (Chapter 8) or the quality of leader-subordinate relations (Chapters 9 and 10). In short, in this chapter many of the theoretical topics presented earlier are pulled together into applications that take the form of OD interventions designed to try to help complex organizations deal with complex issues and problems.

So far, we have studied work behavior at a number of levels. We looked at work behavior at the individual level, examining the processes by which individual workers are selected and assigned to jobs, trained, and evaluated. We have studied some of the internal processes that affect the behavior of individual workers, including the factors that influence worker motivation, job satisfaction, and stress. We have also explored work behavior at the group level, examining the ways workers communicate with one another, how workers coordinate their activities to pull the group members together, and how conflict can operate to try to pull the group apart. We also looked at the important roles members play in work groups and the special role of leadership, as well as how leaders can be a major force in determining the effectiveness of work groups. Finally, we investigated the processes of influence, power, and politics, exploring how these strong forces affect the behavior of group members. It is now time to look at work behavior from a larger perspective—the *organizational* level. This larger perspective will allow an exploration of how the structure and dynamics of the organization itself can affect the behavior of its work groups and individuals.

We will begin by studying the structure of organizations, or how they are designed and operate. We will consider how factors both inside and outside of the organization affect its structure, focusing on how different structures affect behavior within the organization. Finally, we will look at how organizations can change and develop to meet the demands placed on them from both within and without. In particular, we will study some of the various techniques used to help organizations change in order to become more productive and effective.

ORGANIZATIONAL STRUCTURE

organizational structure
the arrangement of positions in an organization and the authority and responsibility relationships among them

Organizational structure refers to the arrangement of positions in an organization and the authority and responsibility relationships among them. This means that every organization is made up of persons holding particular positions and that specific authorities and responsibilities are associated with each position. The organization's structure is then determined by the interrelationships among the responsibilities of the various positions. Consider, for example, a simple mail order business that has three positions. The first is the director of operations, who has authority over the other two positions. The director's responsibilities include selecting and acquiring the products that will be offered through the business and handling the organization's finances. The second position is the marketing specialist, whose responsibilities consist of designing the advertisements for the organization's products and placing the ads in various publications. In terms of authority, the marketing specialist is subordinate to the director but superior to the third position: the shipping clerk.

The clerk's responsibilities are solely to package and mail orders. In this very small organization, positions and responsibilities are clearly defined, and the responsibilities are linked in such a way that all functions of the company are handled smoothly and efficiently.

Of course, most work organizations are extremely complex, made up of dozens, hundreds, or thousands of workers. Each has an arrangement of positions and responsibilities that is in some way unique. However, all organizations can be classified under a general continuum of structure that ranges from the very formal and traditional to the completely informal and nontraditional. We will begin by exploring the extremes.

Max Weber, a German sociologist, defined the characteristics of a bureaucracy.

TRADITIONAL ORGANIZATIONAL STRUCTURES

Traditional organizations have formally defined roles for their members, are very rule driven, and are stable and resistant to change. Jobs and lines of status and authority tend to be clearly defined in traditional structures, which means that much of the work behavior tends to be regulated and kept within organizational guidelines and standards.

The traditional organizational structures arose around the turn of the century, when advancements in technology had led to the growth of manufacturing organizations and the increase in their output. As these manufacturing organizations became larger and larger, there was greater need for establishing rules to coordinate the various activities of the growing numbers of workers in each organization. These traditional structures began to replace the small, family-type manufacturing organizations, and today many work organizations, such as major manufacturers and service organizations, including banks, the Internal Revenue Service, the department of motor vehicles, and your college or university administration, are based, more or less, on what is called the bureaucratic model.

The bureaucracy. The prototypical traditional organizational structure is the **bureaucracy,** which is characterized by a well-defined authority hierarchy with strict rules for governing work behavior. The bureaucratic organization is often represented as a pyramid, with the few members with highest status on the top, leading directly down to the bottom-level workers who carry out the organization's goal of producing goods or services. The bureaucratic model was developed around the turn of the century by the German sociologist Max Weber, who formulated a theory of organizational structure that was based on formality and authority (Weber, 1947). Weber was concerned with the fact that growing organizations were becoming chaotic places to work. There were few rules governing such aspects as job procedures and personnel actions, including job placements, promotions, and disciplinary actions. Weber designed the bureaucracy to establish order in the work setting and to increase productivity by reducing inefficiencies in organizational operations. According to him, a true bureaucratic organization should possess six characteris-

bureaucracy
a traditional organizational structure typified by a well-defined authority hierarchy and strict rules governing work behavior

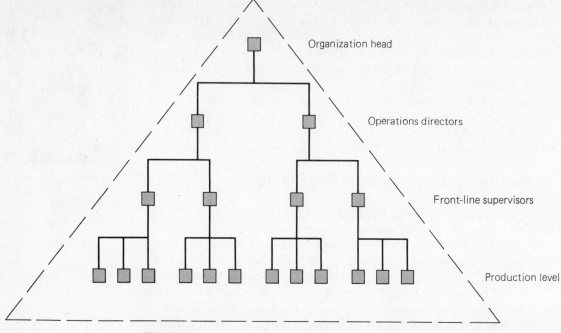

Organization head

Operations directors

Front-line supervisors

Production level

Figure 12.1
A BUREAUCRACY
A bureaucratic organization is arranged like a pyramid, with decreasing authority levels leading down to the production line.

tics: the division or specialization of labor, a well-defined authority hierarchy, formal rules and procedures, impersonality, merit-based employment decisions, and an emphasis on written records.

The first characteristic is the division or *specialization of labor,* which means that the complex goals or outputs of the organization are broken down into separate jobs with simple, routine, and well-defined tasks. In this way, each person becomes a specialized expert at performing a certain task. For example, if the manufacturing organization builds barrels, some workers cut the slats for the barrels, others bend and form the slats, some assemble the barrels, and finally other job specialists make sure that they are watertight.

The second characteristic of a bureaucracy, one that can be easily seen in an organizational chart, is a *well-defined authority hierarchy.* Bureaucracies are characterized by a pyramid-type arrangement in which each lower position is controlled and supervised by the next higher level. Every position is under the direct supervision of someone higher up, so that there is no confusion about who reports to whom (see Figure 12.1).

Bureaucracies are also distinguished by their emphasis on *formal rules and procedures.* Strict adherence to these formalities is expected to ensure uniformity and to regulate work behavior. Because of these extensive rules and procedures, there should never be any doubt about what a particular worker is supposed to be doing. Everyone's job is well defined, and procedures for coordinating activities with other workers should be clearly established.

Another characteristic of bureaucracies, according to Weber, is the notion of *impersonality:* this means that personal preferences and emotional factors do not have a place in any work-related decisions. Behavior is based on logical rather than emotional thinking. For example, a bureaucratic service organization would never give preferential treatment to one customer over another.

Developing from their impersonality characteristic, bureaucracies also *base employment decisions on merit.* Hiring and promotion decisions are based on who is best qualified for the job rather than on the personal preferences of those making the personnel decisions. In a true bureaucracy people who are effective workers should be the only ones advancing to higher-level positions.

A final and very distinguishable characteristic of a true bureaucracy is a strong *emphasis on written records.* To ensure uniformity of action, and fair and equitable treatment of employees, bureaucracies keep meticulous records of past decisions and actions. All behaviors occurring in the organization are recorded, which contributes to the image of bureaucrats as compulsive "paper-shufflers."

Weber believed that the bureaucracy represented the *ideal* organizational structure, and, in his day, it did represent a great advancement in increasing the efficiency of manufacturing organizations. Of course, it is important to bear in mind that when Weber developed his theory, most organizations were not very complex. Even the largest organizations in his time would be quite small by today's standards. For modern organizations, however, which can be fantastically large and complex, the bureaucratic model may not be the ideal type of structure. While some of the bureaucratic characteristics are well suited for present-day organizations, others restrict their ability to grow and innovate. For example, complex organizations must have formal rules and procedural guidelines, but operating too much "by-the-book" can stifle creativity and innovation. Many of the characteristics of the bureaucratic model have both strengths and weaknesses. For example, bureaucracies are impersonal and do not play favorites, which is very admirable indeed. However, this same characteristic creates the impression that bureaucracies are cold and insensitive. Similarly, bureaucracies' emphasis on keeping written records of all behaviors gives the impression that they are inefficient, slow, cumbersome, and full of "red tape." In reality however, bureaucracies can be quite efficient, particularly for organizations whose tasks involve high volume and repetitive procedures.

Manufacturing organizations and those providing simple customer service are the most likely candidates for bureaucratic structure, which with its emphasis on job specialization, tends to lead to greater productiv-

To many people modern bureaucracies seem overly large and impersonal, with a dismaying amount of paperwork and "red tape."

ity when the manufacturing of goods or the delivery of services is routine. Think about it. Many of the bureaucracies you deal with, such as the post office, supermarkets, department stores, and fast-food restaurants, are efficient organizations. Each must serve hundreds or thousands of customers each day. In spite of occasional problems, they get the job done. However, the formal nature of the bureaucratic organization, with inflexible rules that stifle individual creativity and initiative, may be negatively related to worker satisfaction.

The line-staff organizational structure. As organizations grew in complexity, a variation of the traditional bureaucratic model began to emerge. This structure was designated the **line-staff organizational structure** (see Figure 12.2). This traditional structure is made up of two groups of employees, each with different goals. The first group is the **line,** or those workers who are directly engaged in the tasks that accomplish the primary goals of the organization. For example, in manufacturing organizations, line employees are the ones making products on the assembly lines or shop floors. In service organizations, line workers are involved in the distribution of services to customers. The second group of employees is designated as **staff,** which consists of specialized positions designed to support the line. In today's complex organizations, many organizational members hold staff positions that have very little to do directly with the primary goals of the organization. For example, in a computer assembly plant, many employees' jobs involve functions that have nothing to do with assembling computers, such as bookkeeping, plant maintenance, public relations, marketing research, maintaining employee records, and providing personnel services.

In essence, all organizational members who are not directly involved in accomplishing the company's primary goal, whether it be building computers or providing services, are staff. In some organizations, line-staff distinctions are obvious. However, in other companies the distinctions between line and staff are often blurred (Nossiter, 1979). This is particularly true in very large and complex organizations, whose goals might involve a variety of services. For example, in an automobile manufacturer, the line workers are easy to spot: They are dealing with the primary production goals of the organization: assembling cars. The staff consists of the various departments, such as accounting, advertising, and maintenance, that do not play a direct role in auto assembly. However, in a university, the line-staff distinctions may not be as clear-cut. The line in a university is the professors, because they are directly involved in fulfilling the organization's mission: providing education. The staff is the administrators, building maintenance workers, and groundskeepers. There may be some positions in a university, however, in which the line-staff distinctions are blurry. For example, the student services personnel, such as academic counselors, and the doctors and nurses working in the student health center might be viewed, in terms of the educational goal of the

line-staff organizational structure
a traditional organizational structure composed of one group of employees (the line) who achieve the goals of the organization and another group (the staff) who support the line

line
employees in an organization who are engaged directly in tasks that accomplish its goals

staff
specialized employee positions designed to support the line

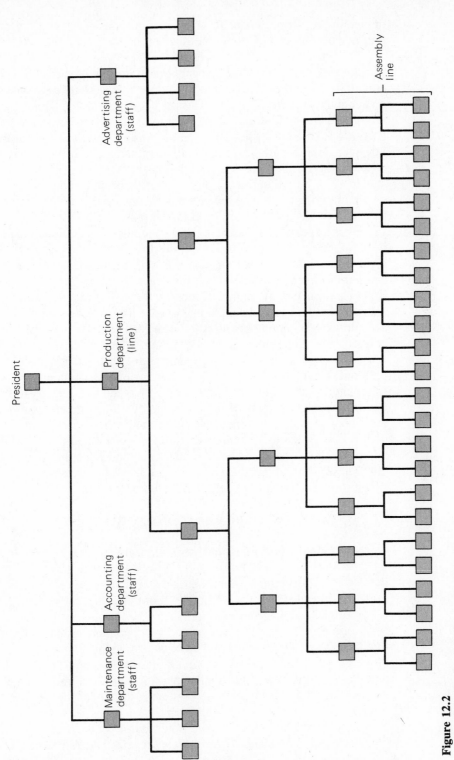

Figure 12.2

LINE-STAFF ORGANIZATIONAL STRUCTURE

In a manufacturing organization, the line is represented by production line workers. The staff consists of specialized positions or departments designed to support the line.

President

Advertising department (staff)

Maintenance department (staff)

Accounting department (staff)

Production department (line)

Assembly line

university, as supporting staff. However, in terms of the goals of providing specific services to students, they can be viewed as line workers.

The line-staff structure represents an improvement on the traditional bureaucratic model, because the supporting staff takes care of the peripheral activities in the organization so that the line workers can concentrate on achieving its primary goals. This means that in today's complex work world, the line-staff structure can help to increase organizational productivity through greater specialization of worker functions. One difficulty, however, in line-staff structures is the confusion that can result in terms of the authority hierarchy. In certain instances, it may not be clear who should have formal authority, line managers or staff managers. For example, in hiring new line employees, a line manager may insist on having the final say, while the personnel manager—a staff manager who is regarded as a specialist in assessing and selecting the most qualified personnel—might want to have the final authority. This can lead to potential disruptive conflict between the line and staff. In addition, the orientations and perspectives of line and staff members are often different, and may lead to some line-staff conflict. Generally, the line tends to be more practical in its concerns and orientation, because line members are focused on accomplishing concrete organizational goals. The staff, on the other hand, is often more theoretical in its orientation, which is also reasonable because many of the tasks of staff members are abstract. Because of these different orientations, the line and staff may not always agree, and organizational conflict can result. For example, in manufacturing organizations the production line tends to be concerned with a concrete goal such as producing as many components as quickly and efficiently as possible. The quality control staff has a more abstract goal of evaluating the products, accepting those that meet certain standards and rejecting those that do not. These differing perspectives can produce considerable conflict between the production line and the quality control staff.

NONTRADITIONAL ORGANIZATIONAL STRUCTURES

Nontraditional organizational structures are characterized by less formalized work roles and procedures. As a result, they tend to be rather flexible and adaptable, without the rigid status hierarchy characteristic of more traditional structures. Generally, nontraditional organizations have fewer employees than the traditional structures and may also occur as a small organization that is a subunit of a larger, more traditionally structured organization. For example, an organization that manufactures state-of-the-art jet airliners may be made up of a nontraditional organizational unit that is responsible for designing new aircraft and a traditional organizational unit that is charged with producing dozens of the new jets.

matrix organization
a nontraditional organizational structure consisting of a team of members permanently organized around a particular project or product

The matrix organization. The nontraditional approach to organizational structure is typified by the **matrix organization.** A matrix organiza-

Film crews, with many different specialists working together, are an example of a matrix organization.

tion is a permanent team of members who are organized around a particular project or product line and are responsible for all aspects of the job. The most well-known examples of matrix organizations are the National Aeronautic and Space Administration (NASA) teams that developed the various space projects, from the early Gemini and Apollo programs to the more recent space shuttle and space station programs. These, and many other matrix organizations, are made up of groups of professionals of varying types of expertise who pool their knowledge and talents to develop the project. Motion picture production crews are another example of a matrix organization. Film crews contain a number of types of experts—camerapersons, actors/actresses, lighting specialists, editors— who work together to produce a creative, quality product. Although a relatively new type of organizational structure, matrix organizations have also been set up in hospitals and health care agencies, financial institutions, and government (Kolodny, 1979). Matrix organizations typically have four important characteristics: high flexibility and adaptability, collaboration among workers, less emphasis on organizational status, and group decisionmaking.

Because matrix organizations are designed to adapt rapidly to changing conditions, they are characterized by high flexibility and adaptability. Workers have broadly defined jobs, not the narrowly specialized positions common to traditionally structured organizations. Workers in a matrix structure thus know a great deal about the product or goals of the organization and tend to possess a variety of work-related skills. This enables both the workers and the organization to adopt new technology readily, to take on new projects, and to develop innovative work strategies.

A second characteristic of matrix organizations is the collaboration among workers. Rather than each worker independently contributing a "piece" to the final product, as in a traditional organization, employees in matrix organizations share skills and resources, working collaboratively to get the job done. Because of this tendency to work together, a great deal of communication in the form of meetings, problem-solving groups, and conferences goes on in matrix organizations.

Matrix organizations also place much less emphasis on organizational status than do traditional structures. Although matrix organizations may have a formal project leader and supervisors or managers, these workers do not typically possess the "ultimate" authority that leaders or managers have in traditional organizations. Each worker is viewed as a knowledgeable and skilled professional who is expected to be self-motivated and committed to the goals of the organization.

A final characteristic of matrix organizations is the tendency toward group decisionmaking. Matrix members have considerable input into organizational decisionmaking. Often matrix organizations make important decisions by consensus. This increase in group decisionmaking means that there is bound to be a great deal of conflict in matrix organizations. However, this intragroup conflict is usually turned to productive, functional outcomes. The lack of both hierarchy and formally designated roles means that the structure of a matrix organization is radically different from the pyramidal shape of traditional organizations (see Figure 12.3).

Matrix organizations will not work well with all types of tasks or workers. They tend to be best suited for projects and products that require creativity and innovation, but are not well suited for routine tasks that can be easily broken down into specialized components. Routine tasks are better handled in traditional organizational structures. Moreover, because matrix structures lack rigid operating procedures and guidelines, members must be competent, motivated professionals who bring valuable energy and resources to the work group. To contribute, matrix organizational members need to be able to take the initiative rather than waiting to be told what to do by someone in authority. Because of these restrictions, there are relatively few matrix organizations in comparison to more traditional structures.

Matrix organizations tend to have high levels of performance in dealing with complex, creative work products. Also, because of the amount of interaction among members in matrix structures, and the high levels of responsibility they possess, matrix organizations usually have greater worker job satisfaction.

As mentioned, both traditional and nontraditional structures may exist within large organizations. For example, a toy manufacturer may have

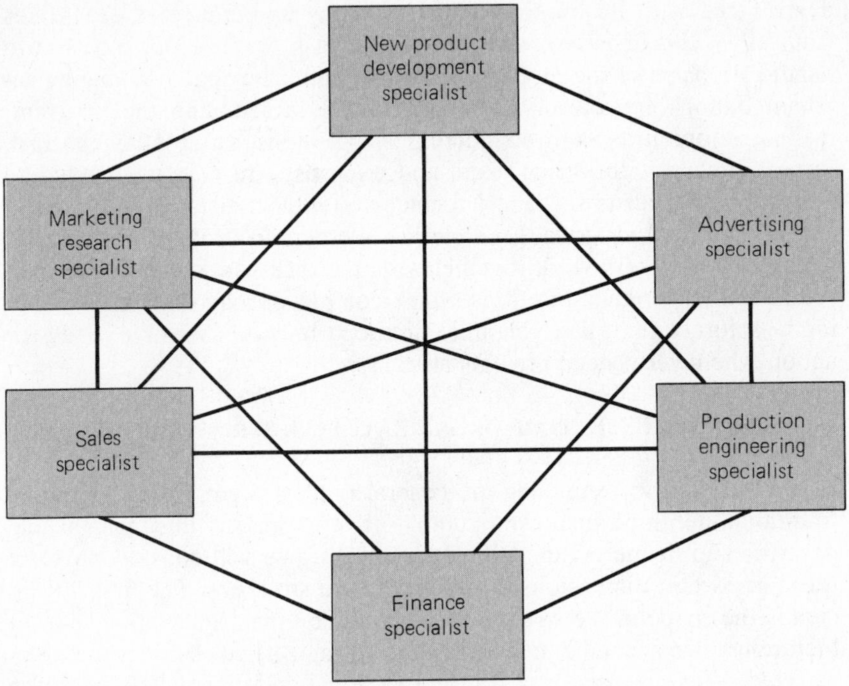

Figure 12.3
A SIMPLE MATRIX
ORGANIZATIONAL
STRUCTURE

a matrix-type of organization for developing new products. This involves a team of research and development specialists, marketing professionals, and budgeting experts whose task it is to create a new, appealing, and profitable toy. However, while this matrix organization is responsible for developing the prototype of the new toy, when it comes to actual production, the task may be transferred to the assembly plant, an organization that is more traditional and bureaucratic, and thus better suited to producing mass quantities of the new toy.

The project task force.   Another type of nontraditional organizational structure, which usually only occurs in the context of larger, more traditional organizations, is the **project task force.** Typically, a project task force is a temporary, nontraditional organization of members from different departments or positions within a traditional structure who are assembled to complete a specific job or project. Traditional lines of status or authority do not usually operate in such a task force, whose structure is more like a "temporary" matrix organization. All members are viewed as professionals who will contribute collaboratively to the group's output. As in matrix organizations, decisions are made through democratic or consensus decisionmaking, and members are expected to take on responsibility and be self-motivated.

A project task force might be created in an organization that is sud-

project task force
a nontraditional organization of workers who are assembled temporarily to complete a specific job or project

denly faced with hosting the annual two-day conference of executives from all of the divisions and affiliates. A task force is put together to handle all facets of the meeting, including obtaining space, arranging accommodations for out-of-town participants, assembling the program, mailing information, and conducting the sessions. In creating the task force, persons with varied skills and expertise are selected, including budgeting specialists to handle finances, graphic artists to produce designs for printed programs, and clerical workers to deal with correspondence. All members work together until the task is completed and then return to their original positions. Some companies may even have standing task forces that, like volunteer fire departments, assemble ready for action whenever special projects arise.

OTHER DIMENSIONS OF ORGANIZATIONAL STRUCTURE

In addition to examining the general type of organization along the traditional-nontraditional continuum, other important dimensions help describe and define organizational structures. We will consider three of these important dimensions of organizational structure. The first dimension is the shape of the structure, as defined by the organization's status hierarchy. The second dimension is how organizational subunits are constructed. We will consider both the functional and divisional structuring of subunits. The third dimension is whether organizational decisionmaking power is centralized or decentralized.

Chain of command and span of control. Traditional organizational structures are characterized by an authority hierarchy that is represented in the organizational chart, or organigram. The organigram depicts graphically the various levels of status or authority in a traditional organization and the number of workers that report to each position of authority. The **chain of command** is the number of authority levels in a particular organization. The chain of command follows the lines of authority and status vertically through the organization. The **span of control** is the number of workers who must report to a single supervisor. An organization with a wide span of control has many workers reporting to each supervisor; an organization with a narrow span has few subordinates reporting to each superior. Based on these dimensions of chain of command and span of control, traditional organizations are often described as being either "tall" or "flat" in structure (see Figure 12.4). A tall organizational structure has a long chain of command—many authority levels—and a narrow span of control. A flat organizational structure has a short chain of command but a wide span of control. It is important to note that both dimensions are more descriptive of traditional rather than nontraditional structures. Very nontraditional organizations, such as matrix organizations, may have a very small chain of command or none at all, because they deemphasize authority levels.

chain of command
the number of authority levels in an organization

span of control
the number of workers who must report to a single supervisor

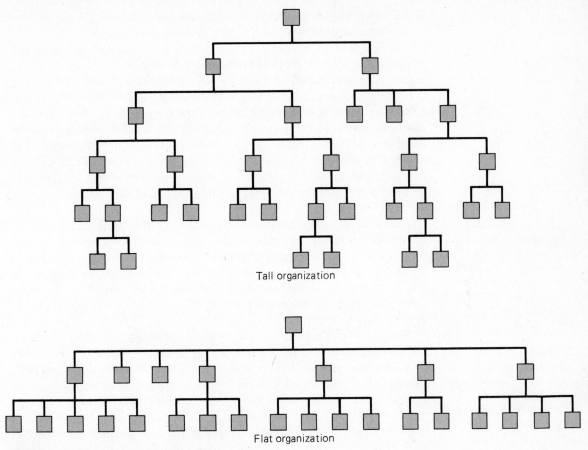

Figure 12.4
TALL AND FLAT ORGANIZATIONAL STRUCTURES

An organization's shape, either tall or flat, can have important implications for worklife in the organization. For example, in tall organizational structures, workers at the bottom levels may feel cut off from those above, because they are separated by many levels of middle-ranking superiors. On the positive side, tall organizations may offer lower-level employees many different promotional opportunities throughout their careers. Another advantage of such structures is that there is usually adequate supervision because the span of control is narrow; each supervisor is only responsible for a few employees. However, tall organizational structures can become "top heavy" with administrators and managers, because the ratio of line workers to supervisors is very low. Conversely, in a flat structure few levels separate top-level managers from bottom-level workers, possibly leading to greater interaction between the top and bottom of the organization. However, flat structures offer few promotional opportunities to workers, and supervision may not always be adequate, because many workers report to the same supervisor.

Although there has been considerable research on how the two types of structures, tall and flat, affect important outcomes such as productivity and worker satisfaction, the results have been inconclusive. It does not appear that one type of structure is better than the other (Gray & Starke, 1984). It is more likely that the shape of the organization follows from its functions and goals. For example, flat organizational structures may be more common when the task is routine or repetitive, thus requiring a large number of workers who need minimal supervision. Organizations with complex and multifaceted goals or products may have taller structures, with different levels handling the various aspects of the company's goals.

Functional versus divisional structure. Organizations can also be structured by either functions or divisions. **Functional structure** divides the organization into departments based on the functions or tasks performed. For example, a manufacturing firm may be made up of a production department, sales department, and finance department. An amusement park might be divided into operations, publicity, and maintenance departments.

Divisional structure is based on types of products or customers. Each division may perform the same range of functions, but those functions only serve the goals of the particular division. In other words, each division operates almost as if it were a separate organization. For example, a computer manufacturer may have three types of computers—a ''super'' multi-use computer designed for large businesses or educational institutions, a small business computer, and a home or personal computer—each of which is represented by a separate division. Within each division are people who handle manufacturing, marketing, and financing, but only for their particular product. Figure 12.5 provides examples of organizations structured by function and division.

A primary advantage of functional structure is that it creates job specialists, such as experts in marketing or finance, and eliminates duplication of functions. One disadvantage of functional structure is that workers may become overly focused on their own department and area of specialization, and this may breed interdepartmental rivalry and conflict. Another disadvantage is that work must move from one large department to another to be completed, which may decrease productivity, particularly when work is lost in the shuffle or when one department is particularly slow in accomplishing its functions, thereby creating a bottleneck.

Divisional structure has positive and negative aspects as well. One advantage is that the company can easily expand products or services merely by adding a new division. Also, since each division operates as a separate entity, with its own production goals and profit picture, there is greater accountability. It is easy to determine which units are performing

functional structure
an organizational
structure that divides
the organization into
departments based on
the functions, or tasks,
they perform

divisional structure
an organizational
structure that divides
the organization
according to types of
products or customers

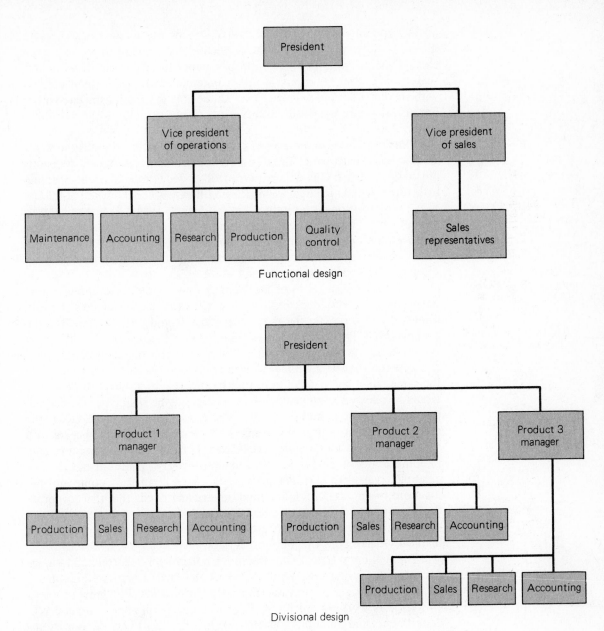

Figure 12.5
FUNCTIONAL AND DIVISIONAL ORGANIZATIONAL DESIGNS

at exceptional or substandard levels. One of the major drawbacks to divisional structure concerns the duplication of areas of expertise, since each division contains its own departments for production, sales, research, and other functions. Another potential weakness is that workers with similar skills and expertise may not be able to benefit from each other because they are housed in different divisions.

Centralized versus decentralized structure. Another dimension of organizational structure deals with how important work-related decisions are made, which can be either centralized or decentralized. **Centralization** is the degree to which decisionmaking authority is concentrated at the top of the organizational hierarchy (Fry & Slocum, 1984). In highly centralized organizations, the decisionmaking power is firmly held by the top levels of the organization. **Decentralization** is the process of taking the decisionmaking power out of the hands of the top level and distributing some of it to lower levels.

For example, a chain of ice cream parlors could have either a very centralized or a very decentralized structure. In the centralized structure, top-level executives in the corporate office would control all of the decisionmaking. They would decide what flavors of ice cream should appear in the stores each month, the number of personnel each store can hire, and how the advertising budget for each store will be spent. In contrast, if the same chain had a decentralized structure, each of the store managers would be allowed to make decisions concerning the selection of ice cream flavors, advertising, and personnel. The centralized organization has the advantage of uniformity, which means that each store should operate with some average level of quality and efficiency. However, this structure may limit the ability of individual stores to adjust to special circumstances. For example, one store manager in the centralized chain may complain that his store has special personnel and advertising needs that the corporate decisionmakers do not consider. In the decentralized company, each store can make its own decisions, but this could backfire if the store managers make poor or uninformed decisions.

Today there is a general trend moving from more centralized to more decentralized structures. This is partly fueled by the increased emphasis on worker participation in decisionmaking discussed in Chapters 9 and 10. Also, as work organizations become larger with greater diversity in departments and functions, decentralization is likely to occur. For example, it is unlikely that a few top managers of a huge, international manufacturing conglomerate that has different divisions producing products as diverse as household appliances, missile guidance systems, and business machines are going to make decisions for all of the company's components. Such giant corporations have no choice but to decentralize the decisionmaking by dispersing the power to the various divisions and locations.

centralization
the degree to which decisionmaking power rests at the upper levels of the organizational hierarchy

decentralization
the process of taking the decisionmaking authority away from the top level of the organization and distributing it to lower levels

CONTINGENCY MODELS OF ORGANIZATIONAL STRUCTURE

It is clear that no one type of structure is appropriate for all work organizations. Organizations differ on many factors, including the number and type of goods or services they produce, their size, their customers, their employees, and the environment in which they reside. All these factors can help determine which structure is "best" for an organization. Many theorists argue that organizational structure is best addressed with contingency models. Recall that these models look at the interaction of characteristics of the individual—in this case the organization—and characteristics of the situation—in this case the setting in which the organization operates. We will consider three contingency models of organizational structure, two focusing on how structure adjusts to fit with characteristics of work technology and one considering how structure is made to fit aspects of the external environment.

Organizational structure and work technology. The earliest contingency models of structure emphasized the role that technology plays in influencing organizational structure. The technology that an organization uses—the tools, machines, and computer systems—is closely related to its goals and to how the organization works to achieve these goals. For example, an automobile manufacturer that wants to stay competitive must utilize state-of-the-art, computer-assisted, auto assembly technology. This sophisticated technology shapes the organization's structure. If modern auto manufacturing equipment consists of robot welders and assemblers, this is going to affect the number of human assembly-line workers that are needed, and the number and type of highly skilled personnel required to operate and maintain the technology. The shift from large numbers of line workers to specialized technicians will require a change in the traditional organizational hierarchy.

One of the earliest contingency models of organizational structure was proposed by sociologist Joan Woodward (1965), who predicted that the complexity of the technology used in an organization would place different kinds of demands on the workers and that an effort to meet these demands efficiently would then influence the structure of the organization. She examined how the type of technology used in manufacturing organizations influenced organizational structure in terms of the span of control in front-line supervision and the chain of command. Organizations were classified as possessing one of three types of production technologies: small-batch production, mass production, and continuous-process production. The simplest technology was in organizations that produced small batches of specialty products, such as specialized electronic components or construction equipment. If these producers were to be productive and efficient, the span of control needed to be moderate in size, with about twenty to thirty workers reporting to a supervisor, and the chain of command had to be short. Mass-production organizations, referred to as "large batch" companies, used a more complex technology than "small batch" producers. Examples of mass-production organizations are automobile assemblers and manufacturers of household appliances. For these types of organizations to be successful, the span of control tended to be very large, with forty to fifty workers per supervisor, and the chain of command fairly long, with several levels in the organizational hierarchy. Finally, the technology is most complex in organizations involved in continuous-process manufacturing, such as producing chemicals or refining oil, in which output must occur continually. In such organizations, the span of control was most limited, with ten to twenty workers per supervisor, due to the complexity of the process and the emphasis on high quality. Also, the chain of command was very long, involving many levels in the organizational hierarchy.

In short, Woodward's theory maintained that for manufacturing organizations to be productive, there had to be a proper match between the complexity and sophistication of their organization's technology and its organizational structure. When organizational structures fit the level of technological complexity, the organizations were productive. When there was a mismatch between technological complexity and the appropriate structures designated by Woodward's model, productivity suffered (Woodward, 1965; Zwerman, 1970).

The one obvious limitation to Woodward's structural contingency model is that it deals only with manufacturing organizations. A theory proposed by Perrow (1970) looked at the relationship between technology and structure in all types of organizations. Rather than focusing solely on production technology, Perrow examined what he called "information technology," which refers to all aspects of jobs, including the equipment and tools used, the decisionmaking procedures followed, and the information and expertise needed. This is a much broader definition of work technology than the relatively simplistic categorization of manufacturing technology used by Woodward. Perrow classified work-related technology along two dimensions: whether the technology was analyzable or unanalyzable and whether the work contained few or many exceptional work situations requiring creative problem solving. Analyzable-nonanalyzable work refers to whether the technology can be broken down into simple, objective steps or procedures. Work with few exceptions is predictable and straightforward—presenting few novel problems. Work with many exceptions has unfamiliar problems turning up often in the work process.

The interaction of these two technology dimensions leads to Perrow's model of four categories of organizational technology: routine, engineering, craft, and nonroutine (see Figure 12.6). Routine technology consists of analyzable work tasks with few exceptions; examples are assembly-line production or the work of grocery store clerks. Engineering technology consists of analyzable tasks with many exceptions; examples are the

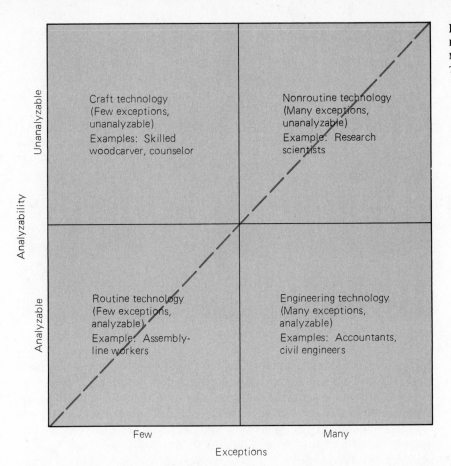

Figure 12.6
PERROW'S CONTINGENCY
MODEL OF ORGANIZA-
TIONAL STRUCTURE

Craft technology
(Few exceptions,
unanalyzable)
Examples: Skilled
woodcarver, counselor

Nonroutine technology
(Many exceptions,
unanalyzable)
Example: Research
scientists

Routine technology
(Few exceptions,
analyzable)
Example: Assembly-
line workers

Engineering technology
(Many exceptions,
analyzable)
Examples: Accountants,
civil engineers

Unanalyzable

Analyzable

Analyzability

Few

Many

Exceptions

work of lawyers or civil engineers, which involves tasks that are analyzable but ones that also present workers with novel problems that need to be solved. The lawyer dealing with unique legal cases or an engineer encountering problems in constructing a specific bridge are examples. Craft technology uses technology that is unanalyzable, with no discrete steps, and has few exceptions; examples include the jobs of a skilled woodcarver and a social worker. Both these jobs involve specialized experience and knowledge, but both present workers with similar types of problems. Finally, nonroutine technology is represented by the work of scientific researchers or professional artists and musicians in which there are no clearly defined steps to follow yet there are many unique problems to be solved.

According to Perrow's model, the structure of the organization adjusts to the technology. For example, organizations with routine technology tend to be formal, highly rule driven, and centralized in structure. Nonroutine technology leads to a less formal, more flexible structure,

Because performing artists face many unique problems with no clearly defined steps to follow, they require a nonroutine technology.

such as a matrix organization. The craft and engineering technologies tend to result in structures that are neither completely traditional nor completely nontraditional but rather a combination of both (Lynch, 1974; Van de Ven & Delbecq, 1974; Withey, Daft, & Cooper, 1983).

Both Woodward's and Perrow's contingency models emphasize that organizational structure must adjust to fit the technology used by the organization. Woodward's theory focused on the different forms of technology used in manufacturing organizations, while Perrow's model expanded the definition of technology to look at all forms of organizations.

Organizational structure and the external environment. While it is clear that the structure of an organization can be greatly affected by the technology used, the organization is also affected by *external* factors— elements in the outside world that exert some influence on the work organization, affecting its operations and its structure. Some common environmental factors that have an impact on work organizations include economic forces, competitors, consumer demand, the supply of raw materials, the supply of human resources, and government regulations. Lawrence and Lorsch (1967) have developed a contingency model of organizational structure that looks at how structure must adapt to fit changing environmental conditions. They assert that two processes determine a company's ability to keep up with external changes: differentiation and integration. **Differentiation** is the complexity of the organizational structure: the number of units, the various orientations and philosophies of the managers, and the goals and interests of the organization's members.

differentiation
the complexity of an organization's structure, which is based on the number of units, the orientations of managers, and the goals and interests of members

Integration is the amount and quality of collaboration among the various units of the organization. As the external environment becomes more complex and turbulent, the organization must increase its differentiation and integration to match its internal complexity to the external complexity.

integration
the amount and quality of collaboration among the divisions of an organization

For example, in today's marketplace, a manufacturer of photocopiers must be highly differentiated, with a number of departments designed to meet certain organizational goals. The engineering and research and development departments must keep up with the latest technology in developing improved office and home copier machines, the advertising department must be able to develop eye-catching and convincing ads to rival those of the competition, the sales department must maintain high sales rates, and the service department must provide courteous and efficient service to customers. As environmental conditions change, with consumers demanding better-quality photocopiers and the competition continuing to present new product lines and new advertising and sales campaigns, the organization with its various departments must innovate in order to survive. The organizational complexity must increase to meet more complex environmental demands. This means that there must be good integration among the various departments, to be able to work together to achieve shared goals. Therefore, the organization must use a great deal of its resources to make sure that the various departments are well integrated, for it would do no good to have the best copiers on the market if the servicing of the machines is so poor that it drives away customers.

To test their theory, Lawrence and Lorsch studied three industries, each faced with different levels of environmental complexity: plastics manufacturers, manufacturers of cardboard and metal containers, and food manufacturers. At the time, the plastics industry was experiencing great external complexity: Technology was constantly changing, the demand for new products increased daily, and the field was highly competitive. In contrast, the container industry existed in a relatively simple, nondemanding environment. The products had not changed in years, demand was steady, and the level of competition was low. Midway between these two extremes was the food industry, which was in a moderately complex environment. To be successful, organizations in the plastics industry needed to be very high in both differentiation and integration; organizations in the container industry operated most efficiently with low levels of internal complexity; and the most successful organizations in the food industry tended to have moderate levels of both differentiation and integration. Thus, this research found support for Lawrence and Lorsch's contention that to be effective, organizational complexity must increase to meet the increased external demands placed on the organization.

The Lawrence and Lorsch model makes us aware of the effect of the external environment on the organization, its structure, and its ability to meet its goals. Organizations today exist in a constantly changing world. The work organization that fails to keep up with evolving consumer trends, technology, and industrial developments may have a tough time surviving. This notion that organizations can be structured to adapt to environmental changes is a central tenet of the area of behavioral science known as *organizational development*.

ORGANIZATIONAL DEVELOPMENT

In recent years, many organizations have had to cease operating because they were unable to change to keep up with the times. Companies that did not use the latest marketing or production techniques lost out to competitors who took advantage of such state-of-the-art technology. Retail stores that were unable to keep pace with changing consumer tastes have gone out of business. Furthermore, organizations have to adapt not only to external conditions but also to internal factors. For example, as new generations of workers enter the work force with different types of skills and different ideas about what they want from their jobs, the organization must adjust to utilize their skills and to meet their demands. Otherwise, the better workers will leave the organization, or disgruntled employees may be able to slow down productivity through costly work stoppages and strikes. In short, the ability to change is critical to an organization's survival.

organizational development (OD)
the process of assisting organizations in preparing for and managing change

The study of organizational change and the use of certain interventions to help organizations prepare for and manage such change are the concerns of **organizational development (OD).** Organizational development often involves altering the organization's work structure or workers' attitudes or behavior to help the organization to adapt to fluctuating external and internal conditions. OD typically takes place in a series of phases. The first phase is usually a diagnosis of the organization to identify significant problems. In the next phase, appropriate interventions are chosen to try to deal with the problems. The third phase is the implementation of the interventions, or OD techniques. Finally, the results of the interventions are evaluated (Burke, 1987). Organizational development is not one theory or approach but rather a variety of orientations and methods for managing change.

Organizational development is both a general philosophy about the nature of modern organizations as well as a discipline that studies ways to help organizations be more effective. Most OD programs are oriented toward long-term organizational improvement rather than focusing on solving immediate problems. In fact, most OD practitioners believe that their role is not to solve the organization's problems but to improve the organization's ability to solve its own problems. Typically, employees of all levels collaborate in the development and implementation of the OD program. Moreover, many OD programs use team approaches to deal with problems at the group or organizational level, rather than focusing on

How to Develop Effective Work Teams

Many innovative strategies for improving work performance involve the development and use of work teams. If work teams or committees are to be effective in solving organizational problems, certain criteria must be met. Care must be taken to select appropriate participants for problem-solving teams and to ensure that certain procedures are followed. Galbraith (1973; 1977) has developed a set of rules for making high-level, decisionmaking work teams effective:

1. *Team members should perceive their participation as important and personally rewarding.* To build commitment to the team, members must view their work as beneficial. One way to do this is to offer some sort of formal rewards for contributions to the team.
2. *The work team should include some persons of organizational power who will be responsible for helping to implement any decisions made by the group.* If a team is to develop innovative strategies, it is important that these efforts are implemented. It is important to have some managers with organizational power as part of the work team to make sure that team suggestions are listened to and implemented.
3. *Team members should have knowledge and information relevant to the decision.* In any problem-solving work team, it is critical that members have job-related knowledge relevant to the decisions that are being made. This involves including lower-level workers who have first-hand experience with the job.
4. *Team members should have the authority to commit their respective departments to the decision.* The work team participants must be able to commit valuable resources (human and otherwise) to help in the successful implementation of the strategies developed by the team.
5. *Team members should represent and inform nonteam workers.* If the problem-solving work team or committee is a select group of a larger body of workers, it is crucial that the team members inform nonteam members about the committee tasks and decisions.
6. *The influence of team members on decisions should be based on expertise.* This is especially important when members come from various levels in the organization. Work-related decisions should be based on relevant knowledge, not on organizational politics.
7. *Work team conflict should be managed to maximize the problem-solving process.* The conflict that arises in problem-solving committees should be functional and help to develop a high-level and highly critiqued course of action. It is important that such conflict be controlled to avoid dysfunctional outcomes.
8. *Team members should have good interpersonal skills and adequate leadership.* The success of a work team is going to be directly related to the smooth flow of communication among members. The better their interpersonal skills, the better the group's ability to reach high-quality decisions. It is also important for the team leader to take an appropriate but not too dominant role to facilitate team interaction and help to resolve nonproductive conflicts.

problems associated with individual workers (see Up Close). One goal of such programs is to help the organization become aware of its own operations and problems (Friedlander, 1980). Often this is done by opening up organizational communication channels and increasing members' involvement in the planning and execution of work activities. The rationale is that workers who are more involved in and have a better understanding of important organizational processes will be more committed to helping the organization to achieve its goals (French, 1969).

Organizational development is an applied, practice-oriented area of the behavioral sciences. The OD practitioner is oriented toward helping the organization design and implement a program for dealing with change-related problems. The OD practitioner is often referred to as a **change agent,** one who coaches or guides the organization in developing problem-solving strategies. The change agent, however, is not a problem solver. The change agent works with the various levels of the organization, developing or deciding on problem-solving techniques. The change agent is a behavioral scientist, often an industrial/organizational psychologist, who is expert at assisting organizations in diagnosing problems and skilled in helping organizational members to deal with sensitive situations. The change agent will have some special knowledge of particular OD interventions that may be used to help solve the organization's problems. The change agent also acts as an educator who trains the organization to implement strategies for coping with future problems (Burke, 1987).

Organizational development programs usually follow one of several procedural models, all of which typically use an OD consultant, or change agent, and go through the four phases outlined earlier. One popular OD model is **action research,** which is the process of applying social science research methods to collect relevant data within the organization to study an organization and to help it understand and solve its problems (Frohman, Sashkin, & Kavanagh, 1976). The application-oriented goal of action research means that it is somewhat different than the traditional hypothesis-testing research discussed in Chapter 2. While hypothesis-testing research attempts to find new knowledge that is applicable to a wide range of organizations, action research tries to solve problems specific to a particular organization. Action research involves some of the same tools used by hypothesis-testing research, namely objective observation and the collection and analysis of research data. However, their goals and scope are quite different, for action research is oriented toward producing some specific results.

The first step in the action research process is data gathering and problem diagnosis. Here, the OD consultant collects data in order to diagnose the problem situation. In the next step, feedback is given as the data, and the OD consultant's interpretation of the data, are presented to the organization's members. The next step is joint action planning. Here the OD consultant and the organizational members design a problem-solving program, which might be one of a variety of OD interventions that we will discuss later. Once the program is implemented, the action research process repeats itself. Now, however, the data gathering is an attempt to determine the effectiveness of the OD program. If it is successful, the organization and the OD consultant might discuss ways to make it a regular part of the organization's operations. If unsuccessful, the pro-

change agent
a name for an OD practitioner that refers to the person's role as a catalyst who helps organizations through the process of change

action research
an OD methodological model that applies social science research methods to collect relevant data in an organization that are used as the basis for solving organizational problems

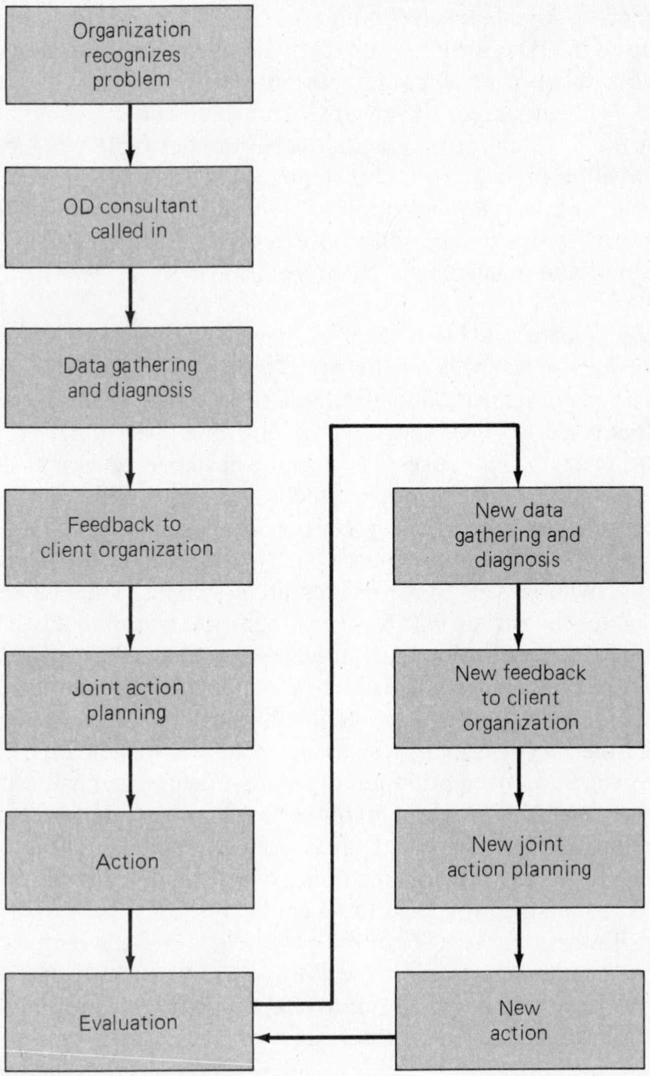

Figure 12.7
STEPS IN THE ACTION
RESEARCH PROCESS

```
┌─────────────────┐
│  Organization   │
│   recognizes    │
│     problem     │
└────────┬────────┘
         ↓
┌─────────────────┐
│  OD consultant  │
│    called in    │
└────────┬────────┘
         ↓
┌─────────────────┐
│  Data gathering │
│  and diagnosis  │
└────────┬────────┘
         ↓                      ┌─────────────────┐
┌─────────────────┐             │    New data     │
│   Feedback to   │             │  gathering and  │
│client organization│           │   diagnosis     │
└────────┬────────┘             └────────┬────────┘
         ↓                               ↓
┌─────────────────┐             ┌─────────────────┐
│  Joint action   │             │  New feedback   │
│    planning     │             │    to client    │
│                 │             │  organization   │
└────────┬────────┘             └────────┬────────┘
         ↓                               ↓
┌─────────────────┐             ┌─────────────────┐
│     Action      │             │   New joint     │
│                 │             │ action planning │
└────────┬────────┘             └────────┬────────┘
         ↓                               ↓
┌─────────────────┐             ┌─────────────────┐
│   Evaluation    │←────────────│      New        │
│                 │←────────────│    action       │
└─────────────────┘             └─────────────────┘
```

gram might need some alterations, or a different program might be tried.
Figure 12.7 graphically depicts the steps in the action research model.

ORGANIZATIONAL DEVELOPMENT TECHNIQUES

In solving organizational problems, OD programs use a wide variety
of established techniques, some of which we have already discussed. For
example, recall from Chapter 6 that job enrichment is a process of increasing the levels of responsibility associated with jobs to improve
worker satisfaction and commitment to the work effort. Although job

enrichment was presented in Chapter 6 as a motivational technique, it can also be used in OD efforts because it involves the collaboration of workers in work teams that play an important part in solving change-related problems that may affect the groups' work performance. Organizational behavior modification programs that reinforce desirable work behaviors can likewise be used as an OD technique. Of the other procedures that have been used by OD practitioners, we will discuss five of the more popular: survey feedback, sensitivity training, team building, process consultation, and management by objectives.

survey feedback
an OD technique whereby the consultant works with the organization to develop and administer a survey instrument to collect data that are then fed back to organizational members and used as the starting point for change

Survey feedback.   The use of employee surveys is a common OD strategy. **Survey feedback** is the process by which the OD consultant works with the organization to develop a survey instrument to collect data that is then used to solve specific problems or to institute a program for managing change. The survey is usually designed to assess employee attitudes about important work-related issues such as the organization in general, company policies and practices, quality of leadership, and coordination among work units. Once constructed, the survey is distributed either to all workers or to a representative sample. The OD consultant then tabulates the survey data and puts them into a form that will be easily understood by organizational members. Next the results are presented to organizational members. This feedback can be done in a number of ways: in written form, in small or large group discussions, or in a general meeting. Since the survey is merely an assessment tool to indicate which areas of the organization need attention or improvement, the final, crucial step in a survey feedback program involves developing strategies to deal with any problems or concerns that arise from the results. The survey is a starting point for solving organizational problems or for instituting future programs for planned organizational change.

One of the direct benefits of the survey is that it can increase the upward flow of communication from lower-level workers to management. The survey may also have a positive effect on workers' attitudes, as they perceive that management is interested in hearing their views and concerns. This will only occur, however, if steps are taken to address problems. If not, workers may develop negative attitudes about management and the survey process. Finally, the survey results can show workers that they are not alone and that others share their attitudes and concerns.

Research indicates that survey feedback is an effective OD technique, if followed by some positive actions (Bowers, 1973; Bowers & Hauser, 1977). Surveys have additional advantages as well. They are an efficient way of collecting a large amount of information from a large number of workers. Also, since surveys can be conducted anonymously, lower-level workers feel that they can safely voice their opinions, which can lead to very honest appraisals of work situations. Since it requires considerable training to create valid and reliable employee surveys and to analyze and interpret the results, I/O psychologists or other social science professionals are most often involved in survey feedback programs.

Sensitivity training. The OD strategy termed **sensitivity training** actually refers to the use of unstructured group interaction to help workers gain insight into their motivations and their behavior patterns in dealing with others. In sensitivity training, also known as encounter or training groups (t-groups), small groups of workers meet in a nonwork setting for an unstructured discussion of their attitudes and beliefs concerning their work, the work environment, and their interactions with supervisors and co-workers. The eventual goals of sensitivity training are for participants to gain insight concerning their own behavior, to develop greater openness, and to improve skills in understanding and dealing with others. Typically, a professional serves as group leader, although the leader usually plays a nondirective role in merely keeping the goals of the session in everyone's minds and keeping the discussion from getting out of hand. An effective leader will usually prevent problems such as "psychological casualties," which occur when the group targets one or more persons for intense criticism or when participants suffer from airing sensitive personal information in a public forum.

Sensitivity training was very popular in the 1960s and early 1970s, when interest in self-exploration and group encounters was at its height. Although it is not as popular today, this method is still used by some OD practitioners who report very positive results, particularly in improving the communication skills of managers. However, research on the effectiveness of sensitivity training has been inconclusive. There is some evidence that managers can achieve insight into their behavior and develop interpersonal skills through the process, although there is some concern over whether the insights and skills gained from sensitivity training generalize to actual work settings (Campbell & Dunnette, 1968; Mirvis & Berg, 1977). Specifically, it is not clear that gaining insight about one's own behavior, and developing communication skills in the "safe" setting of the t-group, will then translate into changes in a worker's behavior in the actual work setting.

Team building. **Team building** is an OD intervention in which groups of workers meet to discuss ways to improve their performance by identifying strengths and weaknesses in their interaction with one another. In some ways, team building is similar to sensitivity training, although the focus is no longer on individual growth and skill development but on improving team functioning and goal attainment. Although some emphasis is put on improving members' abilities to communicate with one another, greater stress is placed on helping the team to achieve performance-related goals.

Team building can use existing groups of workers or construct new

sensitivity training
an OD technique that uses unstructured group interaction in assisting workers to achieve insight into their own motivations and behavior patterns in dealing with other organizational members

team building
an OD technique in which teams of workers discuss how to improve team performance by analyzing group interaction

*In team building,
groups of employees
discuss methods of
improving their work.*

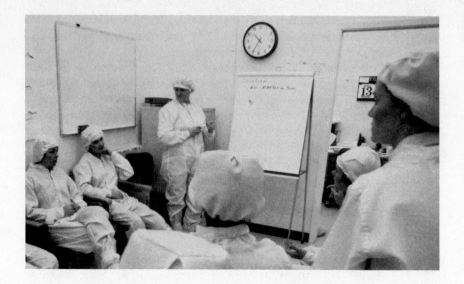

work teams. The first session is a diagnostic meeting. The OD consultant serves as moderator, while the team discusses its current level of functioning in an unstructured setting similar to that used in sensitivity training. Each team member is allowed to present personal views and suggestions for improving the team's performance. Through this process, the group should eventually agree upon strategies for implementing positive changes. Subsequent sessions involve evaluating and "fine-tuning" new procedures or suggesting alternate approaches.

Because of its emphasis on the group, rather than the individual, team building does not have the threat of psychological casualties that may exist in sensitivity training. Also, because team building is focused clearly on performance-related goals, it may be connected to improved job performance (Woodman & Sherwood, 1980).

Process consultation. **Process consultation** is an OD technique in which a consultant helps a client organization to "perceive, understand, and act upon process events which occur in the client's environment" (Schein, 1969, p. 9). In process consultation, the OD consultant helps the organization to learn how to solve its own problems. In many ways, process consultation epitomizes many of the central themes of organizational development. It uses a change agent, the process consultant, who works as a teacher to assist the client-organization in learning how to use objective methods, such as survey instruments, structured interviews, or the collection of relevant performance data, to diagnose and solve its own problems. The consultant also instructs organizational members in how to implement specific OD problem-solving techniques. The goal is for the organization to become self-reliant by knowing how to deal with change-related problems once the process consultant is gone.

*process consultation
an OD technique in
which a consultant
helps a client-organiza-
tion to study its prob-
lems objectively and
thus to learn to solve
them*

To understand the specific steps in process consultation outlined by Schein (1969), we will use the example of a consultant who is working with CDE company, which produces and sells cosmetics. The first step is the *initial contact* with the client-organization, which is usually initiated by someone in the organization who realizes that problems exist and is willing to try to solve them. In the case of CDE, the vice president of sales called in the process consultant, Dr. Io, because of what he considers to be high turnover of sales personnel and managers.

The second step is *developing the contract*. In initial, exploratory meetings, the vice president of sales meets with top decisionmakers—the other vice presidents and the company president—to determine the problems, explain the consultant's role, and formulate actions to be taken. A formal contract is drawn up to determine matters such as client time and compensation. A "psychological" contract, which includes the expectations and goals of the organization as well as Dr. Io's goals, is also formulated: The company wants to reduce costly turnover, and Dr. Io wants the organization to take steps not only to reduce turnover but also to ensure that the company can deal with future turnover problems. But she also wants the organization to explore any related problems that the consultation uncovers.

The third step is the *selection of a setting and a method of work*. A site for study is selected collaboratively with the client and is usually a unit near the top of the organization. Those workers who are being observed by the consultant must be made aware of her presence and purpose. Together, Dr. Io and the CDE decisionmakers choose the largest regional headquarters as the site for study. Because this office is adjacent to corporate headquarters, Dr. Io will have easy contact with the company's top-level executives.

The fourth step is *data gathering and diagnosis*. By using interviews (particularly exit interviews), direct observation, and surveys of employees, Dr. Io tries to obtain an in-depth picture of the organization and its internal processes. She works with certain CDE personnel, instructing them in data collection methods. Through analysis of these data and consultation with relevant CDE personnel and executives, specific problem areas are targeted. The data reveal that turnover is linked to three factors: (1) Salespersons perceive their sales commissions rates to be lower than those in other sales positions; (2) salespersons feel they do not receive enough attention from sales managers; and (3) some salespersons are hired without much experience, and CDE provides little specific training of new personnel.

The next step is the *intervention*. A variety of intervention strategies are used in process consultation. Some are as simple as providing feedback of the consultant's observations to workers. Others may involve counseling work groups or individuals or setting agendas to increase a group's awareness of its own internal processes. In the case of CDE, Dr. Io and company executives jointly decide to develop a "sales force improvement task force," composed of both management personnel and salespersons, who will formulate a proposal to improve the hiring and training procedures for new salespersons. Other goals of the task force will be to conduct a survey of sales commission rates in other companies and to develop a program for improving sales managers' supervision.

The final step in process consultation is the *evaluation of results and disengagement*. According to Schein (1969, p. 123), successful process consultation improves organizational performance by "changing some of the *values* of the organization and by increasing the *interpersonal skills* of key managers." If these goals are met, CDE should see some changes in the organization's perception of the value of the sales force and in the selection, training, and treatment of sales personnel. There will also likely be some improvement in the interpersonal skills of sales managers. The relationship between consultant and client is terminated by mutual agreement. In the case of CDE, Dr. Io may or may not work with the organization in implementing and evaluating the various new programs. Sometimes, a slow disengagement process is used whereby the consultant gradually lessens involvement with the client-organization. This is likely in the case of Dr. Io, since the programs for organizational improvement will probably take a long time to design and implement, and their evaluation will likely initially require her assistance.

Process consultation is a detailed OD program, involving an extensive and long-term relationship between the consultant and the client-organization. Some authors have likened this technique to the psychotherapeutic process in which a therapist works with a client over a long period of time to diagnose and work toward solving the client's problems (Landy, 1989).

Management by objectives (MBO). **Management by objectives,** or **MBO,** is a goal-setting technique that is often used as an OD intervention. In MBO, subordinates work with superiors in jointly setting performance goals. The basic rationales behind the procedure are that work-related goals must be clearly specified and measurable, and that employees should participate in setting them to become committed to their fulfillment. MBO is closely related to the goal-setting techniques of motivation discussed in Chapter 6. Management by objectives can also be used as an alternative to traditional rating methods of performance appraisal, because successful MBO programs must accurately and objectively measure the attainment of performance goals (see Chapter 3). At the end of the goal period—usually three to six months and occasionally twelve months—employees again meet with supervisors and receive feedback concerning the goal attainment. If the goals have not been met, suggestions for improvement are made. If they have been attained, new and perhaps even more challenging goals are set.

management by objectives (MBO)
a goal-setting OD technique in which supervisors and subordinates jointly set performance goals; at the end of the goal period, their attainment is evaluated and new goals are set

The MBO technique actually predates the organizational development movement. Developed in the 1950s by Drucker and his associates (Drucker, 1954), it has been a very popular method for improving worker performance. Unfortunately, MBO has also been widely misused. Often any type of goal setting is labeled MBO, even though it does not follow the MBO model (McConkie, 1979). For MBO to be implemented correctly, the following criteria must be met:

In management by objectives, employees and supervisors work together to set specific performance goals.

· *Employees must participate in setting personal performance goals*. However, a potential weakness of MBO goal-setting is that workers may take advantage of the freedom they are afforded and set goals that are much too easy and do not represent a motivating challenge. Alternatively, if the supervisor too strongly influences the setting of goals, MBO may not be effective because employees may feel that they have no real voice in the goal-setting process.
· *Feedback concerning goal attainment must be provided*. As in any performance appraisal system, the strength of the appraisal depends on the ability to assess performance objectively. Objective measurement of goal attainment must take place, and this information must be presented to the employees.
· *Guidelines for improvement must be provided*. In the case of the failure to reach goals, supervisors should provide suggestions for improving work performance. Otherwise, employees may become frustrated and unmotivated by their inability to achieve set goals.
· *Goals must be realistic*. They must neither be too high nor too low. If goals are unrealistically high, the workers will be frustrated. If they are too low, the employees are not challenged.
· *The upper levels of the organization must support the program*. Since MBO is a time-consuming process for supervisors, their efforts must be recognized. The best way to do this is to include effective participation in the MBO program as part of the supervisors' own performance goals.
· *Individual, work group, and organizational goals must be equally emphasized*. If jobs involve cooperation with other employees (and most jobs do), overemphasis on individual goals may inhibit the group's ability to work together. Thus, workers must be oriented toward achieving not only their own goals but also those of the group and the organization as a whole.

Management by objectives is one of the most widely used OD techniques, partly because it can be implemented in just about any work organization and with almost any type of job (see On the Cutting Edge for discussion of some other OD techniques).

Quality Circles and Other Organizational Development Imports from Japan

In recent years, several management techniques popular in Japan have been imported to American companies for use as part of an OD program. This interest arose because of the high levels of productivity and product quality among Japanese manufacturers. It is believed that much of their success is related to their effective use and development of their human resources, especially their great concern over selecting the best employees and building employee commitment to the organization and the work group (Hatvany & Pucik, 1981). This purportedly leads to higher production and higher levels of quality than are typically seen in U.S. manufacturing companies.

The Japanese management technique that has been most widely adopted in the United States is the concept of **quality circles,** which are small groups of volunteer employees from the same work areas who meet regularly to identify, analyze, and solve quality- and other work-related problems (Munchus, 1983). In the initial meetings, members are trained in quality control, work on developing communication skills, and learn problem-solving techniques. They then select a particular problem to study and use a variety of methods to gather information pertinent to the issue. Finally, a recommendation is made to management about how to solve the problem. The goal of quality circles is to get employees more involved in their jobs and to increase their feelings of having some control over their work. This increased employee involvement should lead to greater worker satisfaction, work quality (and perhaps productivity), and worker commitment to the organization. The important question, however, is whether quality circles work in American companies.

Although it is difficult to give a firm answer, very recent evaluations indicate that quality circles can indeed lead to increased quality and productivity in American manufacturing organizations, and may enhance participants' job satisfaction (Marks, Mirvis, Hackett, & Grady, 1986). However, in certain instances American applications of quality circle programs have failed, although analysis suggests that the failures have more to do with poor implementation than to any inherent flaws in the theory underlying quality circles. The failure of quality circle programs, and indeed of other OD programs, can often be traced to the lack of support from management and/or workers, or to poor training and preparation of participants (Marks, 1986).

THE EFFECTIVENESS OF ORGANIZATIONAL DEVELOPMENT

quality circles
small groups of volunteer employees from the same work areas who meet regularly to solve work-related problems

A variety of techniques have been used as interventions in organizational development programs. However, the important question is, "Does OD work?" There is no firm answer to this question. A number of factors make it difficult to determine the effectiveness of OD programs. One difficulty concerns the variety of OD techniques that can be used as part of OD programs. Some of these techniques may simply be better than others. For example, evidence suggests that MBO and survey feedback are moderately successful (Kondrasuk, 1981; Miner, 1983), whereas there is some question about the effectiveness of sensitivity training (Odiorne, 1963; Miner, 1983). A second reason lies in the nature of the organization that conducts the OD program. What works in one organization may not

An Organizational Development Program "Develops" at Polaroid

Several years ago, at one of Polaroid's film-manufacturing plants near Boston, employees were becoming increasingly frustrated and angry with the treatment they were getting from management (see Albrecht, 1983). The main problem was their dissatisfaction with a plant manager who was considered to be an "oppressive, inconsiderate tyrant" with little concern for workers' needs or concerns. The situation had gone so far that an employee complaint was delivered to the division vice president, asking that the plant manager be replaced or reoriented. An OD consulting team was called in. The OD consultants used interviews, questionnaires, and reviews of the plant's performance to gather relevant data. Interestingly, the plant was one of the most productive Polaroid facilities. According to questionnaire and interview results, employees' dissatisfaction centered on the issue of trust in management.

Working with workers at all levels, the OD consultants, together with Polaroid employees, developed a set of strategies, including sending the plant manager to a leadership training program, conducting communication and problem-solving workshops for various supervisors and key employees, and holding regular meetings between the plant manager and various employee groups.

As a result of the OD program, employees' satisfaction and the social climate in the organization improved greatly. More importantly, the program's benefits extended to other problems identified during the diagnosis, including improvements in the relationship between managers and hourly workers, the establishment of quality-of-worklife focus groups, and the development of joint productivity-improvement projects that were Polaroid's version of quality circles.

Not only did the OD intervention work to solve immediate problems at this specific Polaroid plant, but the OD diagnosis and assessment uncovered other potential problems that were addressed in subsequent programs. Thus, the first OD intervention led to subsequent OD interventions in other areas of the plant. Furthermore, the success of the OD program in this plant led to the use of OD techniques in other plants within the company.

---

be effective in another because of differences in the attitudes of organizational members or in their commitment to OD efforts. Furthermore, determining the effectiveness of organizational development is hard because of difficulties in conducting good evaluations. Because OD intervention usually takes place on a large scale, often involving an entire organization, much of the evidence for its effectiveness is based on case studies. The unit of measurement—the subject in the evaluation of an OD program—is the organization. It is very difficult to combine the results of a specific OD strategy with those of the same method used in other companies because the circumstances may be very different. This often leaves us with only a series of case studies as evidence for the effectiveness of OD programs (see Applying I/O Psychology).

Overall, the results of evaluations of organizational development programs are mixed. There have been some reports of glowing successes, and other reports of failures (Bennis, 1969; French & Bell, 1978; Porras & Berg, 1978). Bass (1983) proposes that the positive effects may be greater in job satisfaction and organizational commitment than in increased organizational productivity. Moreover, he suggests that many of the successes of OD programs may be long-term changes that do not show up for months or years, long after the evaluation of the OD program is completed. Until more rigorous evaluation research of OD programs is routinely conducted, it will be very difficult to draw firm conclusions about their effectiveness. However, organizational development remains quite popular, largely because its underlying theory—that organizations must adapt to keep up with the rapid changes in the world at large—makes sense.

SUMMARY

Organizational structure is the arrangement of positions in an organization and the relationships among them. Organizational structures can be generally classified into traditional and nontraditional forms. The *bureaucracy* and the *line-staff organization* typify the traditional structure. The bureaucracy is a structure based on authority relationships among organizational members that operate through a system of formal rules and procedures. The line-staff organization is a formal structure in which the *line* executes organizational objectives, while the *staff* is designed to support the line. Nontraditional organizational structures are exemplified by the *matrix organization,* a permanent team of competent workers designed for maximizing organizational adaptability. Traditional organizational structures tend to be stable and rule driven, while nontraditional structures are characterized by their flexibility, adaptability, and lack of formal authority lines.

Other important dimensions of organizational structure are the number of authority levels in an organization, or *chain of command,* and the number of workers reporting to a single work supervisor, or the *span of control*. Organizations can also be divided by the kinds of tasks performed—a *functional structure*—or by the types of products produced or customers served—a *divisional structure*. Decisionmaking power can either be concentrated at the top levels of the organization (*centralization*), or dispersed throughout the organization (*decentralization*). The most recent approaches to organizational structure are contingency models whereby the most effective type of structure depends on the fit between structure and the external or internal environment of the work organization.

Organizational development (OD) is the process of preparing for and managing change in organizations. OD programs use a consultant who is commonly called a *change agent*. OD programs usually occur in phases. One model for such a program is *action research,* which involves collecting data, diagnosing organizational problems, and developing strategies to take action to solve them. A variety of interventions are used in OD programs, including *survey feedback,* a technique of using data about organizational members' feelings and concerns as the basis for planned change; *sensitivity training,* a process of increasing workers' awareness of their own and other members' behavior; *team building,* the development of teams of workers to focus on ways to improve group performance; *process consultation,* a long-term method of helping an organization to develop problem-solving strategies; and *management by objectives (MBO),* a goal-setting technique designed to increase worker commitment to the attainment of personal and organizational goals. Evaluation of OD programs indicates that they can be effective for improving certain aspects of organizational effectiveness, although neither their implementation nor their evaluation is easy.

STUDY QUESTIONS AND EXERCISES

1. Consider an organization with which you have had some contact. Describe the structure of this organization using the dimensions of traditional-nontraditional, functional-divisional, and centralized-decentralized. If you have access to the organization's chart, describe its chain of command and span of control.

2. Based on what you know about traditional and nontraditional organizational structures, contrast the work life of the typical worker in a bureaucracy with that of a worker in a matrix organization.

3. Compare and contrast the contingency models of organizational structure.

4. Consider a common problem in classrooms, such as a difficulty in communication between professor and students or an unclear grading policy. How might an OD consultant solve this problem? What OD techniques might be used?

5. What are the difficulties in evaluating the success of OD programs?

SUGGESTED READINGS

Albrecht, K. (1983). *Organizational development: A total systems approach to positive change in any business organization.* Englewood Cliffs, NJ: Prentice-Hall. *A straightforward introduction to organizational development written primarily for practicing managers.*

Burke, W. W. (1987). *Organization development: A normative view*. Reading, MA: Addison-Wesley. *Another brief overview of OD.*

Miller, D., & Friesen, P. H. (1984). *Organizations: A quantum view*. Englewood Cliffs, NJ: Prentice-Hall. *A summary of research on organizational structure, structural change, and entrepreneurial behavior within organizations.*

Van de Ven, A. H., & Joyce, W. F. (Eds.) (1981). *Perspectives on organization design and behavior*. New York: John Wiley & Sons. *A collection of readings on topics relating to organizational structure.*

13

PART FIVE

HUMAN FACTORS IN WORK DESIGN

CHAPTER OUTLINE

Human Factors: Seeing the Big Picture

This chapter introduces the specialty within I/O psychology known as human factors, which focuses on the relationship between the worker, the work environment, and the work task. The material presented here is thus quite different from that of other chapters, which concentrated on characteristics of the worker and the relationships among workers. In this chapter there is much less theorizing than in many of the previous chapters on other areas of I/O psychology, because human factors is more "problem-focused." In other words, human factors psychologists are often concerned with solving specific problems, such as reducing errors in a particular work system or improving efficiency in the performance of some work task.

However, this chapter does have important links to other chapters. Most importantly, since human factors psychologists study workers and their jobs, the topics of job analysis and job performance (Chapter 3) are central. When human factors psychologists study jobs, they typically begin with a job analysis to obtain detailed knowledge of the work tasks. This is the starting point for designing work machinery, equipment, and environments to be compatible with the people using them. Of course, human factors psychologists are also quite involved in training workers how to operate complex machine systems efficiently (Chapter 5). Finally, this chapter fits together with Chapter 14, with the present chapter concentrating on the worker-machine relationship, which is known as the operator-machine system, and the next chapter emphasizing the relationship between the worker and the more general work environment.

While some of the basic principles and procedures of human factors introduced in this chapter may appear to be commonsensical, don't be fooled, for they are actually much more complex. Principles of human factors are based on a thorough understanding of human capabilities and limitations (such as perceptual processes and cognitive and physical abilities), the technical capabilities of machines, and the relationship between the two.

The key to success in human factors psychology is the same as that in other areas of I/O psychology: a solid grounding in basic research methodology. Using established principles and knowledge, the human factors professional strives to improve and innovate. These new developments in technology or procedures are then thoroughly and systematically tested before they are ever put into operation. Human factors psychologists spend a great deal of time testing and evaluating what works and what does not in a particular operator-machine system.

In previous chapters, we have explored the social environment of the work place, focusing on communication processes, work group dynamics, various relationships and roles at work, and how these relationships and roles are interrelated and structured. In this section, we will turn away from the social relationships at work and look at the relationship between the worker and the work task. This chapter will begin by examining how the worker, the work environment, and work tools and machinery all interact to enable the worker to perform a job. We will look at how industrial/organizational psychologists have played an important role in designing work environments, tools, and machines that are compatible with the humans who use them, thus leading to increased productivity and efficiency in work operations. In Chapter 14, we will examine how characteristics of the work environment affect worker safety and well-being. We will close that chapter, and the book, with a discussion of how the work environment plays a part in determining the quality of worklife.

To start the discussion of how the physical work environment affects worker behavior, we need to consider the various ways in which the work world is and will be changing. For example, in the very near future, workers will be spending much of their work day interacting, not with another person, but with a very sophisticated machine. Tremendous advances in technology have led to the development of extremely complex computers designed to perform or assist in various work tasks. The computer has revolutionized much of the working world and human lives in general. Secretaries who once used typewriters and file cabinets now use word processors and computerized filing systems. Factory workers who formerly performed assembly work by hand are now assisted by robots that execute some of the more physically demanding (and tedious) tasks. Even retail clerks ring up sales on computer systems that reduce pricing errors and keep inventories of merchandise under control. The tools, machines, and systems that workers use are becoming increasingly complex and sophisticated. The area of I/O psychology that is concerned with issues such as the design and operations of these complex work systems and work environments is known as human factors.

HUMAN FACTORS

Industrial/organizational psychologists have played an important role in the design and development of complex work machines and systems. This specialty within the field is called **human factors.** Also known as ergonomics or engineering psychology, this area is concerned with designing tools, machines, work systems, and work places to provide an optimal fit between characteristics of work machinery and environments and the skills and abilities of workers. Human factors is concerned with engineering machine systems and work environments to try to increase

human factors
the specialty area of I/O psychology concerned with designing tools, machines, work systems, and work places to fit the skills and abilities of workers

efficiency by making the machine more compatible with human capabilities and limitations. Additional goals of human factors are to help teach workers to use the machines and systems that have been designed and to protect their safety and comfort while they interact with the machine work system. This latter concern will be discussed more fully in Chapter 14.

Human factors, one of the most exciting and rapidly growing areas of I/O psychology, draws on research and information from a number of areas of psychology, including the study of sensation and perception, psychophysiology, and cognitive psychology. It also interacts with other disciplines, particularly engineering and architecture, to try to improve work systems and environments. To gain a better understanding of the field, it is important to look at its history.

A BRIEF HISTORY OF HUMAN FACTORS

The roots of human factors psychology lie in the work of Frederick Taylor and his followers (see Chapter 1). Recall that Taylor, the "father" of scientific management, wanted to redesign manual labor jobs to make them more efficient and productive. He and his followers such as the Gilbreths achieved this by using time-and-motion studies to break jobs down into smaller, well-defined tasks and then devising a better, more efficient way to perform the same jobs. To some extent, the methods used by human factors psychologists still follow Taylor's methods of breaking down complex jobs into their basic components. However, the job of a computer operator or an air traffic controller is much more complex than the simple mechanical jobs studied by the Taylorists. Human factors has progressed enormously since the early days of time-and-motion studies.

Even though Taylor and his followers did improve the productivity and efficiency of many jobs, their methods and concerns did not catch on very quickly. It was not until late in World War II that the idea of designing complex equipment and machinery to fit the capabilities of the human operator became clear. For instance, during the war, the emphasis of the Army Air Corps (which would later become the Air Force) was on training pilots to fly airplanes rather than on designing efficient airplane controls. It was not until it was discovered that even very experienced pilots were prone to making serious errors with poorly designed control systems that concern was given to creating cockpits with controls that maximized the pilot's ability to operate the craft. For example, similar-looking controls operating the landing gear and steering flaps on some B-25 bombers were placed next to each other. As a result, several B-25s landed on their bellies because the pilots had believed that they had operated the landing gear control when they were really operating the steering flaps control (Mark, Warm, & Huston, 1987).

As World War II progressed, the need for more sophisticated war machinery meant not only improving the speed, quality, and firepower of the machinery but also creating better operating systems so that the persons controlling these machines could operate them quickly and safely, with a minimum of errors. Near the end of the war, human factors laboratories were created by the American armed forces to meet this challenge. Interestingly, the need for state-of-the-art war machinery has continued to increase, as has the need for human factors professionals to assist in designing even more efficient operating systems. Moreover, in nearly every industry, as machines and equipment have become more complex, there is concern with producing efficient and safe systems. In the past four decades, human factors has played a significant and an increasing role in the design of equipment, machinery, work environments, and products in industries as diverse as the military, the space industry, the automotive industry, pharmaceuticals, the nuclear energy industry, and the computer industry.

OPERATOR-MACHINE SYSTEMS

A topic of central concern for human factors psychologists is the design and improvement of the **operator-machine system,** which is the interaction of one or more persons with one or more tools or devices to perform some task. These systems can be as simple as a worker using a hammer to drive a nail or as complex as an astronaut flying the space shuttle. However, as technology advances, a greater percentage of workers are operating fairly sophisticated machine systems as an everyday part of their jobs. These sophisticated work machines include delivery trucks, word processors, telephone systems, automated assembly lines, and computers.

The human factors psychologist views the operator and the machine as engaged in a two-way interaction. With sophisticated machinery, such as a computer system, this notion is quite appropriate, because the operator receives information from a sophisticated work machine through various machine displays. The operator then processes this information and makes some decisions about what the machine should do. The operator communicates these decisions to the machine by using certain controls—the buttons, levers, or knobs that control its functioning. The machine responds to the controls and produces the desired operation. The new operating status of the machine is then communicated to the operator via the machine displays (see Figure 13.1). For example, someone working with a personal computer looks at its display: the video screen. Seeing a blank screen, the operator knows that the power to the machine is off. The operator decides to turn on the computer and flips a control switch that causes the computer to "boot up," ready for operation. This computer operation is communicated to the operator by some message on the video screen and with a flashing cursor that lets the operator know that

operator-machine system
the interaction between workers and tools or devices to perform a task

Today's work places abound in sophisticated, complex machinery.

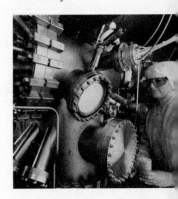

Figure 13.1

AN OPERATOR-MACHINE
SYSTEM

Source: A. Chapanis,
"Engineering Psychology," in
M. D. Dunnette (Ed.), *Hand-
book of Industrial and
Organizational Psychology*
(Chicago: Rand McNally,
1976), p. 701.

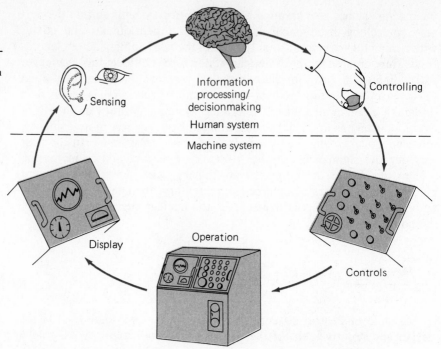

the computer is waiting for the next command. All of this—machine display output, sensory reception by operator, interpretation, decision-making, and operator action—may take only a fraction of a second. Moreover, this process occurs hundreds or even thousands of times in a typical workday as humans and machines engage in ongoing interaction.

To design an operator-machine system, a human factors psychologist often begins with a detailed job analysis, using methods quite similar to those discussed in Chapter 3. A basic starting point is breaking the job down into its component tasks. Decisions are made concerning which tasks the human operator should perform and which the machine should be required to do. In making these decisions, psychologists take into account the respective strengths of both the human operator and the machine system (see Table 13.1). For example, unlike people, machines can perform numerous repetitive actions without fatiguing, while humans can judge the quality of an object and solve problems through inductive reasoning, which are beyond the capabilities of even the most sophisticated computer.

Once the various tasks have been allocated to the operator and to the machine, the next step is for the human factors psychologist to coordinate these activities. For operators and machines to coordinate their respective tasks, they must have some way of communicating with each other. As mentioned, the model of an operator-machine system is the interaction

Table 13.1 STRENGTHS OF THE HUMAN OPERATOR AND THE MACHINE SYSTEM

Operator Characteristics	Machine Characteristics
Is adaptable/flexible; can handle unexpected events	Does not fatigue
Can think and be creative	Makes few processing errors
Can easily pull together information from a variety of sources	Can store great amounts of information efficiently
Can learn to correct own mistakes	Can perform several tasks at once
Can perceive and make sense out of ambiguous stimuli	Can perform in a dangerous environment (such as extreme heat, cold, or radiation)
Has low initial costs, high long-term costs (such as salary and benefits)	Has high initial costs, low long-term costs (maintenance)

between two beings, which psychologists typically speak of in terms of the inputs and outputs of both parties. In an operator-machine system, the machine outputs information concerning operating status via its displays. This information becomes the operator's input. The operator processes this information, makes decisions, and then outputs the decisions by manipulating machine controls. The manipulation of the controls becomes the machine's input, which causes the machine to perform the requested action. We will examine each of the specific elements in this interaction, first focusing on machine displays, then looking at operator information processing and decisionmaking, and finally investigating machine controls.

DISPLAYS

Machine systems communicate with human operators through a variety of **displays,** or mechanical means of communicating information about their operating status to the operator. Some of these displays are visual, such as the radar screen an air traffic controller uses or the lights on your automobile dashboard. Others are auditory: bells, buzzers, and horns that are often used to attract the operator's attention. In rare instances, tactile displays that are sensed by touch and olfactory displays that are sensed by smell are used to inform operators. Tactile displays might include differently shaped knobs to assist in the rapid identification of controls or tiny buttons on the *f* and *j* or *d* and *k* keys of a typewriter to help the operator find the "home row." An example of an olfactory display is the noxious scent mixed with natural gas that warns of possible leaks. Some underground mines in the United States also use a distinguishable odor released into the ventilation system to signal miners to evacuate the mine. Regardless of the type of display, speed and accuracy are often of utmost importance when considering which to use in an efficient operator-machine system. Of the various modes, visual and auditory displays are by far the most common.

displays
mechanical means of communicating information about a machine's operating status to an operator

The effectiveness of a display—its speed, accuracy, arrangement, and the type of information it provides—can be crucial to an operator's success, as in this air traffic control room.

Visual displays. Visual displays on machines can be of three types: quantitative, qualitative, and check reading. Quantitative displays are those that give precise numerical values, such as heat gauges, speedometers, and counters. In the past, they have taken a variety of forms, including the circular or "clock-face" displays and the horizontal or vertical scales seen on radios and older stereos. However, with the rapid advances in technology, including development of the LED (light-emitting diode) and LCD (liquid crystal) displays, many of these older, mechanical quantitative displays are being replaced by digital displays. With digital displays, operators generally make more precise readings and fewer reading errors (Sinclair, 1971). However, there may be some specific errors in reading certain kinds of digital displays, such as confusing 3s and 8s or 1s and 7s because of how these digits are formed. Moreover, persons who are trained to read one type of mechanical display may have difficulty quickly reading the digital displays that are replacing many of the older-type quantitative displays. For example, drivers who are used to a semicircular speedometer may have a hard time adapting to digital speed displays.

Qualitative visual displays provide less precise information to the operator—feedback dealing with certain "qualities" or characteristics of machine operation. For example, the temperature gauge on an automobile or on an automated drillpress may be divided into sections of "cold," "normal," or "hot" operating ranges. Qualitative displays are used when the operator does not need to know precise numerical values. For a truly efficient operator-machine system, it is important to provide the operator with enough information to do the job, but not give *too much* information that might overload the operator or delay response time.

Check-reading displays, which merely tell whether a machine system is on or off, or operating normally or abnormally, provide even less information to the operator. The warning lights on most automobile dashboards that signal low oil pressure or an overheated engine are check-reading displays. They replaced the old quantitative and qualitative gauges, which gave more information than the typical driver needed. After turning on the ignition, the driver merely needs to scan the dashboard display panel; if there are no check-reading displays illuminated, the automobile is safe to drive. Industrial machinery also has check-reading displays to tell the operator when something in the system is malfunctioning.

In addition to the type of visual display, a human factors psychologist must also be concerned with where displays are located and how they are arranged. Consider, for example, the cockpit of a modern jet. The pilot, copilot, and flight engineer are presented with a great number and variety of visual displays that inform them about their altitude, speed, location, and operating status of the aircraft. If displays are not placed so that they can be easily scanned and read, the crew may not receive data needed to fly the jet safely. There are some basic rules for the arrangement of visual displays. First, place displays within the line of the operator's sight. If displays are put in places where the operator cannot easily see them, the operator may not receive the information and it may inhibit performance and efficiency of the operator-machine system. Second, put displays that provide similar or related information next to one another. Third, displays that are to be read sequentially should be placed in reading order, most often left to right or up to down. For example, on machinery controlling an automated assembly line, displays that indicate that power is on are placed in a horizontal sequence to the far left of the operator's field of vision. Displays indicating proper hydraulic pressure in each of the line's units are placed next. Gauges that present the speed of line operations are to the immediate right of the pressure gauges, with counters indicating unit production to the right of the speed gauges. With a sweep of the head from left to right, the operator can receive all necessary information about the line's operation, from information about whether or not the system is operating, to a count of finished products.

Auditory displays. Many machine systems have auditory as well as visual displays to communicate information to the human operator. Auditory displays, which most commonly take the form of bells, horns, buzzers, or other sounds designed to get the operator's attention, are used as warning systems because they usually communicate information faster and more efficiently than visual displays. An operator who is not looking at the display might miss a visual warning, while an operator's ears are always open to receive auditory input. Of course, in noisy work environments, there may be a reliance on visual warnings because auditory displays may go unnoticed.

Recent advancements in auditory communication systems, such as computer-generated, or synthetic, speech, have increased the complexity of auditory information displays from machine systems. For example, many telecommunication systems and certain personal computers use synthetic speech to send messages to system users. While such synthetic speech displays are helpful for the visually impaired or for those who cannot read printed text, for the average operator they may be less efficient than printed displays because the time it takes an operator to receive and process information through the auditory channel may be much greater than the time to process the same information presented in a visual text. In other words, it usually takes longer to listen to a message than to read it. Another problem lies with the quality of computer-generated speech. Although it has been improving, synthetic speech is more difficult to understand than natural speech. Until further technological advancements are made, there may be some problems with operators misunderstanding information presented by synthetic speech (Waterworth & Thomas, 1985). Sometimes, this advanced auditory display technology is used not because it is more efficient or more effective but merely because it represents state-of-the-art technology. For example, a popular sports car has an auditory display system consisting of a recorded message of a woman's voice saying, "The door is ajar," in place of the warning buzzer and red light used in earlier models. It is unclear that this is an improvement over the old system.

Human factors psychologists use certain basic rules to determine when visual displays and auditory displays are appropriate for operator-machine systems (see Table 13.2). Generally, visual displays are used when information is lengthy, complex, or abstract or when a permanent record is needed. Visual displays can include such things as computer printouts or the graphed readouts on medical equipment that provide a detailed, permanent copy of a machine's output. Auditory displays tend to be used when the message is short and simple or urgent. However, if

Table 13.2   GUIDELINES FOR THE USE OF VISUAL AND AUDITORY MACHINE DISPLAYS

Use Visual Displays When:	Use Auditory Displays When:
The message is complex or abstract.	The message is simple and short.
A permanent record is needed.	The message will not be referred to later.
The environment is too noisy to hear.	The environment is too dark to see.
The operator's attention is focused on displays.	The operator is required to move in all directions.
The message is not particularly urgent.	The message is urgent.
The message deals with location in space.	The message deals with a specific moment (e.g., a gun fired to start a race).
	The visual system is overloaded.

the work environment is too noisy, a visual display will be required, and if the environment does not allow for normal operator vision, an auditory display is needed. Auditory displays will also be used if the operator's visual system is overloaded with too many visual displays.

OPERATOR INFORMATION PROCESSING AND DECISIONMAKING

Once the machine displays output information about operating status, it is time for the human part of the system to go to work. The operator receives information through the senses: the eyes receive visual input, the ears take in auditory data. The operator's attention to the information is an important variable here. If the operator is distracted, inattentive, or overloaded with other stimuli, some of the critical information may not be received. However, the sensory input that does reach the operator must then be classified and interpreted.

Any information provided by a machine display represents some form of code that is shared by the machine and the operator. For example, a computer system may give data to the operator by using a computer language, and an automobile displays speed in terms of miles per hour, a code that every driver can understand. The trained operator will readily classify and interpret these machine displays. The various classifications of information parallel the types of information presented in the display. That is, the information can be *quantitative* or *qualitative,* or give some *status,* or provide a *warning.* Information can also be presented in a more complex code, such as written or spoken language, mathematical formulas, or graphed representations. For example, a certain reading on a gauge may be classified as status information and interpreted as a sign that the machine is functioning at normal capacity. The sound of a bell may be classified as a warning signal and interpreted as indicating that it is time for the operator to change some machine operation. To classify and interpret the incoming information, the operator relies on memory, calling on past experience with the machine system. Through experience and training, the operator has learned the specific language that this particular system uses, which then serves as a reference for interpreting whatever messages the machine displays are outputting.

Once the operator has received the information, the next step is decisionmaking, an extremely complex process in which the operator also relies heavily on memory or training. A variety of decisionmaking situations can arise in operator-machine interactions. The most basic is whether or not an operator action is needed. For example, if the operator interprets a message about a machine's operational status to mean that all is going smoothly, the decision will be that no operator action is necessary. If, on the other hand, the message is interpreted as a warning of a machine overload, a decision to slow or shut down the machine will be made. A more complex form of operator decisionmaking would involve deciding which of several courses of action should be taken. The operator

Early Video Games: Problems in the Design of Machine Controls

In the late 1970s, the country was swept by a video game craze. Advances in computerization led to the development of these new entertainment devices. Although the early video games were fairly sophisticated in technical design, they often lacked human factors sophistication, particularly in their controls. These games can thus be analyzed from the standpoint of a human factors psychologist in an effort to spot weaknesses in their operator-machine system design and suggest means of improvement.

One of the very first video arcade games was called Pong. It consisted of two vertical bars of light, which represented the two players' paddles, and a bouncing ball. The object of the game, a video version of Ping Pong, was for the players to hit the ball with the paddles to keep it in play. If one player missed hitting the ball, the opponent received a point. The problem with Pong was that the players' control knobs did not match the functions that they performed. The video paddles were controlled by knobs that were twisted. A clockwise twist made the paddle go up, whereas a counter-clockwise twist made it go down (see Figure 13.2, *left*). It took players quite a while to learn to control the paddles because the knobs violated the principle that a control should imitate the movement it produces. If the Pong paddle controls had been slide switches mounted so that an upward movement on the switch produced an upward movement in the paddle and a downward slide caused a downward movement, there would have been much less operator error.

Asteroids was another early video game. It consisted of a video spaceship (a triangle) that could be rotated to fire at and destroy asteroids before they collided with the ship. Again there was a problem in the control design. The ship was rotated by pressing one of two buttons. Pressing the button on the left caused the spaceship to rotate counter-clockwise; pressing the button on the right created a clockwise rotation (see Figure 13.2, *right*). Novice operators had trouble pushing the correct button and releasing it at the appropriate time to be able to hit the approaching asteroid targets. Imagine a redesign with a knob (like the ones controlling the paddles on Pong) that when twisted to the right creates a clockwise rotation and when twisted to the left causes the spaceship to rotate counter-clockwise. The game would be made more efficient from the operator's perspective because the control actions more closely resemble the movements they produce. (Of course if these video games had been made more efficiently, it might have taken the challenge out of them.) Today's video games have more sophisticated controls that produce more complex actions. For the most part, video game controls have been improved following the human factors guidelines for control design. However, it is still possible to find inefficient mismatches between the controls in certain video games and the specific actions they cause.

---

might rely on memories of how this situation was handled in the past or try to recall what the "normal" procedure is in this instance. When a decision is made, the operator communicates it to the machine by manipulating machine controls.

MACHINE CONTROLS

controls
mechanical devices
that an operator uses
to control machine
functions

Controls are the various knobs, switches, buttons, pedals, levers, and the like that are connected to the operation of the machine. The correct type of control is necessary if operator decisions are to be quickly and efficiently communicated to the machine. Controls such as an on-off switch or a forward-reverse lever cause very general changes in machine

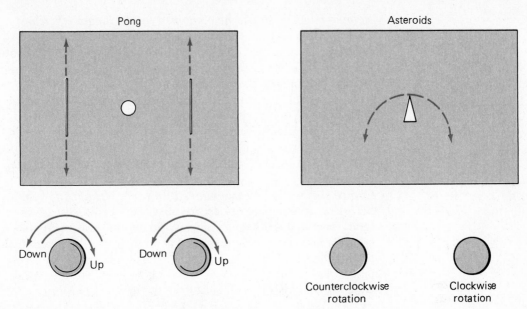

Figure 13.2
TWO EARLY VIDEO GAMES, PONG AND ASTEROIDS

operations, whereas others, such as a volume dial or a channel/frequency selector on a radio, can be designed to make very precise changes. If operator-machine systems are to be efficient, the design and selection of appropriate controls should follow certain basic principles, as outlined:

· *Controls should be matched to the operator's body.* Because humans have greater dexterity with their hands than with their feet, controls requiring precision must be hand operated. To prevent the operator's hands from being overloaded with too many controls, some simple operations can be allocated to foot pedals or switches. An automobile is a good example of how controls can be spread out so that the operator's feet and hands can simultaneously operate different controls.

· *Control movements should mirror the machine actions they produce.* For example, if you turn the steering wheel of an automobile to the left, the car should then turn to the left. This is why people have difficulty learning to drive a forklift forward. Because the steering wheel operates the back rather than the front wheels, when the steering wheel is turned to the left, the front of the forklift turns to the right, and vice versa. Of course, a forklift is designed this way because when it is loaded, the driver will be moving backward. Turned around, the vehicle now follows the "correct" steering pattern: Turn the wheel to the left and the loaded forklift goes left, and vice versa (see Applying I/O Psychology).

· *Related controls should be combined for maximum efficiency.* Two controls that have similar functions should be combined so that in one action, the operator can change the operation of both systems. A simple example is the combined on-off and volume switches on radios. If you turn the volume down completely, you have effectively turned off the radio. Another little turn and a click is heard to indicate that the power has also been shut off. The combined telescopic lens and lens focus on most movie and video cameras is another example. As the camera operator zooms in or out, the focus is automatically changed to keep the image clear.

· *Controls should be clearly marked for rapid identification.* Many industrial accidents have occurred because operators inadvertently operated the wrong controls. To cut down on such errors, controls must be clearly identified as to their use. Many controls are identified with written labels, such as "hot," "cold," "volume," and "tone." However, language barriers and the worldwide distribution of machinery have led to the increasing use of picture-coded controls, such as the light bulb picture on the switch controlling automobile headlights.

On certain sophisticated operator-machine systems, marking controls to be visually recognized may not be enough, since an operator who must quickly operate a variety of controls may not even have time to glance at the control to make sure that the correct one is being operated. Human factors psychologists have thus developed a number of shape-coded controls that can be identified rapidly by touch (see Figure 13.3). The operator merely

Figure 13.3
TACTILE-CODED CONTROLS: STANDARDIZED SHAPE-CODED KNOBS FOR UNITED STATES AIR FORCE AIRCRAFT

Source: United States Air Force, *Air Force System Command Design Handbook 1-3: Human Factors Engineering,* 1980.

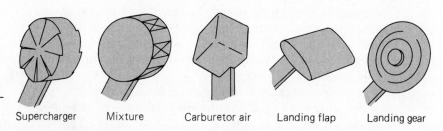

Supercharger   Mixture   Carburetor air   Landing flap   Landing gear

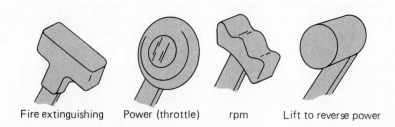

Fire extinguishing   Power (throttle)   rpm   Lift to reverse power

needs to put a hand on the control and knows immediately what machine function is regulated by the control. These controls are used in jet fighter aircraft, where split-second actions can mean the difference between life and death.

· *Placement of controls on similar machine systems should be standardized.* Have you ever borrowed a friend's car? It takes a little while to get oriented to the new machine. You need to find all of the important controls, such as the ignition switch, headlight control, and mirror and seat adjustments. These controls may be placed in very different locations than in your car. Although there is general standardization of some controls, such as the steering wheel and gearshift, there is still some variation in automobile control design and placement. Standardization of controls is especially important when an operator is required to switch back and forth among similar types of machinery.

· *Controls should be adequately spaced and arranged to avoid unintentional activation.* Controls need to be spaced apart from each other so that operating one control does not accidentally activate an adjacent control. Emergency controls should also be clearly labeled and protected either by covering with a shield, by being recessed, or by requiring some force to operate it. This prevents accidental activation that might prove costly or have irreversible results.

Keyboard controls. An increasing percentage of jobs today involve processing information. More and more, workers in the United States must interact with computer systems, communicating either in some written code, often the English language, or in some numeric code. Therefore, the controls that allow workers to enter commands and data into computer systems are becoming increasingly important. The primary control device for most computer systems is some type of alphabetic or numeric keyboard. Much of the information that is entered into a computer system takes the form of alphanumeric characters, such as strings of numerals, words, or alphabetic codes. Generally, the most efficient way to enter this information is through a keyboard. There are three principle arrangements for numeric keyboards. The simplest is the arrangement common to most typewriter keyboards: a simple string of numbers at the top row of the keyboard. A more efficient keyboard arrangement, which is common to calculators and numeric data entry pads, consists of three rows of three digit keys, with the lowest numerals on the bottom row and the zero beneath the third row. Another efficient arrangement, which is typical of push-botton telephones, has the numerals in ascending order, with the lowest numerals on the top row (see Figure 13.4).

There are also two types of alphabetic keyboards, although only one is in widespread use. The standard typewriter keyboard, often called the QWERTY keyboard after the arrangement of keys on the first line of

Figure 13.4
COMMON NUMERIC
KEYBOARDS

Calculator

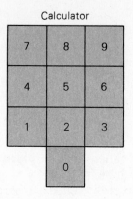

Telephone

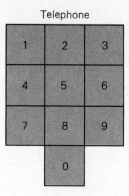

letter characters, is clearly the accepted standard. However, as anyone familiar with touch typing can tell, its letter arrangement is not very efficient. For example, vowels, which are very common in English, are scattered throughout the traditional keyboard. Because of these difficulties, more efficient keyboards, such as the Dvorak keyboard (Dvorak, Marrick, Dealey, & Ford, 1936), have been designed (see Figure 13.5). On the Dvorak keyboard, vowels are centrally located on the home row and are all activated by the left hand. The problem, however, is that so many typists have learned the QWERTY system that the Dvorak arrangement has never really caught on, even though it may increase typing speed by anywhere from 5 to 20 percent (Sanders & McCormick, 1987).

Computer controls.   Many workers now operate some form of computer or computer-assisted machinery as part of their jobs. One of the goals of human factors psychologists has been to make computer systems that can be controlled by the novice. These simple-to-operate systems are often described as "user-friendly."

Among the earliest developments designed to make computer systems more efficient and user-friendly was the ability to activate specific computer functions by hitting certain coded keys instead of typing an entire command. For example, some text keys may allow for editing procedures: removing or replacing a single character, an entire word, or a string of characters. Other keys control the cursor, or pointer, moving it from one place on the computer screen to another. Another innovation was the touch screen control, which enables the user simply to touch some portion of the screen to activate computer functions. For example, a group of boxes with command words appears on the video screen, and a touch on one of the boxes activates that function. Other computer control developments include the "joystick," which is a stick attached to a box that can be moved in all directions to position a pointer on the video screen. A similar device is the "mouse," a hand-held control with a ball or wheels underneath that is rolled on the desk top to move the cursor in

Figure 13.5
ALPHABETIC KEYBOARDS

QWERTY keyboard

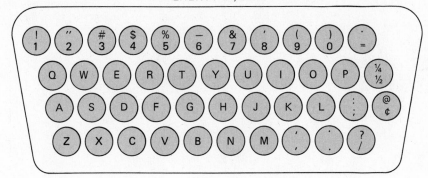

Dvorak simplified keyboard

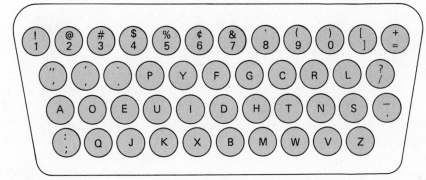

any direction on the screen. These different types of computer controls can be used for a variety of tasks, from editing text to producing computer drawings. One study compared four types of computer controls—the mouse, joystick, text keys, and step keys (up, down, left, and right)—in a text-editing task (see Figure 13.6). The mouse was found to be the fastest and to have the lowest rate of errors (Card, English, & Burr, 1978). Of course, a number of factors affect the speed and efficiency of interacting with a computer system using different controls. For example, individual differences in users' preference for, and familiarity and experience with, specific controls will influence how well they can be used in performing tasks.

Advanced control systems. Two special and very sophisticated machine control systems are teleoperators and speech-activated controls. These advanced controls are currently in limited operation in certain work situations, but as their technology improves, they may become more widespread. **Teleoperators** are sophisticated control systems that act

teleoperators
sophisticated control systems that act as an extension of the human operator

Figure 13.6

COMPUTER CONTROLS FOR TEXT EDITING

Source: S. Card, W. English, and B. Burr, "Evaluation of Mouse, Rate-Controlled Isometric Joystick, Step Keys, and Text Keys for Text Selection on a CRT," *Ergonomics, 21* (1978).

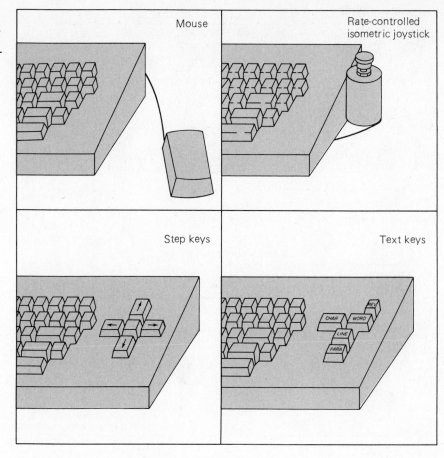

as an extension of the human operator. Usually teleoperators are used in environments that would be dangerous for humans, such as underwater, in outer space, or in radioactive environments. A common teleoperator system is the mechanical arms used for delicate handling of radioactive material. The operator sits in one room, separated by a safety shield from the mechanical arm and radioactive materials in the adjacent room. The operator places his hands in a complicated control apparatus while the mechanical arms, with fingerlike prongs, imitate each of the movements of the operator, whose own arms and fingers are harnessed in the control devices. If the operator's left hand makes a pinching motion, the mechanical arm will make a similar motion to grip an object. The operator can watch the process of the mechanical arm either directly through a window or on a television screen.

speech-activated control machine controls that respond to the sounds of human voices

An even more advanced control system, which has been shown frequently in science fiction movies but is actually in the early stages of development, is **speech-activated control.** In sophisticated speech-

In dangerous environments such as outer space, teleoperators allow humans to control the work from a safe distance.

activated control systems, such as speech-recognition computer systems, the verbal commands of the operator substitute for the keyboard to enter data directly into the system. Although these controls permit the quick entry of information and free the operator's hands for other activities, the current state of speech-activated technology is such that there are some severe limitations. For instance, each word or command must be programmed into the system, which means that words must be uttered clearly and consistently. The operator must learn to use the same speech patterns, pitch, and voice inflections each time a word or command is uttered. Also, extraneous sounds such as coughing, clearing the throat, or stammering will not be recognized and may produce errors in the system operation. Speech-activated control systems need further development before they can be put into everyday work use (it will probably be a long time before you and I can actually "speak" to our computers). Currently, however, they are successfully used with certain tasks, such as simple data recording in situations in which the operator's hands are occupied by other activities. Speech-activated controls are also being used on a limited basis by handicapped individuals who are unable to operate manual controls. For example, persons paralyzed from the neck down can use speech-activated controls to have a computer handle such tasks as dialing telephone numbers and doing simple word processing.

Accidents Lead to Increased Attention to Human Factors in Industry

In earlier times, a worker who made a mistake might spoil a piece of work or waste some time. Today, however, a worker mistake can lead to dire consequences. Consider, for example, the disasters in the nuclear energy industry—Three Mile Island (TMI) and Chernobyl—or Union Carbide's chemical accident in Bhopal, India. In each of these cases, errors in operator-machine systems led to devastating consequences not only for the workers themselves but also for people in the surrounding communities. Specifically, in each case, operators were unaware of the seriousness of the system malfunctions because warning displays were poorly designed or located and operators had not been sufficiently trained in dealing with these emergency situations. The Chernobyl nuclear disaster caused many deaths and exposed thousands to deadly radiation. The Bhopal tragedy—the worst industrial crisis in history—resulted in thousands of deaths and injuries to over a quarter of a million people living around the chemical plant (Morehouse & Subramaniam, 1986). While the TMI incident is classified as a "near disaster," without any direct deaths or injuries, the toll in terms of stress to the nearby residents was considerable (Hartsough & Savitsky, 1984).

The near disaster at TMI has received one of the most extensive investigations into the safety of operations of an industrial plant (Sills, Wolf, &

Shelanski, 1982). All of the evidence points to serious human factors flaws in the design and operation of the plant. For example, control panels presented operators with an overwhelmingly complex amount of information—more than 1,600 gauges and windows that had to be scanned to find where a malfunction was occurring! Moreover, many warning devices were slow to display emergency information and difficult for operators to read (a problem not limited to TMI). The net result was the near avoidance of a potentially catastrophic nuclear accident.

It is unfortunate, but it took disasters such as these to force governments and organizations to consider human factors more fully in the design and operations of complex operator-machine systems. In fact, before the TMI accident, there were virtually no human factors psychologists on the staffs of the Nuclear Regulatory Commission (NRC) nor of the firms hired to design, build, and operate nuclear power plants (Cordes, 1983). Since then, considerable attention has been given to human factors issues in the design and operation of American nuclear power plants. The NRC now has dozens of human factors psychologists on staff. Unfortunately, there is still not enough concern given to human factors in complex plant operations, as evidenced by the Chernobyl and Bhopal disasters, each attributed in part to human factors deficiencies.

ERRORS IN OPERATOR-MACHINE SYSTEMS

Many of the advancements in operator-machine systems are the result of investigation of systematic errors that occur in specific systems. For example, in recent years there seems to have been an alarming increase in airline accidents and near accidents ("near misses"). While much of this is due to the increased volume of air traffic and occasional mechanical malfunctions, such mishaps are frequently said to be due to "human error," the mistakes made by airline pilots or by air traffic controllers. However, such errors are usually not the fault of the human operator alone. Sometimes there is a breakdown in the total system, some mismatch or miscommunication between the machine and the individual operating the machine. Rather than attributing these errors simply to pilot or controller inattention or incompetency, a human factors psychologist may want to examine whether certain mistakes might be caused by faults in the design of the operator-machine systems. For example, perhaps an air traffic controller was overloaded with information, or maybe the system and work load were too complex for a single operator to handle. Maybe information was misread. The pilot may have misread a gauge because it was not placed where he expected it to be on the instrument panel or it was not illuminated enough. Perhaps the pilot tried to correct an initial error, but the system did not respond quickly enough to his adjustment. Whatever the reason for error, the human factors approach to examining such unfortunate instances looks not only at the machine system or the human operator but rather at the interaction of the two (see Up Close: Accidents Lead to Increased Attention to Human Factors in Industry). To study errors in operator-machine systems, some system of categorization is needed. One simple classification examines four types of error that can be investigated in terms of the total operator-machine system (Swain & Guttmann, 1983):

- *Errors of omission:* the failure to do something. An example would be an electrician's failure to shut off the power before working on electrical circuitry. While the worker might be at fault, there could also have been some miscommunication between the operator and the machine system. For example, the power switch may not have been labeled correctly, so that the electrician thought that the power was off when it really wasn't.
- *Errors of commission:* performing an act incorrectly. For example, a worker editing a computer database is presented with the on-screen message, "Hit 'enter' to begin printing." Instead of continuing to edit, the worker strikes the "enter" key and accidentally begins printing the unfinished data.
- *Sequence errors:* performing a task or a step in a task out of order. A salesperson may make a sequence error when entering a price into the cash register before entering the merchandise identification number.
- *Timing errors:* performing an action either too quickly or too slowly. For example, a worker operating a drill press may activate the press via a foot switch before her hands are removed from the work piece. Better coordination between the operator and the machine system, perhaps by having the press activated by a hand switch, would cut down on such timing errors.

There are basically two approaches to dealing with the human errors that will inevitably occur in the work place. The first is the personnel approach, which involves selecting only those workers whose skills and

Robots like this painting arm have taken over many routine manual tasks in industry.

abilities are suited to the operation of the machines and equipment needed to perform the job, or developing training programs to teach workers to perform the job safely with a minimum number of errors. (We will discuss safety training programs more fully in Chapter 14). The second strategy, which is more likely to be used by human factors psychologists, is the design approach. This involves designing equipment, procedures, and environments that reduce the likelihood of errors or the consequences of errors that do occur. This approach should help develop safe and efficient operator-machine systems. Unfortunately, poor design in an operator-machine system is often not discovered until there is a serious accident or breakdown in the system (see On the Cutting Edge).

The two approaches can work together. That is, some poor designs in equipment and machinery can be overcome by training the operators to take these weaknesses into account and compensate for them. For example, a baker can be taught that when an oven door is opened frequently, the oven's temperature will drop and baking time must be adjusted accordingly, because the temperature gauge does not accurately register the change. However, certain poor machine system designs may not be overcome by training. For example, the operator of an air traffic radar screen that has a blind spot will be unable to view air traffic in the blind area. No amount of training can compensate for this weakness.

AUTOMATION AND OPERATOR-MACHINE SYSTEMS

There is no doubt that operator-machine systems are becoming more complex. Greater sophistication in technology means that machines are being constructed that can do more and more. Tasks that were previously performed by humans are being taken over by sophisticated machine systems. While computers have taken over some of our "thinking" tasks, such as bookkeeping, mathematical calculations, and record keeping, robots and robotic devices have taken over some of the manual tasks. **Robots** are automatic, programmable devices that can carry out tasks that are typically performed by humans. Although humanlike robots, such as C3PO from *Star Wars,* have been made famous in science fiction movies and literature, the industrial robots that are currently in use bear little resemblance to human beings. These industrial robots are used quite extensively in the automobile assembly industry, where they perform tasks such as welding and painting.

Some manufacturing plants, such as oil refineries and chemical plants, are completely automated, with all manufacturing operations carried out by robotic devices. The human operators' jobs are simply to watch the system, making sure that it is operating properly, troubleshooting when problems arise, and taking care of some routine maintenance tasks. While such fully automated factories inevitably replace line work-

robots
automatic, programmable devices that can perform tasks typically done by people

Measuring Employee Concerns About the Introduction of Robots into the Work Place

Increasingly, manufacturing workers are being replaced by industrial robots that can perform assembly work more quickly and efficiently than their human counterparts. The introduction of robots into the work place is supposed to be a technological breakthrough, because these sophisticated machines can take on the monotonous, boring, and physically demanding tasks, thereby freeing the people to perform higher-level and more challenging work operations. However, not all workers view industrial robots as a blessing. Employee reactions range from the very positive views that robots will improve work quality, efficiency, and safety to the very negative attitude that they will cause a loss of jobs and will dehumanize the work place.

To better understand worker reactions to robots, researchers have developed a fifty-eight-item questionnaire that measures employee perceptions of robots in four areas: (1) *job security,* perceptions about the jobs that will be lost to robots; (2) *expected changes,* expectations concerning the way robots will change worklife; (3) *management concern,* workers' perceptions of how management views the use of industrial robots; and (4) *general robotics orientation,* employee perceptions of the role of robots in industry (Chao & Kozlowski, 1986). Employees were asked to respond to statements such as the following using the scale of strongly disagree, disagree, neutral, agree, or strongly agree.

Job Security

- Robots seriously threaten my future with this company.
- Robots will make me less useful as a worker.
- As a result of robots in the work place, I will have a smaller and smaller part in the operation of the plant.

Expected Changes

- Robots probably won't change the way work is done here very much.
- Robots will mean fewer and fewer promotions.
- I'm excited about the prospect of working with robots.

Management Concerns

- Management's interest in robots is to improve productivity without much concern for the employees.
- Management is genuinely concerned about the welfare of employees who will be affected by robots.
- Management has a responsibility to inform workers in advance about all robotics programs.

General Robotics Orientation

- New automation and robots should reduce the drudgery associated with many jobs.
- In the long run, automation and robots will result in a higher standard of living for my family and me.
- Robots will help American companies keep up with the pace of foreign competitors.

The questionnaire was administered to 461 hourly workers in a large manufacturing plant that used an assembly line process. The plant was planning to introduce robots into the assembly line. The results indicated that low-skilled workers, such as the assembly line workers, had negative reactions toward the implementation of robots, perceiving them as a threat to job security. Workers with higher levels of skills, such as plant electricians, reacted more positively toward the robots and perceived robots as providing opportunities to expand their skills.

It is important to consider employee perceptions and attitudes toward robots in order to prevent possible resistance to implementation of the new technology, as illustrated in the following case in which employees were not notified that a robot was being delivered to the plant. "Before the robot was unpacked it was accidentally dropped. After repairs, the robot was mysteriously moved from its installation site, fed twice the required voltage, and had sand placed in its hydraulic system" (Sullivan, 1982, cited in Chao & Kozlowski, 1986, p. 71). This example shows how important it is to consider employees' perceptions of robots as part of the strategy for implementing robots in the work place.

ers, the operators of the systems are upgraded; they have high levels of responsibility and the sophisticated skills needed to monitor, control, and maintain the complex machine systems. The situation is thus a trade-off: While workers may lose lower-level positions, the operator positions are enriched.

Whenever automated systems are introduced into a company, there is likely to be some resistance from employees. After all, some tasks that were formerly performed by the human workers are now allocated to machines, which means that there may be some loss of line positions. Moreover, there is a general tendency to be wary of (and perhaps resist) any changes in usual work operations. To ease the transition, certain basic guidelines can be followed to increase worker acceptance of the new technology (see Weiner & Curry, 1980):

> · *Involve workers in the decision to adopt automation.* Because needs and desires for automation may vary from department to department and from individual to individual, workers should be behind any decisions to automate. To overcome worker resistance to automation, they must be informed of its potential benefits to them, including increased productivity and efficiency, upgraded skills as workers learn to control the sophisticated technology, and the freedom for workers to take on higher-level responsibilities since the machines now handle the repetitive and physically demanding work tasks.
> · *Workers must understand how the automated system works.* If workers are to be in ultimate control of the automated system, it is critical that they know how the system works. Workers will be more accepting of the new technology if they understand how it works, and how they themselves fit into the new operator-machine system. This typically involves considerable training and education of operators, leading to an upgrading of workers' skills and job knowledge.
> · *The automated system should be designed to be compatible with the human operator.* Any automated system should be designed so that it performs tasks in a way that is similar to the procedures a human operator would use. For example, a computerized filing system should index and retrieve information in a fashion that is compatible with how the operator would perform these operations by hand. This will create greater operator understanding and acceptance of the machine system.

No doubt the future will see even greater increases in the automation of the work place. Therefore, consideration must be given to how automation is introduced to workers and its impact on their work lives. The compatibility of operator and machine must be considered a principal goal if the two components are to work together in an efficient and harmonious relationship.

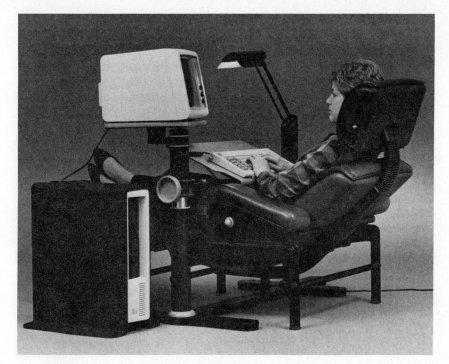

A reclining office chair is one small example of recent advances in workspace design.

THE WORK ENVIRONMENT: WORKSPACE DESIGN

While much of human factors psychology involves the design and improvement of operator-machine systems, psychologists are also concerned with the design and improvement of the larger work environment. A great deal of attention has been given to **workspace design,** the physical layout of individual work stations, and the design and arrangement of space and equipment within factories and offices. Workspaces are designed with considerations of work performance efficiency, operator comfort and safety, operator abilities and limitations, and characteristics of the machines, tools, and products kept firmly in mind. Workspace design considers how individual work stations are designed, and how work stations are linked together to form entire work environments. This section will focus primarily on the design of individual work stations and the equipment used in the station.

*workspace design
the design and arrangement of equipment, space, and machinery in a work environment*

There are three categories of individual work stations: seated, standing, and combination, in which the worker must both stand and sit (see Figure 13.7). Seated work stations are most often used when all of the tools, machines, and supplies needed can be placed comfortably within the reach of the seated worker and when the work requires no heavy lifting or forceful movements. Most typically, they are found in fine as-

Figure 13.7
WORK STATION DESIGNS

Sitting work station

Standing work station

Combination work station

sembly work, clerical tasks, and writing/word processing. Standing work stations are used when heavy objects are handled, when the worker must reach extensively, and when the worker must frequently move from place to place. They are commonly found in large assembly work, such as automobile factories, and in packaging and wrapping operations. Combination sitting-standing work stations are set up for work that requires multiple tasks, some best performed seated, others performed best while standing, and when the worker is doing seated work but must repeatedly reach to high or low distances. An example of a sitting-standing job is a draftsperson working with large blueprints or an individual doing layout designs for a newspaper or large advertisement. In combination work stations, workers are often given a high stool to make changing positions easier.

Certain basic principles governing the location and arrangement of equipment, tools, and space should be followed whether designing an individual work station or an entire workspace (McCormick & Sanders, 1982):

· *Importance principle:* The most important functions or operations should take place in a central location. Similarly, crucial displays, such as warning lights, should be directly in front of the operator. For example, a work station for a graphic artist should have a centrally placed drawing table with drawing supplies nearby. An air traffic controller's seated work station should have the radar screen positioned directly in front of the controller, with other important displays surrounding it.

· *Frequency-of-use principle:* Machines, tools, or controls that are used often should be conveniently located. For example, a worker soldering computer circuit boards should have soldering iron and solder on the work table, with frequently used pliers and clamps in holders so that they can be reached without looking up from the work. In office design, workers who play a central coordinating role for other workers, such as a supervisor or a pooled secretary, should be in a central location so that workers have easy access to this person.

· *Functional principle:* Components should be grouped together according to their function. For example, temperature displays and controls should be grouped together. Different machine punch presses should be located together, as should similar types of tools or parts.

· *Sequence-of-use principle:* Items should be placed in the order in which they will be used. Most assembly work follows this principle. Indeed, in an assembly line the product moves from station to station as it approaches completion.

Human factors psychologists have also played an important role in the design of work tools and equipment. One area that has made many advancements in recent years is the human factors specialty of **engineering anthropometry,** which is the measurement of the physical characteristics of the human body and the development of equipment designed to fit the characteristics of the human user (Kroemer, 1983; Sanders & McCormick, 1987). Since body measurements such as stature and arm reach can vary as a function of sex, age, and ethnic populations, certain work equipment, particularly work stations and seats, should be designed to fit the

engineering anthropometry
the measurement of physical characteristics of the human body and the development of equipment to fit those characteristics

How to Design an Efficient Student Work Environment

The same principles that govern the design of work stations and work environments can be used in creating a functional and efficient environment for school-related tasks such as studying and writing term papers. The first step is to set aside a certain portion of your living area, such as a dormitory room, bedroom, or office, as a study-work space. It is important to have a consistent work area so that when you are in this space you develop an expectation that whenever occupying this space you are going to be working on school-related activities.

Borrowing from research in human anthropometry and work station design, choose a chair that is comfortable, neither too low nor too high in relation to your work table or desk. Make sure that all work machinery (such as typewriter, computer, or calculator), tools, and supplies (such as pens, writing pads, stapler, and paper clips) are within close and comfortable reaching distances. Try to avoid cluttering your workspace. Label and systematically file different documents and put them in a drawer or cabinet that can be easily accessed. The better organized the work station, the less likely that you will experience frustration or fatigue caused by spending needless effort trying to find supplies, documents, or information.

The initial design of your work station is important because people tend to accommodate and adapt themselves to their workspace (Sundstrom, 1986). If the work station is poorly designed, poor work habits may soon emerge. Slow, inefficient work methods may become commonplace and well practiced. They will later be difficult to break, and discomfort and dissatisfaction with the work station and the work itself may develop.

Perhaps the most important decision to be made in the creation of a student work station involves the work machinery that will be used. Today, as the price of personal computing systems continues to decline while their power and ease of use continues to increase, it is almost impossible to be an efficient and productive student without the assistance of word processing and mathematical calculating equipment. A great deal of thought and critical analysis should go into the decision of which computer system to use. A personal needs analysis can be conducted to determine the types and frequencies of tasks that you will likely be required to perform during your college years. For example, will you need only word processing capabilities or a more sophisticated computer that can handle large data sets and perform statistical analyses? Another important concern is your level of computer sophistication. Consider your background in working with computers. If you are a novice, it may be important to select a system and accompanying software that are user friendly and easy to learn to operate. A more sophisticated computer user might select a more powerful but more difficult system to use. A final but crucial consideration is a cost-benefit analysis. Should you purchase your own computer system or share one with others? (Is there easy access to the college's computers?)

Taking the time to consider the design and implementation of a student work station will not only improve your productivity and efficiency but also help you understand the tasks of industrial/organizational psychologists who design work stations and systems for a wide range of workers in various jobs and industries.

characteristics of the user. A tremendous amount of time and energy has gone into developing functional and comfortable seats for various work stations, including seats for working at computer terminals, and for automobiles and other vehicles. These seats are designed so that the operator is at the proper height and distance to operate the machine, displays are at eye level, and hand and foot controls can be easily reached. Seats are also fashioned so that operators who are seated for long periods do not experience back or leg strain (see Up Close: How to Design an Efficient Student Work Environment).

Thus not only should workspaces be designed for functional efficiency, but their characteristics must appeal psychologically to the worker. That is, the workspace should be reasonably pleasant and comfortable, with adequate space, lighting, and privacy, as we will see in Chapter 14.

SUMMARY

The area of industrial/organizational psychology called *human factors* deals with the design of tools, machines, work systems, and work places for human use. A great deal of the work of human factors psychologists has involved the development of efficient and productive *operator-machine systems* that coordinate the activities of the worker and the machines and tools the worker uses. In an operator-machine system, the operator and the machine are engaged in two-way interaction, collaborating to perform some work task.

Machine *displays* give the operator information about the machine's operating status in a variety of ways. Visual and auditory displays are the most common. Visual displays, such as gauges, counters, or lights, can provide detailed and complex information to the operator. Auditory displays, such as bells, buzzers, and horns, are most often used as warnings. Once the machine displays have presented data to the operator, the operator must process the information and make some operating decisions, which the operator communicates to the machine through *controls*, or the levers, switches, knobs, or keyboards that are used to input information into the system. A number of principles govern the proper shape, movement, and placement of controls needed for the quick and efficient operation of machine systems.

An important consideration is the reduction of errors in operator-machine systems. Errors that appear to be caused solely by the human operator may actually be due to some incoordination between the operator and the machine system. Human factors psychologists take one of two approaches for dealing with such errors. The personnel approach involves the selection of only those individuals who have the skills and expertise to operate the system flawlessly. The design approach is an attempt to create operator-machine systems that minimize the chance for error.

The tremendous advancements in computer technology and the development of *robots*—automatic, programmable devices that can perform human tasks—have led to increased automation of factories and work operations. Today and in the future, operators will need to be more sophisticated, because they will be overseeing the operations of increasingly complex automated machinery.

Human factors psychologists are also concerned with *workspace design*. A great deal of energy, time, and research has gone into the creation of working environments that are efficient, productive, and comfortable settings for the workers. One related area is *engineering anthropometry,* which is the design of work equipment, such as chairs and tables, to fit the actual physical measurements of the users.

STUDY QUESTIONS AND EXERCISES

1. What are the links between the time-and-motion studies of the scientific management practitioners in the early part of the century and the procedures of human factors professionals of today?

2. Consider the configuration of an automobile dashboard, with its various displays and controls. What do you suppose are the reasons behind their placement? Are there any controls or displays that you might change to make the car easier or more efficient to operate? Why or why not?

3. What are the four categories of errors outlined by Swain and Guttman (1983)? How might a counterperson in a fast-food restaurant, working with both a cash register and a soft drink machine, commit each of these errors?

4. In what ways have technological advancements, including machine automation, changed how people work? What factors should be considered before introducing new technology or advanced automated equipment into a work place?

5. Often factors such as status, economics, or personal preferences help determine how a workspace is configured. For example, high-status workers might have work stations near the windows, or lack of funds may lead to the purchase of cheap and uncomfortable office furniture. How might such factors conflict with basic principles of workspace design?

SUGGESTED READINGS

Sanders, M. S., & McCormick, E. J. (1987). *Human factors in engineering and design* (6th ed.). New York: McGraw-Hill. *This is the psychology textbook on human factors. It is a comprehensive overview of all areas of concern to human factors psychologists.*

Oborne, D. J. (1985). *Computers at work: A behavioural approach.* Chichester, England: John Wiley & Sons. *A comprehensive text on the impact of computers in work situations.*

Rasmussen, J., Duncan, K., & Leplat, J. (Eds.). (1987). *New technology and human error*. Chichester, England: John Wiley & Sons. *A book of readings on recent research on the errors associated with sophisticated, high-tech operator-machine systems.*

Sills, D. L., Wolf, C. P., & Shelanski, V. B. (Eds.). (1982). *Accident at Three Mile Island: The human dimensions*. Boulder, CO: Westview Press. *A detailed analysis of the Three Mile Island nuclear accident with special attention given to the human factors problems at TMI and other nuclear power plants. A collaborative effort with a variety of social scientists (sociologists, human factors specialists, psychologists, anthropologists, and philosophers) contributing chapters and different perspectives.*

14

WORK CONDITIONS AND WORK SAFETY

Coming Full Circle: The Effects of Work Conditions on the Worker

With this chapter, we have come full circle. Some of the earliest work in the field of industrial/organizational psychology examined how physical working conditions could affect worker behavior. For example, the original goal of Mayo and his Hawthorne studies was to determine the effects of physical conditions in the work setting, such as illumination levels and rest break length, on productivity. This chapter directly examines the effects of such environmental conditions on worker behavior and attitudes. However, we will go beyond the influence of physical conditions such as illumination, temperature, and noise to consider psychological conditions of the work environment such as privacy, crowding, and employees' sense of control over the setting. We will also look at the temporal conditions of the work environment—how work is scheduled—and explore the dangers that workers are exposed to in the work place.

The topics of work conditions and work safety are related to the human factors issues that we studied in Chapter 13 because an important goal of human factors psychologists is to create a machine that is easy and safe for the worker to operate. This chapter, however, expands the discussion of the worker-task relationship to include the context in which workers perform their jobs. In addition, issues of psychological conditions of the work setting, such as privacy and control over the work environment, and work dangers are both connected to the topics of work stress and job satisfaction presented in Chapter 7. For instance, experiencing crowding or the threat of injury from a work setting can lead to job stress. Similarly, having a sense of control over some aspects of the work environment may promote job satisfaction by making workers feel as if they are an important and influential part of the work organization. Finally, because many work safety programs emphasize safety training, there is a connection between this chapter and Chapter 5, which is devoted to personnel training, for the same issues regarding implementation apply to both forms of training.

The effects of work conditions on work behavior is a longstanding topic in I/O psychology but one that continues to have relevance. Because work conditions have been shown to affect workers' job performance and satisfaction with their jobs, and because extreme work conditions may present life-threatening dangers, the protection and well-being of workers has been and will continue to be an important goal of I/O psychology.

I n this chapter, we will continue to explore how factors in the work
environment affect work behavior. We will begin by looking at how
work conditions influence important outcomes such as work performance
and job satisfaction. In particular, we will see how physical conditions,
such as lighting, temperature, and noise, and psychological factors, such
as feelings of privacy and a sense of control over the job environment,
affect worker behavior. We will also examine how temporal factors—
work shifts and work-week structures—influence job performance and
satisfaction. We will next consider safety in the work place, outlining
specific work-related dangers and safety programs. Finally, we will explore the use and abuse of alcohol and drugs in the work place and
consider programs designed to reduce such abuse at work and improve
worker health and well-being.

WORK CONDITIONS

Although many workers' ideal might be a comfortable, quiet, and
elegant office, complete with the latest in office equipment and technology, in reality people often work under less than perfect conditions. In
fact, for some the work environment is quite hostile, hampering the ability
to get the job done and threatening their health and well-being. Workers
exposed to extreme weather conditions, dangerous and noisy machinery,
and potentially harmful chemicals all face great difficulty in doing the job
efficiently. Industrial/organizational psychologists have long been concerned with the conditions under which people work, particularly the role
that the physical work environment plays in affecting worker performance, satisfaction, and health (Oborne & Gruneberg, 1983).

PHYSICAL CONDITIONS OF THE WORK ENVIRONMENT

Among the more obvious factors that can affect the behavior of workers are the physical conditions of the work environment, including the
levels of lighting, the usual temperature, the levels of noise, the amounts
and types of airborne chemicals and pollutants, and aesthetic features
such as the colors of walls and floors and the presence (or absence) of
artwork, music, plants, or decorative items. While some of these factors,
such as extreme noise, high or low temperature, and very low illumination, can greatly hamper work performance, others, such as music and
colors, have more subtle effects on workers.

Illumination. As you may recall, level of illumination was one of the
variables manipulated in the classic Hawthorne studies conducted by
psychologist Elton Mayo and his associates. In those studies, Mayo was
trying to determine the optimal level of lighting for high worker productiv-

Table 14.1 LEVELS OF ILLUMINATION RECOMMENDED FOR CERTAIN
WORK TASKS AND SETTINGS

Task	Illuminance (lx)[a]
Living rooms (general lighting)	50
Furnace rooms in glassworks	150
General office work, mainly clerical and typing	500
Motor vehicle assembly	500
Proofreading in printing works	750
Color matching in paint works	1,000
Fine assembly work, such as electronics assembly	1,000
Inspection of hosiery and knitwear	1,500
Inspection and testing shops of detailed work or small instruments	2,000
Jewelry and watchmaking	2,000
Hospital operating rooms	10,000–50,000

[a]lx = lux, a standard measure of illuminance
Source: Chartered Institution of Building Services Engineers, *CIBSE Code for Interior Lighting* (1984).

ity; he discovered instead the Hawthorne Effect. Of course, level of illumination can significantly facilitate or detract from performance of most tasks. Research generally indicates that increasing the level of illumination tends to improve performance. However, there is a point at which improvement will level off; precisely where this occurs depends on the type of task, particularly the amount of fine visual discrimination demanded (Sanders & McCormick, 1987). It has also been reported that too much lighting can lead to distraction and eye problems in some workers (Nemecek & Grandjean, 1973).

Sometimes a simple change can vastly improve work conditions, as in this auto plant where a lower floor allows workers to bend less often.

While bright light is necessary for the adequate performance of many work tasks, it is also important to use energy efficiently by not overlighting a work area. The key seems to be to find an optimal level of illumination that is bright enough to perform a particular job but does not use energy inefficiently. Research has led to the development of *Lighting Handbooks* that list appropriate levels of illumination for particular tasks (see, e.g., Kaufman & Christensen, 1984). Also, switching from incandescent to fluorescent lighting provides increased illumination, better light distribution, and considerable energy and dollar savings, which is why many work places, schools, and public buildings have fluorescent lights (see Table 14.1).

Lighting can also produce adverse effects, such as the visual fatigue caused by the distracting glare from direct light. Glare can be uncomfortable and dangerous, and can inhibit performance of tasks, as any driver who has tried to control a car while facing into the sun or the headlights of oncoming traffic can testify. Efforts have been made to reduce glare in work settings by the use of light shields, visors, and surfaces that diffuse light such as wall paper and flat paint. Such use of indirect lighting not only cuts down on glare but also more uniformly illuminates the work area.

A great deal of energy has also gone into trying to reduce the types of

Workers subjected to prolonged doses of very loud noise need to wear hearing protection.

glare and reflections that occur on computer and video display screens. These methods have included the use of etched or frosted screens and screen filters. Persons who work at video display terminals are especially prone to visual fatigue and eyestrain because of the large amounts of time they spend focusing on small, illuminated characters (Dainoff, Happ, & Crane, 1981). Recent advancements in the design of display screens and display characters are attempting to alleviate some of these problems.

Temperature. Workers who labor under extreme heat or cold may exhibit some decrease in performance. Realizing this, many offices and factories have installed adequate heating and cooling systems. However, some industrial work places still remain too hot in the summer and too cold in the winter. Moreover, it is impossible to escape the heat or cold in certain types of jobs, such as those in steel mills, boiler rooms, and refrigeration plants; or jobs that require working outside in extreme temperatures, such as construction work and road repair.

Research on the effects of temperature on work performance indicates that when workers are exposed to extreme temperatures—greater than 90°F or lower than 32°F—there are some decrements in both manual and cognitive work performance (Kobrick & Fine, 1983). In general, hot and humid conditions tend to increase the demands of heavy physical work, causing excessive fatigue and reducing work output. Extreme cold may impair performance of tasks that require fine hand-motor movements. There is also some evidence that exposure to less extreme temperatures—slightly warm or cool conditions—for prolonged periods may also affect task performance adversely due to worker fatigue or discomfort (Enander, 1984; 1987). However, a number of factors, such as workers' adaptation to the extreme temperatures, the duration of exposure to heat or cold, individual differences in the tolerance of extreme temperatures, and the type of clothing worn, make straightforward interpretations of the effects of extreme temperatures on work performance difficult (Bell, 1981; Vickroy, Shaw, & Fisher, 1982). Moreover, simple measurement of temperature is not easy, since a variety of atmospheric factors can interact with temperature to produce conditions that are more or less extreme in terms of their effects on the human body. For example, raising the humidity in a room that is 79°F from 50 to 90 percent will increase the feeling of discomfort four times (Fanger, 1970). Other factors, such as air velocity and the radiant heat of furnaces, lamps, or the sun, can also affect how temperature is experienced in a particular situation. Table 14.2 presents some typical strategies for reducing worker discomfort caused by extreme temperatures.

Noise. Noise is difficult to define. Consider, for example, the sounds of a heavy metal rock concert. One person's noise may be another person's nirvana. However, most definitions agree that noise is some unwanted, distracting sound, which may interfere with work performance.

Table 14.2 TECHNIQUES TO REDUCE WORKER DISCOMFORT CAUSED
BY EXTREME TEMPERATURES

Heat Discomfort	Cold Discomfort
Decrease the temperature	Raise the temperature
Increase the air velocity	Reduce the air velocity
Reduce the work load	Increase or even out the work load
Adjust the clothing	Increase the amount of clothing insulation
Provide shields against radiant heat	Increase the amount of radiant heat
Reduce the humidity	

Source: Eastman Kodak Company, *Ergonomic Design for People at Work,* Vol. 1 (Belmont, CA: Lifetime Learning Publications, 1983), pp. 254–262.

In any work setting, there are a wide variety of sounds, some of which may be interpreted by workers as noise. Although noise does not have to be loud to be distracting, it is louder noises that are more often considered to be stressful by workers (see Chapter 7). One common way for measuring loudness is to express the sound in terms of **decibels**. For example, a relatively quiet home or office produces noise of about 40 decibels, the average factory has noise of about 100 decibels, while a rocket launch produces noise of a very loud 180 decibels (see Table 14.3). Not only is noise a source of distraction and stress, but repeated or prolonged exposure to loud noises may result in permanent hearing damage or loss (see Loeb, 1986).

decibels
a measure of sound loudness

Although we often associate noise in the work place with manufacturing plants or heavy construction work, any level of sound can be distracting, depending on the persons and the type of tasks in which they are engaged. Research shows that while even low levels of noise can lower the performance of cognitive tasks, there is tremendous individual variation in terms of distractibility. For example, some students have no trouble studying with the TV or radio turned up loud, while others must have absolute quiet to study effectively. Similarly, in one computer manufacturing plant, workers in a "clean room," where air is filtered to eliminate all forms of airborne dust and particles, had to listen to the loud, steady sounds of the air filtration system. It was found that only a certain per-

Table 14.3 SOUNDS AND ASSOCIATED LEVELS OF NOISE IN DECIBELS

Noise Source	Loudness in Decibels
Quiet home or office	42
Ventilating fan	56
Automobile, 50 feet away	68
Quiet factory area	76
Average factory area	100
Punch press	103
Nail-making machine	111
Pneumatic riveter or hammer	128
Jet airplane at takeoff	150
Rocket at launch	180

centage of workers were able to concentrate on performing the very detailed microassembly of computer components under these conditions of constant noise.

On the other hand, noise does not necessarily detract from performance and in some instances may actually enhance performance. Particularly when a worker is performing a simple or boring task, noise may serve as an arousing stimulus to keep the worker aware and attentive (Michael & Bienvenue, 1983). In a summary of research on the effects of environmental noise on cognitive performance, the Environmental Protection Agency (1974) reached the following conclusions:

1. Noise does not generally impair performance unless it exceeds ninety decibels.
2. Intermittent or unpredictable noises are more disruptive than steady noises.
3. High-pitched (or high-frequency) noises interfere with performance more than low-frequency noises.
4. Noise is more likely to increase work error rates than to lower rates of performance.

Noise can also interfere with worker-to-worker communication, which can lead to breakdowns in coordinated work activities, reduce the important social interactions in the work place, and produce worker dissatisfaction with the job and the work place. There is also some evidence that the breakdown in worker communication due to noise as well as inability to hear feedback from machines is partially responsible for the increased incidence of accidents in noisy industrial settings (Cohen & Weinstein, 1981; Sundstrom, 1986).

Noise seems to be a particular problem in open-plant offices—those with a number of workers in a large room, separated by partitions. While these offices offer the advantage of providing workers with easy access to one another, the constant noise and lack of privacy can distract workers, which may impair job performance. A number of environmental features, including fabric-covered panels, thick carpeting, and acoustical ceilings, have been designed to cut down on noise in open-plan offices and in workspaces generally. Obviously, a goal of human factors psychologists and of work-place architects is to design work environments in such a way to reduce distracting noise levels. This includes designing enclosures that muffle noisy machinery as well as using structural barriers with porous surfaces that absorb noise.

Motion. Some workers conduct their work activities while seated behind the controls of vehicles that move them about on the ground, in the air, and in outer space. The accompanying vibrations, feelings of movement, accelerations, and decelerations (and in outer space, feelings of weightlessness) mean that human factors psychologists must consider motion as a working condition.

The most common motion condition is vibration. All modes of transportation subject occupants to some degree of vibration. Certain machines and tools, such as jackhammers, industrial machinery, and handheld power tools, cause considerable vibrations to operators. What are the effects of continual exposure to vibration? There is some evidence that workers subjected to vibration over long periods may develop problems in their backs and joints. Vibrations may also adversely affect task performance, particularly in activities that involve visual tracking and steady hand movements. More common are the subjective effects of vibration, such as the distraction and discomfort caused by vibration and motion, which may lead to feelings of annoyance, disorientation, and motion sickness (Sanders & McCormick, 1987).

Motion is a particular problem in jobs that involve moving at high speeds. Jet pilots and astronauts are subjected to extreme acceleration and deceleration effects that can seriously impair performance. The weightlessness that accompanies working in outer space creates a host of problems, including motion sickness, dizziness, and disorientation, that human factors psychologists are studying intensely, both in actual space flights and in simulated conditions (see Applying I/O Psychology: Dealing with Hostile Work Conditions: Worker Safety and Health in Outer Space).

Pollution. Because of the wide range of chemicals used in industrial work places and the variety of substances used in constructing and furnishing working areas, many workers are exposed to a surprising number of potentially harmful substances. Among the many workers who are particularly prone to chemical pollutants are miners, who are exposed to potentially lethal gases; farm workers, who may come into contact with dangerous insecticides or fertilizers; industrial workers, who may have to use toxic chemicals; and even surgical teams, who may be exposed to harmful gases released from anesthetic equipment. While in most of these jobs exposure to the pollutants is a known, job-related risk, many workers may be unaware of the potentially harmful chemicals present in almost any work place.

Certain building materials used in most offices may contain toxic chemicals. For example, some insulation materials in older buildings contain deadly asbestos. Chemicals used in certain paints and substances intended to make drapes and furniture fire retardant may give off airborne pollutants. The situation can be particularly dangerous if there is not adequate ventilation. Some work materials, such as cleaning fluids, glues and adhesives, and copying machines (which produce ozone, a chemical that can cause eye and throat irritation), can be dangerous if used in an enclosed area. Although there have been some efforts to remove certain pollutants, such as asbestos, from work environments, a surprising number of harmful substances are not regulated or controlled. For example, current concerns include the potential cancer-causing effects of insec-

Dealing with Hostile Work Conditions: Worker Safety and Health in Outer Space

Outer space, with its extreme temperatures ranging from subfreezing to broiling (literally), exposure to radiation, and a total lack of atmosphere and gravity, is the most hostile work environment imaginable. To allow human beings to live and work in outer space, human factors psychologists have had to develop equipment, clothing, and tools to help cope with these conditions.

The spacesuits that astronauts wear when working outside of their vehicles provide breathable air and protection against temperature extremes. State-of-the-art insulation materials and a system of circulating liquid help keep them cool or warm, depending on whether they are directly exposed to the superhot rays of the sun or are floating in the frigid shade of the earth. A tinted safety shield over the face protects against the bright, radioactive rays of the sun. However, even with all of this protection, astronauts can only remain in this very hostile environment for an hour or two at a time.

The various life-support systems required for the astronaut simply to survive in space make the spacesuit very bulky, thus greatly restricting the astronaut's movement. While working, care must

be taken not to puncture the suit or damage any life-support systems. Therefore, human factors specialists have had to develop various tools specifically designed for use by a spacesuited human working in space. Moreover, because of weightlessness, all loose tools and parts must have some means of being attached to the spacesuit so they do not float away. While the lack of gravity is beneficial because it allows the astronaut to lift and move loads that would be very heavy on earth, it also makes it difficult to get leverage or to provide a stable floor for working on large objects.

Inside the space vehicle are other hazardous and bothersome work conditions. Although sophisticated filtration systems keep the air fresh and clean, a special form of atmospheric pollution still occurs as particles of food, debris, and droplets of water accumulate and float about the interior. Astronaut clean-up chores include the occasional use of a special vacuum to clean the air!

Work stations must be created to fit an astronaut who is maintaining what is called a "zero-gravity neutral" body position rather than a seated or standing position. Standing in a weightless envi-

---

ticides used on fruit crops that may be endangering farm workers, and the potential harmful effects of certain chemical substances used in manufacturing the Stealth Bomber aircraft. Moreover, the introduction of new products and substances, such as synthetic plastics, adhesives, and building materials, may mean that we are increasing the variety of possible pollutants in the work environment. We will consider the topic of harmful pollutants more fully in the discussion of work safety.

Evidence of the effects of airborne pollution on job performance is scanty. Most of the research has examined the effects of carbon monoxide and found that exposure has led to decreases in attention, sensorimotor coordination, memory, and problem-solving ability (Evans & Jacobs, 1981). Carbon monoxide pollution may be a particular problem for persons working around automobiles and gasoline-powered machinery, and employees in smoggy and polluted urban centers.

A controversial type of air pollution is that caused by cigarette smoke. Nonsmokers are likely to be more irritated by cigarette smoke in

ronment is impossible, and remaining seated puts strain on the stomach muscles. However, one of the benefits of designing for a weightless work environment is that both the ceiling and floor can be used as working space.

Astronauts must contend not only with a hostile physical environment but also with a difficult social work environment in a confined space vehicle. Crowding and lack of privacy are always going to be problems in space. Moreover, workspace and living space overlap, and astronauts must live and work together for extended periods. In long-term assignments, such as working in a space station for several months, the confined and crowded conditions coupled with a sense of lack of control over much of the environment can be quite stressful. A human factors specialist describes such an assignment as follows:

> Imagine that you buy a medium-sized motor home, and we put you inside with two to four other people and lock the door. You can look out the windows, but you can't drive. We drive the motor home for you, we refuel it, and we pass food through the door. You're living and working with those same people for 237 days (Reichardt, 1986)

The boredom of an extended space flight is a problem. Space workers may lose motivation and make costly and dangerous errors because of inattention or fatigue. There must be time set aside for diversions, such as movies, TV communication with families on earth, and games. Also, because there is no night and day in space, schedules must be set up to regulate waking and sleep patterns.

Maintaining the physical health of space crews is also a concern. Because of weightlessness, muscles that stay in shape by "wrestling" with earth's gravity may weaken unless they are exercised. The cardiovascular system may also deteriorate for the same reasons. However, exercising is not easy because the astronaut does not have gravity to work against and must be strapped into the exercise apparatus.

In the future, as more and more humans are sent to work in space, industrial/organizational psychologists will be challenged to develop better procedures, equipment, and tools to help deal with the hostile working conditions of outer space.

the work environment and be more sensitive to the potential health hazards of breathing another's smoke. In recent years, more and more work places are eliminating smoking, or confining it to selected locations in an effort to both clean up the air and ease the irritation of nonsmokers (also see On the Cutting Edge).

Aesthetic factors: Music and color. In the 1950s and 1960s strong claims were made for the positive effects of certain kinds of music and certain colors on work performance. Many businesses and industries began to pipe in industrial background music (Muzak, the nondescript instrumental music frequently heard in elevators) or had the walls painted in "motivating" colors. Despite such claims, there is little sound research on the effects of such aesthetic factors on work performance. However, it is possible that factors such as music and an aesthetically-pleasing environment may have subtle, but complex, effects on work behavior. There is some evidence that music played in offices and that certain office color-

Negative Ions: A New Help or Hazard in the Work Environment?

Researchers have recently uncovered a new potential hazard in the work environment: atmospheric electricity. There is evidence that the use of certain types of electronic equipment can greatly increase or decrease the atmospheric concentration of negative or positive ions in the work place. Studies are showing that unusually high concentrations of negative or positive ions in the air may influence human behavior. This is interesting because claims are being made that negative ions in the air are associated with enhanced mood and psychological well-being in work settings, which has led some businesses to purchase "negative ion generators." On the other hand, an increased concentration of positive ions in the air has supposedly been linked to incidence of industrial accidents (Baron & Byrne, 1987).

A series of controlled laboratory studies have investigated the effects of negative ions on a variety of human behaviors, such as cognitive performance, aggressiveness, and mood (see, for example, Baron, 1987; Baron, Russell, & Arms, 1985). The results are not conclusive. Although atmospheric electricity does seem to influence human behavior, the effects are complex. For example, it appears that rather than having across-the-board beneficial effects on behavior, as the manufacturers of negative ion generators claim, increased concentrations of negative ions may simply enhance the behaviors that are dominant in a given situation. Thus if a worker is concentrating on a job, increased negative ionization may make the person more productive. However, if the worker is feeling frustrated or stressed, worrying rather than working, this behavior might be intensified by the increased negative ions. Moreover, there is some evidence that some people may be more affected by negative ions than others. For example, men may be more susceptible to the effects of atmospheric electricity than women (Baron, 1987).

Regardless of the actual effects of atmospheric ionization, the investigations of this environmental phenomenon illustrate the scope and detail of the research being conducted on work behavior. Industrial/organizational psychologists are concerned not only with environmental variables that can be easily seen and measured but also with the unseen factors that may affect human work behavior.

ings may increase attention to work tasks, and that most (but not all) employees view music played in offices favorably (Sundstrom, 1986). Office decorations, such as plants and posters, and tidiness also tend to have positive effects on office visitors (Campbell, 1979; Morrow & McElroy, 1981).

It is more likely that aesthetic factors affect employees' perceptions of the work environment rather than having any direct effects on their behavior. For example, nobody wants to work in a stark, dingy environment. Pleasant colors and music may increase worker satisfaction with the work setting. Likewise, companies that put effort into sprucing up the work setting and businesses that play music may be telling their workers that they care about maintaining the quality of their surroundings. Of course, if a great deal of company money is invested in lavish office decorations, employees may feel that the owners are spending *too much* money on the work environment—money that might be better spent on employee wages and benefits.

Individual preferences are of prime importance in determining the effects of aesthetic factors. While many workers may find music in the

Microchip Plants: Maintenance of a "Superclean" Work Environment

The creation of the computer microcircuit—the "microchip"—has revolutionized work technology. These microcircuits have been getting tinier and tinier in an effort to make smaller and more powerful computers. Their manufacture requires an extremely clean work environment, free from airborne particles of dust or moisture. Microchip factory "clean rooms" have elaborate air filtration systems that rid the air of any such pollutants. These clean rooms are one thousand times cleaner than a hospital's operating room! Workers in the clean rooms must wear suits that cover their entire bodies to eliminate the introduction of dust. In these superclean environments, a worker's dandruff or a sneeze may introduce pollutants that can ruin an entire day's production of microchips. In the newest microchips, even microscopic particles such as bacteria or viruses are large enough to block the tiny microcircuit lines that have been re-

duced to the width of one micron, which is roughly equivalent to 1 percent of the diameter of a human hair. This need for a superclean work environment has challenged human factors psychologists to design equipment and procedures to maintain a productive manufacturing setting.

An additional problem that microchip clean rooms face is vibrations. Even the slight vibration from a truck passing on the street or the heavy footsteps of someone running down an adjacent hall can throw off the sensitive manufacturing equipment. Therefore, clean rooms need to be isolated from outside vibrations and noises, and many are built with vibration-damping seals in the floors. As microchips continue to shrink in size, one possible alternative is to create microchip factories in outer space, where there will be no airborne pollutants (and no air) and few possibilities for vibrations.

Source: O. Port, "Superchip Plants: Where 'Clean' Has a Whole New Meaning," *Business Week*, September 26, 1988.

work setting pleasing, others may find it irritating. Moreover, different types of music may appeal to different workers. In spite of the lack of evidence for the beneficial effects of background music and color on work behavior, millions are spent each year on work place decorations and music. (See Applying I/O Psychology.)

PSYCHOLOGICAL CONDITIONS OF THE WORK ENVIRONMENT

Research has shown that the physical layout and design of a work setting, the amount of workspace available, and the types of furnishings can all affect worker behavior by creating psychological conditions such as feelings of privacy or crowding, a sense of status and importance, or perceptions of anonymity and unimportance. For example, the layout of a work area can govern the amount of contact and interaction that workers have with one another. Work areas designed to facilitate social interaction typically have positive influences on workers' job satisfaction and performance. However, work areas that are congested and allow too much socializing and too little privacy may be detrimental to important organizational outcomes such as productivity (Canter, 1983). The amount of workspace allocated to a particular worker and the privacy of that space are also linked to notions of status and importance within the organization. Top-level executives usually have large, private offices, while lowly clerical workers, assemblers, or data processors might be lined up, nearly shoulder-to-shoulder, in a huge, open room. Research has compared the traditional closed-office designs (workers in private office spaces) versus open-office designs (workers in a large, open room with partitions). While open-office designs allow ease of interaction among employees and greater opportunity for supervisors to observe and interact with workers, the evidence indicates that workers may sense a lack of privacy and control over their space in such settings (Sutton & Rafaeli, 1987). This may lead to dissatisfaction with the work environment and may negatively affect work behavior (Sundstrom, Burt, & Kamp, 1980). However, the psychological effects of the physical layout of the workspace are complex, and may vary depending on the level of the employees and their status in the organization. For example, lower-level clerical workers may welcome the open-office design because it provides chances to interact informally with co-workers. On the other hand, managers and executive administrators may be dissatisfied with open designs since they lack the status associated with private offices, and afford little privacy and insulation from noisy distractions and interruptions (Zalesny & Farace, 1987). Previous exposure to different office designs will also likely influence worker satisfaction with the amount of privacy or socialization opportunities provided by open versus closed designs.

Recent research has shown that physical and psychological conditions of the environment work together to have an important impact on worker behavior and attitudes. One study assessed the effects of four workspace characteristics on the attitudes and behaviors of office workers: (1) the number of workers in an office, which constituted the measure of crowding; (2) the measured seating distance between workers, another index of crowding; (3) the number of enclosures or partitions surrounding each individual work station; and (4) office darkness. The results showed a link between these four variables and rates of employee job dissatisfaction and turnover. When the office was perceived as dark and crowded, and had few partitions, workers tended to be dissatisfied and were more likely to quit than workers who were not exposed to these conditions (Oldham & Fried, 1987).

As we saw when studying stress in Chapter 7, control significantly affects job satisfaction and perceived work stress. Research indicates that giving an employee some sense of control over the work environment goes a long way toward reducing distress and dissatisfaction (Zimring, 1981). This can include control over the amount of openness and privacy in the workspace, over some aspects of the decorating, and if possible over the thermostat. Prolonged and uncontrollable exposure to aversive environmental factors may have detrimental effects on work attitudes and behaviors; a sense of control over aspects of the work environment may have positive effects on work attitudes and work performance.

TEMPORAL CONDITIONS OF THE WORK ENVIRONMENT: WORK SCHEDULES

Industrial/organizational psychologists are concerned not only with the physical and psychological conditions of work but also with the temporal conditions—the time structure of the work day. Although the vast majority of employees work a nine-to-five schedule (give or take an hour on either end and an hour for lunch), more and more people are working on alternative types of schedules. There are some important reasons why nontraditional work schedules exist. First, many production-oriented organizations must operate round-the-clock to meet the demand for the goods or services they produce. This necessitates the use of three eight-hour shifts. Second, over the years stores, restaurants, and other service industries have extended their hours of operation into the evening (some even to twenty-four hours), which means that more than one crew of workers is needed. More recently, in the large urban centers, traffic congestion has led to alternative work schedules to allow workers to commute at nonpeak times. Finally, some of the more flexible work schedules have developed in an effort to give workers a greater sense of control over the planning and timing of their work days. We will examine several types of work schedules and their effects on the worker.

Shift work. Work **shifts** are any sort of scheduling in which groups of employees alternate working times to keep the work place in extended or continuous operation. A three-shift day might typically consist of a morning or day shift from 6 A.M. to 2 P.M., an afternoon or "swing" shift from 2 P.M. to 10 P.M., and a night or "graveyard" shift from 10 P.M. to 6 A.M. Shifts may also vary in terms of the days worked. Typically, employees work five days and have two days off, although a number of variations are possible. For example, one schedule might be 3 days on, 1 day off followed by 3 on, 2 off; 6 on and 2 off, 4 on and 2 off, and so on.

shifts — employee schedules designed to alternate work times to keep the work place in extended or continuous operation

Research indicates that night shifts may disrupt the natural sleep and waking cycles of workers' bodies, often referred to as "circadian rhythms," and may lead to problems such as high rates of stress, fatigue, job dissatisfaction, and performance errors (Landy, 1985; Zedeck, Jackson, & Marca, 1983). This may be particularly true when workers are rotated from day to night shifts during a month, which does not allow their bodies to adapt to a regular schedule.

Compressed work weeks. Work organizations have also tried **compressed work weeks,** in which the number of work days is decreased while the number of hours worked per day is increased. Most common are four ten-hour days, although there have been some attempts at scheduling three twelve-hour shifts. What are the potential costs and benefits of these compressed work weeks?

compressed work weeks — schedules that decrease the number of days in the work week, while increasing the number of hours worked per day

On the positive side, the extra day off allows workers time to take care of tasks that need to be done Monday through Friday, such as going to the doctor, dentist, or tax accountant. Usually compressed work weeks include a three-day weekend, which allows workers more free time to take weekend vacations. Both of these benefits cut down on absenteeism, since workers previously might have called in sick to take an extra day of "vacation" or to run errands. An extended shift might also allow a worker to miss peak traffic times. However, a drawback is that working mothers might have difficulty finding child care for the extended work day. Also on the negative side, a ten-hour (or twelve-hour) work day is more exhausting than the typical eight-hour day (Ronen & Primps, 1981). This fatigue may lead to decreases in work productivity and concern for work quality (although many people say that the extra couple of hours are not necessarily tiring).

For the work organization, the shorter work week can reduce overhead costs when the plant is shut for the fifth day. Company savings are also realized in terms of decreased "start-up" time. Furthermore, certain compressed work schedules, such as twelve-hour shifts, are particularly effective for the staffing of organizations that must maintain continuous operation, twenty-four hours a day, seven days a week (Breaugh, 1983).

Research on the effects of compressed work weeks are inconclusive. The one general finding is that most (although not all) workers are satisfied with the system (Cohen & Gadon, 1978; Ronen & Primps, 1981). Moreover, one study found that workers had more favorable attitudes toward compressed work schedules if they had participated in the decision to implement the schedule change (Latack & Foster, 1985). There is little evidence, however, that compressed work weeks increase overall work performance (Ivancevich & Lyon, 1977).

Flextime. **Flextime** is a scheduling system whereby a worker is committed to a specified number of hours per week (usually forty) but has some flexibility concerning the starting and ending times of any particular work day. Often flextime schedules operate around a certain core of hours during which all workers must be on the job (such as 10 A.M. to 2:30 P.M.). However, the workers can decide when to begin and end the work day as long as they are present during the core period and work an eight-hour day. Some flextime schedules even allow workers to borrow and carry hours from one work day to the next or, in some extremely flexible programs, from one week to another. The only stipulation is that an average of forty hours per week is maintained.

What are the primary advantages of flextime? For the worker, it affords a sense of freedom and control over planning the working day (Hicks & Klimoski, 1981). Workers can sleep in and begin work later in the morning, as long as they make up the time by staying late. Employees who want to leave work early to do some late afternoon shopping can arrive early to work that day. Advantages for the company include reduced rates of absenteeism and the virtual elimination of tardiness (Ro-

flextime
a schedule that commits an employee to working a specified number of hours per week but offers flexibility in regard to the starting and ending times for each day

nen, 1981). Research indicates that flextime programs increase employee satisfaction and morale, and are sometimes but not always positively related to worker productivity (Kim & Campagna, 1981; Narayanan & Nath, 1982; Ralston, Anthony, & Gustafson, 1985; Schein, Mauner, & Novak, 1977).

Obviously, only certain types of companies can institute flextime. It is not possible if a task requires employees to work together, as in assembly-line work, or when there must be some guarantee of minimum staffing, as in a service organization. Also, not all positions are amenable to flextime schedules. For example, in a library, book shelvers and catalogers might be able to work on such schedules, while workers staffing the check-out and information desks may not be able to work on flextime since they have to cover the desks during the hours when the library is open. However, in many organizations, especially in government and civil service, flextime has been quite successful and is very popular with employees (Kirk, 1981; Walker, Fletcher, & McLeod, 1975).

In general, alternative work schedules can be effective when they meet the needs of both the worker and the organization. Careful consideration of the costs and benefits, including the employees' needs and scheduling preferences, should be made before the introduction of any changes (Dunham, Pierce, & Castaneda, 1987).

Under a flextime system this employee starts work at 7:30 in the morning in order to come home early to her family.

WORK SAFETY

The conditions of the work environment include more than just physical, psychological, and temporal elements. The work environment can also present many dangers to workers. In extreme situations, these dangers may be seriously health injuring and even life threatening. Each year hundreds of thousands of workers are seriously injured on the job, and tens of thousands are killed or permanently disabled from industrial accidents and hazards in the work environment. The toll in human lives, pain, and suffering is staggering. There are also tremendous economic costs associated with work place accidents and hazards, including productivity losses, worker compensation, employee health insurance, and medical benefits. Federal agencies estimate that these combined costs total about $100 billion annually. An important goal of organizations and of I/O psychologists is to protect the worker and to reduce health costs by preventing accidents in the work place and removing health hazards.

In modern times, safety legislation has helped to cut down on the number of work-related accidents and injuries by setting standards for safe and healthful work conditions. The main federal agency involved in administering and enforcing these standards is the **Occupational Safety and Health Administration (OSHA),** established in 1970. Not only is OSHA responsible for establishing safety guidelines, but it also keeps

Occupational Safety and Health Administration (OSHA)
the government agency that administers and enforces health and safety standards in work organizations

statistics on work-related accidents and injuries. OSHA guidelines and standards include a number of safety rules and regulations for a wide variety of industries that govern such matters as the use of power tools and machinery, the containment and handling of toxic substances, the use of compressed gases, and the handling of flammable materials. OSHA inspectors conduct unannounced inspections of industrial work sites and have the power to issue warnings and citations for safety violations. They may also levy fines for serious or repeated offenses. Unfortunately, in spite of this safety legislation and OSHA's efforts to enforce it, the typical work place can still be very dangerous. One reason is that OSHA employs only a few hundred inspectors for the millions of work places in the United States. It is impossible for these few OSHA inspectors to enforce and maintain safety standards in all of these work places. Also, in spite of companies' attempts to maintain safe work environments, accidents and exposure to health-threatening conditions still happen because of the dangers inherent in some jobs. For example, working with heavy equipment and machinery may result in some accidents regardless of the safeguards taken to prevent them.

To understand the dangers in the work place, it is important to consider their sources. Some of these dangers are caused by conditions of the work environment that may harm workers' health and cause work-related diseases. Other dangers stem from errors in operator-machine system design that can cause industrial accidents, as we saw in Chapter 13. Still other dangers result from the workers themselves—from tendencies to engage in risky or dangerous work behaviors or from fatigue and stress.

DANGERS IN THE WORK ENVIRONMENT

The conditions under which people are required to work can expose them to various dangers. We have already seen that work conditions can vary greatly, from extremely hot to extremely cold, from quiet and bright offices to noisy and dim factories. Variables such as inadequate illumination, extremes of temperature, and noise and distractions can lead to accidents and health hazards. For example, workers may experience eye strain and thus be prone to making dangerous errors if levels of illumination are too low or if the glare is too great. Laboring in extremely hot or cold weather can cause harmful increases or decreases in body temperature. Noisy work environments can cause permanent hearing damage unless proper protection is used. Work place pollution can also increase the incidence of employee health problems (see Table 14.4). For example, workers in the nuclear industry are exposed to cancer-causing radiation; miners are susceptible to a wide variety of respiratory diseases caused by airborne particles; metalworkers come into contact with toxic substances such as mercury, arsenic, and lead; and many workers in a variety of industries work with chemicals that can cause severe burns through ex-

Table 14.4 SOME COMMON OCCUPATIONAL DISEASES

Disease	Causes	Symptoms	Occupation/Victims
Angiosarcoma	Inhaling vinyl chloride	Liver or brain cancer	Plastics workers
Anthrax	Bacteria from animals	Fever, pneumonia	Agricultural workers, ranchers
Asbestosis	Inhaling asbestos	Lung irritation or cancer	Miners, workers exposed to asbestos insulation
Black lung disease	Inhaling coal dust	Lung irritation or cancer, emphysema	Coal miners
Byssinosis	Inhaling cotton dust	Bronchitis, emphysema	Textile workers
Lead poisoning	Exposure to lead	Kidney disease, anemia, birth defects	Metal workers
Radiation	Exposure to radiation	Thyroid, lung, or bone cancer; leukemia; genetic damage	Medical technicians, nuclear plant workers, uranium miners
Silicosis	Inhaling silica	Bronchitis, emphysema, pneumonia	Miners, quarriers, glassworkers

Source: K. A. Pelletier, *Healthy People in Unhealthy Places: Stress and Fitness at Work* (New York: Delacorte Press, 1984).

plosions, fires, or skin contact. In short, the work environment presents many potential hazards to workers.

An additional source of danger in the work place stems from a lack of maintenance. Oil or water spills that are not cleaned up can cause workers to slip and injure themselves. Piles of boxes or clutter in hallways or exits can lead to accidents or block workers' escape in case of a fire. Worn-out protective gear and malfunctioning safety equipment are other sources of accidents and injuries. For example, protective eye gear that becomes scratched and clouded can dangerously impair a worker's vision.

Work procedures themselves can also cause injury, as when workers are required to lift heavy loads or to remain in unnatural positions or postures for extended periods. For example, major league baseball catchers tend to have shorter careers than outfielders, because catchers spend a great deal of time crouching, and are more prone to injury from batted or thrown balls.

DANGERS IN MACHINE SYSTEMS

Many complex and sophisticated machine systems present certain dangers to workers. Moving assembly lines, heavy industrial machines that move and rotate, and motor vehicles can all injure workers. Work machinery and equipment can become extremely hot and burn careless operators.

Some employees, such as those in the hazardous waste industry, need special clothing and equipment because of work place dangers.

As we saw in Chapter 13, one of the primary concerns of human factors psychologists in the design of operator-machine systems is operator safety. Poor human factors design has been responsible for many industrial accidents and injuries, particularly when machine systems have inadequate safety guards.

Safety guards or shields are especially important features for industrial machinery in order to protect the operator from harm. These safety guards are designed to minimize the chances that an operator's hands or limbs will get caught in moving machinery and protect the operator from flying objects. Booth (1986) lists five common types of dangers that must be guarded against in designing and operating industrial machinery. One is *traps,* components whose movements could trap the operator's limbs, such as a hydraulic press that could crush fingers or rotating gears that could pinch skin. Another danger results from *impact* with moving machines or parts. For example, some industrial equipment moves at high speed, such as a forklift or a product moving on an elevated conveyor, and could cause injury if the operator gets in the way. A third danger is *contact* with machine parts that are sharp, abrasive, hot, cold, or electrically charged. A fourth danger is *entanglement* with moving machine parts that can catch clothing, hair, gloves, and the like. A final machine danger results from the *ejection* of objects from the machine, such as splinters of metal from a grinding wheel.

Besides safety guards, machine systems must have well-designed warning displays that immediately inform the operator of any potential problems. For instance, a worker could be severely burned by escaping steam if a boiler overheats without warning and explodes. Safety control devices, such as emergency shut-off switches, also need to be placed so that they can be quickly activated. For example, the operator of a metal-stamping machine had a hand seriously injured when his sleeve became entangled in the machine feeder and he was unable to reach the emergency shut-off switch.

In summary, machine systems can be quite dangerous to operators and thus require built-in safeguards. Moreover, workers must be trained to follow proper safety procedures when working with potentially dangerous machinery and equipment to minimize the risk of injury.

DANGERS IN WORKER CHARACTERISTICS AND BEHAVIOR

In some cases it is the worker rather than the environment or the machinery who is primarily responsible for work-related accidents and injury. Inattention, fatigue, and stress as well as other personal variables are all related to the incidence of work accidents.

Lack of job-related experience is often linked to work accidents. An experienced and quick-thinking worker may be able to avert an accident. Workers who lack insight into machine procedures and work operations may not be able to predict when systems are out of line and an accident is likely. Generally, the more experienced a worker is with a particular task, the less likely he or she is to have an accident. That is why it is important that workers be properly trained, particularly in regard to safety procedures. There is also a tendency for younger workers to have higher accident rates than older workers, due perhaps to lack of maturity and a more carefree or reckless attitude.

Because of the role of the individual in accident rates, many researchers have searched for ways to measure **accident proneness,** or the existence of certain personality characteristics that may predispose a person to work accidents. If there is such a thing as accident proneness, industries need only screen out accident-prone individuals from high-risk jobs in order to reduce the number of work-related accidents. Unfortunately, research has been unable to find any firm evidence of accident-prone personality characteristics. It thus does not appear that there are certain types of worker personalities that are to blame for the majority of work accidents.

accident proneness
the presence of certain
personality characteris-
tics that may predis-
pose a person to work
accidents

Individuals may interact with other workers, creating a climate that encourages or discourages safe work practices. Research has investigated the roles that the leader and the social climate of the work group play in influencing accident rates. One study found that a combination of certain leader practices, such as a lack of planning and structuring of work assignments, little concern about whether work groups were coordinating efforts, and leader inexperience was related to greater incidence of work accidents than work groups who had experienced and organized leaders (Butler & Jones, 1979). Another study discovered that work groups with a ''safety climate'' had safer work areas than work groups without such a climate. This safety climate was determined by measuring workers' attitudes toward such matters as the perceived importance of safety training programs, management's attitudes toward safety promotion, and the status and importance given to the work group's safety committee and safety officer (Zohar, 1980). Clearly, these results indicate that groups and their leaders who consider safety a priority can significantly increase safe work behaviors and reduce work accidents.

As we have seen, accidents can be caused by a number of variables: errors in operator-machine design, work conditions, or worker behavior. Knowing more about the causes of work accidents can help us to develop safety programs to try to prevent them.

PROGRAMS TO INCREASE WORK SAFETY

A variety of programs are designed to increase work safety. Many encourage employees to engage in routine safe work behavior and to follow established safety procedures. Too often, accidents occur because employees disregard proper safety procedures. In fact, it has been estimated that as much as 75 percent of all machinery accidents could have been prevented if proper precautions had been taken (Booth, 1986). These precautions include such things as wearing protective garb such as goggles to protect eyes from flying debris; following proper procedures, for example, shutting off a machine and/or the electrical current before beginning maintenance operations; or remembering to engage safety guards or locks when machines are not in operation. Such precautions are not taken for a variety of reasons. One is that workers may not be aware of them, usually because of poor employee training. Another reason is the inconvenience of the procedures. For example, workers may not wear protective goggles or hard hats because they are hot and uncomfortable. Others may not bother to shut off power to a machine before working on it or may neglect to raise a safety guard because such procedures inhibit work speed and productivity. Finally, workers may ignore safety procedures because certain work group norms develop that say that following safety procedures indicates that a worker is not "courageous" or "manly" ("*Real* construction workers don't wear hard hats!"). The goal of work safety programs is to try to overcome these impediments and encourage safe work behavior.

Of the various programs designed to improve work safety, by far the majority have concentrated on employee training and education. Most companies have some formal programs of lectures or workshops to encourage safe worker behavior. However, although workers may learn about safe and unsafe behaviors, that knowledge may not always translate into safe actions. Workers may still neglect to take proper safety precautions if they are uncomfortable, inconvenient, or cause them to be less productive. Also, unless safety education is an ongoing process, workers may abandon safe procedures out of negligence or in an effort to cut corners. For example, unless safety checks are continually emphasized, employees may begin to ignore routine safety inspection procedures in order to save time and to be able to keep up with backlogged work.

Industrial/organizational psychologists have had considerable success in reducing accident rates by applying organizational behavior modification principles. Primarily, this involves providing incentives for reducing the incidence of work-related accidents or rewarding employees for engaging in safe work behaviors or for developing new safety strategies. These programs seem to be effective because they emphasize the positive consequences of engaging in safe behavior—rewards and incentives—rather than the negative consequences, such as inconvenience or decreased productivity and efficiency. In one such program, the accident rates of bus drivers for a large, urban transit authority were reduced by the development of a safety behavior modification program. The program consisted of three components. The first was *performance feedback*. Drivers' daily safety records were posted in the lunchroom for all drivers to see. The second element was a *team competition*. Drivers were put into teams that competed against each other's safety records. The goal was to move the focus of reinforcement contingencies from the individual to the group. Both of these components were designed to develop group norms

Aircraft carrier person-nel improve work safety by competing with each other to spot debris that might damage a jet engine.

to encourage safety. The third aspect was *incentives*. Winning drivers and teams received cash or prizes for outstanding safety records. The result was a 25 percent reduction in accident rates. Importantly, the program incentives were paid for by the savings in accident claims (Haynes, Pine, & Fitch, 1982).

In another program, workers in a food manufacturing plant attended a training session at which they received information about safe and unsafe work practices and the reasons why it was important to engage in safe work behaviors. Following the session, departmental safety records were posted. Employees who engaged in safe work behaviors were merely given public recognition by management. The results showed a significant decline in work-related accidents for twenty-five weeks. When the program was discontinued, the accident rate rose to the earlier high level. The program was finally reinstated, and the accident rate decreased dramatically and remained low for a long-term follow-up period. In fact, the plant that had had the worst safety record of the company's many manufacturing plants went from last to first place following this fairly simple and straightforward safety program (Komaki, Barwick, & Scott, 1978).

These results indicate that monitoring the incidence of unsafe work behaviors, alerting workers to these behaviors, and recognizing safe work behaviors are often enough to reduce work-related accident rates. In recent years, companies have tried to reduce accidents and injuries by combining safety training programs, the monitoring of work-related injuries and accidents, and safety incentive programs (see, for example, Reber & Wallin, 1984). Others have set up work safety task forces or committees to develop strategies for keeping the work place safe.

The Wizard of Id

Two newer safety training programs are aimed specifically at reducing operator errors in complicated and potentially dangerous operator-machine systems. The first trains workers in problem-solving strategies for dealing with machine emergencies or malfunctions. They are taught to: (1) recognize and define the problem, (2) generate alternative courses of action for solving the problem, (3) evaluate the alternative courses, (4) select and implement the chosen strategy, and (5) evaluate the effectiveness of the strategy for solving the problem. Although this type of problem-solving training has not been widely used in industry, it is expected that this type of training might be effective in helping nuclear power plant operators, air traffic controllers, and others who work with complex machine systems to deal with potential crisis situations. The second innovative safety program is called *stress inoculation training,* which is designed to keep system operators from panicking when faced with an emergency. The two major components of these programs are helping workers to: (1) prepare cognitively for potential stressful events, such as a malfunction in a nuclear power plant; and (2) learn and rehearse coping strategies for dealing with various types of crises. The goal is to teach workers to ignore the distracting stimuli, such as their own arousal, panicking co-workers, and noise, and focus on the emergency. Stress inoculation training has been used successfully in combat training and may prove useful in helping machine system operators deal with dangerous crisis situations (Spetell & Lebert, 1986).

ALCOHOL AND DRUG USE IN THE WORK PLACE

A growing problem—one that is of increasing concern to businesses and to industrial/organizational psychologists—is employee use and abuse of alcohol and drugs. No doubt a great many industrial accidents occur because of worker intoxication. The combination of alcohol or drugs and heavy machinery or motor vehicles is deadly. Drug and alcohol abuse is also directly responsible for decreased productivity and increased absenteeism and turnover, not to mention all the problems that it can cause in the home life of workers. The costs of all of this is staggering. A conservative estimate is that substance abuse in a company of 1,000 employees costs more than a half million dollars per year in lost work time and productivity (Axel, 1986).

In an effort to combat substance abuse, many companies are developing **employee assistance programs (EAPs),** programs that offer counseling for a variety of employee problems. Of particular concern is counseling for drug and alcohol abuse, although EAPs also help employees to deal with work stress and personal problems that may adversely affect their performance and well-being (Cairo, 1983). Although employee counseling has long been offered by companies, only in the past dozen years have comprehensive EAPs become commonplace in large organizations. This increase is likely due to the growing concern over the devastating consequences of substance abuse in terms of harming worker health and organizational productivity. The majority of large American companies today have some type of formalized employee assistance program.

employee assistance programs (EAPs) counseling provided for a variety of worker problems, specifically drug and alcohol abuse

While industrial/organizational psychologists are greatly concerned about the adverse impact of substance abuse and work stress on employee productivity and well-being, clinical and counseling psychologists, social workers, and drug rehabilitation counselors, rather than I/O psychologists, typically staff EAPs. However, I/O psychologists may have a hand in the design, implementation, and evaluation of EAPs.

Employee assistance programs usually take one of two forms. External programs are those in which the company contracts with an outside agency to provide counseling services for its employees. Internal EAPs offer services at the work site. The advantage of an internal program is its convenience for the employees, although they are expensive to maintain. Only large organizations can usually afford internal EAPs. The main advantages of external programs are the lower costs and the increased employee confidentiality.

In spite of the increasing popularity of employee assistance programs, there has been surprisingly little research on their effectiveness (Weiss, 1987). The problem results partly from the difficulty of evaluating *any* counseling program, because it is not always clear which variables will best determine a program's "success" (Mio & Goishi, in press). For example, some programs measure success by the number of workers treated, whereas others may use some standard of recovery or "cure." Furthermore, it is difficult to determine how EAP counseling affects bottom-line variables such as employee performance. It is also difficult to determine the effectiveness of EAPs because the large number of external agencies that offer counseling services for businesses usually conduct their own evaluations, and it is unclear how objective and accurate these self-assessments are. Although there are questions about the effectiveness of employee assistance programs in general, it is likely that even a few cases of employee recovery would lead an employer to label an EAP a success because of the severity of drug and alcohol addiction. Moreover, there is some evidence that EAPs do help reduce long-term

What Will Work Conditions Be Like in the Next Century?

Based on what we know about both the changes that have taken place in work technology and working conditions and the advancements in industrial/organizational psychology, what will the working world look like in the next century?

The biggest change in office technology will be a movement away from printed documents to a paperless, electronic office. No office will be without a video display terminal (VDT) from which a worker can send and receive mail and memos, call up documents, view an appointment calendar, and access various databases. With advances in graphics, there will be more pictorial representations of information and less emphasis on written descriptions. For example, rather than telling someone about a new product or piece of equipment, you will be able to show it in graphic detail. The refinement of the videophone, along with video-computer interfaces, will mean that many executives will be able to see as well as hear telephone callers on the VDT screen. With access to numerous databases workers will never have to leave the office to go to a library to research a topic or to examine voluminous company documents and records. In state-of-the-art offices, receptionists will be replaced by computers who will answer and screen calls, and busy executives will be able to dictate directly into a speech-activated word processor that creates memos or documents instantaneously.

The office building of the next century may have advanced environmental monitoring and control equipment to allow each individual to control the environmental conditions of the individual workspace. The temperature will remain constantly pleasant, with humidity controlled, and the air will be filtered to remove all pollutants. The amount and quality of lighting will also be adjusted to suit the worker's needs. More and more workers will also be involved in the design and equipping of their workspace—creating a physical environment that suits them, as well as choosing the work equipment they prefer (Sundstrom, 1986).

Advances in communication will allow a greater number of workers to telecommute, that is, to work at home while tapping into the company's computer-communication network via telephone lines. Although it is expected that the majority of workers will still perform their jobs at a central site due to the importance placed on face-to-face social contact in the work setting (Naisbett, 1982), undoubtedly there will be greater flexibility in work hours. As urban commuting traffic becomes worse and worse, employers will have to allow workers more flexibility in beginning and ending their workdays.

Perhaps the greatest changes in work conditions will occur in factories, where more operations will be performed by computers and robots. As factories become more automated, the worker's job will change from manual tasks to those involving the programming, overseeing, and maintenance of the sophisticated machine systems. The physical environment for factory workers will become more like a comfortable office, with environmentally regulated control rooms. The monitoring and inspection of manufacturing processes will be done remotely through videocameras or sophisticated electronic feedback systems. Safety concerns will be put to rest since the more dangerous operations will be handled by robots or teleoperator systems.

The sweeping changes occurring in the world of work mean that industrial/organizational psychologists will be even more involved in creating a more productive, harmonious, comfortable, and safe work environment while they help organizations accept and adapt to the rapid and inevitable changes that occur.

health care costs for employees (Cummings & Follette, 1976). One critic of current substance abuse EAPs argues that they focus primarily on treating alcohol and drug problems after they have reached the problem stage but give little attention to their prevention (Nathan, 1983). In spite of the uncertainty of the effectiveness of employee assistance programs, it is likely that they will become a mainstay in most work organizations and another service that will be considered an essential part of any employee benefit package (see Up Close).

SUMMARY

I/O psychologists are greatly concerned with how the physical, psychological, and temporal (or scheduling) conditions of work can affect worker performance, satisfaction, and health. Physical conditions, such as levels of illumination, temperature, noise, motion and vibration, airborne pollutants, and aesthetics, can influence worker behavior. Research indicates that more illumination is positively associated with job performance up to an optimal point at which increased brightness no longer influences performance. Because lighting glare can also detract from effective job performance, steps are taken to try to reduce it. Extreme heat or extreme cold can decrease performance, although appropriate clothing can protect against the adverse effects of temperature. While excessive noise can adversely affect job performance, the label of "noise" can be quite subjective. Extremely loud, high-pitched, intermittent, or unpredictable noise may have more negative effects than steady, low-volume noise. In jobs involving transportation of heavy machinery or equipment, motion may adversely affect work performance. The effects of airborne pollution in the work place is also a particular hazard to performance as well as to worker safety and health. Finally, aesthetic factors, such as the presence of music and certain colors or decorations, may have subtle effects on workers, particularly on satisfaction with the job and the work environment.

The psychological conditions of the work environment that can affect work performance include feelings of privacy or crowding, the status associated with the amount or location of workspace, and the amount of control over the work environment. Industrial/organizational psychologists have also had a hand in influencing the time structure of the typical working day. The effects of various *shifts* (such as day, afternoon, and night) on the productivity and well-being of the worker has received considerable attention. Experiments have also been conducted with *compressed work weeks,* or weeks that are shortened by lengthening each work day, and *flextime,* a scheduling system that gives workers a great deal of control over structuring their own work schedules.

In considering work conditions, a critical concern is safety, for work accidents and injuries are very costly in terms of both the pain and suffering of the victims and the financial losses to the organization. The *Occu-*

pational Safety and Health Administration (OSHA) is the federal agency responsible for establishing safety guidelines in work organizations. However, in spite of OSHA's efforts, work places still present many dangers from a variety of sources. Some dangers stem from qualities of the physical work environment, such as inadequate illumination, temperature extremes, or noisy distractions. Lack of work place maintenance can also lead to accidents and injury. Another major source of dangers is the unsafe design of operator-machine systems. Systems with inadequate warning displays, poor placement of controls and displays, and inadequate safety guards can cause serious injury. Finally, accidents may occur because of certain worker characteristics or behaviors. Untrained or inexperienced workers may have more accidents than those who are more expert. Although attempts have been made to distinguish individuals who demonstrate *accident proneness,* or a predisposition to accidents created by certain personality characteristics, no such characteristics have yet been identified.

A variety of programs attempt to increase work safety. Behavior modification programs have been quite successful in reducing accident rates and in increasing attention to safe work behaviors. The monitoring of the incidence of unsafe work behaviors to alert workers to their existence, the recognition of safe work behaviors, emergency problem-solving training, stress inoculation training, and the introduction of incentives for increased work safety have all also been successful strategies.

A growing problem related to worker safety and health is the use and abuse of alcohol and drugs in the work place. Many companies have created *employee assistance programs (EAPs)* to provide counseling for employees trying to deal with substance abuse. EAPs can be in-house, internal programs or the organization can contract with an outside agency for provision of counseling services. In spite of the tremendous growth and popularity of EAPs, there has been little systematic evaluation of their effectiveness.

STUDY QUESTIONS AND EXERCISES

1. In what occupations are workers exposed to extreme or aversive physical conditions? What are some of the steps that can be taken to help deal with them?

2. Psychologists have attempted to uncover the characteristics that lead to an accident-prone personality. Although there has been no confirmation of such a personality, what personal attributes might be linked to higher accident rates?

3. In spite of federal legislation and agencies such as OSHA, accident rates in industry are still at unacceptable levels. Based on what you have learned in this course, how can I/O psychologists help to create a safer work place?

4. Ten or twenty years ago, employee assistance programs in industry were rare. What changes in the attitudes of society and employers have led to their introduction?

SUGGESTED READINGS

Connors, M. M., Harrison, A. A., & Akins, F. R. (1986). Psychology and the resurgent space program. *American Psychologist, 41,* 906–913. *Reviews some of the roles that industrial/organizational psychologists will play in the space program by helping to make conditions more livable on long space flights.*

Myers, D. (1984). *Establishing and building employee assistance programs.* Westport, CT: Quorom. *A resource book covering the creation and maintenance of EAPs in organizational settings.*

Oborne, D. J., & Gruneberg, M. M. (Eds.). (1983). *The physical environment at work.* Chichester, England: John Wiley & Sons. *A collection of articles on various facets of the physical environment of work and how they affect worker behavior. A fairly technical reference that is part of the Wiley Series in Psychology and Productivity at Work.*

Ridley, J. (1986). *Safety at work* (2nd ed.). London: Butterworths. *A comprehensive textbook on work safety. Although the safety legislation covered applies primarily to Great Britain, the discussion of safety procedures, techniques, and guidelines applies to the United States as well.*

APPENDIX A

CAREERS IN INDUSTRIAL/
ORGANIZATIONAL PSYCHOLOGY

This appendix will present information about careers in industrial/organizational psychology. We will begin by discussing what I/O psychologists do on the job and explore career possibilities for persons with training in the field. Next, we will look at what students need to do to prepare for a career in I/O psychology. We will also explore professional organizations for I/O psychologists and provide sources for further information about the field and about career possibilities.

WHAT DO INDUSTRIAL/ORGANIZATIONAL PSYCHOLOGISTS DO?

Industrial/organizational psychologists perform a wide variety of tasks. As you can tell from the topics covered in this book, they are involved in such diverse activities as personnel selection and placement, employee training and development, performance assessment and appraisal, the design of work environments and operator-machine systems, organizational development, the implementation of motivational and safety programs, and the assessment of employee attitudes and job satisfaction. As in all professions, there is a great deal of specialization in the field. I/O psychologists typically specialize in one or a few of the topic areas presented in this book.

I/O psychology has both a research and a practical emphasis, which means that some I/O psychologists are primarily teachers and/or researchers, others are primarily practitioners, while still others divide their time between research and applied practice. Of I/O psychologists holding Ph.D.s, approximately one-third are employed in colleges and universities, about one-third are employees of businesses and industries, about 20 percent work in research or consulting firms, and about 10 percent are employed in federal, state, or local government (Thayer, 1988).

I/O psychologists work for a variety of major American and international corporations, including Bell Telephone, United Airlines, Xerox Corporation, Unisys Corporation, Dow Chemical, IBM, and Standard Oil. They can hold job titles such as director of human resources, vice

Brief Biographical Sketches of I/O Psychologists

I/O psychologists come from a variety of backgrounds and engage in a vast range of activities, as the following profiles of actual I/O psychologists reveal:

Dr. M is an I/O psychologist working for a large aerospace firm. Her main area of expertise is sophisticated robot systems, and she has helped design and test several sophisticated robotlike systems for use in outer space. Her latest project involves working on the development of a proposed orbiting space station in which much of the construction is done by robots. Dr. M maintains that her training in research methods, which allows her to approach work problems systematically, was the most valuable part of her academic education.

Dr. C received his Ph.D. in I/O psychology in the early 1970s. His first job was conducting research for the General Telephone and Electronics Laboratories on the organizational processes in some of the company's operational units, including assessing job satisfaction, facilitating communication, and helping to resolve conflicts. Some years later, Dr. C joined a large consulting firm, and currently is employed by an international consulting company where he conducts survey feedback and other organizational development programs for a variety of businesses and organizations.

Dr. H is an I/O psychologist who is in the United States Navy. His responsibilities include developing and researching placement systems for certain Navy personnel. Dr. H is active in the American Psychological Association's divisions of I/O Psychology (Division 14) and Military Psychology (Division 19), and regularly reports his research at national and regional professional conferences. Much of his work involves personnel selection within the military—trying to fit new recruits to the types of positions for which they are best suited.

Dr. R is an I/O psychologist who owns a private consulting practice in a small midwestern city. Before becoming an independent consultant, Dr. R worked for a large consulting firm in a metropolitan area, where he conducted job analyses and ran training seminars for businesses. His decision to move to a less urban area was primarily responsible for his decision to start an independent practice. Dr. R specializes in personnel selection, job analysis, and the design of training and development programs, although he occasionally engages in other activities such as conducting attitude and marketing surveys and serving as an expert witness in labor-related legal cases. In a sense, he has had to become an industrial/organizational "jack-of-all trades," because he is one of the few I/O psychologists in his region. Dr. R claims that the most

---

president of employee development, manager of employee relations, senior employment specialist, director of human factors department, testing specialist, and staff industrial psychologist (see Box A-1).

TRAINING FOR CAREERS IN INDUSTRIAL/ORGANIZATIONAL PSYCHOLOGY

The usual professional degree in industrial/organizational psychology, as in all areas of psychology, is the doctorate (Ph.D.). However, a growing number of programs offer master's degrees in psychology with an emphasis in I/O psychology, and a handful of college programs even offer a bachelor's degree with a major in I/O psychology (Peters, 1985). The master's degree (M.A. or M.S.) can also qualify one as a practitioner of psychology, although licensing requirements may vary from state to state. In recent years, the employment picture for I/O psychologists, particu-

valuable training he received was in statistics, psychology, and the business courses that he took after receiving his Ph.D., so that he could become more knowledgeable about various business operations and learn business terminology.

Ms. O received a master's degree in industrial/organizational psychology just a few years ago. She is an assistant director of marketing research for a national chain of fast food restaurants. Her duties include researching the sites for new restaurants, and designing and organizing customer satisfaction surveys. Ms. O also teaches I/O psychology and marketing courses at a local junior college.

Dr. P, an I/O psychologist, is a professor in the school of management in a large state university. He previously held academic positions in university psychology departments. Dr. P is quite well-known and respected for his research in I/O psychology, particularly in the areas of motivation and job satisfaction. He is the author of several books and numerous journal articles, some of which are considered classics in the field. In addition to his research and teaching, Dr. P has served as a consultant for several large corporations, including many *Fortune* 500 companies.

Mr. K, who has a master's degree in organizational psychology, is the director of human resources for a fairly large insurance company, which means that he is responsible for the administration of all facets of human resources for his organization. Mr. K oversees payroll, benefits, compensation, and personnel activities such as the development of job descriptions, employee selection, and personnel training. He also has an active internship program that uses undergraduate and graduate students as interns who help set up special human resource programs for his employees. For example, one group of interns helped develop and administer a survey of employee attitudes and created and implemented a stress management program.

Although she is not an I/O psychologist, Ms. F received a bachelor's degree with a major in psychology and worked as an administrative intern with a publishing company in her senior year. Her internship led directly to her employment as assistant manager of employee training with a competitor firm immediately after graduation. Through climbing the "career ladder," Ms. F has held a succession of higher and higher administrative positions. Five years after graduation, she is the director of college recruiting for a large computer software company. One of her duties is overseeing the on-campus personnel recruiting program for the company. Ms. F plans to continue her academic career by taking a two-year leave of absence from her job to obtain a master's degree in business administration.

larly those with a Ph.D., has been very good, with salaries among the highest in the field of psychology.

Of course, the theories and principles of I/O psychology are not only used by I/O psychologists. These concepts are applicable to many areas of work behavior, and the wise manager makes good use of some of them. However, many of the more complex areas of I/O psychology, including the use of tests and the application and interpretation of certain measurement tools and techniques, require a trained professional.

PROFESSIONAL ORGANIZATIONS FOR INDUSTRIAL/ORGANIZATIONAL PSYCHOLOGISTS

The largest American professional organization for psychologists is the American Psychological Association (APA), with more than 65,000 members (not all psychologists are members of APA). The APA has a number of divisions, each representing a specialty within the field. The division with which I/O psychologists are most likely to affiliate is Division 14—the Society for Industrial and Organizational Psychology, Inc.—which has more than 2,500 members. Three other divisions also include I/O psychologists in their membership: Division 19 (Military Psychology), Division 21 (Applied Experimental and Engineering Psychologists), and Division 23 (Consumer Psychology). More recently, a group of psychologists who are primarily scientists or scientist-practitioners have created the American Psychological Society (APS) to promote the advancement of psychology as a scientific endeavor. Because I/O psychologists are trained in *both* the science and practice of psychology, many are affiliating with this newer organization. Both groups help to coordinate activities, determine standards of professional behavior, and provide forums for psychologists to interact with colleagues. For example, the Society for Industrial and Organizational Psychology (1987) has established principles for the validation and use of personnel selection procedures, while both the Society and the APA have set up guidelines for ethical standards for practicing psychologists (APA, 1981; Lowman, 1985). Each also holds annual research conferences where I/O psychologists can meet colleagues and share information. Many I/O psychologists may also choose to affiliate with other organizations of professionals from other disciplines who also study work behavior. This provides I/O psychologists an opportunity to interact with colleagues who are not psychologists, but who may be interested in many of the same issues that I/O psychologists are concerned with. For example, some organizational psychologists are members of the Academy of Management, the professional organization for scientists and practitioners in the field of management. Personnel psychologists may belong to one or more of the many professional societies in that area, such as the International Personnel Management Association or the American Society of Personnel Administrators, and human factors psychologists may belong to the Human Factors Society. Participation in these professional organizations allows I/O psychologists employed in a number of different settings the chance to interact with their counterparts in other organizations in various parts of the country or the world.

EXPLORING CAREER POSSIBILITIES IN INDUSTRIAL/ORGANIZATIONAL PSYCHOLOGY

To explore a possible career in industrial/organizational psychology, in any other specialty within psychology, or in related fields, you can do a number of things *now*, including the following:

- Go to your university's career guidance office and find out what information is available on careers in I/O psychology. Talk to your psychology department advisor about careers that previous psychology graduates have pursued.

· Arrange a short "information interview" with a practicing I/O psychologist in your area. Ask for a few minutes of the professional's time to find out firsthand what she or he does for a living. You might talk to several such professionals, since individuals' job duties can vary greatly. Again, the career guidance office may be able to help you locate practicing I/O psychologists.

· The American Psychological Association and especially Division 14 also have information on careers in I/O psychology. For this information write: American Psychological Association, 1200 17th Street NW, Washington, DC 20036.

· Read beyond the textbook. Examine some of the suggested readings at the end of each chapter. Go to the library and scan through some of the journals that publish research in I/O psychology. (There is a list of these journals in Appendix B.)

PREPARING FOR GRADUATE STUDY IN INDUSTRIAL/ORGANIZATIONAL PSYCHOLOGY

If you are definitely headed toward graduate school and a career in I/O psychology, there are steps that you can take to find out about graduate programs and to prepare yourself for graduate study:

· Early in your preparation, talk to your psychology advisor in depth about the process of applying to graduate programs, including the alternatives available, the requirements for admission, the deadlines, letters of recommendations, and the like.

· The APA publishes two important handbooks for additional information: (1) the annual guide to graduate schools entitled *Graduate Study in Psychology,* and (2) a handbook designed to help prepare for graduate study, *Preparing for Graduate Study: NOT for Seniors Only!* by B. R. Fretz and D. J. Stang (1980). Both can be purchased by writing to: APA Publications, 1400 North Uhle Street, Arlington, VA 22201.

· Become active in the field. Student affiliate memberships in both the APA and Division 14 are offered at decreased rates and include subscriptions to the newsletters of the societies. For information write to: APA, 1200 17th Street, NW, Washington, DC 20036; Society for Industrial and Organizational Psychology, Inc., Administrative Office, 617 East Golf Road, Suite 103, Arlington Heights, Illinois 60005. Also, keep abreast of the developments in I/O psychology through journals (see Appendix B). Finally, try to become involved in a faculty research project to develop your basic research skills and gain valuable experience.

CAREERS IN BUSINESS AND INDUSTRY FOR PSYCHOLOGY MAJORS

If you are not considering graduate school but are interested in business careers, recent studies have shown that the bachelor's degree in psychology is good preparation (Carducci et al., 1987; Takooshian et al., 1985). In fact, results of a recent series of studies indicate that undergraduate majors in the social sciences and humanities have very high managerial potential and tend to be successful practicing managers (Howard, 1986). In particular, psychology graduates tend to have fairly well-developed problem-solving skills, written and verbal communication skills, and a knowledge of human behavior that helps them to make an easy transition to a career in management (Carducci, 1985).

To find a job that will allow you to use some of the psychological knowledge and skills you have learned as an undergraduate, you must approach your job search systematically. Again, utilizing campus resources such as the career guidance office, find out about the types of jobs available to you. Go on "information interviews" to find out firsthand what particular jobs are like. Consider an internship or cooperative education course, if one is available on your campus. Cooperative education combines academic knowledge with relevant work experience, thus allowing students to gain valuable on-the-job experience in a variety of careers. Many students use this experience as a stepping stone to finding a full-time career. The combination of work experience from an internship or other employment, a knowledge of human behavior gained from psychology courses, and good academic performance that indicates a motivation and willingness to work hard can open a number of doors for a successful career in business and industry.

Regardless of the career path chosen, the topics studied by I/O psychologists pertain to just about any job in any work setting. A knowledge of principles of industrial/organizational psychology can help facilitate understanding of human behavior and organizational processes occurring in the work place.

REFERENCES

American Psychological Association. (1981). *Ethical principles of psychologists*. Washington, DC: Author.

Carducci, B. J. (1985, August). Help wanted: Psychology majors interested in business careers. In H. Takooshian et al., *Employment with a psychology B.A.* Symposium conducted at the meeting of the American Psychological Association, Los Angeles.

Carducci, B. J., Deeds, W. C., Jones, J. W., Moretti, D. M., Reed, J. G., Saal, F. E., & Wheat, J. E. (1987). Preparing undergraduate psychology students for careers in business. *Teaching of Psychology, 14*, 16–20.

Howard, A. (1986). College experiences and managerial performance. *Journal of Applied Psychology, 71,* 530–552.

Lowman, R. L. (Ed.). (1985). *Casebook on ethics and standards for the practice of psychology in organizations.* College Park, MD: Society for Industrial and Organizational Psychology, Inc.

Peters, L. H. (1985). Undergraduate programs in I/O psychology: Survey results. *The Industrial-Organizational Psychologist, 23,* 37–39.

Society for Industrial and Organizational Psychology, Inc. (1987). *Principles for the validation and use of personnel selection procedures* (3rd ed.). College Park, MD: Society for Industrial and Organizational Psychology, Inc.

Takooshian, H., Matthews, J. R., Ware, M. E., Carducci, B. J., Furumoto, L., & Nadien, M. B. (1985, August). *Employment with a psychology B.A.* Symposium conducted at the meeting of the American Psychological Association, Los Angeles.

Thayer, P. W. (1988). Some things non-psychologists should know about I/O psychology. *The Industrial-Organizational Psychologist, 26,* 55–65.

APPENDIX B

JOURNALS PUBLISHING RESEARCH IN INDUSTRIAL/ ORGANIZATIONAL PSYCHOLOGY AND RELATED AREAS

Academy of Management Executive
Academy of Management Journal
Academy of Management Review
Administrative Science Quarterly
American Psychologist
Annual Review of Psychology
Applied Ergonomics
Applied Psychological Measurement
Ergonomics
Human Factors
Human Relations
Industrial Engineering
The Industrial-Organizational Psychologist
Journal of Applied Psychology
Journal of Business Research
Journal of Industrial Psychology
Organizational Behavior and Human Decision Processes
Organizational Dynamics
Personnel
Personnel Journal
Personnel Psychology
Psychological Bulletin
Psychological Review
Training and Development Journal

GLOSSARY

A

accident proneness   personality characteristics believed to predispose a person to work accidents. To date, they have not been uncovered by research.

accommodation   giving in or making sacrifices to resolve a conflict

achievement-motivation theory   McClelland's model of motivation that emphasizes the importance of three needs—achievement, power, and affiliation—in determining worker motivation

achievement-oriented behavior   in the path-goal theory of leadership, leader behavior that is focused on specific work outcomes

action research   a methodological model that applies social science research methods to collect relevant data in an organization and then use the information as the basis for taking action to solve organizational problems

actor-observer bias   in social perception, the tendency for the observer to overattribute cause to characteristics of the actor and the tendency for the actor to overattribute cause to situational characteristics

adverse impact   some form of discrimination against a protected group in personnel actions

affirmative action   voluntary organizational decision to develop policies that attempt to ensure that jobs are made available to qualified persons regardless of sex, age, or ethnic background

apprenticeship   an employee training technique, often lasting several years, that combines on-the-job experience with classroom instruction

assessment center   a detailed, structured assessment of job applicants using a variety of measurements and techniques

audience factors   characteristics of the receiver of information that influence the way the communication is perceived and thus the effectiveness of the communication process

audiovisual methods   personnel training procedures using films, videotapes, audiotapes, or slide presentations

autocratic decisionmaking   a decisionmaking strategy whereby the leader makes decisions based primarily on information that the leader possesses

avoidance   in conflict situations, a strategy of withdrawing from or avoiding the conflict

B

behaviorally anchored rating scales (BARS)   a performance appraisal method using a rating scale with labels reflecting examples of poor, average, and good behavioral incidents

behavioral observation scales   a performance appraisal method that requires evaluators to recall how often a worker has been observed performing key work behaviors

bell-shaped curve   a graphic representation of a normal distribution of scores. It is assumed that many variables are normally distributed and thus would be graphed in this form.

biographical information blanks (BIBs) a personnel screening form that assesses basic applicant biographical information, attitudes, and values to predict those who are best able to perform certain jobs

bureaucracy Weber's theory that illustrates a traditional organizational structure, characterized by a well-defined authority hierarchy and strict rules governing work behavior

burnout a syndrome resulting from prolonged exposure to work stress that can lead to decreased performance and eventually withdrawal from the organization. Burnout typically occurs in three phases: emotional exhaustion, depersonalization, and feelings of low personal accomplishment.

C

case study a descriptive research investigation involving a one-time assessment of behavior usually with a single individual, a group, or an organization

causal attribution the process by which people ascribe cause to events or behaviors

censoring in the communication process, a purposeful omission of information from a message or a decision not to transmit particular information

centralization the degree to which decision-making power is concentrated in the top levels of the organizational hierarchy.

centralized networks systematic lines of communication among organizational members by which the flow of information is directed through specific members

central tendency error the tendency to give all workers the midpoint rating in performance appraisals

chain of command the authority levels in an organizational hierarchy

change agent an organizational development practitioner or consultant who serves as a catalyst to help organizations through the process of change

channel in the communication process, the vehicle through which a message flows from a sender to a receiver. Channels may include the written or spoken word, nonverbal communication, pictures, or graphs.

channel factors characteristics of the vehicle of transmission of a message that affect the accuracy and/or perception of the communication

checklists a performance appraisal method consisting of a series of statements about job performance that are checked off by the evaluator

classical conditioning a theory of learning based on the notion that two events, experienced together in space and time, become associated with each other (also called Pavlovian conditioning)

coalition in power dynamics, the uniting of individuals to combine power

coercive power the use of punishment or the threat of punishment to affect the behavior of others

cognitive psychology the specialty area of psychology that studies how people think and process information

cohesiveness the degree of attraction group members feel for one another

collaboration a conflict resolution strategy whereby the parties cooperate so they can attain their respective goals

communication the transmission of information from one person or group to another person or group

communication networks systematic lines of communication linking various senders and receivers

comparable worth the notion that jobs that require equivalent levels of knowledge and skills should be compensated equally

comparative methods a performance appraisal method that compares one worker's performance with the performance of others

comparison others persons who are used as a basis for comparison in making judgments of equity-inequity. A key element in the equity theory of motivation.

compensable factors the job elements or dimensions that are used to determine appropriate compensation

competition the process whereby group members work against one another to achieve individual goals

competition (as a conflict resolution strategy) the perpetuation of a conflict situation until one party attains personal goals at the expense of the other party's goal attainment

compressed work weeks work schedules that shorten the number of days in the work week while increasing the number of hours worked per day

compromise a conflict resolution strategy whereby both parties give up some part of their goals

computer assisted instruction (CAI) programmed instruction using computers to present material and to test trainees

conference a forum where participants share ideas, information, and problems. Often used as a management training technique.

conflict behavior by a person or group that inhibits the attainment of goals by another person or group

conformity the process of adhering to and following group norms

consensus a decisionmaking strategy that requires all group members to reach full and complete agreement

consideration leader behavior that shows a concern for the feelings, attitudes, and needs of subordinates

content validity in personnel screening, a form of validity that is concerned with whether the items in a measurement instrument adequately assess the characteristics necessary to perform the job

contingency theories theories that look at the interaction of the characteristics or behaviors of individuals (such as leaders) and the qualities of the situation

control group in an experimental investigation, a comparison group that receives no treatment

controls the mechanical devices used to operate machine functions

correlational method the research method that examines the relationship between or among variables as they naturally occur

correlation coefficient a statistical technique that determines the strength of a relationship between two variables. Expressed as numerical values ranging from $+1.00$ to -1.00.

criterion-related validity in personnel screening, a method of establishing the accuracy of a measurement instrument by determining the relationship between scores on the instrument and some criterion of job success

critical incidents technique a method of job analysis that uses as its basis instances of particularly successful or unsuccessful job performance

D

decentralization the process of taking the decisionmaking power away from the top level of an organization and distributing it to lower levels

decentralized networks communication networks that allow messages to originate at any point, without having to be directed through certain, central members

decibels a standardized measure of sound loudness

decision-making model (Vroom and Yetton's) a theory that matches characteristics of the work decision situation with leader decision-making strategies

decoding in the communication process, the act of translating a message so that it can be understood

democratic decisionmaking a decisionmaking strategy whereby group members are allowed to participate, usually by majority-rule voting

dependent variable the measured outcome variable in an experimental investigation. Changes in the dependent variable are presumably caused by manipulation of the independent variable.

descriptive model a theory that simply provides an objective account of the behavior being studied

descriptive statistics arithmetical formulas for summarizing and describing research data. The mean, standard deviation, and frequency distribution of scores are all examples

Dictionary of Occupational Titles (DOT) a reference guide that classifies and provides job descriptions of over 40,000 jobs

differentiation the complexity of an organizational structure based on the number of units or departments, the different orientations of managers, and the different goals and interests of members

directive behavior in the path-goal theory of leadership, leader behavior that provides instructions and suggestions for getting the job done

displays mechanical means of communicating information about a machine's operating status to an operator

divisional structure an organizational structure in which divisions are made based on types of products or customers

downward communication the flow of messages from superiors to subordinates in an organizational hierarchy, usually in the form of orders, directives, or requests for information

dysfunctional politics political behaviors that detract from an organization's ability to attain its goals

E

Employee Assistance Programs (EAPs) programs offering counseling for a variety of worker problems, especially drug and alcohol abuse

employee ownership a concept whereby employees own all or part of an organization, typically through stock purchases

empowerment the process by which organizational members are able to increase their sense of power and personal control in the work environment. Workers can be empowered by

managers or may be able to empower themselves through increasing important work-related skills or responsibilities.

encoding in the communication process, the act of preparing a message for transmission by putting it into some recognizable form or code

engineering anthropometry the measurement of physical characteristics of the human body in order to develop equipment designed to fit those characteristics

Equal Employment Opportunity Commission (EEOC) the federal agency created to protect against discrimination in employment

equity theory a motivation theory that states that workers are motivated to reduce perceived inequities between work inputs and outcomes

ERG theory (existence, relatedness, and growth) Alderfer's motivation model that classifies needs into categories of existence (basic physiological requirements), relatedness (social interaction), and growth (the development of one's full potential)

exaggeration in communication, the distortion of information through the elaboration or overestimation of certain aspects of the message

exceptioning the practice of ignoring pay discrepancies between particular jobs with equivalent duties and responsibilities

expectancy the perceived relationship between an individual's effort and the performance of a behavior. One of the three components of the VIE theory of motivation.

experimental method a research design characterized by a high degree of control over the research setting, which allows the determination of cause-and-effect relationships as the researcher manipulates one aspect of the situation and measures its effect on another aspect

expert power power that results from the possession of some special work knowledge or skill

external validity whether research results obtained in one setting will generalize to other settings

extraneous variables variables other than the independent variable that may influence the dependent variable. Also referred to as "third variables."

F

feedback in the communication process, an acknowledgment that a message has been received and understood

Fiedler's contingency model a leadership theory that maintains that effective leadership depends on a match between the leader's style and the degree to which the work situation gives that person control and influence

filtering the selective presentation of the content of a communication

fixed interval schedule a reinforcement schedule in which reinforcement follows the passage of a specified amount of time

fixed ratio schedule a reinforcement schedule in which reinforcement is contingent on performance of a fixed number of behaviors

flextime a schedule in which an employee works a specified number of hours per week but has flexibility in the starting and ending times for work days

frequency distribution a descriptive statistical technique that arranges scores by categories and often takes a graphic form such as bar graphs or histograms

functional job analysis (FJA) a job analysis technique that examines the sequence of tasks in a job and the processes by which the worker completes the task

functional politics political behaviors that assist the organization in attaining its goals

functional structure an organizational structure that divides the organization into departments based on the functions or tasks they perform

G

gainsharing a compensation system based on effective group rather than individual performance

goal-setting theory the motivational theory that emphasizes the setting of specific and challenging performance goals

grapevine the informal communication network in an organization

graphic rating scale a job evaluation method using a predetermined scale to rate the worker on important job dimensions. Graphic rating scales can take a variety of forms.

great-man-woman theory a universalist theory of leadership that maintains that great leaders are born, not made

group two or more individuals who engage in social interaction to achieve some goal

group polarization the tendency for groups to make more extreme decisions than individuals

groupthink a syndrome, proposed by Janis, characterized by a concurrence-seeking tendency that overrides the ability of a cohesive group to make critical decisions

growth need strength the need and desire for personal growth on the job that is a key element in the job characteristics model

H

halo effect in social perception, an overall positive evaluation of a person based on one known positive characteristic or action

hardiness the notion that some people may be more resistant to the health-damaging effects of stress

Hawthorne effect changes in behavior that occur because subjects know that they are being observed, and because of subjects' expectations concerning their role as research participants

human factors the specialty area of I/O psychology focusing on the relationship between the worker and the work task. Human factors is concerned with designing tools, machines, work systems, and work places to fit the skills and abilities of the workers who will be using them. Also referred to as engineering psychology and ergonomics.

human relations movement a movement begun by Mayo that emphasizes the influence of social factors on worker performance

hygienes elements related to job context that, when absent, cause dissatisfaction. A key idea in Herzberg's two-factor theory of motivation.

hypotheses statements, used in research methods, concerning the supposed relationships between or among variables

I

independent variable the variable that is manipulated by the experimenter as part of the experimental method of research. The independent variable is the presumed cause of changes in the dependent variable.

individual coping strategies techniques such as exercise or meditation that individuals can use to deal with work stress

individual power power derived from personal characteristics, such as expertise or leadership ability, that are of value to an organization

industrial/organizational (I/O) psychology the branch of psychology that studies behavior in work settings and applies psychological principles to changing work behavior

inferential statistics statistical techniques used for analyzing data in order to test research hypotheses

influence the ability to use social forces, such as persuasiveness, flattery, or manipulation, to affect the behavior of others

ingratiation influencing others by increasing one's personal appeal by using flattery or doing favors

initiating structure leader behaviors that define, organize, and structure the work setting

inputs elements that a worker invests in a job, such as experience, knowledge, and effort. A key factor in the equity theory of motivation.

instrumentality the relationship between performing a behavior and the expected likelihood of receiving a particular outcome. An important factor in the VIE theory of motivation.

integration the amount and quality of collaboration among the various units or departments within an organization

intergroup conflict conflict that results when two groups interfere with one another's goal attainment

interindividual conflict conflict that arises when two individuals are blocking one another's goal attainment

internal consistency a common method of establishing the reliability of a test by examining the intercorrelation of the various items

interorganizational conflict conflict occurring between two organizations with incompatible goals

interpersonal stress stress that arises from difficulties with relations with others in the work site

intragroup conflict conflict that results when a person or faction within a group is attempting to attain a goal and interferes with the group's goal attainment

intraindividual conflict conflict that occurs when an individual is faced with two sets of incompatible goals and working to attain one goal interferes with the attainment of the other goal

J

jargon specific language developed in connection with certain jobs. Also referred to as technical language.

job analysis the systematic study of the tasks, duties, and responsibilities of a job and the knowledge, skills, and abilities needed to perform it

job characteristics model a theory that emphasizes the role that certain aspects of jobs, or job characteristics, play in influencing work motivation

job description a detailed account of job tasks, procedures, and responsibilities; requisite tools and equipment; and output

Job Descriptive Index (JDI) a standardized, self-report job satisfaction rating scale that measures five job facets

Job Diagnostic Survey (JDS) a questionnaire measure of core job characteristics used in conjunction with the job characteristics model

job enlargement expansion of a job to include additional, more varied work tasks

job enrichment a program that involves redesigning jobs to give workers greater responsibility in the planning, execution, and evaluation of their work

job evaluation an assessment of the relative value of jobs to determine appropriate compensation

job rotation a method of moving workers among a variety of jobs or tasks to increase their breadth of knowledge or to alleviate boredom and monotony

job satisfaction the positive and negative feelings and attitudes about one's job

job specification a statement of the human characteristics required to perform a job, such as experience, knowledge, and training

job uncertainty stress that results from ambiguity in the job and in work tasks

K

knowledge-based pay a system of compensation whereby workers receive pay based on their knowledge and skills rather than on the positions they hold

L

lack of control a feeling of having little input or effect on the job and work environment. Research indicates that a sense of lack of control is a significant source of stress

lateral communication communication between two parties at the same status level in an organizational hierarchy

leader-member exchange model a leadership theory that defines effective leadership by the quality of the interaction between the leader and particular group members

leader-member relations the quality of the relationship between leader and followers. A key element in Fiedler's contingency model of leadership.

leadership the ability to direct a group toward the attainment of goals

learning a relatively permanent change in behavior that occurs as a result of experience

least preferred co-worker (LPC) a measure that assesses a leader's task- or relationship-orientation by having the leader rate his or her least preferred co-worker

lecture a personnel training method in which an expert provides job-related information in a classroom setting

legitimate power an individual's formal rights or authorities that derive from the person's position in an organization

leniency errors the tendency to give all workers the midpoint rating in performance appraisals

life events significant events in a person's recent history that can cause stress. Measuring them is one way of assessing a person's stress level.

line employees directly engaged in tasks that accomplish the primary goals of an organization

line-staff organizational structure a traditional organizational structure made up of one group of employees—the line—who achieve the goals of the organization and another group—the staff—who support the line

M

management by objectives (MBO) a goal-setting organizational development technique in which supervisors and subordinates jointly set performance goals and, at the end of a certain period, evaluate goal attainment and set new goals

management games a management training technique that uses scaled-down enactments of the operations and management of organizations

matrix organization a nontraditional organizational structure consisting of a permanent team of members organized around a particular project or product

mean a statistical measure of central tendency calculated by taking the sum of scores and dividing by the number of scores. Also referred to as the average.

mentoring a personnel training program in which an inexperienced individual develops a working relationship with an experienced worker who serves as an advisor

merit pay a compensation system whereby employees receive a base rate and additional pay that is based on individual performance

meta-analysis a statistical technique that allows the results from several research investigations to be combined and summarized

Minnesota Satisfaction Questionnaire (MSQ) a standardized, self-report measure of job satisfaction that breaks satisfaction down into 20 job facets

modeling learning that occurs by observing and imitating the behavior of others

motivation the force that energizes, directs, and sustains behavior

motivators elements related to job content that lead to job satisfaction. Used in Herzberg's two-factor theory of motivation.

multiple cutoff a personnel selection model that uses a minimum cutoff score on each of several predictors

multiple hurdle a personnel selection model that requires that an acceptance or rejection decision be made at each of several stages in a screening process

multiple regression model a personnel selection method that statistically combines separate predictors to determine how they, in combination, indicate an applicant's potential success at a job

N

need-hierarchy theory Maslow's motivation model that arranges needs in a hierarchy from lower, more basic needs to higher-order needs

needs physiological or psychological deficiencies that an organism is driven to satisfy

negative reinforcers events that strengthen a behavior through the avoidance of an existing negative state

noise physical or psychological distractions that can disrupt the flow of communication or cause stress. In extremes, physical noise can cause permanent hearing damage and is a work environment hazard.

nonverbal communication messages sent and received through means other than the spoken or written word

normal distribution a distribution of scores along a continuum with known properties. The normal distribution is often represented as a bell-shaped curve.

normative (prescriptive) model a type of theory that suggests a certain intervention to obtain desired results

norms rules that groups adopt to govern appropriate and inappropriate behavior for members

O

objectivity the principle that research methods involve unbiased observations and interpretations of behavior

obtrusive observation research observation in which the presence of the observer is known to the participants

Occupational Safety and Health Administration (OSHA) the governmental agency that administers and enforces health and safety standards in work organizations

on-the-job training a personnel training method of placing a worker in the work place to learn firsthand about a job

operant conditioning a learning process whereby behaviors are followed by reinforcement or punishment to obtain desired outcomes

operationalize the process of defining a variable so that it can be measured or manipulated

operator-machine system the interaction of one or more persons with one or more tools or devices to perform a work task

organigram a diagram of an organization's hierarchy representing the formal lines of communication within the organization. Also known as an organizational chart

organizational behavior modification the application of conditioning principles to obtain desired work outcomes

organizational commitment employees' feelings and attitudes concerning the entire work organization

organizational coping strategies techniques and programs that organizations can use to try to reduce stress levels for all or most employees

organizational development (OD) the process of assisting organizations to prepare for and manage change

organizational politics self-serving actions used to affect the behavior of others in order to achieve personal goals

organizational power power derived from a person's position in an organization and from the control over important organizational resources afforded to the person because of the position

organizational psychology the specialty area of I/O psychology that studies relationships among workers

organizational socialization the process by which new employees learn group and organizational roles and norms, and develop specific work skills and abilities

organizational structure the arrangement of positions in an organization, and the authority and responsibility relationships among the positions

outcomes in the equity theory of motivation, those things that a worker expects to receive from a job, such as pay and recognition

overpayment inequity in the equity theory of motivation, workers' perceptions that outcomes are greater than inputs

P

parallel forms a method of establishing the reliability of a measurement instrument by correlating scores on two different but equivalent versions of the same instrument

participant observation an unobtrusive observation research method in which the observer becomes a member of the organization or group being studied

participative behavior in the path-goal theory of leadership, leader behavior that encourages members to take an active role in group planning and decisionmaking

path-goal theory a leadership theory that states that a leader's job is to help the work group attain their desired goals

performance appraisals the process of assessing worker performance in comparison to certain predetermined organizational standards

performance feedback the process of providing information to a worker regarding performance level along with suggestions for improvement

personality tests instruments that measure psychological characteristics of individuals

personnel psychology the area of I/O psychology that deals with the study and analysis of people and jobs

personnel recruitment the process by which organizations attract potential workers to apply for jobs

personnel screening the process of reviewing information about applicants to select individuals for jobs

personnel selection the process of choosing applicants for employment

polygraphs tests of honesty that measure physiological reactions, such as heart rate or respiration, presumed to accompany deception

Position Analysis Questionnaire (PAQ) a job analysis technique that uses a structured questionnaire to analyze jobs in terms of 187 elements grouped into six categories

position power a leader's authority to punish or reward subordinates. A key concept in Fiedler's contingency theory of leadership.

positive reinforcers desirable events that follow certain behaviors and strengthen the tendency to perform them again

power   the use of some aspect of a work relationship to compel another to perform a certain action despite resistance

power bases   individuals' sources of power in an organization

power corollary   the idea that for every exercise of power, there is a tendency for the subject to react with a "return" power play

practitioner model   a method of applying psychological principles to change work behavior through a process of diagnosis, intervention, and evaluation

predictive model   a category of theories that attempt to specify cause-and-effect relationships among variables

pretest-posttest   the evaluation of a program by comparing criterion measures collected before and after the introduction of the program

problem-solving case study   a management training technique that presents a description of a real or hypothetical organizational problem that trainees attempt to solve

process consultation   an organizational development technique in which a consultant helps a client-organization to study its problems objectively and learn how to solve them

profit-sharing   a system whereby employees obtain a share of an organization's profits based on the organization's economic success

programmed instruction   self-paced, individualized training whereby trainees are provided with training materials and can test themselves on how much they have learned

project task force   a nontraditional organizational structure of workers assembled temporarily to complete a specific job or project

protected groups   groups that have been identified as previous targets of employment discrimination, including women and certain ethnic and racial minority groups

psychology   the study of behavior and mental processes

punishment   unpleasant consequences following the performance of a behavior that reduce the tendency to engage in that behavior in the future

Q

quality circles   small groups of volunteer employees from the same work areas who meet regularly to solve quality-related work problems

quality of work life   the evaluative state of all aspects of work

R

random assignment   a method of assigning research subjects to groups to control for the effects of extraneous variables. Each subject has an equal chance of being assigned to any of the groups.

random sampling   selecting research participants from a population so that each individual has an equal probability of being chosen

realistic job previews (RJPs)   an honest presentation of the prospective job and the organization given to applicants

receiver   the recipient of a communication. Also referred to as the decoder, since the receiver decodes the message.

recency effect   the tendency in performance appraisals to give greater weight to recent performance and lesser weight to earlier performance

reciprocity rule   the tendency for persons to feel indebted and for them to want to "pay back" others for their assistance

referent power   power resulting from the fact that an individual is respected, admired, and liked by others

reinforcement theory   the theory that behavior is motivated by its consequences

relationship-oriented behaviors   a leader orientation that focuses on maintaining interpersonal relationships on the job

reliability   the stability of a measurement device over time

reward power   power that results from having the ability to give others something positive, such as money and praise

robots automatic, programmable devices that can carry out tasks typically performed by humans

role pattern of behavior that is adopted based on expectations about the functions of a position

role differentiation the process by which group members take on various roles

role expectations beliefs concerning the responsibilities and requirements of a particular role

role-playing personnel training exercises that require trainees to act out situations that often occur at work

rumors information that is presented as fact but may actually be either true or false

S

sampling the selection of a representative group from a larger population for study

scientific management begun by Taylor, a method of applying scientific principles to improve job productivity and efficiency through procedures such as time-and-motion analyses

self-efficacy the belief that a person has the abilities and energy to accomplish a particular task or goal

self-report techniques methods of assessment relying on the reports of research subjects concerning their own behavior

sender the person who encodes and transmits a communication. Also referred to as the encoder.

sensitivity training an organizational development technique that uses unstructured group interaction to help workers gain insight into their own motivations and behavior patterns in dealing with other organizational members

severity errors the tendency to give all workers very negative evaluations in performance appraisals

shifts alternate employee work times scheduled to keep the work place in extended or continuous operation

simulation training that replicates job conditions without placing the trainee in the actual work setting

situational exercises assessment tools that require the performance of tasks that approximate actual work tasks. Often used as part of an assessment center.

social learning theory a learning theory that emphasizes observational learning of behavior

sociogram a diagram of the informal lines of communication among organizational members

Solomon four-group design a very thorough method of program evaluation using two treatment and two control groups

source factors in the communication process, characteristics of the sender that influence the effectiveness or accuracy of a message

span of control the number of workers that must report to a single supervisor in an organization's structural hierarchy

speech-activated controls machine controls that respond to the sounds of human voices

staff in line-staff organizational structures, specialized employee positions designed to support the line

standard deviation a measure of variability of scores in a frequency distribution

statistical significance a method for calculating the probability that a particular research result could have occurred by chance. A statistically significant result is unlikely to have occurred by chance and is thus presumed to have been caused by some other factor, such as an intervention.

stratified sampling selecting research participants based on categories that represent important distinguishing characteristics of a population

stress the physiological, emotional, and psychological reactions to threatening environmental events

stressor an environmental event that causes a stress reaction

superordinate goal a goal that both parties in a conflict situation are attracted to and are willing to work to attain

supportive behavior in the path-goal theory of leadership, leader behavior focusing on interpersonal relationships and showing concern for workers' well-being

survey a common, self-report measurement technique that asks subjects to report on their attitudes, beliefs, or behaviors

survey feedback an organizational development technique in which the consultant works with the organization to develop and administer a survey instrument to collect data about the organization, which are then fed back to organizational members and used as the starting point for change

T

task-oriented behavior leader behavior focused on the work task

task structure an assessment of the amount of structure associated with a group's work task. An important component in Fiedler's contingency theory of leadership.

team building an organizational development technique in which teams of workers meet to discuss ways to improve team performance through improved group interaction and coordination of efforts

teleoperators sophisticated control systems that act as an extension of the human operator

test battery in personnel testing, a combination of tests that are used together to increase the accuracy of the prediction of job performance

test-retest reliability a method of determining the reliability of a measurement instrument by administering the same measure to the same individuals at two times, and then correlating the two scores

test utility the value of a screening test in helping to affect important outcomes, such as dollars gained through its use

Thematic Apperception Test (TAT) a projective test consisting of ambiguous pictures used to assess psychological motivation

theory the organization of certain beliefs into a representation of the factors that affect behavior. Also known as a model.

Theory X a leader orientation, proposed by MacGregor, characterized by the view that workers are basically unmotivated and disinterested in work, and need to have their activities directed and controlled

Theory Y a leader orientation, proposed by MacGregor, characterized by respect and trust in subordinates, and a belief that workers are self-motivated and desire to take on responsibility

time-and-motion studies studies in which work tasks are broken down into simple, component movements and each is timed to develop a more efficient method of performance. Developed by Taylor, time-and-motion studies are an important part of scientific management.

traits consistent and enduring attributes associated with an individual's personality

trait theory theoretical attempts to discover the characteristics, or traits, shared by all effective leaders

treatment group the group in an experimental investigation that is subjected to the change in the independent variable

_t_-test a test of the statistical significance of the difference between the means of two groups of scores, which is expressed as a numerical value representing the size of the difference between the two means

two-factor theory Herzberg's motivational theory that proposes that two factors—motivators and hygienes—are important in determining worker satisfaction and motivation

two-tier wage structure a cost-saving compensation system whereby top rates of pay for new employees are lower than those for older employees

Type A behavior pattern a pattern of behavior characterized by excessive drive, competitiveness, impatience, and hostility that has been linked to higher incidence of coronary heart disease

U

underpayment inequity according to equity theory, the situation that exists when workers perceive that their inputs are greater than work outcomes

underutilization a source of stress that results when workers feel that their knowledge, skills, or energy are not being used fully

universalist theories leadership theories that look for the key characteristic or group of characteristics common to all effective leaders

unobtrusive observation research observation in which the presence of the observer is not known to the participants

upward communication messages flowing upward in an organizational hierarchy, usually taking the form of feedback

V

valence in the VIE theory of motivation, the desirability of a particular outcome to an individual

validity the accuracy of a measurement instrument

validity generalization the ability of a measurement instrument to predict performance in a job or setting different from the one in which the test was validated

variable interval schedule a schedule of reinforcement in which the reinforcement follows the passage of a specified amount of time, with the exact time of reinforcement varying

variable ratio schedule a schedule of reinforcement in which the reinforcement is contingent on the performance of a specified but varying number of behaviors

variables the elements that are measured in research investigations

vestibule training training that uses a separate area adjacent to the work area to simulate the actual work setting

VIE theory a rational theory of motivation that states that workers weigh expected costs and benefits of a particular course of action before they are motivated to take action

W

weighted application form a job application form that assigns different values or "weights" to the various information requested

we-they feeling intragroup cohesiveness created when a group is faced by a common threat, typically another group

work samples a job skill test that measures applicants' abilities to perform brief examples of important job tasks

workspace design the design and arrangement of equipment, space, and machinery in a work environment

REFERENCES

Abelson, R. P., & Levi, A. (1985). Decision making and decision theory. In G. Lindzey & E. Aronson (Eds.), *The handbook of social psychology* (3rd ed, pp. 231–310). New York: Random House.

Adams, J. S. (1965). In L. Berkowitz (Ed.), *Advances in experimental social psychology* (Vol. 2, pp. 267–299). New York: Academic Press.

AFSCME v. State of Washington, 578 F. supp. 846 (W. D. Wash., 1983).

Albemarle Paper v. Moody, 74-389 (1975).

Albrecht, K. (1983). *Organization development: A total systems approach to positive change in any business organization.* Englewood Cliffs, NJ: Prentice-Hall.

Alderfer, C. P. (1972). *Existence, relatedness, and growth: Human needs in organizational settings.* New York: Free Press.

Allen, R. W., & Porter, L. W. (Eds.). (1983). *Organizational influence processes.* Glenview, IL: Scott, Foresman.

Ansari, M. A., & Kapoor, A. (1987). Organizational context and upward influence tactics. *Organizational Behavior and Human Decision Processes, 40,* 39–49.

Argyris, C. (1980). Some limitations of the case method: Experiences in a management development program. *Academy of Management Review, 5,* 251–298.

Arnold, H. J., & Feldman, D. C. (1982). A multivariate analysis of the determinants of job turnover. *Journal of Applied Psychology, 67,* 350–360.

Arvey, R. D. (1979). *Fairness in selecting employees.* Reading, MA: Addison-Wesley.

Arvey, R. D., & Campion, J. E. (1982). The employment interview: A summary and review of recent research. *Personnel Psychology, 35,* 281–322.

Ashour, A. S. (1973). The contingency model of leadership effectiveness: An evaluation. *Organizational Behavior and Human Performance, 9,* 339–355.

Astley, W. G., & Sachdeva, P. S. (1984). Structural sources of intraorganizational power: A theoretical synthesis. *Academy of Management Review, 9,* 104–113.

Atkin, R. S., & Goodman, P. S. (1984). Methods of defining and measuring absenteeism. In P. S. Goodman & R. S. Atkin (Eds.), *Absenteeism: New approaches to understanding, measuring, and managing employee absence* (pp. 47–109). San Francisco: Jossey-Bass.

Axel, H. (Ed.) (1986). *Corporate strategies for controlling substance abuse.* New York: The Conference Board.

Bacharach, S. B., & Lawler, E. J. (1980). *Power and politics in organizations: The social psychology of conflict, coalitions, and bargaining.* San Francisco: Jossey-Bass.

Bachman, J. G., Bowers, D. G., & Marcus, P. M. (1968). Bases of supervisory power: A comparative study in five organizational settings. In A. S. Tannenbaum (Ed.), *Control in organizations* (pp. 229–238). New York: McGraw-Hill.

Baird, J. E. (1977). *The dynamics of organizational communication.* New York: Harper & Row.

Baldwin, T. T., & Ford, J. K. (1988). Transfer of training: A review and directions for future research. *Personnel Psychology, 41,* 63–105.

Balkin, D. B., & Gomez-Mejia, L. R. (Eds.). (1987). *New perspectives on compensation.* Englewood Cliffs, NJ: Prentice-Hall.

Bandura, A. (1977). *Social learning theory.* Englewood Cliffs, NJ: Prentice-Hall.

Bandura, A. (1986). *Social foundations of thought and action: A social-cognitive view.* Englewood Cliffs, NJ: Prentice-Hall.

Barker, L. L., Wahlers, K. J., Watson, K. W., & Kibler, R. J. (1987). *Groups in process: An introduction to small group communication* (3rd ed.). Englewood Cliffs, NJ: Prentice-Hall.

Baron, R. A. (1986). *Behavior in organizations: Understanding and managing the human side of work* (2nd ed.). Boston: Allyn & Bacon.

Baron, R. A. (1987). Effects of negative ions on cognitive performance. *Journal of Applied Psychology, 72,* 131–137.

Baron, R. A., & Byrne, D. (1987). *Social psychology: Understanding human interaction* (5th ed.). Boston: Allyn & Bacon.

Baron, R. A., Russell, G. W., & Arms, R. L. (1985). Negative ions and behavior: Impact on mood, memory, and aggression among Type A and Type B persons. *Journal of Personality and Social Psychology, 48,* 746–754.

Barrett, G. V., & Kernan, M. C. (1987). Performance appraisal and terminations: A review of court decisions since Brito v. Zia with implications for personnel practices. *Personnel Psychology, 40,* 489–503.

Bass, B. M. (1954). The leaderless group discussion. *Psychological Bulletin, 51,* 465–492.

Bass, B. M. (1981). *Stogdill's handbook of leadership (rev. and enl. ed.).* New York: Free Press.

Bass, B. M. (1983). Issues involved in relations between methodological rigor and reported outcomes in evaluations of organizational development. *Journal of Applied Psychology, 68,* 197–199.

Bateman, T. S., & Strasser, S. (1984). A longitudinal analysis of the antecedents of organizational commitment. *Academy of Management Journal, 27,* 95–112.

Bavelas, A. (1950). Communication patterns in task-oriented groups. *Journal of Acoustical Society of America, 22,* 725–730.

Bazerman, M. H., Giuliano, T., & Appleman, A. (1984). Escalation of commitment in individual and group decision making. *Organizational Behavior and Human Performance, 33,* 141–152.

Beehr, T. A. (1985). Organizational stress and employee effectiveness. A job characteristics approach. In T. A. Beehr & R. S. Bhagat (Eds.), *Human stress and cognition in organizations: An integrated perspective* (pp. 57–81). New York: John Wiley & Sons.

Beehr, T. A. (1986). The process of retirement: A review and recommendations for future investigation. *Personnel Psychology, 39,* 31–55.

Beehr, T. A., & Bhagat, R. S. (Eds.). (1985). *Human stress and cognition in organizations: An integrated perspective.* New York: John Wiley & Sons.

Bell, P. A. (1981). Physiological, comfort, performance, and social effects of heat stress. *Journal of Social Issues, 37,* 71–94.

Benne, K. D., & Sheats, P. (1948). Functional roles of group members. *Journal of Social Issues, 4,* 41–49.

Bennett, G. K. (1980). *Bennett Mechanical Comprehension Test.* San Antonio, TX: The Psychological Corporation.

Bennett, G. K. (1981). *Hand-Tool Dexterity Test*. San Antonio, TX: The Psychological Corporation.

Bennis, W. G. (1969). *Organization development: Its nature, origins, and prospects*. Reading, MA: Addison-Wesley.

Ben-Shakhar, G., Bar-Hillel, M., Bilu, Y., Ben-Abba, E., & Flug, A. (1986). Can graphology predict occupational success? Two empirical studies and some methodological ruminations. *Journal of Applied Psychology, 71,* 645–653.

Bernardin, H. J., & Beatty, R. W. (1984). *Performance appraisal: Assessing human behavior at work*. Boston: Kent.

Bernardin, H. J., & Bulkley, M. R. (1981). Strategies in rater training. *Academy of Management Review, 6,* 205–242.

Berryman-Fink, C. (1985). Male and female managers' views of the communication skills and training needs of women in management. *Public Personnel Management, 14,* 307–313.

Bhagat, R. S. (1983). Effects of stressful life events on individual performance effectiveness and work adjustment processes within organizational settings: A research model. *Academy of Management Review, 8,* 660–671.

Bhagat, R. S. (1985). The role of stressful life events in organizational behavior and human performance. In T. A. Beehr & R. S. Bhagat (Eds.), *Human stress and cognition in organizations: An integrated perspective* (pp. 205–212). New York: John Wiley & Sons.

Blake, R. R., & Mouton, J. S. (1985). *The managerial grid III*. Houston: Gulf.

Blake, R. R., Mouton, J. S., & Sloma, R. L. (1964). An actual case history of resolving intergroup conflict in union-management relations. In R. R. Blake, H. A. Shepard, & J. S. Mouton, *Managing intergroup conflict in industry* (pp. 155–195). Houston: Gulf.

Blake, R. R., Shepard, H. A., & Mouton, J. S. (1964). *Managing intergroup conflict in industry*. Houston: Gulf.

Block, P. (1987). *The empowered manager*. San Francisco: Jossey-Bass.

Booth, R. T. (1986). Machinery hazards. In J. Ridley (Ed.), *Safety at work* (2nd ed., pp. 549–571). London: Butterworth.

Borman, W. C. (1986). Behavior-based rating scales. In R. A. Berk (Ed.), *Performance assessment: Methods and applications* (pp. 100–120). Baltimore: The Johns Hopkins University Press.

Boroson, W. (1976, June). The workaholic in you. *Money,* pp. 32–35.

Bouchard, T. J., Barsaloux, J., & Drauden, G. (1974). Brainstorming procedure, group size, and sex as determinants of the problem-solving effectiveness of groups and individuals. *Journal of Applied Psychology, 59,* 135–138.

Bowers, D. G. (1973). OD techniques and their results in 23 organizations: The Michigan ICL study. *Journal of Applied Behavioral Science, 9,* 21–43.

Bowers, D. G., & Hauser, D. L. (1977). Work group types and intervention effects in organizational development. *Administrative Science Quarterly, 22,* 76–94.

Bray, D. W., Campbell, R. J., & Grant, D. L. (1974). *Formative years in business: A long-term AT&T study of managerial lives*. New York: John Wiley & Sons.

Breaugh, J. A. (1981). Relationships between recruiting sources and employee performance, absenteeism, and work attitudes. *Academy of Management Journal, 24,* 142–147.

Breaugh, J. A. (1983). The 12-hour work day: Differing employee reactions. *Personnel Psychology, 36,* 277–288.

Brief, A. P., & Motowidlo, S. J. (1986). Prosocial organizational behaviors. *Academy of Management Review, 11,* 710–725.

Brito v. Zia Company, 478 F.2d 1200 (1973).

Burgess, R. (1968). Communication networks: An experimental reevaluation. *Journal of Experimental Social Psychology, 4,* 324–337.

Burke, M. J., & Day, R. R. (1986). A cumulative study of the effectiveness of managerial training. *Journal of Applied Psychology, 71,* 232–245.

Burke, W. W. (1987). *Organization development: A normative view.* Reading, MA: Addison-Wesley.

Butler, M. C., & Jones, A. P. (1979). Perceived leader behavior, individual characteristics, and injury occurrence in hazardous work environments. *Journal of Applied Psychology, 64,* 299–304.

Cairo, P. C. (1983). Counseling in industry: A selected review of the literature. *Personnel Psychology, 36,* 1–18.

Camara, W. J. (1988). Senate approves bill to ban polygraph testing in the workplace. *The Industrial-Organizational Psychologist, 25*(4), 57–58.

Campbell, D. E. (1979). Interior office design and visitor response. *Journal of Applied Psychology, 64,* 648–653.

Campbell, J. P., & Dunnette, M. D. (1968). Effectiveness of t-group experiences in management training and development. *Psychological Bulletin, 70,* 73–104.

Campbell, J. P., Dunnette, M. D., Lawler, E. E., & Weick, K. E. (1970). *Managerial behavior, performance, and effectiveness.* New York: McGraw-Hill.

Campion, M. A., Pursell, E. D., & Brown, B. K. (1988). Structured interviewing: Raising the psychometric properties of the employment interview. *Personnel Psychology, 41,* 25–42.

Cann, E., Siegfried, W. D., & Pearce, L. (1981). Forced attention to specific applicant qualifications: Impact on physical attractiveness and sex of applicant biases. *Personnel Psychology, 34,* 65–76.

Canter, D. (1983). The physical context of work. In D. J. Oborne & M. M. Gruneberg (Eds.), *The physical environment at work* (pp. 11–38). Chichester, England: John Wiley & Sons.

Card, S., English, W., & Burr, B. (1978). Evaluation of mouse, rate-controlled isometric joystick, step keys, and text keys for text selection on a CRT. *Ergonomics, 21,* 601–613.

Carrell, M. R. (1978). A longitudinal field assessment of employee perceptions of equitable treatment. *Organizational Behavior and Human Performance, 21,* 108–118.

Carroll, S. J., Paine, F. T., & Ivancevich, J. J. (1972). The relative effectiveness of training methods: Expert opinion and research. *Personnel Psychology, 25,* 495–510.

Carsten, J. M., & Spector, P. E. (1987). Unemployment, job satisfaction, and employee turnover: A meta-analytic test of the Muchinsky model. *Journal of Applied Psychology, 72,* 374–381.

Cartwright, D. (1968). The nature of group cohesiveness. In D. Cartwright & A. Zander (Eds.), *Group dynamics: Research and theory* (3rd ed., pp. 91–109). New York: Harper & Row.

Cascio, W. F. (1976). Turnover, biographical data, and fair employment practice. *Journal of Applied Psychology, 61,* 576–580.

Cascio, W. F. (1987). *Applied psychology in personnel management* (3rd ed.). Englewood Cliffs, NJ: Prentice-Hall.

Cascio, W. F., & Phillips, N. F. (1979). Performance testing: A rose among thorns? *Personnel Psychology, 32,* 751–766.

Cattell, R. B. (1986). *Sixteen Personality Factors Questionnaire.* Champaign, IL: Institute for Personality and Ability Testing.

Cavanagh, G. F., Moberg, D. J., & Velasquez, M. (1981). The ethics of organizational politics. *Academy of Management Review, 6,* 363–374.

Cederblom, D. (1982). The performance appraisal interview: A review, implications, and suggestions. *Academy of Management Review, 7,* 219–227.

Chao, G. T., & Kozlowski, S. W. J. (1986). Employee perceptions on the implementation of robotic manufacturing technology. *Journal of Applied Psychology, 71,* 70–76.

Chapanis, A. (1976). Engineering psychology.

In M. D. Dunnette (Ed.), *Handbook of industrial and organizational psychology* (pp. 697–744). Chicago: Rand-McNally.

Cherniss, C. (1980). *Staff burnout: Job stress in human services*. Beverly Hills: Sage.

Chesney, M. A., & Rosenman, R. H. (1980). Type A behaviour in the work setting. In C. L. Cooper & R. Payne (Eds.), *Current concerns in occupational stress* (pp. 187–212). Chichester, England: John Wiley & Sons.

Cialdini, R. B. (1984). *Influence: How and why people agree to things*. New York: William Morrow.

Cialdini, R. B. (1988). *Influence: Science and practice* (2nd ed.). Glenview, IL: Scott, Foresman.

Close, G. C. (1960). *Work improvement*. New York: John Wiley & Sons.

Cobb, A. T. (1984). An episodic model of power: Toward an integration of theory and research. *Academy of Management Review, 9*, 482–493.

Cohen, A. R., & Gadon, H. (1978). *Alternative work schedules: Integrating individual and organizational needs*. Reading, MA: Addison-Wesley.

Cohen, S. (1980). Aftereffects of stress on human behavior and social behavior: A review of research and theory. *Psychological Bulletin, 88*, 82–108.

Cohen, S., & Weinstein, N. (1981). Nonauditory effects of noise on behavior and health. *Journal of Social Issues, 37*, 36–70.

Colarelli, S. M. (1984). Methods of communication and mediating processes in realistic job previews. *Journal of Applied Psychology, 69*, 633–642.

Collins, E. G. C., & Scott, P. (1978). Everyone who makes it has a mentor. *Harvard Business Review, 56*, 89–101.

Collins, N. W. (1983). *Professional women and their mentors*. Englewood Cliffs, NJ: Prentice-Hall.

Conger, J. A., & Kanungo, R. N. (1988). The empowerment process: Integrating theory and practice. *Academy of Management Review, 13*, 471–482.

Cordes, C. (1983). Human factors and nuclear safety: Grudging respect for a growing field. *APA Monitor, 14*, 1, 13–14.

Cotton, J. L., & Tuttle, J. M. (1986). Employee turnover: A meta-analysis and review with implications for research. *Academy of Management Review, 11*, 55–70.

Crawford, J. (1981). *Crawford Small Parts Dexterity Test*. San Antonio, TX: The Psychological Corporation.

Cummings, L. L., & Schwab, D. P. (1978). Designing appraisal systems for information yield. *California Management Review, 20*, 18–25.

Cummings, N. A., & Follette, W. T. (1976). Brief psychotherapy and medical utilization: An eight-year follow-up. In H. Dorken (Ed.), *The professional psychologist today: New developments in law, health, insurance, and health practice*. San Francisco: Jossey-Bass.

Dainoff, M. J., Happ, A., & Crane, P. (1981). Visual fatigue and occupational stress in VDT operators. *Human Factors, 23*, 421–438.

Dalton, D. R., Krackhardt, D. M., & Porter, L. W. (1981). Functional turnover: An empirical assessment. *Journal of Applied Psychology, 66*, 716–721.

Dansereau, F., Graen, G., & Haga, B. (1975). A vertical dyad linkage approach to leadership within formal organizations: A longitudinal investigation of the role making process. *Organizational Behavior and Human Performance, 13*, 46–78.

Davis, K. (1968). Success of chain-of-command oral communication in a manufacturing management group. *Academy of Management Journal, 11*, 379–387.

Davis, K. (1972). *Human behavior at work*. New York: McGraw-Hill.

Davis, L. E., & Cherns, A. B. (Eds.). (1975).

The quality of working life (Vols. 1 and 2). New York: Free Press.

Davis, T. R. V., & Luthans, F. (1980). A social learning approach to organizational behavior. *Academy of Management Review, 5,* 281–290.

Decker, P. J. (1982). The enhancement of behavior modeling training of supervisory skills by the inclusion of retention processes. *Personnel Psychology, 35,* 323–332.

Decker, P. J., & Cornelius, E. T. (1979). A note on recruiting sources and job survival rates. *Journal of Applied Psychology, 64,* 463–464.

Decker, P. J., & Nathan, B. R. (1985). *Behavior modeling training: Principles and applications.* New York: Praeger.

DePaulo, B. M., Stone, J. I., & Lassiter, G. D. (1985). Deceiving and detecting deceit. In B. R. Schlenker (Ed.), *The self and social life* (pp. 323–370). New York: McGraw-Hill.

Diehl, M., & Stroebe, W. (1987). Productivity loss in brainstorming groups: Toward the solution of a riddle. *Journal of Personality and Social Psychology, 53,* 497–509.

Dienesch, R. M., & Liden, R. C. (1986). Leader-member exchange model of leadership: A critique and further development. *Academy of Management Review, 11,* 618–634.

Dipboye, R. L. (1982). Self-fulfilling prophecies in the selection-recruitment interview. *Academy of Management Review, 7,* 579–587.

Dipboye, R. L. (1985). Some neglected variables in research on discrimination in appraisals. *Academy of Management Review, 10,* 116–127.

Dipboye, R. L., Fontenelle, G. A., & Garner, K. (1984). Effects of previewing the application on interview process and outcomes. *Journal of Applied Psychology, 69,* 118–128.

Dobbins, G. H., & Platz, S. J. (1986). Sex differences in leadership: How real are they? *Academy of Management Review, 11,* 118–127.

Doppelt, J. E., Hartman, A. D., & Krawchick, F. B. (1986). *Typing Test for Business.* San Antonio, TX: The Psychological Corporation.

Downey, H. K., Sheridan, J. E., & Slocum, J. W. (1976). The path-goal theory of leadership: A longitudinal analysis. *Organizational Behavior and Human Performance, 16,* 156–176.

Drucker, P. F. (1954). *The practice of management.* New York: Harper & Row.

Duchon, D., Green, S. G., & Taber, T. D. (1986). Vertical dyad linkage: A longitudinal assessment of antecedents, measures, and consequences. *Journal of Applied Psychology, 71,* 56–60.

Dunham, R. B., Pierce, J. L., & Castaneda, M. B. (1987). Alternative work schedules: Two field quasi-experiments. *Personnel Psychology, 40,* 215–242.

Dunnette, M. D., Campbell, J. P., & Hakel, M. D. (1967). Factors contributing to job satisfaction and dissatisfaction in six occupational groups. *Organizational Behavior and Human Performance, 2,* 143–174.

Dvorak, A., Marrick, N., Dealey, W., & Ford, G. (1936). *Typewriting behavior: Psychology applied to teaching and learning typewriter.* New York: American Book.

Eastman Kodak Company. (1983). *Ergonomic design for people at work* (Vol. 1.). Belmont, CA: Lifetime Learning Publications.

Eisenberg, E. M., & Witten, M. G. (1987). Reconsidering openness in organizational communication. *Academy of Management Review, 12,* 418–426.

Enander, A. (1984). Performance and sensory aspects of work in cold environments: A review. *Ergonomics, 27,* 365–378.

Enander, A. (1987). Effects of moderate cold on performance of psychomotor and cognitive tasks. *Ergonomics, 30,* 1431–1445.

Environmental Protection Agency. (1974). *Information on levels of environmental noise requisite to protect public health and wel-*

fare with an adequate margin of safety (Tech. Rep.). Washington, DC: Author.

Equal Employment Opportunity Commission. (1974). *Uniform guidelines on employee selection procedures*. Washington, DC: U.S. Government Printing Office.

Equal Employment Opportunity Commission. (1978). *Uniform guidelines on employee testing procedures*. Washington, DC: U.S. Government Printing Office.

Erez, M., & Arad, R. (1986). Participative goal-setting: Social, motivational, and cognitive factors. *Journal of Applied Psychology, 71,* 591–597.

Erez, M., & Zidon, I. (1984). Effect of goal acceptance on the relationship of goal difficulty to performance. *Journal of Applied Psychology, 69,* 69–78.

Evans, G. W., & Jacobs, S. V. (1981). Air pollution and human behavior. *Journal of Social Issues, 37,* 95–125.

Fanger, P. O. (1970). *Thermal comfort, analysis, and applications in environmental engineering*. Copenhagen: Danish Technical Press.

Farrell, D., & Petersen, J. C. (1982). Patterns of political behavior in organizations. *Academy of Management Review, 7,* 403–412.

Feild, H. S., & Holley, W. H. (1982). The relationship of performance appraisal system characteristics to verdicts in selected employment discrimination cases. *Academy of Management Journal, 25,* 392–406.

Feldman, D. C. (1976a). A contingency theory of socialization. *Administrative Science Quarterly, 21,* 433–454.

Feldman, D. C. (1976b). A practical program for employee socialization. *Organizational Dynamics, 57,* 64–80.

Feldman, D. C. (1981). The multiple socialization of organization members. *Academy of Management Review, 6,* 309–318.

Feldman, D. C. (1984). The development and enforcement of group norms. *Academy of Management Review, 9,* 47–54.

Feldman, J. M. (1981). Beyond attribution theory: Cognitive processes in performance appraisal. *Journal of Applied Psychology, 66,* 127–148.

Ferris, G. R., Yates, V. L., Gilmore, D. C., & Rowland, K. M. (1985). The influence of subordinate age on performance ratings and causal attributions. *Personnel Psychology, 38,* 545–557.

Fiedler, F. E. (1965). Engineer the job to fit the manager. *Harvard Business Review, 43,* 115.

Fiedler, F. E. (1967). *A theory of leadership effectiveness*. New York: McGraw-Hill.

Fiedler, F. E. (1973). How do you make leaders more effective? New answers to an old puzzle. *Organizational Dynamics, 54,* 3–18.

Fiedler, F. E., & Chemers, M. M. (1984). *Improving leadership effectiveness: The Leader Match concept* (rev. ed.). New York: John Wiley & Sons.

Field, R. H. G. (1982). A test of the Vroom-Yetton normative model of leadership. *Journal of Applied Psychology, 67,* 523–532.

Fine, S. A., & Wiley, W. W. (1971). *An introduction to functional job analysis*. Kalamazoo, MI: W. E. Upjohn Institute.

Flanagan, J. C. (1954). The critical incidents technique. *Psychological Bulletin, 51,* 327–358.

Fleishman, E. A. (1960). *Leader opinion questionnaire*. Chicago: Science Research Associates.

Fleishman, E. A., & Harris, E. F. (1962). Patterns of leadership behavior related to employee grievances and turnover. *Personnel Psychology, 15,* 43–56.

Fodor, E. M. (1976). Group stress, authoritarian style of control, and use of power. *Journal of Applied Psychology, 61,* 313–318.

Forbes, R. J., & Jackson, P. R. (1980). Nonverbal behaviour and the outcome of selection interviews. *Journal of Occupational Psychology, 53,* 65–72.

Ford, J. K., & Noe, R. A. (1987). Self-assessed training needs: The effects of attitudes toward training, managerial level, and function. *Personnel Psychology, 40,* 39–53.

Forsyth, D. R. (1983). *An introduction to group dynamics.* Monterey, CA: Brooks/Cole.

Forsythe, S., Drake, M. F., & Cox, C. E. (1985). Influence of applicant's dress on interviewer's selection decisions. *Journal of Applied Psychology, 70,* 374–378.

Franke, R. H., & Kaul, J. D. (1978). The Hawthorne experiments: First statistical interpretation. *American Sociological Review, 43,* 623–643.

Frease, M., & Zawacki, R. A. (1983). Job-sharing: An answer to productivity problems? In K. M. Rowland, G. R. Ferris, & J. L. Sherman (Eds.), *Current issues in personnel management* (2nd ed.) (pp. 296–300). Boston: Allyn & Bacon.

Fredericksen, N. (1962). Factors in in-basket performance. *Psychological Monographs, 76* [Entire issue no. 541].

French, J. L., & Rosenstein, J. (1984). Employee ownership, work attitudes, and power relationships. *Academy of Management Journal, 27,* 861–869.

French, J. R. P., & Caplan, R. D. (1972). Organizational stress and individual strain. In A. J. Marrow (Ed.), *The failure of success* (pp. 30–66). New York: AMACOM.

French, J. R. P., & Raven, B. H. (1959). The bases of social power. In D. Cartwright (Ed.), *Studies in social power* (pp. 150–167). Ann Arbor: University of Michigan Press.

French, W. L. (1969). Organization development objectives, assumptions, and strategies. *California Management Review, 12,* 23–46.

French, W. L., & Bell, C. H. (1978). *Organization development: Behavioral science interventions for organization improvement* (2nd ed.). Englewood Cliffs, NJ: Prentice-Hall.

Fried, Y., & Ferris, G. R. (1987). The validity of the job characteristics model: A review and meta-analysis. *Personnel Psychology, 40,* 287–322.

Friedlander, F. (1980). The facilitation of change in organizations. *Professional Psychology, 11,* 520–530.

Friedman, H. S., & Booth-Kewley, S. (1987). The "disease-prone personality": A meta-analytic view of the construct. *American Psychologist, 42,* 539–555.

Friedman, M., & Rosenman, R. H. (1974). *Type A behavior and your heart.* New York: Alfred A. Knopf.

Frohman, M. A., Sashkin, M., & Kavanagh, M. J. (1976). Action-research as applied to organization development. *Organization and Administrative Sciences, 7,* 129–142.

Fry, W., & Slocum, J. W. (1984). Technology, structure, and workgroup effectiveness: A test of a contingency model. *Academy of Management Journal, 27,* 221–246.

Gaines, J., & Jermier, J. M. (1983). Emotional exhaustion in a high stress organization. *Academy of Management Journal, 26,* 567–586.

Gaines, J. H. (1980). Upward communication in industry: An experiment. *Human Relations, 33,* 929–942.

Galbraith, J. (1973). *Designing complex organizations.* Reading, MA: Addison-Wesley.

Galbraith, J. (1977). *Organization design.* Reading, MA: Addison-Wesley.

Gandz, J., & Murray, U. V. (1980). The experience of workplace politics. *Academy of Management Journal, 23,* 237–251.

Ganster, D. C., Mayes, B. T., Sime, W. E., & Tharp, G. D. (1982). Managing organizational stress: A field experiment. *Journal of Applied Psychology, 67,* 533–542.

Garland, H. (1984). Relation of effort-performance expectancy to performance in goal-setting experiments. *Journal of Applied Psychology, 69,* 79–84.

Gherman, E. M. (1981). *Stress and the bottom line: A guide to personal well-being and corporate health.* New York: AMACOM.

Ghiselli, E. E. (1973). The validity of aptitude tests in personnel selection. *Personnel Psychology, 26,* 461–477.

Ghorpade, J. V. (1988). *Job analysis: A handbook for the human resource director.* Englewood Cliffs, NJ: Prentice-Hall.

Gibb, J. R. (1961). Defensive communication. *Journal of Communication, 11,* 81–84.

Gilbreth, F. B. (1916). Motion study in surgery. *Canadian Journal of Medicine and Surgery, 1,* 1–10.

Gillet, B., & Schwab, D. P. (1975). Convergent and discriminant validities of corresponding Job Descriptive Index and Minnesota Satisfaction Questionnaire scales. *Journal of Applied Psychology, 60,* 313–317.

Gist, M. E. (1987). Self-efficacy: Implications for organizational behavior and human resource management. *Academy of Management Review, 12,* 472–485.

Goldman, R. B. (1976). *A work experiment: Six Americans in a Swedish plant.* New York: Ford Foundation.

Goldstein, I. L. (1986). *Training in organizations: Needs assessment, development, and evaluation* (2nd ed.). Monterey, CA: Brooks/Cole.

Goldstein, I. L., & Sorcher, M. A. (1974). *Changing supervisory behavior.* New York: Pergamon.

Golembiewski, R. T., Munzenrider, R. F., & Stevenson, J. G. (1986). *Stress in organizations: Toward a phase model of burnout.* New York: Praeger.

Gottfredson, L. S. (Ed.). The *g* factor in employment. *Journal of Vocational Behavior, 29,* 293–450.

Gough, H. G. (1984). A managerial potential scale for the *California Psychological Inventory. Journal of Applied Psychology, 69,* 233–240.

Gough, H. G. (1985). A work orientation scale for the *California Psychological Inventory. Journal of Applied Psychology, 70,* 505–513.

Gough, H. G. (1987). *California Psychological Inventory.* Palo Alto, CA: Consulting Psychologists Press.

Gouldner, A. W. (1960). The norm of reciprocity: A preliminary statement. *American Sociological Review, 25,* 161–178.

Graen, G. (1976). Role making processes within complex organizations. In M. D. Dunnette (Ed.), *Handbook of industrial and organizational psychology* (pp. 1201–1245). Chicago: Rand McNally.

Graen, G., Novak, M., & Sommerkamp, P. (1982). The effects of leader-member exchange and job design on productivity and satisfaction: Testing a dual attachment mode. *Organizational Behavior and Human Performance, 30,* 109–131.

Graen, G. B. (1969). Instrumentality theory of work motivation: Some experimental results and suggested modifications. *Journal of Applied Psychology Monograph, 53* (Vol. 2, Pt. 2).

Graen, G. B., Scandura, T. A., & Graen, M. R. (1986). A field experimental test of the moderating effects of growth need strength on productivity. *Journal of Applied Psychology, 71,* 484–491.

Gray, B., & Ariss, S. S. (1985). Politics and strategic change across organizational life cycles. *Academy of Management Review, 10,* 707–723.

Gray, J. L., & Starke, F. A. (1984). *Organizational behavior: Concepts and applications* (3rd ed.). Columbus, OH: Charles E. Merrill.

Greenberg, J. (1982). Approaching equity and avoiding inequity in groups and organizations. In J. Greenberg & R. L. Cohen (Eds.), *Equity and justice in social behavior.* New York: Academic Press.

Greenberg, J., & Ornstein, S. (1983). High status job title as compensation for underpayment: A test of equity theory. *Journal of Applied Psychology, 68,* 285–297.

Greenberger, D. B., & Strasser, S. (1986). Development and application of a model of personal control in organizations. *Academy of Management Review, 11,* 164–177.

Griggs v. Duke Power Co. (1971). 401 U.S. 424, 3EPD p8137, 3 FEP Cases 175.

Guion, R. M. (1965). *Personnel testing.* New York: McGraw-Hill.

Guion, R. M., & Gibson, W. M. (1988). Personnel selection and placement. *Annual Review of Psychology, 39,* 349–374.

Guion, R. M., & Gottier, R. J. (1965). Validity of personality measures in personnel selection. *Personnel Psychology, 18,* 135–164.

Gupta, N., & Beehr, T. A. (1979). Job stress and employee behaviors. *Organizational Behavior and Human Performance, 23,* 373–387.

Gutteridge, T. G. (1986). Organizational career development systems: The state of the practice. In D. T. Hall and Associates, *Career development in organizations* (pp. 50–94). San Francisco: Jossey-Bass.

Gyllenhammer, P. (1977). *People at work.* Reading, MA: Addison-Wesley.

Hackett, R. D., & Guion, R. M. (1985). A reevaluation of the absenteeism–job satisfaction relationship. *Organizational Behavior and Human Decision Processes, 35,* 340–381.

Hackman, J. R., & Oldham, G. R. (1975). Development of the Job Diagnostic Survey. *Journal of Applied Psychology, 60,* 159–170.

Hackman, J. R., & Oldham, G. R. (1976). Motivation through the design of work: Test of a theory. *Organizational Behavior and Human Performance, 16,* 250–279.

Hakstian, A. R., & Cattell, R. B. (1975–1982). *Comprehensive Ability Battery.* Champaign, IL: Institute for Personality and Ability Testing.

Hall, D. T., & Hall, F. S. (1976). What's new in career management? *Organizational Dynamics, 5,* 62–72.

Halpin, A. W., & Winer, B. J. (1957). A factorial study of the leader behavior descriptions. In R. M. Stogdill & A. E. Coons (Eds.), *Leader behavior: Its description and measurement.* Columbus: Ohio State University Bureau of Business Research.

Hammer, T. H., & Landau, J. C. (1981). Methodological issues in the use of absence data. *Journal of Applied Psychology, 66,* 574–581.

Hammer, T. H., Landau, J. C., & Stern, R. N. (1981). Absenteeism when workers have a voice: The case of employee ownership. *Journal of Applied Psychology, 66,* 561–573.

Hamner, W. C., & Hamner, E. P. (1976). Behavior modification on the bottom line. *Organizational dynamics, 4,* 8–21.

Hanson, T. J., & Balestreri-Spero, J. C. (1985). An alternative to interviews. *Personnel Journal, 64,* 114–123.

Hare, A. P. (1976). *Handbook of small group research* (2nd ed.). New York: Free Press.

Harrison, T. M. (1985). Communication and participative decision making: An exploratory study. *Personnel Psychology, 38,* 93–116.

Hartsough, D. M., & Savitsky, J. C. (1984). Three Mile Island: Psychology and environmental policy at a crossroads. *American Psychologist, 39,* 1113–1122.

Hathaway, S. R., & McKinley, J. C. (1970). *MMPI: Minnesota Multiphasic Personality Inventory.* Minneapolis: University of Minnesota Press.

Hatvany, N., & Pucik, V. (1981). An integrated management system: Lessons from the Japanese experience. *Academy of Management Review, 6,* 469–480.

Haynes, R. S., Pine, R. C., & Fitch, H. G. (1982). Reducing accident rates with organizational behavior modification. *Academy of Management Journal, 25,* 407–416.

Heilman, M. E., & Saruwatari, L. R. (1979). When beauty is beastly: The effects of appearance and sex on evaluations of job applicants for managerial and nonmanagerial jobs. *Organizational Behavior and Human Performance, 23,* 360–372.

Heneman, H. G. (1975). The impact of interviewer training and interview structure on the reliability and validity of the selection interview. *Proceedings of the Academy of Management, 231–233.*

Heneman, R. L., & Wexley, K. N. (1983). The effects of time delay in rating and amount of information observed in performance rating accuracy. *Academy of Management Journal, 26,* 677–686.

Henley, N. M. (1977). *Body politics: Power, sex, and nonverbal communication.* Englewood Cliffs, NJ: Prentice-Hall.

Herrick, N. Q., & Maccoby, M. (1975). Humanizing work: A priority goal of the 1970's. In L. E. Davis & A. B. Cherns (Eds.), *The quality of working life* (Vol. 1, pp. 63–77). New York: Free Press.

Hersey, R. (1966). Grapevine—Here to stay but not beyond control. *Personnel, 43,* 62–66.

Herzberg, F. (1966). *Work and the nature of man.* Cleveland, OH: World.

Herzberg, F., Mausner, B., & Snyderman, B. B. (1959). *The motivation to work.* New York: John Wiley & Sons.

Hicks, W. D., & Klimoski, R. J. (1981). The impact of flexitime on employee attitudes. *Academy of Management Journal, 24,* 333–341.

Hickson, D. J., Hinings, C. R., Less, C. A., Schneck, R. E., & Pennings, J. M. (1971). A strategic contingencies theory of intraorganizational power. *Administrative Science Quarterly, 16,* 216–229.

Hill, G. W. (1982). Group versus individual performance: Are N + 1 heads better than one? *Psychological Bulletin, 89,* 517–539.

Hogan, R., & Hogan, J. (1985). *Hogan Personnel Selection Series.* Minneapolis: National Computer Systems.

Hollander, E. P. (1978). *Leadership dynamics: A practical guide to effective relationships.* New York: Free Press.

Hollander, E. P. (1985). Leadership and power. In G. Lindzey & E. Aronson (Eds.), *The handbook of social psychology* (3rd ed.) (pp. 485–538). New York: Random House.

Hollenbeck, J. R., & Williams, C. R. (1986). Turnover functionality versus turnover frequency: A note on work attitudes and organizational effectiveness. *Journal of Applied Psychology, 71,* 606–611.

Holmes, T. H., & Rahe, R. H. (1967). The Social Readjustment Rating Scale. *Journal of Psychosomatic Research, 11,* 213–218.

House, R. J. (1971). A path-goal theory of leader effectiveness. *Administrative Science Quarterly, 1,* 321–338.

House, R. J., & Dessler, G. (1974). The path-goal theory of leadership: Some post hoc and a priori tests. In J. G. Hunt & L. L. Larsen (Eds.), *Contingency approaches to leadership* (pp. 29–55). Carbondale: Southern Illinois University Press.

House, R. J., & Mitchell, T. (1974). Path-goal theory of leadership. *Journal of Contemporary Business, 3,* 81–98.

Howard, G. S., & Dailey, P. R. (1979). Response-shift bias: A source of contamination of self-report measures. *Journal of Applied Psychology, 64,* 144–150.

Hunt, G. T. (1980). *Communicaton skills in the organization.* Englewood Cliffs, NJ: Prentice-Hall.

Hunter, J. E., & Hunter, R. F. (1983). Validity and utility of alternative predictors of job performance. *Psychological Bulletin, 96,* 72–98.

Hunter, J. E., & Schmidt, F. L. (1982). Fitting people to jobs: The impact of personnel selection on national productivity. In M. D. Dunnette & E. A. Fleishman (Eds.), *Human performance and productivity: Human capability assessment* (pp. 233–284). Hillsdale, NJ: Lawrence Erlbaum.

Huseman, R. C., Hatfield, J. D., & Miles, E. W. (1987). A new perspective on equity theory: The equity sensitivity construct. *Academy of Management Review, 12,* 222–234.

Iaffaldano, M. T., & Muchinsky, P. M. (1985). Job satisfaction and job performance: A meta-analysis. *Psychological Bulletin, 97,* 251–273.

Ilgen, D. R., Fisher, C. D., & Taylor, M. S. (1979). Consequences of individual feedback on behavior in organizations. *Journal of Applied Psychology, 64,* 349–371.

Ilgen, D. R., & Hollenback, J. H. (1977). The role of job satisfaction in absence behavior. *Organizational Behavior and Human Performance, 19,* 148–161.

Illuminating Engineering Society. (1977). *IES code for interior lighting.* London: Author.

Imada, A. S., & Hakel, M. D. (1977). Influence of nonverbal communication and rater proximity on impressions and decisions in simulated employment interviews. *Journal of Applied Psychology, 62,* 295–300.

Ivancevich, J. M. (1979). Longitudinal study of the effects of rater training on psychometric error in ratings. *Journal of Applied Psychology, 64,* 502–508.

Ivancevich, J. M. (1982). Subordinates' reactions to performance appraisal interviews: A test of feedback and goal-setting techniques. *Journal of Applied Psychology 67,* 581–587.

Ivancevich, J. M., & Lyon, H. L. (1977). The shortened workweek: A field experiment. *Journal of Applied Psychology, 62,* 34–37.

Jackson, S. E. (1983). Participation in decision making as a strategy for reducing job-related strain. *Journal of Applied Psychology, 68,* 3–19.

Jackson, S. E., Schwab, R. L., & Schuler, R. S. (1986). Toward an understanding of the burnout phenomenon. *Journal of Applied Psychology, 71,* 630–640.

Jacobs, R. R. (1986). Numerical rating scales. In R. A. Berk (Ed.), *Performance assessment: Methods and applications* (pp. 82–99). Baltimore: The Johns Hopkins University Press.

Jago, A. G., & Ragan, J. W. (1986). The trouble with Leader Match is that it doesn't match Fiedler's contingency model. *Journal of Applied Psychology, 71,* 555–559.

Janis, I. L. (1972). *Victims of groupthink: A psychological study of foreign-policy decisions and fiascoes.* Boston: Houghton Mifflin.

Janis, I. L., & Mann, L. (1977). *Decision making: A psychological analysis of conflict, choice, and commitment.* New York: Free Press.

Jette, M. (1984). Stress coping through physical activity. In A. S. Sethi & R. S. Schuler (Eds.), *Handbook of organizational stress coping strategies* (pp. 215–231). Cambridge, MA: Ballinger.

Jochim, T. C. (1979). Employee stock ownership programs: The next economic revolution? *Academy of Management Review, 4,* 439–442.

Jones, E. E., & Nisbett, R. E. (1972). The actor and the observer: Divergent perceptions of the causes of behavior. In E. E. Jones, D. E. Kanouse, H. H. Kelley, R. E. Nisbett, S. Valins, & B. Weiner (Eds.), *Attribution: Perceiving the causes of behavior* (pp. 79–94). Morristown, NJ: General Learning Press.

Judd, K., & Gomez-Mejia, L. R. (1987). Comparable worth: A sensible way to end pay discrimination or the "looniest idea since looney tunes." In D. B. Balkin & L. R. Gomez-Mejia (Eds.), *New perspectives on compensation* (pp. 61–79). Englewood Cliffs, NJ: Prentice-Hall.

Kabanoff, B. (1981). A critique of Leader Match and its implications for leadership research. *Personnel Psychology, 34,* 749–764.

Kahn, R., & Katz, D. (1960). Leadership practices in relation to productivity and morale. In D. Cartwright & A. Zander (Eds.), *Group dynamics: Research and theory,* (2nd ed.). Elmsford, NY: Row, Peterson, & Co.

Kaplan, A. (1964). *The conduct of inquiry.* New York: Harper & Row.

Katz, D., & Kahn, R. L. (1966). *The social psychology of organizations.* New York: John Wiley & Sons.

Katz, D., & Kahn, R. L. (1978). *The social psychology of organizations* (2nd ed.). New York: John Wiley & Sons.

Kaufman, J., & Christensen, J. (Eds.). (1984). *IES lighting handbook* (reference vol.). New York: Illuminating Engineering Society of North America.

Kennedy, J. K. (1982). Middle LPC leaders and the contingency model of leadership effectiveness. *Organizational Behavior and Human Performance, 30,* 1–14.

Kenny, D. A., & Zaccaro, S. J. (1983). An estimate of variance due to traits in leadership. *Journal of Applied Psychology, 68,* 678–685.

Kerr, S., & Jermier, J. M. (1978). Substitutes for leadership: Their meaning and measurement. *Organizational Behavior and Human Performance, 22,* 375–403.

Kerr, S., & Schriesheim, S. (1974). Consideration, initiating structure, and organizational criteria: An update of Korman's 1966 review. *Personnel Psychology, 27,* 555–568.

Kim, J. S., & Campagna, A. T. (1981). Effects of flexitime on employee attendance and performance: A field experiment. *Academy of Management Journal, 24,* 729–741.

Kipnis, D. (1976). *The powerholders.* Chicago: The University of Chicago Press.

Kipnis, D., Schmidt, S. M., & Wilkinson, I. (1980). Intraorganizational influence tactics: Explorations in getting one's way. *Journal of Applied Psychology, 65,* 440–452.

Kirk, R. J. (1981). *Interim report to the President and Congress: Alternative work schedules experimental program.* Washington, DC: Office of Personnel Management.

Kirkpatrick, D. (1976). Evaluating in-house training programs. *Training and Development Journal, 32,* 6–9.

Kirkpatrick, D. L. (1959–60). Techniques for evaluating training programs. *Journal of the American Society of Training Directors, 13,* 3–9, 21–26; *14,* 13–18, 28–32.

Klein, K. J. (1987). Employee stock ownership and employee attitudes: A test of three models. *Journal of Applied Psychology, 72,* 319–332.

Klimoski, R. J., & Strickland, W. J. (1977). Assessment centers—Valid or merely prescient? *Personnel Psychology, 30,* 353–361.

Knight, G. P., & Dubro, A. F. (1984). Cooperative, competitive, and individualistic social values: An individualized regression and clustering approach. *Journal of Personality and Social Psychology, 46,* 98–105.

Knowlton, W. A., & Mitchell, T. R. (1980). Effects of causal attributions on a supervisor's evaluation of subordinate performance. *Journal of Applied Psychology, 65,* 459–466.

Kobasa, S. C. (1982). The hardy personality: Toward a social psychology of stress and health. In J. Suls & G. Sanders (Eds.), *The social psychology of health and illness* (pp. 3–32). Hillsdale, NJ: Erlbaum.

Kobasa, S. C., & Puccetti, M. C. (1983). Personality and social resources in stress resistance. *Journal of Personality and Social Psychology, 45,* 839–850.

Kobrick, J. L., & Fine, B. J. (1983). Climate and human performance. In D. J. Oborne & M. M. Gruneberg (Eds.), *The physical environment at work* (pp. 69–107). Chichester, England: John Wiley & Sons.

Koehler, J. W., Anatol, K. W. E., & Applbaum, R. L. (1981). *Organizational communication: Behavioral perspectives* (2nd ed.). New York: Holt, Rinehart and Winston.

Kolodny, H. F. (1979). Evolution to a matrix organization. *Academy of Management Review, 4,* 543–553.

Komaki, J., Barwick, K. D., & Scott, L. R. (1978). A behavioral approach to occupational safety: Pinpointing and reinforcing safe performance in a food manufacturing plant. *Journal of Applied Psychology, 63,* 434–445.

Kondrasuk, J. N. (1981). Studies in MBO effectiveness. *Academy of Management Review, 6,* 419–430.

Krackhardt, D., & Porter, L. W. (1986). The snowball effect: Turnover embedded in communication networks. *Journal of Applied Psychology, 71,* 50–55.

Kraiger, K., & Ford, J. K. (1985). A meta-analysis of ratee race effects in performance ratings. *Journal of Applied Psychology, 70,* 56–65.

Kram, K. E. (1983). Phases of the mentor relationship. *Academy of Management Journal, 26,* 608–625.

Krau, E. (1981). Turnover analysis and prediction from a career developmental point of view. *Personnel psychology, 34,* 771–790.

Kraut, R. E. (1980). Humans as lie detectors: Some second thoughts. *Journal of Communication, 30,* 209–216.

Kroemer, K. H. E. (1983). Engineering anthropometry: Work space and equipment to fit the user. In D. J. Oborne & M. M. Gruneberg (Eds.), *The physical environment at work* (pp. 39–68). Chichester, England: John Wiley & Sons.

Landy, F. J. (1985). *Psychology of work behavior* (3rd ed.). Homewood, IL: Dorsey Press.

Landy, F. J. (1989). *Psychology of work behavior* (4th ed.). Pacific Grove, CA: Brooks/Cole.

Landy, F. J., & Farr, J. L. (1983). *The measurement of work performance: Methods, theory, and applications.* New York: Academic Press.

Landy, F. J., & Sigall, H. (1974). Beauty is talent: Task evaluation as a function of the performer's physical attractiveness. *Journal of Personality and Social Psychology, 29,* 299–304.

Larwood, L., & Wood, M. M. (1977). *Women in management.* Lexington, MA: Lexington Books.

Latack, J. C., & Foster, L. W. (1985). Implementation of compressed work schedules: Participation and job redesign as critical factors for employee acceptance. *Personnel Psychology, 38,* 75–92.

Latane, B., & Darley, J. (1970). *The unresponsive bystander: Why doesn't he help?* New York: Appleton-Century-Crofts.

Latham, G. P. (1988). Human resource training and development. *Annual Review of Psychology, 39,* 545–582.

Latham, G. P., & Saari, L. M. (1979). Application of social-learning theory to training supervisors through behavioral modeling. *Journal of Applied Psychology, 64,* 239–246.

Latham, G. P., & Saari, L. M. (1984). Do people do what they say? Further studies on the situational interview. *Journal of Applied Psychology, 69,* 569–573.

Latham, G. P., Saari, L. M., Pursell, E. D., & Campion, M. A. (1980). The situational interview. *Journal of Applied Psychology, 65,* 422–427.

Latham, G. P., & Wexley, K. N. (1977). Behavioral observation scales for performance appraisal purposes. *Personnel Psychology, 30,* 225–268.

Lawler, E. E. (1982). Strategies for improving the quality of work life. *American Psychologist, 37,* 486–493.

Lawler, E. E. (1986). *High-involvement management: Participative strategies for improving organizational performance.* San Francisco: Jossey-Bass.

Lawler, E. E. (1987). Paying for performance: Future directions. In D. B. Balkin & L. R. Gomez-Mejia (Eds.), *New perspectives on compensation* (pp. 162–168). Englewood Cliffs, NJ: Prentice-Hall.

Lawrence, D. G., Salsburg, B. L., Dawson, J. G., & Fasman, Z. D. (1982). Design and use of weighted application blanks. *Personnel Administrator, 27,* 47–53.

Lawrence, P. R., & Lorsch, J. (1967). *Organization and environment.* Cambridge: Harvard University Press.

Leavitt, H. J. (1951). Some effects of certain communication patterns on group performance. *Journal of Abnormal and Social Psychology, 46,* 38–50.

Leibowitz, Z. B., Farren, C., & Kaye, B. L. (1986). *Designing career development systems*. San Francisco: Jossey-Bass.

Leister, A., Borden, D., & Fiedler, F. E. (1977). Validation of contingency model leadership training: Leader Match. *Academy of Management Journal, 20,* 464–470.

Leiter, M. P., & Maslach, C. (1988). The impact of interpersonal environment on burnout and organizational commitment. *Journal of Organizational Behavior, 9,* 297–308.

Levi, L., Frankenhaeuser, M., & Gardell, B. (1986). The characteristics of the workplace and the nature of its social demands. In S. G. Wolf & A. J. Finestone (Eds.), *Occupational stress: Health and performance at work* (pp. 54–67). Littleton, MA: PSG Publishing.

Levine, E. L., Ash, R. A., & Bennet, N. (1980). Exploratory comparative study of four job analysis methods. *Journal of Applied Psychology, 65,* 524–535.

Levine, E. L., Ash, R. A., Hall, H., & Sistrunk, F. (1983). Evaluation of job analysis methods by experienced job analysts. *Academy of Management Journal, 26,* 339–347.

Lewin, K. (1935). *Dynamic theory of personality*. New York: McGraw-Hill.

Lewis, P. V. (1987). *Organizational communication: The essence of effective management* (3rd ed.). New York: John Wiley & Sons.

Likert, R. (1961). *New patterns of management*. New York: McGraw-Hill.

Likert, R. (1967). *The human organization*. New York: McGraw-Hill.

Locke, E. A. (1968). Toward a theory of task motivation and incentives. *Organizational Behavior and Human Performance, 3,* 157–189.

Locke, E. A. (1976). The nature and causes of job satisfaction. In M. D. Dunnette (Ed.), *Handbook of industrial and organizational psychology* (pp. 1297–1350). Chicago: Rand-McNally.

Locke, E. A., & Latham, G. P. (1984). *Goal setting: A motivational technique that works*. Englewood Cliffs, NJ: Prentice-Hall.

Locke, E. A., & Schweiger, D. M. (1978). Participation in decision making: One more look. In B. M. Staw (Ed.), *Research in organizational behavior* (pp. 265–339). Greenwich, CT: JAI Press.

Locke, E. A., Shaw, K. N., Saari, L. M., & Latham, G. P. (1981). Goal-setting and task performance: 1969–1980. *Psychological Bulletin, 90,* 125–152.

Loeb, M. (1986). *Noise and human efficiency*. Chichester, England: John Wiley & Sons.

Loher, B. T., Noe, R. A., Moeller, N. L., & Fitzgerald, M. P. (1985). A meta-analysis of the relation of job characteristics to job satisfaction. *Journal of Applied Psychology, 70,* 280–289.

Lord, R. G., DeVader, C. L., & Alliger, G. M. (1986). A meta-analysis of the relation between personality traits and leadership perceptions: An application of validity generalization procedures. *Journal of Applied Psychology, 71,* 402–410.

Lounsbury, J. W., & Hoopes, L. L. (1986). A vacation from work: Changes in work and nonwork outcomes. *Journal of Applied Psychology, 71,* 392–401.

Lowry, S. M., Maynard, H. B., & Stegemerten, G. J. (Eds.). (1940). *Time and motion study and formulas for wage incentives* (3rd ed.). New York: McGraw-Hill.

Luthans, F., McCaul, H. S., & Dodd, N. G. (1985). Organizational commitment: A comparison of American, Japanese, and Korean employees. *Academy of Management Journal, 28,* 213–219.

Lynch, B. P. (1974). An empirical assessment of Perrow's technology construct. *Administrative Science Quarterly, 19,* 338–356.

Machlowitz, M. M. (1976, October 3). Working the 100-hour week—and loving it. *The New York Times.*

Mann, R. B., & Decker, P. J. (1984). The effect of key behavior distinctiveness on generalization and recall in behavior modeling training. *Academy of Management Journal, 27,* 900–909.

Manz, C. C. (1986). Self-leadership: Toward an expanded theory of self-influence processes in organizations. *Academy of Management Review, 11,* 585–600.

Manz, C. C., & Sims, H. P. (1980). Self-management as a substitute for leadership: A social learning perspective. *Academy of Management Review, 5,* 361–367.

Margerison, C., & Glube, R. (1979). Leadership decision-making: An empirical test of the Vroom and Yetton model. *Journal of Management Studies, 16,* 45–55.

Mark, L. S., Warm, J. S., & Huston, R. L. (1987). *Ergonomics and human factors: Recent research.* New York: Springer-Verlag.

Markham, S. E., Dansereau, F., & Alutto, J. A. (1982). Female vs. male absence rates: A temporal analysis. *Personnel Psychology, 35,* 371–382.

Marks, M. L. (1986). The question of quality circles. *Psychology Today, 20,* 36–46.

Marks, M. L., Mirvis, P. H., Hackett, E. J., & Grady, J. F. (1986). Employee participation in a quality circle program: Impact on quality of work life, productivity, and absenteeism. *Journal of Applied Psychology, 71,* 61–69.

Markus, H., & Zajonc, R. B. (1985). The cognitive perspective in social psychology. In G. Lindzey & E. Aronson (Eds.), *The handbook of social psychology* (3rd ed., pp. 137–230). New York: Random House.

Marlowe, H. A. (1986). Social intelligence: Evidence for multidimensionality and construct independence. *Journal of Educational Psychology, 78,* 52–58.

Martin, J. E., & Peterson, M. M. (1987). Two-tier wage structures: Implications for equity theory. *Academy of Management Journal, 30,* 297–315.

Martin, T. N., & Schermerhorn, J. R. (1983). Work and nonwork influences on health: A research agenda using inability to leave as a critical variable. *Academy of Management Review, 8,* 650–659.

Marx, R. D. (1982). Relapse prevention for managerial training: A model for maintenance of behavior change. *Academy of Management Review, 7,* 433–441.

Maslach, C. (1982). *Burnout: The cost of caring.* Englewood Cliffs, NJ: Prentice-Hall.

Maslow, A. H. (1965). *Eupsychian management.* Homewood, IL: Richard D. Irwin.

Maslow, A. H. (1970). *Motivation and personality* (2nd ed.). New York: Harper & Row.

Matsui, T., Kagawa, M., Nagamatsu, J., & Ohtsuka, Y. (1977). Validity of expectancy theory as a within-person behavioral choice model for sales activity. *Journal of Applied Psychology, 62,* 764–767.

Mathis, R. L., & Jackson, J. H. (1985). *Personnel: Contemporary perspectives and applications.* St. Paul, MN: West.

Matteson, M. T., & Ivancevich, J. M. (1982). *Managing job stress and health.* New York: Free Press.

Matteson, M. T., & Ivancevich, J. M. (1987). *Controlling work stress: Effective human resource and management strategies.* San Francisco: Jossey-Bass.

Mayes, B. T., & Allen, R. W. (1977). Toward a definition of organizational politics. *Academy of Management Review, 2,* 672–678.

Mayo, E. (1933). *The human problems of an industrial civilization.* Cambridge: Harvard University Press.

McClelland, D. C. (1961). *The achieving society.* New York: Van Nostrand.

McClelland, D. C. (1975). *Power: The inner experience.* New York: Irvington Press.

McClelland, D. C. (1980). Motive dispositions: The merits of operant and respondent measures. In L. Wheeler (Ed.), *Review of personality and social psychology* (Vol. 1, pp. 10–41). Beverly Hills: Sage Press.

McClelland, D. C., Atkinson, J. W., Clark, R. A., & Lowell, E. L. (1953). *The achievement motive*. New York: Appleton-Century-Crofts.

McClelland, D. C., & Boyatzis, R. E. (1982). Leadership motive pattern and long term success in management. *Journal of Applied Psychology, 67,* 737–743.

McClelland, D. C., & Burnham, D. H. (1976). Power is the great motivator. *Harvard Business Review, 54,* 100–111.

McClintock, C. G., Messick, D. M., Kuhlman, D. M., & Campos, F. T. (1973). Motivational bases of choice in three-choice decomposed games. *Journal of Experimental Social Psychology, 9,* 572–590.

McConkie, M. L. (1979). A clarification of the goal setting and appraisal processes in MBO. *Academy of Management Review, 4,* 29–40.

McCormick, E. J. (1979). *Job analysis: Methods and applications*. New York: AMACOM.

McCormick, E. J., Jeanneret, P. R., & Mecham, R. C. (1969). *Position analysis questionnaire*. West Lafayette, IN: Occupational Research Center, Purdue University.

McCormick, E. J., & Sanders, M. S. (1982). *Human factors in engineering and design* (5th ed.). New York: McGraw-Hill.

McEvoy, G. M., & Cascio, W. F. (1985). Strategies for reducing employee turnover: A meta-analysis. *Journal of Applied Psychology, 70,* 342–353.

McGregor, D. (1960). *The human side of enterprise*. New York: McGraw-Hill.

McIntyre, R. M., Smith, D. E., & Hassett, C. E. (1984). Accuracy of performance ratings as affected by rater training and perceived purpose of rating. *Journal of Applied Psychology, 69,* 147–156.

Mechanic, D. (1962). Sources of power of lower participants in complex organizations. *Administrative Science Quarterly, 7,* 349–364.

Meehl, P. (1954). *Clinical vs. statistical prediction*. Minneapolis: University of Minnesota Press.

Mehrabian, A. (1981). *Silent messages* (2nd ed.). Belmont, CA: Wadsworth.

Meyer, H. H., & Raich, M. S. (1983). An objective evaluation of a behavior modeling training program. *Personnel Psychology, 36,* 755–761.

Michael, P. L., & Bienvenue, G. R. (1983). Industrial noise and man. In D. J. Oborne & M. M. Gruneberg (Eds.), *The physical environment at work* (pp. 179–209). Chichester, England: John Wiley & Sons.

Milkovich, G. T., & Newman, J. M. (1987). *Compensation* (2nd ed.). Plano, TX: Business Publications.

Miner, F. C. (1984). Group versus individual decision making: An investigation of performance measures, decision strategies, and process losses/gains. *Organizational Behavior and Human Performance, 31,* 112–124.

Miner, J. B. (1983). The unpaved road from theory: Over the mountains to application. In R. H. Kilmann, K. W. Thomas, D. P. Slevin, R. Nath, & S. L. Jerrel (Eds.), *Producing useful knowledge for organizations* (pp. 37–68). New York: Praeger.

Miner, J. B. (1984). The unpaved road over the mountains: From theory to applications. *The Industrial-Organizational Psychologist, 21,* 9–20.

Mintzberg, H. (1973). *The nature of managerial work*. New York: Harper & Row.

Mintzberg, H. (1984). Power and organization life cycles. *Academy of Management Review, 9,* 207–224.

Mio, J. S., & Goishi, C. K. (in press). The employee assistance program: Raising productivity by lifting constraints. In

P. Whitney & R. B. Ochman (Eds.), *Psychology and productivity*. New York: Plenum Press.

Miron, D., & McClelland, D. C. (1979). The impact of achievement motivation training on small businesses. *California Management Review, 21,* 13–28.

Mirvis, P. H., & Berg, D. N. (1977). *Failures in organization development and change: Cases and essays for learning.* New York: John Wiley & Sons.

Missarian, A. K. (1982). *The corporate connection: Why executive women need mentors to help them reach the top.* Englewood Cliffs, NJ: Prentice-Hall.

Mitchell, T. R., & Kalb, L. S. (1982). Effects of job experience on supervisor attributions for a subordinate's poor performance. *Journal of Applied Psychology, 67,* 181–188.

Mobley, W. H. (1982). Some unanswered questions in turnover and withdrawal research. *Academy of Management Review, 7,* 111–116.

Mobley, W. H., Griffeth, R. W., Hand, H. H., & Meglino, B. M. (1979). Review and conceptual analysis of the employee turnover process. *Psychological Bulletin, 86,* 493–522.

Morehouse, W., & Subramaniam, M. A. (1986). *The Bhopal tragedy: What really happened and what it means for American workers and communities at risk.* New York: Council on International and Public Affairs.

Moriarty, S. E., & Scheiner, E. C. (1984). A study of close-set text type. *Journal of Applied Psychology, 69,* 700–702.

Morrisby, J. R. (1955). *Mechanical Ability Test.* London: Educational and Industrial Test Services.

Morrow, P. C., & McElroy, J. C. (1981). Interior office design and visitor response: A constructive replication. *Journal of Applied Psychology, 66,* 646–650.

Morse, N. C., & Reimer, E. (1956). The experimental change of a major organizational variable. *Journal of Abnormal and Social Psychology, 52,* 120–129.

Moscovici, S. (1985). Social influence and conformity. In G. Lindzey & E. Aronson (Eds.), *Handbook of social psychology* (3rd ed., pp. 347–412). New York: Random House.

Motowidlo, S. J., Packard, J. S., & Manning, M. R. (1986). Occupational stress: Its causes and consequences for job performance. *Journal of Applied Psychology, 71,* 618–629.

Mowday, R. T. (1979). Equity theory predictions of behavior in organizations. In R. M. Steers & L. W. Porter (Eds.), *Motivation and work behavior* (2nd ed.). New York: McGraw-Hill.

Mowday, R. T., Koberg, C. S., & McArthur, A. W. (1984). The psychology of the withdrawal process: A cross-validational test of Mobley's intermediate linkages model of turnover in two samples. *Academy of Management Journal, 27,* 79–94.

Mowday, R. T., Steers, R., & Porter, L. W. (1979). The measurement of organizational commitment. *Journal of Vocational Behavior, 14,* 224–247.

Muchinsky, P. M. (1977a). A comparison of within- and across-subjects analyses of the expectancy-valence model for predicting effort. *Academy of Management Journal, 20,* 154–158.

Muchinsky, P. M. (1977b). Organizational communication: Relationships to organizational climate and job satisfaction. *Academy of Management Journal, 20,* 592–607.

Muchinsky, P. M. (1979). The use of reference reports in personnel selection: A review and evaluation. *Journal of Occupational Psychology, 52,* 287–297.

Muchinsky, P. M. (1987). *Psychology applied to work* (2nd ed.). Chicago: Dorsey.

Munchus, G. (1983). Employer-employee based quality circles in Japan: Human resource policy implications for American firms. *Academy of Management Review, 8,* 255–261.

Munsterberg, H. (1913). *Psychology and industrial efficiency*. Boston, MA: Houghton Mifflin.

Myers, D. G., & Lamm, H. (1976). The group polarization phenomenon. *Psychological Bulletin, 83,* 602–627.

Naisbett, J. (1982). *Megatrends: Ten new directions transforming our lives*. New York: Warner.

Narayanan, V. K., & Nath, R. (1982). A field test of some attitudinal and behavioral consequences of flexitime. *Journal of Applied Psychology, 67,* 214–218.

Nathan, P. E. (1983). Failures in prevention: Why we can't prevent the devastating effect of alcoholism and drug abuse. *American Psychologist, 38,* 459–467.

Nemecek, J., & Grandjean, E. (1973). Results of an ergonomic investigation of large-space offices. *Human Factors, 15,* 111–124.

Newman, J. E., & Beehr, T. A. (1979). Personal and organizational strategies for handling job stress: A review of research and opinion. *Personnel Psychology, 32,* 1–43.

Nieva, V. F., & Gutek, B. A. (1981). *Women and work: A psychological perspective*. New York: Praeger.

Nisbett, R. D., & Wilson, T. D. (1977). The halo effect: Evidence for unconscious alteration of judgments. *Journal of Personality and Social Psychology, 35,* 250–256.

Noe, R. A. (1986). Trainees' attributes and attitudes: Neglected influences on training effectiveness. *Academy of Management Review, 11,* 736–749.

Noe, R. A. (1988). An investigation of the determinants of successful assigned mentoring relationships. *Personnel Psychology, 41,* 457–479.

Noe, R. A., & Schmitt, N. (1986). The influence of trainee attitudes on training effectiveness: Test of a model. *Personnel Psychology, 39,* 497–523.

Nossiter, V. (1979). A new approach toward resolving the line and staff dilemma. *Academy of Management Review, 4,* 103–106.

Oborne, D. J., & Gruneberg, M. M. (Eds.). (1983). *The physical environment at work*. Chichester, England: John Wiley & Sons.

O'Connor, F. (1977). *O'Connor Finger Dexterity Test*. Lafayette, IN: Lafayette Instruments.

Odiorne, G. (1963). The trouble with sensitivity training. *Training Directors Journal, 17,* 12–19.

Oldham, G. R., & Fried, Y. (1987). Employee reactions to workspace characteristics. *Journal of Applied Psychology, 72,* 75–80.

O'Reilly, C. A. (1978). The intentional distortion of information in organizational communication: A laboratory and field approach. *Human Relations, 31,* 173–193.

O'Reilly, C. A. (1980). Individuals and information overload in organizations: Is more necessarily better? *Academy of Management Journal, 23,* 684–696.

O'Reilly, C. A., & Roberts, K. H. (1976). Relationships among components of credibility and communication behaviors in work units. *Journal of Applied Psychology, 61,* 99–102.

Osborn, A. F. (1957). *Applied imagination*. New York: Charles Scribner's Sons.

Otis, A. S. (1929). *Self-Administering Test of Mental Ability*. Tarrytown-on-Hudson, NY: World.

Owen, G., & Arnold, B. (1958). *Purdue Blueprint Reading Test*. West Lafayette, IN: Purdue University.

Owens, W. A. (1976). Background data. In M. D. Dunnette (Ed.), *Handbook of industrial and organizational psychology* (pp. 609–644). Chicago: Rand-McNally.

Owens, W. A., & Schoenfeldt, L. F. (1979). Toward a classification of persons. *Journal of Applied Psychology, 65,* 569–607.

Parasuraman, S., & Alutto, J. A. (1984). Sources and outcomes of stress in organizational settings: Toward the development of a structural model. *Academy of Management Journal, 27,* 330–350.

Parsons, H. M. (1974). What happened at Hawthorne? *Science, 183,* 922–932.

Patterson, M. L. (1983). *Nonverbal behavior: A functional perspective*. New York: Springer-Verlag.

Pearce, J. L., Stevenson, W. B., & Perry, J. L. (1985). Managerial compensation based on organizational performance: A time series analysis of the effects of merit pay. *Academy of Management Journal, 28*, 261–278.

Pearlman, K., Schmidt, F. L., & Hunter, J. E. (1980). Validity generalization results for tests used to predict job proficiency and training success in clerical occupations. *Journal of Applied Psychology, 65*, 373–406.

Pelletier, K. A. (1984). *Healthy people in unhealthy places: Stress and fitness at work*. New York: Delacorte Press.

Perrow, C. (1970). *Organizational analysis: A sociological perspective*. Belmont, CA: Wadsworth.

Peter, L. J., & Hull, R. (1969). *The Peter principle*. New York: William Morrow.

Peters, L. H., Hartke, D. D., & Pohlmann, J. T. (1985). Fiedler's contingency theory of leadership: An application of the meta-analysis procedures of Schmidt and Hunter. *Psychological Bulletin, 97*, 274–285.

Petty, M. M., McGee, G. W., & Cavender, J. W. (1984). A meta-analysis of the relationships between individual job satisfaction and individual performance. *Academy of Management Review, 9*, 712–721.

Pfeffer, J. (1981). *Power in organizations*. Boston: Pitman.

Porras, J. I., & Berg, P. O. (1978). The impact of organization development. *Academy of Management Review, 3*, 249–266.

Port, O. (1988, September 26). Superchip plants: Where "clean" has a whole new meaning. *Business Week*.

Porter, L. W., Allen, R. W., & Angle, H. L. (1981). The politics of upward influence in organizations. In B. Staw (Ed.), *Research in organizational behavior* (pp. 109–149). Greenwich, CT: JAI Press.

Porter, L. W., & Lawler, E. E. (1968). *Managerial attitudes and performance*. Homewood, IL: Richard D. Irwin.

Porter, L. W., & Roberts, K. H. (1976). Communication in organizations. In M. D. Dunnette (Ed.), *Handbook of industrial and organizational psychology*. Skokie, IL: Rand-McNally.

Porter, L. W., & Steers, R. M. (1973). Organizational, work, and personal factors in employee turnover and absenteeism. *Psychological Bulletin, 80*, 151–176.

Porter, L. W., Steers, R. M., Mowday, R. T., & Boulian, P. V. (1974). Organizational commitment, job satisfaction, and turnover among psychiatric technicians. *Journal of Applied Psychology, 59*, 603–609.

Premack, S. L., & Wanous, J. P. (1985). A meta-analysis of realistic job preview experiments. *Journal of Applied Psychology, 70*, 706–719.

Pritchard, R. D., Hollenback, J., & DeLeo, P. J. (1980). The effects of continuous and partial schedules of reinforcement on effort, performance, and satisfaction. *Organizational Behavior and Human Performance, 25*, 336–353.

Pritchard, R. D., Leonard, D. W., Von Bergen, C. W., & Kirk, R. J. (1976). The effects of varying schedules of reinforcement on human task performance. *Organizational Behavior and Human Performance, 16*, 205–230.

Psychological Corporation. (1986). *Computer Competence Tests*. San Antonio, TX: The Psychological Corporation.

Pulakos, E. D. (1984). A comparison of rater training programs: Error training and accuracy training. *Journal of Applied Psychology, 69*, 581–588.

Pulakos, E. D. (1986). The development of training programs to increase accuracy with different rating tasks. *Organizational Behavior and Human Decision Processes, 38*, 76–91.

Rafaeli, A., & Klimoski, R. J. (1983). Predicting sales success through handwriting analysis: An evaluation of the effects of training and handwriting sample content. *Journal of Applied Psychology, 68,* 212–217.

Ralston, D. A., Anthony, W. P., & Gustafson, D. J. (1985). Employees may love flextime, but what does it do to an organization's productivity? *Journal of Applied Psychology, 70,* 272–279.

Rasmussen, J. (1986). *Information processing and human-machine interaction: An approach to cognitive engineering.* New York: North-Holland.

Rasmussen, K. G. (1984). Nonverbal behavior, verbal behavior, resume credentials, and selection interview outcomes. *Journal of Applied Psychology, 69,* 551–556.

Rauschenberger, J., Schmitt, N., & Hunter, J. E. (1980). A test of the need hierarchy concept by a Markov model of change in need strength. *Administrative Science Quarterly, 25,* 654–670.

Reber, R. A., & Wallin, J. A. (1984). The effects of training, goal setting, and knowledge of results on safe behavior: A component analysis. *Academy of Management Journal, 27,* 544–560.

Reichardt, T. (1986, January). Sociology on the space station: An interview with B. J. Bluth. *Space World,* pp. 8–10.

Reichers, A. E. (1987). An interactionist perspective on newcomer socialization rates. *Academy of Management Review, 12,* 278–287.

Reilly, R. R., & Chao, G. T. (1982). Validity and fairness of some alternative employee selection procedures. *Personnel Psychology, 35,* 1–62.

Rice, B. (1982). The Hawthorne defect: Persistence of a flawed theory. *Psychology Today, 16*(2), 70–74.

Rice, R. W. (1978). Construct validity of the least preferred co-worker (LPC) score. *Psychological Bulletin, 85,* 1199–1237.

Rice, R. W., Instone, D., & Adams, J. (1984). Leader sex, leader success, and leadership process: Two field studies. *Journal of Applied Psychology, 69,* 12–31.

Richman, L. S. (1987, June 8). Software catches the team spirit. *Fortune.*

Riggio, R. E. (1986). Assessment of basic social skills. *Journal of Personality and Social Psychology, 51,* 649–660.

Riggio, R. E., & Throckmorton, B. (1988). The relative effects of verbal and nonverbal behavior, appearance, and social skills on evaluations made in hiring interviews. *Journal of Applied Social Psychology, 18,* 331–348.

Risher, H. (1984). Job evaluation: Problems and prospects. *Personnel, 61,* 53–66.

Ritchie, R. J., & Moses, J. L. (1983). Assessment center correlates of women's advancement into middle management: A 7-year longitudinal analysis. *Journal of Applied Psychology, 68,* 227–231.

Robbins, S. P. (1974). *Managing organizational conflict: A nontraditional approach.* Englewood Cliffs, NJ: Prentice-Hall.

Robbins, S. P. (1979). *Organizational behavior: Concepts and controversies.* Englewood Cliffs, NJ: Prentice-Hall.

Roche, G. R. (1979). Much ado about mentors. *Harvard Business Review, 57,* 14–19.

Rock, M. L. (1984). *Handbook of wage and salary administration* (2nd ed.). New York: McGraw-Hill.

Roethlisberger, F. J., & Dickson, W. J. (1939). *Management and the worker.* Cambridge: Harvard University Press.

Ronen, S. (1981). Arrival and departure patterns of public sector employees before and after implementation of flexitime. *Personnel Psychology, 34,* 817–822.

Ronen, S., & Primps, S. B. (1981). The compressed work week as organizational change: Behavioral and attitudinal outcomes. *Academy of Management Review, 6,* 61–74.

Rosen, C., Klein, K. J., & Young, K. M. (1986). *Employee ownership in America: The equity solution.* Lexington, MA: Lexington Books.

Rosenman, R. H. (1978). The interview method of assessment of the coronary-prone behavior pattern. In T. M. Dembroski, S. M. Weiss, J. L. Shields, S. G. Haynes & M. Feinlib (Eds.), *Coronary-prone behavior* (pp. 55–69). New York: Springer-Verlag.

Rusbult, C. E., & Farrell, D. (1983). A longitudinal test of the investment model: The impact on job satisfaction, job commitment, and turnover on variations in rewards, costs, alternatives, and investments. *Journal of Applied Psychology, 68,* 429–438.

Russell, J. S. (1984). A review of fair employment cases in the field of training. *Personnel Psychology, 37,* 261–276.

Rynes, S. L., Heneman, H. G., & Schwab, D. P. (1980). Individual reactions to organizational recruiting: A review. *Personnel Psychology, 33,* 529–542.

Sackett, P. R., & Harris, M. M. (1984). Honesty testing for personnel selection: A review and critique. *Personnel Psychology, 37,* 221–245.

Sackett, P. R., Zedeck, S., & Fogli, L. (1988). Relations between measures of typical and maximum job performance. *Journal of Applied Psychology, 73,* 482–486.

Salancik, G. R., & Pfeffer, J. (1977). Who gets power and how they hold on to it: A strategic-contingency model of power. *Organizational Dynamics, 5,* 3–21.

Sallis, J. F., Johnson, C. C., Trevorrow, T. R., Hovell, M. F., & Kaplan, R. M. (1985). *Worksite stress management: Anything goes?* Paper presented at the meeting of the American Psychological Association, Los Angeles.

Sanders, M. S., & McCormick, E. J. (1987). *Human factors in engineering and design* (6th ed.). New York: McGraw-Hill.

Scandura, T. A., & Graen, G. B. (1984). Moderating effects of initial leader-member exchange status on the effects of a leadership intervention. *Journal of Applied Psychology, 69,* 428–436.

Scarpello, V., & Campbell, J. P. (1983). Job satisfaction: Are all the parts there? *Personnel Psychology, 36,* 577–600.

Schachter, S., & Burdick, H. (1955). A field experiment of rumor transmission and distortion. *Journal of Abnormal and Social Psychology, 50,* 363–371.

Schein, E. H. (1968). Organizational socialization and the profession of management. *Industrial Management Review, 34,* 171–176.

Schein, E. H. (1969). *Process consultation: Its role in organization development.* Reading, MA: Addison-Wesley.

Schein, V. E. (1977). Individual power and political behaviors in organizations: An inadequately explored reality. *Academy of Management Review, 2,* 64–72.

Schein, V. E., Mauner, E. H., & Novak, J. F. (1977). Impact of flexible working hours on productivity. *Journal of Applied Psychology, 62,* 46–56.

Schmidt, F. L. (1973). Implications of a measurement problem for expectancy theory research. *Organizational Behavior and Human Performance, 10,* 243–251.

Schmidt, F. L., & Hunter, J. L. (1977). Development of a general solution to the problem of validity generalization. *Journal of Applied Psychology, 62,* 529–540.

Schmidt, F. L., & Hunter, J. E. (1981). Employment testing: Old theories and new research findings. *American Psychologist, 36,* 1128–1137.

Schmidt, F. L., Hunter, J. E., McKenzie, R. C., & Muldrow, T. W. (1979). Impact of valid selection procedures on work-force productivity. *Journal of Applied Psychology, 64,* 609–626.

Schmidt, F. L., Hunter, J. E., Outerbridge, A. N., & Trattner, M. H. (1986). The economic impact of job selection methods on size, productivity, and payroll costs of the federal work force: An empirically based demonstration. *Personnel Psychology, 39,* 1–29.

Schmidt, S. M., & Kipnis, D. (1984). Managers' pursuit of individual and organizational goals. *Human Relations, 37,* 781–794.

Schmied, L. A., & Lawler, K. A. (1986). Hardiness, Type A behavior, and the stress-illness relation in working women. *Journal of Personality and Social Psychology, 51,* 1218–1223.

Schmitt, N. (1976). Social and situational determinants of interview decisions: Implications for the employment interview. *Personnel Psychology, 29,* 79–101.

Schmitt, N., Gooding, R. Z., Noe, R. A., & Kirsch, M. (1984). Meta-analyses of validity studies published between 1964 and 1982 and the investigation of study characteristics. *Personnel Psychology, 37,* 407–422.

Schnake, M. E. (1986). Vicarious punishment in a work setting. *Journal of Applied Psychology, 71,* 343–345.

Schneider, B. (1985). Organizational behavior. *Annual Review of Psychology, 36,* 573–611.

Schneider, D. J., Hastorf, A. H., & Ellsworth, P. C. (1979). *Person perception.* Reading, MA: Addison-Wesley.

Schneider, J., & Locke, E. A. (1971). A critique of Herzberg's incident classification system and a suggested revision. *Organizational Behavior and Human Performance, 6,* 441–457.

Schriesheim, C. A., Bannister, B. D., & Money, W. H. (1979). Psychometric properties of the LPC scale: An extension of Rice's review. *Academy of Management Review, 4,* 287–290.

Schriesheim, C. A., & Kerr, S. (1974). Psychometric properties of the Ohio State leadership scales. *Psychological Bulletin, 81,* 756–765.

Schriesheim, C. A., & Kerr, S. (1977). Theories and measures of leadership: A critical appraisal of current and future directions. In J. G. Hunt, & L. L. Larson (Eds.), *Leadership: The cutting edge* (pp. 9–45). Carbondale: Southern Illinois University Press.

Schriesheim, C. A., & Murphy, C. J. (1976). Relationship between leader behavior and subordinate satisfaction and performance: A test of some situational moderators. *Journal of Applied Psychology, 61,* 634–641.

Schwab, D. P., Olian-Gottlieb, J. D., & Heneman, H. G. (1979). Between-subjects expectancy theory research: A statistical review of studies predicting effort and performance. *Psychological Bulletin, 86,* 139–147.

Scott, K. D., & Taylor, G. S. (1985). An examination of conflicting findings on the relationship between job satisfaction and absenteeism: A meta-analysis. *Academy of Management Journal, 28,* 599–612.

Scott, W. D. (1908). *The psychology of advertising.* New York: Arno Press.

Scott, W. G., Mitchell, T. R., & Birnbaum, P. H. (1981). *Organizational theory: A structural and behavioral analysis.* Homewood, IL: Richard D. Irwin.

Selye, H. (1976). *The stress of life* (rev. ed.). New York: McGraw-Hill.

Sethi, A. S. (1984). Meditation for coping with organizational stress. In A. S. Sethi & R. S. Schuler (Eds.), *Handbook of organizational stress coping strategies* (pp. 145–165). Cambridge, MA: Ballinger.

Shaw, M. E. (1964). Communication networks. In L. Berkowitz (Ed.), *Advances in experimental social psychology* (Vol. 1). New York: Academic Press.

Shaw, M. E. (1978). Communication networks fourteen years later. In L. Berkowitz (Ed.), *Group processes.* New York: Academic Press.

Shaw, M. E. (1981). *Group dynamics: The psychology of small group behavior* (3rd ed.). New York: McGraw-Hill.

Sherif, M., Harvey, O. J., White, B. J., Hood, W. R., & Sherif, C. W. (1961). *Intergroup conflict and cooperation: The Robbers Cave experiment.* Norman, OK: Institute of Group Relations.

Sills, D. L., Wolf, C. P., & Shelanski, V. B. (Eds.). (1982). *Accident at Three Mile Island: The human dimensions.* Boulder, CO: Westview Press.

Silverman, S. B., & Wexley, K. N. (1984). Reaction of employees to performance appraisal interviews as a function of their participation in rating scale development. *Personnel Psychology, 37,* 703–710.

Sims, H. P., Szilagyi, A. D., & Keller, R. T. (1976). The measurement of job characteristics. *Academy of Management Journal, 19,* 195–212.

Sinclair, H. J. (1971). Digital versus conventional clocks—A review. *Applied Ergonomics, 2,* 178–181.

Smith, C. A., Organ, D. W., & Near, J. P. (1983). Organizational citizenship behavior: Its nature and antecedents. *Journal of Applied Psychology, 68,* 653–663.

Smith, P. C. (1976). Behavior, results, and organizational effectiveness: The problem of criteria. In M. D. Dunnette (Ed.), *Handbook of industrial and organizational psychology* (pp. 745–766). Skokie, IL: Rand-McNally.

Smith, P. C., & Kendall, L. M. (1963). Retranslation of expectations: An approach to the construction of unambiguous anchors for rating scales. *Journal of Applied Psychology, 47,* 149–155.

Smith, P. C., Kendall, L. M., & Hulin, C. L. (1969). *The measurement of satisfaction in work and retirement.* Chicago: Rand-McNally.

Smith, P. C., et al. (1987). The revised JDI: A facelift for an old friend. *The Industrial-Organizational Psychologist, 24*(4), 31–33.

Snyder, R. A., & Morris, J. H. (1984). Organizational communication and performance. *Journal of Applied Psychology, 69,* 461–465.

Solomon, R. L. (1949). An extension of control group design. *Psychological Bulletin, 46,* 137–150.

Spetell, C. M., & Liebert, R. M. (1986). Training for safety in automated person-machine systems. *American Psychologist, 41,* 545–550.

Spool, M. D. (1978). Training programs for observers of behavior: A review. *Personnel Psychology, 31,* 853–888.

Staw, B. M., & Ross, J. (1985). Stability in the midst of change: A dispositional approach to job attitudes. *Journal of Applied Psychology, 70,* 469–480.

Steers, R. M. (1977). Antecedents and outcomes of organizational commitment. *Administrative Science Quarterly, 22,* 46–56.

Steers, R. M., & Porter, L. W. (Eds.). (1983). *Motivation and work behavior* (3rd ed.). New York: McGraw-Hill.

Stein, B. A. (1983). *Quality of work life in action: Managing for effectiveness.* New York: American Management Associations.

Stogdill, R. M. (1948). Personal factors associated with leadership: A survey of the literature. *Journal of Psychology, 25,* 35–71.

Stogdill, R. M. (1963). *Manual for the leader behavior description questionnaire—Form XII.* Columbus: Ohio State University, Bureau of Business Research.

Stogdill, R. M., & Coons, A. E. (Eds.). (1957). *Leader behavior: Its description and measurement.* Columbus: Ohio State University Bureau of Business Research.

Strube, M. J., & Garcia, J. E. (1981). A meta-analytic investigation of Fiedler's contingency model of leader effectiveness. *Psychological Bulletin, 90,* 307–321.

Stumpf, S. A., & Dawley, P. K. (1981). Predicting voluntary and involuntary turnover using absenteeism and performance indices. *Academy of Management Journal, 24,* 148–163.

Stumpf, S. A., & Hartman, K. (1984). Individual exploration to organizational commitment or withdrawal. *Academy of Management Journal, 27,* 308–329.

Stumpf, S. A., & London, M. (1981). Management promotions: Individual and organizational factors influencing the decision process. *Academy of Management Review, 6,* 539–549.

Sundstrom, E. (1986). *Work places: The psychology of the physical environment in offices and factories*. Cambridge: Cambridge University Press.

Sundstrom, E., Burt, R. E., & Kamp, D. (1980). Privacy at work: Architectural correlates of job satisfaction and job performance. *Academy of Management Journal, 23,* 101–117.

Sutton, R. I., & Rafaeli, A. (1987). Characteristics of work stations as potential occupational stressors. *Academy of Management Journal, 30,* 260–276.

Swain, A., & Guttmann, H. (1983). *Handbook of human reliability analysis with emphasis on nuclear power plant applications.* Washington, DC: Nuclear Regulatory Commission.

Swaroff, P. G., Barclay, L. A., & Bass, A. R. (1985). Recruiting sources: Another look. *Journal of Applied Psychology, 70,* 720–728.

Taylor, D., Block, C., & Berry, P. (1958). Does group participation when using brainstorming facilitate or inhibit creative thinking? *Administrative Science Quarterly, 3,* 23–47.

Taylor, F. W. (1911). *The principles of scientific management.* New York: Harper.

Taylor, M. S., & Bergmann, T. J. (1987). Organizational recruitment activities and applicants' reactions at different stages of the recruitment process. *Personnel Psychology, 40,* 261–285.

Taylor, M. S., & Schmidt, D. W. (1983). A process-oriented investigation of recruitment source effectiveness. *Personnel Psychology, 36,* 343–354.

Thomas, K. W. (1976). Conflict and conflict management. In M. Dunnette (Ed.), *Handbook of industrial and organizational psychology* (pp. 889–936). Chicago: Rand-McNally.

Thornton, G. C. (1980). Psychometric properties of self-appraisals of job performance. *Personnel Psychology, 33,* 236–271.

Tiffin, J. (1968). *Purdue Pegboard.* West Lafayette, IN: Science Research Associates.

Tjosvold, D. (1984a). Effects of crisis orientation on managers' approach to controversy in decision making. *Academy of Management Journal, 27,* 130–138.

Tjosvold, D. (1984b). Effects of leader warmth and directiveness on subordinate performance on a subsequent task. *Journal of Applied Psychology, 69,* 222–232.

Tosi, H., & Tosi, L. (1987). What managers need to know about knowledge-based pay. In D. B. Balkin & L. R. Gomez-Mejia (Eds.), *New perspectives on compensation* (pp. 43–48). Englewood Cliffs, NJ: Prentice-Hall.

Treiman, D. J., & Hartmann, H. I. (Eds.). (1981). *Women, work and wages.* Washington, DC: National Academy Press.

Tubbs, M. E. (1986). Goal setting: A meta-analytic examination of the empirical evidence. *Journal of Applied Psychology, 71,* 474–483.

Tucker, F. D. (1985). A study of the training needs of older workers: Implications for human resources development planning. *Public Personnel Management, 14,* 85–95.

Tziner, A. (1982). Differential effects of group cohesiveness types: A clarifying overview. *Social Behavior and Personality, 10,* 227–239.

United States v. City of Chicago. (1977). 549 F.2d 415, *cert. denied,* 434 U.S. 875 (1977).

United States Air Force. (1980). *Air Force System Command design handbook 1–3: Human factors engineering* (3rd ed.).

U.S. Department of Labor. (1977). *Dictionary of occupational titles* (4th ed.). Washington, DC: U.S. Government Printing Office.

Vale, C. D., & Prestwood, J. S. (1987). *Minnesota Clerical Assessment Battery.* San Antonio, TX: The Psychological Corporation.

Vance, R. J., Kuhnert, K. W., & Farr, J. L. (1978). Interview judgments: Using external criteria to compare behavioral and graphic scale ratings. *Organizational Behavior and Human Performance, 22,* 279–294.

Van de Ven, A. H., & Delbecq, A. (1974). A task contingent model of work-unit structure. *Administrative Science Quarterly, 19,* 183–197.

Vecchio, R. P. (1977). An empirical examination of the validity of Fiedler's model of leadership effectiveness. *Organizational Behavior and Human Performance, 19,* 180–206.

Vecchio, R. P. (1982). A further test of leadership effects due to between-group and within-group variation. *Journal of Applied Psychology, 67,* 200–208.

Vickroy, S. C., Shaw, J. B., & Fisher, C. D. (1982). Effects of temperature, clothing, and task complexity on task performance and satisfaction. *Journal of Applied Psychology, 67,* 97–102.

Vroom, V. H. (1964). *Work and motivation.* New York: John Wiley & Sons.

Vroom, V. H., & Jago, A. G. (1978). On the validity of the Vroom-Yetton model. *Journal of Applied Psychology, 63,* 151–162.

Vroom, V. H., & Yetton, P. W. (1973). *Leadership and decision-making.* Pittsburgh: University of Pittsburgh Press.

Wahba, M. A., & Bridwell, L. T. (1976). Maslow reconsidered: A review of research on the need hierarchy theory. *Organizational Behavior and Human Performance, 15,* 212–240.

Walker, J., Fletcher, C., & McLeod, D. (1975). Flexible working hours in two British government offices. *Public Personnel Management, 4,* 219.

Wallach, M. A., Kogan, N., & Bem, D. J. (1962). Group influence on individual risk taking. *Journal of Abnormal and Social Psychology, 65,* 75–86.

Walton, R. E. (1972). How to counter alienation in the plant. *Harvard Business Review, 50,* 22.

Walton, R. E. (1975). Criteria for quality of working life. In L. E. Davis & A. B. Cherns (Eds.), *The quality of working life* (Vol. 1, pp. 91–104). New York: Free Press.

Walton, R. E., & Dutton, J. M. (1969). The management of interdepartmental conflict: A model and review. *Administrative Science Quarterly, 14,* 73–84.

Wanous, J. P. (1980). *Organizational entry: Recruitment, selection, and socialization of newcomers.* Reading, MA: Addison-Wesley.

Wanous, J. P., Keon, T. L., & Latack, J. C. (1983). Expectancy theory and occupational/organizational choices: A review and test. *Organizational Behavior and Human Performance, 32,* 66–86.

Wanous, J. P., Reichers, A. E., & Malik, S. D. (1984). Organizational socialization and group development: Toward an integrative perspective. *Academy of Management Review, 9,* 670–683.

Wanous, J. P., Stumpf, S. A., & Bedrosian, H. (1979). Job survival of new employees. *Personnel Psychology, 32,* 651–662.

Wasik, B. (1984). *Teaching parents effective problem solving: A handbook for professionals.* Chapel Hill: University of North Carolina Press.

Waters, L. K., & Roach, D. (1979). Job satisfaction, behavioral intention, and absenteeism as predictors of turnover. *Personnel Psychology, 32,* 393–397.

Waterworth, J. A., & Thomas, C. M. (1985). Why is synthetic speech harder to remember than natural speech? *Human factors in computing systems proceedings* (pp. 201–206). New York: Association for Computing Machinery.

Weaver, C. N. (1980). Job satisfaction in the United States in the 1970's. *Journal of Applied Psychology, 65,* 364–367.

Weber, M. (1947). *The theory of social and economic organizations* (A. M. Henderson & T. Parsons, Trans.). New York: Free Press.

Wechsler, D. (1981). *Wechsler Adult Intelligence Scale-Revised.* New York: Psychological Corporation.

Weiner, E. L., & Curry, R. E. (1980). Flight

deck automation: Promises and problems. *Ergonomics, 23,* 995–1012.

Weiss, D. J., Dawis, R. V., England, G. W., & Lofquist, L. H. (1967). *Manual for the Minnesota Satisfaction Questionnaire* (Minnesota Studies on Vocational Rehabilitation Vol. 22). Minneapolis: University of Minnesota Industrial Relations Center.

Weiss, H. M., Ilgen, D. R., & Sharbaugh, M. E. (1982). Effects of life and job stress on information search behaviors of organizational members. *Journal of Applied Psychology, 67,* 60–66.

Weiss, R. M. (1987). Writing under the influence: Science versus fiction in the analysis of corporate alcoholism programs. *Personnel Psychology, 40,* 341–356.

Wexley, K. N. (1986). Appraisal interview. In R. A. Berk (Ed.), *Performance assessment: Methods and applications* (pp. 167–185). Baltimore: The Johns Hopkins University Press.

Wexley, K. N., & Baldwin, T. T. (1986). Post-training strategies for facilitating positive transfer: An empirical exploration. *Academy of Management Journal, 29,* 503–520.

Wexley, K. N., & Latham, G. P. (1981). *Developing and training human resources in organizations.* Glenview, IL: Scott, Foresman.

Wexley, K. N., Sanders, R. E., & Yukl, G. A. (1973). Training interviewers to eliminate contrast effects in employment interviews. *Journal of Applied Psychology, 57,* 233–236.

Wexley, K. N., & Yukl, G. A. (1984). *Organizational behavior and personnel psychology* (rev. ed.). Homewood, IL: Richard D. Irwin.

Wheeler, D. D., & Janis, I. L. (1980). *A practical guide for making decisions.* New York: Free Press.

Wickens, C. D. (1984). *Engineering psychology and human performance.* Columbus, OH: Charles E. Merrill.

Williams, L. J., & Hazer, J. T. (1986). Antece-dents and consequences of satisfaction and commitment in turnover models: A reanalysis using latent variable structural equation methods. *Journal of Applied Psychology, 71,* 219–231.

Withey, M., Daft, R. L., & Cooper, W. H. (1983). Measures of Perrow's work unit technology: An empirical assessment and a new scale. *Academy of Management Journal, 26,* 45–63.

Wolf, F. M. (1986). *Meta-analysis: Quantitative methods for research synthesis.* Beverly Hills, CA: Sage Press.

Wolf, S. G. (1986). Common and grave disorders identified with occupational stress. In S. G. Wolf & A. J. Finestone (Eds.), *Occupational stress: Health and performance at work* (pp. 47–53). Littleton, MA: PSG Publishing.

Wonderlic, E. F. (1983). *Wonderlic Personnel Test.* Northfield, IL: Wonderlic and Associates.

Woodman, R. W., & Sherwood, J. J. (1980). Effects of team development intervention: A field experiment. *Journal of Applied Behavioral Science, 16,* 211–227.

Woodward, J. (1965). *Industrial organization: Theory and practice.* London: Oxford University Press.

Work in America: Report of a special task force to the Secretary of Health, Education, and Welfare. (1973). Cambridge, MA: MIT Press.

Yeager, S. J. (1981). Dimensionality of the Job Descriptive Index. *Academy of Management Journal, 14,* 205–212.

Yetton, P. W., & Bottger, P. C. (1982). Individual versus group problem solving: An empirical test of a best-member strategy. *Organizational Behavior and Human Performance, 29,* 307–321.

Yorks, L. (1979). *Job enrichment revisited.* New York: AMACOM.

Youngblood, S. A. (1984). Work, nonwork, and withdrawal. *Journal of Applied Psychology, 69,* 106–117.

Yukl, G. (1971). Toward a behavioral theory of leadership. *Organizational Behavior and Human Performance, 6,* 414–440.

Zalesny, M. D., & Farace, R. V. (1987). Traditional versus open offices: A comparison of sociotechnical, social relations, and symbolic meaning perspectives. *Academy of Management Journal, 30,* 240–259.

Zaremba, A. (1988, July). Communication: Working with the organizational grapevine. *Personnel Journal,* pp. 83–84.

Zedeck, S. (1977). An information processing model and approach to the study of motivation. *Organizational Behavior and Human Performance, 18,* 47–77.

Zedeck, S., Jackson, S. E., & Marca, E. S. (1983). Shift work schedules and their relationship to health, adaptation, satisfaction, and turnover intention. *Academy of Management Journal, 26,* 297–310.

Zimring, C. M. (1981). Stress and the designed environment. *Journal of Social Issues, 37,* 145–171.

Zohar, D. (1980). Safety climate in industrial organizations: Theoretical and applied implications. *Journal of Applied Psychology, 65,* 96–102.

Zussman, Y. M. (1983). Learning from the Japanese: Management in a resource-scarce world. *Organizational Dynamics, 11,* 68–80.

Zwerman, W. L. (1970). *New perspectives on organizational theory.* Westport, CT: Greenwood Press.

Acknowledgments

TEXT CREDITS

CHAPTER 3

60 Reprinted by permission of the publisher from *Job Analysis: Methods and Applications,* by E. J. McCormick. © 1979 AMACOM, a division of American Management Association, New York. All rights reserved.

61 From Jai V. Ghorpade, *Job Analysis: A Handbook for the Human Resource Director,* © 1988, p. 6. Adapted by permission of Prentice Hall, Inc., Englewood Cliffs, New Jersey.

67 From E. J. McCormick, P. R. Jeanneret, and R. C. Meacham, *Position Analysis Questionnaire,* copyright 1969 by Purdue Research Foundation, West Lafayette, Indiana 47907. Reprinted with permission.

70 From *Psychology of Work Behavior,* 3rd Edition by Frank J. Landy. Copyright © 1985 by Wadsworth, Inc. Adapted by permission of Brooks/Cole Publishing Company, Pacific Grove, CA 93950; and adapted from *Handbook on Wages and Salary Administration,* 2nd ed., by M. L. Rock. © 1984. Used with permission of McGraw-Hill Publishing Company.

74 Table from F. J. Landy and J. L. Farr, *The Measurement of Work Performance: Methods, Theory, and Applications.* Adapted by permission of Academic Press.

80 From R. R. Jacobs, "Numerical Rating Scales" in R. A. Berk, ed., *Performance Assessment: Methods and Applications.* The Johns Hopkins University Press, Baltimore/London, 1987, pp. 82–99.

81 From *Psychology of Work Behavior,* 3rd Edition by Frank J. Landy. Copyright © 1985 by Wadsworth, Inc. Adapted by permission of Brooks/Cole Publishing Company, Pacific Grove, CA 93950.

82 From R. M. Guion, *Personnel Testing.* Copyright 1965. Reprinted by permission of the author.

83 From W. C. Borman, "Behavior-Based Rating Scales" in R. A. Berk, ed., *Performance Assessment: Methods and Applications.* The Johns Hopkins University Press, Baltimore/London, 1987, p. 103.

CHAPTER 4

107 From G. K. Bennett, *Test of Mechanical Comprehension.* Bennett Mechanical Comprehension Test. Copyright © 1942, 1967–1970, 1980 by The Psychological Corporation. Reproduced by permission. All rights reserved.

109 From H. G. Gough, *California Psychological Inventory.* Reproduced by special permission of the Publisher, Consulting Psychologists Press, Inc., Palo Alto, CA 94306, from the *California Psychological Inventory* by Harrison G. Gough. © 1986. Further reproduction is prohibited without the Publisher's consent.

121   From Wayne F. Cascio, *Applied Psychology in Personnel Management*, 3e, © 1987, p. 282. Adapted by permission of Prentice Hall, Inc., Englewood Cliffs, New Jersey.

CHAPTER 5

146   From Zandy B. Leibowitz, C. Farren, and B. L. Kaye, *Designing Career Development Systems*, p. 7 (Table 2). Reprinted by permission of Jossey-Bass, Inc.

147   From T. G. Gutteridge, "Organizational Career Development Systems: The State of the Practice" in D. T. Hall and Associates, *Career Development in Organizations*, pp. 82–85. Adapted by permission of Jossey-Bass, Inc. and the author.

CHAPTER 6

162   From D. C. McClelland and R. S. Steele, Motivation Workshops. Copyright © 1972 General Learning Press.

168   From J. R. Hackman and G. R. Oldham, "Motivation Through the Design of Work: Test of a Theory," from *Organizational Behavior and Human Performance*. Reprinted by permission of Academic Press.

CHAPTER 7

189   Adapted from *The Minnesota Satisfaction Questionnaire*. Reproduced by permission of Vocational Psychology Research, University of Minnesota. Copyright 1977.

190   From P. C. Smith, L. M. Kendall, and C. L. Hulin, "Job Descriptive Index," from *The Measurement of Satisfaction in Work and Retirement*. Revised, 1985, Bowling Green State University. Copyright 1975, 1985, Bowling Green State University.

191   From Robert A. Baron, *Behavior in Organizations: Understanding and Managing the Human Side of Work*, Second Edi-

tion. Copyright © 1986 by Allyn & Bacon. Used with permission.

193   From R. T. Mowday, R. Steers, and L. W. Porter, "The Measure of Organizational Commitment," in *Journal of Vocational Behavior*, p. 228. Reprinted by permission of Academic Press.

206   From T. H. Holmes and R. H. Rahe, "The Social Readjustment Rating Scale," in *Journal of Psychosomatic Research*, vol. 11, pp. 213–218. Reprinted by permission of The American Psychosomatic Society, Inc.

208   Based on Sheldon Cohen, "Aftereffects of Stress on Human Performance and Social Behavior: A Review of Research and Theory," in *Psychological Bulletin*, 88, 1980, p. 85. Copyright 1985 by the American Psychological Association. Adapted by permission.

214   Reprinted with permission of The Free Press, a Division of Macmillan, Inc. from *The Quality of Working Life*, Volume 1, Louis E. Davis and Albert B. Cherns, Eds. Copyright © 1975 by Louis E. Davis and Albert B. Cherns.

CHAPTER 8

223   From P. V. Lewis, *Organizational Communication: The Essence of Effective Management*, 3rd Edition. Copyright © 1987 John Wiley & Sons, Inc. Reprinted by permission.

CHAPTER 9

250   From K. D. Benne and P. Sheats, "Functional Roles of Group Members," *Journal of Social Issues*, Vol. IV, No. 2, pp. 41–49. Reprinted by permission of The Society for the Psychological Study of Social Issues.

CHAPTER 10

284   Reprinted by permission from *Leadership Opinion Questionnaire* by Edwin A.

Fleishman. Copyright 1960 Science Research Associates, Inc.

286 Adapted from Robert A. Baron, *Behavior in Organizations: Understanding and Managing the Human Side of Work,* Second Edition, pp. 288–289. Copyright © 1986 by Allyn & Bacon. Used with permission.

289 The Managerial Grid figure from *The Managerial Grid III: The Key to Leadership Excellence,* by Robert R. Blake and Jane Srygley Mouton. Houston: Gulf Publishing Company, Copyright © 1985, page 12. Reproduced by permission.

290 From F. E. Fiedler, *A Theory of Leadership Effectiveness,* pp. 40–41. Copyright 1967. Reprinted by permission of the author.

296 Reprinted from *Leadership and Decision-Making,* by Victor H. Vroom and Philip W. Yetton, by permission of the University of Pittsburgh Press. © 1973 by University of Pittsburgh Press.

297 Reprinted from *Leadership and Decision-Making,* by Victor H. Vroom and Philip W. Yetton, by permission of the University of Pittsburgh Press. © 1973 by University of Pittsburgh Press.

CHAPTER 11

312 From D. Kipnis, S. M. Schmidt, and I. Wilkinson, "Intraorganizational Influence Tactics: Explorations in Getting One's Way," in *Journal of Applied Psychology,* 65, pp. 445–448. Copyright 1980 by the American Psychological Association. Reprinted by permission.

324 From Stephen P. Robbins, *Organizational Behavior,* © 1979, p. 404. Reprinted by permission of Prentice Hall, Inc., Englewood Cliffs, New Jersey.

331 From A. T. Cobb, "An Episodic Model of Power: Toward an Integration of Theory and Research," in *Academy of Management Review,* 9, 1984, pp. 482–493. Reprinted by permission of the Academy of Management.

CHAPTER 13

376 From A. Chapanis, "Engineering Psychology," from *Man-Machine Engineering,* Brooks/Cole Publishing Co.; as it appeared in M. D. Dunnette, ed., *Handbook of Industrial and Organizational Psychology,* John Wiley & Sons, Inc.

388 From S. Card, W. English, and B. Burr, "Evaluation of Mouse, Rate-Controlled Isometric Joystick, Step Keys, and Text Keys for Text Selection on a CRT," in *Ergonomics,* 21, 1978. Reprinted by permission of Taylor & Francis Ltd., Hampshire, UK.

CHAPTER 14

405 Adapted from *CIBSE Code for Interior Lighting* (1984) by permission of The Chartered Institution of Building Services Engineers.

407 From *Ergonomic Design for People at Work,* Vol. I, pp. 254–262. Copyright © 1983 Eastman Kodak, Company. Adapted by permission.

419 From K. R. Pelletier, *Healthy People in Unhealthy Places: Stress and Fitness at Work.* Reprinted by permission of Robert Briggs Associates.

PHOTO CREDITS

Unless otherwise acknowledged, all photographs are the property of Scott, Foresman and Company.

CHAPTER 1

6 © Taro Yamasaki

7 Historical Pictures Service, Chicago

12 © Adam Bartos

15 © Rick Browne

19 © Andy Freeberg

CHAPTER 10

280 AP/Wide World Photos
284 AP/Wide World Photos
285 © Brent Jones
287 © Nancy Ellison/Sygma
293 AP/Wide World Photos (*top and bottom*)
295 AP/Wide World Photos
298 AP/Wide World Photos
299 AP/Wide World Photos
301 AP/Wide World Photos

CHAPTER 11

310 © Jim Pickerell 1985
317 © McConnell McNamara & Company 1980
318 Drawing by Dana Fradon; © 1977 The New Yorker Magazine, Inc.
325 AP/Wide World Photos
326 © Punch/Rothco
330 © Jim Pickerell 1985

CHAPTER 12

337 Historical Pictures Service, Chicago
339 Photo copyright 1985, U.S. News & World Report, Inc. Credit: Gary L. Kieffer, U.S. News & World Report
343 © Robert Landau/West Light
354 © 1984 Jack Vartoogian. All rights reserved
362 © Charles Harbutt
365 © Jim Pickerell 1985

CHAPTER 13

375 © McConnell McNamara & Company 1982
378 © Jim Pickerell 1989
389 NASA
392 © McConnell McNamara & Company 1981
395 Niels Diffrient

CHAPTER 14

405 Dennis Cox for INSIGHT Magazine
406 © Ron Watts/West Light
417 © John McGrail 1988. All rights reserved
420 © McConnell McNamara & Company 1988
423 Photo © 1989 by Dan Lamont. All rights reserved
424 © North American Syndicate 1986. By permission of Johnny Hart and NAS, Inc.

Name Index

A

Abelson, R. P., 16, 455
Adams, J., 302, 475
Adams, J. S., 169, 455
Albrecht, K., 367, 369, 455
Alderfer, C. P., 158, 160, 180, 455
Allen, R. W., 310, 323, 331, 333, 455, 470, 474
Alliger, G. M., 300, 469
Alutto, J. A., 196, 209, 470, 473
American Psychological Association, 434, 436
Anatol, K. W. E., 231, 467
Angle, H. L., 331, 474
Ansari, M. A., 313, 455
Anthony, W. P., 417, 475
Applbaum, R. L., 231, 467
Appleman, A., 271, 456
Arad, R., 175, 461
Argyris, C., 143, 455
Ariss, S. S., 331, 463
Arms, R. L., 412, 456
Arnold, B., 105, 473
Arnold, H. J., 192, 455
Aronson, E., 455, 465, 470, 472
Arvey, R. D., 114, 116, 117, 125, 229, 455
Ash, R. A., 60, 68, 469
Ashour, A. S., 293, 455
Astley, W. G., 315, 455
Atkin, R. S., 195, 218, 455
Atkins, F. R., 429
Atkinson, J. W., 161, 471
Axel, H., 425, 455

B

Bacharach, S. B., 317, 455
Bachman, J. G., 319, 456
Baird, J. E., 231, 239–241, 456

Baldwin, T. T., 133, 456, 481
Balestreri-Spero, J. C., 118, 464
Balkin, D. B., 199, 456, 466, 468, 479
Bandura, A., 131, 322, 456
Bannister, B. C., 293, 477
Barclay, L. A., 95, 471
Bar-Hillel, M., 111, 457
Barker, L. L., 226, 456
Baron, R. A., 85, 194, 227, 286, 412, 456
Barrett, G. V., 88, 456
Barsaloux, J., 271, 457
Barwick, K. D., 423, 467
Bass, A. R., 95, 479
Bass, B. M., 114, 284, 287, 302, 306, 367, 456
Bateman, T. S., 195, 456
Bavelas, A., 238, 456
Bazerman, M. H., 271, 456
Beatty, R. W., 75, 457
Bedrosian, H., 144, 480
Beehr, T. A., 146, 204, 208–210, 456–457, 464, 473
Bell, C. H., 367, 462
Bell, P. A., 406, 456
Bem, D. J., 275, 480
Ben-Abba, E., 111, 457
Benne, K. D., 249–250, 456
Bennet, N., 60, 469
Bennett, G. K., 105–107, 456–457
Bennis, W. G., 367, 457
Ben-Shakhar, G., 111, 457
Berg, D. N., 361, 472
Berg, P. O., 367, 474
Bergmann, T. J., 96, 479
Berk, R. A., 80, 83, 457, 466, 481
Berkowitz, L., 455, 477
Bernardin, H. J., 75, 89, 457
Berry, P., 271, 479
Berryman-Fink, C., 136, 457
Bhagat, R. S., 205, 208, 456–457
Bienvenue, G. R., 408, 471

Gandz, J., 317, 462
Ganster, D. C., 211, 462
Garcia, J. E., 53, 293, 478
Gardell, B., 205, 469
Garland, H., 175, 462
Garner, K., 116, 460
Gherman, E. M., 208, 218, 462
Ghiselli, E. E., 108, 463
Ghorpade, J. V., 60, 61, 463
Gibb, J. R., 235, 463
Gibson, W. M., 118, 464
Gilbreth, F. B., 8–9, 374, 463
Gilbreth, L., 8–9, 374
Gillet, B., 189, 463
Gilmore, D. C., 86, 461
Gist, M. E., 322, 463
Giuliano, T., 271, 456
Glube, R., 298, 470
Goishi, C. K., 425, 471
Goldman, R. B., 166, 463
Goldstein, I. L., 140, 142, 148, 154, 463
Golembiewski, R. T., 203, 463
Gomez-Mejia, L. R., 71, 199, 456, 466, 468, 479
Gooding, R. Z., 114, 477
Goodman, P. S., 195, 218, 455
Gottfredson, L. S., 104, 463
Gottier, R. J., 108, 464
Gough, H. G., 105, 108–109, 463
Gouldner, A. W., 257, 463
Gradous, D., 92
Grady, J. F., 366, 470
Graen, G. B., 168, 171, 298–299, 459, 463, 476
Graen, M. R., 168, 463
Grandjean, E., 405, 473
Grant, D. L., 113, 457
Gray, B., 331, 463
Gray, J. L., 259, 348, 463
Green, S. G., 299, 460
Greenberg, J., 170, 463
Greenberger, D. B., 322, 463
Griffeth, R. W., 197, 472
Gruneberg, M. M., 404, 429, 458, 467, 468, 471, 473
Guion, R. M., 82, 108, 118, 195, 464
Gupta, N., 209, 464
Gustafson, D. J., 417, 475
Gutek, B. A., 302, 473
Gutteridge, T. G., 147, 464
Guttmann, H., 390, 400, 479
Gylenhammer, P., 166, 464

H

Hackett, E. J., 366, 470
Hackett, R. D., 195, 464

Hackman, J. R., 166–168, 464
Haga, B., 298, 459
Hakel, M. D., 165, 229, 460, 466
Hakstian, A. R., 105, 464
Hall, D. T., 147, 154, 218, 464
Hall, F. S., 464
Hall, H., 68, 469
Halpin, A. W., 283, 464
Hammer, T. H., 195, 201, 464
Hamner, E. P., 177, 464
Hamner, W. C., 177, 464
Hand, H. H., 197, 472
Hanson, T. J., 118, 464
Happ, A., 406, 459
Hare, A. P., 255, 464
Harris, E. F., 284, 465
Harris, M. M., 110, 476
Harrison, A. A., 429
Harrison, T. M., 233, 464
Hartke, D. D., 293, 474
Hartman, A. D., 105, 460
Hartman, K., 192, 478
Hartmann, H. I., 69, 479
Hartsough, D. M., 390, 464
Harvey, O. J., 266, 477
Hassett, C. E., 85, 471
Hastorf, A. H., 229, 477
Hatfield, J. D., 171, 465
Hathaway, S. R., 108, 464
Hatvany, N., 366, 464
Hauser, D. L., 368, 457
Haynes, R. S., 423, 464
Haynes, S. G., 476
Hazer, J. T., 197, 481
Heilman, M. E., 117, 464
Henderson, A. M., 480
Heneman, H. G., 96, 116, 173, 464, 476, 477
Heneman, R. L., 85, 465
Henley, N. M., 229, 465
Herrick, N. Q., 214, 465
Hersey, R., 241, 465
Herzberg, F., 163–165, 180, 184, 465
Hicks, W. D., 416, 465
Hickson, D. J., 319, 465
Hill, G. W., 270, 465
Hill, K. D., 306
Hinings, C. R., 319, 465
Hogan, J., 105, 109, 465
Hogan, R., 105, 109, 465
Hollander, E. P., 281–282, 300, 465
Hollenback, J. H., 177, 195, 466, 474
Hollenbeck, J. R., 43, 465
Holley, W. H., 88, 461
Holmes, T. H., 205–206, 465
Hood, W. R., 266, 477

Porter, L. W., 43, 97, 157, 171, 182, 190–193, 195, 197, 199, 241–242, 309, 331, 333, 455, 459, 468, 472, 474, 478
Premack, S. L., 97, 474
Prestwood, J. S., 105, 479
Primps, S. B., 416, 475
Pritchard, R. D., 177, 474
Psychological Corporation, 106, 474
Puccetti, M. C., 207, 467
Pucik, V., 366, 464
Pulakos, E. D., 85, 89, 144, 474
Pursell, E. D., 116, 458, 468

R

Rafaeli, A., 111, 414, 474, 479
Ragan, J. W., 294, 466
Rahe, R. H., 205–206, 465
Raich, M. S., 140, 471
Ralston, D. A., 417, 475
Rasmussen, J., 401, 475
Rasmussen, K. G., 229, 475
Rauschenberger, J., 159, 475
Raven, B. H., 315, 320, 462
Reber, R. A., 423, 475
Reed, J. G., 436
Reichardt, T., 411, 475
Reichers, A. E., 253, 475, 480
Reilly, R. R., 98, 475
Reimer, E., 285, 287, 472
Rice, B., 46, 56, 475
Rice, R. W., 289, 302, 475
Richman, L. S., 258, 475
Richter, J., 218
Ridley, J., 429, 457
Riggio, R. E., 117, 300, 475
Risher, H., 72, 475
Ritchie, R. J., 38, 475
Roach, D., 197, 480
Robbins, S. P., 264, 320, 324, 475
Roberts, K. H., 225, 241, 473, 474
Roche, G. R., 138, 475
Rock, M. L., 70, 475
Roethlisberger, F. J., 10, 475
Ronen, S., 416–417, 475
Rosen, C., 201, 475
Rosenman, R. H., 209, 459, 462, 475
Rosenstein, J., 201, 462
Rosow, J. M., 154
Ross, J., 194, 478
Rowland, K. M., 86, 461–462
Rusbult, C. E., 195, 476
Russell, G. W., 412, 456

Russell, J. S., 150, 476
Rynes, S. L., 96, 476

S

Saal, F. E., 436
Saari, L. M., 116, 148, 174, 468, 469
Sachdeva, P. S., 315, 455
Sackett, P. R., 38, 110, 476
Salancik, G. R., 331, 476
Sallis, J. F., 211, 476
Salsburg, B. L., 98, 468
Sanders, G., 467
Sanders, M. S., 386, 397, 401, 405, 409, 471, 476
Sanders, R. E., 116, 481
Saruwatari, L. R., 117, 464
Sashkin, M., 358, 462
Savitsky, J. C., 390, 464
Scandura, T. A., 168, 299, 463, 476
Scarpello, V., 186, 476
Schachter, S., 241, 476
Schein, E. H., 252, 362–364, 476
Schein, V. E., 321, 417, 476
Scheiner, E. C., 35, 472
Schermerhorn, J. R., 205, 470
Schlenker, B. R., 460
Schmidt, D. W., 95, 479
Schmidt, F. L., 112, 173, 465, 474, 476
Schmidt, S. M., 312–313, 467, 476
Schmied, L. A., 207, 477
Schmitt, N., 114, 133, 159, 473, 475, 477
Schnake, M. E., 36, 477
Schneck, R. E., 319, 465
Schneider, B., 186, 477
Schneider, D. J., 229, 477
Schneider, J., 164, 477
Schneier, C. E., 92
Schoenfeldt, L. F., 98, 473
Schriesheim, C. A., 284–285, 293, 295, 477
Schriesheim, S., 284, 467
Schuler, R. S., 209, 466, 477
Schwab, D. P., 89, 96, 173, 189, 459, 463, 476, 477
Schwab, R. L., 209, 466
Schweiger, D. M., 284, 469
Scott, K. D., 195, 477
Scott, L. R., 423, 467
Scott, P., 138, 459
Scott, W. D., 6, 477
Scott, W. G., 255, 477
Selye, H., 202, 477
Sethi, A. S., 210, 466, 477
Sharbaugh, M. E., 205, 481
Shaw, J. B., 406, 480
Shaw, K. N., 174, 469

T

U

V

W

Wahba, M. A., 159, 480
Wahlers, K. J., 226, 456
Walker, J., 417, 480
Wallach, M. A., 275, 480
Wallin, J. A., 423, 475
Walton, R. E., 166, 214–215, 261, 480
Wanous, J. P., 95, 97, 144, 173, 253, 474, 480
Ware, M. E., 437
Warm, J. S., 374, 470
Wasik, B., 212, 480
Waters, L. K., 197, 480
Waterworth, J. A., 380, 480
Watson, K. W., 226, 456
Weaver, C. N., 194, 480
Weber, M., 337–339, 480
Wechsler, D., 105, 480
Weick, K. E., 143, 458
Weiner, B., 466
Weiner, E. L., 394, 480
Weinstein, N., 408, 459
Weiss, D. J., 188, 481
Weiss, H. M., 205, 481
Weiss, R. M., 425, 481
Weiss, S. M., 476
Wexley, K. N., 84, 85, 88, 116, 133, 137, 142, 149, 465, 468, 478, 481
Wheat, J. E., 436
Wheeler, D. D., 273, 481
Wheeler, L., 470
White, B. J., 266, 477
Whitney, P., 471
Wickens, C. D., 16, 481
Wiley, W. W., 63, 461
Wilkinson, I., 312, 467
Williams, C. R., 43, 465
Williams, L. J., 197, 481

Wilson, T. D., 85, 473
Winer, B. J., 283, 464
Withey, M., 354, 481
Witten, M. B., 243, 460
Wolf, C. P., 390, 401, 477
Wolf, F. M., 53, 481
Wolf, S. G., 469, 481
Wonderlic, E. F., 104–105, 481
Wood, M. M., 302, 468
Woodman, R. W., 362, 481
Woodward, J., 351–353, 481

Y

Yates, V. L., 86, 461
Yeager, S. J., 189, 481
Yetton, P. W., 271, 287, 295–298, 300, 480, 481
Yorks, L., 166, 481
Young, K. M., 201, 475
Youngblood, S. A., 196, 481
Yukl, G., 116, 137, 149, 284, 482

Z

Zaccaro, S. J., 300, 467
Zager, R., 154
Zajonc, R. B., 16, 470
Zalesny, M. D., 414, 482
Zander, A., 277, 458, 466
Zaremba, A., 241, 482
Zawacki, R. A., 40, 462
Zedeck, S., 38, 174, 415, 476, 482
Zidon, I., 174, 461
Zimring, C. M., 414, 482
Zohar, D., 421, 482
Zussman, Y. M., 16, 482
Zwerman, W. L., 352, 482

SUBJECT INDEX

A

Absenteeism, 43–44, 195
Abstract models, 28
Academy of Management Journal, 15
Academy of Management Review, 15
Acceleration, 408–409
Accident proneness, 421
Accident reduction, 422–424
Accidents, 390
Accommodation, 253, 265
Achievement-motivation theory, 160–163
Achievement-oriented behavior, 294
Achievement training program, 162
Action research, 358–359
Actor-observer bias, 86–87
Adaptability, 343
Administrative Science Quarterly, 15
Advanced control systems, 387–389
Adverse impact, 122
Aesthetic factors, 411–413
Affirmative action, 123
AFSCME v. State of Washington, 72, 455
Air velocity, 406
Airborne pollutants, 410–411, 413
Albermarle Paper v. Moody, 88, 455
Alcohol use in the work place, 424–427
Alderfer's ERG theory, 160
Alphabetic keyboards, 385–387
Altruistic behavior, 258
American versus Japanese, 194
  levels of production, 194
  levels of satisfaction and commitment, 194
Analysis of Variance (ANOVA), 50
Annual Review of Psychology, 15
Anticipatory socialization, 253
Antidiscrimination laws, 122
Application forms, 98–99
Applications, 97–98

Apprenticeship, 137
Army Air Corps, 374
Army Alpha, 12
Army Beta, 12
Army General Classification Test, 12
Artificiality of experimental method of research, 35
Asbestos, 409
Assessment center, 112–114
Asteroids, 383
Astronaut, 410–411
Atmospheric electricity, 412
Atmospheric ionization, 412
Attribution errors, 85–86
Audience factors, 227
Audioconferencing, 226
Audiovisual instruction, 139–140
Auditory displays, 379–380
Authority hierarchy, 338
Autocratic decisionmaking, 268
Autonomy, 167
Average, 48
Avoidance, 265

B

B-25 bombers, 374
Bay of Pigs invasion, 273
Behavior modeling training, 140
Behavioral criteria, 148
Behavioral observation scales, 84
Behavioral theories of leadership, 283–285, 287
  evaluation of, 287
Behaviorally anchored rating scales (BARS), 81–84, 88
Bell-shaped curve, 49
Benefit programs, 200–201
Bennett Mechanical Comprehension Test, 105–107
Bhopal, India, 390

Bias of responses, 42
Biofeedback, 210
Biographical information blanks (BIBs), 98
Bottom line variables, 42–44
Brainstorming, 271
Brito v. Zia Company, 88, 457
Buffalo Mining Company, 273
Bureaucracy, 337–340
　characteristics of, 338–339
　definition of, 337
　examples of, 339–340
Bureaucratic model, 337
Burnout, 209

C

California Psychological Inventory, 105, 108
Carbon monoxide pollution, 410
Career counseling, 147
Career development, 146–148
　benefits of, 146
　systems, 146–147
Career forum, 147
Career planning workshops, 147
Career resources library, 147
Case study, 38–39
Case study method, 38–40
　definition of, 38–39
　examples of, 39–40
Causal attribution, 85–86
Cautious shift, 275
Censoring, 233–234
Central tendency error, 85
Centralization, 350
Centralized networks, 236–237
Centralized structure, 350
Chain of command, 346–348
Chain network, 236–237
Change agent, 358
Channel, 222
Channel factors, 225–226
Checklists, 79–80
Check-reading displays, 379
Chemical pollutants, 409
Chernobyl nuclear disaster, 390
Cigarette smoke, 410–411
Circadian rhythms, 415
Circle networks, 237
Civil Rights Act of 1964, 13, 122
Classical conditioning, 130–132
Clean rooms, 413
Closed-office designs, 414
Coalition, 318–319
Coercive power, 315

Cognitive ability tests, 104–106
Cognitive explosion, 16–17
Cognitive psychology, 16
Cohesiveness, 255–256
Collaboration, 265, 343–344
Collection of data, 28–29
Collective rationalizations, 273–274
Color, effect of, on work performance, 411–413
Comcon network, 237
Commitment and consistency, 314
Communication, 4, 221–243
　barriers, 231–235
　breakdowns, 234
　flow, 230–235
　model, 221–224
　networks, 236–238
　and work outcomes, 241–243
Comparable worth, 69–72
Comparative methods of performance appraisal,
　77–79
Comparative ranking, 77–79
Comparison others, 169
Compensable factors, 69
Compensation for inadequacies, 329
Compensatory model, 119
Competition, 259, 265
　for power and resources, 328
Compliance professionals, 314
Comprehensive Ability Battery, 105
Compressed work weeks, 415–416
Compromise, 265
Computer assisted instruction (CAI), 141–142
Computer Competence Tests, 106
Computer controls, 386–387
Computer-generated speech, 380
Concrete models, 28
Concurrent validity, 103
Conditioned response, 130
Conditioned stimulus, 130
Conference, 143
Conflict, 259–268
　definition of, 259
　levels of, 260–261
　management of, 264–266
　outcomes of, 262–264
　resolution of, 265–267
　sources of, 261–262
　stimulation of, 266, 268
Conflict resolution strategies, 266, 268
Conflict stimulation strategies, 265–267
Conformity, 254–255
Consensus, 269
Consequence, 131
Consideration, 283–285
Content validity, 102

Contingency approaches to power and politics, 331
Contingency models of organizational structure, 351–356
Contingency theories of leadership, 287–301
    comparison of, 300–301
Continuing education, 144
Continuous-process production, 351–352
Contrast effects, 117
Control group, 34
Control systems, 374
Controls, 382–389
Cooperation, 257–258
Coping skills, 212
Coronary-prone behavior pattern, 163
Correlation and causality, 37
Correlation coefficient, 50–51
Correlational method, 37–38
    definition of, 37
    examples of, 37–38
Cost effectiveness of personnel testing, 112
Craft technology, 352–353
Crawford Small Parts Dexterity Test, 106
Credibility, 225
Criterion contamination, 75
Criterion deficiency, 75
Criterion relevance, 75
Criterion usefulness, 76
Criterion-related validity, 102–103
Critical evaluators, 275
Critical incidents technique (CIT), 66–69
Crowding, 413–414

D

Dangers, 418–421
    in machine systems, 419–420
    in work environment, 418–419
    in worker characteristics and behavior, 420–421
Deceleration, 408–409
Decentralization, 350
Decentralized networks, 237–238
Decentralized structure, 350
Decibels, 407
Decision making model, 295–298
Decision tree framework, 296–297
Decoder, 221–224
Decoding, 221–222
Defensiveness, 234
Delay in measuring work outcomes, 328–329
Delegating, 286
Democratic decisionmaking, 268–269
Dependent variable, 34, 42–44
Depersonalization, 209
Descriptive model, 31–32

Descriptive statistics, 45, 47–48
Diagnosis, 5
Dictionary of Occupational Titles (DOT), 63–65
Diet plans, 210–211
Differentiation, 354
Digital displays, 378
Direct conformity pressure, 273–274
Direct ownership, 201
Directive behavior, 294
Discrimination
    in intelligence testing, 104, 106
    in recruitment, 97
Disease-prone personality, 207
Disneyland Career Development System, 147
Displays, 377–380
    arrangement of, 379
    types of, 378–380
Distress, 203
Division of labor, 338
Divisional structure, 348–350
Downward communication, 230–231
Drug testing, 111
Drug use in the work place, 424–427
Dvorak keyboard, 386–387
Dysfunctional politics, 323

E

Edsel, 273
Efficiency experts, 8
Ejection, 420
Emotional exhaustion, 209
Empirical approach, 17–18
Employee Assistance Programs (EAPs), 425–427
    definition of, 425
    effectiveness of, 425, 427
Employee career development, 146–148
Employee ownership, 201
Employee referrals, 95
Employee stock ownership, 201
Employee suggestion systems, 232
Employee surveys, 233
Employee training, 4, 213
Employee-owned companies, 201
Employee-sponsored child care, 200
Employment applications, 97–99
Empowerment, 322
Empowerment process, 322
Encoder, 221–224
Encoding, 221
Encounter groups, 361
Engineering anthropometry, 397–398
Engineering psychology, 3–4, 373
Engineering technology, 352–353

Hogan Personnel Selection Series, 105
Horns effect, 85
Human anthropometry, 398
Human Communication Research, 15
Human error, 390
Human factors, 373–399
  definition of, 373–374
  history of, 374–375
Human factors design flaws, 374–375, 390–392
Human factors psychology, 3–4, 373–399
Human relations, 9–11
  principles of, 11
  shortcomings of, 11
Human Relations, 15
Human relations movement, 9–11
Human resources, 59
Humidity, 406
Hygienes, 164
Hypotheses, 28
Hypothesis testing, 45, 48–52

I

Illumination, 404–406, 418
Illumination levels, 405
Illusion of invulnerability, 273–274
Illusion of morality, 273–274
Illusion of unanimity, 273–274
Impersonality, 338–339
Importance principle, 397
Impoverished manager, 288
In-basket test, 113–114
Independent variable, 34, 42
Individual coping strategies, 210–211
Individual power, 315
Individual-administered tests, 104
Inferential statistics, 45, 48–49
Influence, 309–313
  definition of, 309–310
  tactics of, 312–314
Informal communication, 238–241
Information technology, 352
Industrial/organizational psychology
  careers in, 431–436
  definitions of, 3
  future of, 13–16, 19
  future trends in, 16–19
  graduate study in, 435–436
  journals, 15
  multidisciplinary nature of, 14–16
  objective of, 5
  professional organizations in, 433–434
  training for, 433
Ingratiation, 312–313

Ingroup, 298
Initiating structure, 283–285
Inputs, 169–170
Insecticides, 410
Instrumentality, 172
Integration, 355
Intelligence tests, 104–106
Interdependence, 261–262
Intergroup conflict, 260–261
Interindividual conflict, 260
Intern programs, 147
Internal consistency, 102
Interorganizational conflict, 261
Interpersonal sources of conflict, 262
Interpersonal stress, 204
Interpretation of research results, 30, 52–59
Intervention, 5
Interviewer biases, 117
Interviewer training, 116
Intragroup conflict, 260
Intraindividual conflict, 260
Involuntary absenteeism, 195–197
Involuntary turnover, 196–197

J

Jargon, 225
Job analysis, 4, 59–72
  definition of, 4, 59
  interview methods of, 62
  methods of, 60–69
  observational methods of, 62
  standardized techniques of, 63–69
  survey methods of, 62–63
Job characteristics model, 166–169
Job description, 59
Job Descriptive Index (JDI), 188–190
Job design theories of motivation, 163–169
Job Diagnostic Survey (JDS), 168
Job dissatisfaction, 163–164
Job enlargement, 198–199
Job enrichment, 164, 166, 168, 215, 359–360
Job evaluation, 59
  and comparable worth, 59
  definition of, 59
Job knowledge tests, 106–108
Job posting, 147
Job redesign, 303
Job relatedness, 116
Job rotation, 138–139, 197–198
Job satisfaction, 4, 185–201
  definition of, 186
  and employee absenteeism, 43–44, 195–197
  and employee attendance, 43–44, 195–197

and employee turnover, 43–44, 195–197
facet approach to, 186
global approach to, 186
increasing, 197–201
and job performance, 189–192
measurement of, 186–189
and organizational commitment, 192–195
Job skills tests, 106–108
Job specification, 59
Job uncertainty, 204
Johnson administration, 273
Journal of Applied Psychology, 15
Journal of Communication, 15
Journal of Occupational Psychology, 15
Journal of Organizational Behavior, 15
Joystick, 386–387

K

Kalmar, Sweden, 166
Kennedy administration, 273
Keyboard controls, 385–387
Knowledge-based pay, 199
Korean War, 273

L

Lack of control, 204
Lateral communication, 231
Lawrence and Lorsch model, 354–355
Leader Behavior Description Questionnaire
    (LBDQ), 284
Leader effectiveness, 280, 286
Leader Match, 293–294, 301, 303
Leader Opinion Questionnaire (LOQ), 283–284
Leader role, 249
Leaderless group discussion, 114
Leader-member exchange model, 298–299
Leader-member relations, 291
Leadership, 4, 280–303
    definition of, 280
    sex differences in, 302
Leadership theories, 281–301
    applications of, 301–303
Leadership training, 301–302
Leadership traits, 300
Learning, 129–130
Learning criteria, 148
Least preferred co-worker (LPC), 288–290
Lecture, 139
Legitimate power, 316
Leniency errors, 84–85, 89
Letters of recommendation, 118

Lie detectors, 109–110
Life events, 205
Life events stress index, 205–206
Lighting handbooks, 405
Line, 340–341
Line-staff organizational structure, 340–341

M

Machine characteristics, 377
Machine control design, 382–383
Machine controls, 382–389
Management by objectives (MBO), 175, 364–365
Management games, 143
Management potential scales, 108–109
Management training methods, 142–143
Management-union conflict, 267
Managerial Grid, 288
Managerial Grid training, 288
Maslow's need-hierarchy theory, 158–160
Mass production, 351–352
Matrix organization, 342–345
    characteristics of, 343–344
    definition of, 342–343
    examples of, 344
McClelland's achievement motivation theory, 160–163
McGregor's Theory X and Theory Y, 282
Mean, 48–49
Measurement of job performance, 73–76
Measurement of variables, 40–45
Measures of central tendency, 48–49
Measures of variability, 48–49
Mechanical Ability Test, 105
Mechanical ability tests, 105–106
Median, 49
Meditation, 210
Mentoring, 137–138
Merit pay, 199
Merit-based employment decisions, 339
Meta-analysis, 53
Microchip plants, 413
Middle management potential, 40
Mindguards, 273–275
Minnesota Clerical Assessment Battery (MCAB), 105
Minnesota Multiphasic Personality Inventory
    (MMPI), 108
Minnesota Satisfaction Questionnaire (MSQ), 188–189
Model, 28, 30–33
Modeling, 131–132
Motion, 408–409
Motion sickness, 409

Motivating potential score (MPS), 167
Motivation, 4, 156–180
  definition of, 157
  and performance, 177–180
  theories of, 157–177
Motivational profiles, 162
Motivators, 164
Motor tests, 105–106
Mouse, 386–387
Multiple cutoff model, 120
Multiple hurdle model, 120
Multiple performance evaluation, 89
Multiple regression, 51–52
Multiple regression model of personnel selection, 119
Multivariate analysis of variance (MANOVA), 59
Music, effect of, on work performance, 411–413
Muzak, 411

N

Narrative methods, 84
Near misses, 390
Need for achievement, 160–161, 163
Need for affiliation, 161
Need for power, 160–161, 318
Need theories of motivation, 158–162
Need-hierarchy theory, 158–160
Needs, 158
Negative consequences, 131
Negative correlation, 50–51
Negative ion generator, 412
Negative ions, 412
Negative reinforcement, 175
Negative reinforcers, 175
Network centrality, 315
New employee orientation and training, 144
Noise, 223–224, 406–408, 418
  and work performance, 407–408
Nonroutine technology, 352–353
Nontraditional organizational structures, 342–346
Nonverbal communication, 228–230
  functions of, 228–229
Normal distribution, 48–49
Normative model, 32–33, 295
Norms, 251–252
Nuclear Regulatory Commission (NRC), 390
Numeric keyboards, 385–386

O

Objectivity, 26
Observational techniques, 41–42

Obtrusive observation, 41
Occupational diseases, 419
Occupational Safety and Health Administration (OSHA), 417–418
O'Connor Finger Dexterity Test, 105
Office decorations, 412
Office of Strategic Services (OSS), 12, 114
Off-site methods, 139–142
Ohio State behavioral approach, 285
Ohio State leadership studies, 283–285
Olfactory displays, 377
One best method, 7
On-site methods, 136–139
On-the-job training, 136–137
Open-door policies, 233
Open-office designs, 414
Open-plan offices, 408
Operant conditioning, 131–132
Operationalization, 40–41
Operator characteristics, 377
Operator decisionmaking, 381
Operator information processing, 381
Operator-machine system, 375–394
  definition of, 375–376
  design of, 375–377
  errors in, 390–392
Organigram, 239–240
Organizational Behavior and Human Decision Processes, 15
Organizational behavior modification, 177, 360
Organizational chart, 239
Organizational commitment, 192–195, 201
Organizational Commitment Questionnaire (OCQ), 192–193
Organizational coping strategies, 211–213
Organizational development (OD), 356–368
  definition of, 356
  effectiveness of, 366–368
  techniques of, 359–365
Organizational Dynamics, 15
Organizational issues, 3
Organizational politics, 311, 321–331
  causes of, 327–330
  definition of, 311, 323–324
Organizational power, 314–315
Organizational psychology, 3
Organizational socialization, 252–253
Organizational structure, 336–356
  definition of, 336
  and the external environment, 354–356
  types of, 337–350
  and work technology, 351–354
Otis Self-Administering Test of Mental Ability, 104–105

Outcome variables, 42–44
Outcomes, 42–44, 169–170
Outer space, 410–411
Outgroup, 298
Overpayment inequity, 170
Ozone, 409

P

Paired comparisons, 78
Panel interviews, 116
Paper and pencil tests, 104
Parallel forms, 102
Participant observation, 41
Participative behavior, 294
Participative decisionmaking, 233
Path-goal theory, 294–295
Pavlovian conditioning, 130–131
Pay structure, 199
Pay-for-performance systems, 199–200
Performance appraisal, 72–89, 329
  interviews, 88–89
  legal concerns in, 87–88
  problems and pitfalls of, 84–87
  process, 88–89
Performance assessment, 88
Performance feedback, 88
Performance measurement, 73–76
Performance ratings, 76–84
Performance self-appraisals, 77
Performance tests, 104
Perrow model, 352–354
Personal biases, 86–87
Personality tests, 108–109
Person-job fit, 211, 213
Personnel issues, 3
Personnel planning, 60
Personnel psychology, 3, 13, 58–59
Personnel Psychology, 13, 15
Personnel recruitment, 95–97
Personnel screening, 97–118
Personnel screening tests, 103–111
  effectiveness of, 111–112
Personnel selection, 4, 119–123
Personnel testing, 12–13, 100–114
Personnel training, 129
Personnel training methods, 136–143
Peter principle, 329
Physiological needs, 158
Piecework, 176–177
Polaroid, 367
Political behaviors, 324–327

legitimate versus illegitimate, 326–327
  types of, 324–327
Pollution, 409–411, 418–419
Polygraphs, 109–110
  definition of, 109
  validity of, 110
Pong, 383
Porter and Lawler model, 190–191, 199
Position Analysis Questionnaire (PAQ), 64–69
Position power, 291
Positive consequences, 131
Positive correlation, 50–51
Positive ions, 412
Positive reinforcement, 175
Positive reinforcer, 175
Power, 4, 310–311, 313–321
  definition of, 310–311
  and dependency relationships, 319
  increasing, 318–319
  and leadership, 320–321
  sources of, 314–316
  and work outcomes, 319–320
Power bases, 315–316
Power corollary, 320
Power distribution, 317–318
Power dynamics, 317–321
Power tests, 104
Practitioner model, 5
  definition of, 5
  steps in, 5
Predictive model, 32
Predictive validity, 102–103
Preexperimental designs, 149
Prescriptive model, 32–33, 295
Present employee method, 103
Pretest-posttest, 149
Privacy, 413–414
Probability, 48
Problem-solving case study, 142–143
Process consultation, 362–364
Production-oriented behaviors, 285
Profit sharing, 200–201
Programmed instruction, 141
Project task force, 345–346
Projective test, 161
Prosocial behavior, 258
Protected groups, 122
Protective garb, 422
Psychological casualties, 361–362
Psychological effects of stress, 208
Psychology, definition of, 3
Punishments, 131, 175–176
Purdue Blueprint Reading Test, 105
Purdue Pegboard, 106

Q

Qualitative display, 378
Quality circles, 215, 366–367
Quality of work life, 214–216
Quality of work life improvement, 215–216
Quality of work life movement, 214
Quantitative display, 378
QWERTY keyboard, 385–387

R

Radiation, 418
Random assignment, 35
Random sampling, 28
Ranking technique, 77–78
Rate setting, 11
Rater training, 144–145
Rational theories of motivation, 169–174
Reaction criteria, 148
Realistic job previews (RJPs), 96–97
Receiver, 221–224
Recency effects, 85
Reciprocity rule, 257, 314
Recruitment methods, 95–97
References, 118
Referent power, 316
Reinforcement theory, 175–177
Reinforcers, 131, 175
Relatedness needs, 160
Relationship-oriented behaviors, 285
Relationship-oriented leaders, 291–292
Relaxation, 210–211
Reliability, 44–45, 101–102
Research designs, 33–40, 46
Research process, steps in, 27–30
Resource control, 315
Results criteria, 148
Résumés, 97–98
Retirement planning, 145–146
Retirement plans, 200
Retraining, 144
Reverse halo effect, 85
Reward power, 315–316
Rewards, 131
Risky shift, 275
Robots, 392–394, 426
Role conflict, 251
Role differentiation, 249
Role expectations, 248
Role management, 253
Role playing, 143
Roles, 248

Routine technology, 352–353
Rumors, 241
Rusty halo effect, 85

S

Safety behavior modification program, 422–423
Safety control devices, 420
Safety guards, 420
Safety incentive programs, 424
Safety needs, 158
Safety procedures, 421
Safety programs, 421–424
Safety task force, 424
Safety training programs, 423–424
Sampling, 28–29
Scarcity principle, 314
"Science of coal shoveling," 7
Scientific management, 7–9, 374
    applications of, 7–9
    definitions of, 7
    principles of, 7
    shortcomings of, 8
Scientific management versus human relations, 11–12
Selection and placement of World War II military personnel, 12–13
Self-actualization needs, 158
Self-censorship, 273–274
Self-centered roles, 250–251
Self-efficacy, 322
Self-report techniques, 42
Sender, 221–224
Sense of control, 213, 414
Sensitivity training, 361
Sensory ability tests, 105–106
Sequence errors, 391
Sequence-of-use principle, 397
Severity errors, 85, 89
Sex discrimination in employee compensation, 71–72
Shape-coded controls, 384
Shared negative stereotypes, 273–274
Shields, 420
Shifts, 415
Shiftwork, 415
Simulation training, 140–141
Situational exercises, 114
Situational interview questions, 116
Situational tests, 12–13
Sixteen Personality Factors Questionnaire (16 PF), 105
Skill training program, 212
Skill variety, 167

Skills inventory, 147
Small-batch production, 351–352
Snap judgments, 117
Snellen Eye Chart, 106
Snowball effect, 242
Social cognition, 16–17
Social competence, 300
Social control, 16, 311–313
Social debts, 258
Social influence tactics, 314
Social intelligence, 300
Social learning theory, 131–132
Social needs, 158
Social Readjustment Rating Scale, 206
Social scientific research methods, 26–54
    goals of, 26–27
Sociogram, 239
Soft performance criteria, 73–75
    advantages and disadvantages of, 74
    definition of, 73–74
Solomon four-group design, 149–150
Source factors, 224–225
Spacesuits, 410–411
Span of control, 346–348
Speech-activated control, 388–389
Speed tests, 104
Split-half reliability, 102
Staff, 340–341
Standard deviation, 48–49
Statistical analyses, 29, 45–52
Statistical significance, 48
Stratified sampling, 29
Stress, 202. *See also* Work stress
Stress history, 205
Stress inoculation training, 424
Stressor, 202
Stress-related illness, 207–208
Structured interviews, 116
Student work environment, 398
Subject contamination, 46
Subjective performance appraisals, 328
Superordinate goal, 266
Supportive behavior, 294
Survey feedback, 360–361
Surveys, 42
Symptoms of groupthink, 273–275
Synthetic speech, 380
Systematic biases, 86
Systematic relaxation training, 210–211

T

Tactile displays, 377
Tall organizational structure, 346–348

Task identity, 167
Task significance, 167
Task structure, 291
Task-oriented behaviors, 285
Task-oriented leaders, 291–292
Team building, 361–362
Team managers, 288
Technical language, 225
Teleconferencing, 226
Teleoperators, 387–389
Temperature, effect of, on work performance, 406, 418
Temperature extremes, 406
Temporal conditions, 415–417
Test battery, 111
Test utility, 112
Test-retest reliability, 101–102
Text keys, 386–387
Thalidomide, 273
Thematic Apperception Test (TAT), 161–162
Theorizing, 28
Theory, 28
Theory X, 282
Theory Y, 282
Threats, 320
Three Mile Island (TMI), 390
Time management, 211
Time-and-motion procedures, 7, 9, 374
Timing errors, 391
Title VII of the Civil Rights Act of 1964, 69, 122
Touch screen control, 386
Toxic substances, 418–419
Traditional organizational structures, 337–342
Trainee readiness, 133
Training feedback, 133
Training groups (t-groups), 361
Training needs assessment, 134–136
    demographic analysis, 135–136
    organizational level analysis, 134
    person analysis, 135
    task level analysis, 134–135
Training program
    evaluation of, 148–150
    structure of, 133
Trait theory of leadership, 281–282
Traits, 281
Transfer of training, 133
Traps, 420
Treatment group, 34
Truman administration, 273
Turnover, 43–44
Two-factor theory, 163–165
Two-tier wage structure, 171
Type A behavior pattern, 163, 207
Type A personality, 207

Type B personality, 207
Types of research models, 30–33
Typing Test for Business (TTB), 105

U

Unconditioned response, 130
Unconditioned stimulus, 130
Underpayment inequity, 169
Underutilization, 203
Unhardy persons, 207
Uniform Guidelines on Employee Selection Procedures, 122–123
Union Carbide, 390
United States Department of Labor, 63
United States Office of Strategic Services (OSS), 12, 114
United States v. City of Chicago, 88, 479
Universalist theories, 281–282
University of Michigan leadership studies, 285
Unobtrusive observation, 41
Upward communication, 231–233
User friendly computer systems, 16, 386

V

Valence, 171–172
Validity, 44–45, 101–103
Validity coefficient, 111
Validity generalization, 111–112
Variable interval schedule, 176
Variable ratio schedule, 177
Variables, 28
Vestibule training, 137–138
Vibration, 408–409, 413
Video games, 382–383
Videoconferencing, 226
VIE theory of motivation, 171–174
Vietnam War, 273
Visual displays, 378–379
Visual fatigue, 405
Voluntary absenteeism, 43–44, 195–197
Voluntary turnover, 196–197
Volvo automobile assembly plant, 166
Vroom and Yetton's decision making model, 295–298

W

Walton model, 215
Warning displays, 420
Wechsler Adult Intelligence Scale–Revised (WAISR), 105
Weighted application forms, 98
Weightlessness, 408–411
Western Electric Company, 9
We-they feeling, 256, 262
Wheel network, 237
Wonderlic Personnel Test, 104–105
Woodward model, 351–352
Work conditions, 4, 404–417
Work environment issues, 4
Work in America, 302, 481
Work overload, 203
Work place maintenance, 419
Work safety, 417–427
Work safety programs, 421–424
Work samples, 106, 108, 114
Work schedules, 415–417
Work station design, 395–398
Work stations, 395–397, 410–411
Work stress, 4, 202–213
    and absenteeism and turnover, 208–209
    coping with, 210–213
    definition of, 202
    effects of, 207–210
    sources of, 203–207
    and work outcomes, 208–209
Work stress management program, 212
Work teams, 215, 357
Workaholic, 163
Worker issues, 3
Worker morale, 10
Work-orientation scales, 108–109
Workspace design, 395–399
Written records, 339

Y

Y-network, 237

Z

Zero-gravity neutral body position, 411